Encyclopedia of
AMERICAN
EDUCATION

Harlow G. Unger

Facts On File, Inc.

Encyclopedia of American Education

Facts On File, Inc.
11 Penn Plaza
New York NY 10001

Library of Congress Cataloging-in-Publication Data

Unger, Harlow G., 1931–
    Encyclopedia of American education / by Harlow G. Unger.
        p. cm.
    Includes bibliographical references and index.
    ISBN 0-8160-3458-3 (vol. 1)
        0-8160-3459-1 (vol. 2)
        0-8160-3505-9 (vol. 3)
        0-8160-2994-6 (set) (alk. paper)
    1. Education—United States—Encyclopedias. I. Title.
    LBI7.U54   1996
    370′973—dc20   95-41694

CONTENTS

R

race In education, a class of people with common, identifiable and presumably inherited characteristics. Most anthropologists classify humans into three races: Caucasoid (whites), Mongoloid (Asiatics) and Negroid (blacks). The U.S. Department of Education and other American government agencies, along with the entire educational establishment, keep detailed academic and other records, categorized by race, as well as by certain national and ethnic origins, such as data for Hispanics, American Indians (q.v.) and Pacific Islanders. For the first 250 years of white settlement in North America, the vast majority of blacks were enslaved by whites. After emancipation in 1863, state laws in much of the United States segregated them for an additional century from white life and opportunities.

Although legally free, blacks continue to suffer far higher rates of economic and cultural deprivation in the United States than do whites. During the last quarter of the 20th century, almost one-third of American blacks remained consistently below the poverty (q.v.) level, while the percentage of whites below the poverty level dropped steadily from nearly 18% in 1960 to about 11% in 1991. During those same years, the poverty rate for the nation as a whole dropped from 22% to about 14.5%.

Black educational achievement mirrors economic conditions, with a rate of functional illiteracy of more than 12% among blacks, compared to less than 2% among American whites. According to recent U.S. Department of Education figures, more than one-third of all black Americans had failed to complete high school, compared to 21% of all whites. Only 7.5% of blacks held bachelor's degrees from college, compared to 11.9% of whites. In 1991, 24% of blacks 18 to 24 years old were enrolled in college, compared with 34% of whites, Moreover, proficiency of black elementary and secondary school students in reading, writing, mathematics, science and other academic courses was substantially lower than that of whites. The scores of college-bound black high school students on verbal and mathematics Scholastic Assessment Tests (q.v.) are more than 20% lower than those of white students, while scores of Asian Americans (q.v.) are only 6.8% below those of white students on the verbal tests and 8.4% higher than those of white students on the mathematics tests.

In an effort to smooth out such differences in academic achievement, and ultimately reduce the economic deprivation perceived as the cause, the federal and state governments, along with the entire educational establishment, began establishing a broad array of compensatory educational programs (q.v.) 1963, the 100th anniversary of the Emancipation Proclamation. At the most elementary level, the federal government sponsored the establishment of the huge Head Start (q.v.) program of preschool education to lift the level of school-readiness skills of culturally disadvantaged children. At the elementary and secondary school levels, a wide array of remedial instruction is now a standard element of the school curriculum in disadvantaged areas. At the college level, most community colleges, as well as state colleges, have adopted variations of open-enrollment admission policies that admit all applicants, regardless of high school grades and entrance examination scores and, where necessary, provide remedial instruction to help the culturally disadvantaged cope with college-level courses. Although academically selective private and public colleges maintain high academic standards for admission, most also have affirmative action (q.v.) admission policies that apply lower standards for black applicants "in the interests of diversity." Indeed, institutions as notable as Duke University, the University of Virginia, Washington University in St. Louis, Rice University in Houston and many others have established merit scholarships awarded on the basis of race alone.

Rutgers, the State University of New Jersey, has the largest race-based system of merit scholarships, awarding between 200 and 250 such grants to minority high school seniors who finished in the top 10% of their classes and had a combined score of 1,100 on the SATs.

(See also AFRICAN AMERICANS; RACE-BASED SCHOLARSHIPS.)

References: DES; NYT; *Race and Races,* Richard A. Goldsby (1977); *Human Variation: Races, Types and Ethnic Groups,* Stephen Molnar (1991).

race-based scholarships Financial grants awarded by a college or university to a student primarily on the basis of race, rather than academic, athletic or other abilities. Race-based scholarships are permitted under U.S. federal regulations as long as they are granted to help "remedy past discrimination" and promote diversity on the campus. Race-based scholarships account for about 4% of the more than $3.5 billion in scholarships awarded by four-year colleges each year. In 1995, the U.S. Supreme Court refused to review a lower court ruling that race-based scholarships funded with public money at the University of Maryland were unconstitutional because they discriminated against white students. Race-based scholarships funded with private money, however, are part of a long tradition of privately funded scholarships for students from a wide variety of special groups, including American Indians, Chinese Americans, Italian Americans, Jews, foreign students, women, men, Christians, lineal descendants of Confederate soldiers and "students of Huguenot ancestry," among others.

Although entirely legal and ethical, many colleges hesitate to publicize the availability of race-based scholarships for fear of provoking reverse-discrimination lawsuits by white students who are refused admittance in favor of less qualified blacks (see UNIVERSITY OF CALIFORNIA REGENTS V. BAKKE). Most such scholarships are, therefore, awarded without fanfare, usually to black students who might otherwise forgo op-

portunities to attend a prestigious college because of financial need.

Among the most prestigious institutions that admit awarding race-based scholarships are the University of Virginia, Duke University, Washington University in St. Louis and Rice University. Emory University has two race-based scholarship programs for the top graduates of Atlanta's public schools, whose student bodies are predominantly black. The largest provider of race-based scholarships is Rutgers University, New Jersey's state university, which awards upward of 200 scholarships annually to minority students who finish in the top 10% of their high school classes and have combined SAT scores of at least 1,100. Called the Carr scholarships, the $5,000 awards cover about two-thirds of the annual cost for tuition, room and board for New Jersey residents.

Reference: NYT.

racial balance In public education, a student population whose racial and ethnic makeup reflects the racial makeup of the general community. Thus, racial balance in a community whose population is 40% white, 30% Hispanic and 30% black would see the student population made up of roughly the same percentages of each group.

Racial balance in American public schools has been a primary goal of the U.S. federal courts since 1954, when the U.S. Supreme Court outlawed racial segregation in public schools in the case of *Brown v. Board of Education of Topeka* (q.v.). At that time, the Court ordered public schools to desegregate "with all deliberate speed." Although the decision and subsequent federal legislation outlawed de jure segregation, de facto segregation, based on residential patterns, has persisted. Thus, all-black neighborhoods tend to have all-black schools; all-white neighborhoods, all-white schools. Although reflective of neighborhood population, such schools are not considered racially balanced if they do not reflect a broader population of the town, city or county and area beyond the immediate district boundaries. Some communities instituted mandatory, inter-district busing (q.v.) of schoolchildren to achieve a modicum of racial balance in schools of all-white and all-black districts, but such forced busing was subsequently declared unconstitutional, and racial imbalances persist to this day in neighborhoods where de facto segregation exists.

Reference: *Desegregation: How Schools Are Meeting Historic Challenge,* National School Public Relations Association, Arlington, Virginia (1973).

racism The belief that race is the primary cause of human characteristics and abilities and that some races are inherently superior to others, intellectually, psychologically and physically. There are two broad forms of racism: institutional, practiced by government or business, educational and social organizations; and individual, practiced by one or more persons against a member or members of a different race. Both forms have influenced American education since the first white settlers arrived in the New World. From earliest colonial days, institutional racism barred blacks, American Indians and Asians from most schools. Southern states made it a crime, punishable by fines and imprisonment, to teach blacks to read. Although the Civil War ended legalized slavery in the United States, southern states passed laws that segregated blacks from whites in public schools for nearly a century, while federal government regulations and local or state ordinances forced most American Indians to attend segregated schools on their reservations.

In 1954, the U.S. Supreme Court ruled that racially segregated schools were inherently unequal and unconstitutional, and it ordered an end to legalized, state-sponsored institutional racism in American education in its 1954 decision in *Brown v. Board of Education of Topeka* (q.v.). Institutional racism in private colleges and universities, however, continued until the U.S. Congress passed the Civil Rights Act of 1964 (q.v.), outlawing all institutional racism in public facilities in the United States. Passage of subsequent federal, state and local laws discouraged overt institutional racism in education, although some subtle forms inevitably persisted. Among these was the failure of some schools to achieve racial balance in their faculties and thus give students of each race adequate numbers of adult role models. At the individual level, some teachers and their instructional materials failed to recognize the achievements of minorities in history, literature, science and other fields. The subtlest form of racism, however, often took the form of lower teacher expectations for poor and minority students. By demanding less of such students, teachers got exactly what they expected.

References: *The Retreat of Scientific Racism,* Elazar Barkan (1992); *Racism in the United States: An American Dilemma,* David M. Reimers, ed. (1972); *Equal Educational Opportunity: More Promise Than Progress,* Institute for the Study of Educational Policy, Washington, D.C.

radio The wireless transmission of sound, or "wireless telephone," as it was first called, following its invention in Europe in the late 19th century. Radio did not become an educative medium in the United States until the early 1920s, when the industry expanded from two local transmitters that reached a few thousand listeners in Pittsburgh and Detroit, to 530 stations broadcasting to more than one million American homes in 1924. Among the station owners were newspapers, which broadcast news; churches, which broadcast their varied interpretations of "the word"; and universities, which offered home study courses and certificates from what was loosely called the "university of the air."

By 1940, there were 847 American stations broadcasting to more than 28 million households—80% of all the households in the United States at that time. Radio became the most effective public medium of the day, reaching the unlettered as well as the educated with the informative, regular "fireside chats" of President

Franklin D. Roosevelt; up-to-the-minute news of local, regional, national and international interest and news analysis by various experts; weekly concerts of the New York Philharmonic and the NBC Symphony; live opera from the Metropolitan Opera House; the weekly "Invitation to Learning," which brought readings of classical literature to more than a million listeners; and, of course a wide variety of entertainment, including comedy, popular music, variety shows and quiz programs. A 1945 survey found that Americans thought more of radio than they did of their churches and schools, saying that radio provided them with substantial general knowledge and practical information and cultural opportunities. Moreover, they said they preferred programs with advertising to those without, arguing that commercials provided them useful information and shopping guidance.

Reference: *A History of Broadcasting in the United States,* Erik Barnouw (3 vols., 1966–70).

Rainbow Curriculum

Rainbow Curriculum   A controversial series of short texts introduced in New York City schools in the early 1990s to inculcate in children a spirit of acceptance of a wide range of people of different races, religions, ethnic backgrounds and sexual preferences. It was the last element—illustrated by titles such as "Heather Has Two Mommies"—that triggered a barrage of attacks and parent demonstrations against the New York Board of Education and its chancellor, Joseph A. Fernandez. The texts were withdrawn as a mandatory part of the elementary school curriculum. The booklets explaining "alternative lifestyles" remain available to the city's schoolchildren as a counseling tool.

Reference: NYT.

rational counting   The counting of specific, concrete objects, as opposed to the simple mastery of the sequence of numbers. Also called enumeration, rational counting is the standard method of teaching students to count. Rational counting replaced rote memorization, which was the conventional method of learning numbers in the 19th century, before the development of the progressive education concept of moving from the concrete to the abstract. Rational counting gives each number name a meaning—as in "one book" or "two pencils," instead of simply one, two, three and four. Teachers of young children routinely use rational counting as a pedagogical tool, asking one child to count the number of students, another to count books and others to count blocks. Teachers report that physical touching of the objects counted quickens number mastery.

References: *Teaching and Learning in the Elementary School,* John Jarolimek and Clifford D. Foster (1985); *The Elementary School Handbook,* Joanne Oppenheim (1989).

raw score   The actual number of correct answers on a test, unadjusted and unconverted to conventional grading systems or to relative positions in a distribution curve. Thus, the raw, or, as it is sometimes called, crude, score for six questions answered correctly on a test made up of 12 questions is six. As a percentage grade, it would be 50%. Graded by position on a distribution curve, it might, if it were the highest grade in the class, merit an adjusted grade of 90%.

Reference: *Measuring and Evaluating School Learning,* Lou M. Carey (1988).

"reach" school   A colloquialism referring to a college whose empirical qualifications for admission appear somewhat higher than the academic qualifications of an applicant, thus making it an academic "reach" for that student. College-bound students usually apply to at least one such "reach," or "dream," school that they would most like to attend, but for which their academic qualifications are below those of the average student accepted to that institution. In addition to one "reach" school, college-bound high school students usually apply to at least one "safety" school for which they appear somewhat over-qualified academically, in comparison to the majority of applicants.

Reference: *A Student's Guide to College Admissions,* Harlow G. Unger (1995).

readability The degree of reader understanding of written material. Readability is an essential measure for publishers of educational materials to determine, prior to publication and distribution to specific student age groups. Materials too easy or too difficult to understand are of little educational value in the classroom, and teachers, as well as publishers, attempt to determine readability before distributing written materials to students. Vocabulary, syllabic structures, sentence structure, average sentence length, number of prepositional and participial phrases, page design and format, average paragraph length and type size and design are all elements taken into account in measuring readability. There are, however, a variety of different formulas and systems for measuring readability, none of which are accepted as entirely valid or reliable.
References: *Teaching Them to Read,* Dolores Durkin (1989); *How to Measure Readability,* W. B. Gray Jr. (1975).

readiness skills (for school) A body of knowledge and abilities that provide a preschool or kindergarten child with a foundation for the formal school experience and academic learning. A child who cannot read the individual letters of the alphabet, for example, lacks the readiness skills for learning to read. School readiness heads the list of educational priorities of the U.S. Government's Goals 2000 (q.v.) program to make American education the world's best.

The basic readiness skills required for learning in the school situation can be categorized as social, oral, interpretive and mathematical:

- Social readiness skills: ability to listen to others, take turns talking, and not interrupt or distract others.
- Oral skills: ability to identify rhyming words (e.g., cat, bat), position words (front, back, beginning, end, etc.), upper case and lower case letters, and the sounds and names of letters.
- Interpretive skills: ability to understand the overall form of a story—i.e., beginning, middle, end—and analyze the traits of characters and predict what may happen to them after the story ends; ability to recount a story from a picture; ability to differentiate between real and make-believe.
- Mathematical skills: ability to sort and compare objects by color, kind, size, shape, details; ability to count from 1 to 10, backwards and forwards and starting from any number within the sequence; ability to estimate quantities and determine which of two groups is probably larger.

About 35% of American children started first grade in 1991 unprepared to learn, according to a study by the Carnegie Foundation for the Advancement of Teaching. Entitled *Ready to Learn: A Mandate for the Nation,* the study traced lack of school readiness skills to a number of causes, including poor health care, inattentive or overworked parents, scarce child-care and preschool opportunities, unsafe neighborhoods, mindless television programming and isolation from adults. It said about a half-million American children under six suffered from malnourishment.
Reference: *The School-Smart Parent,* Gene I. Maeroff (1989).

readiness tests Examinations administered to preschoolers and kindergartners to measure their readiness for the formal elementary school, educational process. The three most commonly used readiness tests in the early 1990s were the Metropolitan Readiness Test, the Lee-Clark Reading Readiness Test and the Murphy Durrell Reading Readiness Test. Readiness tests are usually required for applicants to highly selective, private elementary schools, with far more applicants than available seats. Administered somewhat less routinely by public schools, readiness tests are far from reliable and are often invalid, because of built-in cultural biases that can obscure the educational promise of perfectly healthy or even gifted children. A rural child from a home with a huge, covered porch might fail to select the tricycle from a picture question that asks, "Which of these toys do you never use in the house?"

Reference: *The Elementary School Handbook,* Joanne Oppenheim (1989).

reading The perception, comprehension and intellectual integration of printed letters or symbols, words and groups of words. The most basic element of formal education and the school curriculum, reading is generally defined as a four-part sequence: word perception, or recognition of a word and the understanding of its meaning; comprehension, or grasp of ideas from word groupings; reaction, or intellectual, emotional or physical effect or response; and integration, or absorption of all or parts of the material into one's own body of knowledge and experience.

In broadest terms, reading instruction consists of three stages: development of a sense (sight or, in the case of Braille, touch); development of word-attack skills (learning to sound-out, learning meanings by their context, etc.); and integration of reading and thinking. Ironically, learning to read does not begin with instruction in letters, but in the absorption of ideas and concepts during the preliterate years of infancy and early childhood. To begin to learn to read, infants and young children must first hear language, associate meanings to words and gradually intuit that words are composed of sounds, represented by printed symbols, or letters. "Play" with words and sounds is an essential element in acquiring reading readiness skills, by focusing the child's attention on word sounds as well as meaning. A second important element is parental reading to children, to help them learn new words and meanings, expand vocabulary, provide contact with letters and words and build awareness that printed words tell stories and provide information. Some reading instruction also begins before preschool, as the child observes and, with parental assistance, recognizes large-print logos—e.g., "PIZZA"—and engages in pretend-reading from books whose stories he or she already knows from parental readings. Depending on the individual child's stage of development, formal instruction in reading readiness skills may begin in preschool, but certainly no later than kindergarten, when children are taught to read, recite and write the alphabet and match capital and small letters.

Kindergarten reading instruction begins with elementary phonics, with children taught to make letter-sound associations, sound out and name letters at the beginning of short, monosyllabic words, and to read and rhyme short words such as man and ran. Teacher-directed storytime takes up a significant part of the kindergarten day. Children have read-along copies of many stories and poems and are encouraged to read aloud, according to their abilities. Cross-disciplinary stories introduce children to subjects such as history and science. Children also learn to differentiate between real and make-believe, and to dictate their own words and stories to the teacher, who slowly transcribes them on the chalkboard. Teacher transcriptions of children's words into written words are a basic teaching technique for kindergarten-aged children and are critical to their learning to read. Some children learn to write short words—spelled phonetically, correctly or incorrectly (immaterial at this age)—and all learn to write their own first and last names correctly.

As simplistic as such reading-readiness skills may appear, they are essential to the development of basic reading skills, which, in turn, are essential to academic success throughout primary, secondary and higher education and to economic and professional success in adult life. Better-than-average readers are generally higher-than-average achievers; those in power have traditionally sought to preserve their authority by limiting the literacy of the populace.

In the Western world, the development of reading as a popular skill got under way only after 1382, when a group of dissident Oxford

University students, followers of John Wycliffe, first translated the Vulgate, or Latin Bible, into the vernacular. Until then, only priests and a minority of the nobility, fluent in Latin, had direct access to the contents of the Bible, which they could interpret as best served their interests. Wycliffe broke with the papacy over his belief in a direct relationship between humanity and God, without the mediation of popes, prelates and the church. Denouncing many of the beliefs and practices of the Catholic Church as non-scriptural, he called the Scriptures the sole religious truth; a translation of the Bible brought that truth to an expanded audience, who were encouraged not only to follow the text but also to interpret it. The development of the printing press during the 15th century and the Renaissance contributed further to the climate of literacy.

Wycliffe's efforts helped bring about the Protestant Reformation that split the Catholic Church in 1517 and also sowed the seeds of a popular education movement, which had begun in England as a struggle between Wycliffe's followers and those loyal to the papacy. The struggle grew more violent following Henry VIII's break with the Pope in 1532. In an attempt to resolve the conflict, Henry forced Parliament to pass the Act of Supremacy declaring him the head of the English church. Recognizing the continuing strength of Catholics in England, his daughter, Elizabeth I, forced Parliament in 1562 to add "all teachers of children" to those required to take the oath of supremacy.

The object, of course, was not to spread education in the modern sense, but to produce a generation of Englishmen loyal to the Crown and its version of Protestantism, the Church of England. The result, however, was an unprecedented expansion of schooling throughout the end of the 16th and beginning of the 17th centuries. Instead of cementing popular loyalty to Crown and church, however, reading opened the door to knowledge, and knowledge produced an endless array of intellectual and religious rebellions that, in turn, produced a civil war in Britain and sent many Britons fleeing to the American colonies.

The majority of schools produced by the Tudor educational revolution were petty schools (q.v.), which concentrated on learning to read Scripture. The study of reading began with the alphabet and syllables, taken from a hornbook (q.v.), or ABC, and then proceeded sequentially to a primer (q.v.), a catechism, a Psalter, the Old Testament and the New Testament. For wealthier students, education progressed from petty school to grammar school (q.v.), where they studied Latin, mathematics and other advanced subjects. It was this type of education that the first English settlers brought to the American colonies.

After independence, some leaders of the new nation, such as Thomas Jefferson, James Madison and Benjamin Franklin, recognized that the ability to read was essential for democratic self-government. Northern industrialists and southern plantation owners feared that education might provoke worker rebellions and deprive them of their cheapest labor—children and black slaves. Again, reading was seen as a danger to the powers of the ruling class, and southern states passed laws making it a crime, punishable by fines and imprisonment, to teach blacks how to read. The creation of state public school systems following the Civil War legally opened education and reading to all American children, but pervasive child labor prevented almost half the children in the United States from attending school. It was not until the passage of the last of the state compulsory education laws in the early 1920s that every American child was given the right to learn how to read.

In today's schools, children equipped with reading-readiness skills begin in first grade to learn to recognize whole words, read complete sentences, paragraphs and short stories and, above all, to understand the meaning of the texts they read. Although some schools preface whole-word instruction by phonics (q.v.)—i.e., the "sounding" out of individual letters, letter combinations, then words—most teachers combine phonics and whole-word instruction, followed by the basal reader (q.v.) program, a group of instructional materials consisting of readers and workbooks.

In the later elementary school and middle school years, reading instruction gradually shifts from development of basic recognition skills to vocabulary expansion and the development of a variety of subskills, including understanding word meanings from their context, finding the main idea in a sentence, paragraph or passage, distinguishing between fact and opinion and summarizing and interpreting complex written materials. By the end of elementary school, learning to read has evolved into reading to learn, with the learning of new reading skills limited to subskills such as scanning, finding meanings through context, comprehending abstract materials and acquiring a larger, more technical vocabulary.

References: EB; *Teaching Them to Read*, Dolores Durkin (1989); *Literacy: Reading the Word and the World*, Paolo Freire and Donaldo Macedo (1987).

reading accelerator Any of a variety of mechanical devices developed in the 1960s to increase the reading speed of slow readers and students with reading disabilities. One device uses a flat bar, about an inch and a half wide, that lies across the page and moves down it at a speed that can be adjusted mechanically, forcing the reader to stay ahead of the bar. Another device covering the entire page is equipped with a moving shutter mechanism that moves downward, exposing one line at a time. By shortening the time of exposure, the teacher can force the student to read faster. Comprehension is tested after each page is read. Somewhat effective with ''lazy,'' but otherwise normal readers, the device can prove extremely anxiety provoking.

Reference: *Corrective Reading*, Miles V. Zintz (1977).

reading age The age-equivalent level of a student's reading ability as measured by stan-dardized, norm-based examinations. Reading age does not take chronological age into account. Thus, a student with a reading age of 10 may actually be 6, 10 or 20 years of age.

(See also READING LEVELS.)

Reference: *Teaching Them to Read*, Dolores Durkin (1989).

reading clues A variety of elements in a written passage that indirectly suggest the meaning of a word, of a character's personality or feelings, or of story content and plot. Teaching students how to identify reading clues—probable story content from a title or the meaning of a word from its context—is an essential element of reading instruction in elementary school education.

References: *Teaching Them to Read*, Dolores Durkin (1989); *Principles and Practices of Teaching Reading*, Arthur W. Heilman, Timothy R. Blair and William H. Rupley (1986).

reading comprehension The ability to infer meaning from a printed passage. There are four levels of reading comprehension that develop sequentially: literal, interpretive, critical and creative. The first limits understanding of written materials to words, phrases, sentences and explicitly stated ideas. Interpretive comprehension allows the reader to understand ideas implied, but not specifically stated, in a printed passage. Critical comprehension allows the reader to evaluate the accuracy and aesthetic value of a passage, while creative comprehension allows the reader to relate and apply ideas expressed or implied in a passage to the world beyond that described in the reading. An essential part of the reading instruction program is to teach students to progress from one level of comprehension to the next. although the rate of progress is determined in part by individual development and sociocultural and economic background.

References: *How to Increase Reading Ability*, Albert J. Harris and Edward R. Sipay (1985); *Principles and Practices of Teaching Reading*, Arthur W. Heilman,

Timothy R. Blair and William H. Rupley (1986); *Reading Comprehension: New Directions for Classroom Practice,* John D. McNeil (1987).

reading games Any of a variety of entertaining activities that require students to read. Some reading games such as crossword puzzles, picture riddles, rebuses and card games are commercially prepared; others are prepared by teachers. By associating reading with "fun," reading games are designed as conditioning experiences that, presumably, help students develop a lasting interest in reading. There are no valid or reliable studies to support that assumption, however, and experienced teachers are careful to keep games to a minimum and to select only those that focus on the acquisition of specific skills. One disadvantage of reading games is their failure to teach children that learning often requires serious, albeit rewarding, concentration. Overuse of games can dissuade some children from learning efforts that fail to entertain and provoke a "that's-no-fun" response.
Reference: How to Increase Reading Ability, Albert J. Harris and Edward R. Sipay (1985).

reading levels A broad-based measure of individual reading achievement, valid only when related to the reader's age and the level of difficulty (or readability) of the material. There are three basic evaluative levels, as determined by an Informal Reading Inventory (q.v.):

- Dependent level. Reader needs no assistance, makes fewer than 2% oral reading errors and comprehends more than 90% of the material.
- Instructional level. Oral reading errors reach 5%, while comprehension, or comprehension "capacity," drops to about 75%, and reader needs some teacher assistance.
- Frustration level. Oral reading errors climb to more than 10%, while comprehension falls to less than 50%; a level detrimental to instructional progress and one at which materials are withdrawn in favor of easier reading.

Teacher evaluation of a student's reading level and comprehension capacity is essential in the selection of appropriate materials for basal reading instruction of early elementary school students.
References: *How to Increase Reading Ability,* Albert J. Harris and Edward R. Sipay (1985); *Reading Comprehension: New Directions for Classroom Practice,* John D. McNeil (1987).

reading lists In education, any roster of books and other reading materials deemed appropriate in terms of content, language and readability for a youngster at a specific age or grade in elementary or secondary school. Publishers of children's and young adult (adolescent) books generally specify the age groups for which each book is most appropriate. There are myriad reading lists prepared by libraries, teachers' associations, religious organizations and publishers. Some lists are inclusive, in that they include all literature generally regarded by scholars as classical along with newly published works deemed appropriate by teachers of reading and English; others are exclusive, in that they exclude materials—classical or not—deemed objectionable to a particular community or group within that community. Although there are no universally accepted reading lists, in 1988 then-secretary of education William J. Bennett developed reading lists of appropriate literature for every grade from kindergarten through high school. The New York Public Library and various teachers' associations also produce annual reading lists largely related to new books published in that year.
References: New York Public Library; *James Madison Elementary School* and *James Madison High School,* William J. Bennett, U.S. Department of Education, Washington, D.C. (1988).

reading rate The speed at which one reads orally and silently, expressed in words per minute. Normal oral and silent reading rates for a 10-year-old child at the beginning of fourth grade are about 130 words per minute. Although oral reading rates remain relatively stable at that level, silent reading rates climb to about 250 words a minute by the time students graduate from high school. Silent reading rates are affected by reader interest, reader familiarity with the context of the material, reading environment (lighting, noise levels, etc.) and the reader's physical and psychological condition.

References: *How to Increase Reading Ability,* Albert J. Harris and Edward R. Sipay (1985); *Principles and Practices of Teaching Reading,* Arthur W. Heilman, Timothy R. Blair and William H. Rupley (1986).

reading readiness   That level of physical, intellectual, emotional and sociocultural development at which a child is most susceptible to successful acquisition of reading skills. Most normal children do not know how to read when they enter kindergarten at five years old, but they are ready to learn to read. Reading readiness is evident by a number of distinct, measurable characteristics: sight recognition of familiar words such as one's own name, product names and road signs; ability to recite all or most of the alphabet and to point out and name letters and numbers; the knowledge of how books "work," from left to right and top to bottom on each page and from front to back and that the printed symbols on each page represent spoken sounds and words; the knowledge of story form, with a beginning, middle and end.

Most schools generally try to measure reading readiness with one of three commonly used tests: Metropolitan Readiness Test, Lee-Clark Reading Readiness Test and Murphy Durell Reading Readiness Analysis. The tests measure alphabet and letter recognition, whole-word recognition, vocabulary and visual discrimination (the ability to distinguish between p and b, for example). Although the tests correctly predict that children with high scores do indeed progress quickly in reading instruction and achieve superior reading proficiency by third grade, they have relatively little validity in predicting the future progress of children with low scores. Indeed, they may simply evaluate the child's level of development at the time of the test rather than any real reading "aptitude." Experienced first grade teachers maintain they can determine a child's reading aptitude far more accurately than tests, through observation of a child's drawings, body language, listening skills, reaction to stories, participation in classroom discussions, and interaction with peers, adults and classroom materials.

Reading readiness is largely a function of a child's socioeconomic and cultural background during the preliterate years. Children acquire such skills both by direct instruction and by simply observing their surroundings and absorbing knowledge independently. Acquisition of the first reading readiness skills begins when the infant first hears language spoken. Gradually, the child begins to associate meanings to words and eventually to intuit that words are composed of sounds, represented by printed symbols, or letters. "Play" with words and sounds are an essential element in acquiring reading readiness skills, by focusing the child's attention on word sounds as well as meaning. A second important element is parental reading, which teaches new words and meanings, provides contact with letters and words and builds awareness that printed words tell stories and provide information.

Some reading instruction begins before preschool, as the child observes and, with parental assistance initially, but eventually independently, recognizes large-print logos—e.g., "PIZZA"—and engages in pretend-reading from books whose stories he or she already knows from parental readings. The process continues in day-care, nursery school and preschool, with acquisition of alphabet and limited word recognition skills and other reading "building blocks."

(See also PRESCHOOL; READING.)

Reference: *The Elementary School Handbook,* Joanne Oppenheim (1989).

reading reversals   A perceptual dysfunction whereby the reader sees similarly shaped letters and words in reverse—*b*, for example, instead of *d* or *p*, and *saw* instead of *was*. Relatively common among preschool children and beginning readers, reading reversals, if they persist, can be one symptom of more serious visual perception problems or learning disorders in reading letters, words or sentences. For normal reading-reversal problems, many teachers introduce multisensory instruction, whereby children trace each letter with their fingers, while reading and reciting the letter aloud.

(See also LEARNING DISABILITIES; DYSLEXIA; GILLINGHAM METHOD.)

Reference: *Teaching Reading to Slow and Disabled Learners,* Samuel A. Kirk et al. (1978).

reasoning skills The ability to infer or reach conclusions, in an orderly, rational way, on the basis of a group of facts and applicable principles or laws. Often called higher-order thinking skills, reasoning skills are generally defined as the ability to identify a problem, to determine what information is needed to solve it, to generate possible solutions from such information, to evaluate each solution and select the correct one, to implement the solution and to describe and defend the reasons behind the implementation. In short, reasoning skills require students to arrive at the correct solution and explain how and why they arrived at it.

Reasoning skills have been at the center of a highly charged educational debate over the apparent failure of American public schools to teach such skills to most students. Much of the failure is ascribed to the pervasive use of objective tests requiring only rote answers and memory skills, instead of written essay-style tests and assignments requiring original thought.

Generally required for academic proficiency, beginning in the fifth grade, reasoning skills are essential to academic success at the high school and college level. Although many students acquire problem-solving skills and strategies intuitively or by imitating others, some educators believe that instruction in reasoning skills should be an integral part of the curriculum throughout the elementary and middle school years. Instruction in reasoning skills begins with extensive use of teacher questioning and problem-raising, followed, initially, by teacher guidance in and discussion about identifying, evaluating and selecting problem-solving strategies. In solving problems for the class, teachers intent on teaching reasoning skills carefully describe the reasoning skills and problem-solving strategies they used in arriving at a solution, rather than simply providing the solution.

References: *Successful Problem Solving Technique,* Carole E. Greenes et al. (1977); *The School-Smart Parent,* Gene I. Maeroff (1989).

rebus A common reading game (q.v.) that combines pictures and other symbols with printed letters and words in a sequence that permits a young reader to decode a complete sentence by sequentially pronouncing the name of each picture, letter or word. Thus, the number 2 might be used as a symbol for the words to or too, as well as two, while a picture of a bee might be used to symbolize the word be. The word rebus is derived from the Latin word *res,* or thing.

References: *Teaching Reading to Slow and Disabled Learners,* Samuel A. Kirk et al. (1978); *Peabody Rebus Reading Program,* Richard W. Woodcock and Charlotte R. Clark (1970).

recital In education, the public demonstration of a student's skills in the performing arts, either alone or in concert with one or more other students. Recitals are often required in performing arts courses in lieu of the traditional final examination of academic courses. They are generally required, as well, as auditions for admission to specialized schools for the performing arts. Recitals may also be an extracurricular activity, in which students perform for the entertainment of fellow students, parents, faculty and friends. In all cases, they are essential instructionally for future public performers, who require preparation and emotions far different from that of instrumentalists who perform alone.

Reference: *Music Talks: Conversations with Musicians,* Helen Epstein (1987).

Reconstruction The decade (approximately) following the Civil War, during which normal relations were restored between the Union and the secessionist southern states. For education, Reconstruction meant the introduction of formal schooling of African Americans for the first time in their history. Moreover, Reconstruction also saw the first extension of the northern common, or public, school system to the South, thus introducing poor white children to their first formal schooling.

Reconstruction consisted of three phases: The first was a two-year period of relative self-rule, during which the southern states passed laws that all but restored slavery, in the guise of runaway-apprentice and contract-labor laws reminiscent of pre–Civil War fugitive slave laws. The second phase began with congressional passage of the First Reconstruction Act of 1867, dividing the South into five military districts, each under the control of a Union general charged with ensuring that each state draw up and ratify a constitution guaranteeing all citizens the right to vote, regardless of race, and mandating schools for all children, thus guaranteeing everyone the right to a public education. The

Reconstruction saw schools overflowing with African Americans of all ages hungry for education, after more than two centuries of slavery, during which the teaching of reading and writing to blacks was a crime in the South. (Library of Congress)

third phase began in 1868, with the readmission of the secessionist states to the Union, the restoration of self-rule, and ratification of the Fourteenth Amendment to the U.S. Constitution that declared everyone born in the United States a citizen thereof and thus guaranteed the privileges and protection of the federal Constitution. It thus extended to each state government all the constitutional restrictions that applied to the federal government. Reconstruction proper may be said to have ended in March 1870, with passage of the Fifteenth Amendment to the Constitution giving all citizens the right to vote and stripping states of the power to deny such rights on the basis of race, color or previous condition of servitude.

Within the framework of Reconstruction, public education generally and African-American education specifically spread southward by four methods: by church missionaries from the North, who opened schools for former African-American slaves; by fiat of the military governors, such as Gen. Samuel Chapman Armstrong (q.v.), who opened schools for former slaves on military bases; by order of Congress, which established the Freedman's Bureau (q.v.), charged inter alia with establishing free public schools and institutions of higher education for African Americans in the South; and by southern state governments themselves.

The end of Reconstruction and a return to self-rule saw southern states gradually reimpose tight restrictions on African Americans. Using every device from discriminatory taxes to terrorism, the states gradually deprived blacks of both the right to vote and the right to a minimal education. By 1874, white supremacy had been reestablished throughout the South, and schools were segregated along racial lines. Eager to restrict popular power, the states slashed educational budgets, effectively limiting comprehensive education to wealthy families who could afford to send their children to private schools. Reconstruction may thus be said to have brought public education and common school systems to the South, but, by the end of the 19th century, those schools ranked as the poorest in the United States, with Louisiana at the bottom.

References: *Northern Schools, Southern Blacks, and Reconstruction: Freedmen's Education, 1862–75,* Ronald E. Butchart (1980); *Reconstruction After the Civil War,* John Hope Franklin (1961); *Schools for All: The Blacks and Public Education in the South, 1865–1877,* William Preston Vaughan (1974).

reconstructionism A philosophy of education based on social reform and the spread and preservation of democracy as essential elements of formal schooling. An outgrowth of John Dewey's (q.v.) philosophy, reconstructionism grew as a movement in the 1930s, as the Depression devastated the United States, and a group of Columbia University Teachers College scholars—all disciples of Dewey—declared a need to reconstruct American society and the American economic system, through a redistribution of wealth. They further called for reconstruction of the educational system. They began their program by urging teachers to indoctrinate students in democratic principles, converting classrooms into laboratories of democratic behavior and social change. Among the reconstructionists were Teachers College professors Harold O. Rugg and George S. Counts (qq.v.). Counts was the first to articulate the reconstructionist program in a widely read pamphlet entitled "Dare the School Build a New Social Order?" Rugg translated the program into social studies texts that were widely distributed in public schools across the United States, until they were ordered burned by the American Legion and other patriotic groups.

Although reconstructionist ideas and pamphlets were the center of considerable discussion and debate among educators in graduate schools of education, they had little long-term, practical effect on elementary and secondary schoolteachers, desperately trying to teach basic academics while maintaining a semblance of order in overcrowded classrooms. While still of interest, reconstructionism has had little lasting effect on American education.

References: *Toward A Reconstructed Education,* Theodore Brameld (1956); *Introduction to the Philosophy of Education,* George Kneller (1971).

recreation In education, any structured or unstructured period of nonacademic activities organized for the relaxation and amusement of students. Generally used to describe the unstructured school playground or gymnasium activities of kindergarten and early elementary school children, recreation is absorbed by more structured physical education (q.v.) in the later elementary school years.

Reference: *Fundamentals of Recreation,* Thomas S. Yukic (1970).

redshirting A colloquialism, usually referring to the practice of some college football coaches of keeping younger players out of varsity competition for a year, to extend their eligibility while allowing them to develop more fully physically and thus be less prone to injuries. The term refers to the red shirts worn by members of the practice squad in scrimmages against the regular varsity players. National Collegiate Athletic Association rules permit students to play only four years of any given varsity sport. A redshirted freshman can thus postpone playing for the varsity until sophomore year and extend his varsity years into graduate school at age 23 or 24. The practice has led to widespread abuses that reach back into high school sports, with some parents and football coaches encouraging talented 13- and 14-year-olds to repeat their last year of middle school and thus enter high school stronger and better developed physically. The practice was first reported in the 1980s, in Alabama and Texas, where football often takes precedence over academic achievement. At the college level, some coaches ask potential players to repeat their senior year of high school for the same reason.

Ironically, redshirting, which was designed to improve school athletic records, has now spilled over into the academic sector, where some parents purposely extend preschool years to give their children a developmental advantage when they enter first grade. In Texas, an estimated 27% of five-year-olds were being retained in preschools in some districts, thus starting kindergarten at six years old and first grade at seven, according to a survey by the state board of education in 1990.

Reference: NYT; *College Sports Inc.,* Murray Sperber (1990).

Reeve, Tapping (1744–1823) American lawyer, jurist, educator and founder of the nation's first law school (q.v.). Born in Long Island, New York, he graduated from the College of New Jersey (now, Princeton University [qq.v.]) in 1763. Like most aspiring lawyers before the modern era, he studied law as an apprentice in a law firm, learning his trade through a combination of self-study, copying legal documents, informal association with and formal instruction from practicing lawyers and, eventually, limited practice under supervision.

In 1772, he opened a practice in the then-important town of Litchfield, Connecticut, where his skills quickly earned him a national reputation and drew more students than he could possibly train. To avoid repeating himself and to improve his teaching efficiency, he devised and opened what was the nation's first "law school" in 1774. The Litchfield Law School was a simple free-standing structure he built in his backyard. It was devoted entirely to instruction and study, and it quickly became the nation's preeminent institution of its kind. Reeve eventually worked out a curriculum consisting of a carefully planned series of lectures on 139 different areas of the law. Among his most notable students was the young Horace Mann (q.v.), who would later found the nation's first public school system in Massachusetts.

When Reeve was appointed to the Connecticut Superior Court in 1798, he called on a former student to help him run the school until 1820, when two more former students joined the faculty. It remained the nation's premier law school until its closure in 1833, when it could no longer compete with the expanded law departments at Harvard, Yale and Columbia colleges. Reeve went on to become chief justice of the Connecticut Supreme Court of Errors. He retired from the bench and public life in 1816. He devoted the rest of his life to writing definitive law texts, although he continued teaching until 1820.

References: DAB; *The Litchfield Law School, 1775–1833,* Samuel H. Fisher (1933).

reflective teaching A teacher-training program aimed at making public school teachers more insightful in their approaches to teaching and to problem solving. Started in the late 1960s, reflective teaching was designed to counter criticisms that public school teachers have few insights into why they teach given material and that they are mere automatons. Most teachers, it was said, merely fed students whatever materials were prescribed by state regents or district boards of education and referred all student problems to guidance counselors or administrators charged with problem solving.

There are a variety of complex approaches to reflective teaching. In broadest terms, these approaches call for careful description of a problem, with all its contributory elements, including self-evaluation and examination of the teacher's own contributions to the problem. In the academic sector, reflective teaching calls for a broad knowledge of the reasons for teaching a particular topic—the "why" of teaching as well as the "what." Reflective teaching practices are usually developed during in-service training, in conjunction with a supervisory mentor or master teacher.

Reference: *The Reflective Practitioner: How Professionals Think in Practice,* Donald A. Schon (1983).

Reformation The 16th-century ecclesiastical revolution in the Roman Catholic Church that created Protestantism and began the movement in the Western world toward universal public education. Although the Reformation had vast historical consequences, its implications for the history and evolution of education can be traced to one event: the translation of the Bible into a vernacular that permitted public access to a document that had hitherto been the closely guarded purview of the priesthood. The church hierarchy had used the Scriptures to justify despotic papal civil rule across western Europe, papal taxation, lavish spending by clerics at all levels for their personal pleasures, the sale of indulgences to laic transgressors and all the excesses and oppression that are ubiquitous elements of autocracies.

Resentment against papal taxation and rule by a distant, foreign papacy first made its appearance in England in the 14th century, when a dissident priest, John Wycliffe, saw the Bible translated into English and began preaching sermons in English rather than Latin. His teachings coincided with a peasants' revolt in England and were ultimately responsible for provoking nationalist uprisings in Bohemia in the 15th century and Germany in the 16th century. Moreover, Wycliffe's work influenced the young German priest Martin Luther, who finally rebelled against papal authority in 1517 and began the establishment of the first of the Protestant sects.

Swept up in the fervor of the Reformation was a young English priest, William Tyndale, who in 1524 retranslated the Bible into an English vernacular more accessible to the English masses than Wycliffe's translation. Banned in England and printed in Germany in 1525, copies began streaming into England. The fortuitous invention of the printing press in the 15th century produced new copies as quickly as church authorities could seize and burn them. By 1537, the bishop of Hereford, Edward Fox, warned a conference of bishops, "Make not yourselves the laughing-stock of the world; light is sprung up, and is scattering all the clouds. The low people know the Scriptures better than many of us.''

By then, Henry VIII had split with the Roman Catholic Church and declared himself the head of the Church of England, thus creating another Protestant church. In 1538, just two years after Tyndale had been executed for heresy, Henry ordered English Bibles placed in every church in England. Henry's proclamation was reconfirmed and honored during the subsequent regency, by the Catholic Queen Mary, and then by Henry's daughter, Elizabeth I.

Tyndale's Bible thus became a powerful instrument of popular education. It was written in a style that was particularly readable, and it therefore served as a basis for all subsequent English translations, including the Great Bible of 1539, published under the authority of Thomas Cranmer and Thomas Cromwell, and the King James Bible of 1611. Translated into the language of the laity, the Bible became an incentive to literacy the basis for all instruction in the English world, allowing ordinary people as well as an appointed few to become students for the first time in history. Intellectually, it gave the people, as well as an appointed clerical elite, access to ''The Word of God.'' By substituting individual textual examination, study and discussion for dogmatic doctrine, the translated Bibles provoked intellectual and religious freedoms that spawned an endless variety of Protestant sects. Ultimately, the translation of the Bible implied a trust in human reason from which the concept of universal public education was a natural outgrowth.

References: *The Reformation of the Sixteenth Century,* Roland H. Bainton (1952); *The English Reformation,* A. G. Dickens (1964); *The Protestant Mind of the English Reformation, 1570–1640,* Charles H. George and Katherine George (1961); *The Christian Scholar in the Age of the Reformation,* E. Harris Harbison (1955).

reformatory A custodial institution designed to reeducate and rehabilitate individuals deemed deviant or dependent and in need of spiritual, educational and physical care. Originally the purview of private, charitable organizations, reformatories gradually evolved into quasi-public and, finally, publicly operated institutions over the first half of the 19th century. It is only in the second half of that century that they became penal institutions. A group of New York City Protestant evangelical churches was responsible for founding the first reformatory. Called the Orphan Asylum, it was a shelter that provided instruction in reading, writing, arithmetic and domestic affairs, along with ''a sound moral education in a homelike atmosphere, presided over by a pious and respectable man and his wife.'' Ten years later, the New York Society for the Prevention of Pauperism set out to determine the causes of poverty in order to eliminate it in New York City. After nearly a decade of investigation, it established the House of Refuge in 1825, as a residential facility to provide homeless boys with moral rehabilitation and training in mechanical skills. By 1840, it had become the official New York State agency in New York City for the rehabilitation of juvenile delinquents, giving a reformatory the connotation of a penal institution for the first time.

State and federal reformatories, or training schools, as they are often called, remain penal institutions for young offenders, usually ranging in age from 16 to 25 years, depending on state law. Unlike prisons, which are designed to punish, reformatories continue to be concerned with the physical, psychological and moral development and rehabilitation of inmates, and they continue to provide academic and vocational education. Inmates are usually given indeterminate sentences, with release determined by behavior and developmental progress.

References: EB; *House of Refuge: Origins of Juvenile Reform in New York State, 1815–1857,* Robert S. Pickett (1969).

Reformed churches Protestant Calvinist churches with their origins on the Continent rather than in England and Scotland. Similar in many respects to Puritanism, Congregationalism, Presbyterianism and other reformed churches that originated in the British Isles, the Continental Reformed churches bear the name of their countries of origin—Dutch Reformed, German Reformed, etc.

(See individual churches for their influence on American education.)

Reference: *The Encyclopedia of American Religions,* Gordon J. Melton (1992).

regents Members of a governing board with policy-setting powers and authority over the operations of public education. The term is variously used to mean members of the governing board for all state education, as in the New York State Board of Regents, or simply the board of trustees of a state university, as in the Board of Regents of the University of California. The term is a carefully chosen one, referring back to regents who ruled with the full authority of the king in his absence. Thus, regents in American education were originally appointed by and ruled with the full authority of the state executive or governor, although regents in some states are now elected. Their role and powers differ somewhat from those of trustees, who are entrusted with authority over private schools and are elected on the basis of their proven commitment to long-range institutional goals rather than to the goals of a single governor or constituency.

Reference: ERIC.

Regents Examinations Standardized competency examinations required of all public elementary and secondary school students by a state board of regents for promotion to the next higher grade or for graduation from high school. In 1913, New York State's Board of Regents established the first such examinations in core subjects such as English, mathematics, social studies, science and foreign languages.

Reference: *History of the State Education Department,* F. P. Graves (vol. 9 of *History of the State of New York,* 1937).

regional educational research laboratories In education, a nationwide network of geographically dispersed centers funded by the U.S. Government under Title IV of the Elementary and Secondary Education Act of 1965 (q.v.), to improve the quality of education in public elementary and secondary schools. Although 20 such laboratories were funded by the act, only nine remained after 20 years: Appalachia Educational Laboratory, Charleston, West Virginia; CEMREL, Inc., St. Louis, Missouri; Far West Laboratory for Educational Research and Development, San Francisco, California; Mid-Continent Regional Educational Laboratory, Aurora, Colorado; The Network, Inc., Andover, Massachusetts; Northwest Regional Educational Laboratory, Portland, Oregon; Research for Better Schools, Philadelphia, Pennsylvania; Southwest Educational Development Laboratory, Austin, Texas; SWRL Educational Research and Development, Los Angeles, California. Notable for massive amounts of monographs and educational design proposals, the laboratories produced few practical reforms or improvements in education in their regions. The regional laboratories had no direct, administrative ties to the 14 Research and Development Centers (q.v.) of the Office of Educational Research and Improvement at the U.S. Department of Education, although the latter did provide some funding for some regional-laboratory research projects.

Reference: Office of Educational Research and Improvement, U.S. Department of Education, Washington, D.C.

registrar A college or university official charged with officially registering and keeping the rolls—including course-enrollment records and grades—of all students attending the institution.

Reference: *Handbook of College and University Administration,* Asa S. Knowles, ed. (1970).

registration In higher education, a term with two meanings, namely, the annual process of entering one's name on the official record of students attending an educational institution and the process of enrolling in specific classes or courses. Institutions of higher education have varied registration requirements, with some requiring only annual registration and others requiring it at the beginning of each semester. In primary and secondary schools, registration is usually required only once at any single school, when the child first enrolls. The single registration is valid until the child either graduates to a higher level school or moves to a new community and enters a new school.

Reference: *Handbook of College and University Administration,* Asa S. Knowles, ed. (1970).

regression In education, a temporary reversion to an earlier level of behavior by an otherwise normal child experiencing normal developmental progress. Not to be confused with the more serious, psychological term, regression is a normal aspect of child and adolescent development. Two kinds of regression are most common in the classroom: intellectual and behavioral. The former manifests itself in memory lapses: A student temporarily forgets or is suddenly unable to perform or demonstrate routine material he or she had apparently mastered. Usually, such regression disappears after adequate repetition and achievement of true mastery. Behavioral regression manifests itself in conduct that is inappropriate for the particular student's age and is usually the consequence of a particular event. Teachers can often help students overcome such problems by quiet, one-to-one discussions designed to elicit the cause of the regression. The more serious, psychological regression usually involves long-term, infantile behavioral problems requiring professional psychological or psychiatric help.

References: *Educational Psychology: An Introduction,* Gary S. Belkin and Jerry L. Gray (1977).

regular education initiative An approach to mainstreaming that integrates special education and other resources, teachers and specialists into regular classrooms to provide special help to regular students as well as to special education students with chronic extra needs. The goal of the regular education initiative is to avoid labeling students with special needs and isolating them from their classmates in special-resource classrooms. By working as a team, special education and regular teachers integrate all daily instruction—special and regular—into a single, unified educational program. While filling the needs of special education students, such teams also provide the occasional, extra, in-classroom help that almost all regular students also need from time to time.

Reference: *Making the Best of Schools,* Jeannie Oakes & Martin Lipton (1990).

Rehabilitation Act of 1973 A landmark federal law that prohibited discrimination on the basis of physical handicaps by any public or private organization receiving federal funds, directly or indirectly, and mandated the elimination of architectural barriers that interfered with access by the handicapped to a publicly used building. The law opened all schoolhouse and college doors to the physically handicapped for the first time in American history. The law specifically barred discrimination in hiring on the basis of physical handicaps, and it barred handicap-based discrimination in admissions by all schools and social-service organizations. The law also required federal contractors, including educational institutions fulfilling federal contracts, to "take affirmative action to employ and advance handicapped individuals." The act was amended in 1984 and again in 1986 to require expanded services, including rehabilitative vocational education, for the severely handicapped. As a result of the various acts, the number of physically handicapped children attending American public elementary and secondary schools climbed from a negligible amount when the first act was passed in 1973 to nearly 3 million students, or more than 7% of the school-aged population, 20 years later.

Reference: *Free Appropriate Public Education: The Law and Children with Disabilities,* H. Rutherford Turnbull III (1986).

reinforcement A psychological term referring to rewards (positive reinforcement) or punishments (negative reinforcement) that encourage or discourage repetition of a particular type of behavior. In the classroom, teachers routinely use praise, high grades, and extra privileges and responsibilities to reinforce positive social and academic behavior.

Reference: *Educational Psychology: Mastering Principles and Applications,* Janice T. Gibson and Louis A. Chandler (1988).

released time A specific period, usually toward the end of the school day, during which a student, at the request of his or her parents, is permitted to leave school to attend religious instruction at a nonschool site. Released time does not relieve the student of responsibility for learning the work covered in the regular classroom and for all homework assignments. Released time affects only individual students, and nonparticipating students must remain in school until regular dismissal.

Released time represents a compromise between two groups with diametrically opposed, but nonetheless sincere interpretations of the First Amendment of the Constitution (q.v.). On the one side are those for whom any religious practice in school represents a violation of the First Amendment's Establishment Clause (q.v.) mandating separation of church and state. Opposed to them are those who see any ban on religious practice as a violation of First Amendment guarantees of freedom to practice religion. In 1948, the U.S. Supreme Court ruled in *McCollum v. Board of Education* (q.v.) that clerics could not come into public schools to offer religious instruction, but in 1952 it ruled in *Zorach v. Clauson* (q.v.) that students had a constitutional right under the First Amendment's guarantee of freedom of worship to obtain religious instruction off school premises. The state, in other words, could not forbid a student from leaving school to practice his or her religion. Moreover, released time did not violate the principal of church-state separation so long as the school was neutral and nonparticipatory and spent no funds to facilitate such religious instruction and held all students responsible for the schoolwork they missed.

Reference: U.S. Supreme Court proceedings.

religion In American education, an institutionalized set of beliefs based on a power or being superior to humans and ultimately responsible for the creation and governing of humanity and the universe. Religions—for the most part Protestant Christian religions—were the basis of all education in the American colonies. With independence, Americans and their educators ignored the Establishment Clause (q.v.) of the First Amendment that was aimed at separating church and state. Indeed, six states (New Hampshire, Massachusetts, Connecticut, Maryland, Virginia and South Carolina) had official religions and mandated or permitted taxes for the support of public teachers of the Christian religion. It was not until 1833 that the last of these six states, Massachusetts, disestablished its official religion. Disestablishment did not end the continuing conflict between constitutionalist defenders of the First Amendment and those who seek to introduce religion into public education and American life generally. Although state after state has sought to introduce daily prayers into their elementary and secondary public school curricula, the U.S. Supreme Court has consistently ruled such efforts a violation of the Establishment Clause.

(For a fuller discussion, see ABINGTON SCHOOL DISTRICT V. SCHEMPP; CHILD BENEFIT THEORY; CHURCH-STATE CONFLICTS; RELEASED TIME.)

Reference: *The Uneasy Boundary: Church and State,* Dean M. Kelly and Richard D. Lambert (1979).

Religious Education Association An association of religious educators founded in 1903 to promote broad programs of Christian education in the home, the church, the Sunday school and the public school. Guided in its early years by George Albert Coe, it failed in its attempts to introduce prayer and religious instruction in the public school curriculum, but did spearhead the widespread practice of church-sponsored released time (q.v.), whereby public schools permit students to leave school early to obtain off-premises religious instruction.

Reference: *Education in Religion and Morals,* George A. Coe (1904).

religious schools   A wide variety of part-time and full-time schools sponsored by or affiliated directly or indirectly with individual churches and religious groups. Part-time religious schools, such as Sunday schools, usually offer instruction devoted entirely to religion. Although instruction at some full-time religious schools is intensively religious, the majority of such schools offer a general academic as well as religious instruction. There are more than 21,000 full-time religious elementary and secondary schools, with just over 4 million students. They constitute nearly 18% of all elementary and secondary schools in the United States and hold almost 7.4% of the total student population. Religious schools make up 80% of all private schools and have 86% of the private school population. Roman Catholic schools make up the largest percentage of religious schools, with nearly 43% of the total number. Of the 3,573 institutions of higher education in the United States in 1992, 933, or about 26%, were religiously affiliated, and their nearly 1.4 million students made up more than 9.4% of the nearly 14.5 million students in all institutions of higher education.

Religious schools do not necessarily limit their enrollments to students of the faith with which the school is affiliated. Indeed, many are open to students of all faiths, although they include clergy on their faculties and some, at the elementary and secondary levels, require all students to attend services and classes in religious instruction.

(See also PAROCHIAL SCHOOL.)

Reference: DES.

remedial reading   A program of special instruction to correct deficiencies in a student's previous reading development. Not designed for students with learning disabilities or other incapacities, remedial reading is simply corrective instruction for normal students whose previous reading development was in some way stunted or impaired by external factors such as cultural deprivation or a late start in school. Remedial reading programs merely provide one-to-one "catch-up" instruction by a remedial specialist. As in normal reading programs, remedial reading instruction teaches visual and sound discrimination, letter recognition, sound recognition, sound blending, recognition of word meanings and word-attack skills (q.v.).

References: *How to Increase Reading Ability,* Albert J. Harris and Edward Jr. Sipay (1985); *Diagnostic and Remedial Reading for Classroom and Clinic,* Robert M. Wilson and Craig J. Cleland (1989).

remediation program   A broad-based instructional program to correct multiple deficiencies in a student's educational development. Such remediation may include remedial reading, remedial mathematics and special assistance in a variety of other subjects such as science or foreign languages. Designed to focus on the student's entire academic development, remediation programs range from "extra help" during a free period or after school to complex prescriptive programs that may involve modifying course content, introduction of unorthodox instructional methods, instruction in learning skills, possible changes in the student's home or school learning environment, and even behavior modification.

Reference: *The Handbook of Special Education: Research and Practices,* Margaret C. Wang, M. C. Reynolds and Herbert J. Walberg, eds. (1988).

Renaissance   Literally a rebirth, referring roughly to the period in European history, from 1300 to 1600, that saw the flowering of Europe's first universities and colleges and explosive advances and changes in art, science, technology, philosophy and political systems. Considered by many scholars a turning point in

Western civilization, the Renaissance was a period of intellectual ferment that encouraged the emergence of humanists who tested medieval conceptions of the universe that had, with the support of the Catholic Church, dominated all Western thought. The humanists reexamined man's role in the universe and concluded that man shared control over nature with God. The humanists rediscovered and celebrated such pre-Christian human achievements as the art and architecture and the literary, historical, philosophical and scientific works of ancient Greece and Rome. One result of this expansion of intellectual frontiers, was a broadening of education. Secular education—including classical literature, the sciences and mathematics—began to infiltrate the hitherto all-religious curricula of schools and colleges. By the 17th century, when the first schools and colleges opened in the American colonies, primary and secondary education was extended to nontheological students. By the beginning of the next century, even theological colleges such as Harvard and Yale (qq.v.) had expanded their curricula and were welcoming students of the sciences and the humanities, as well as future clerics.

(See also REFORMATION.)

References: *Renaissance and Reformation,* Trevor Cairns (1987); *Classics of Western Thought: Middle Ages, Renaissance and Reformation,* Karl F. Thompson, ed. (1988).

Rensselaer Institute

The first private college in the United States devoted exclusively to instruction of engineering and the sciences. Founded in 1824 in Troy, New York, Rensselaer was actually the second American college to teach engineering; the first, West Point, was not only a government institution but also limited its instruction to building fortifications and other military installations. A growing need for engineers to work on civil projects led to the opening of Rensselaer (now, Polytechnic) Institute in Rensselaer County, which had been part of the tract of land owned by Killian van Rens-

selaer, the Dutch gem merchant who was a founder and director of the Dutch West India Company, which colonized the area. In addition to engineering, the Rensselaer Institute's original curriculum included chemistry, botany, zoology and the teaching of agricultural techniques and the use of fertilizer in the cultivation of vegetables. Along with West Point, Rensselaer pioneered the development of advanced mathematics, chemistry, physics and laboratory instruction in the natural sciences. When liberal arts colleges later added sciences and engineering to their curricula, they used the instructional models developed at West Point and Rensselaer.

An all-male institution when founded, RPI is now a coeducational institution, with women comprising about 20% of the undergraduate student body of about 4,400. In addition to undergraduate and graduate science and engineering, which continue to be the centerpieces of its curriculum, RPI now offers undergraduate and graduate programs in architecture, management, the humanities and social sciences. RPI also has five graduate schools.

References: *Barron's Profiles of American Colleges* (new edition); *Engineering in American Society,* Raymond H. Merritt (1969); Rensselaer Polytechnic Institute Library, Troy, New York.

report card

A record of a student's grades for the marking period, term or school year. Report card (or grade card) formats vary from school to school and according to the level of education. In preschool and the early elementary school years, "grades" are usually in the form of general assessments, such as "unsatisfactory" (or "needs improvement," in the gentler schools), "satisfactory" and "excellent." Letter or percent grades for each subject replace such designations as the student progresses to the later elementary years and to middle or high school. At the preprimary, elementary and secondary school levels, report cards invariably include teacher comments on the student's academic and social progress.

In higher education, the report card is replaced with the "transcript," which is simply a running record of grades and courses studied, along with accumulated credits toward graduation.

Reference: ERIC.

republican (style of) education A term used by scholars to describe the basis of American education, which predicated the preservation of the new Republic on state-sponsored, universal public education. First articulated by John Adams and Thomas Jefferson in the 1760s and 1770s, republican education was based on four beliefs: that the survival of the future nation would depend on responsible exercise of citizenship; that the responsible exercise of such citizenship was possible only with universal education of the citizenry; that the most effective way of educating the citizenry was through a system of hierarchal schools open to all—primary schools, academies, colleges and universities—and through which citizens would progress according to their abilities; and that the system would be tied to and controlled by public financial support and be supervised by public officials.

Quite simply, Jefferson believed, "If a nation expects to be ignorant and free, in a state of civilization, it expects what never was and never will be." A proponent of a nationally controlled system of education, Jefferson had the strong support of Adams, Benjamin Rush, Benjamin Franklin and James Madison. ". . . a people who mean to be their own Governors," said Madison, "must arm themselves with the power which knowledge gives."

Madison and Jefferson's pleas for constitutional creation of a national system of education were rejected by northern industrialists who depended on child labor for their profits and southern plantation owners who depended on slaves of all ages for theirs. Although a republican style of education eventually emerged in the United States, it required more than a century to evolve on a state-by-state basis—often (especially in the south) in forms that seemed as travesties to what Jefferson, Adams and Madison had envisioned.

References: *American Education: The National Experience, 1783–1876,* Lawrence A. Cremin (1979); *Liberalism and American Education in the Eighteenth Century,* Allen Oscar Hansen (1926); *Essays on Education in the Early Republic,* Frederick Rudolph, ed. (1965).

ReQuest A "shorthand" title for a reading-instruction technique called requestioning, in which teacher and students all read the same passage silently, then pose questions to each other and initiate involved discussion and analysis of the passage and its implications. At first, most questions are teacher-initiated, but the technique is designed to encourage increasingly active student ideation, questioning and in-depth analysis that provide the basis for answering the questions of others.

Reference: *ReQuest in Prereading Activities for Content Area Reading and Learning,* David W. Moor, John E. Readance and Robert J. Rickelman (1982).

Research and Development Centers A group of 14 educational research centers established by the federal government in 1963 at major universities across the United States. Designed to bring groups of scholars from various disciplines together to work on educational improvement projects, the centers had a record of mixed success in producing major educational reforms in public education. Three decades after their founding, only half remained in existence—at Ohio State and Stanford universities, at the universities of Oregon, Pittsburgh, Texas and Wisconsin and at the University of California at Los Angeles (UCLA). However, the surviving centers—most notably Oregon, Stanford and UCLA—were responsible for developing a number of impressive and far-reaching programs such as Stanford's Accelerated Schools Project (q.v.) for improving educational quality of American public schools.

(See also EDUCATION REFORM.)

References: Office of Educational Research and Improvement, U.S. Department of Education, Washington, D.C.; *Educational Research: An Introduction,* Walter R. Borg and Meredith D. Gall (1989).

"research" companies   Commercial firms that sell students essays and term papers. A widespread industry, with mail-order facilities and branches near most four-year colleges and universities, research firms have catalogs containing as many as 20,000 research reports—usually of poor quality —on virtually every topic covered in college courses. The firms generally charge between $5 and $10 a page for stock reports selected from their catalogs. They charge $25, $50 or even more per page for custom-made reports prepared to a client's specifications and written by free-lance writers. Although some states, such as New York and New Jersey, outlaw the sale of papers submitted to meet course or degree requirements, research firms skirt such laws by requiring purchasers to sign disclaimers that state they do not intend to submit their purchases to academic institutions. Moreover, many research firms stamp each page with a statement: "Prepared by (name of firm), for research and reference use only." Students simply rewrite such reports on their own paper before submission. No statistics exist on the number of such companies, the number of papers they provide students or the frequency of student reliance on such firms.

Reference: NYT.

research university   A university whose overall educational goals include development of new knowledge as well as the teaching of existing knowledge. Thus, faculty and staff at research universities generally divide their time (not necessarily evenly) between classroom instruction (in the sciences and arts) and laboratory and field experimentation and exploration (in the sciences) and historical and critical investigation (in the arts).

Reference: *Handbook of College and University Administration,* Asa S. Knowles, ed. (1970).

Reserve Officers Training Corps (ROTC)

The generic term for a variety of programs, such as the Air Force Reserve Officers Training Corps, the Army Reserve Officers Training Corps and the Naval Reserve Officers Training Corps (qq.v.), which prepare college students for commissions in the Armed Services. The ROTC programs were successor organizations to the Army Specialized Training Program and V-12 (qq.v.) programs of World War II, which trained college students as officers at a time when the military academies could not fill the needs of the Armed Services. A once-ubiquitous presence on the larger college campuses, ROTC was forced off many campuses during the Vietnam War, when students protested its presence as an arm of the United States Department of Defense, which the students perceived as an agency that was pursuing an illegal war. Harvard student protestors forced the college to shut down in the spring of 1969, and students at Kent State University (q.v.) in Ohio burned down the ROTC building on their campus in May of the following year. Two days later, National Guard troops that had been called on campus to quell the disturbances fired on students, hitting 13 protesters and killing four. One by one, colleges across America began severing their ties with ROTC until, by the mid-1990s, fewer than 200 colleges were still offering one or more ROTC programs.

References: U.S. Department of Defense, Arlington, Virginia.

residence halls   Those buildings on a school, college or university campus where students live during the school year.

Reference: *Handbook of College and University Administration,* Asa S. Knowles, ed. (1970).

residency requirement   In education, a state or local ordinance requiring that students attending free public schools be residents of the school district. At the higher education level, all state universities require that students be residents of the state to be eligible for reduced tuition fees. Residency requirements may or may not include durational qualifications, depending on the level of education. Most state laws require that every elementary and secondary public school provide education to every child in their district immediately after the child's family establishes residency. Most state colleges and universities, however, require that students spend at least one academic year in the state before granting the tuition reductions to which resident students are entitled.

References: ERIC; *Handbook of College and University Administration*, Asa S. Knowles, ed. (1970).

residential academy In modern education, a state-financed boarding school for gifted high school students. Public residential academies are open to any students who pass qualifying entrance examinations or, in the case of schools of music and art, have successful auditions or present acceptable portfolios. Residential academies were founded to meet the needs of widely scattered rural students too far from any major city to attend day magnet schools (q.v.). Attendance is usually limited to high school juniors and seniors mature enough to live away from home for long periods of time.

The North Carolina School for Science and Mathematics, in Durham, was the first such state-financed residential academy; like other, similar facilities, it is located near a thriving university and industrial research area, where the school can take advantage of skilled mentors and where students can avail themselves of advanced study and research facilities. Founded in 1980, it became a model for similar schools in many other states. By the mid-1990s, nine other states had such academies and still others, including New York and Massachusetts, were preparing to establish similar institutions. Among the earlier state residential academies (with the years of their founding) are the Louisiana School for Math, Science and the Arts (Natchitoches, 1983); Illinois Math and Science Academy (Aurora, 1985); Texas Academy of Mathematics and Science (Denton, 1987); Indiana Academy for Science, Mathematics and Humanities (Muncie, 1988); Mississippi School for Mathematics and Science (Columbus, 1988); South Carolina Governor's School for Science and Mathematics (Hartsville, 1988); and Oklahoma School of Science and Mathematics (Oklahoma City, 1990).

References: ERIC; NYT.

residential school In modern education, any educational institution that provides room and board as well as regular instruction. Now usually synonymous with boarding school (q.v.), the term is occasionally used to mean an institution where children are committed involuntarily either for custodial care, in the case of the severely handicapped (mentally or physically), or for treatment of severe health or behavioral problems. Custodial residential institutions have largely been replaced by so-called halfway houses (q.v.), where small groups of youngsters live in homelike conditions within a community. Moreover, the federal Education for All Handicapped Children Act of 1975 (q.v.) requires education of the handicapped in the least restrictive environment appropriate for their needs.

References: ERIC; *Residential Facilities for the Mentally Retarded*, Alfred A. Baumeister and Earl Butterfield, eds. (1970).

resident student In higher education, a state university student who is a legal resident of the state and therefore entitled to a lower tuition rate than nonresident students. To qualify as a resident student, the individual must usually have been a legal resident of the state for at least one academic year prior to enrolling at the state college or university. The term resident student differs from residential student, referring to any student who lives on campus during part or all of the school year.

Reference: *Handbook of College and University Administration*, Asa S. Knowles, ed. (1970).

resistance training Instruction of elementary school children in techniques of rejecting temptations to participate in immoral or illegal behavior, ranging from name-calling or racism to chemical substance abuse or premature sex. Far from a proven approach, resistance training replaced traditional scare tactics aimed at frightening children with graphic representations of the possible effects of substance abuse and other self-destructive behavior (quite simply, too many youngsters were aware of some peers who had successfully survived drugs with few ill effects). Resistance training is based on teaching children decision-making skills to cope with a variety of stress situations, including peer pressure. While stressing the benefits of physical activity and fitness, resistance training uses role playing to give children practice in resisting the temptations of unacceptable behavior.

Reference: *The Elementary School Handbook,* Joanne Oppenheim (1989).

resource room Any classroom equipped for the special education (q.v.) of students with specific learning disabilities, mental or physical handicaps or emotional or behavioral problems. Staffed by specially trained resource, or special education, teachers, resource rooms are usually equipped to handle no more than four students at a time. Students meet for 30 to 120 minutes a day for individualized instruction—either in lieu of regular classroom work, in the case of elementary school students, or, in the case of secondary school students, during free periods or in lieu of one or more courses. Designed to supplement the regular classroom instruction of special-needs students, resource rooms contain special projectors, charts, screens and other devices that help retrain students to learn in ways that bypass specific learning disabilities. Thus, one type of projector may cast the letters C, A, T three feet apart on a screen—a distance too great for most dyslexics to see them in reverse order. By gradually bringing the letters together, the dyslexic learns to differentiate the letters in ever-closer proximity, until at last the word is perceived as an entity rather than in constantly shifting symbols.

Reference: *The Organization and Management of the Resource Room: A Cookbook Approach,* Howard Drucker (1976).

resource teacher A teacher trained in special education (q.v.) to meet the instructional needs of the learning disabled, the mentally or physically handicapped and the emotionally or behaviorally unadjusted. Resource teachers test, evaluate and design individualized instructional programs and techniques and provide instruction, either in the regular classroom, in cooperation with regular teachers, or in a special resource room (q.v.).

Reference: *The Resource Teacher: A Guide to Effective Practice,* J. Lee Wiederholt (1978).

retention The forced repetition, for whatever reason, of a school year; the opposite of promotion (q.v.). Retention is also sometimes used to refer to the penalty of detention at school for a specific period after the end of the school day, as penance for misbehavior.

Reference: ERIC.

retirement The voluntary or involuntary termination of service. Retirement in education is usually mandatory at a specific age, depending on the state and whether the institution is part of the public elementary and secondary education system or the state college and university system. The vast majority of school systems permit voluntary retirement with benefits for vested teachers at age 60. Public school systems require all teachers to participate in retirement programs that provide lifetime income and various benefits, including health insurance, disability insurance and death benefits for family survivors. Retirement programs vary from state to state, with some reserved for teachers only, others open to all workers in education, and still others open all state employees, including teachers. Funding also varies, with some programs funded entirely by the state and others funded partially by state contributions and partially by teachers themselves. Unvested plans are not portable from one state to another. Although always entitled to recover the funds they invested in their pension plans, teachers are not entitled to state contributions until such plans become vested after the teacher has worked a specified number of years. The number varies from fewer than five to as many as 20 years, depending on the state; until a teacher has worked public schools in the state for the required number of years, he or she loses all claim to the state contributions in their plan if they move to a job in another state. In addition to income from the teacher's retirement program, teachers are also entitled to Social Security income and benefits. Retirement programs for faculty at colleges, universities and independent private schools are usually provided through the Teachers Insurance and Annuity Association and College Retirement Equities Fund (TIAA-CREF) (q.v.).

Reference: American Federation of Teachers, Washington, D.C.; National Education Association, Chicago, Illinois.

return sweep   The shift of a reader's eyes from the end of one line to the beginning of the next. Inaccurate return sweep often causes readers to skip lines and lose the meaning of the passage they are reading. To overcome inaccurate return sweep, teachers often give students an opaque straight-edge to block out all but the subsequent line.

Reference: *How to Increase Reading Ability*, Albert J. Harris and Edward Jr. Sipay (1985).

Revolutionary War   The war in which the American colonies declared and won their independence from England. For education, the Revolutionary War—or War of Independence, as it's called in Britain—was a source not only of immediate disruption, but also of pivotal, long-term changes. Colleges were especially disrupted. Indeed, of all the colleges standing in the colonies, only newly chartered Dartmouth, in

the forests of faraway New Hampshire, was left unscathed.

Harvard's (q.v.) buildings were appropriated, forcing faculty and students to move to Concord. Yale (q.v.) had to move to three inland towns because of food shortages. Although classes resumed in New Haven in 1778, the faculty and students were forced to join in the defense of the city against invading British troops the following year. King's College (now Columbia [q.v.]) was the target of mob violence in New York and later occupied by British troops. It discreetly changed its name to Columbia after the war. Queen's College (now Rutgers) in New Jersey was, unfortunately, located in the center of the British stronghold in New Brunswick, and was forced to move eight miles west during the war. The College of New Jersey (q.v.) in nearby Princeton was used alternately as barracks for British and Continental troops, and the successive battles to keep or regain control of the town left Nassau Hall in ruins at the end of the war. The College of Philadelphia (q.v.) (later the University of Pennsylvania) experienced similar changes of control and suspended all operations in 1777, as did the College of Rhode Island (q.v.) (Brown University), in Providence. The College of William and Mary (q.v.) suspended operations during the battle of Yorktown, which left the president's house badly damaged by French troops.

Education at the primary and secondary level, whether held in churches or in free-standing schools, also came to a halt wherever troops passed through or were stationed, because such structures were the first to be commandeered as barracks. But when education resumed, following a battle or the war itself, it included an entirely new curriculum based on a new American history and ideology of individual liberty and freedom from the tyranny of state and church and the doctrine of predestination. The Revolutionary War, in short, produced a revolution in American education as well as in the political system: It gave rise to notions of republican education (q.v.), based on the belief that, if the people were to govern themselves effectively, they would have to be universally educated—that the survival of the republic depended on an educated electorate. Thus, the Revolution promoted the concept of universal public education, a concept that would take nearly a century to implement, but one that nevertheless became an integral part of American life.

The Revolution also opened the door to secular education. No longer was the Bible the sole reason for learning one's letters; mechanics, agriculture and the practical skills of building a new nation became the highest educational priorities. When Thomas Jefferson (q.v.) founded the University of Virginia (q.v.), he purposely omitted all theological courses from the curriculum, which concentrated on architecture, mathematics, engineering, law, the sciences and arts. Divinity, which had been the primary purpose of pre-Revolution colleges, was nowhere mentioned. God and king would not govern the United States; man would have to do the job. Even the English language was revolutionized, with the postwar publication in 1783 of Noah Webster's (q.v.) new American spelling book, which threw off as many orthographical ties to England as possible.

Reference: *The American Revolution Considered as a Social Movement,* J. Franklin Jameson (1926); *The American Revolution Reconsidered,* Richard B. Morris (1967).

reward and punishment training   The application of behavioral theory, or behavior modification techniques, to instruction, providing the learner with pleasure for desirable behavior and pain for undesirable behavior. For some pre-school learning, such as lining up to leave the playground at the sound of a whistle, quieting down when a teacher raises a hand and other behavior that requires minimal cooperation or understanding, reward and punishment can be effective teaching techniques. Praise, a teacher's smile, good grades (or their equivalent), extra time for play and public recognition, and frowns, threats, ostracism and loss of privi-

leges are all relatively effective techniques for teaching certain types of behavior. But all studies of early learning techniques indicate that rewards and punishments do not help children learn more or get better academic grades. Reward and punishment training may even encourage cheating. All indications are that the link between learning and the eventual reward or punishment (high or low grades, promotion or retention, etc.) is too obscure for preschool and early elementary school children to recognize. Moreover, in associating punishment and reward with academic work, children learn to substitute gratification from grades for the pleasure of learning and mastering new skills and knowledge—a concept that can render the youngster a disservice in secondary school and higher education.

Reference: *Making the Best of Schools,* Jeannie Oakes & Martin Lipton (1990).

rhetoric   The art or skill of oratory that was an essential and required element of American and Western education until the last half of the 20th century. Derived from the Greek word *rhetor,* or orator, rhetoric (with grammar and logic) was one of the three preliminary subjects in the trivium (q.v.), which, together with the four advanced subjects in the quadrivium, formed the traditional core curriculum of the seven liberal arts (q.v.) in Western medieval universities.

Rhetoric's routes go back to the establishment of democracy in ancient Athens in 510 B.C. and the requirement that all male citizens participate in the assembly and the making of laws. Oratory became essential to success, influence and power in the assembly, and a group of teachers, known as the Sophists, immediately began developing and teaching rhetoric. The scholar Plato mocked the Sophists for corrupting rhetoric and focusing on persuasion rather than truth. Aristotle's *Rhetoric* supported Plato's ideas, saying that the function of rhetoric was not to appeal to listener emotions to persuade but to present a logical sequence of ideas that inevitably led listeners to the truth. He called rhetoric the sister art of logic.

Rhetoric remained essential in universities throughout the Middle Ages and well into the 18th century, so long as Western Europe, England and the American colonies comprised what was essentially an oral culture. In colleges and universities, pedagogy was based on the lecture, the declamation and the disputation, with the master using the lecture as an oral textbook to expose a body of knowledge and pose questions about each element. Students, in turn, were expected to read all available books on the subject and "declaim," or display that knowledge orally before the class. In the disputations that followed, students engaged in formal arguments or debates about questions raised by a moderator. Rhetoric was essential to successful declamation and disputation, and it was an integral part of the required curriculum at Harvard College, the first college founded in the American colonies in the early 17th century. Successful rhetoric required clarity of expression, style, quick wit and a depth of intellect and knowledge. As late as 1950, rhetoric remained a requirement at many of the most selective independent private secondary schools and colleges. As American educational culture became more audiovisual than oral, rhetoric gradually disappeared as a requirement—replaced with short, elective courses in "public speaking."

References: EB; *Expression and Meaning,* J. R. Searle (1985).

Rhode Island   Last of the original 13 states to join the Union and one of the first to establish a free, universal public education system. Officially named the State of Rhode Island and the Providence Plantations, Rhode Island by itself is a large island county in the middle of Narragansett Bay. "Discovered" by the Dutch explorer Adriaen Block (Block Island) and named Roode Eylandt (perhaps for its red clay), it was settled by the religious leader Roger Williams, who founded Providence in 1636 as a haven of religious tolerance. A deep believer in individual freedom of religion, he repudiated both the Church of England, in which he had taken orders, and the Puritans of Massachusetts, whom he had later joined, for using the powers of civil government to enforce religious principles. Banished from Massachusetts, he made Providence the first colony (and the first state) to impose complete separation of church and state and guarantee religious and racial toleration. As the first president of Rhode Island, Williams not only respected the rights of American Indians, he also saw to it that the colony provided a safe haven for Jews, Quakers and other persecuted religious groups. The oldest standing Jewish house of worship built in the Americas, Touro Synagogue, still stands in Providence.

In 1840, Newport became the first Rhode Island community to establish a free school. Because of religious tolerance, however, no single church was able to establish a statewide system of education, as the Puritan churches were able to do in Massachusetts, for example. The result was a more haphazard educational establishment, based largely on the willingness of a churchman here or there to teach the children of his congregation or on the desire of a community to read, write and calculate. One early teacher was the Baptist minister James Manning, who organized a Latin School in Warren, Rhode Island, in 1764. In 1765, he expanded and changed its name to the College of Rhode Island (q.v.). In 1770, he moved it to Providence, where it eventually was renamed Brown University (q.v.).

Nevertheless, the development of education was slow, and by 1843 the state had so few schools and so illiterate a population that it faced an exodus of industry and trade to better cultured areas, such as Boston, New Haven and New York, which were training literate labor forces. At the suggestion of Horace Mann, who had founded the public school system in neighboring Massachusetts, the governor of Rhode Island and the legislature invited Henry Barnard (q.v.) to establish a statewide system of public schools and a teacher training school.

Rhode Island has just under 300 public elementary and secondary schools, with about

135,000 students. An additional 20,000 students attend private school. Rhode Island public schools rank about average for the nation in terms of academic quality. The state has two public and nine private four-year institutions of higher education. In addition to Brown, the state's private colleges include the renowned Rhode Island School of Design, which houses one of the foremost art collections of any college or university in the United States. Rhode Island has only one two-year college, a public institution.

References: EB; DES.

Rhodes Scholarship

Rhodes Scholarship   A grant awarded annually to select college and university students from the nations of the British Commonwealth and from the United States, South Africa and Germany, for two years of study at the University of Oxford, England. The scholarships were established in 1902 under the will of Cecil Rhodes, the British statesman who, by the time he was 19, had accumulated a fortune as a diamond prospector in South Africa. In 1873, he returned to England and began studying part-time, dividing his year between his studies and further prospecting in the South African diamond fields. He eventually received his degree in 1881, by which time he had also amalgamated a large number of diamond claims into the giant De Beers Mining Co., which still controls South Africa's diamond production and trade. He spent the rest of his life engaged in South African politics and willed most of his personal fortune to the establishment of the Rhodes Scholarships.

Reference: EB.

Rice, Joseph Mayer (1857–1934)

Rice, Joseph Mayer (1857–1934)   New York pediatrician whose 1893 book, *The Public-School System of the United States,* galvanized the first major, educational reform movement in the United States. His concerns over health conditions in New York City public schools and disease prevention among children provoked an interest in child development and modern pedagogy. He abandoned his practice to embark on an eight-year study of more than 100 school systems in Europe and the United States, focusing on the length of time different teachers with different pedagogies spent teaching children the same materials. After studying pedagogy in Germany from 1888 to 1890, he returned to the United States and spent the first half of 1892 studying the American public school system, visiting schools, talking with teachers, students and parents and attending school board meetings in 36 cities. Rice published his findings in the influential journal *Forum* and showed that a nationwide pattern existed of mindless teaching, dependence on rote learning, low academic achievement, administrative ineptitude, political corruption and public apathy.

He found several oases of educational reform, however. Minneapolis teachers displayed warmth and took individual differences into consideration. Indianapolis teachers tied learning in one subject to materials taught in all other subjects, while LaPorte, Indiana, teachers taught children to collaborate instead of compete in the classroom. In Chicago, the "father of progressive education," Francis W. Parker (q.v.), was training teachers to use maps, drawings, models, stuffed animals and other concrete objects to teach literature, the arts and the sciences.

Rice urged the citizens across the United States to demand adoption of similarly "progressive" teaching methods in their own schools. Coining the phrase "progressive education," Rice predicted continued decline in educational quality unless public schools were "absolutely divorced from politics in every sense of the word." Although Rice himself was never directly involved in teaching, his book was the first to define educational problems as national in scope. As such, it became the definitive policy statement that coalesced a wide range of educators and educational theorists into a single, nationwide "progressive education" movement. Rice exploded the myth that the more time allotted to teaching a subject each day, the more rapidly a child would learn. He conducted studies on how children learned to spell, then wrote *The Rational Spelling Book* (1898) for teachers. In 1903, he founded the Society of Educational Research and, a decade later, wrote *Scientific Management in Education*.

References: BDAE; NYT; *The Public-School System of the United States,* J. M. Rice (1893).

Rickover, Admiral Hyman George (1900–1986)

United States Navy admiral and "father of the nuclear navy" and the U.S. nuclear submarine fleet. An engineer and scientist, as well as a Navy officer, Rickover veered into the field of education in the late 1950s, when he established nuclear-power schools for the United States Navy in Connecticut and California. Lamenting what he considered the poor educational foundations of American students in mathematics and science, he published a controversial book entitled *Education and Freedom* (1959), which warned that declining educational standards would threaten the preservation of freedom in American society. A strong advocate of the back-to-basics movement (q.v.), he heralded the need to train more engineers and scientists as essential to national defense.

References: DAB; NYT; *Education and Freedom* (1959), *Swiss Schools and Ours: Why Theirs Are Better* (1962) and *American Education: A National Failure* (1963), Hyman Rickover.

Right to Read

A federal program established by Congress in 1974 to improve the reading skills of American citizens and to eliminate illiteracy. The elements of the program included establishing and underwriting improved reading instruction in preschools and elementary schools, establishment of special reading programs for illiterate youths in and out of schools, and expansion of the use of reading specialists in public schools. In 1978, Right to Read was absorbed into the more far-reaching, federal Basic Skills and Educational Proficiency Program (q.v.) to improve all the basic academic skills of American citizens, in mathematics and in oral and written communications, as well as in reading.

Reference: U.S. Department of Education, Washington, D.C.

Robinson, James Harvey (1863–1936)

American historian, educator and champion of the "humanization of knowledge"—the writing and presentation of complex, often esoteric knowledge so that it can be more easily understood by the average student (and average citizen). As compulsory, universal education was spreading across the United States at the end of the 19th and the beginning of the 20th century, a few educators had become aware that textbooks in many complex subjects, including history, had been written for scholars and not for the ordinary student or citizen. A graduate of Harvard, the Illinois-born Robinson obtained his Ph.D. in Germany and returned to teach at the University of Pennsylvania in 1891. In 1895, he was appointed professor of European history at Columbia University, where he joined educator John Dewey (q.v.) and historian Charles Beard (1874–1948) in reforming the study and teaching of history by transforming it from a narrow, dull, chronological compilation of political, military and economic facts into a vibrant, comprehensive study of social, cultural, intellectual and scientific events that tied the lives and achievements of the past to the everyday lives of modern man. Responsible for developing a humanized "new history," Robinson also led the development of a broader, humanized education movement that eventually affected the presentation of the social sciences, the sciences and even mathematics.

"It has become apparent that we must fundamentally reorder and readjust our knowledge before we can hope to get into the current of our daily thought and conduct," Robinson declared in *The Humanizing of Knowledge* (1923), the most important of his 24 books. "It must be re-synthesized and re-humanized. It must be made to seem vitally relevant to our lives and deeper interests." It must "bring home to the greatest number of readers as much knowledge as possible, in the most pleasing, effective, and least misleading manner." In 1919, Robinson left Columbia to help Dewey and others found the New School for Social Research (q.v.) in New York City. Two years later, he left teaching and devoted the rest of his life to research and writing.

References: BDAE; DAB; *The Humanizing of Knowledge,* James Harvey Robinson (1923).

Rochester Method A system of instruction for the hearing impaired (q.v.) that combines the simultaneous use of finger spelling (q.v.) with speech.

Reference: *A Handbook of Readings in Education of the Deaf and Postschool Implications,* Irving S. Fusfeld, ed. (1967).

Rochester Plan A much-heralded but largely unsuccessful 1987 program to reform public school education in Rochester, New York. The scheme began by giving teachers a 40% pay increase over three years and raising top salaries after 11 years of service, to $45,000 a year. Special veteran teacher positions paying $70,000 a year were established as part of a broad plan to establish school-based management, with faculty and administrators in full charge of the program for their school and its students, unhindered by the city's central school-board bureaucracy. The high pay, however, was accompanied by a new system of teacher accountability.

At the time, most of the system's 33,000 students were from poor families, and half were from single-parent homes. The city's black and Hispanic students were far worse off economically than their white classmates. Each teacher, however, was to counsel 20 students and get to know each student's family and become as involved as possible in personally assuring the student's progress. After parents, the school board and teachers agreed to the program, major corporations, such as Eastman Kodak, agreed to fund innovative programs and provide schools with teacher support and individual students with mentors.

Initially, the program produced some impressive results, especially for learning-disabled students, who received individual attention to a degree never seen before. Similarly, gifted students profited from the company mentorship programs that helped raise math scores. But on the whole, the program proved a dismal example of how and why educational reform programs have historically been doomed to failure in U.S. public school systems.

Parents resented teacher-mentors intruding in family life. Teachers, too, balked at their new counseling roles. Many feared they would lose merit pay raises when one of their students dropped out of school. Others claimed they lacked proper training as counselors and refused to be accountable for the actions of recalcitrant adolescents. Teachers also refused to take on additional responsibilities or invest the time and research to develop new, imaginative curricula. Parents and school board members, in turn, grew concerned that they had no adequate system of accountability with proof positive that each teacher earning a merit pay increase actually deserved it. Moreover, they could not agree on whether to base teacher assessments on how well the students did or how much they tried.

The results of the Rochester Plan were decidedly mixed. After three years, the number of graduating high school seniors applying to college climbed from 41% to 48%, while the number of students taking regents exams climbed from 4,100 to 6,000. But the percentage of third and sixth graders achieving mastery of reading and math tests fell from 60% to 46%, and Rochester's high school dropout rate actually climbed during the first three years, from about 13% in the first year, to 14.1% the second, before settling at 13.8% in 1990. Educational researchers who studied the Rochester Plan's successes and failures agreed that its overall failure stemmed from the faulty assumption that four varied groups with sharply diverging interests—parents, teachers, administrators and school board officials and bureaucrats—could work in harmony.

Reference: *Parenting Our Schools, A Hands-On Guide to Education Reform,* Jill Bloom (1992).

Rockefeller, John D. (1839–1937)

Oil magnate whose personal fortune reached $1 billion and whose philanthropic contributions totaled about $550 million, of which 80% went to four organizations: the Rockefeller Foundation (q.v.); the General Education Board (q.v.), which promoted universal education in the South and improved the quality of black education; the Rockefeller Institute for Medical Research (now, Rockefeller University [q.v.]); and the Laura Spelman Rockefeller Memorial, to promote worldwide child-welfare and social-science studies. Born in Richford, New York, Rockefeller attended public school in Cleveland until he was 16, when he went to work as a bookkeeper. At the age of 23, in 1862, he went into partnership with Samuel Andres, the inventor of an inexpensive oil refining process that helped the two men build the massive Standard Oil Co. By 1878, Rockefeller, at the age of 39, controlled 90% of the oil refineries in the United States and, soon after, all the distribution and marketing facilities as well. He retired in 1911 to devote the rest of his life to philanthropy. In that same year, the U.S. Supreme Court ruled that the Standard Oil Co. had violated anti-trust regulations and ordered it split into the constituent corporations we know today.

References: EB; DAB; Rockefeller Foundation, New York, New York.

Rockefeller Foundation

A philanthropic organization founded in 1913 by John D. Rockefeller Sr. "to promote the well-being of mankind around the world." Originally funded with about $250 million in personal Rockefeller funds, its endowment grew to about $1.7 billion by 1990, and it was awarding more than $60 million a year in annual grants and fellowships. Its broad areas of work are: Arts, Humanities and Contemporary Values, through which it has made major contributions to American colleges, universities, museums and other educative institutions; Conquest of Hunger; Equal Opportunity; International Relations; and Population and Health. In 1918, the foundation absorbed the Laura Spelman Rockefeller Foundation to encourage worldwide child-welfare and social science studies.

Reference: Rockefeller Foundation, New York, New York.

Rockefeller University

A unique graduate university in New York City, founded by oil magnate John D. Rockefeller in 1901 to conduct medical research. Originally called the Rockefeller Institute for Medical Research, it became a graduate institution in 1954, with programs leading to the Ph.D. It changed its name to Rockefeller University in 1965 and now offers a combined six-year graduate program leading to an M.D. and Ph.D., with nearby Cornell University Medical College. Rockefeller University's primary mission, however, remains research. It has a full-time faculty of about 250 and enrolls only about 100 graduate students. There are few formal courses, and most instruction is tutorial. The university is organized into about 60 laboratories, instead of departments, with each laboratory headed by a senior professor and staffed by other faculty members, as well as postdoctoral and graduate fellows. Student progress is described in annual reports rather than measured with conventional grades. The primary task of each laboratory is original research in the biological, behavioral and medical sciences, with a range of diseases under investigation at any one time. The university operates a small, private research hospital. Rockefeller University scientists have won nearly two dozen Nobel prizes.

Reference: Rockefeller University, New York, New York.

Rodriguez v. San Antonio School District

A 1974 U.S. Supreme Court decision upholding the right of states to finance public school systems with local property taxes. The decision was a devastating setback for representatives of minority groups and the poor, who contended that the funding of public schools led to inequitable spending on education. Schools in wealthy districts with high property values obtained far more funding and therefore provided better education than schools in poor districts, where property values were low. The suit was filed against the state of Texas by parents in San Antonio, where property taxes provided only $26 per pupil for schools in poor districts and $333 per pupil in wealthy districts. The plaintiffs argued that such inequity violated the U.S. Constitution's guarantee of equal protection under the law.

The Supreme Court, however, ruled against the plaintiffs on the grounds that the Constitution makes no mention of education and offers no specific guarantee of any right to education. "Education . . . is not among the rights afforded explicit protection under our federal constitution. Nor do we find any basis for saying it is implicitly so protected." Moreover, the Court declared that "where wealth is involved the equal protection clause does not require absolute equality of precisely equal advantages." The Court also said that the plaintiffs had failed to prove that disparities in funding had deprived their children of an "opportunity to acquire minimum basic skills necessary for the full enjoyment of rights of free speech and full participation in the political process."

The irony of the decision is that it followed by three years a California State Supreme Court decision in *Serrano v. Priest* (q.v.) that required the state to develop a more equitable distribution of public school funds to reduce the discrepancies in quality of education between poor and rich districts. Subsequently, more than 30 states have issued similar rulings. The difference in these rulings, however, is that they are based on state constitutions that do mention education and insist on equity in education for all the state's children. The U.S. Supreme Court did not rule against equity in education. It merely said that such equity was not guaranteed by the federal constitution.

References: *School Finance in Transition: The Courts and Educational Reform,* John Pincus, ed. (1974); U.S. Supreme Court proceedings.

role playing A common technique used by psychologists and, with the permission and supervision of the school psychologist, by teachers attempting to give students a broad understanding of major social problems. Role playing is often used in resistance training to teach children not only to "just say no," but also how to do it and feel comfortable about doing it. Reciting a list of "don'ts" and "dangers" is seldom as effective as staging a drama with student participants—one urging another, "Just try it," and the other, on stage, in front of his peers, learning the confidence to say, "Get out of my face! Drugs are dumb! I didn't think you were that dumb!" Similarly, role playing, under careful professional guidance, can be an effective method of teaching youngsters how to deal with such problems as race relations, teen suicide, sex and other social problems. Moreover it can serve as an effective cathartic for feelings about racial tensions, parent-child tensions and teacher-student tensions.

References: *Group Counseling,* Merle M. Ohlsen (1977); *Using Role Playing in the Classroom,* John Thompson (1978).

rolling admissions A system whereby a college sets no fixed date for its admissions decisions, accepting applications at any time during the school year and responding to applicants within 30 days. Upon receipt of an acceptance, the student is usually given 30 days to decide whether to attend and to send in the appropriate deposit. Rolling early decision operates in much the same way, with colleges responding to applications within 30 days. As with conventional early decision (q.v.) applicants, however, an applicant accepted under a rolling early-decision program is under a moral obligation to withdraw all other college applications. The only difference between conventional and rolling early decision is that applications are not reviewed at a fixed time.

Reference: *A Student's Guide to College Admissions,* Harlow G. Unger (1995).

Roman Catholic Church

The largest, single, organized Christian church, made up of nearly 1 billion communicants who acknowledge the supreme authority of the bishop of Rome—the Pope (or father)—in matters spiritual and, for many, temporal. Derived from the Greek word *katholikos,* meaning "universal," the "Catholic" Church of Rome was, with few exceptions, the only Christian religion recognized by Western believers until the 12th century, when the first Protestants challenged papal authority. At the time, Catholic leaders were the temporal as well as spiritual rulers of Western Europe. The Waldensians in France, under the leadership of Peter Waldo (1140–1217), were first to criticize the Catholic leadership publicly. Waldo declared that the excessive temporal practices of the Catholic Church had no basis in the Scriptures and was simply the product of greed and arrogance. Although fiercely persecuted, the Waldensians survived in parts of France and Switzerland. Similarly minded Lollards, followers of John Wycliffe in France and England in the 1380s, and Hussites in 15th-century Bohemia followed the Waldensians in the spreading Protestant movement. The protests grew until 1517, when Martin Luther's grievances against the church triggered a massive rebellion against it; within a century, dozens of Protestant sects had severed connections with Rome and challenged the need for priestly intermediaries in the relationship between God and humanity.

Wounded and somewhat weakened, the Catholic Church held on to whatever temporal powers it could, but gradually recognized that its future growth lay not in sending military armies to conquer the world but in sending spiritual armies to convert the world. Education slowly replaced force as the church's primary weapon.

As early as 1493, when military conquest was still very much in favor, 12 priests accompanied Christopher Columbus on his second voyage and established the first see in the New World at Santo Domingo (in what is now the Dominican Republic), the first European settlement in the New World. The second American see was established at Santiago de Cuba in 1522 and the third in Mexico in 1532. Between the middle of the 16th century and the end of the 18th century, Spanish Franciscan, Dominican and Jesuit missionaries emanating from those three sees established communities in what later became Florida, Texas, New Mexico and California. At the same time, French missionaries were establishing settlements in present-day Maine, in northern New York and around the Great Lakes and upper Mississippi. The Catholic population reached about 30,000 by the time of the Revolutionary War, increased to 250,000 by 1820 and 1 million by 1840.

Like other Americans after the Revolutionary War, most Catholic families were content to send their children for secular education in Protestant-dominated common schools and for spiritual training to their local priest on weekends. Like other minority groups of the day, Roman Catholics were largely scattered across the rural United States and far from any central diocesan control.

A wave of Catholic immigrants from Europe that settled in major cities following the Civil War provoked a change in the thinking of the Catholic hierarchy. Fearful that Protestant-dominated common schools would, in the process of "Americanizing" immigrant children, also "Protestantize" them, the Third Plenary Council of Baltimore in 1884 ordered the construction of a national Catholic school system. The church decreed that within two years, a parochial school was to be built near each Catholic church. It decreed that all parents would be obliged to remove their children from secular schools and send them to parochial schools. The decree called for the construction of Catholic high schools, academies and colleges and the establishment of diocesan boards of education. It also crowned this system with the construction of Catholic University, in Washington; and from that point until the middle 1960s, the official goal of the Catholic Church in the United States was to send every Catholic child to Catholic schools and colleges and thus preserve Catholicism in America. In addition to founding Catholic University of America, by 1960 the Catholic Church had been responsible for establishing 13,000 elementary and secondary schools and nearly 400 colleges in the United States.

(See also CATHOLIC SCHOOLS.)

References: EB; DES; National Catholic Education Association; *American Education,* Lawrence A. Cremin (3 vols., 1970, 1979, 1987).

romance languages A group of modern languages derived primarily from Low Latin and spoken by about 400 million people, largely in Europe. Spanish and French are by far the most widely spoken. They are also the most studied in fulfillment of American secondary school and college foreign language requirements. Other romance languages include Italian, Ladin and Fiulian, all spoken in Italy; Portuguese; Ladino, a Judaeo-Spanish language originally spoken in Spain; Catalan and Valencian, spoken in Spain; Andorran; Romansch, spoken in Switzerland; and Rumanian.

References: *Native Tongues,* Charles Berlitz (1984); *The World's Major Languages,* Bernard Comrie (1990).

Roosevelt, Franklin Delano (1882–1945)
Thirty-second president of the United States and the only president to be elected to four terms in office. More than any president before him, he involved the federal government in the creation of broad educative institutions through agencies to provide grants for the fine arts, theater, music and literature. His efforts did not grow out of his personal love of the arts, but from a need to get millions of unemployed people back to work during the Great (economic) Depression of the

1930s—including the thousands of unemployed writers, artists, actors and dancers.

Born to wealth in Hyde Park, New York, Roosevelt was educated at the elite Groton School and Harvard University and earned his law degree at Columbia University. His political career began in 1910 and carried him to the New York governorship, in 1928 and in 1930, and to the presidency, in 1932, as the nation cried out for help in the midst of its economic agonies. In his first, famous "100 Days" in office, he enacted sweeping economic and social reforms—the "New Deal"—that reorganized the American political, financial, economic, industrial, agricultural and social systems. In effect, the New Deal transformed a laissez-faire economy and social system into a modified socialist state, with myriad Washington agencies regulating key industries and providing the American people with annual stipends designed to keep them fed, clothed and housed.

A primary thrust of the New Deal was to put as many as possible of the nation's 13 million unemployed back to work. Roosevelt's first effort came in 1933, when he issued an executive order creating the Civilian Conservation Corps (q.v.), putting young men 18 to 25 to work on conservation projects and providing subsistence funds to keep youngsters 16 to 24 in school. Funds were also provided so that needy young people who had quit school could be put to work on neighborhood projects. By 1935, more than a half-million young men were working in the CCC, not only contributing to the conservation needs of their country, but also earning money for themselves and learning useful trades they could take back to civilian life after their year of service expired. World War II ended the need for the CCC nine years later, by which time it had enrolled some 2.5 million men, who had planted billions of trees, halted the erosion of millions of acres of soil and created hundreds of parks and recreation areas.

Recognizing that unemployed artists and writers were just as entitled to work as any other segment of the unemployed, Roosevelt backed the establishment in 1933 of the Public Works of Art Project, which hired 3,000 artists across the United States to decorate public buildings with murals depicting American history. The project exposed millions of otherwise isolated rural Americans to fine art and history lessons. With the establishment of the Works Progress Administration (q.v.) (later, the Works Project Administration) in 1935, the Roosevelt administration incorporated the Public Works of Art Project into a broader Federal Art Project (q.v.) that included commissions for artists, musicians, dancers, playwrights, poets and other unemployed artists. In all, the Federal Art Project engaged more than 100,000 writers, artists, musicians, dancers and other artists, who not only earned subsistence incomes to carry them through the Depression, but also brought culture to some of the most remote areas of the nation. The program marked the beginning of massive federal government sponsorship of the arts. It shifted its focus during World War II to sponsorship of massive programs of entertainment for American service personnel throughout the world. After the war, the program continued with the establishment of the National Foundation on the Arts and Humanities (q.v.).

References: DAB; *Roosevelt: The Lion and the Fox,* James MacGregor Burns (1956); *FDR,* Kenneth S. Davis (3 vols., 1985–86).

ROTC The popularly used abbreviation (along with "Rot-C") for the Reserve Officers Training Corps (q.v.), which prepares college and university students for commissions in the armed services.

rote counting A recital of numbers in order and by memory, with little or no understanding of the meaning of each number. The words one, two, three, four may have as little meaning to a child as fee, fie, fo, fum—simply a series of sounds the child has memorized in a specific order. Although rote learning can often be a first step in learning, the actual learning process does not begin until the child can associate each sound with a specific, concrete object.

Reference: *Teaching and Learning in the Elementary School,* John Jarolimek and Clifford D. Foster (1985).

rote learning The acquisition of information by memorization. Often the beginning of knowledge—and often essential to the acquisition of knowledge, understanding and higher-order conceptualization—rote learning does not encourage the development of reasoning and other problem-solving skills. It can, however, place the necessary facts at the learner's immediate disposal for the solution of complex problems. At the simplest level, for example, a thorough knowledge of the multiplication tables gives a student all the tools necessary for solving complex multiplication problems, once the student has mastered adequate problem-solving and higher-order reasoning skills. Exclusive use of rote learning, however, can interfere with development of higher-order reasoning and problem-solving skills, especially in abstract mathematics and science courses.

References: *American Memory,* Lynn V. Cheney (1987); *Learning How to Learn,* Bob Gowin and Joseph Novak (1984); *Education and Learning to Think,* Lauren B. Resnick (1987); *Mathematical Problem Solving,* Alan Schoenfeld (1985).

Rough Rock Demonstration School One of several schools that the Bureau of Indian Affairs (q.v.) operated on Indian Reservations for American Indian children in the 1960s. Located in Lukachukai, Arizona, on the Navajo Reservation, the school was used by BIA as an instrument of Indian education reform. Responding to a barrage of criticism that it was keeping Indian children buried in ignorance, BIA obtained extra funding from the Office of Economic Opportunity in 1964 and introduced many standard public school methods of instruction at the school. It brought Navajo parents into the school planning process, incorporated Navajo culture into the social studies program, opened the school to adult education, encouraged formation of PTAs and other home-school ties, and opened school services and facilities to all community residents.

Although praised by Navajo leaders for improving school-community relations, the BIA was ridiculed for doing nothing more than using conventional public school methods to update what were essentially backward, 19th-century schools. The program produced no substantial improvements in student academic achievement. In 1972, the BIA effort became superfluous, with passage of the Indian Education Act authorizing a battery of new educational programs for Indians, including grants to local educational agencies and special literacy and job-training programs for Indian adults. The programs reached about 78% of the more than 400,000 Indian children in the United States.

Two subsequent laws also improved Indian education. The Indian Self-Determination and Education Assistance Act of 1975 and the Indian Education Act of 1978, which together stripped the Bureau of Indian Affairs of many of its powers and turned control of education over to Indians.

(See also AMERICAN INDIANS.)

References: *American Indian Education,* R. Merwin Deever et al., eds. (1974); *Education and the American Indian: The Road to Self-Determination Since 1928,* Margaret C. Szasz (1977).

Rousseau, Jean-Jacques (1712–1778)

Swiss-born philosopher, author, political scientist, musicologist and one of the most influential minds in the so-called Age of Enlightenment. In the field of education, his novel *Emile, ou l'Education* (1762) proved one of the most influential documents in 18th- and 19th-century education, offering a new theory of education based on the principles of natural child development and the futility of attempting to treat children as small adults. In the novel, the boy Emile learns by experience and natural observation, using his senses to acquire new knowledge and acquiring new skills as he becomes developmentally ready.

In 1775, the pioneer Swiss educator Johann Pestalozzi attempted to apply the educational techniques of *Emile* on his estate, where he opened a school for poor children, who would ordinarily have gone uneducated. After five years of experimenting with "Emilian" educational methods, he closed the school for lack of funds. Apparently he had enjoyed relatively little progress in educating the children, but he later applied his methods successfully in a well endowed school he founded for wealthier children. Pestalozzian methods, derived in part from Rousseau's *Emile,* became the foundation of modern elementary education in Europe, England and the United States. Ironically, as insightful as Rousseau was to the educational needs of his fictional Emile, he abandoned his own children, leaving them to grow up in orphanages.

References: *Emile, ou l'Education* (1762) and *Confessions* (posthumously, 1788), Jean-Jacques Rousseau.

Roxbury, Massachusetts

Site of one of the first schools in the American colonies, with a free school having been established by consensus of the residents in 1645, 10 years after the first school had been established in Boston. The school was free, however, only to the children of subscriber families who agreed to contribute to the £20 annual stipend for the schoolmaster. Now called the Roxbury Latin School, it is a private day school for boys.

(See also MASSACHUSETTS.)

References: *Old School Book,* manuscripts, records, Roxbury Latin School, Roxbury, Massachusetts.

Royal Society of London for Improving Natural Knowledge

A scientific organization officially founded in 1660, but convening informally beginning in 1645 at regular meetings of England's leading scientists. It rivaled Oxford and Cambridge universities as a source of the latest scientific advances, simply because it did not restrict members to the stifling rules and regulations of a university. Its membership included the foremost thinkers and scientists from

the American colonies, as well as England, and its findings formed the basis of much of the early science curriculum of American academies and colleges. Among its members were Robert Boyle (1627–91), Francis Bacon (q.v.), John Locke, Isaac Newton and Connecticut Governor John Winthrop Jr. (qq.v.), who was also a chemist and mineralogist and who provided a steady flow of materials and learned observations to the society from America. Cotton Mather, William Penn and John Morgan (qq.v.), the pioneer of American medical education, were all members of the Royal Society, and Benjamin Franklin (q.v.) used the society as a model for forming the American Philosophical Society (q.v.).
Reference: EB.

Rugg, Harold O. (1886–1960)

American educator, author and leader of the reconstructionism movement (q.v.) that sought to use education to reform the American social system during the devastating economic depression of the 1930s. Born in Massachusetts, he received his advanced degrees at Dartmouth College before teaching at three universities in Illinois and eventually becoming a professor of education at Teachers College, Columbia University, in 1920—joining a faculty that included John Dewey and a crowd of Dewey disciples who believed formal education should imbue all children in the principles of democracy.

Rugg and his colleague George S. Counts (q.v.) attempted to translate reconstructionism into practical terms. While Counts tried to whip American teachers into a reconstructionist frenzy, Rugg and his Teachers College students spent the years from 1921 to 1928 producing the 12-volume Rugg Social Science Pamphlets, which became the most popular social-studies texts of their day. Both critical and appreciative of the United States, the pamphlets were distributed to more than 5 million American schoolchildren in about 5,000 school systems—until 1940, when patriotic and business groups attacked them as subversive and effectively banned

them from almost all American schools. A group in Bradner, Ohio, even burned them.

A veteran of World War I and a prolific author, Rugg wrote the influential *The Child-Centered School* (1930), *Culture and Education in America* (1931), *American Life and the School Curriculum* (1936), *Progressive Education at the Crossroad* (1938), *That Men May Understand* (1941), *Foundations for American Education* (1941), *The Teacher in the School and Society* (1950) and *The Teacher of Teachers* (1952).
Reference: BDAE.

rules and regulations

A codification of permissible and impermissible student behavior and academic effort in a school or college and the consequent rewards and discipline for such behavior. According to U.S. Department of Education studies, the most effective elementary, middle and high schools have clearly defined, strictly enforced rules of academic conduct and social behavior. Rules catalogs issued to students and parents usually indicate in clearest terms the school's policies for handling misconduct, absenteeism, lateness, disruptive behavior, cheating, vandalism, violence, physical threats or verbal abuse, theft, weapons possession, racism or bigotry, gambling, use of tobacco, drugs or alcohol, and even use of radios and tape players with headphones. The rules state whether there is a dress code and describe it and whether there is a code of conduct for students when they are not in school. Rules booklets also state clearly the discipline and possible punishments for all infractions.
Reference: "What Did You Learn in School Today?" Harlow G. Unger (1991).

runaways

A social problem that is largely ignored by government, by schools and, at times, by parents—often because of helplessness or ignorance. The U.S. Department of Health and Human Services estimates upward of 2 million children run away from their homes each year—36% because of physical or sexual abuse,

44% because of long-term problems and 20% because of temporary crises. About 25% are labeled "incorrigible, hard-core street kids," of whom three-quarters engage in some kind of chronic criminal activity and half in prostitution. An unmeasurable number are so-called "throwaways," who have been abandoned by their families or literally expelled from the family home. Approximately 5,000 unidentified bodies of murdered children and youths are found each year. There is no gender, racial, ethnic or economic pattern to the runaway population.

Most communities have few government-operated facilities for runaways seeking help, although volunteer groups and some state agencies maintain about 2,300 shelters, hotline agencies, foster-care organizations and other community-based agencies in all 50 states and Puerto Rico. Towns and states with shelters, however, usually do not have enough beds to accommodate children and youths seeking help. Few have any support services other than bathing facilities, clean beds, food and fresh clothes. In 1984, Congress enacted the Runaway and Homeless Youth Act, which provided funds for the Department of Health and Human Services to underwrite costs at 260 runaway and homeless youth shelters across the United States. With an average of 500 students under his care, the average high school guidance counselor is particularly ill-equipped to identify potential runaways and provide preventative counseling or turn a youngster over to a social worker or psychologist.

References: U.S. Department of Health and Human Services, Washington, D.C.; *An Introduction to Guidance: The Professional Counselor,* E. L. Tolbert (1982).

rural education   An increasingly archaic term referring to the imagined disparities between educational quality in isolated rural communities and small towns and in larger suburbs and cities. Small student populations, low tax bases, high teacher turnover rates and lack of adequate technological facilities and equipment did indeed reduce educational quality of some rural schools for many decades. Until the 1980s, many rural communities in the United States continued to rely on one- or two-room schoolhouses, with one or two instructors teaching kindergarten through twelfth grade in a single room. In 1980, there were more than 1,000 such schools still in operation, but more than half disappeared over the ensuing decade, and they are expected to become extinct by the year 2000, as the rural population declines. In 1900, 40% of the American population lived on farms. By 1940, the percentage had dropped to 15%. By 1980 it was 3% and in 1990, 2.5%.

Most rural states have now reorganized their educational systems to eliminate the need for one- and two-room schoolhouses. Buses drive students to and from centrally located schools, and even the most isolated schools have access to a wide array of electronic systems that permit use of videotapes and other forms of instruction in the classroom. Interactive television systems allow one teacher to instruct and react with students at a number of schools within the same region. Moreover, many states now provide fleets of portable classrooms for schools whose student populations are not large enough to justify investment in costly, specialized facilities for computer training or woodworking or foreign-language study. Specially equipped portable classrooms bring such facilities, along with special teachers, to a school for one term, then move on to another school. In some states, portable classrooms move computers from school to school in outlying areas; in other states they carry science labs, fine arts programs and specialized vocational training facilities to schools that would otherwise lack such programs.

Much of the statistical evidence for the poor quality of rural education can be traced to what is now recognized as a largely invalid, 20-year study of 440,000 high school students, started in 1960 and called Project Talent (q.v.). It found that seniors in large high schools performed better in mathematics and science than seniors in small high schools and that student achievement tended to increase with teacher salaries. According to 1994 studies, however, students in schools with fewer than 300 students registered higher mathematics, science and SAT scores than students in larger schools. The same studies found that students in several relatively rural states—Iowa, Kansas, Minnesota, Montana, Nebraska, North Dakota, South Dakota, Utah, Wisconsin and Wyoming—obtained the highest average scores in the United States.

References: U.S. Department of Education, Washington, D.C.; *Profile in Excellence: Katahdin High School,* Richard Elwell, U.S. Department of Education (1984); *The Career Data Book: Results from Project Talent's Five-year Follow-Up Study,* John C. Flanagan et al. (1973).

Rush, Benjamin (1745–1813) American physician, statesman, signer of the Declaration of Independence and champion of universal public education. A founder of Dickinson College in 1773, Rush's long-term influence on American education was in his articulation and perpetuation of a liberal educational ideology that he would never live to see implemented.

Born in Philadelphia and educated at the College of New Jersey (now Princeton), he earned his M.D. after six years as an apprentice to a Philadelphia physician and two years of study at the University of Edinburgh, in Scotland. He returned to Philadelphia in 1768, became the first chemistry professor ever at the College of Philadelphia (now the University of Pennsylvania), and in 1770 published the first American chemistry text, based on his lectures. He also entered private practice and, because of his location, began treating and establishing friendships with the most important colonial leaders, who were gathering in Philadelphia to declare independence from England. He welcomed and entertained John Adams, George Washington and Thomas Paine and inoculated Patrick Henry against smallpox. Through such

Benjamin Rush. (Library of Congress)

associations, he won election to the Second Continental Congress in time to sign the Declaration of Independence.

Named to the medical department of the Continental Army, he fought constantly with superiors over unhealthy conditions in military hospitals and finally resigned his commission in 1778. After the Revolution, he spent the next decade on ''a one-man crusade to remake America,'' campaigning for free schools, a national university, prison reform, free postage for newspapers, churches for blacks, temperance, emancipation, education of women and abolition of capital punishment.

He was a staunch proponent, along with Adams, Jefferson, Franklin and Madison of the republican style of education (q.v.) and espoused establishment of a national system of universal education. His—and their—efforts to include educational rights in the Constitution were defeated by the fierce opposition of northern mill owners who depended on children for cheap labor and southern plantation owners who depended on slavery for free labor. Like Jefferson, he turned his attention to his native state, Pennsylvania, where he attempted to establish a three-level system of schooling, with free district, or township, schools to teach reading, writing, arithmetic, English and German (for the Pennsylvania "Dutch"—that is, Deutsch). The state would have four regional colleges to teach higher mathematics and the sciences, and a university in Philadelphia would teach law, medicine, divinity, politics, economics and natural philosophy. "The university will in time furnish masters for the free schools, while the free schools, in their turns, will supply the colleges and university with scholars, students and pupils," said Rush. "The same systems of grammar, oratory and philosophy, will be taught in every part of the state . . . Our schools of learning, by producing one general and uniform system of education, will render the mass of people more homogeneous, and thereby fit them more easily for uniform and peaceable government."

Rush saw colleges as "true nurseries of power and influence," and favored establishment of a national university that graduates of state universities would be required to attend to receive training for public service. Rush also believed that women should be educated as wives and mothers in schools that would teach reading, writing, grammar, arithmetic and bookkeeping, geography, history, astronomy, chemistry, natural philosophy, vocal music, dancing and the Christian religion. He called for establishment of post offices and urged free distribution of newspapers as "vehicles of knowledge and intelligence" and "sentinels of the liberties of our countries." He protested corporal punishment, denounced slavery and espoused a belief in the perfectibility of human beings through education. In 1786, he established the nation's first free dispensary.

In 1791, he rejoined the faculty of the University of Pennsylvania and helped organize its medical school, the first in the United States. A leader in the battle against the Yellow Fever epidemic in 1793, he devoted the rest of his life to teaching and research. Often called the "father of American psychiatry," he wrote the first discourse on mental illness published in the United States, *Medical Inquiries and Observations Upon the Disease of the Mind* (1812).

References: DAB; *The Autobiography of Benjamin Rush*, George W. Corner, ed. (1948); *Benjamin Rush: Philosopher of the American Revolution*, Donald J. D'Elia (19740; *Benjamin Rush and His Services to American Education*, Harry G. Good (1918); *Benjamin Rush: Physician and Citizen, 1746–1813*, Nathan G. Goodman (1934).

S

sabbatical Also called sabbatical leave; a year's leave every seven years for teachers in institutions of higher learning, to rest, travel or pursue research. Institutions generally limit the number of sabbaticals granted in any given year. Although some offer sabbaticals with full pay, others offer full pay for only a half-year's sabbatical or half-pay for a full year's leave. Some institutions offer no pay for such leaves, although the institution offices and research facilities remain at the disposal of the professor on leave. The term derives from the Mosaic law of ancient Judea under which farmers traditionally left each acre of land fallow for a year after six consecutive harvests.

References: *The Personnel Function in Educational Administration,* William B. Castetter (1976); *Webster's Ninth New Collegiate Dictionary.*

safe havens Locally organized programs under a variety of names whereby storekeepers and individual homeowners post identifying signs such as "SAFE HAVEN" and pledge to provide temporary harbor to any fearful, troubled or endangered child on his or her way to or from school (or at any other time, for that matter) until parents or authorities can be summoned. In communities with safe haven programs, parents and teachers routinely walk their children along the safest routes home, pointing out and stopping to visit safe-haven volunteers. The latter pledge to remain at their posts, watching the nearby streets and sidewalks for specific hours each morning before school opens and for a similar period after school closes.

Reference: *The Elementary School Handbook,* Joanne Oppenheim (1989).

safety education An amorphous form of instruction relating to accident prevention and minimization at all levels of human activity, ranging from play at preschool and school to vehicle operation to activities in the workplace.

Formal safety education began in Massachusetts, which passed a law in 1867 forcing industry to provide paid factory inspectors in each plant. In the 1920s, safety education was integrated into employee training at most plants throughout the United States,.

In American schools, safety education begins with fire drills in some preschools and in all kindergartens. Students walk in pairs, hands clasped, in double file behind the teacher, who leads them out of the school building to a safe vantage point. Practice crossing streets in the presence of school crossing guards, recognition of safe haven (q.v.) facilities and learning to travel in pairs or groups are all basic elements of early safety education at elementary schools. In middle school and high school, safety education includes hygiene, social and sexual education, and driver education. Methods of preventing venereal diseases, AIDS, premature pregnancy, abstinence from drugs and chemical substances, and careful methods of driving vehicles all fall under the broad category of safety education.

References: *Safety Education,* A. E. Floria, et al. (1979); *Safety: Concepts and Instruction,* Alton L. Thygerson (1976).

safety patrols School-organized groups of older elementary and middle-school students at least 10 years old who are charged with ensuring the safety of students at street crossings near the school, by instructing, directing and controlling car and pedestrian traffic. Usually accompanied by adult crossing guards, with large, appropriately colored "stop" and "go" signs, school patrol members wear brightly colored, phosphorescent Sam Browne belts. Use of school patrols must be approved by each district and state and is not without some controversy over the question of district liability in the case of injuries. The children patrollers are not employees and, therefore, not covered by employee compensation insurance. The question of protecting such chil-

dren has been resolved differently from community to community, depending on state laws.
Reference: *Policies and Practices for School Safety Patrols,* American Automobile Association.

"safety" school A school or college where a student applicant's academic and other qualifications would clearly rank the student in the top third or quarter of existing classes. In effect, a safety school is one for which the applicant is clearly overqualified and likely to gain admission with ease—especially if the student is asking for no financial aid. Many students make the mistake of selecting such schools quite casually, solely on the basis of ease of admission. For any given student, however, there are myriad safety schools that can provide exciting, challenging college careers, and most authorities on college admissions urge applicants to select their safety schools with as great, if not greater, care than their so-called "dream" or "reach" schools for which they may be underqualified.
Reference: *A Student's Guide to College Admissions,* Harlow G. Unger (1995).

St. George's Episcopal Church (New York City)

Pioneering institutional church (q.v.) that responded to the influx of poor immigrants by converting itself into a free, educative institution, open to all on a nonsectarian basis. The Reverend William S. Rainsford assumed the rectorship of St. George's on Stuyvesant Square in January 1883. An Irish-born, Cambridge-educated veteran of mission work in the poor East End of London, he brought with him a new vision of a church dedicated to the promotion of social justice and the fulfillment of the physical and educational, as well as the spiritual, needs of its parishioners. It was a new concept for New York and, indeed, for the United States.

Before accepting his post, Rainsford demanded that the vestry declare St. George's "a truly democratic church," with all pews free. He insisted that all committees be appointed by him, and he demanded an annual discretionary fund of $10,000 for evangelistic work. Astounded, the members of a tense and silent vestry eyed each other angrily until banker J. P. Morgan Sr. forcefully intoned, "Done!" Rainsford proceeded to transform the church into one of New York City's most remarkable social and educative institutions. He declared St. George's a free church, open to all, and preached an expansive evangelical message that declared all equal in the eyes of God, with equal access to His word.

He opened the church from 8 A.M. to 5 P.M. daily and acquired an adjunct building called Memorial House, where young people flocked to read, dance, play games and listen to music. He organized a trade school for boys to learn carpentry, printing, mechanical drawing, electrical and metal work and applied design. The public schools of New York, he declared, "are lamentably behind the times, and what the church should do is set an example of a higher standard for growing boys and girls."

Rainsford did not ignore spiritual training. He reorganized Sunday School into graded classes and chose well-trained teachers with warm personalities as well as a knowledge of the Scriptures. He set up a circulating library and organized a Battalion Club for boys 14 to 18, with a program of military exercises, a rifle range, and a summer camp. He also organized a Girls' Friendly Society, with a program of handicrafts, cooking, sewing, dressmaking, calisthenics and reading. He set up a Men's Club, with a billiard room, a common room and a gymnasium, and a Women's Society, with an instructional program on child-rearing and homemaking. For the poor, he established a program of relief, with a grocery department, a clinic, a summer camp and an emergency fund for the impoverished.

By the end of the decade, the church counted more than 4,000 parishioners, including Morgan, who worked unceasingly as a warden and volunteer. By 1899, more than a dozen institutional churches had been established in New York, along the line of the St. George's model. Across America, there were 173 such institutions. Many similar institutions emerged else-where in the United States in the decades that followed, but the range of offerings gradually shrank, as quasi-religious organizations such as the YMCA, secular organizations such as the Boys Clubs, and school organizations began offering similar social services.

To one degree or another, however, the institutional church and religious center survives to this day. It is a uniquely American educative institution, whose roots stretch back to St. George's Episcopal Church and the 1883 arrival of the Reverend William S. Rainsford as its minister.

References: St. George's Episcopal Church, New York, New York; *The Administration of an Institutional Church: A Detailed Account of the Operation of St. George's Parish in the City of New York,* George Hodges and John Reichert (1906); *The Story of a Varied Life: An Autobiography,* W. S. Rainsford (1922).

salutatorian Usually the student who ranks second academically in the graduating high school or college class. A peculiarly American honor, the salutatorian traditionally gives an opening salutation, or short speech, welcoming guests to graduation ceremonies. Until the mid-19th century, the salutary address was usually delivered by the head of the school or faculty. For reasons unknown, the salutation began to be turned over to the second student in the class at some American colleges as a form of formal recognition, second only to that of the valedictorian (q.v.). The latter is usually the graduating class's top student, who delivers the valedictory, or farewell address. Often, the honor of delivering the salutatory was given to the highest ranking student of the junior class who, on behalf of the student body, bid farewell to the graduating seniors. This custom seems largely to have disappeared.

Reference: *Webster's Ninth New Collegiate Dictionary.*

Salvation Army An international religious and social service organization and one of the most far-reaching educative institutions among the American poor during the late 19th and early 20th centuries. The Salvation Army began in Cornwall as an informal effort of Methodist evangelists William and Catherine Booth, moving to the slums of London's East End during the 1860s. Their purpose was to supplement efforts of traditional churches by replacing preachments with a variety of social services. These included home visitation, distribution of Bibles and tracts, instruction in mothering, relief for the poor, reading rooms, and evening classes in reading, writing and arithmetic.

Called the East London Christian Mission, it evolved into an independent quasi-church that won converts by the thousands. It was reorganized in 1878 into a hierarchal organization along military lines and renamed the Salvation Army. William Booth assumed the general superintendency and was called "General." A year later, the first Salvationists arrived in the United States, and in 1880 Booth sent a trusted aide, F. Scott Railton, and seven women to New York City as an "invasion force" to evangelize the United States. As the movement spread through the Middle Atlantic states and midwest, disagreement developed over the question of loyalty to the British organization. In 1884, Major Thomas E. Moore, who had replaced Railton, established the Salvation Army of America, independent of Booth's authority. In 1887, General Booth sent his son Ballington and Ballington's wife Maud to take charge of the American Army, but in 1896 they resigned and started the competitive Volunteers of America.

In 1904, General Booth's daughter Evangeline assumed command of the Army of the United States, by which time there were 741 corps and outposts across North America, with more than 2,500 officers and cadets. By 1934, when she returned to England to become commander of the worldwide Army, she had built the U.S. organization to 1,640 corps and outposts and 4,477 officers and cadets. Using open-air meetings, parades and communal singing, they promised instant salvation and a simplified theology to the poor, the unchurched, the unschooled and all those who simply took the "oath" and promised to lead a better, more Christian life. In exchange, the Army provided food, shelter, clothing, work and an enormous variety of formal and informal schooling, instruction and broad-based education that was unavailable to the of poor immigrants swarming through American cities. In addition, Salvationists joined the small, but growing army of secular settlement-house workers in lobbying government authorities at all levels to assume more responsibility for feeding, housing and educating the poor.

Reference: *Soldiers Without Swords: The History of the Salvation Army in the United States,* Herbert A. Wisbeym Jr. (1955).

Sankey, Ira D. (1840–1908) American evangelist, hymn writer and singer whose inspiring musical offerings transformed a partnership with fellow evangelist Dwight L. Moody (q.v.) into the most successful and influential fundamentalist Christian organization in the world in the late 19th and early 20th centuries. The charismatic Moody reached tens of thousands of converts through his preachings, prayers, publications and missions, but Sankey's church hymns and gospel songs extended their combined audience to millions. As charismatic as Moody was, Sankey's appeals to audiences to join in the singing made responders feel at one with the movement. Sankey's music turned the Moody revivals into gatherings of historic size, by adding inspiring, participatory music that excited audiences in a way that listening passively to mere words could never do.

Born to a Methodist family in western Pennsylvania, Sankey involved himself in local church affairs and Sunday-school education. He became president of a local YMCA in Pennsylvania in 1867 and introduced singing services; Moody, meanwhile, had become deeply involved in YMCA affairs in Chicago. When the two met at a YMCA convention in Indianapolis, Moody recognized that the dramatic effect of Sankey's singing on audiences represented the missing element in his own evangelistic approach. They immediately formed a partnership that saw Sankey's catchy, repetitive tunes with simple harmonies lure huge audiences into massive responsive singing that left them easy prey to Moody's scriptural passages, anecdotes, parables and exhortations. Like Moody, Sankey had no formal theological training, but he knew instinctively how to arouse audiences through song.

The educational results of the Moody-Sankey partnership were a network of Sunday schools across the United States, a Bible Institute in Chicago, and a far-reaching Student Volunteer Movement that sent college students as missionaries across the United States and the world.

Reference: *Modern Revivalism: Charles Grandison Finney to Billy Graham,* William G. McLoughlin Jr. (1959).

satellite schools Any of a variety of small, ancillary schools providing education to students drawn from a variety of nearby comprehensive schools. Still highly experimental, the satellite school concept can serve a variety of functions. One type of satellite school provides specialized or advanced forms of vocational or academic education that would attract too few students to be cost effective at a conventional comprehensive high school. By setting up a single facility for an entire city or region at a satellite school, the latter can serve students from all comprehensive high schools in the area. The students continue to take their core academic courses in their home schools but complete upper-level, specialized courses at the satellite school. Some cities have upwards of a half-dozen such separate specialty schools.

A second type of satellite school is designed to ease overcrowding in a public school system by establishing ancillary facilities in cooperation with new local industries whose arrival causes a sudden ballooning in the school population. A natural extension of company day-care programs, the concept began in Miami, Florida, in the 1980s, when a huge expansion of Miami International Airport threatened existing public schools with overcrowding. To relieve the problem, the airport authority agreed to convert an administrative building into the Miami International Airport Satellite School, where 60 children of airport workers enrolled in kindergarten and first grade classes staffed by Miami public school teachers and administrators. At least five similar satellite schools were later established, either in portable classrooms or at company-built schoolhouses, with the sponsoring firms paying costs of maintenance, electricity and security, while the local school system paid all other educational costs. Companies sponsoring such schools reported that absenteeism among workers with children at a satellite school dropped 30%, while job turnover declined 4%, to 5%.

References: Dade County Board of Education, Miami, Florida; NYT; *High School,* Ernest L. Boyer (1983).

save harmless A legal term referring to the indemnification that many school districts and states afford to teachers in the performance of their stated duties. Under the concept, some states are required to defend teachers against charges of negligence and pay any judgments awarded.

Reference: *The Law of Public Education,* E. Edmund Reutter Jr. and Robert R. Hamilton (1976).

scale In education, a statistically graduated series of grades or scores that relates each individual's score to the scores of all others in the same group. Unlike raw scores, which might include zeros and 100 percents, a scale bases all scores on aggregate measurements, such as a mean, and compares each score to that mean rather than any absolute figure. Scales based on means and standard deviations thus convert raw scores into practical, relative scores. I.Q. and Scholastic Assessment Tests are but two of a wide variety of scales for grading various types of tests. Neither scale has a zero. Instead, 500 is arbitrarily selected as the mean of all raw scores for SAT tests, while 100 is the mean for I.Q.

scores. Conversion of all raw scores to an appropriate scale thus allows them to be compared to each other and to a norm. Fifty correct answers on a SAT test of 100 questions, for example, has no broad meaning until it is converted to a scale in which it can be compared to other test results. If the mean score for all test takers is 50 correct answers, then 50 would convert to 500 on the SAT scale. Depending on the number of raw scores above or below 50%, each score could convert to any level on the scale above or below the mean. Indeed, a 50/100 raw score could conceivably convert to a 200, the lowest score on the SAT scale, or an 800, the highest score, depending on how all the other raw scores place on the scale.

Reference: *Educational Measurement,* Robert L. Thorndike, ed. (1971).

SCAT (Cooperative School and College Ability Tests) A battery of tests, requiring about an hour to measure the anticipated ability of students to complete the work of the next higher middle school, high school or community college grade successfully. Published by the Educational Testing Service, different SCAT batteries are available for grades 4–6, 7–9, 10–12 and 13–14.

Reference: Educational Testing Service, Princeton, New Jersey.

Schall v. Martin A significant but little known U.S. Supreme Court decision in 1984, in which the Court held it constitutional for states to hold juvenile criminal suspects in preventive detention before bringing them to trial. The case involved a New York State law that gave a judge the option of ordering a juvenile (15 years or younger) held in custody for up to 17 days if the suspect was charged with a serious crime, and up to six days for a minor crime. Aimed at preventing suspects from committing additional crimes, the ruling is relatively unknown to the majority of public school teachers, who often feel they have no legal options in the face of juvenile crime in their schools and classrooms.

Although lawyers for juveniles argued that young people should have the same rights to habeas corpus and bail as adults, the Court ruled that "juveniles, unlike adults, are always in some form of custody . . . Children by definition, are not assumed to have the capacity to take care of themselves. They are assumed to be subject to the control of their parents, and if parental control falters, the state must play its part."

According to most polls of teachers, a large proportion fear retaliation for reporting students for criminal conduct in classrooms and school buildings, and few are aware of the Schall decision.

References: *Law Enforcement and the Youthful Offender*, Edward Eldefonso (1983); *The Child Savers: Juvenile Justice Observed*, Peter S. Prescott (1981); U.S. Supreme Court Proceedings.

Schechter, Solomon (1847–1915)

Romanian-born religious leader and educator whose influence spanned the Middle East, eastern and western Europe and, eventually, the United States, where he became the leader of Conservative Judaism. Educated at the universities of Vienna and Berlin, he taught rabbinics at Cambridge University in England and became a professor of Hebrew at London University. In 1896, his archaeological excavations in Cairo uncovered an archive of some 50,000 manuscripts, including the original Hebrew text of Ecclesiasticus.

In 1902, the world-renowned scholar was asked to come to New York City to serve as president of the Jewish Theological Seminary and help revive its deteriorating fortunes. At the time, enormous tensions had developed between the recently arrived, relatively poor and ignorant Jews from eastern Europe and the totally Americanized, well educated, prosperous German Jews. The latter had fanned out across the United States, assimilated with Christian Americans and practiced a Protestantized form of Reform Judaism. They sought to lure the European Orthodox Jews away from their old ways into the new, through organizations such as the Educational Alliance, which sought to Americanize them and bring them into the fold of Reform Judaism. The resistance was enormous, and a group of conciliatory German Jews established Conservative Judaism as a compromise theology that would eschew the use of the English language in services and adhere instead to a modernized practice of Orthodoxy.

Although the Jewish Theological Seminary had been established in 1886, it had met with little success. Seeking peace among the Jews, however, a group of wealthy Reform Jews— Jacob Schiff, Daniel and Simon Guggenheim, Leonard Lewisohn, among them—raised a half-million dollars to restore the seminary and lure the scholar Schechter to New York to head it. A brilliant scholar and mediator, he not only recruited an equally brilliant faculty, he was also able to mediate between the Orthodox and Reform communities. Located at the edge of the Columbia University (q.v.) campus, the seminary, under Schechter's leadership, immediately established links with Teachers College at Columbia University, thus allowing rabbinical students to study the new progressive pedagogies of John Dewey and William Heard Kilpatrick (qq.v.).

Schechter never achieved his original goal of uniting all American Jews into a single movement, but he did manage to create a strong bridge between the Orthodox and the Reform movement that has permitted generations of American Jews to shift their views and religious practices, according to their spiritual needs at the time—much as many Protestants often shift from one sect to another, according to their particular needs.

Schecter's work reached far beyond Jewish Theological Seminary, which remains the most important Conservative rabbinical and cantorial school in the world. In 1913, he founded the United Synagogue of America, which is the central Conservative synagogue in the United States. By the 1970s, the synagogue had grown to more than 800 congregations, each with Sunday and day schools. Schechter was also editor of the first edition of the *Jewish Encyclo-paedia* in 1901, editor of the *Jewish Quarterly Review* and author of numerous books on Judaism.

References: DAB; Jewish Theological Seminary, Archives, New York.

schedules of reinforcement An instructional plan that includes the regular review of previous learning. Reinforcement schedules may be rigid or not, according to the teacher's own approach to reinforcement. Usually, the simplest form of reinforcement begins with the words, "Remember when we talked about X (this morning, yesterday, last week)? What did we say about it?" Fixed-time reinforcement, usually a fixture of mathematics training, calls for a schedule of reinforcement after a specific amount of time has elapsed. Variable-time reinforcement schedules are usually based on a teacher's instinctive skills in selecting appropriate times to relate current materials to materials taught earlier. "Surprise" quizzes are often used as a form of variable-time reinforcement.

Reference: *The Theory of Reinforcement Schedules*, William N. Schoefeld, ed. (1970).

schema theory The belief that the brain organizes all thoughts and experiences in a highly codified way and that all new experiences and learning are absorbed to the extent that they can find an appropriate fit into the student's existing schema. It is the student's schema that permits comprehension and absorption of all new reading material. Without any experience or knowledge with which to relate to a body of reading, the reader would literally see and absorb nothing. To see, for example, t g@l on a printed page produces no understanding unless an instructor can tie each symbol and the total expression to experiences and concepts that form part of the reader's schema. Relating new symbols, words and concepts to children's schema lies at the heart of the complex process of teaching developing children.

Reference: *Theoretical Models and Processes of Reading*, Harry Singer and Robert B. Ruddell, eds. (1985).

Scholar of the House (1) An honorary designation awarded at some colleges and universities to that undergraduate or graduate student who has achieved the highest levels of academic achievement among his or her colleagues during the previous academic year or other designated period. Depending on the institution, the designation may carry a stipend. (2) An honorary title for a faculty member of renowned scholarship or a similar fellow at a particular residential college or graduate school.

References: Yale University Archives, New Haven, Connecticut.

scholarship A word with several meanings, the most common being financial aid (q.v.) in the form of a monetary award to a student, originally granted for exceptionally high academic achievement. Scholarships vary from symbolic stipends to full costs of tuition and are usually granted on the basis of merit. In recent years, however, the "purity" of scholarships in higher education has been sullied by intensified competition among many colleges for top scholars. Used as a lure, scholarships often no longer reflect the actual academic merit of scholar recipients. Moreover, many colleges now routinely award scholarships for achievements outside the realm of academics, such as athletics. Numerous reference books list the tens of thousands of scholarships awarded. In the 1991–1992 academic year, American colleges and universities awarded more than $9 billion in scholarships and fellowships out of a total educational expenditure of more than $121 billion.

A second meaning for the word scholarship is simply the demonstration of academic ability—i.e., to exhibit scholarship or knowledge.

References: *Barron's Handbook of American College Financial Aid* (updated periodically); *The College Blue Book: Scholarships, Fellowships, Grants and Loans*, Lorraine Mathies and Elizabeth I. Dixon (updated periodically).

Scholastic Aptitude Tests An obsolete term for a battery of college entrance examinations that was reformulated in 1993 and renamed Scholastic Assessment Tests (q.v.). The Scholastic Aptitude Tests consisted of two parts: the SATs and the Achievement Tests. The SATs (now called the SAT I) measured verbal and mathematical skills, while the Achievement Tests (now called the SAT IIs) were made up of one-hour examinations on specific high school subjects.

Reference: *A Student's Guide to College Admissions,* Harlow G. Unger (1995).

Scholastic Assessment Tests (SATs)

A battery of tests designed to determine a high school student's ability to do college work. Scholastic Assessment Tests are divided into two parts: SAT I and SAT II. Once called the Scholastic Aptitude Test, SAT I is a reasoning test consisting of two parts, the first of which deals with verbal skills and the second with mathematical skills. The verbal section measures vocabulary and verbal aptitude. Readings with several layers of meaning test the student's ability to interpret and to reason logically. The three parts of the verbal test—sentence completion questions, analogy questions and reading comprehension questions—last 30, 30 and 15 minutes, respectively. Similarly, the mathematics section tests the student's ability to reason logically and to apply mathematical concepts to problems in order to arrive at appropriate solutions. Although there are some multiple-choice questions, success in the test depends on the student's own reasoning skills. Calculators are permitted. The three parts of the mathematics test—multiple-choice questions, quantitative comparison questions and student-produced response questions—last 25, 25 and 25 minutes, respectively. The tests are usually given in January, March, May, June, October, November and December each year.

The SAT IIs test academic knowledge of specific subjects. Once called Achievement Tests, they last one hour each and consist of multiple-choice questions, with one test available for various levels or types of writing, litera-

ture, history (American, European, etc.), mathematics, the sciences and foreign languages. Not all colleges require SAT IIs, but most of those that do use them not only to determine whether to accept the student, but also at what level to place the student in each subject. A high score in a particular subject may exempt the student from the freshman requirement in that subject and allow enrollment at a higher level. A very high score might even exempt the student from the entire college requirement in that subject.

SATs were originated in 1926 by the College Entrance Examination Board (q.v.), a nonprofit organization of 2,400 four-year colleges, founded in 1900 to establish common standards of higher education and common qualification standards for admission. The consensus on these standards forced American high schools to adopt a common core curriculum of English, mathematics, science, social studies and foreign languages.

SATs are graded on a scale of 200 to 800, with 500 the absolute mean, or average. The average is adjusted each year to reflect the distribution of student scores rather than the number of correct and incorrect answers on the test. In any given year, the average score in the nation—500—might indeed reflect a 50% raw score, but another year might see students obtain the average score of 500 by answering only 45% of the questions correctly or, perhaps, 55%. The raw score remains immaterial. Students who score the average number of correct answers on the test for that year receive a 500.

The new scoring was designed to remove SATs from the center of controversy over educational quality in American public schools. Over the 25 years from 1967 to 1992, average SAT scores of college-bound seniors dropped 42 points, or 9%, on the verbal SAT and 14 points, or 2.8%, on the mathematics SAT. Leading critics of American education argue that the decline in SAT scores reflects a decline in educational quality of American public schools. The drop, however, may have been less a reflection of educational quality than of the size and makeup of the pool of college-bound students taking SATs. In the decade from 1980 to 1990, the number of students taking SATs climbed 5% to more than one million. In 1972, whites made up 87% of that pool. By 1991, however, they made up only 72%, while minority groups with less developed English language skills—one-third of them were Hispanic and another one-third Asian—made up 28%.

Critics of the SATs allege that many questions are replete with a cultural bias that produces consistently lower scores among minority groups, especially African Americans. College Board officials insist that the lower scores are the result not of cultural bias but of lower-quality primary and secondary school education in schools serving African Americans. The College Board has been at a loss, however, to explain the consistently lower average scores of girls, who just as consistently obtain higher grade-point averages than boys in both high school and college. In a concession to critics, the College Board redesigned the Scholastic Aptitude Tests and in 1994 renamed them Scholastic Assessment Tests. The new tests replaced some of the multiple-choice questions that had made up 100% of the old tests with questions requiring greater analytical ability. In the mathematics sections, for example, about 20% of the questions on the new test were open-ended, requiring students to calculate their answers from scratch, rather than guessing from a group of choices provided by the test. Similarly, the verbal test presented longer reading passages and more questions aimed at measuring comprehension of themes rather than simple facts.

Reference: Educational Testing Service, Princeton, New Jersey.

school An institution or a group of scholars that provides instruction. The ultimate root of the word school is the Greek word *schole,* meaning leisure. In ancient Greece, as in the United States until passage of compulsory education laws, education—most especially secondary and higher education—was largely reserved for young men whose families were wealthy enough to afford their sons the leisure of attending school. However, the more modern connotation of the word school is derived from the Latin *schola,* meaning discussion or lecture. The English word has two meanings: (1) any institution organized to educate children (minors, as opposed to college-aged students) and (2) a group of thinkers or philosophers dedicated to promoting a specific point of view, way of thinking or philosophy, as in a school of thought.

Schools of thought date back to ancient Greece and the various approaches to thinking about and interpreting the world (see SOCRATES, PLATO and ARISTOTLE). Subsequent schools of thought have emerged with philosophers, scientists, authors, poets, historians, artists, statesmen and religious or social leaders who have presented points of view or interpretations of the world around them that differed in part or in substance from the ideas of their predecessors.

The school as a formal instructional institution of bricks and mortar first emerged in the English-speaking world with the arrival in England of the Roman missionary Saint Augustine in 597. Supported by King Ethelbert, Augustine and his monks established themselves at Canterbury. Intent on converting the English to Christianity, he and his monks fanned out across southern England, scoring huge successes they had not anticipated. The Augustinians soon needed help from a native clergy fluent in Latin, thoroughly familiar with Christian literature and grounded in Catholic liturgy. To educate such a clergy required schools. Within 200 years, the Augustinians had established schools at their diocesan seats. By the end of the medieval period, there were schools at every church, monastery, hospital and charitable institution.

By the end of the 12th century, the first universities had evolved to train and provide England with a highly educated native clergy. The lower-level schools largely became geared to preparing children for eventual entry into university and the clergy. Regardless of their ultimate intent, however, all the lowest-level "petty" schools began with systematic instruction in reading, writing and arithmetic, along with study of the arts and languages. Some were more religious in character than others and prepared children for service in choirs and as altar boys, teaching them "to say, to sing and to read." Others were more secular and sent most of their children into the world of work as apprentices. Between petty school and university, a secondary "grammar" school provided the educational bridge to collegiate scholarship. When the first English settlers arrived in the American colonies, they brought their three-part system of schooling with them. Its development into a purely American system of education is detailed in the article, history of education.

Reference: *Educational Charters and Documents, 598 to 1909,* Arthur F. Leach (1911).

school audit An ill-defined measure of school performance, aimed at making schools more accountable for the academic achievements and failures of students. Somewhat akin to accreditation (q.v.), it differs in its focus on student performance as a measure of the quality of teaching methods and school administration. Whereas accreditation is based on the degree to which a school achieves its stated goals, school audits compare student academic performance at a school with that of previous students and with students elsewhere in the school district, the state and the nation. Any deficiencies are then traced to their sources, either at the district level, the individual school or the classroom, to determine whether the fault lies in the curriculum, the school's administrative leadership or the instructional methods of individual teachers. A school audit presumes that students in each grade should be performing at least as well as the national average for students in the same grade.

In addition to relying on standardized tests, school audits may survey students, teachers and administrators to obtain a clearer picture of the sources of any deficiencies. Thus, one nationwide survey of students by the U.S. Department of Education in 1990 found that only 61% of eleventh graders reported that their teachers routinely marked errors on written papers, and only 31% said their teachers routinely pointed out what was well done. The survey found that only 28% of the same eleventh graders were capable of writing an adequate letter to a senator supporting a position on the space program.

Depending on the individual district or state, school audits may include school-by-school comparisons of dropout rates, student attendance, achievement test results, percentage of students who go on to college and Scholastic Assessment Test (q.v.) scores. Such audits, however, tend to ignore nonschool factors that can affect school performance—namely, the social and economic differences of student families and of the surrounding neighborhood. Income, occupation and education of students' parents, and family stability all have a strong bearing on Scholastic Assessment Test scores, for example. A College Board study in the early 1990s found that students from the poorest families, with incomes under $10,000 a year, scored about 120 points lower than students from families with incomes over $70,000. In recent years, as a result, school audits in some areas have been taking family income of students into account in assessing school performance. Pioneered in New York City and South Carolina, such "school performance scales" have been the target of critics who maintain that factoring student family income into school audits automatically lowers academic standards and expectations for poor students, forming the basis for a self-fulfilling prophecy. The historic goal of American common schools, say critics of such school audits, is to overcome the strong relationship between a child's ancestral economic status and that child's ability. The lowering of academic standards in school audits obscures that goal.

Reference: National Assessment Governing Board, Washington, D.C.

school-based management A system of school administration that places all functional responsibilities—education, curriculum selection and design, teaching methods, textbook and equipment selection, discipline, purchasing, business management, etc.—on school administrators, staff and teachers. School-based management minimizes and often obviates the need for a central board of education and limits the duties of the school superintendent and school board to broad policy determinations and fund raising. Once a policy has been established, the school board's work is limited to hiring the best agents—superintendents and school principals—it can afford to implement that policy.

U.S. Department of Education studies have demonstrated that school districts with the strongest schools academically hire the best professional educators they can find and give them complete autonomy to run schools free of interference from nonprofessionals—local politicians, school board members and parents. "The most successful public schools," said one department study in 1990, "all give teachers a great deal of autonomy in doing their work." Such autonomy, in turn, "produces respect, dignity, deference and esteem . . . [from] colleagues, students and community members." The study found that students invariably function better academically when they know their teachers have authority.

Teachers, in turn, function better when they participate in decisions that affect their work. In general, school-based management allows teachers to design their own courses, select their own textbooks and teaching materials, and teach them in the ways they consider best. Educators agree that decisions regarding a youngster's education should be made by those who know the youngster best and can tailor decisions to individual needs—i.e., the teacher or teachers who work with that youngster six hours a day, five days a week, 35 weeks a year. Although the principal in each school has the ultimate authority, teacher authority over student behavior and student retention or promotion is a mark of well-run schools offering high-quality education. Twenty-one state governments, however, dictate the choice of textbooks for all teachers in all grades in those states. Some even impose lesson plans on teachers. Few school boards give teachers the authority to retain or promote students or impose direct discipline.

School-based management has long been the standard approach in almost all academically selective, private boarding schools and many private day schools, where boards of trustees leave education to professional educators and concern themselves with fiscal matters. Often viewed as an approach to reform in public school systems, school-based management has won little favor among parents and the general public, who have long believed they have a right to determine what is taught in schools and are unwilling to cede that right to teachers.

References: DES; *A Place Called School,* John I. Goodlad (1984); *School Site Management,* Lawrence C. Pierce (1977); *"What Did You Learn in School Today?"* Harlow G. Unger (1991).

school board   An alternative title for board of education (q.v.); an elected body of school district residents charged with ultimate responsibility for all school operations within the district.

school bond   A public or private loan obtained by a school district to pay for capital expenditures over 5, 10, 20 or 30 years, or other extended period. With property taxes only barely covering the costs of current school expenditures, most school districts have little choice but to float bonds and borrow money from the public or from private sources when they require capital sums to build new buildings or renovate existing facilities. Bonds are issued in minimum denominations of either $1,000 or $5,000 and pay tax-free interest quarterly or semi-annually. Most are sold to the general public through local banks. Like all bonds, school bonds are rated by credit-rating agencies who label the bonds AAA (prime), AA (high grade), A (upper medium grade), BBB (medium investment grade), BB (lower medium grade), B (speculative), CCC and CC (highly speculative). Interest rates paid on such issues climb according to the degree of risk: The higher the risk, the higher the interest rate. C, DDD and DD ratings indicate degrees of default, with the school district temporarily unable to pay interest on its debts.

Most school bond issues in middle- and upper-income districts are rated quite highly, because they are backed by the local property owners and, indirectly, by the state. Poor districts are usually unable to obtain approval to float such issues and are, therefore, heavily dependent on state government for capital funds.

References: Standard & Poor's Corporation, New York; *Financing Education in a Climate of Change,* Percy E. Burrup, Vern Brimsley Jr. and Rulon R. Garfield (1988).

school-business partnerships Any of a wide variety of formal or semi-formal relationships between a company and its employees and one or more nearby schools and their teachers and students. Although many companies had been helping students and nearby schools for more than a century, the school-business partnership did not grow into a national movement until Labor Secretary Willard Wirtz berated American industry in a speech at the National Manpower Institute in 1975. Wirtz castigated industry for constantly harping about the declining quality of education while conspicuously refusing to get involved. "Although business leaders have a stake in education," he said, "in no sense do they become full partners in the joint enterprise . . . Virtually every community in the country has an untapped reservoir of personnel and information. What is lacking is the requisite collaborative process."

Wirtz triggered a nationwide movement that saw major companies contribute funds and services to various public school educational programs. By 1992, direct corporate financial contributions to public schools reached $6.2 billion. The school-business partnership movement spread into more than 100 cities in 42 states,

building bridges between industry and schools. The almost endless varieties of relationship include the following:

- Adopt-a-School programs (q.v.) in which a large company underwrites projects at a school, endowing teaching chairs or funding specific purchases of capital equipment such as computers.
- Helping disadvantaged students and preventing dropouts by sending qualified employees to donate their time as tutors, mentors or counselors.
- Establishing enrichment programs for the gifted, sending highly qualified personnel into schools as volunteer teachers and inviting gifted students to corporation facilities for scientific or technological training.
- Helping teachers by offering advanced courses and training in mathematics, science, technology, computers and other areas and by providing grants to teachers for advanced study in nearby colleges and universities.
- Preparing students for the workplace with cooperative education programs, with students spending a half-day in school and the rest of the day at in-plant, worker-training programs.
- Training school administrators in management and leadership techniques. In 1992, 80 firms sent teams of executives to more than 200 schools, resulting in an average savings of $100,000 a year in each school district since the visits.

References: *How to Start a School/Business Partnership,* Carol O'Connell.

school calendar An adaptation of the traditional yearly calendar to include the dates of all pertinent events at an individual school or school district. Published annually before the beginning of the school year in August or September, a typical school calendar would include the school's opening and closing dates, school holidays, vacation dates, dates of board meetings, teacher conferences, PTA meetings, parents' days, athletic events, school plays and community events that might affect school activities. At the beginning of the 1990s, the typical American school year averaged about 180 days—a target of school critics because it is the shortest school year in most of the industrialized world. The average school year at four-year colleges was only 156 days. In contrast, the Japanese school year lasts 243 days; the West German, 226 to 240, depending on the province; the South Korean, 220; the Israeli, 216; the Russian, 211; the English, 192. Spain and Sweden, like the United States, have 180-day school years.

The relatively short length of the American school calendar and the school day itself has been the subject of criticism for some time. In 1994, a National Education Commission on Time and Learning, created by Congress, called for a longer school year and a longer school day. Its report called for a school year of 220 days, with children devoting at least 5 1/2 hours a day to core academic subjects, instead of the three hours they now spend. The commission found that gym classes, pep rallies and sessions on topics such as personal safety and AIDS now absorb as much as 60% of the school day. At the time, about 2,250 schools—with 1.6 million students, or about 4% of the nation's schools—had converted to year-round schooling, with 20 to 30 additional days, and vacations never lasting more than four weeks but staggered regularly throughout the year. About 7% of the schools that tried year-round schooling eventually abandoned it.

Supporters of year-round schooling maintain that shorter summer vacations help students retain more from year to year and provid more flexibility for extra tutoring, field trips and other academic enhancements. In addition, more frequent breaks help prevent both teacher and student burnout, and schools get fuller utilization of their buildings. Opponents say year-round schooling actually costs more, necessitating the operation and sometimes installation of air-conditioning. Critics argue that family chaos can result for siblings of different ages with different schedules. Year-round schooling can also disrupt plans of students who want to participate in seasonal sports or other extracurricular activities. In addition, shortened vacations prevent many teachers from updating their own studies.

References: NYT; United States Department of Education, Washington, D.C.; *Introduction to Educational Administration,* Roald F. Campbell et al. (1966).

school census A count of all school-age and preschool-age children residing within a specific school district. Usually conducted at the end of each school year and during the summer by volunteers in smaller communities and by paid enumerators in large cities, a school census is essential to school budgetary and personnel planning. The school census provides data on student population increases and decreases as well as shifts from one area of the district to another. Essential for establishing school bus transportation routes, the census is also necessary for enforcement of compulsory education laws.

Reference: *Introduction to Educational Administration,* Roald F. Campbell et al. (1966).

school choice The right of parents to select whatever elementary or secondary school they prefer their child to attend. A reversal of traditional state and local authority to assign children to specific schools, school choice began as one of many proposed reforms to improve public school education in the 1980s. It quickly grew into one of the most controversial legal, as well as academic, issues in American education. Adopted or proposed by more than 25 states by the early 1990s, the goal of school proponents was to introduce capitalistic competition into public school systems by allowing consumer-parents to select the best schools for their tax dollars and leave schools with poor-quality education with the choice of either improving or closing. Opponents of school choice countered that only the most aggressively concerned parents (often the wealthiest, best educated) would take advantage of school choice, leaving children from the poorest, most dysfunctional families—the children who most need education—in the worst schools with the lowest quality education. There was some truth to both arguments, depending on the type of school choice and the community that adopted it.

There is a wide variety of school choice, of which the three most basic are intra-district school choice, inter-district school choice and extra-system, or parochial/private school choice. Intra-district school choice allows children to attend any public school within the school district where they live—but nowhere else—at public expense, including costs of transportation to and from school. In effect, intra-district school choice limits choices to elementary and middle schools in most areas of the country, because most districts are served by a single, comprehensive central high school (q.v.).

Inter-district choice permits students to attend any public school in or out of their home district (within state lines), although not necessarily entirely at public expense. Under inter-district choice, the total amount of tax dollars allocated for the child's education in, and public transportation to, the home-district school is simply transferred to the district school the child plans to attend. The parents usually must bear all additional costs.

Extra-system choice, with the child transferred to a private or parochial school, operates in much the same way as inter-district choice, with parents issued school vouchers (q.v.) equal to the tax dollars that would have been spent on the child's education in and transportation to the home-district public school. The vouchers may be used toward paying the costs of private or parochial school.

One irony of the school-choice debate is that all varieties of school choice have been legally available to every American family since 1954. Unfortunately, wealthy or aggressively involved parents have usually taken the most advantage of school choice. Obviously, any American family is legally (though not necessarily financially) free to relocate to any school district it believes offers

its children the highest quality education. Indeed, one of the motivating thrusts of the mass migration from cities to suburbs in the decades following World War II was the quest for better schools in the suburbs. Any family is just as legally free to transfer its children from the public school system to any state-accredited private or religious school or to educate its children at home. Indeed, 25% of American schools are private, and 12% of American children attend them. About 300,000 students, or 0.1% of the student population, are educated at home. In addition, even the poorest children are eligible for free education at (and transportation to) public "magnet" schools, which are specialized schools in the arts, sciences, mathematics, etc., for academically gifted students.

Most children are excluded from these options for a wide variety of reasons, including economic status, less-than-gifted intelligence and distance from better schools. Proponents of school choice insist it would give the poor and the average the same freedom now enjoyed by the wealthy to select the best schools for their children. Over the long term, say school-choice proponents, poor-quality schools will be forced to improve dramatically or face a total exodus of students and eventual extinction, with consequent loss of jobs for the very teachers and administrators who allowed their schools to decline. School choice, in other words, would result in an evolutionary "cleansing" process after which only the fittest public schools, teachers and administrators would survive—and that indeed is exactly what has happened in a handful of free-choice areas.

In one New York City slum, 1,000 students transferred out of the poor-quality public schools in the district after free choice was instituted. Facing loss of state funds, the district immediately began rebuilding its system, adding magnet schools and innovative instructional programs that have reversed the exodus. Another, similar district has won back 6,000 of the 8,000 students it lost to private schools under free choice. Similarly, in Cambridge, Massachusetts, the percentage of students switching from public to private schools dropped from 30%, when free choice first went into effect, to 10%, after the public schools responded to the exodus with educational improvements.

But school choice in other areas of the United States, including Minnesota, which pioneered statewide school choice, has produced little or no general improvement in educational quality or student achievement—at considerable extra cost. Indeed, a 1992 study by the Carnegie Foundation for the Advancement of Teaching found that, while "choice" students moved up from the 30th to 34th percentile in national reading tests, they fell from the 33rd to the 30th percentile in math, leaving them approximately where they started before moving to better public or private schools. In those districts where student achievement had improved following institution of school choice—New York's Harlem and Cambridge, Massachusetts, for example—the programs that produced such improvements were largely the result of huge infusions of federal funding for innovative educational experiments. Those funds are not generally available to the vast majority of schools.

Even more disturbing, the report seemed to bear out most arguments of school-choice opponents. In the first place, school choice had little general, public support. Indeed, 62% of parents polled opposed it, and only 32% supported it. In 1994, voters turned down school choice in a referendum in California, where school choice seemed to have had the most popular support. Many supporters there and elsewhere in the United States, it turned out, were middle-income parents struggling to send their children to religious schools and eager to pay for that education with vouchers for funds they were already paying in local taxes for public schools. Most suburban parents with children in public schools opposed school choice. Although many parents classed as "urban poor" supported school choice, few took advantage of it. In the

13 states that had approved school choice at the time of the report, fewer than 2% of students actually took advantage of it. Moreover, most of the parents who had opted for school choice had done so for nonacademic reasons, such as safety, convenience to the parent's place of work and sports programs. In Minnesota, where only 1.8% of students took advantage of school choice, only 16% of parents cited academic reasons for the decision to change schools. Most of those who took advantage of school choice were white and came from better educated, higher economic groups, thus confirming fears of school-choice opponents that academically laggard children of color from troubled or poor families were most likely to remain in the worst schools. Making that eventuality a near-certainty in most school-choice areas was the freedom of schools to reject or accept out-of-district applicants on the basis of academic qualifications or, as in most cases, space limitations.

Moreover, the report found that school choice not only left the worst schools with less funding and, therefore, less able to improve educational quality, it also added to the overall cost of public education by adding to expenditures on transportation to carry children out of their school districts. State funding of local schools is based on student enrollment, and any loss of enrollment reduces school income. The Carnegie Foundation report cited the case of Brockton, Massachusetts, which lost 135 students—and $1 million in state aid—to nearby Avon. Brockton had to lay off teachers and squeeze 40 students into each classroom.

Opponents of school choice contend it will ensure the perpetuation of what is already a two-tier system of public education in the United States, based on the economy of the particular school district. Funds spent on transferring students from poor to better schools, say school-choice opponents, would be better spent improving education in the poor schools and allowing students to go to school near their homes.

References: NYT; Carnegie Foundation for the Advancement of Teaching, Princeton, New Jersey; *Politics, Markets and America's Schools,* John E. Chubb and Terry M. Moe (1989).

school-college partnership programs

Any of several thousand formal or informal arrangements in which colleges, elementary and secondary schools and their respective faculties collaborate to enhance the education of elementary and secondary school students. From fewer than 10 in 1970, the number of partnerships had grown to more than 2,000 by 1995, with much of the growth spurred by school-reform reports such as *A Nation at Risk* (q.v.) in the early 1980s. Found in every state, each partnership, or articulation program, targets a grade level, with some targeting more than one. About half the programs are designed for high schools, about 28.5% for middle schools and almost 22% for elementary schools.

About two-thirds of the participating colleges are public and one-third private. Although many colleges began their programs to spur public school educational reforms, many other motives contributed to the growth of the partnership movement. One was to halt the decline in college enrollments in the 1980s by providing high school students with stimulating college-level programs that would encourage them to continue their education beyond high school. Another was to improve high school teaching to prepare students better for college-level work. At the time, many students entered college so ill-prepared that colleges found themselves introducing remedial reading and mathematics programs and preparatory, high school-level courses in languages, sciences and the arts. And still another motive for cooperative education was to halt the frightening, accelerating school dropout rates among minority "at-risk" students who would constitute the majority of the population in some states by the end of the 20th century.

There are four basic types of partnership, almost all of which overlap to some degree:

programs and services for students; programs and services for educators; coordination, development and assessment of curriculum instruction; and programs to mobilize, direct and promote sharing of educational resources.

1. Programs and services for students. There are four categories of programs for students:
   a. Early-intervention programs for "underrepresented" and "at risk" students, usually sixth-through-ninth graders but sometimes younger children. Most involve tutoring, mentoring and encouraging interest in education through hands-on activities and field trips. Many offer the promise of college scholarships.
   b. College courses for high school students who have finished the standard high school curriculum. Courses are offered either at high school or at nearby college.
   c. Enrichment and gifted-and-talented programs at elementary, middle and high schools, at colleges or at summer institutes. Among the most prominent college programs for gifted youngsters is the Johns Hopkins University (q.v.) Center for the Advancement of Academically Talented Youth.
   d. Middle and early colleges. A relatively new type of institution for high school students ready for college-level work. Most integrate high school and college courses into a seven-year program taught by a faculty of specially trained high school and college instructors in classes at the two institutions. Simon's Rock of Bard College, Great Barrington, Massachusetts, is the only free-standing middle college for high school students. Most matriculate after tenth or eleventh grade.
2. Programs and services to improve the skills of teachers in the elementary, middle and high schools
3. Development of new curricula and teaching and testing materials. Among the most no-

table outcomes of this type of program were the tech-prep, two-plus-two and coordinated vocational-technical programs (qq.v.) that combined the last two years of high school vocational education and community college technical training into a single, four-year program leading to an associate degree.

4. Programs to promote sharing of educational resources. One result has been the development of new magnet schools that can use college science laboratories and other facilities that would be too costly to build.

(See also PROJECT ADVANCE.)

References: American Association for Higher Education, Washington, D.C.; *Linking America's Schools and Colleges,* Franklin Wilbur and Leo M. Lambert (1991).

school colors The specific hue or combination of hues used to identify a particular school, college or university. School colors date back to the formation of the first schools, colleges and universities of the Middle Ages, when almost all were associated either with the church or a noble or royal sponsor or with a specific merchant guild or trade, and therefore bore the colors of their sponsors. Of little significance in most countries of the world, school colors, often selected arbitrarily, grew in importance in the United States as secondary schools and colleges began fielding athletic teams, whose uniforms and, later, pennants sported identifying colors.

Reference: *The Universities of Europe in the Middle Ages,* Hastings Rashdall (1936).

school design The external and internal architecture of educational institutions. The product of specialists, school design is determined by a variety of often conflicting goals, each of which is determined by the needs and philosophies of various constituencies. A school must not only meet the needs of its users—students, teachers and administrators—it must also satisfy the tastes of the community that commissions it. Exterior design must, therefore, conform to community standards and be pleasing aesthetically, while providing a large enough shell in which to house the facilities required by school administrators and teachers. Underconstruction, based on failure to predict future school population accurately, can often force communities to spend unnecessarily large sums building additions or new schools or using unsightly portable classrooms (q.v.).

Even more than exterior design, interior design must fulfill the needs of a variety of conflicting constituencies—namely, students, teachers, administrators, school boards and taxpayers—while fulfilling the overriding goal of all: educating children. Childless taxpayers might, for example, opt for the least costly, most austere school design with as many students packed into classrooms as humanely possible, while some students might be more concerned with inclusion of recreation facilities such as swimming pools and tennis courts. Administrators invariably demand adequate office space, and teachers seek teachers' lounges and, if possible, individual offices. Science teachers press for lavish laboratories; mathematics teachers for individual computers; language teachers for language laboratories; coaches for athletic facilities; and other faculty for specially equipped art rooms, music rooms and theaters.

In resolving the various conflicts, school designers must keep two overriding concerns in mind. 0ne is the purpose or, in architectural terminology, the program of the building—to educate children as efficiently as possible and to permit movement from class to class in the minimum time. At the same time, they must confront the appalling reality that all the costly facilities of the school will lie empty and unused for an average of 185 full days each year and 17 hours a day of the remaining 180 days of the year, when school is in session. In other words, whatever the designer includes in the final structure may lie idle 85% of the year. From the standpoint of cost effectiveness, it becomes even more essential that school design maximize educational effectiveness during the 15% of the time in which the school is in use.

Although all constituents of the school community agree in principle that school design should permit construction of the best possible school at the lowest cost, the definition of "best" differs widely from one constituency tothe next. Choice of materials alone can produce enormous variations in near-term capital costs and long-term spending on heat, lighting, soundproofing and security. In general, interior design must provide adequate classroom and laboratory space for each student—usually about 30 square feet—and passageway space to permit students to move relatively quickly from activity to activity. Student traffic determines the size of principal and secondary passageways and stairways. Aesthetics and teaching philosophy also enter into interior design. Large windows, for example, allow more light in the classrooms but also produce avenues of distraction for students. Large, open teaching spaces divided by movable partitions are less costly, but elevated noise levels can often interfere with the teaching and learning process. Modern school design tends to leave classroom layout as flexible as possible. Depending on school philosophy and individual teacher preferences and abilities, some classrooms may contain traditional rows of individual desks to encourage classroom discipline. Other classrooms may simply contain long seminar tables for teachers who are able to control the freer give-and-take of group discussions.

Making modern design more complex is the legal necessity of making schools barrier-free to permit access to physically handicapped students, teachers and staff members. In budget-constrained communities, the added cost of ramps and elevators can often preclude special facilities for arts, music, drama and other programs often considered inessential to the typical school program.

Reference: *Guide for Planning Educational Facilities,* Council of Educational Facility Planners.

school directories Any of a wide variety of bound compilations of information about educational institutions. Available in many bookstores and libraries, school directories cover the entire range of institutions: public schools at all grade levels, private and parochial schools, community colleges, four-year colleges, universities and graduate schools and nontraditional schools and colleges. Most provide complete descriptions of each institution's facilities, along with requirements for admission, academic ranking, and all other pertinent information.

(See also PETERSON'S GUIDES; BARRON'S EDUCATIONAL SERVICES, INC.)

Reference: American Library Association, Chicago, Illinois.

school district The most basic, local administrative unit in public elementary and secondary education, with all schools governed by a single school board and under the ultimate administrative jurisdiction of a single school superintendent. Depending on the state, a school district may also be an independent fiscal unit, with its own budget, responsible for annual public disclosure of its finances. It may also have tax-levying authority and the authority to borrow independently. In an effort to promote fiscal and administrative efficiency, most states reduced and consolidated the number of school districts as much as possible during the latter half of the 20th century—from more than 100,000 in the 1930s and 1940s to about 15,000 in the mid-1990s.

References: DES; American Association of School Administrators, Washington, D.C.

School District of Abington Township, Pennsylvania, et al. v. Schempp et al. A 1963 U.S. Supreme Court decision making prayers and Bible readings in public schools unconstitutional, even when unwilling students were excused from such classes. The Court said that in holding such prayers and readings, the Abington School District had violated the "Establishment Clause" of the First Amendment to the Constitution, which states, "Congress shall make no law respecting an establishment of religion or prohibiting the free exercise thereof.'' The clause has been the rationale for every Supreme Court decision enforcing the concept of complete separation of church and state, including any arm of the state, such as public schools.

References: PDK; *The Supreme Court and Education,* David Fellman (1976); *Education and the Law: Cases and Materials on Public Schools,* William R. Hazard; *Constitutional Rights and Student Life: Value Conflict in Law and Education,* Frank R. Kemerer and Kenneth L. Deutsch; U.S. Supreme Court proceedings.

School District of the City of Grand Rapids v. Ball

A 1985 U.S. Supreme Court decision that declared it unconstitutional to pay public school teachers from public funds to teach special programs in religious schools—even when the programs, such as remedial reading, were nonreligious.

Reference: U.S. Supreme Court proceedings.

school enrollment The student population officially registered in American educational institutions. Total enrollment in all levels of education is expected to grow from the approximately 17 million of 1900 to a projected 70 million in 2000. Here are the U.S. Department of Education's actual and projected enrollment figures for various levels of education in 1900 and 2000:

	1900	*2000*
Elementary & secondary school, total	16,855,000	54,412,000
Public schools, total	15,503,000	48,345,000
Public schools, grades K–8	14,984,000	34,441,000
Public schools, grades 9–12	519,000	13,904,000
Private schools, total	1,352,000	6,067,000
Private schools, grades K–8	1,241,000	4,688,000
Private schools, grades 9–12	111,000	1,379,000
Higher education, total	238,000	15,462,000

No breakdown between public and private colleges and universities is available before 1940.

Reference: DES.

school funding The revenues needed to underwrite costs of operating educational institutions. Nationally, of the approximately $250 billion in annual, public elementary and secondary school receipts in the mid-1990s, 46.4% came from state governments, 44.3% came from local school districts and local governmental entities, 6.6% from the federal government and 2.7% from private contributions. The sources of private and parochial secondary school funding varied so widely that no meaningful averages have been developed.

Local school-district funding of public schools became the center of a nationwide controversy in the 1990s, and its future grew unclear. Most district monies originate from taxes levied on local property values, and courts in many states deemed the system unconstitutional because it automatically favored schools in wealthy districts with high property values and low student populations. In 1994, Michigan responded by abolishing the use of property taxes to fund local public education. Instead, the state legislature adopted a new system of funding based on annual appropriations by the state, with funds distributed equally to each school district on a per-capita student basis. Prior to the change, per-pupil funding ranged from $2,300 a year, in the poorest school districts, to $9,900 in the wealthiest. The new Michigan plan attempted to guarantee every school district a minimum of $4,200 per student for 1994–1995, the first school year of the plan.

Though well-intentioned, the Michigan plan, and similar plans adopted elsewhere, did not equalize spending between poor and rich schools as much as legislators had hoped—largely because parents' associations in wealthier school districts can raise substantial sums privately to cover the cost of programs that the tax-based budgets cannot cover. Many such associations raise upward of $100,000 annually to pay for such amenities as full-time art teachers, extra science teachers, full-time nurses and kindergarten aides. In comparison, schools in economically deprived areas, with the same state-mandated, tax-based budget, have no kindergarten aides, no art or science teachers and part-time nurses.

Although the official Michigan plan ended the debate over equalized government spending for education in rich and poor districts, it did not end the debate over whether the increased spending in poor districts would have any effect on educational quality. That second debate had been raging since 1966, when the United States Department of Education published a study of 600,000 students in 3,000 public schools and concluded that family and student attitudes, rather than spending, determined educational achievement. The report was largely ignored. Declining Scholastic Aptitude Test (now, Scholastic Assessment Test) (qq.v.) scores of college-bound high school seniors prompted parents, politicians and educators to call for more spending on education, and, over the next 25 years, per pupil spending across the United States rose from an average of $2,700 a year to $4,900, the highest of any nation in the world, except Switzerland. Average class size was reduced from 25 to 18, while the percentage of teachers with master's degrees rose from 25% to 50%, and median teacher experience went from 8 to 15 years.

Ironically, scores on SAT tests fell by another 5%, with states that spent the most on education having the lowest SAT scores and those that spent the least producing the highest scores. The results fueled a new debate over whether increased spending had any effect on academic achievement. The "ayes" insisted that much of the spending increases over the previous quarter-century had not been on academics, but on federally mandated programs to expand educational opportunities for the handicapped. Moreover, they pointed out the decline in SAT scores was less a reflection of lower academic achievement than of the increased pool of college applicants, which included far more immigrants and poor students than it had 25 years earlier.

The states that spent most on education, such as New York, New Jersey and the District of Columbia, but had the lowest SAT scores, also had the highest proportion of poor and immigrant students, while states with low spending rates and high SAT scores—Utah, for example—had relatively easy-to-educate, homogeneous populations. In other states (mostly in the Deep South) with similar results to those of Utah, college-bound students who took SATs were largely limited to affluent whites. The black colleges and state colleges of the Deep South seldom require SAT or other entrance examinations.

Two Princeton University economists, David Card and Alan Krueger, attempted to end the debate over the relationship between school funding and academic achievement by insisting that the ability to answer multiple-choice questions (on SAT examinations) is not an accurate measure of the quality of public education. Instead, they proposed measuring educational quality by the earning capacity of high school graduates; after an intensive study of state-by-state averages for teacher pay and class size, they found that every extra dollar spent on education produced an increase of 10 cents in the average annual wage of the student beneficiary—a not inconsiderable 10% return. Subsequent studies by other researchers were unable to replicate the Princeton study, however, and the debate over the relationship between spending on public education and academic achievement (and earning capacity) continues to this day.

In higher education, the debate is far more muted, with almost all studies consistently showing an increase in earning power with each additional year of higher education. In higher education, revenues of public institutions approached $110 billion in the mid-1990s, while revenues of private institutions had climbed above $65 billion. Funding of public and private institutions, however, differed sharply, as the following figures from the U.S. Department of Education indicate.

Revenue source (by percent)	Public	Private
Tuition and fees	17.1	40.7
Federal government	10.6	15.3
State governments	38.3	2.5
Local governments	3.7	0.7
Private gifts, grants, contracts	4.0	8.3
Endowment income	0.6	4.8
Sales and services	23.2	23.3
Educational activities	2.9	2.6
Auxiliary enterprises (sports events, etc.)	9.5	10.3
Hospitals	10.9	10.3
Other sources	2.5	4.4

(See also SCHOOLING AND INCOME.)

References: DES; NYT; *Handbook of College and University Education,* Asa S. Knowles, ed. (1970).

schooling and income The relationship between years of formal education and annual personal earnings. Although median incomes tend to climb steadily, the relationship between schooling and income has remained relatively constant. Assuming 1.00 as the median income of all American men aged 25 and over, the median income of men with less than a ninth grade education is only .54, or about half the median income for all men, while the median income for men with professional degrees is 2.37, or more than twice that of all men.

Here are the relationships of schooling and income, for men and women, listed as a percentage of the median income for men aged 25 and over.

Educational attainment	Men	Women
Median income, all ages, 25 and over	1.00	.72
Less than 9th grade	.54	.40
9th to 12th grade (no diploma)	.67	.45
High school graduate (includes equivalency)	.85	.61
Some college, no degree	1.00	.72
Associate degree	1.04	.80
Bachelor's degree	1.29	.95
Master's degree	1.55	1.12
Professional degree	2.37	1.44
Doctorate	1.80	1.42

Although the relationships between median incomes of people with different educational backgrounds have changed little over the years, the actual dollar revenues represented by each median figure for any group have changed substantially. Largely because more men and women are graduating from college with four-year degrees than ever before, their average earnings have declined, because the expansion of jobs requiring such education has not kept pace with the available number of prospective workers. Thus, from 1898 to 1993, the median wage of a man with a bachelor's degree fell, in 1993 dollars, from $18.16 to $17.16 an hour.

Reference: U.S. Department of Commerce, Bureau of the Census, Washington, D.C.

school management The control and supervision of noneducational functions of educational institutions, including plant maintenance, construction, purchasing and finance. One of the most controversial and costly areas of education, school management is given little attention in the curricula of most departments of education and teacher-training institutions. Indeed, the vast majority of school administrators—many of them former teachers who rose through the ranks—have virtually no formal training in business management and usually rely entirely on business managers and school superintendents to handle noneducational functions. The latter, however, usually have no training or background in education, and the result for most public schools is a dysfunctional enterprise in which managers of the educational division and managers of the financial division know nothing about each other's operations and, despite their interdependency, have no controls over each other.

Nationally, costs of this dysfunction in public elementary and secondary schools rose to a staggering $100 billion by 1995, with 39% of all public school funds flowing into noneducational functions. According to the United States Chamber of Commerce's Center for Workforce Preparation and Quality Education, which did a comprehensive study of school-district finances in 1993, 75% to 80% of funds earmarked for public school education should flow into educational functions, such as teacher salaries, instructional support, and instructional equipment and educational services.

In major cities such as New York, public schools were rocked by financial scandals with astonishing regularity throughout the 1970s, '80s and '90s, as unsupervised custodians, purchasing agents, business managers and school board officials pocketed supplies, services and funds, while classrooms and school buildings languished in disrepair, and schoolchildren and their teachers struggled with inadequate or outdated equipment and supplies. In 1990, only 33% of funds earmarked for New York City public school education found their way into the classroom in the form of educational services. Some cities have acted to correct the situation by turning over some or all management functions to private school management companies (q.v.) on a contract basis.

Reference: United States Chamber of Commerce Center for Workforce Preparation and Quality Education, Washington, D.C.

school management companies   Any of a variety of private firms specializing in the financial, administrative and educational management of educational institutions. Operating under contract with public school boards or private school boards of trustees, school management companies are usually called upon to rectify failing schools. The majority of school management firms operate on a consultancy basis, usually focusing on specific failures in educational results, administrative operations or finances. A handful of firms, however, have adopted a more comprehensive approach, taking complete control of individual schools and even entire school systems. Most notable of these was the Minneapolis-based Education Alternatives, Inc., which in 1992 took over management of nine public schools in Baltimore, Maryland, and in 1994 added the entire 32-school, Hartford, Connecticut, public school system.

Contracts with total-management firms such as Education Alternatives usually give the management firm full discretion on all aspects of school management, including the right to hire and fire teachers, nonteaching staffs and school administrators. Such firms usually operate under five-year contracts, agreeing to accept as their fee the annual funds budgeted for education in each school. Education Alternatives and comparable firms claim they can earn profits by a variety of cost-cutting measures to eliminate waste and improve operational efficiency—all, while improving educational quality. Most of the savings are generated by eliminating unnecessary nonteaching school and school board functions, which absorb an average of about 40% of all public school budgets in the United States. Successful private schools funnel 20% or less of their budgets into nonteaching functions such as overhead costs, administration and building maintenance, while providing a level of education that is clearly superior to that available in the average American public school. Much of the higher educational quality of conventional private schools, however, can be traced to selective student admission policies and lower student-teacher ratios. Even the most efficient private schools, however, are nonprofit institutions that rarely finish their fiscal years with money to spare; after its first five years of operation, Education Alternatives lost about $8.5 million. Moreover, there was scant evidence that the company had succeeded in lifting student academic achievement to any significant degree. Indeed, Dade County, Florida, refused to renew its contract with Educational Alternatives, and after only a year Hartford cut the number of schools assigned to Educational Alternatives from 32 to 8.

References: NYT; ERIC.

school nurse   Usually, a registered nurse on a school's noneducational staff, charged with managing student health services. The nurse obtains certification that all students have received their proper inoculations and immunizations each year, renders emergency first-aid and performs superficial diagnoses to determine whether a student requires professional medical attention. The nurse may also check to verify the validity of student medical absences.

Reference: *Redesigning School Health Services,* Annette Lynch (1983).

school phobia An overwhelming, persistent, irrational fear of attending school. Also known as "school refusal," the condition must be treated psychiatrically. Although its exact causes remain unknown, some clinicians associate it with fear of separation from or abandonment by the child's parents. Symptoms include refusal to attend or remain in school and frequent physical illnesses such as nausea, diarrhea, stomach pains and migraine headaches that preclude the child's leaving home.

Reference: *Truancy and School Phobias,* A. H. Denney (1974).

school plant The physical structure of a school and all permanently affixed instructional and noninstructional equipment therein and on the school grounds.

Reference: National School Boards Association, Alexandria, Virginia.

school recognition programs An effort by the U.S. Department of Education to call attention to the successes of outstanding American elementary and secondary schools. The effort began in 1982 in the face of mounting criticism of educational quality and student achievement in American public schools. In addition to balancing public criticism with ample examples of outstanding schools and high-quality public education, the recognition programs provide models for less successful schools to emulate. First limited to public secondary schools, the recognition programs subsequently expanded to include private secondary schools and, by 1985, elementary public and private schools.

After being nominated for the programs, schools are reviewed by an external panel that examines all the school's documents and conducts a two-day on-site visit to determine if it meets detailed lists of "indicators of success" and "attributes of success." About 300 elementary and 300 secondary schools are recognized annually, although no specific number is sought. Schools may be nominated from all 50 states, Bureau of Indian Affairs schools, Department of Defense dependents schools, and schools in the District of Columbia, Puerto Rico and the Virgin Islands.

Schools selected as "unusually successful" generally share these characteristics:

- Clear academic goals, with a clearly stated school mission and a strong emphasis on academics.
- High academic expectations for students, with students taking rigorous courses, and high standards in grading. There is a greater press in such schools for students to go to college and to work at their full potential. There is great concern for those experiencing academic difficulties.
- Order and discipline, with clear guidelines for student behavior. Students are responsible for personal behavior and school duties. Discipline is infrequent but fair and firm. Such schools generally have fewer disciplinary problems and exceptionally low class cutting and absentee problems. Such schools offer a safe, orderly, caring, but regulated environment that promotes close teacher-student relations.
- Rewards and incentives for students, with frequent use of praise and direct performance feedback. Formal prizes were found relatively ineffective, while availability of teachers for personal assistance and consultation proved highly effective.
- Regular and frequent monitoring of student progress through frequent performance feedback to students and regular homework, clearly marked and graded to reflect high standards.
- Opportunities for meaningful student responsibility. High proportion of children in positions of responsibility; high participation in extracurricular activities; many routes to success and diverse experiences for students.

- Teacher efficacy. Respect for teachers and teaching, recruitment of high-quality teachers, great autonomy for teachers, pleasant working conditions for staff.
- Concentration on academic learning time. Students actively engage in learning; classes begin on time; students do more homework; higher rates of attendance and less class cutting.
- Positive school climate, with greater teacher interest in students and shared activities between staff and students under pleasant working conditions. Teachers show high regard for adolescents and awareness of their values, producing a sense of community. Reciprocity in human relations and an orderly, caring environment were characteristic of superior schools.
- Administrative leadership, with consistent policies and procedures and clear authority to solve problems and create means of coordination. Administrators in the most successful schools displayed strong instructional leadership and displayed ''vision'' about school goals and direction.
- Well-articulated curriculum that translates the school's goals and philosophy, supported by appropriate texts. Superior schools often used team teaching (q.v.) to promote curriculum development and articulation.
- Evaluation of instructional improvement. Standardized tests used for diagnosis and justification of curricular decisions such as emphasis on basics.

Reference: U.S. Department of Education, Office of Research and Improvement, Washington, D.C.

school security The men, women and equipment charged with protecting the on-campus safety of students and personnel and the integrity of campus property, buildings and equipment. Although teachers and staff have always been responsible for the security of students in their charge, security grew in importance at the secondary school level in the mid-1950s, with the emergence of armed, teenaged gangs. Security concerns rose during the 1980s and 1990s, as the percentage of murders committed by children under 18 climbed from about 9% in the early 1980s to a startling 15% by 1992. School crime is highest in crowded urban schools, many of which are now patrolled full-time by uniformed, and sometimes armed, security officers and equipped with metal detectors at each doorway. Since the early 1970s, when growing numbers of students began experimenting with chemical substances—and bringing them onto school premises to share with or sell to other students—almost all schools now conduct random locker searches while classes are in session.

At the college and university level, security is largely concerned with protecting students and the campus complex from crimes initiated by persons from the surrounding community. Federal law requires all colleges to disclose campus crime rates to prospective applicants. Most colleges have installed extensive safety and security measures, including locked gates and entry doorways and 24-hour security guards stationed in various dormitory entryways to check IDs. Pathways and sidewalks are usually brilliantly lighted, and emergency telephones and alarm buttons are placed strategically almost every 50 feet. In addition, many campuses provide campus shuttle-bus and escort services after dark, and all colleges indoctrinate students regularly on the dangers of crime, through seminars, pamphlets, posters and self-defense education. Nevertheless, stereo sets, TVs, cameras, computers and other costly electronic equipment in student rooms will tempt burglars. In 1993, for example, Yale University was the target of 1,150 burglaries and larcenies. University of Pennsylvania students suffered 47 car thefts and 45 robberies or attempted robberies in that year, while Harvard was the scene of 39 aggravated assaults.

(See also CAMPUS SECURITY ACT OF 1990.)

References: NYT; *Barron's Profiles of American Colleges* (published periodically); *Yale Alumni Magazine* (December 1994).

school social worker A trained professional with a degree in social work and specializing in counseling needy or socially maladjusted children and their families. Usually a full-time staff worker responsible to the principal, the social worker intervenes when a student's personal, social and emotional problems are having adverse effects on the student's work and behavior at school. Intervention may take the form of direct, one-to-one counseling, or group and individual work with the student's family, teachers or fellow students. The social worker might also counsel the family to obtain outside medical, psychological or psychiatric services.

Reference: *The Practice of Social Work in Schools,* Wendy G. Winters and Freda Easton (1983).

school songs Those melodies and lyrics that, like school colors (q.v.), are particularly associated with and symbolic of specific schools and colleges. Seldom associated with elementary schools, they have their origins in the first schools and colleges of the Middle Ages. At the time, almost all schools and colleges were associated with the church or crown, and all processions and recessions were accompanied by the singing of a particular hymn. Processionals and recessionals remained in the realm of church music until secularization began eroding the theological structure of universities. Harvard University was the first American college to adopt a secular hymn, or alma mater, as the principal school song is usually called. In 1836, Samuel Gilman, Harvard class of 1811, introduced "Fair Harvard," sung to a traditional Irish air, to commemorate the 200th anniversary of Harvard's founding. Student songs, unrelated to their particular school or college, predate school songs by many centuries. Usually sung at celebrations, the most renowned is "Gaudeamus igitur" (q.v.), which may date from as early as the 13th century and has been sung by generations of students throughout the world at festive occasions. Still sung by many college glee clubs (q.v.), its opening measure, "Gaudeamus igitur, Juvenes dum sumus," calls on students to "be merry while we are young," to wish their teachers long life ("Vivat academia, Vivat pro-

fessores") and to pray that the school that educated them will flourish ("Alma Mater floreat, Quae nos educavit").

School songs proliferated in the United States toward the end of the 19th century, as schools and colleges sponsored sporting events, and students cheered, and ultimately sang songs, to urge their school teams to triumph. Many school songs were written and composed by students who later went on to great fame as song writers. As an undergraduate, Cole Porter wrote two of Yale's famous football songs, "Bulldog" and "Bingo," which are still sung at Yale football games. At the end of the 19th century, the composer-to-be Charles Ives composed Yale's still-popular drinking song, "Here's to Good Old Yale."

References: *Yale University Song Book,* Yale University Library (published periodically).

school staffing ratios Any of a variety of ratios that relate the number of students to the number of full-time teachers (student-teacher ratio), counselors to students, administrators to teachers, etc. Such ratios are particularly important in school evaluations that seek empirical measurements to compare one school to national norms and to other schools in the area and in the state. The average national student-teacher (or pupil-teacher) ratio in public schools in 1994 was 17.6:1, compared to a national average of 15.0:1 for private schools. Public elementary schools had a student-teacher ratio that averaged 19.0:1, while the average student-teacher ratio of public high schools in the United States was 15.4:1. The student-teacher ratio of private schools averaged 16.5:1 in elementary schools and 11.4:1 in secondary schools. University of Chicago School of Education studies in 1993 indicated that the quality of education and student achievement increase in inverse proportion to the student-teacher ratio.

References: DES; NYT.

schools-within-a-school An administrative system in large schools whereby the student body is divided into smaller, semi-autonomous administrative units of 500 or fewer students each. Usually applied at the secondary school level, the concept developed in the late 1950s, as huge urban and suburban comprehensive schools grew overcrowded and virtually ungovernable. Suburban schools used the luxury of open areas to build freestanding middle schools where the seventh, eighth and ninth grades were combined in a setting away from the high school. Urban high schools had little choice but to reserve specific physical areas within the building—either a wing or a specific floor—for the exclusive use of students assigned to a particular "school" within a school, or "house," as it is often called. Each house has its own administrators, counselors and faculty. Specific classes or groups may go beyond the physical boundaries of each house to share certain common facilities that might otherwise lie idle most of the time—science laboratories, for example—but never to use those facilities at times when they might commingle with students of another house. Some interschool contacts may occur in varsity athletics, the school band or dramatics, but the thrust is to give students the advantages of the atmosphere, warmth and individual attention inherent in small schools, along with the consequent decrease in violence, conflict, loss of individual identity, class absenteeism and other ills inherent in all large institutions.

A 1993 study of Philadelphia schools measured differences in scholastic achievement of high school students in schools-within-a-school, each with a maximum of 400 students, against comparable students in conventional high schools with nearly 2,000 students. The schools-within-a-school saw 76.7% of their students pass English achievement tests, 76.4% pass social studies, 70.5% pass math and 77.2% pass science. In contrast, only 71.3% of students in the larger, conventional schools passed, while 75.8% passed social studies, 65.5% passed math and 71.3% passed science. Average daily student attendance at the smaller schools was 83.8%, compared with 80.4% at the larger schools,

while the percentage of students suspended at least once was 1% lower—16% versus 17%.

Schools-within-a-school may be organized vertically or horizontally, with vertical schools made of students in a single grade and horizontal schools made up of students from all grades. Vertical schools-within-a-school tend to be more effective, because they accommodate individuality by giving students the flexibility to move up or down a half-grade, according to their ability. There is, in other words, more overlapping, with faster students able to move ahead and slower students able to take their time with the majority of their classmates, while a handful of their peers are simply accommodated in a class of slightly older students. But in essence they remain together as a class. In the horizontal schools-within-a-school, all students must remain at grade level, when some could easily master more advanced work in certain subjects. Still another advantage of vertical schools-within-a-school is the opportunity to grow socially by mingling with students of different ages.

References: *The Schools-Within-A-School Program: A Modern Approach to Secondary Instruction and Guidance,* Robert D. Ramsey et al. (1965).

schools without walls So-called "open-space" schools, with few interior partitions, allowing groups of students to work in separate areas of a huge, open space. An outgrowth of open education (q.v.), or open classroom techniques, that developed in preschools of the 1930s and 1940s, schools without walls provided enormous appeal to both progressive educators and to taxpayers and school boards eager to cut the escalation in school construction costs in the decades following World War II. Especially effective in elementary schools, schools without walls are particularly conducive to team teaching. Seated in different parts of a huge room, on carpeted floors that minimize noise, groups of students and their teachers work on one topic at a time, and, when appropriate, a second teacher specializing in another subject may arrive to introduce applications of the first subject to a second subject. Groups of students will join or separate, according to what they are studying. In simplest terms, a group studying Egyptian history with one teacher would learn the plane and solid geometry of the pyramid from another, the origins of language and hieroglyphics from a third teacher, art from a fourth and geography and political science from a fifth. Various groups might work together or apart, according to a schedule of team teaching determined by the faculty.

From the construction point of view, schools without walls eliminate all costs of partitions and their attendant insulation and wiring. When needed, portable folding partitions, portable chalkboards and other movable equipment can substitute for all materials that conventional walls might support. White-taped ''alleyways'' solve the problems of student traffic flow during and between classes.

Reference: *Profiles of Significant Schools: Schools Without Walls,* Educational Facilities Laboratories (1971).

School-to-Work Opportunities Act A

$300 million federal program enacted by Congress in 1994 to fund public school programs to integrate the teaching of work skills with the teaching of academics. Designed to improve the preparation of non-college-bound students for jobs and the marketplace, the act is a two-pronged program, with both elements requiring linkages between schools and local businesses. The first combines traditional academic classroom work with special work in which students are paired with professional volunteers from local business, who show students how the classroom work is directly related to practical work. A volunteer stockbroker in the school-to-work program might tie the study of fractions to the workings of American financial markets and even to the national or world economy. The second thrust of the program asks the non-college-bound student to select a ''career major'' at the beginning of the eleventh grade and, with

the help of cooperating businesses, obtain work in that field after school hours and receive a year's training after graduation.

Reference: U.S. Department of Education, Washington, D.C.

school visits Visits by parents and their children to evaluate a school and determine whether it is appropriate for one or more of their children. Evaluative parental visits are usually somewhat unwelcome in public schools, where administrators believe that parents have little choice but to send their children to a particular school. However, parents do have a wide range of school choice (q.v.), and, as in visits to private schools, visits to public schools can simplify that choice by providing such information as whether the school is accredited by the appropriate regional accreditation association (q.v.), how students are doing academically and the colleges to which the school's graduates have been admitted. Visits also elicit such information as the quality of the school neighborhood, the physical condition of the school and grounds, the classroom teaching methods and atmosphere, the adequacy of the school library facilities, sports and extracurricular activities, special education programs, psychological services and guidance departments, and school security. A school visit may also include an interview with the principal or headmaster to determine the school's educational philosophy and how that philosophy is translated into concrete results in the form of student achievement.

Reference: *''What Did You Learn in School Today?''— A Parent's Guide for Evaluating Your Children's School,* Harlow G. Unger (1991).

school voucher A certificate valid for a fixed sum of tuition funds that parents may withdraw from the funds set aside for educating their children in public school and use toward payment of education in any other public or private school in the state or district. A highly controversial form of school choice (q.v.), vouchers were first introduced in 1990 by the city of Milwaukee, which passed a scheme whereby low-income students were provided with funds to attend other, nonreligious schools. About 900 students participated in the program annually, but the system was under challenge, and the U.S. Supreme Court had yet to rule on its constitutionality.

Although California voters rejected a voucher plan, Puerto Rico became the second school system to introduce a voucher system in 1993, when it offered vouchers worth up to $1,500 a year at any private or public school for children from families earning less than $18,000 a year. The system came under immediate attack in the courts by the island's three teachers' unions who claimed that dollars spent on vouchers siphoned badly needed funds from public schools. Proponents of vouchers maintained it would force the poorest public schools to compete with better schools or go out of business. Opponents said it was illegal to use public funds to support private schools and that the voucher system was designed to provide public financial underpinnings for a flagging parochial school system.

References: NYT; ''Educational Vouchers: The Private Pursuit of the Public Purse,'' R. Freeman Butts, *Phi Delta Kappan* (September 1979); *Education Vouchers: A Report on Financing Education by Payments to Parents,* Center for the Study of Public Policy, Cambridge, Massachusetts (1970); *Educational Vouchers: Concepts and Controversies,* George R. La Noue, ed. (1970).

science A broad term meaning, collectively, all verifiable knowledge and, specifically, any single body of verifiable knowledge—literally, knowledge in contrast to ignorance. In education, however, the term has taken on a more specific meaning, namely, those bodies of systemized knowledge concerned with the physical world and its observable and measurable phenomena. Although the term may be applied accurately to virtually any area of knowledge— the science of writing, of theology or of football—science in education is generally limited to

the natural sciences, as opposed to the arts, in that accepted knowledge in the natural sciences is largely derived from laws obtained through observation and experiment.

The first efforts to systematize scientific knowledge can be traced to paleolithic times and to designs on the walls of caves. Mesopotamian civilizations produced records of astronomical observations, chemical substances, disease symptoms and mathematical tables. Babylonian mathematicians knew the Pythagorean theorem, solved quadratic equations and developed an elaborate system of measurement as early 2000 B.C. Scientific knowledge spread through the Nile Valley, with the development of early systems of solid geometry and astronomy. The Greek philosopher Thales explored natural phenomena in the 6th century B.C., while Pythagoras systematized mathematics into a fundamental tool for scientific investigation. In the 4th century B.C., Plato developed deductive reasoning and mathematical representation, while Aristotle developed a system of inductive reasoning and qualitative description and classification that combined to form the core of scientific investigation for the next 20 centuries.

Astronomy, geometry, mechanics, hydrostatics, botany, anatomy and physiology made great strides during the so-called Hellenistic Age following the death of Alexander the Great, but scientific progress came to a virtual halt after the Roman destruction of Carthage and Corinth in 146 B.C. Although progress continued in other cultures—particularly the Arabic, Hindu and Chinese—disciplined scientific inquiry in the modern sense began to see a revival in Western Europe only with the publication of the works of Copernicus in astronomy and of Vesalius in anatomy in 1543. Two years later, Italian mathematician Geronimo Cardano (1501–76) modernized algebra. The seminal work of Galileo Galilei (1564–1692) in mathematics, astronomy and physics may be said to have opened the way for the development of all modern science.

In the English-speaking world, science of a

sort was first taught at Oxford and Cambridge universities in England in the 1250s. This was a result of Papal authorizations that permitted the teaching of Boethiusian arithmetic, Euclidean geometry, Ptolemaic astronomy, Galenian and Hippocratic medicine and the three philosophies—mental, moral and natural—the last referring to a broad scientific study. During the 13th century, Roger Bacon (?1220–92) at Oxford expanded the frontiers of Aristotelian science (arithmetic, geometry, music and astronomy), incorporating Arabic learning, observation and controlled experiment, but scientific activity—apart from alchemy—was largely suppressed by religion and superstition until the 17th century, when England's Sir Francis Bacon (q.v.) provoked a shift of intellectual focus from the supernatural to the natural. A non-academic humanist, Bacon developed a startling new theophilosophy that contested the Old Testament dictum that "in much wisdom is much grief." Although ambivalent about knowledge, he nevertheless recognized the universe as God's creation and believed that knowledge of the universe produced a more profound knowledge of God. Francis Bacon revitalized the discipline of observation and refined the inductive method (q.v.).

The Age of Enlightenment that followed Bacon saw a spectacular growth in the body of the sciences and their study in schools and universities in England and in the colonies, with the opening of the first American institutions such as Harvard College and the College of William and Mary. At first, the four basic Aristotelian sciences—arithmetic, geometry, music and astronomy, along with such subtopics as mechanics, optics, physics, meteorology, zoology and botany—were studied as a totality, usually called "natural philosophy." The Age of Enlightenment, however, saw the sciences accumulate too much remarkable new information to be studied as one all-encompassing subject. The work of Robert Boyle in the 17th century and chemist Antoine Lavoisier (*Traite elementaire*

de chimie, or Treatise on Chemical Elements) in the 18th century led to the spin-off of chemistry as a separate scientific subject. In the 19th century, the works of British physicists John Dalton, James Faraday, James Clerk Maxwell and Hames Prescott Joule and others separated physics from the broad science curriculum as a separate course of study. And the work of Charles Darwin added so much to the scientific literature as to necessitate spinning off biology as a separate course.

Although still taught at the elementary and secondary school level as a superficial overview in the form of "general science," the natural sciences at the beginning of the 20th century had been divided into the physical and biological, or earth, sciences, with the former including physics, chemistry, astronomy and geology, while the latter included botany, biology and zoology. At the college level, each was taught as an individual course. Subsequent subdivisions, mostly in the last half of the 20th century, saw the physical sciences subdivided into mechanics, cosmology, physical chemistry and meteorology and the biological sciences further subdivided into physiology, embryology, anatomy, genetics and ecology.

By the 1970s, the standard elementary school science curriculum consisted of a basic one-year "general science" course with its traditional overview of the entire science curriculum, followed in secondary school by specialized one-year courses in biology, chemistry, physics, astronomy and geology, with only one or two of the specialized courses required for graduation. Ironically, in the 1980s the primary school and secondary school study of the sciences began reverting to the 17th and 18th century principle of an all-encompassing course that tied each of the scientific branches together into a single, interrelated, cross-disciplinary unit. Comparable in its curricular format only to the old "natural philosophy" curriculum, the current curricular approach is to study the sciences as an interrelated group for three years. Under the new, unified curriculum, chemistry, physics, biology, geology and astronomy studies are conducted as intensively as they might have been in individual courses, but their relationship to each other and to life beyond the laboratory is now integrated into the course.

References: ERIC; EB; *The Scientific Renaissance, 1450–1630,* Marie Boas (1962); *The Enlightenment: An Interpretation,* Peter Gay (2 vols., 1969); *The Pursuit of Science in Revolutionary America, 1735–1789,* Brooke Hindle (1956); *Scientific Thought in the American Colleges, 1638–1800,* Theodore Hornberger (1945); *The Appreciation of Ancient and Medieval Science During the Renaissance (1450–1600),* George Sarton (1955).

Science: A Process Approach (SAPA)

An elementary school science curriculum developed in the early 1960s that replaced rote memorization of scientific facts, figures and formulae with a reasoned, hands-on, sensory approach to learning. The K-through-6 curriculum was developed by a team of teachers, psychologists and scientists working under the auspices of the American Association for the Advancement of Science. Although the content of the curriculum remained unchanged, the approach to learning was shifted to an activities-oriented process involving experiment and reasoning as the primary method of developing a permanent understanding of scientific phenomena. The program was divided into two broad segments, one for K-3 students and the other for grades 4-6. K-3 students learned to observe, classify, measure, infer, predict and formulate basic experiments, using numbers and time-space relationships. The curriculum for older students involved formulating hypotheses, defining procedures, controlling variables, interpreting data and, in effect, participating in simplified versions of the experimental processes they would encounter in secondary school and college. SAPA used no specific textbooks, depending instead on kits and on materials available at home, school and in the environment.

Reference: *Teaching Science Through Discovery,* Arthur A. Carin and Robert B. Sund (1975).

Science Curriculum Improvement Study (SCIS)

A widely used, commercially available, elementary school science curriculum developed at the University of California, Berkeley, in 1961. A highly structured, hands-on, laboratory-oriented curriculum, the ready-to-use program consists of 12 units, one each in life science and physical science for each of the six elementary grades. In addition to teachers' guides and appropriate printed materials, SCIS sells all the supplies, animals and living organisms required for student experiments. The juxtaposition of life science and physical science is the key to the program. In fourth grade, for example, the physical science curriculum deals with measurement, motion, change and spatial relationships, using the solar system, time and weather phenomena as primary examples. The life science segment, meanwhile, deals with the effects of seasonal change, temperature, weather and time on living organisms and the environment.

Reference: *Building Bridges,* American Chemical Society.

science education centers

Educational organizations specializing solely in science instruction to student groups of all ages, from kindergarten children to senior citizens. Located in federal parks, forests, refuges and recreation areas, the centers are operated, variously, by private research organizations, educational foundations and the National Park Service. All, however, offer formal, specialized courses in a wide variety of sciences related to wilderness areas, such as wildlife, plants, ecology, geology and forestry. Classes are grouped by age and are usually conducted in conjunction with school and college curricula, with full course credit. Most centers have campsites, some with rustic cabins to lodge students. Courses for kindergarten and other early elementary students usually last only about two days. Classes are held in the wild, using the land itself, along with its flora and fauna, as a laboratory to demonstrate lecture materials. Courses for the youngest and oldest students are less specialized than those for high school and college students, whose courses might well center on, say, hoofed mammals, the trumpeter swan or wolf recovery. Although a handful of centers are scattered in such eastern areas as Florida, Pennsylvania, New York and New England, most science education centers are in the west, in or near major national parks in California, Oregon, Washington, Montana, Wyoming, Colorado, Utah and New Mexico.

Reference: National Park Service, Department of the Interior, Washington, D.C.

science kit A packaged collection of items needed to conduct and complete a science experiment. Commercially or teacher-prepared, kits may be designed for use by students in the classroom laboratory or by the teacher as a classroom demonstration project.

Reference: *Teaching Elementary Science,* William K. Esler (1977).

Science Research Associates A major educational publisher that produces standardized textbooks, prepackaged instructional materials and widely used achievement tests in reading, mathematics, language arts, social studies, work-study skills and science. Designed for students in grades one through nine, the achievement tests are norm-referenced for rural and small-town schools, nonpublic schools and high-level socio-economic schools, thus yielding appropriately scaled scores for students from different types of schools. Originally an arm of International Business Machines, SRA is a subsidiary of McGraw-Hill Publishing Co.

Reference: Science Research Associates, Chicago, Illinois.

scope and sequence Curriculum development terms referring to the horizontal and vertical placement and relationship of materials to be taught. The scope of any portion of the curriculum envelops the horizontal or side-by-side positioning of materials, as in the elements of history, physics, geometry, art and

language development that will be included in the study of the Egyptian pyramids in a single year. Curricular sequence, on the other hand, deals with vertical positioning of topics—the "when" of teaching—as in the positioning of biology, chemistry and physics in various grades of high school or within the context of an elementary school general science course.

Reference: *Curriculum: Principles and Foundations,* Robert S. Zais (1976).

Scopes Monkey Trial The colloquial, newspaper-headline title of the near-legendary court case of 1925, when a high school science teacher, John Thomas Scopes, was charged with violating Tennessee's law banning the teaching of Darwin's theory of evolution. The case gained worldwide notoriety, not for the facts or background of the case, but for the cast of characters, among whom Scopes himself was, perhaps, the least important.

The saga began on March 21, 1925, when Tennessee's Governor Austin Peay signed into law the Butler Bill, which made it illegal for any state public school or university "to teach any theory that denies the story of the Divine Creation of man as taught in the Bible, and to teach instead that man has descended from a lower order of animals." It imposed a fine of $100 to $500 on any teacher who violated the law.

After the American Civil Liberties Union decided to challenge the law, its representative, a local mining engineer, persuaded Scopes, a 24-year-old science teacher and football coach at Dayton High School, to join the challenge. Ironically, all that Scopes did was to do what he had always done—assign students the state's own, prescribed biology textbook, George William Hunter's *A Civic Biology* (1914), which explained the theory of evolution. Formal charges were filed against Scopes, who was arrested on May 7, 1925, and charged in a preliminary hearing on May 10. It was then that the major characters in the plot moved onto center stage. The gifted orator William Jennings Bryan, a three-time candidate for the U.S. presidency and a staunch Christian fundamentalist, agreed to represent the World's Christian Fundamentals Association (q.v.) serve as associate counsel in the case with the state's prosecutors. Clarence Darrow, the world-renowned trial lawyer and gifted orator, agreed to serve as co-counsel for Scopes.

The appearance of the two "stars" on the same stage drew hordes of spectators and more than 100 reporters from around the world. At stake was nothing less than the legal supremacy of the American Constitution over the Bible, with Darrow assembling a cast of distinguished legal scholars and scientists to argue that the Butler Law was unconstitutional in that it established a state religion. In any case, they argued, using the Bible as a substitute for scientific truth was nothing less than irrational, because even biblical scholars disagreed over interpretations of Scripture. Bryan's argument rested not only on biblical inerrancy, but also on the question of the parental right to determine whose truths their children would be taught—the truths of parents or the truths of professional experts. After six days, the judge ruled such testimony irrelevant to the case, which, he said, hinged only on whether Scopes had violated the law, not on whether the law was constitutional or valid.

On the seventh day, however, Darrow shocked the world by calling Bryan to the stand; surprisingly, neither the judge nor Bryan objected. Darrow destroyed Bryan, asking such questions as whether Jonah really remained in the whale's belly for three days; whether the great flood occurred in 4004 B.C.; whether the Earth was really created in six days; and how the serpent moved from point to point before being condemned to crawl on the ground eternally on its belly. Bryan's attempts to support a literal interpretation of the Bible drew gasps of disbelief from the audience. As the formerly heroic figure grew confused and dazed, the judge tried intervening: "What is the purpose of this examination?" he thundered. "We have the purpose," Darrow fired back, "of preventing bigots and ignoramuses from controlling education of the United States and you know it, and that is all." Even Bryan's supporters withdrew from the public eye, as the absurdity of his literal scriptural interpretations became evident.

Ironically, on the eighth day of the trial, the jury deliberated only nine minutes before returning a guilty verdict, whereupon the judge fined Scopes $100. The Supreme Court of Tennessee upheld the Butler Act, but reversed the fine because the state constitution mandated that all fines of more than $50 had to be imposed by a jury rather than a judge. Bryan died five days after the original trial, a beaten man, leaving the Christian fundamentalist movement in leaderless disarray until after World War II. But the greatest irony of the trial is that it produced none of the great constitutional interpretations that its main characters—and indeed, all Americans—had hoped for. In the end, the case involved only the question of whether Scopes had violated the Butler Law. The jury decided he had.

The law remained in effect until the Tennessee legislature repealed it in 1967, and it was not until 1968 that the U.S. Supreme Court handed down the first decision declaring anti-evolution legislation unconstitutional.

(See also EPPERSON V. ARKANSAS.)

References: *Bryan and Darrow at Dayton,* Leslie Allen, ed. (1925); *The World's Most Famous Court Trial, State of Tennessee v. John Thomas Scopes,* John Scopes (1971).

Scottish "common sense" philosophy

A school of philosophy founded by Thomas Reid (1710–96), who argued that human sensory impressions are accurate, valid and reliable impressions of the natural world. Published in 1764 in his *Inquiry into the Human Mind on the Principles of Common Sense,* Reid's philosophy was in direct opposition to that of British philosopher David Hume, who maintained that human reasoning, based on sensory impressions, was inobjective. Even more far-reaching in its consequences, Reid's man-centered philosophy undermined the validity of many basic church premises and God-centered teachings: It implied that many spiritual elements of church doctrine may not exist, because man cannot see, hear, feel, smell or taste them.

Reid was born in Strachan, Kincardine, Scotland, and was a professor of philosophy at King's College, Aberdeen, and later at the University of Glasgow. He influenced an entire generation of presbyterian minister-scholars who migrated to the American colonies and, in their turn, influenced American higher education in the late 18th and throughout the entire 19th century. First and foremost of these was John Witherspoon (q.v.), the sixth but by far the most influential of the early presidents of the College of New Jersey (now Princeton University). Indeed, in his 25 years as president he reshaped the college into a secular, albeit pious, school that produced leaders of the new American republic and shaped secular education for the next 100 years. Among Witherspoon's students were the future president James Madison, the future vice president Aaron Burr, 10 future cabinet officers, 60 future members of Congress, three future justices of the Supreme Court and his own successor at Princeton, Samuel Stanhope Smith. In his lectures, Smith summed up the Scottish "common sense" school by saying that "the testimony of our senses and of all our simple perceptions . . . ought to be admitted as true, and no ulterior evidence be required of the reality, or the nature of the facts which they confirm."

In education, Smith expanded on the Scottish common-sense realism he had learned from Witherspoon by enlarging the Princeton curriculum to include the widest range of secular courses of any college in the colonies. Smith's students, in turn, went on to head the universities of Pennsylvania, North Carolina and others, thus carrying the influence of Scottish common-sense philosophy to every corner of the new nation in the early 1800s. Indeed, Scottish realism, according to one historian, "overran the country" during the revolutionary era "and had

an exclusive and preponderant influence well beyond the centennial of the country's independence." It was not until the development of the laboratory sciences at the end of the 19th century that the reliability of raw, sensory observations came into question once again.

References: *Princeton College During the Eighteenth Century,* Samuel Davies Alexander (1872); *Inquiry into the Human Mind on the Principles of Common Sense* (1764), *Essays on the Intellectual Powers of Man* (1785) and *Essays on the Active Powers of Man* (1788), Thomas Reid.

screening test   Any of a wide variety of written, oral or other form of examination used to accept and reject specific individuals or groups of individuals from a specific activity. Thus, screening tests may be used to eliminate ineligible applicants for teaching or staff positions—or prospective students. Screening tests may also be used to identify a variety of learning or physical disabilities requiring special education—or to identify specific skills and skill levels required for participation in a variety of academic and nonacademic school activities, such as the school orchestra or football team. Screening tests use a variety of criteria, including minimum test scores and demonstration of specific aptitudes, abilities and skills.

Reference: ERIC.

sea-grant colleges   A group of colleges in five coastal states that trains professional officers for the United States Merchant Marine. Created by Congress under the 1966 National Sea Grant and Program Act, the sea-grant colleges are somewhat akin to the land grant colleges (q.v.) that Congress created in the 19th century to train students for agriculture and mechanics (engineering). Like the land-grant colleges, the sea-grant colleges are public and are one of many academic programs or "schools" in what are otherwise conventional state university systems. Funded in part by the federal government, the sea-grant colleges duplicate the curriculum and training offered by the U. S. Merchant Marine

Academy (q.v.). The five sea-grant colleges are the California Maritime Academy, the Maine Maritime Academy, the Massachusetts Maritime Academy, the State University of New York Maritime College and Texas A & M University at Galveston.

References: *Barron's Profiles of American Colleges;* NYT.

searches of students In education, the physical inspection by school authorities of the person and property of minor students and the equipment they use. A highly controversial legal and social issue, student searches became increasingly essential in many American elementary and secondary schools in the last half of the 20th century, as minors gained access to drugs and weapons. There is no question of school authorities ever searching students who have reached the age of majority and are, therefore, fully protected by the Fourth Amendment of the U.S. Constitution, guaranteeing the "right of the people to be secure in their persons, houses, papers, and effects, against unreasonable searches and seizures." To search the person or property of a college student, for example, college officials would have to turn to the police, file formal charges and obtain a warrant, or provide evidence that a crime was being or was about to be committed.

Children, however, were chattel at the time of the writing of the Constitution, and, for the first 150 years of the republic's existence, teachers and school administrators routinely searched any student's person or property when it seemed in the best interests of school discipline. In the last decades of the 20th century, however, an increasing number of parents have filed civil suits and even brought criminal complaints against teachers who so much as touched their children, and the courts have been hesitant to provide educators, parents or students with a definitive set of rulings on student searches. A few state courts have ruled that school authorities have the right to search student desks and lockers, which are legally the property of the school. Some states, however, insist that such searches be conducted only with student permission and with the student and at least one adult witness present. Most states now require that schools include in their published school rules their policy with regard to desk and locker searches.

As for searches of the student's person and property, the first, somewhat definitive U.S. Supreme Court decision on the subject came in 1985, in *New Jersey v. T.L.O.* (q.v.). In that case, the Court ruled it legally permissible for public school officials and teachers to search a student's property as long as the scope of the search was proper and there were "reasonable grounds" to believe the search would yield evidence of a violation of the law or school rules. Although the Court said that students were covered by Fourth Amendment protection against "unreasonable searches and seizures," it said that school officials could conduct certain types of searches without a warrant as long as they fulfilled two important prerequisites: they based the search on grounds of reasonable suspicion, and they limited the scope of the search to one that was appropriate for the circumstances.

In the case of "T.L.O." (the initials of a girl whose name was kept confidential), the student was caught smoking in the school bathroom. School officials searched her pocketbook and found drug paraphernalia and evidence of recent drug sales. They called police, and she was arrested. She challenged her eventual conviction on the grounds that the evidence against her had been seized illegally, but the Court ruled against her.

Noting that violent crime and drug use in schools had become "major social problems," the Court declared that "the school setting requires some easing of the restrictions to which searches by public authorities are ordinarily subject." The Court failed, however, to provide specific, in-school search-and-seizure rules and left most educators unclear about the extent of their rights in this area. "The legality of a search of a student," said the Court, "should depend simply on the reasonableness, under all the circumstances, of the search."

References: National Education Association, Washington, D.C.; U.S. Supreme Court proceedings.

secondary education A generic term referring to all formal education between elementary school and college, usually seventh through twelfth grades. Secondary education usually consists of two programs: junior high, or middle, school, with seventh and eighth grades; and senior high, or simply high school, with grades 9-12, offering general, technical, vocational or college-preparatory curricula. Often housed in separate buildings and even on different campuses, both differ from elementary education in that the faculty is made up of specialist teachers, each conducting courses in a specific subject, with students moving from classroom to classroom throughout the school day to study each subject. In contrast, elementary school teachers are usually generalists, each of whom teaches almost the entire curriculum to a specific age group in the same classroom throughout the school day.

Unlike elementary education, secondary education was slow to develop in the United States. Long reserved for a relatively small, wealthy, academic elite preparing for college, secondary education has its roots in the early, colonial grammar schools—the first having been Boston Latin, which was founded in 1635. At the time, primary education in petty schools (q.v.) consisted of about three years of education in basic reading, writing and calculating for five- to seven-year-olds. Secondary education, which lasted about seven years, was reserved for wealthy or particularly talented boys and progressed to Latin, Greek and occasionally Hebrew, along with a thorough study of the Scriptures. From grammar school, students who wanted to continue their education either enrolled at Harvard College, the only college in the colonies in the early 17th century, or crossed the Atlantic to enroll at an English, Scottish or continental university.

As the grammar school curriculum expanded in the 18th and early 19th centuries to include the sciences, modern languages, philosophy and other courses, another type of secondary school, the academy (q.v.), evolved. Academy education varied widely, with some offering little more instruction than the traditional grammar school and others a range of education comparable to any college in the colonies. With the advent of public education in the 19th century, primary and secondary education underwent a radical structural change, with primary schools gradually evolving into elementary schools and expanding their curricular reach from kindergarten through sixth grade. Grammar schools and academies metamorphosed into junior and senior high schools, offering instruction from grades seven through twelve.

Until well into the 20th century most American children ended their education after elementary or junior high school. As late as 1940, only 50.8% of American 17-year-olds actually finished high school. The earliest available figures show that only 2% of American 17-year-olds graduated from high school in 1870, 2.5% in 1880, 3.5% in 1890 (half of them from private schools, however) and 6.4% in 1900 (one-third from private schools). By 1930, 29% of American 17-year-olds were graduating from high school, with nine-tenths of them emerging from public schools. In 1994, 73.1% of American 17-year-olds were graduating from secondary schools.

Reference: *Secondary Education: An Introduction,* David G. Armstrong and Thomas V. Savage (1983).

Secondary School Admission Test (SSAT) A standardized test used by more than 500 American private, independent secondary schools to measure verbal and mathematical skills of applicants for admission to grades six through eleven. A multiple-choice test that measures student ability to use words, understand written materials and solve mathematical problems, the SSAT is administered about a half-dozen times a year, on Saturday mornings, at about 250 test sites across the United States. Administered by the Educational Testing Service (q.v.), the test is sponsored by the Secondary School Admission Test Board, an organization of more than 600 independent secondary schools. The test is, however, only one of dozens of criteria for evaluating candidates for admission.

Reference: Educational Testing Service, Princeton, New Jersey.

Secondary School Science Project (SSSP)

An earth-science course developed by a group of geologists in the 1960s for high school students. Like many courses and curricula developed to encourage student interest in the sciences, SSSP replaced traditional textbook study with a sequence of student experiments and investigations, through which students compiled textbooks of their own from their accumulated notes and observations.

Reference: McGraw-Hill Book Company, New York.

Secretary of Education (U.S.)

The administrative head of the U.S. Department of Education (q.v.), a cabinet-level department that administers and coordinates most federal aid to education and compiles statistics on and disseminates the vast majority of data on American education. Appointed by the president of the United States, with the approval of the U.S. Senate, the secretary of education, like all cabinet officers, serves at the pleasure of the president and may be removed by the president at will or by congressional censure or impeachment. Charged with carrying out presidential policies, the secretary—again, like all cabinet officers—has no executive function. The first secretary of education was Shirley Hufstedler, appointed by President Jimmy Carter in 1979, when the department was created. She was succeeded by Terrel Bell (1981–85), William J. Bennett (1985–88) (qq.v.) and Lauro F. Cavazos (1988–89), all of whom served in President Ronald Reagan's administration. Cavazos

(1989–91) and Lamar Alexander (1991–93) served in President George Bush's administration, and Richard W. Riley took office at the beginning of President Bill Clinton's administration.

Prior to elevation to cabinet rank, the administration of the federal government's education functions had been headed by a commissioner of education in the Department of Health, Education and Welfare—prior to 1953, in the Department of Interior. The first commissioner of education was the renowned American educator Henry Barnard (q.v.), who was named to the post in 1867. His successors had few duties and were relatively impotent figures who, at best, could use their small and powerless agency only as a "bully pulpit" to preach the tenets of progressive education and school reform.

References: EB; ERIC.

segregation

The involuntary separation of people according to various characteristics such as race, religion, national origin, gender, physical or mental disadvantages or other definable differences. There are two broad types of segregation: de jure and de facto, the former referring to segregation by law and the latter to segregation by actuality.

Until 1954, de jure segregation of African Americans was the law in states throughout the American South and parts of the Southwest, where blacks and whites lived in separate neighborhoods, sent their children to separate schools and, in many respects, lived their lives separately. The law required that they stay in separate hotels, ride in different sections of trains, buses and other transit facilities, go to separate parks, swim in separate public pools, use separate public washrooms and eat in separate restaurants. There was little question that such segregation forced poor racial minorities into inadequate living conditions, where they received little or no education or other resources with which to emerge from poverty.

Although African-American segregation was most pervasive, American Indians were segregated on reservations in the West, while women were barred by law from male universities until late in the 19th century and from the voting booth until 1919. Jews were barred by town ordinances from living in many towns, and hotels and restaurants throughout the United States had the legal right to exclude them if they so chose. Legal discrimination enabled industries to bar blacks, women, Jews, Roman Catholics, Asians and a host of other qualified men and women from a wide variety of jobs. Members of certain professional or occupational groups, such as professional actors or circus performers, were barred from many hotels and towns.

In 1954, the U.S. Supreme Court declared racial segregation unconstitutional in American public schools, in the world-renowned case of *Brown v. Board of Education of Topeka* (q.v.). Beginning in 1957, Congress passed three sweeping civil rights acts, in 1957, 1960 and 1964, that outlawed all forms of discrimination on the basis of race, religion, national origin, gender, age, physical or mental disadvantages. For the most part, these laws are being enforced as stringently as possible in most areas of the United States.

Elimination of de jure segregation has not, however, eliminated de facto segregation, which remains a pervasive social, economic and educational problem in the United States. Though not the result of any laws, millions of American neighborhoods and small towns are segregated by race or religion from mainstream America—in some cases, self-segregated, in others, segregated by groups who shun other groups and refuse to live with them side by side. Some small Mormon villages in Utah, Idaho and other parts of the Rocky Mountains, for example, seek to remain 100% Mormon and shun non-Mormons who would live among them. Black slums in virtually every American city are often the result of unequal access to good education, to equal job opportunities and to housing in predominantly white areas.

A Harvard University study released in 1993 showed that de facto segregation of schools had actually increased in the four decades following the 1954 *Brown* decision. The report found that 66% of black students in the United States attended predominantly minority schools in the 1991–1992 school year, the highest level since 1968, when the federal government reported the figure at 77%. After dropping to 64% in 1972 and 63% in 1980 and 1986, the figure has climbed since. In addition, the Harvard study found that 74.3% of Hispanic students were attending predominantly minority schools in the 1991–1992 school year, compared to only 55% in 1968, 57% in 1972, 68% in 1980 and 72% in 1986. The study cited higher birth rates and immigration as the causes of increased racial segregation, rather than any white flight to the suburbs. It said poverty and housing patterns in large cities had concentrated black and Hispanic students in districts with few white families. The study predicted that within 30 years, half the public schools in the United States will be predominantly black and Hispanic.

Conducted for the National School Boards Association, the study's findings were startling and ironic. It found that schools in the northeast, which had provided much of the moral thrust to desegregate schools in the south during the Civil Rights Era of the 1950s, were now the most racially segregated schools in the United States, while schools in the south were the most integrated.

In the nation's largest cities, the study found that 15 of every 16 black and Hispanic students were in schools where most of the students were non-white. In medium-sized cities, 63% of African-American and 70% of Latino students attended such schools. The study found that black and Hispanic students were much more likely than white students to be in schools where academic achievement was below national averages. In states with the most racially segregated schools, the percentages of blacks attending schools where minorities made up 90% to 100% of the student bodies were: 59.3% in Illinois, 58.5% in Michigan, 57.5% in New York, 54.6% in New Jersey, 45.7% in Pennsylvania, 37.3% in

Tennessee, 36.8% in Alabama, 36.7% in Maryland, 36.6% in Mississippi and 36.2% in Connecticut. In the states with the most segregated schools for Hispanics, the percentages of Hispanic students in schools where minorities made up 90% to 100% of the student bodies were: 58.1% in New York, 44.4% in New Jersey, 41.7% in Texas, 35.4% in California, 33.7% each in Illinois and Connecticut, 28.0% in Florida, 27.4% in Pennsylvania, 19.6% in Indiana, 18.3% in New Mexico and 16.2% in Arizona.

De facto segregation of economic groups invariably produces lower educational quality in poor districts, where property values are low and yield inadequate property taxes to finance local schools. In contrast, the wealthiest white communities with high property taxes boast public schools that offer a level of education comparable to some of the finest, most elite private independent schools.

(See also AFRICAN AMERICANS; CIVIL RIGHTS ACT OF 1964; DESEGREGATION.)

References: NYT: *School Desegregation*, Harold B. Gerard and Norman Miller (1975); *The Courts and Education*, University of Chicago Press (annual yearbook).

Seguin, Edouard (1812–1880) French-born American physician who immigrated to the United States in 1850 and developed many of the first techniques for successfully teaching mentally retarded children. Seguin had studied under Jean-Marc-Gaspard Itard (1775–1838), the pioneer French military surgeon who specialized in diseases of the ear and developed some of the first techniques for educating deaf-mutes and the mentally retarded. Itard was best known for his work *Rapports sur le sauvage de l'Aveyron* (1801), the story of his attempts to educate a boy found living wild in the forest. Itard insisted that the mentally retarded be treated medically and educationally rather than by imprisoning them as emissaries of the devil. Seguin brought his techniques to the United States in 1850 and strongly influenced the world's educational leaders, including Maria Montessori (q.v.).

References: *Itard, Seguin, and Kephart: Sensory Education—A Learning Interpretation*, Thomas S. Ball (1971).

selection aids for colleges and schools Any of a wide variety of electronic or printed directories, catalogs, guides, brochures and profiles to help prospective candidates for colleges or private elementary and secondary schools choose institutions whose educational goals and policies most suit their individual needs. Independent publishers such as Barron's Educational Series, Inc. (q.v.), of Hauppauge, New York, and Peterson's Guides, Inc. (q.v.), of Princeton, New Jersey, are the largest producers of college directories available to the general public in book stores and libraries. Both publish so-called profiles (q.v.) of a wide range of four-year colleges, universities and two-year colleges, and Peterson's publishes a definitive catalog of profiles of independent secondary schools. The College Entrance Examination Board (q.v.) also publishes a widely used directory containing profiles of four-year colleges, while Wintergreen Orchard House, Inc., of New Orleans, Louisiana, publishes the comprehensive *College Admissions Data Handbook*, which contains the most comprehensive college profiles of any directory, but is so costly as to be available only through high school guidance offices and major public libraries. Other published selection aids are available directly from independent schools and colleges, which annually publish a plethora of course catalogs, guides, brochures, profiles and histories of their institutions and also furnish prospective applicants with videotapes that offer "tours" of their campuses.

Although published materials formed the bulk of selection aids as the 20th century neared its end, they were gradually being replaced with electronic equivalents, in the forms of software and CD-ROM programs that allow prospective applicants to call up complete college-course catalogs and profiles and conduct college or secondary school searches by punching in the characteristics they most seek at their future colleges or schools. The programs search and call up a list of schools that fit those descriptions.

Available in most high school guidance offices or in software shops, the programs, when used on computers with modems, can also order application forms from any colleges the applicants select.

Computers with modems can also obtain information interactively from the College Board and from commercial publishers by simply punching in the name of one or more particular school, college or university. In addition to general information, such interactive selection aids take the student on "guided" tours of the institution chosen, allowing "stops" to obtain detailed information about any department or activity specified by the applicant, along with all details for applying, obtaining financial aid and enrolling. Interactive computer programs allow the user to apply for admission and conduct searches on the basis of special needs and interests. Thus, a user can punch "nuclear physics," "field hockey," "photography" or any other subject, sport or activity and elicit a complete search for and produce a list of institutions with appropriate facilities.

References: *A Student's Guide to College Admissions* (1995) and *How to Pick a Perfect Private School* (1993), Harlow G. Unger.

Selective Service Qualification Test A
standardized verbal and mathematics aptitude test administered by the United States Selective Service System (q.v.) to college and university students from 1951 to 1963 and in 1966 and 1967 to determine whether or not to grant temporary student deferments from universal military conscription. Students who obtained high enough scores on the test and were maintaining passing grades at colleges were usually granted the privilege of completing their work for undergraduate and some professional degrees before being drafted into the armed services.

Although the Selective Service Qualification Test was ridiculed as a relatively undemanding measure of academic skills, it produced a storm of controversy in public education in 1963, when, among the half-million male college stu-dents who took the test, education majors scored the lowest. The findings confirmed those of James Koerner's study of teacher education: By all standards, students in teacher education training programs were the least able academically.

See also teacher education.

References: EB; *High School,* Ernest L. Boyer (1983); *The Miseducation of American Teachers,* by James Koerner (1963).

Selective Service System (SSS) The U.S.
government organization charged with administering universal military conscription. Created by Congress in May 1917 under the Selective Service Act of 1917, the SSS was abolished after the end of World War I in 1918 but was restored in 1940. It remains in existence to this day, although its role has varied in the decades since 1940, depending on the United States military situation. Charged with registering and inducting all physically and mentally able men within 60 days of their eighteenth birthdays, the laws that determined SSS policies directly affected higher education in the United States during World Wars I and II and, beginning in 1951, during the Korean War, when college students were granted deferments from service to complete their undergraduate and professional graduate educations. At the peak of the Vietnam War, it became evident that the college deferment was shielding from military service a disproportionately high number of white, advantaged young men, while a disproportionately high number of poor, black youths were being drafted. Student deferments were abolished in 1971, but, with the end of U.S. involvement in the Vietnam War, the draft itself ended in 1973, and an all-volunteer military took its place. Mandatory SSS registration of all 18-year-old men was reinstituted in 1980, but not compulsory military service.

Reference: EB.

self-actualization The ultimate level of
human fulfillment under Abraham Maslow's

"Hierarchy of Needs," which he described in "A Theory of Human Motivation." In simplest terms, the theory lists five basic, hierarchal needs in human behavior, each of which must be fulfilled before the individual can progress to the fulfillment of the needs at the next level. The first hierarchy of needs is physiological (food, drink, air, etc.); the second, safety (shelter, etc.); the third, belongingness and love; the fourth, esteem (achievement, prestige, status, etc.); and the fifth, self-actualization, or the fulfillment of the person's complete potential. Maslow defined self-actualization as man being true to his own nature. "What a man can be, he must be" to fulfill the needs of self-actualization. Maslow's theory has had widespread direct and indirect influence on modern education to this day, with most schools aware of helping students fulfill each hierarchy of needs, including adequate food, at the lowest level, with the school breakfast and lunch programs.

(See also NEEDS HIERARCHY.)

Reference: "A Theory of Human Motivation," Abraham Maslow, *Psychological Review* (July 1943).

self-concept (self-esteem) A controversial educational goal based on improving an individual's perception and evaluation of himself or herself. There is little debate among psychologists or teachers that a student's judgment of his or her own worth can affect the student's work in school and, indeed, the student's entire social life in and out of school, at home and in the broader community. The debate revolving around self-esteem is whether it should be the focus of all educational efforts in the elementary school years. Some educators believe that students acquire self-esteem by learning such concepts as "black is beautiful," "I love myself" and other nostra from popular curricula that minimize academics. Others insist that students develop more self-esteem through tangible, often difficult accomplishments with a traditional curriculum that emphasizes competency and skill development in language, mathematics, science, music, art and other academic areas. The debate, in other words, centers on whether self-esteem results from "who I am" or "what I can do" and whether skills and competency—"what I can do"—eventually form the core of "who I am."

The self-esteem movement began in the 1980s, with teachers in many public schools praising student accomplishments so indiscriminately that such praise became meaningless. Teachers admitted accepting inadequate work "because there is the fear that kids will not feel good." Some teachers praised students simply for turning in homework, regardless of quality. In some New Mexico schools, the self-esteem movement lifted two-thirds of all students into the honors category. Supporting the self-esteem movement were publishers, who produced a mass of textbooks and tests with such titles as *All About Me* and *We Applaud Ourselves,* and chapters headed "What I Like to Eat," "What I Like to Watch on TV," "What I Want for a Present" and "Where I Want to Go on Vacation."

Critics of the self-esteem movement maintain that teachers who create learning activities in which all children discover that by working hard they can succeed, generally build far more self-esteem in their students than teachers who simply teach children a series of "feel-good" nostra. Lessons that allow children to connect what they do with what they learn—that cutting a piece of wood in half gives two halves; that $\frac{1}{2} + \frac{1}{2} = 1$; and that 1 divided by 2 = $\frac{1}{2}$—give children a sense of control over the learning situation. They thus learn that hard work produces tangible, rewarding results, including a sense of self-esteem born of the acquisition of control over a body of knowledge.

References: *Self-Concept, Self-Esteem and the Curriculum,* James A. Beane and Richard P. Lipka (1984); *Making the Best of Schools,* Jeannie Oakes & Martin Lipton (1990).

self-contained classroom The standard preschool and elementary school classroom, where students from a single grade remain for most or all of the school day under the direction of a generalist teacher who is able to offer instruction in reading, writing, arithmetic, science, history and other subjects and schedule instruction in each as flexibly as student needs dictate. When necessary, specialized resource teachers may be brought into the classroom to teach foreign languages, music, art, dance or drama, although students, in some schools, leave their own classroom to go to specially equipped art, music and drama studios for lessons in those subjects. The advantage of the self-contained classroom is that the teacher gets to know each student more intimately (and vice versa) and can provide individual attention and remedial work when required, while allowing more gifted students to progress at their own pace. From the young child's point of view, the self-contained classroom and the single, all-day teacher provide a sense of security—of having a "home" away from home with a surrogate parent.

Reference: *The Self-Contained Classroom,* Edith R. Snyder, ed. (1960).

self-education The acquisition of skills and knowledge from books and observation, without the intervention of formal instruction in a school or from professional teachers. Until the early 20th century, self-education was the primary source of instruction in North America. In the early colonial era, except for wealthy children destined to enter the clergy or the higher echelons of government service, few children continued their education beyond the common school age of about seven. However, "Poor Richard," in Benjamin Franklin's widely read annual, *Poor Richard's Almanack,* taught that "the doors of the wisdom are never shut," and he made it clear that the greatest profits accrued to those who learned most diligently and continued their education on their own. After only two years of school, Franklin himself began a life of self-education, reading virtually every available tome of didactic literature. His belief in self-education spurred his publishing career, which provided the general public endless peri-

odicals, tracts, pamphlets, booklets and books from which they could study everything from literature to the latest agricultural techniques. He called his *Poor Richard's Almanack* "a proper vehicle for conveying instruction among the common people, who bought scarce any other books." Nearly 10,000 copies were sold annually.

Dozens of other publishers did much the same, producing a tidal wave of printed matter that flooded the colonies and provided the vast majority of American education for more than a century. By 1762, there were about 40 presses across the 13 colonies, with at least one in each of them. Between 1689 and 1783, some 80,000 to 100,000 titles were printed, including broadsides, almanacs, newspapers, magazines, tracts, pamphlets, primers, manuals, textbooks and ordinary books. Virtually every press had an almanac, many producing 60,000 copies a year; although they were popular and often helpful, they were not nearly as practical as the series of self-help booklets that began appearing in the 1730s. Among them were *The Young Secretary Guide, A Speedy Help to Learning, The Poor Man's Help, The Instruction, or Young Man's Companion,* and, eventually, the all-encompassing *The American Instructor,* a veritable encyclopedia for ambitious young tradesmen. It taught proper English, a broad overview of useful cultural knowledge, such as history, geography and astronomy, handwriting, familiar form letters (both social and commercial), elements of arithmetic and bookkeeping, basic shipping documents in commerce, principles of carpentry, of joinery and of bricklaying, basic legal documents, hints on gardening and preserving, value of currencies and the treatment of disease.

The emergence of subscription libraries (q.v.) also spurred the growth of self-education. Again, Franklin promoted their growth, starting the first such library in Philadelphia in 1731. Over the next 15 years, three more libraries opened in Philadelphia, while Germantown, Lancaster, Trenton, New York, Connecticut and Newport,

Rhode Island, also supported libraries based on the Franklin model and designed to foster self-education.

The self-education movement remained strong throughout the 19th century as the only source of instruction and self-improvement for the average person. Although 42% of American children between the ages of five and 19 went to school by 1850, fewer than 1% remained in school beyond the age of seven. Most went to work in the fields, mines and factories. Only 2% of 17-year-olds graduated from high school in 1770, and they were mostly advantaged children in private schools. Even by 1900, only 6.4% of American 17-year-olds graduated from high schools and one-third of those attended private schools. The vast majority of children and adults, therefore, were entirely reliant on self-education to improve their intellectual and economic circumstances. Most relied on periodicals and books, and some turned to a variety of self-help organizations such as the Lyceum (q.v.), founded in 1826 as a mutual, self-help association of adults to promote self-study and self-improvement. The Lyceum movement spread across the nation—as did the Chautauqua movement (q.v.), which began in 1874 as a program to train Sunday School teachers—but the Lyceum soon evolved into a traveling lecture series by some of the nation's most celebrated thinkers, who brought education and a taste of culture to millions of Americans.

With the gradual enactment and enforcement of universal public education laws in the early 20th century, self-education declined somewhat, although autodidacts such as Thomas Edison remained familiar and often towering figures on the American scene. Radio spurred new enthusiasm for self-education, combining the dissemination of knowledge and entertainment into every American home. Adding to the rebirth of self-education was the publication of a variety of encyclopedias and collections of "Great Books" (q.v.), which seemed to offer every less-than-educated American a guaranteed path to knowledge and success. The end of World War II brought strict enforcement of universal public education, with more than 75% of all American 17-year-olds graduating from high school. Full-time schooling all but obviated the need for self-education, and the advent of television and its entertainment-oriented fare all but ended the flow of self-educative materials into the average American home.

References: *How to Read a Book: The Art of Getting a Liberal Education,* Mortimer J. Adler (1940); *The Theory of Education,* William T. Harris (1893); *The Autobiography of Benjamin Franklin,* Leonard W. Labaree, Ralph L. Ketcham, Helen C. Boatfield and Helen H. Fineman, eds. (1964); *The Chautauqua Movement,* John H. Vincent (1886).

self-fulfilling prophecy A meritless, bias-based prediction whose eventual fulfillment stems from the motivation of the prophesier to prove his prediction or bias true. In American public education, the most evident self-fulfilling prophecy is the so-called tracking system (q.v.), which groups high school children according to academic ability, with the least gifted on the general track, the manually skilled on the vocational track and the academically oriented on the college-preparatory track. Both teachers and students on the general track, for example, often have such low initial expectations about student performance that neither group is motivated to excel. Teachers present a variety of unchallenging "personal improvement" courses requiring no student skills or learning effort, and students, recognizing the low teacher expectations and low esteem in which they are held, drop out of school in staggeringly large proportions. Indeed, 63.5% of general education students—more than 2 million students—drop out of high school every year, and they account for about two-thirds of all American high school dropouts.

However, self-fulfilling prophecies are evident in every classroom of almost every school in the world. Teachers who believe youngsters to be slow, average or bright, and treat them on the basis of such premature evaluations, generally motivate such youngsters to fulfill their teachers' expectations. Some psychologists and educators believe the below-average academic performances of poor children and, most especially, poor black and Hispanic children, is partly a result of self-fulfilling prophecies based on low teacher expectations for members of those groups. One experiment with first and second graders found that I.Q. scores of randomly selected students presented to their teachers as "gifted" at the beginning of the school year increased an average of 15 points by the end of the year, regardless of race or ethnic background and regardless of their actual I.Q. scores. Mexican-American children, who, because of their economic status and ethnicity, might otherwise have faced low teacher expectations for success, showed the greatest gains after teacher expectations were raised. Students identified for teachers as average—including some students who were in fact gifted—showed no increase in I.Q. scores. The study is not considered definitive because the findings were not sustained with students in grades three through six, where I.Q. scores remained relatively stable, regardless of teacher expectations.

Thwarting the perpetuation of self-fulfilling prophecies has proved one of the most difficult tasks of educational communities in almost every nation in the world. Teacher sensitivity training and institutional control of classes have produced limited success in combating this problem.

References: "Research on the Self-fulfilling Prophecy and Teacher Expectations," Jere E. Brophy, *Journal of Educational Research* (October 1983); "Teacher Expectations for the Disadvantaged," Robert Rosenthal and Lenore Jacobson, *Scientific American* (April 1968).

semantics The study of the meaning and significance of words. Though complex at the university graduate school level, semantics are nevertheless an integral part of early education, especially as children learn to integrate reading and writing with actual stories. Several instructional techniques are available for teaching semantics:

- Semantic differential technique. A method for displaying the degree of difference in individual perceptions of the meaning of the same word. Usually used to demonstrate the meanings of modifiers, such as adjectives and adverbs, the semantic differential technique asks students to demonstrate the degree of their feelings about a stimulus on a scale of opposites:

Scrooge (stimulus)

Good ——————————————— Bad

The technique demonstrates the imperfect nature of word meanings.

- Semantic mapping. A graphic method of vocabulary building based on tying as many words as possible to a central concept or core word. Thus, the concept "energy" might be written on the chalkboard as a hub-like circle, from which an array of spokes reaches out to lists of various characteristics that describe, detail and explain energy. One spoke, for example, might lead to a list of energy sources, another to energy types, another to uses, another to energy products, another to benefits and still another to dangers. At one and the same time, the technique not only expands vocabulary, but also serves as an important teaching technique in the study of objects, animals and concepts.

- Semantic webbing. A more complex variation of semantic mapping that demonstrates the interrelationships between each of the objects and concepts on a map. A semantic web ties the core object or concept—sun, for example—with specifically identified spokes, such as heat, leading to any number of results, such as plant growth and human survival. In addition, each result is connected to or separated from the others depending on their interrelationships. Plant growth, for example, is also essential to human survival, although the reverse is obviously not true. The web would indicate this.

References: *Teaching Reading in Today's Elementary Schools,* Paul C. Burns, Betty D. Roe and Elinor P.

Ross (1984); *Semantic Mapping: Classroom Application,* by Joan E. Heimlich and Susan D. Pittelman (1986); *Teaching Reading Vocabulary,* D. D. Johnson and P. D. Pearson (1984); *The Management of Meaning,* Charles E. Osgood et al. (1957).

semester One-half of an academic year, usually lasting 15 to 18 weeks. Derived from the Latin *semestris,* or half-yearly, and, in turn, from the Latin *sex* (six) + *mensis* (month), the semester is the most commonly used division of the academic calendar in American colleges and universities.
Reference: *Handbook of College and University Administration,* Asa S. Knowles, ed. (1970).

seminar In education, a meeting of students with a teacher, for a round-table discussion and exchange of ideas about a specific topic, usually proposed by the teacher. Acting as a moderator, the teacher poses questions and stimulates student discussion, with the object of promoting deeper and more thorough understanding of the topic by the entire group. Once limited to colleges and graduate schools, the seminar method has become common at academically demanding secondary schools. At the university level, the seminar often sees students who have done original research compare, exchange and discuss their results and conclusions with their colleagues. The term is derived from the Latin *semen,* or seed, and indeed, the seminary took its name as a seedbed of knowledge, although it now refers exclusively to theological schools. When first introduced in 19th-century German universities, the seminar represented a sharp departure from the scholiocentric lecture that accommodated no discussion or questioning of the professor. A small number of German-trained teachers brought the seminar to American colleges after the Civil War. The seminar is said to have made its first appearance in the United States at the University of Michigan in 1869, with Harvard, Johns Hopkins and Clark universities adopting the approach by the end of the century.

Reference: "The Seminar," Carolyn M. Owen, *Improving College and University Teaching* (Summer 1970).

seminary Literally, a "seedbed" of knowledge and once used to describe theological schools and advanced schools for women. Now used exclusively as a theological school.
Reference: EB.

semi-professions A vague term coined by sociologist Amitai Etzioni, in his book *The Semi-Professions and Their Organizations: Teachers, Nurses, Social Workers* (1969). It is generally used to refer to all those occupations other than the three "learned professions"—theology, medicine and law—that were once accessible with only a high school diploma but now require some college, a college degree or even postgraduate education. A profession was originally a vow made upon entering a religious order. The term was later applied to medicine when, upon completion of their studies, graduates took the Oath of Hippocrates, to serve the sick and "cure your patients." Service in the law in the United States also requires an oath, namely to defend the Constitution and uphold the law as an officer of the court. Although there are other occupations that require as much education as theology, medicine and law, few, if any, require both extensive graduate education and the profession of an oath.

In recent years, however, many occupations that formerly required no education began requiring two or more years of college training, a phenomenon that sociologist Harold L. Wilensky called "the professionalization of everyone." Study for dentistry, optometry, business, engineering, journalism, accounting, teaching and nursing all gradually moved into postsecondary education during the first half of the 20th century, while the post-World War II years saw study for corrections, hotel management, hospital administration, undertaking and other vocations move to associate, bachelor's and even master's degree programs.

In many cases, however, the added education and training did not necessarily lift remuneration to levels that rewarded the years of preparation. The result was unionization in a wide range of new "professions," including teaching, nursing and corrections. Unionization meant labor-management bargaining and strikes, which, in turn, led to the dilution of collegiality and conflicting allegiances to both a profession and organized labor. These conflicting allegiances generated the term semi-profession.

References: *The Semi-Professions and Their Organizations: Teachers, Nurses, Social Workers,* Amitai Etzioni (1969); "The Professionalization of Everyone," Harold L. Wilensky, *American Journal of Sociology* (LXX: 1964–65, **pp. 137–138).

senior In education, a student in his final year of high school or college.

Reference: *Webster's Ninth New Collegiate Dictionary* (1983).

senior high school In the United States, the last four years—i.e., grades nine, ten, eleven and twelve—of the six years of secondary education. Originally, senior high school followed two years of junior high school (grades seven and eight), but the development of the middle school (q.v.), often incorporating grades seven, eight and nine, has lft some high schools with only three years of study. Regardless of the number of grades, the successfull completion of senior high school culminates in the award of a diploma attesting to the student's graduation.

Reference: *The High School,* William N. Alexander et al. (1971).

sensitivity training A professionally directed form of group therapy for providing participants with a better understanding of how to interact with others in the most respectful, productive ways. Designed to give participants a measure of self-understanding, sensitivity training probes the reasons for each participant's insensitivity toward others and, more to the point in educa-

tion, toward individual students or classmates, toward religious, racial or ethnic groups and toward the opposite gender. Based on traditional group therapy methods, sensitivity training follows no formal pattern or procedure. Led by a professional "trainer"—i.e., a psychiatrist, psychologist, social worker or counselor—sensitivity training may be an intensive daylong, multi-day or weeklong project or a once- or twice-weekly meeting for an hour or more over an extended period. Through active communication within the group, sensitivity training seeks to promote an understanding and perhaps elimination of mutual antipathetical feelings of participants. The process also tries to teach participants new techniques of relating to each other.

Reference: *Sensitivity Training: The Scientific Understanding of Individuals,* Henry C. Smith (1973).

separate-but-equal doctrine Until 1954, a legally enforced principle, throughout the American south and elsewhere, that segregated all African Americans and American Indians from whites in separate public facilities, including schools. The separate-but-equal doctrine represented a massive southern rebellion against post-Civil War Reconstruction (q.v.). During the Reconstruction Era, Congress passed the Fifteenth Amendment to the Constitution, giving all citizens the right to vote and stripping states of the power to deny such rights on the basis of race, color or previous condition of servitude. Within the framework of Reconstruction, public education generally and African-American education specifically spread throughout the South for the first time in history.

When the South returned to self-rule in 1870, however, most southern states reimposed tight restrictions on African Americans. Using every device, from discriminatory taxes to terrorism, the states gradually deprived blacks of both the right to vote and the right to a minimal education. By 1874, white supremacy was reestablished throughout the South, and schools and all other public facilities were segregated along racial lines—ostensibly separate but equal. In 1890, Louisiana made the separate-but-equal doctrine state law. Two years later, authorities arrested Homer A. Plessy, an African American who refused to leave a passenger car reserved for whites. Charging a violation of his Fourteenth Amendment rights, Plessy took the case to the U.S. Supreme Court, which in 1896 upheld the separate-but-equal doctrine. It was not until 1954, in *Brown v. Board of Education of Topeka* (q.v.), that the Court reversed itself and ruled the separate-but-equal doctrine unconstitutional, saying that any separation of the races in school produced inherently unequal education.

(See also AFRICAN AMERICANS; CIVIL RIGHTS ACT OF 1964; DESEGREGATION; PLESSY V. FERGUSON; SEGREGATION.)

References: *Landmark Supreme Court Decisions on Public School Issues,* Edward C. Bolmeier (1953); *Simple Justice: The History of Brown v. Board of Education and Black America's Struggle for Equality,* Richard Kluger (1976).

separation anxieties A child's irrational fears of separation from or abandonment by its parents. Not uncommon among young children attending preschool or kindergarten for the first time, separation anxieties usually provoke mysterious aches and other physical symptoms that preclude the child's leaving home and attending school. Often such symptoms escalate to include nausea, diarrhea, stomach pains, migraine headaches and other serious illnesses. At a later age, separation anxieties may trigger rebelliousness, including running away or refusal to attend or remain in school. Persistent separation anxieties may require professional psychiatric help. Often, however, such anxieties may be relieved by the parent simply escorting the child to school for a few days and, with the teacher's permission, spending a few moments in the classroom until formal activities get under way. Separation anxieties often reappear when students must make the transition from elementary to secondary school, when once again children find themselves smallest and youngest at a new school and where they must be independent and find their way from class to class. Lost is the security of a single teacher in a single, all-day classroom. Some anxiety is an inevitable result, but its debilitating effects can be mitigated by frequent preliminary visits to the new school so that students can learn, in advance, what to expect.

(See also SCHOOL PHOBIA).

References: *The Elementary School Handbook,* Joanne Oppenheim (1989).

Serrano v. Priest A landmark California Supreme Court decision in 1971 that ruled that the financing of public schools with property taxes discriminated against the poor and thus violated their constitutional guarantee to equal protection under the law. The court said that taxes based on elevated property values in wealthier, sparsely settled districts produced far better public education and more dollar support per pupil than taxes in poor, overcrowded districts, where property values were low and generated less revenue. The California decision was significant in that it marked the first time that a state declared unconstitutional the traditional system of financing public education with property taxes. In the 25 years that followed, courts in more than 30 states made similar rulings, and Michigan actually outlawed the use of property taxes for financing public schools, choosing instead to finance each public school with state funds, on an equitable, per-capita basis.

Ironically, three years after *Serrano,* the U.S. Supreme Court upheld the right of states to finance public school systems with local property taxes in another case, *Rodriguez v. San Antonio School District* (q.v.). In the 1974 case, the Rodriguez parents filed suit against the state of Texas, claiming that property taxes in San Antonio provided only $26 per pupil for schools in poor districts, compared with $333 per pupil in wealthy districts. The plaintiffs argued that such inequity violated the U.S. Constitution's guarantee of equal protection under the law. The

Supreme Court, however, ruled that the U.S. Constitution makes no mention of education and offers no specific guarantee of any right to education. "Education . . . is not among the rights afforded explicit protection under our federal constitution. Nor do we find any basis for saying it is implicitly so protected." The Court also said that the plaintiffs had failed to prove that disparities in funding had deprived their children of an "opportunity to acquire minimum basic skills necessary for the full enjoyment of rights of free speech and full participation in the political process." Despite the Court's ruling, more than 30 states have used California's *Serrano* ruling to disassociate public school financing from property taxes, because education is indeed among the rights afforded explicit protection under their state constitutions.

References: NYT; U.S. Supreme Court proceedings; *School Finance in Transition: The Courts and Educational Reform,* John Pincus, ed. (1974).

Servicemen's Opportunity Colleges (SOC)

A network of more than 300 community colleges, four-year colleges and universities that provide programs of higher education designed to meet the special needs of men and women in the U.S. armed forces. An outgrowth of a 1970 project to serve the educational needs of returning Vietnam War service personnel, SOC was founded by the American Association of Community and Junior Colleges, whose members offered lower-level college courses on or near military bases and developed nontraditional methods of instruction to accommodate the unpredictable work schedules of active servicemen and women. Funded since 1972 by the Carnegie Corporation of New York and since 1976 by the U.S. Department of Defense, SOC expanded its offerings to include four-year college programs in 1973, when the American Association of State Colleges and Universities and 10 other higher-education associations joined SOC. In addition to its educational programs, SOC also acts as a coordinator to ensure that SOC course credits are transferred to other institutions of higher education when service personnel leave the military and pursue higher education.

Reference: Defense Activity for Non-Traditional Education Support, Pensacola, Florida.

service scholarship An unusual type of partial- or full-tuition merit scholarship awarded at a limited number of colleges to students of high academic standing who agree to perform at least 10 hours a week of community public service work. Often offered at religious colleges such as Xavier University, in Cincinnati, which sees public service training as part of its mission, the program is popular at some secular schools such as Hampshire College, in Amherst, Massachusetts.

References: Xavier University, Cincinnati, Ohio; Hampshire College, Amherst, Massachusetts.

"Sesame Street" The first—and perhaps the most remarkably effective—program to emerge from American educational television (q.v.) for preschool children. A production of Children's Television Workshop, "Sesame Street" first appeared on public television stations in 1969. Financed by the Carnegie Corporation of New York, the Ford Foundation and the federal government, "Sesame Street" was designed for preschool children generally, but most especially for disadvantaged preschoolers who lacked family stability and the economic wherewithal for preschool education. In effect, "Sesame Street"'s actors and puppets, costumed as loving and lovable characters such as the "cookie monster," brought preschool education into the home of even the poorest, most culturally deprived child, providing reading-readiness (q.v.) and math-readiness skills in the exciting, attention-getting, staccato rhythms of television commercials. "Sesame Street" reached 90% of preschoolers in city slums, and studies proved that it not only improved the reading readiness of economically deprived children across the United States, it also succeeded in producing measurable educational gains for middle- and upper-income children.

Reference: *To Serve the Public Interest: Educational Broadcasting in the United States,* Robert J. Blakely (1979).

set induction   Educational jargon equivalent to the show business term "warm-up"—the cultivation of audience (or student) receptiveness for a forthcoming unit of particularly complex work, a new concept, a field trip or any other variation of the usual classroom routine. Designed to avoid the shock of abrupt advances into new, unknown academic territory, set induction is designed to produce a smooth, gradual transition. It relies on careful teacher preparation, tying the new work to the old, and patient discussion with students to allay concerns and anxieties.

References: *Classroom Teaching Skills,* James M. Cooper (1982).

Seton, Saint Elizabeth Ann (1744–1821)   American educator and philanthropist who founded the Roman Catholic school system in the United States. Born Elizabeth Ann Bayley in New York City, she married William M. Seton, a successful merchant, in 1794, and concerned herself with charitable causes. In 1797, she helped found the Society for Relief of Poor Widows with Small Children, New York's first charitable organization. Mother of five, she traveled with her husband to Italy, where he died in 1803. She returned to the United States, converted to Catholicism and in 1809 opened the first parochial free school in the United States— a Catholic elementary school in Baltimore. In the year that followed, she and four nuns organized the Sisters of St. Joseph (later, the Sisters of Charity of St. Joseph), the first such order in the United States. Later, they founded the St. Joseph College for Women, where, as superior of the community, she spent the remainder of her life teaching and helping to found 20 other similar educational communities. In 1856, Seton Hall College (now University) in New Jersey was named in her honor, and in 1975 she became the first American-born Roman Catholic to be canonized.

References: DAB; NAW.

set theory   The core of so-called new math (q.v.), which bases mathematics instruction on recapitulation of its evolution, rather than rote memorization of empirical formulae. Dispensing with numbers, set theory groups all classes of objects, or elements, with common characteristics into sets—cars, insects, Americans, months in a year. Sets may contain no elements (a null set), a few elements, many elements or an infinite number of elements, and be larger, smaller or the same as other sets. Sets may also contain subsets—station wagons are a subset of automobiles, for example, and ants are a subset of insects—and they may be subsets of other sets, as cars are a subset of vehicles. Sets may be related to other sets in unions or partial unions. Instead of relying on numbers to describe such relationships, teachers use easy-to-understand graphic depictions, such as circle A lying within circle B (a union), or circle A partially intersecting circle B, creating a common shaded area, to indicate a partial union.

Set theory was introduced into primary and secondary school mathematics instruction in the late 1950s and early 1960s, to expand student understanding of mathematics by teaching the concepts of the origin and structure of mathematics rather than limiting the emphasis to computation based on memorization. In simplest terms, set theory, for example, is rooted to a preliterate, premathematical era, when man had not yet invented reading, writing or numbers and, therefore, could not count. Presumably he could, however, distinguish the differences between "sets"—i.e., more than, less than or same as. Consider the classic case of the shepherd in a cave with a "set" of goats he releases to graze each morning. As each goat leaves, the shepherd moves a pebble from one side of the cave's entrance to the other, creating a set of pebbles that corresponds numerically to the set of goats in the field. As the goats return, he reverses the process. If the entire set of goats has not returned at dusk, a subset of pebbles is left equal to the subset of missing goats.

In concentrating on the teaching of such abstract mathematical concepts as sets and subsets, equal and equivalent, many teachers failed to give their students the practical arithmetic tools essential for daily life, such as counting correctly and knowing from memory the change due when paying for a 67-cent item with a dollar bill. Insisting that such practical aspects of mathematics would develop as a logical outgrowth of new math, zealots had imposed new math as the standard in elementary schools across the United States by the late 1960s. When, however, the mathematics proficiency of American students showed a dramatic decline in the 1970s, parents and educational reformers demanded a return to traditional instruction. The result was a compromise curriculum in which students, once again, were taught to memorize the multiplication tables and other tools of arithmetic, but were nevertheless taught a modicum of set theory to improve their understanding of the broader concepts on which mathematics is based.

Reference: *Fuzzy Sets and Systems: Theory and Applications,* Didier Dubois and Henri Prade (1979).

Seven Sisters colleges

Seven Sisters colleges   A relatively obsolete term referring to Barnard, Bryn Mawr, Mount Holyoke, Radcliffe, Smith, Vassar and Wellesley colleges, all of them founded as women's colleges in the 1800s, when men's colleges refused to admit women. Although unaffiliated in any formal way, the seven colleges maintained a close working relationship, comparing admission policies and curricular offerings. By the mid-1990s, however, only Mount Holyoke (the first women's college in the world), Smith and Wellesley remained exclusively women's schools, with no direct ties to men's colleges. Although still a women's college, Barnard was directly affiliated with Columbia University (q.v.) from its founding. Radcliffe, always a college of Harvard University, has merged with Harvard College (q.v.). Vassar is coeducational, and Bryn Mawr has long enrolled a handful of male students and maintained cooperative ties to Swarthmore and Haverford colleges, allowing students at each college to cross-register in courses at the other two colleges.

Reference: *Barron's Profiles of American Colleges* (periodically updated).

Seward, William H.

Seward, William H. (1801–1872)   Whig governor of New York State from 1839 to 1843, and an unsuccessful advocate of state support for religious schools and multilingual education in public schools. Better known for his later roles as a senator, as U.S. secretary of state in the Lincoln administration and for his acquisition of Alaska in the Johnson administration, Seward was nonetheless an important governor and, as such, a major influence in the development of public education in New York State. At the time of his accession, New York State politics were dominated by a controversy over state support of religious schools. Prior to 1825, the state had subsidized all schooling within its boundaries, including all denominational schools. In 1825, however, New York City's Common Council voted to restrict its share of school subsidies to nondenominational schools. The move provoked strong protests from the growing number of Roman Catholic schools, whose leaders contended, persuasively, that so-called nondenominational public, or common, schools were, in fact, Protestant (which indeed they were).

Seward not only sided with the Catholic position, he recommended in his inaugural address that immigrant groups be permitted to operate their own state-subsidized public schools, administered and taught by teachers of their own language and religion. ''The children of foreigners,'' he declared, ''are too often deprived of the advantages of our system of public education . . . I do not hesitate, therefore, to recommend the establishment of schools in which they may be instructed by teachers speaking the same language with themselves and professing the same faith.''

The controversy raged at public meetings and in the press until 1841, when the council rejected the Catholic petition for public funds and the entire idea of multilingual, multicultural education. The defeat of the proposal spurred the growth of Roman Catholic parochial and diocesan schools, as well as denominational schools of other religions and of many national groups. Support for Seward's concept would not reemerge until more than a century later, when bilingual education and multicultural education (qq.v.) were introduced into public schools in Hispanic neighborhoods of New York, Los Angeles, Miami and other major American cities.

References: DAB; *American Education: The Metropolitan Experience, 1876–1980,* Lawrence A. Cremin (1987).

sex education A broad-based, highly controversial and widely varying elementary and secondary school curriculum introduced in the late 1960s to provide instruction about human reproduction and the physical, emotional, psychological and social aspects and consequences of human sexuality and sexual behavior. Banned in many schools, the coverage and depth of sex-education varies according to community sentiment. At one end of the spectrum, sex education may be limited to a chapter in a high school biology text containing an empirical study of the human reproductive system. At the other extreme, it may be a comprehensive curriculum, beginning in kindergarten and continuing through elementary, middle school and high school, as part of a broad health-education program. At each stage of such a broad-based study, youngsters are taught to understand their own physical, psychological, emotional and social development and urges. Depending on the age group, explicit information—sometimes subtle, sometimes graphic—is offered on the wide variety of sexual practices, love and the emotions,

the reproductive process, contraception, venereal infections and hygiene. A major thrust of most such programs is to try to teach students to make responsible decisions about sexual contact.

Even in the most accepting communities, however, sex education is seldom free of controversy. Many parents and educators believe strongly that sex education represents a usurpation of parental prerogatives by the state and that schools should limit their instruction to the arts and sciences. Still other critics maintain that most sex-education teachers are not adequately trained or emotionally prepared to deal with preadolescent and adolescent sexuality. And other critics charge that sex education often crosses the line into therapy, for which teachers are certainly untrained and ill-equipped.

Proponents of sex education insist that the opportunities for premature sexual activity in an increasingly promiscuous society make it essential to equip youngsters with adequate knowledge and social skills to act responsibly. Proponents of sex education, however, are themselves involved in heated debates over what sex education should teach. Those in favor of the broadest possible education rely on such explicitly illustrated publications as *Learning About Family Life* (Rutgers University Press, 1993) to teach five-to-eight-year-olds that ''when a woman and a man who love each other go to bed, they like to hug and kiss. Sometimes, if they want to, the man puts his penis in the woman's vagina and that feels really good for both of them. Sperm come out through the man's penis. If one tiny sperm meets a tiny egg inside the woman's body, a baby is started.'' Other titles in the series include *Uncle Seth Has HIV, Learning about Our Genital Parts* and *Talking about Touches,* which urges that masturbation be done in private. A New York City sex education program called ''The Rainbow Curriculum'' promotes tolerance for homosexuality and other types of unconventional sexual behavior.

Such explicit sexual education has come under fire not only from religious and parental organizations, but also from many child psychologists who maintain that premature lessons on sexuality—especially in the classroom arena before the eyes of peers and teachers—often frighten young children and produce serious anxieties about sex and their bodies. As in every other sector, children have different and highly individualized rates of development in the area of sexual curiosity. Critics of school-based sex education maintain that a child's interest in sexual matters is usually best satisfied as the child's own curiosity provokes a question to a parent in the quiet, secure privacy of the home.

Rather than make programs increasingly explicit, some proponents of sex education are introducing the teaching of abstinence as the core of sex education programs in hope of reducing soaring rates of sexual activity among adolescent girls. The percentage of 15-year-olds who report having engaged in premarital sex climbed from less than 5% in 1970 to 30% by 1990; the percentage of 16-year-old girls, from 20% to 30%; 17-year-old girls, from 30% to 50%; and 18-year-old girls, from 40% to 70%.

(See also SIECUS.)

References: NYT: SIECUS, New York, New York; *Discussing Sex in the Classroom: Readings for Teachers,* David R. Stronck, ed. (1982).

sexism Any gender-oriented, discriminatory attitude, belief or behavior. Since the founding of the first school in the Americas, education has continually reflected the sexist attitudes of a society that denied women access to college-level education until 1836 and the right to vote until 1919. Although the Civil Rights Act of 1964 (q.v.) banned overt discrimination of all kinds on the basis of gender inter alia, sexism continued to permeate education at all levels. Until recently, myriad books perpetuated stereotyped women as the weaker sex, destined by nature to be dominated by men, to fulfill specific vocational roles as secretaries, clerks, maids, nurses and elementary school teachers and to accept social roles such as mother and housewife. Moreover, the educational establishment rein-

forced such stereotypes. In 1920, 86% of the teachers in public elementary and secondary schools were females, while their administrative superiors—public school principals—were almost universally men. As late as 1990, women made up almost 72% of all public school teachers but only 30% of public school principals. In addition, many schools continued to perpetuate curricular sexism, with girls steered into home economics courses and boys into industrial arts courses.

(See also GENDER DISCRIMINATION.)

References: DES; *Sexism: New Issue in American Education,* Pauline Gough (1976).

sexual harassment Unwanted or unwelcome, sexually oriented, verbal or physical advances toward a member of the same or opposite sex. A growing problem in American secondary schools, sexual harassment ranges from sexual comments or suggestive looks to rape. Verbal abuse and ogling are by far the most frequent forms of this behavior, with 76% of girls and 56% of boys in grades eight to eleven reporting such harassment, according to a 1993 study conducted by the Louis Harris & Associates polling organization on behalf of the American Association of University Women. Some 65% of girls and 42% of boys reported having been touched, grabbed or pinched in a sexual way; 57% of girls and 36% of boys say they were intentionally brushed up against in a sexual way; 42% of girls and 34% of boys had sexual rumors spread about them; 38% of girls and 28% of boys had their clothing pulled in a sexual way; 31% of girls and 34% of boys were shown, given or left sexual materials; and 20% of girls and 16% of boys had sexual messages written about them in public areas. About 80% of unwelcome sexual behavior was by students directed at other students. The remainder originated with teachers, custodians, coaches and other adults and was directed against students. Two-thirds of the boys surveyed and 52% of the girls admitted to having harassed other students. About 70% of the girls who were harassed said they had been "very

upset" or "somewhat upset," while only 24% of the boys reported similar feelings. Girls clearly responded to harassment far more dramatically than boys, with 33% not wanting to go to school, 32% not wanting to appear in a specific class, 28% finding it hard to pay attention, 23% scoring lower grades, 22% finding it hard to study and 17% thinking about changing schools. Only 6% of boys considered changing schools, and only about 9% to 12% found that it affected their class work or school behavior in any way.
Reference: American Association of University Women, Washington, D.C.

Shanker, Albert (1928-) Prominent American teachers' union leader and long-time president of the American Federation of Teachers (q.v.), AFL-CIO, whose membership he helped increase by more than 50%. A public school teacher in the 1950s, Shanker helped found the United Federation of Teachers (q.v.), the New York City AFT local. After leading several strikes in the 1960s and serving time in jail for violating New York's collective bargaining statutes, he won major improvements in pay, health and welfare benefits, and job protection for both teachers and classroom paraprofessionals in New York City. Indeed, the contracts he won served as models for teacher contracts across the United States and spurred a mass shift in teacher allegiance from the National Education Association to the AFT. Fearful of losing too many teacher-members, the NEA evolved from a professional organization into a quasi-union.

In 1974, Shanker was elected head of the AFT, and in 1981 president of the International Federation of Free Teachers' Unions, headquartered in Brussels, Belgium. The author of a nationally syndicated column on education, Shanker was an outspoken supporter of reform of public education, urging teachers to assume the leadership role in effecting such reforms.
Reference: United Federation of Teachers, New York, New York.

shared facilities and services A cooperative education program whereby two or more private or public schools each use some facilities of the other(s) on a regularly scheduled basis, without charge. An effective money-saving mechanism, such programs allow the students of two or more institutions to use a single set of otherwise underutilized classrooms, laboratories, recreation sites, equipment and services, with a single common charge. Shared-facilities programs require students to be under the supervision of teachers or officials from their own school, while shared-services programs—the use of libraries, for example—do not. Shared-facilities and shared-services programs allow schools in the same or neighboring school districts to avoid the capital costs of building duplicate facilities.
Reference: ERIC.

shared time A cooperative program whereby private and parochial school students may simultaneously enroll in and receive full credit for specific public school courses unavailable at their own schools—laboratory or vocational courses, for example. Also known as dual enrollment, shared time is unrelated to released time (q.v.), whereby public school students are excused from school to obtain religious education elsewhere.
Reference: ERIC.

SHARE Loans A higher-education financing plan of the Consortium on Financing Higher Education. The latter is a group of academically selective, private colleges, such as Yale, Harvard and Princeton, which in the 1980s raised tuition costs beyond the reach of most American families. SHARE allowed parents of students attending the Consortium's member colleges to borrow as much as half the cost of tuition, room and board, at fixed or variable interest rates comparable to those of commercial banks.
Reference: *A Student's Guide to College Admissions*, Harlow G. Unger (1995).

Sheldon, Edward A. (1823–1897) American educator who founded the so-called Oswego Movement, which introduced the teaching methods of Swiss educator Johann Heinrich Pestalozzi (q.v.) to American education. Born and educated in upstate New York, Sheldon organized the Orphan and Free School Association of Oswego in 1848 to help educate poor, immigrant children arriving in Oswego, then a thriving manufacturing city on Lake Ontario. In 1851, he was appointed superintendent of schools in Syracuse, where, over the next two years, he organized the city's graded school system, night schools and public libraries. Returning to Oswego in 1853, he organized the city's public school system and, in 1861, the Oswego Primary Training School to fill the burgeoning demand for teachers. Introduced to Pestalozzian teaching methods at a conference in Toronto, Canada, he brought two Pestalozzian experts from Europe to Oswego to help train students in Pestalozzian teaching techniques. The first institution in the United States to teach Pestalozzian methods, Sheldon's school was renamed the Oswego State Normal and Training School; during his 36 years of leadership, it became one of the most important teacher-training institutions in the United States. By 1867, six other normal schools based on the Oswego model had been established in New York State, and their teachers helped introduce Pestallozian teaching methods in schools across the United States. Essentially, Sheldon stressed so-called object teaching, based on knowledge acquisition through observation and inquiry and the use of the five senses.

Reference: *Oswego: Fountainhead of Teacher Education,* Dorothy Rogers (1961).

sheltered classroom A classroom for non-English-speaking students in which the teacher teaches only in English, using immersion techniques that literally flood students in English and force them to learn the language. Such classes are sheltered when the teacher uses a relatively limited, simple English vocabulary designed to make lessons easier for the students to understand.

Reference: ERIC.

sheltered workshop A usually nonprofit service or manufacturing enterprise that relies largely on physically, mentally or psychologically handicapped workers. Originally custodial institutions when first organized at the beginning of the 20th century, sheltered workshops now provide rehabilitative and training services to help the handicapped become independent, self-sufficient citizens. Workshop participants commute (sometimes independently, sometimes on workshop buses) to and from work. They usually receive minimum or piecework wages for the services they provide or goods they produce. Most workshops provide such services as building or grounds maintenance or engage in light manufacturing requiring relatively few worker skills, such as repairing and processing used clothing or manufacturing and packing candies.

Reference: *Workshops for the Handicapped in the United States: An Historical and Developmental Perspective,* Nathan Nelson (1971).

Shelton v. Tucker A 1960 U.S. Supreme Court decision declaring unconstitutional a 1958 Arkansas law that required teachers to list all organizations to which they had belonged in the previous five years. Declaring the requirement an abridgement of constitutional rights to free association, the Court said the law was particularly egregious because of its unlimited scope. It required teachers to disclose church memberships, political affiliation and "every conceivable kind of associational tie—social, professional, avocational, or religious. Many such relationships could have no possible bearing upon the teacher's occupational competence or fitness." The law's "comprehensive interference with associational freedom," said the Court, "goes far beyond what might be justified in the exercise of the state's legitimate inquiry into the fitness and competency of its teachers . . ."

Reference: U.S. Supreme Court proceedings.

shorthand Any system of rapid notation, using symbols or abbreviations to represent letters, words or phrases. All but rendered obsolete by electronic recording systems and computers, shorthand dates to ancient Rome and a system called *notae Tironianae* (Tironian notes), invented in 63 B.C. by the freedman Marcus Tullius Tiro. Taught in Roman schools, it was used to record speeches of statesmen and proceedings of the Senate and, later, church councils. It remained the primary form of shorthand for more than 1,000 years, when secret writing became associated with witchcraft and Latin had changed so radically as to render it all but useless.

The first modern system of shorthand was invented in 1588 by the English cleric Timothy Bright (1551?–1615). More than a dozen other systems were developed in England, with Europe following suit in the late 17th century. The two most commonly used systems in recent times were developed by British educator and spelling reformer Sir Isaac Pitman (1813–97) in 1837 and by Irish stenographer John Robert Gregg (1867–1948) in 1888. Using symbols or combinations thereof for speech sounds, the two systems were introduced in the United States in 1852 and 1893, respectively, with the Gregg system eventually predominating. About 90% of shorthand instruction in the United States today is in the Gregg system.

In 1924, a radically new kind of shorthand was invented by American educator Emma Dearborn (d. 1937) and revised and improved in 1950 by educator Alexander Sheff (1898–1978). Called speedwriting, it used longhand letters instead of unfamiliar symbols to represent sounds and words. In addition to speedwriting, a third type of shorthand—machine shorthand—was developed in the late 19th century, using small, mechanical keyboards that permitted the imprinting of entire syllables with a single touch. Able to record 200 words a minute, compared to 120 words a minute for written shorthand and speedwriting, machine shorthand became the standard method of transcribing proceedings in courtrooms and government meeting rooms.

Reference: *Business Education Yesterday, Today, and Tomorrow,* Ruth B. Woolschlager and E. Edward Harris (1976).

SIECUS (Sex Information and Education Council of the United States) A private, nonprofit organization founded in 1965 by Mary Steichen Calderone (q.v.) to introduce sex education as a standard element of the K-12 curriculum. The organization outlined a formal curriculum in its *Guidelines for Comprehensive Sexuality Education: Kindergarten-12th Grade,* published in 1991. In addition to promoting sex education and lobbying against efforts to restrict it, SIECUS provides professional training, technical assistance and materials for sex- and health-education teachers, along with extensive, specialized materials for HIV/AIDS education. SIECUS also maintains the most extensive library on sexuality and HIV/AIDS that is open to the public, and it produces a variety of publications for all age groups on sexuality, HIV/AIDS, sex education, sexual rights, contraception and other issues related to human sexuality.

References: SIECUS, New York, New York.

sight reading Usually, a musical term referring to the singing or playing of a composition from its score at first sight. Sight reading can also refer to the translation of an unfamiliar passage into another language.

References: *Piano: Guided Sight-Reading,* Leonhard Deutsch (1977); *Sight-Singing and Related Skills,* Anne M. de Seeuw and Roger E. Foltz (1975).

sight vocabulary A reading-instruction term referring to the totality of words a student is able unhesitatingly to read and understand without help from others or from reference materials.

References: *Teaching Reading in the Elementary School,* Eldon K. Ekwall and James L. Shanker (1989); *Reading Instruction,* Barbara D. Stoodt (1989).

sight word A reading term referring to any word that a student is able to recognize and read unhesitatingly, in its totality, by viewing its overall configuration rather than examining and "sounding out" its letters and syllables.

References: *Teaching Reading in the Elementary School,* Eldon K. Ekwall and James L. Shanker (1989); *Reading Instruction,* Barbara D. Stoodt (1989).

signing A form of communication that depends entirely on the use of finger, hand and arm positions and gestures to represent words, phrases or concepts. There are many signing methods, including Signed English, American Sign Language and finger spelling (q.v.), all of them used primarily by the deaf or hearing impaired. The slow and cumbersome Signed English uses signs in English-language word order, while American Sign Language—the most common and, generally, the swiftest form of signing—has its own syntax that does not reproduce or represent a literal translation of English or any other language. For example, the sentences "People mislabel me as disabled. In fact, I am a member of American deaf culture" would be translated in nine signs meaning, respectively: disabled, people, label me, wrong, true, me, American, deaf, culture.

Reference: Lexington Center for the Deaf, Queens, New York; Gallaudet University, Washington, D.C.

silent reading Reading to oneself, without producing any sound or moving the tongue or lips. A relatively new technique of reading, in historic terms, silent reading contrasts with and has different purposes from oral reading, which is concerned with pronunciation, enunciation, voice control and communication. Until the early 20th century, students universally learned to read orally, because reading was the core of family recreation in the home before radio and television. As a result of eye-movement research just before World War I, silent reading was found to increase reading rates, reading comprehension and the ability to infer word meanings from their context. For several decades thereaf-

ter, silent reading replaced oral reading as the sole goal of reading instruction. More recently, however, most schools have taught both oral and silent reading, each of which provides students with different sets of essential skills.

References: *Teaching Reading in the Elementary School,* Eldon K. Ekwall and James L. Shanker (1989); *Reading Instruction,* Barbara D. Stoodt (1989).

Simon-Binet Scale A pioneering system for measuring human intelligence based on scores achieved in a series of problems of graded difficulty, each corresponding to a different mental level. Developed in 1905 by French psychologists Alfred Binet (q.v.) and Theodore Simon, the Simon-Binet Scale was one of the first efforts to measure human intelligence using standardized tests. It inspired a massive effort by educators and psychologists in the United States to apply the concept of the scale (q.v.) to the measurement of intelligence, aptitude and achievement. Over the next 20 years, testmakers developed endless numbers of scales to measure every imaginable element of educational aptitude and achievement, including arithmetic, handwriting, spelling, drawing, reading, language ability, science skills, vocational skills and, of course, intelligence. In 1916, Lewis M. Terman (q.v.) and his colleagues at Stanford University revised the Binet Scale, converting it into the Stanford-Binet Test (q.v.), a test for measuring what they called the Intelligence Quotient (q.v.), or relationship of an individual's mental and chronological ages.

References: *The Measurement of Intelligence,* Lewis M. Terman (1916); *Alfred A. Binet,* Theta H. Wolf (1973).

simulation A basic method of instruction that reproduces real-life problems and situations under risk-free conditions in the classroom. Developed for all ages of elementary and secondary school instruction, simulation ranges from simple play-acting and role-playing in so-called sociodramas (q.v.) to the use of highly technological equipment such as flight training cockpits. The development of computer-controlled "virtual-reality" devices has expanded the reach of simulation instruction to even the youngest students.

At the simplest level, simulation is used in substance abuse education, sex education and sensitivity training by asking participants to play a specific role in a classroom drama that simulates real-life situations in which students may be tempted by drugs, alcohol, premature sexual activity or participation in bullying or discriminating against other students. By recreating the situation in the classroom, students learn and practice decision-making and problem-solving techniques under teacher and counselor guidance. They can thus make "wrong" decisions risk-free, learn creative thinking habits and gain understanding of the complexity of real-life social problems and the consequences of each decision they make. So-called "debriefing," or evaluation, of each simulative activity provides students with an overview of cause-effect-consequence sequences.

At a different level, mechanical simulation devices are used in a wide range of practical instruction such as driver-training and even in the use of motorized wheelchairs—again, in risk-free devices that reproduce real-life situations on a screen. In the classroom, computers are used to simulate a wide variety of real-life situations to reinforce formal instruction. Software in language laboratories can simulate real-life situations overseas, where students must use their knowledge of the language. Science computers can guide students through simulated laboratory experiments, while social studies computers can escort students through simulated, day-to-day living in societies past and present.
Reference: ERIC.

single-parent families Families in which only one parent lives in the home and is solely responsible for the day-to-day rearing of the children. Single-parent families may result from death of, or abandonment by, a spouse, from divorce and from out-of-wedlock childbearing.

In 1991, about 29% of America's nearly 70 million children (under 18 years old) lived with a single parent (all but about 3% with their mother). When measured by the Department of Education in 1988, the educational achievement of students from single-parent families ranged from 3% to 6% below that of children from two-parent homes. However, the results may be skewed by other factors, such as the economic, social and cultural levels of single-parent homes, for which no breakdown in scores was provided. At the time, half the nearly 20 million students from single-parent homes were either black or Hispanic students, whose academic achievement scores ranked significantly below those of whites and, therefore, may have lowered the overall average of the group. It is possible, therefore, that scores of white students from single-parent homes may not have differed significantly from those of students from two-parent homes.
References: DES; Bureau of Census, U.S. Department of Commerce, Washington, D.C.

single salary schedule A salary scale based solely on training and years of experience, eliminating merit, area of teaching, student ages and hazards or job difficulties as considerations. Thus, an elementary school teacher, a middle school art teacher and a high school chemistry teacher would all receive the same salaries under a school district's single-salary schedule if, for example, they each had a B.A. and one year of teaching experience. Conceived in 1920 to mitigate discrimination on the basis of gender and between elementary and secondary school teachers, the single-salary schedule is calculated graphically by listing years of experience along the vertical axis and teacher-training level (B.A., M.A., M.A. plus 30 credits, doctorate, etc.) along the horizontal. The cell where each teacher's training and experience levels intersect automatically determines his or her salary for the year. The calculation has been modified somewhat since the early 1980s, to account for added extracurricular counseling or administrative duties.

Reference: *The Personnel Function in Educational Administration,* William B. Castetter (1981).

single-sex education The purposeful segregation of students by gender in separate classrooms or in separate schools. Standard in almost all 19th-century colleges and many secondary schools and primary schools, single-sex education all but disappeared from American education in the 1960s and 1970s—largely because of civil rights laws banning gender discrimination and because of the financial advantages of coeducation (q.v.). Until well into the 19th century, however, the common wisdom was to educate boys and girls separately, although "common schools" usually educated five-, six- and seven-

year-old boys and girls together for economic reasons. Aside from fears that children might engage in premature sexual behavior, schools segregated older children by gender because their courses of study differed so dramatically, with males studying arts and sciences, mechanics (engineering) and the professions and females studying the "domestic" and "ornamental" arts in preparation for lives as wives, mothers and homemakers. As males and females began studying a common core curriculum, however, and as sexual mores changed, single-sex education disappeared. By the early 1990s, there were only 84 women's colleges (82 private, two public) left in the United States—down from 228 two decades earlier—and only three major all-

Perceived inequalities in coeducation have spurred renewed interest in single-sex education. Shown here is the Emma Willard School, in Troy, New York, the first women's academy in the United States. (Emma Willard School)

male colleges not devoted to the military arts or theology.

There were, however, more than 200 girls' and nearly 150 boys' day schools and more than 50 girls' and about 75 boys' boarding schools. Although swelled by Roman Catholic institutions, which never conceded to the gender-equality arguments of coeducation, the number of single-sex institutions was not only stabilizing by 1995, it was also actually beginning to expand. Ironically, the very arguments used by the women's equality movement to transform single-sex education into coeducation were now being used to stem and even reverse the process. Indeed, according to an array of studies conducted in the late 1980s and early 1990s by researchers at Wellesley College, George Washington University and American University and by the American Association of University Women, coeducation had failed to promote equality of the sexes. In fact, the opposite had occurred, with all such studies showing that coeducation had perpetuated stereotyping, that in coed classrooms, boys were called on two to 12 times more than girls; that boys were encouraged to challenge, to take risks and were treated as future leaders, while girls were treated as followers; that girls started high school with higher test scores, but finished with lower scores than boys; that coed schools discouraged girls from taking advanced mathematics and science classes.

Meanwhile, all-women's colleges, with a mere 4.5% of all female college graduates in the United States, were producing one-third of all women board members of Fortune 500 companies and one-half the women in Congress. Graduates of five all-women's colleges—Barnard, Bryn Mawr, Mount Holyoke, Smith and Wellesley—accounted for 43% of the math doctorates and 50% of the engineering doctorates earned by American women. Such graduates were also three times more likely than women at coeducational colleges to earn bachelor's degrees in economics and one and a half times as likely to major in science and mathematics. Proponents

of single-sex education say that all-girl schools and women's colleges provide role models, a supportive environment and an opportunity to exercise leadership that all but the most talented would be denied in coeducational environments. In contrast, the most important public events at coeducational schools are often men's athletic contests.

Although studies of single-sex education for girls and women far outnumbered those for boys and men, advocacy of single-sex education for males was also increasing by the mid-1990s. Proponents contended that boys in coeducational situations were less likely to take risks in areas such as singing, dance, drama, design, the fine arts and creative writing, which they viewed as somewhat less than masculine. Moreover, there was a growing perception that coeducational classes provided distracting social and sexual pressures for both boys and girls in all classroom situations.

Although public schools were forbidden by state and federal laws to segregate students by gender, several secular coeducational private schools had experimented with single-sex classes and found that girls' grades did indeed improve significantly, although little change was found in boys' grades. After metamorphosing from single-sex into coeducational schools in the 1960s, 1970s and 1980s, there was a clear indication that a reverse metamorphosis seemed about to begin in the mid-1990s.

(See also GENDER EDUCATION; WOMEN'S EDUCATION).

References: EB; DES; NYT; "How Schools Shortchange Women: The A.A.U.W. Report," American Association of University Women, Washington, D.C.; *A Century of Higher Education for American Women,* Mabel Newcomer (1959); *Failing at Fairness: How America's Schools Cheat Girls,* Myra and David Sadker (1994); *In the Company of Educated Women: A History of Women and Higher Education in America,* Barbara Miller Solomon (1985).

Sipuel v. Board of Regents of the University of Oklahoma

A 1948 U.S. Supreme Court ruling that the state must provide opportunities for legal education for blacks and must do so for one race as soon as for the other. The decision forced the state to choose between providing law faculties and building law schools at black universities or opening the law schools at all-white public universities to black students. *Sipuel,* however, had an importance that would reach beyond the realm of law school education: it proved to be one of a succession of five cases, from 1938 to 1954, that the National Association for the Advancement of Colored People would bring to the Supreme Court in a long-range effort to end racial segregation in American education. That effort culminated in 1954, with the successful prosecution of *Brown v. Board Education of Topeka* (q.v.), in which the Court did indeed declare racial segregation in public schools unconstitutional.

References: *Simple Justice: A History of Brown v. Board of Education and Black America's Struggle for Equality,* Richard Kluger (1975); U.S. Supreme Court proceedings.

Sizer, Theodore S. (1932–   )

American educator, educational reformer, author and developer of the modern concepts of active learning and portfolio (q.v.) assessment of student academic achievement. Educated at Yale University, Sizer served as headmaster of the prestigious Phillips Academy, Andover, Massachusetts, then as dean of the School of Education at Harvard University and then as professor of education at Brown University.

At Brown, he established one of the three major, educational reform movements of the late 20th century: the Coalition for Essential Schools (q.v.), a group of several hundred public high schools where he introduced the concept of active learning. Based in part on the teaching methods of Socrates (q.v.) and in part on those of American educator/philosopher John Dewey (q.v.), active learning calls on teachers to act as "coaches," with students learning from classroom and field experiences and engaging in exchanges of ideas with their teachers. Active learning contrasts with the traditional approach

to education based on the theory that a child's mind was a "clean slate"—a tabula rasa. "If you assume the mind is an empty slate rather than a muscle to be exercised, then you [the teacher] imprint on the kid's mind," Sizer explained. "The notion of schooling as drill comes out of that assumption." Lecture and memorization were effective, he said, until the 1960s, "the first decade when every adolescent was in school. In the 'good old days' people talk about, you didn't have the so-called 'at-risk' students in school. As soon as you get kids in school who don't really want to be there, their boredom and rejection of routine is more obvious, and it forces people to think differently."

Dewey, Sizer points out, proved that children learn from experience, that they are attracted to objects and activities that interest them and learn from direct engagement with those objects and activities. The participation of teacher/coaches should serve to expand learning from such engagements and stimulate additional learning. While Dewey changed elementary education, his ideas had less far-reaching effects on secondary education. Sizer refined Dewey's ideas and applied them to secondary education, where the tabula rasa system of instruction still prevailed, with students listening to and taking notes from teacher lectures, in an atmosphere of what Sizer called "sustained boredom."

"Not only does the notion of the empty slate not square with current research," Sizer pointed out, "it does not square with common sense. A modern example is how we learn to use a computer. You don't just look at the instruction book, memorize it and then turn on the machine. You learn in a series of back-and-forths, where something you need to do compels you to find out how to do it. Yet what we do in [high] school—figuratively speaking—is, say, 'First read the manual front to back, and then apply it.'"

Sizer launched his Coalition of Essential Schools in 1984, also introducing the concept of portfolio assessment "in which a kid's work is collected, and wise people, call them 'educational auditors' can look at these files and make a judgment of the kid's work over time.'' A participant in the landmark *Paideia Proposal* (q.v.), with Mortimer J. Adler (q.v.) and other major American educators and educational reformers, Sizer's major works have included *Secondary Schools at the Turn of Century* (1964) and the seminal *Horace's Compromise: The Dilemma of the American High School* (1984).

References: ERIC; Department of Education, Brown University, Providence, Rhode Island.

skewed distribution   An asymmetrical distribution of scores, with more scores at the negative or positive ends of the scale than in the middle. In a normal distribution (q.v.), or ''bell,'' curve, the majority of scores should fall in the middle, with the median, mode and mean coinciding at the central point. In the classroom, a negatively skewed distribution of scores would indicate that an examination or assignment was too difficult for the students relative to their knowledge and preparation; a positively skewed distribution would indicate that the test material was too easy.

Reference: *Introduction to the Practice of Statistics,* David S. Moore and George P. McCabe (1989).

skill development   The acquisition of productive uses for a child's perceptual, motor and intellectual functions. Skill development varies from age to age, with children normally acquiring the basic elements of perceptual and motor skills between the ages of two and three and thinking skills between three and four, with play (q.v.) being the principle vehicle for skill acquisition. Even in preschool and the early elementary grades, play—or academically oriented variations thereof—remains the primary vehicle for skill development, by maintaining peak student interest. Where interest in a school activity flags, skill development in that area invariably languishes. Basic skill development is usually complete by the end of the elementary years.

Reference: *How Does Your Child Grow and Learn? A Guide for Parents of Young Children,* Missouri Department of Elementary and Secondary Education, Jefferson City, Missouri (1982).

Skinner, B(urrhus) F(redric) (1904–1990)   American behavioral psychologist, educator and inventor of the first teaching machine and of programmed instruction (q.v.). Born in Pennsylvania and educated at Harvard University, Skinner joined the Harvard faculty in 1948, at which time he began applying his theories of behavioral psychology to formal education. He developed the teaching machine, which used programmed instruction to speed and ensure total comprehension in the academic learning process. Now a standard element of all computer-operated learning systems, programmed instruction presented the student with a series of separate, sequentially ordered and incrementally different and more difficult bits of information. Each increment was so small, however, that even a student of minimal intelligence could easily progress. The student had to absorb and understand each bit of information before the machine would proceed to the next bit of information. With the presentation of each bit, the machine would also force the student to review and demonstrate knowledge of all accumulated data bits.

Before inventing the teaching machine for humans, Skinner had invented the Skinner Box, which used reward and punishment to teach a wide variety of animals (including rats, dogs and monkeys) a surprisingly broad range of unusual behavior. Skinner taught pigeons to play ping-pong—and to keep guided missiles on target. (The latter was part of a U.S. Government research project during World War II.) Before returning to Harvard, Skinner had taught at the universities of Minnesota and Indiana. A philosopher as well as a psychologist, Skinner believed that psychology and programmed learning could be used to develop a system of behavioral and social engineering. Aside from technical works for academic audiences, he was author of the widely read *Walden Two* (1948), the tale of a utopian society whose members are products of behavioral engineering that has programmed them to make individual freedom subservient to the common good. A second, similar work, *Beyond Freedom and Dignity* (1971), expanded on the theme, insisting that traditional concepts of individual liberty were obsolete and that societal crises could end only by programming individuals to serve the interests of the group.

References: *Science and Human Behavior* (1953), *The Analysis of Behavior* (with James G. Holland, 1961) and *The Technology of Teaching* (1968), B. F. Skinner; DAB; EB.

Slack's The Instructor: or, Young Man's Best Companion, Mrs. A widely used manual of self-instruction for young men without formal education, published in 1748 by B(enjamin) Franklin (q.v.) and D. Hall and possibly written by Franklin.

Reference: *Benjamin Franklin,* Carl Van Doren (1938).

slavery A social institution with one class of human being the irrevocable property of another class and entirely subject to its will. The owners can use their slaves for whatever purpose—as laborers, servants or sexual objects. Generally, owners may buy, sell, give or pledge their slaves for debt; they may enchain, brand or disfigure their slaves, or do anything they wish—just as they might with livestock. Slavery was an integral part of American life during the colonial era and for the first 75 years after independence. Its effects continue to influence social life and education in the United States to this day.

The practice of slavery dates back to prehistoric times and was normal almost everywhere in the world until the 5th century, when various western European rulers introduced serfdom as a somewhat more humane and less binding form of involuntary servitude. In the 7th century, however, the explosively growing religion of Islam incorporated slavery as a legitimate institution, and the practice once again became universal in all but the relatively small, Christianized areas of western Europe.

In North America, the first slaves—all blacks from Africa—arrived in Jamestown in 1619, and statutory recognition of slavery began in Massachusetts in 1641, in Connecticut in 1661 and in Virginia in 1661. By the time of independence, slavery was the law of the land. Although Britain abolished the slave trade in 1807 and the United States followed suit in 1808, the American Constitution had left the issue of slave traffic and ownership within national boundaries to the individual states. In 1800, there were nearly 900,000 slaves, of whom about 36,500 were in the northern states—used largely as domestic servants. By 1804, however, Vermont, Pennsylvania, Massachusetts, Rhode Island, Connecticut, New York and New Jersey had passed legislation that abolished slavery within their borders. The nearly four million slaves of the 1860 census were almost all in the southern states, which depended on them for cheap labor and refused to abolish slavery until forced to do so by the Civil War.

Fearing that education would stir a rebellion, southern states had made it a crime, punishable by fine and imprisonment, to teach African Americans to read or write. As a result, at the end of the Civil War four million African Americans were not only illiterate and innumerate but also incapable of earning an independent living. Northern white missionaries helped build and staff dozens of vocational and academic schools and colleges for blacks in the south, but, from the end of Reconstruction in the 1870s, southern state governments refused to fund them. When federal courts ordered southern states to provide blacks with public education equal to, albeit separate from, whites, the states reduced funding to all public education to a minimum. The result was a public school system that left southern whites appallingly undereducated well into the 1950s.

The economic effects of poor education were equally disastrous, with industry refusing to build new plants in areas where it could not find a skilled, literate work force. Although major southern cities began a vast and thoroughly successful educational and economic reconstruction movement in the last half of the 20th century, rural areas of the south continue to be among the nation's most backward—educationally, culturally and economically—and their condition is directly traceable to the institution of slavery and the racial divisions that persist to this day.

(For a more complete discussion of the effects of slavery and education, see AFRICAN AMERICANS; CIVIL RIGHTS ACT OF 1964; DESEGREGATION.)

Reference: *History of Black Americans,* Philip S. Foner (3 vols., 1975–83).

Smith, Adam (1723–1790) Scottish economist who developed the science of political economy and in so doing prescribed a system of universal public education that his disciples would introduce in the United States. A professor of theology, ethics, jurisprudence and political institutions at Glasgow University, he resigned in 1764 to travel throughout Europe and meet with leading philosophers and economists. Returning to Scotland in 1767, he spent the next decade working out a theory of the division of labor, money, prices, wages and distribution. The result was his monumental *Inquiry into the Nature and Causes of the Wealth of Nations* (1776), which laid the foundations for the modern science of political economy.

Divided into five parts, the book deals with education in a final section on public institutions and works, including schools. Although he preferred private education, Smith insisted that the state had a responsibility to educate the common people at public expense, to prevent them from slipping into the torpor and stupidity that is symptomatic of those engaged in routine labor. He called an instructed and intelligent people more decent and orderly than an ignorant and stupid people, thus making the state's responsibility to educate the common people even greater in a free society. Smith's books slowly made their way to the United States, where they deeply influenced Franklin, Jefferson, Hamilton, Adams, Madison and others who called for universal primary education to be included in the Constitution as a basic right of all Americans. Southern slave states and northern cotton mill owners who depended on cheap child labor rebuffed them.

Reference: *The Theory of Education in the Political Philosophy of Adam Smith,* Charles Flinn Arrowood (1945).

Smith, William B. (1727–1803) Scottish-born colonial educator whose visionary curricular plan provided the basis for college studies in colonial America and the United States for more than a century. Educated and ordained at the University of Aberdeen, he immigrated to New York in 1751, where he served as a private tutor for two years and prepared a pamphlet, *A General Idea of the College of Mirania,* which received wide circulation among the nation's most prominent citizens, including Benjamin Franklin (q.v.). The pamphlet provided a vision of the fictional utopian province of Mirania, settled in the New World by the English in the early 17th century. By the 1740s, the inhabitants had become "a mighty and flourishing people"—due in part, at least, to their educational system. Designed to meet practical needs rather than as a conduit to the ministry (like the real colleges of the day), Mirania's educational system was divided into two parts, one for young men destined for public service, the "learned professions" (divinity, law and medicine) and agriculture, and the other for students destined for the mechanical professions, skilled trades and all other occupations.

All were educated in common during their first three years of schooling, to prevent development of class prejudices and to establish "indissoluble connections and friendships." Those destined for the trades then enrolled in a six-year mechanics' program, while those bound for the professions enrolled in a five-year Latin school before entering a four-year college. The first-year college curriculum consisted of algebra, geometry, astronomy, chronology, navigation, logic, metaphysics and practical surveying. The second-year curriculum consisted of ethics, physics, natural history and mechanical and experimental philosophy. In the third year, students learned rhetoric, poetry, the precepts of oratory and the canons of taste and criticism as conceived by Cicero, Quintilian, Demosthenes and Aristotle. In the fourth year, the principal taught Miranian college students agriculture, hygiene, chemistry, anatomy, history, ethics and politics.

In 1754 Franklin invited Smith to teach at his academy, which, with Francis Alison (q.v.), he helped convert into the College of Philadelphia (q.v.) (now the University of Pennsylvania). He became the college's first provost (1755–79) and transposed the Miranian curriculum into a three-year bachelor-of-arts program that was by far the broadest, most varied course of study at any college in America. It served as a model for all American colleges for the next century.

References: BDAE; DAB; *William Smith: Educator and Churchman,* Albert Frank Gegenheimer (1943).

Smith College   The largest private college for women in the United States, with more than 2,500 students in its four-year undergraduate program. Founded in Northampton, Massachusetts, in 1871 with an endowment from the American philanthropist Sophia Smith (1796–1870), the college is one of 84 surviving women's colleges—from a group that had numbered in the hundreds several decades earlier. Opened at a time when few women were permitted access to higher education, Smith now has a coeducational graduate school and is a member of a five-college consortium that permits men and women to attend classes and obtain full credit for courses at Smith, Mount Holyoke, Amherst and Hampshire colleges and at the University of Massachusetts at Amherst.

Reference: Smith College Library, Northampton, Massachusetts.

Smith-Hughes Act   A 1917 federal law that provided federal government matching grants for the establishment of vocational education programs in American high schools. The result of intensive lobbying by the National Society for the Promotion of Industrial Education, the act created a federal board of education charged with expanding high school instruction of agriculture, home economics and industrial trades by training more teachers in these fields and subsidizing their salaries. The act was the first incursion into public secondary education by the U.S. Government and the first federal involvement in public education since passage of the two Morrill Acts that created land grant colleges during the late 19th century.

Pressure had been building for several decades for the federal government to intervene in what was seen as a deteriorating and irrelevant public school system in the United States. As late as 1910, only about 10% of American children graduated from high school, and adolescents—many of them children of immigrants—were ill-prepared to function in what had become a highly sophisticated agricultural and industrial society. Indeed, hundreds of thousands of semiliterate, unskilled and unemployed adolescents roamed city streets and country roads with no means of sustenance other than begging, stealing or prostitution. The Smith-Hughes Act was designed to broaden and restructure American public schools and to prepare the next generation of American children for useful work.

(See also GEORGE ACTS.)

Reference: *Foundations of Vocational Education: Social and Philosophical Concepts,* John F. Thompson (1973).

Smith-Lever Act   A 1914 federal law that provided subsidies to land-grant colleges to establish the first cooperative extension programs. The programs were designed to provide "useful and practical information relating to agriculture and home economics" and thus revive the declining American agricultural economy. From their beginnings, extension programs were a cooperative venture between the land-grant (state) colleges (q.v.) and the U.S. Department of Agriculture, which provided agents at each college to set up demonstration programs. The programs covered the gamut of agricultural education: They provided elementary agricultural training for boys in "corn clubs" and for girls in "tomato clubs"; demonstrations in sewing, canning and home gardening for farm women; and demonstration farms to teach farmers techniques of planting, cultivating, fertilization and crop rotation.

At the time, crop yields had dropped disastrously in the wake of several decades of intermittent droughts, dust storms, pest infestations, incessant overplanting and farmer ignorance about modern agricultural methods. The demonstration-farm technique had been used effectively in Texas in 1903, under the leadership of Seaman A. Knapp (q.v.), a scientifically trained farmer who had been a professor of agriculture and then the president of Iowa Agricultural College. He had developed the demonstration-farm technique as a way of teaching modern agricultural methods to local farmers who might have resented formal instruction from college professors but were quick to imitate the evidently successful methods of a farmer-neighbor (who happened to be a professor). Knapp took his demonstration-farm "teaching" technique to ravaged areas of the south, where he received annual grants from the General Education Board (q.v.) from 1906 until 1914, when the Smith-Lever Act was passed and subsidized his approach on a national basis.

References: *Adventure in Giving: The Story of the General Education Board*, Raymond B. Fosdick (1962); U.S. Department of Agriculture, Washington, D.C.

Smithsonian Institution

The world's largest museum complex and a center for scholarly research on a wide range of topics in the sciences and humanities. An agency of the U.S. government, the institution was founded in 1846 by an act of Congress, under the terms of a £100,000 bequest by English scientist James Smithson. The bequest had called for the "founding at Washington, under the name of the Smithsonian Institution, an establishment for the increase and diffusion of knowledge among men." Although Congress received and accepted the legacy in 1836, it took the government a decade to resolve the heated debate between politicians, scholars and ordinary citizens over the exact shape of the institution-to-be. Some called for the establishment of a national university; others suggested a postgraduate educational institution in the arts and sciences, for students who had graduated from college but not yet enrolled in professional schools. There were various calls for the construction of a national astronomical observatory, for a national agricultural school, for a national library, a publications center to publish and disseminate all the works of American researchers, and for a center for scientific research and inquiry. Still others envisioned a center combining almost all these elements, while a few xenophobes insisted that the funds be returned to England as an insult to the new American nation, which, they insisted, was quite capable of building its own cultural institutions.

In the end, Congress created what is essentially a composite institution that maintains scientific and artistic collections, sponsors scientific research and exploration, publishes books and periodicals, provides broad educational opportunities for the American public and maintains a library of about one million volumes dealing with science, natural history and the humanities. The institution is governed by a board of regents, whose members are the vice president of the United States, the chief justice, three members of the Senate, three members of the House of Representatives and nine "illustrious" citizens appointed by Congress. Although based in Washington, D.C., the Smithsonian Institution is actually a complex (indeed, the world's largest) of many institutions scattered across the United States, among them: the Cooper-Hewitt Museum, which is the Smithsonian Institution's National Museum of Design, in New York City; the Smithsonian Astrophysical Observatory, in

Cambridge, Massachusetts; Smithsonian Environmental Research Center, in Edgewater, Maryland; and Smithsonian Tropical Research Institute, on Barro Colorado Island, Gatun Lake, Panama.

The vast majority of the Smithsonian Institution's many units, however, are in Washington, D.C. They include the Arthur M. Sackler Gallery of Asian and Near Eastern Art; the Freer Gallery of Art (oriental art, plus a collection of works—including the "Peacock Room"—by the 19th-century American artist James Whistler); the Hirshhorn Museum and Sculpture Garden (19th- and 20th-century European and American art); the John F. Kennedy Center for the Performing Arts; the National Air and Space Museum, with a comprehensive survey of the development of aviation and astronautics; the National Gallery of Art, one of the world's greatest collections of paintings, spanning many centuries, and including works by Old Masters as well as 19th- and 20th-century artists and sculptors; the National Museum of African Art; the National Museum of American Art, with 25,000 works from the 18th century to the present; the National Museum of Natural History; the National Portrait Gallery, with portraits of great Americans; and the National Zoological Park, with 2,600 living animals.

References: *The Smithsonian Institution, 1846–1896: The History of Its First Half-Century,* George Brown Goode, ed. (1897); *America's Castle,* Kenneth Haffertepe (1984); *The Smithsonian Institution: Documents Relating to Its Origins and History,* William J. Rhees, ed. (1879); Smithsonian Institution, Washington, D.C.; *The Smithsonian Institution: Documents Relative to Its Origins and History, 1835–1899* (2 vols., no author, 1901).

social promotion A term from the 1930s and 1940s referring to the advancement of students to the next higher grade in public elementary and secondary schools on the basis of age rather than academic achievement. Designed to mitigate public humiliation because of academic failure, social promotion was largely eliminated by the introduction of ability grouping and tracking. In both cases, students remained in the appropriate grade with their age mates. Thus, elementary school students would remain with their age mates, but be taught in slower or faster sections, according to their academic abilities. At the high school level, tracking systems placed students in one of three broad curricular "tracks," or programs: an academic track for the college-bound; a general track for slower students unlikely to attend college after graduation; and a vocational track for students interested in learning skilled trades. Within the academic track, ability grouping saw slower students in "regular" sections of each course, with the more gifted students placed in "honors" classes.

Reference: *Promotion or Failure for the Elementary School Pupil?* by Carleton M. Saunders (1941).

social service movement A nationwide thrust to deliver a variety of social, psychological and health services to socioeconomically deprived children in inner-city schools across the United States. Not formally organized as a national program, the movement is actually made up of a variety of independent efforts, with some data-based technical coordination provided by the United States Department of Education.

In 1992, Kentucky mandated establishment of social service centers in every school (a total of more than 300) with more than 20% of its students from families living below the poverty level. New Jersey started a program in 1987, mandating social service centers in at least one school in every county. Iowa did the same two years later.

Some cities, such as Denver, St. Louis, Chicago and Miami Beach, have acted independently of the state and established social service centers in their inner-city schools. In California, several foundations set up a partnership with the state to establish school social service centers. New York, borrowing on the California model, established the largest citywide, in-school social service program, in partnership with the Children's Aid Society (q.v.) and a number of private foundations and corporations. Called the

Beacon Program, it comprises social service centers, each operated by the Children's Aid Society and funded almost entirely with grants from foundations and businesses, in more than three dozen schools. The programs operate before, during and after school and, in many cases, on weekends, offering comprehensive dental and health care and social and psychological services for abused, neglected, violent, addicted or otherwise needy children. Beacon schools also operate before-and-after-school classes and recreation programs. Offering "everything you need outside your house," Beacon schools social service programs are far less costly than conventional social service programs available from hospitals and government social welfare agencies. Indeed, costs per child average only $950 a year, with delivery of services absorbing 90 cents of every dollar, compared to only 65 cents for conventional out-of-school social services. The savings accrue largely from the rent-free basis of Children's Aid Society facilities. Utilizing otherwise idle school space, they pay no rent, utilities, insurance or maintenance, which are all part of the normal costs of operating each school.

In-school social service dates back to the 1890s, when the journalist Jacob Riis (1849–1914) published photographs of the intolerable conditions in New York City's slum schools. In the 1920s and during the Great Depression of the 1930s, many doctors, dentists and social workers set up offices in schools across the nation to treat economically deprived children. Extended, widespread prosperity saw the social service movement all but disappear after World War II. It did not stage a revival until the mid-1980s, when a variety of government studies indicated social and medical neglect as a primary cause of low academic achievement and high dropout rates among inner-city school children.

The social service movement has not been free of controversy. In late 1994, the Committee for Economic Development, an organization of executives at some 25 major American corporations, called for an end to social services in public schools. It urged abandonment of efforts to incorporate mentally and physically handicapped children in regular classrooms and called for an end to social services such as pregnancy counseling, AIDS information and even driver education classes. "America's public schools are being spread too thin," agreed Richard W. Riley, secretary of education at the time. Presenting a report titled "Putting Learning First," Riley contended that schools were failing the business sector. Employers "feel that a large majority of their new hires lack adequate writing and problem solving skills." Even Albert Shanker (q.v.), then president of the American Federation of Teachers, agreed that "you should not get into college just because you're breathing and you're 18."

The report charged that "communities, states and the national government are asking those who manage our classrooms to be parent, social worker, doctor, psychologist, police officer and, perhaps, if there is time, teacher. It seems that whenever a social crisis, such as AIDS, child abuse or drunk driving is perceived, the government looks to the schools to solve it." The report urged schools to limit their services to education and force government to shift social services to better equipped agencies.

References: NYT; United States Department of Education, Washington, D.C.

social settlements A group of private, nonprofit organizations that sought to change the plight of the poor at the turn of the 20th century and grew into one of the most influential social, political and educative forces in American history. They emerged during the 1880s and 1890s, at a time when major American cities were overflowing with millions of illiterate and semi-literate immigrants, some skilled, some not. Those who found work were usually packed into factories, mills, mines and sweat shops, 12 hours a day, seven days a week, earning $3 to $10 a week. To keep labor costs down, farms, mines and factories depended heavily on child labor, with children seven to 14 years of age shipped like cattle from state to state to work in tobacco fields, canneries, mines, meatpacking plants and textile mills. By 1900, more than 1.7 million children were engaged in such labor.

By the late 1890s, several years of drought and dust storms had ravaged the American agricultural economy, while a panic in 1893 had devastated the rest of the economy, closing banks, factories and businesses across the nation. The result was social chaos, with millions of unemployed and homeless—and unattended children—roaming the streets and country roads by the hundreds of thousands. The government was helpless—indeed, it was bankrupt—and so short of cash that it had to borrow funds from private banks to pay its own employees.

Two new institutions evolved out of the social chaos: One was the institutional church (q.v.) and the other was the settlement house. Both were built on similar socio-theological foundations, with the former fearing the death of Christianity if the church did not share its wealth with the destitute and the latter fearing the end of democracy and civilization if the wealthy, educated classes did not share their wealth with the poor and ignorant. Although there were subtle differences in their motives, their goals were the same; but in the end the very secular nature of the settlement house movement drew far more supporters than the institutional church and made it far more powerful and effective.

The social settlement house movement actually began in London in the 1870s, when a group of social reformers that included the elder Arnold Toynbee, among others, determined that the industrial revolution had set in motion a class conflict that was tearing the social fabric of their nation asunder. They appealed especially to young intellectuals at Cambridge and Oxford universities to settle among the poor and bridge the gap that the industrial revolution had created between the urban poor and the larger society. In 1883, clergyman Samuel A. Barnett read two papers to Oxford and Cambridge students. One was "Settlements of University Men in Great Towns," which coined the term "settlement." He urged his student listeners to bring culture and education to working people and, in turn, to learn the horrors of the industrial worker's plight and to bring about social reform. A group of students heeded Barnett's call and on Christmas Eve, 1884, founded Toynbee Hall as the first permanent social settlement and the "spiritual mother house" of the social settlement movement.

In 1886, Stanton Coit, an Amherst College graduate who had spent a few months at Toynbee House, returned home to found a similar settlement in New York City's teeming Lower East Side slums. Known first as the Neighborhood Guild and later as the University Settlement, it was the first settlement in the United States. A year later, a group of Smith College alumnae founded the College Settlements Association, and in 1889 Jane Addams and Ellen Gates Starr (qq.v.) founded Chicago's Hull House (q.v.), the quintessential American settlement house that became the model for the hundreds that followed. By 1891, there were six settlements in the United States. Their number grew to more than 100 by 1900 and more than 400 by 1910, and their leaders and disciples would influence social legislation and education for much of the 20th century. Settlement houses at the turn of the century were the seedbeds for women's suffrage, child labor legislation, progressive labor legislation and social security.

About 60% of all settlement house worker-residents were women and almost 90% were college-educated. Most were committed enough to social service to forgo marriage in favor of a life of educating the poor and the working classes of American slums. Often born of wealth, they relied on family and social ties for funds, acquiring buildings where they brought the advantages of their education and a host of desperately needed social services to working people who lived in the surrounding neighborhoods. Emulating and building on the example of Toynbee Hall, they brought art exhibits, evening and

Sunday concerts, university extension classes, lectures, cooking and sewing classes, adult education and books to the slums; they taught the poor and working classes their political rights and rallied them to support such political causes as library, park, playground and school construction. They provided temporary housing and food for the destitute, reading rooms, recreation facilities, free day nurseries and kindergartens, health clinics, summer camps and, above all, caring institutions for young and old, no matter how desperate.

As the public itself learned the essentiality of the settlement house movement and increased its support, the public sector began absorbing many of the functions of the movement. Public schools gradually absorbed many settlement house children's programs, while public welfare authorities took over such functions as health care, emergency housing and feeding and relief programs. In effect, the settlement house movement taught the monied public its obligation to care for the destitute, and the public sector gradually absorbed those functions. Settlement houses did not, however, disappear. Always in the forefront of public welfare, they were first to establish programs for troubled youth in the 1960s, for inadequately cared-for senior citizens in the 1970s and for the homeless in the 1980s.

Reference: *Spearheads for Reform: The Social Settlements and the Progressive Movement, 1890–1914,* Allen F. Davis (1967).

social studies An amorphous, interdisciplinary course of studies that includes history, geography, political science, civics, economics, culture and sociology. Unique to the American public school system, social studies is, to one degree or another, an integral part of the public elementary and middle school curriculum. Two years of high school social studies are required for graduation in almost every state.

Often called "social slush," social studies has been under attack by educators since it was first introduced into the public school curriculum in 1905. At the time, fewer than 10% of American

youth ever finished high school. Most children attended school during the early elementary grades, barely learning to read, write and calculate before joining the work force. Because of the explosive growth in the number of immigrant children during the last decades of the 19th century, educators feared children would not learn enough American history, geography and culture during their brief sojourn in school to assimilate into American society. The social studies curriculum was an effort to cram into a single course enough basics of the American past and its then-current customs to Americanize immigrant children and help them function effectively in American society.

As public schooling expanded and compulsory education and child labor laws forced most children to continue their education beyond elementary school, the social studies curriculum expanded accordingly. Its content varies so widely from school to school and state to state, however, that there is little uniformity in what American youngsters learn. Until the mid-1990s, most elementary schools still relied on a model developed in the 1930s called "Expanding Horizons," in which pupils studied concepts of the individual and the family in kindergarten, then studied, in successive grades, the community, the state, the nation and the world. United States and world history, however, were condensed into inconsequentially minute overviews for fourth, fifth and sixth graders, with the result that students had little knowledge of history—or any of the other academic areas social studies supposedly covers—as they entered middle school and high school.

In a single year of elementary school, for example, a social studies course might deal with colonial life in New England, life along the Congo River in Africa and Jackie Robinson's successful penetration of organized baseball's racial barriers in the United States in the late 1940s. The pejorative term "social slush" resulted and, critics are quick to point out, along with it the abysmally low scores of American students of all ages in standardized history and geography tests. On a scale of 0 to 500, American twelfth graders scored only 293.1 on geography and 280.7 on history in 1988. Only 4.6% of American twelfth graders and no eighth graders scored 350 or more, a level that demonstrates a "detailed understanding of historical vocabulary, facts, regions and ideas" and an ability to "interpret historical information and ideas." About 41.3% of twelfth graders and 12.6% of eighth graders scored between 300 and 350, a level that demonstrates a "knowledge of basic historical terms, facts, regions and ideas" and "some knowledge of primary texts in U.S. political history." More than 38% of twelfth graders and 54.9% of eighth graders scored between 250 and 300, demonstrating only a "beginning" knowledge of historical information.

Critics insist that social studies be replaced with the type of focused courses taught in academically demanding American private schools (and public schools in Europe and Japan)—i.e., history (ancient, medieval, modern Europe, American, etc.), geography and political science. In the mid-1990s, a handful of publishers were beginning to issue a more focused series of texts in response to low student achievement levels in history, geography and other elements of social studies.

References: *The Social Studies,* Howard D. Mehlinger and O. L. Davis, eds. (1981); *Elementary and Middle School Social Studies,* David T. Naylor and Richard A. Diem (1987).

social utility theory An approach to curricular development designed to make almost all studies provide students with knowledge and skills that will help them function successfully in society. The theory resulted from a series of four reports beginning in 1911, by the National Education Association's Committee on the Economy of Time. NEA was responding to growing demands for educational reform by critics who charged that public schools were ineffective in preparing children for real life.

Reference: National Education Association, Washington, D.C.

Society for the Promotion of Agriculture, Commerce, and Art A mutual-education organization founded in 1781 in New Jersey to help farmers and merchants achieve success in their enterprises. The society served as a model for similar mutual-education groups in Philadelphia, South Carolina and elsewhere. With few schools yet constructed, early American colonials were forced to educate each other, in taverns, inns, Masonic lodges and through a handful of organizations such as Benjamin Franklin's American Philosophical Society (q.v.). In 1748, the Society for the Promotion of Useful Knowledge (q.v.) was formed to improve culture in New York City, and a similar group, the Virginia Society for the Promotion of Useful Knowledge, emerged in Williamsburg in 1773. In 1780, a group of Bostonians established the American Academy of Arts and Sciences, with John Adams and John Hancock among the founding members. The Society for the Promotion of Agriculture, Commerce, and Art differed from these earlier mutual education groups in that its thrust was far more practical, and its appeal was directed to farmers and merchants who were less interested in culture than they were in entrepreneurial success. In effect, the society was the forerunner of the thousands of trade associations and societies that continue to serve as important educative institutions for Americans in business, industry and scientific research.

References: *Scientific Societies in the United States,* Ralph S. Bates (1945).

Society for the Promotion of Useful Knowledge Originally a literary club, founded in New York City in 1748. Later, it became a major force in blocking the establishment of the Church of England as the official religion of the American colonies. The club was formed by three scions of prominent New York families of the day: William Livingston, William Smith Jr. and John Morin Scott. All were Presbyterians; all were educated at Yale; all attended law school; and all served part of their legal apprenticeships in the law office of Smith's father, where they became close friends. They discovered a common disdain for the drudgery of day-to-day legal practice and an equally common love of literature, art, music and other amusements. Deciding to devote their efforts to the cultural expansion of what they considered a culturally barren city, they organized the Society for the Promotion of Useful Knowledge.

A year later they announced plans to publish *The Independent Reflector,* a weekly that was to have been modeled after *The Spectator* in England, with essays for "correcting the taste and improving the minds of our fellow citizens." By the time the first issue went to press in 1752, however, their focus—like that of the entire city—had shifted from the city's cultural development to interdenominational religious bitterness and the question of the city's religious future. At the time, the legislature was just founding the state's first college and, despite a wave of anticlericalism, had appointed trustees who were almost all members of the Church of England.

When Trinity Church proposed deeding some of its lands to the new college, Livingston, Smith and Scott and their society led a massive protest by Presbyterians and other dissenting sects. They warned that the Church of England was planning a "monster tyranny" that would place all the colonies under its control. The first issue of the *Reflector,* now modeled after *The Independent Whig* and *Cato's Letters,* called for a crusade for liberty and reform of "the abuses of my country." Subsequent issues demanded an end to excise taxes and to unrestricted immigration to the colonies—especially for felons. *The Independent Reflector* continued, however, to focus on education and the religious furor surrounding the founding of New York's new college. The *Reflector* urged that admission of

students to the new college be based on parity of all Protestant denominations. It called for the founding of the college by the colonial assembly rather than by a charter from the Crown and for placement of its supervision under civil rather than church authorities. It urged that divinity be eliminated from the curriculum, and it called for establishing county grammar schools to feed students into the new college.

In the end King's College was founded by charter of King George II. Although its first president, Samuel Johnson, was an Anglican clergyman, he was a convert from Congregationalism and apparently sensed the danger that sectarianism presented to the future of the institution. While King's College (later, Columbia) remained officially Anglican until it was closed by the Revolutionary War, religion played a relatively minor role in day-to-day academics. Through the *Reflector,* however, the Society for the Promotion of Useful Knowledge continued to call for secularization of higher education, and it laid the political and philosophical groundwork for the establishment in 1784 of a secular state board of regents, which, though not an actual university, was nevertheless called the University of the State of New York (q.v.) and was under civic control. Livingston, Scott and Smith also contributed greatly to the cultural enrichment of New York City with the founding of the New York Society Library, the city's first library open to the general public by subscription. The library is still in existence.

References: *The Independent Reflector,* Milton M. Klein, ed. (1963); *A Study of the Legal and Political Careers of William Livingston, John Morin Scott, and William Smith, Jr.,* Dorothy Rita Dillon (1949).

Society for Propagation of the Gospel in New England

A charitable organization created by the English Parliament in 1649, to convert American Indians in the Massachusetts Bay Colony to Christianity. A privately run organization, it was financed largely by Puritan merchants and other men of import, including

Oliver Cromwell. The society supported the work of such missionaries as the Rev. John Eliot (q.v.), of Roxbury, Massachusetts, who produced an "Indian Library" consisting of Algonquian translations he made of the Bible, Psalter, a grammar, a primer, a catechism and several other books on piety and religious practices. After the Restoration, the society was reincorporated by a new Parliament as the Company for Propagacion of the Gospell in New England, and the Parts Adjacent in America, but continued its earlier work, buying clothing, building materials and tools for Indians, paying the salaries of ministers and schoolmasters to work among the Indians, and, in 1653, financing construction of the Indian College at Harvard. The latter proved a failure after it was unable to recruit an adequate number of qualified Indian students. By 1675, the society's efforts had nevertheless resulted in the conversion of about 2,500 Indians, or about 20% of the 12,500 Indians in New England.

Reference: *The New England Company, 1649–1776: Missionary Society to the American Indians,* William Kellaway (1961).

Society for the Propagation of the Gospel in Foreign Parts (SPG)

A unique, quasi-public philanthropic organization founded in England in 1701 to strengthen Anglican Christianity and basic education in the American colonies. In its 82 years of existence in colonial America, SPG not only established hundreds of primary schools, it also assured the survival and dominance of the English language, English culture and Protestantism as the framework for American life.

Founded at the urging of the influential Anglican priest Thomas Bray (q.v.), SPG was, from the beginning, unique for England and the Protestant world. In its missionary reach SPG was something of a Protestant counterpart to the Roman Catholic Society of Jesus, or Jesuits (q.v.). Chartered by the Crown, its head was the archbishop of Canterbury, and while undisguisedly furthering the interests of Crown and church, it nevertheless remained independent of

both. A privately funded and managed philanthropy, it was the first such organization in the English-speaking world dedicated to converting other Christians (as opposed to heathens) to a specific Protestant sect.

Bray, who had visited religiously fractious Maryland, had been appalled by the failure of the Church of England to assume a significant role in the religiously and ethnically fragmented American colonies. He warned of "divers Romish priests and Jesuits," spreading atheism, infidelity and "popish superstition and idolatry" in the New World. To counter such influences, SPG recruited a force of more than five dozen missionaries to go to the colonies, establish stations, found churches and schools and recruit schoolmasters and catechists to educate children. Over the following decades, they established 169 missionary stations and more than 180 schools, stretching from New Hampshire to Georgia, and from the Atlantic and New York City to the western frontier.

They distributed thousands of Bibles, prayer books, devotional tracts and school texts in English, German, Dutch and various Indian dialects. From their pulpits, classrooms and libraries, they not only brought Englishmen back to the Church of England, they also converted huge numbers of non-English European settlers and their children to Anglicanism, while at the same time building the loyalties of all to the British Crown. SPG purposely recruited French, Scottish, Irish, German and Dutch missionaries to win the religious and political loyalties of settlements made up of those nationalities. In addition to preaching, they catechized the young and ignorant. SPG schools, with about 40 children each, for a total of 7,200 students during the society's strongest years, taught their charges to read and study the Holy Scriptures and "to write a plain and legible hand, in order to the fitting them for useful employments, with as much arithmetic as shall be necessary to the same purpose."

The SPG effort did not proceed without some setbacks. Settlements were attacked by hostile

Indians, devastated by malaria, dysentery and smallpox epidemics, or denounced by various dissenters—Quakers, Puritans and Methodists particularly—who had fled to the colonies to escape the Church of England. "Is it not enough that they persecuted [us] out of the Old World?" asked the Massachusetts Puritan minister Jonathan Mayhew in his *Observations on the Charter and Conduct of the S.P.G.* (1863). "Will they pursue us into the New to convert us here?—compassing seat and land to make us proselytes, while they neglect the heathen and heathenish plantations?" Despite fierce opposition, SPG scored enormous successes throughout the colonies. In addition to conventional schools, the society founded the first colonial charity schools for the poor, the homeless and the orphaned, in New York City. And, in its longest lasting contribution to American education, in 1754 it was responsible for the chartering of King's College (later, Columbia).

Moreover, SPG did its utmost to convert and educate Indians and slaves, but its efforts among the Indians seldom scored long-lasting successes. In 1702, a year after its founding, SPG established its first mission to the Indians, among the Yamasee in South Carolina, but a Yamasee uprising in 1715 closed the mission. In 1703, the Mohawk nation near Albany, New York, rejected an SPG offer to establish a mission, but in 1712 SPG did establish a school among the Mohawks and apparently attracted about 40 students. A build-up of hostility led to its abandonment in 1719. Undaunted, SPG established other schools among the Indians, including a second among the Mohawks in 1769. Like its predecessor, the school did not endure.

SPG also mounted efforts to instruct and catechize African Americans. In 1704, SPG appointed a French Protestant, Elias Neau, to open a school for blacks in New York City. Neau conducted sessions in his house three evenings a week and went from house to house during the rest of the week to instruct, catechize, comfort and pray. Neau attracted more than 100 students to his school, including Indians and whites

as well as blacks. Although originally charged with provoking a black uprising in 1712, he was declared innocent after authorities found that none of his students had participated. Neau's school continued to thrive until his death in 1722, after which it was gradually absorbed into the SPG charity school in New York City. Still another pioneering SPG effort to educate blacks took place in Charleston, South Carolina, where the botanist Alexander Garden (q.v.) opened a school for Negro children. He purchased his first two students and eventually enrolled about 60 others, teaching them to read so that they might teach other blacks to read. The school closed in 1764 under circumstances that remain unclear.

Although all SPG churches and schools, including King's College, closed during the Revolutionary War, all reopened after the end of the war. The Church of England became the Protestant Episcopal Church in the United States, free of ties to the English Crown and the archbishop of Canterbury, and King's College reopened as Columbia College. SPG ended its work in the former American colonies in 1783. Its missionaries fled to Canada and the West Indies or returned home, and SPG renewed its missionary work in other parts of the world.

Reference: *Two Hundred Years of the S.P.G.: An Historical Account of the Society for the Propagation of the Gospel in Foreign Parts, 1701–1900,* C. F. Pascoe (1901).

sociodrama A type of simulation (q.v.) in which a teacher asks students to reenact spontaneously a real-life problem affecting one or more of the students. Totally unrehearsed, sociodramas are designed to teach participants and observers an understanding of the genesis and consequences of the particular problem they explore.

Reference: *Educational Psychology: Mastering Principles and Applications,* Janice T. Gibson and Louis A Chandler (1988).

Socrates (470–399 B.C.**)** Greek philosopher who developed a method of teaching based on questioning rather than lecturing students. Called the Socratic method and still a fundamental element of Western pedagogy, Socrates feigned ignorance of a problem that he presented to his students. He thus stimulated a student discussion, which he then guided, with rational argumentation, toward eventual discovery of definitions, truth and knowledge. (Such feigned ignorance by a wise teacher is still called Socratic irony.) Often, too, he would simply question an established "truth," thus raising doubts in his students' minds and provoking them into discussions that either proved or disproved the original premise. Socrates, himself, wrote no books or tracts, but his teaching techniques, philosophy and wisdom were recorded in detail by two of his students, the philosopher Plato (q.v.) and the historian Xenophon. In effect, his philosophy called for a ceaseless search for truth, equating ignorance with vice and knowledge with virtue.

Born in Athens, possibly the son of a sculptor, he received the standard elementary education in literature, music and gymnastics, then studied rhetoric, dialectics, philosophy and Athenian culture of the Periclean Age. He was an infantryman in the war with Sparta, serving with conspicuous bravery in two battles. As a member of the legislative council, or *boule,* from 406 to 405, he was familiar with the leading figures of Periclean Athens, but grew convinced he could better serve Athens as a philosopher and teacher. He spent much of his time in the marketplace and public resorts of Athens, luring passersby into dialogue and argument. Ridiculed by the playwright Aristophanes as a corrupter of youthful reasoning in the comedy *The Clouds* (423 B.C.), Socrates was eventually charged by state authorities with blasphemy and corrupting the morals of the young by failing to teach them of the gods. He was sentenced to death. Although his friends, including Plato, arranged for him to escape (a common practice in Athens), he insisted on obeying Athenian law and on dying in defense of his belief in the value of knowledge over ignorance.

Reference: EB; *A History of Greek Philosophy,* W. K. C. Guthrie (6 vols., 1962–86).

Socratic method A teaching technique whereby a carefully constructed series of questions guides students toward accurate definitions of terms and eventual solutions to specific problems. By limiting the scope of each question, the teacher can guide student discussion toward a series of obvious answers, inevitable conclusions and, eventually, a body of knowledge about a particular subject. Originated by Socrates (q.v.) in ancient Greece, the Socratic method is a forerunner of programmed instruction (q.v.), in which a body of knowledge is broken down into a series of small, easy-to-learn bits of information, acquired through correct responses to a series of questions.

References: *Questioning Strategies and Techniques* (1972) and *Involving Students in Questioning* (1976), Francis P. Hunkins.

sodality An organized society, fraternity or sorority. Derived from the Latin *sodalitas,* meaning comradeship or club, sodality is sometimes substituted for the terms fraternity or sorority on some college campuses, especially when the society has been formed for charitable rather than social purposes.

Reference: ERIC.

software All materials associated with computer operations other than the actual machinery (the hardware). Usually recorded on disks, software consists primarily of electronically recorded programs that determine and direct computer operations. In a more general sense, software can also refer to manuals, diagrams and other printed instructions.

Reference: ERIC.

sorority A campus social society or club made up exclusively of women (the Latin *soror,* meaning "sister"). Uniquely American and operationally identical to all-male fraternities (q.v.), sororities are of a more recent origin than fraternities, in part because of the inability of women to gain admission to colleges and universities until the mid-19th century. The earliest sorority, Alpha Delta Pi, was founded at Wesleyan Female College in Macon, Georgia, in 1851. (The earliest American fraternity, a debating and literary society, was founded at Yale College a century earlier.)

In recent years, two new types of fraternity and sorority have emerged, with the traditional ones still bearing Greek-letter names and affiliated with national organizations. A considerable number of independent fraternities and sororities have been organized, and neither their numbers nor memberships are published. The other new group of fraternities limits its operations to black colleges, and its membership rolls are not revealed. An estimated one-third of American college students now belong to some form of residential or nonresidential social fraternity or sorority, but the only accurate membership figures are those kept by the National Interfraternity Conference and National Panhellenic Conference for their member fraternities and sororities, which tend to be traditional, Greek-letter societies. Although a handful of them converted to coeducational societies during the 1970s and 1980s, 72 national men's Greek-letter fraternities and 33 national women's Greek-letter fraternities remained single-sex organizations in the mid-1990s. Their membership totalled about 400,000 fraternity members and more than 200,000 sorority members. Phi Beta Kappa, originally a men's social fraternity, became coeducational in 1875, when the University of Vermont chapter admitted the first two women and the fraternity began converting into an honor society for students graduating college with high academic honors, outstanding character and other achievements.

As in fraternities, membership in sororities plunged during the civil rights movement of the 1950s and 1960s; national revulsion at their often discriminatory policies, even at publicly supported institutions, led some colleges and universities to ban fraternities and sororities en-

tirely. From 1965 to 1972, sorority membership dropped about 40%. The 1970s and 1980s, however, saw a revival in the number of sororities and fraternities. Spurring the revival was the passage of state laws banning the sale of alcoholic beverages to persons under 21, which forced student parties off campus and into private facilities.

Reference: National Panhellenic Conference, Indianapolis, Indiana.

South Carolina Eighth of the original 13 colonies to join the Union, in 1788. South Carolina's first free schools date back to 1710, two years before the Carolinas split into two colonies. The free schools were not, however, a public school system in the modern sense. Established by Anglican missionaries from the Society for the Propagation of the Gospel in Foreign Parts (q.v.), the schools were extensions of an effort to Christianize "heathens." They were few in number in what was essentially a wilderness populated by hostile Indians and ravaged by continual malaria, dysentery and smallpox epidemics. Although the society's first mission to the Indians began in South Carolina in 1702 with the Yamasee tribe, it ended in failure after a Yamasee uprising in 1715. In 1743, another society missionary, the botanist Alexander Garden (q.v.), opened a school for Negro children in Charleston. He purchased the two first children he enrolled and eventually enrolled about 60 others, hoping to teach them to read and send them out to spread literacy among other blacks. The school was closed in 1764 under circumstances that remain unclear.

After national independence, South Carolina joined other southern states in making it a criminal offense to teach blacks to read and write. Although northern military authorities established some public schools during the post-Civil War Reconstruction period (q.v.), state authorities segregated them by race after self-rule was restored. Moreover, legislators representing agricultural interests, which depended heavily on child labor, defeated all efforts to expand the public school system or fund existing schools adequately. The state condoned child labor until federal labor laws barred such practices in the late 1930s. The result was a public school system that was among the poorest in the nation in terms of educational quality, measured by virtually any standard. All efforts to improve the system were blocked by the fears of all-white legislatures that blacks would be the principal beneficiaries. Federal courts forced an end to segregation in the 1950s, but many schools remained segregated, in violation of federal law, until the 1980s, when a new, forward-looking governor, Richard Riley, took control of the state house and organized a concerted effort to lift the quality of the state's education from its abyss.

Rallying a coalition of business interests, labor organizations and educators, Riley, who later became secretary of education in the Clinton administration, pointed out that poor education was the primary cause of economic stagnation and high unemployment in South Carolina. The coalition, in turn, pressured the state legislature to raise spending on education and force schools to raise educational goals and standards. In 1984, the legislature passed the Educational Improvement Act, increasing the sales tax to pay for school improvement, setting higher academic standards, expanding early childhood education and raising teacher salaries. The state's schools and its children scored remarkable improvements. The percentage of eighth graders who passed basic skills tests in reading climbed from 65.2% in 1983 to 74.5% in 1991, while the percentage of those who passed math skills tests soared from 42% to 72.6%. By 1991, teacher salaries had climbed from near-bottom in the nation to 38th, while per-pupil spending rose to 40th in the nation. Although South Carolina did not become an educational mecca, the improvements of the 1980s served as a signal to the rest of the south to put the Civil War, slavery and racial segregation in the past and begin building public school systems that can produce

a work force able to compete in the economic environment of the 21st century.

The state's 1,100 public elementary and secondary schools now enroll more than 600,000 students. The College of Charleston, founded in 1770, is the state's oldest institution of higher education. Although College of Charleston is partially state-supported, Clemson University and the University of South Carolina are the official state universities, along with South Carolina State University, a historically black (it is still 95% black) land-grant college founded in 1895. The University of South Carolina was founded in 1801 and now has four four-year campuses, at Columbia, Aiken, Conway and Spartanburg. Total enrollment is more than 40,000 students, exclusive of the 12,000 students at Clemson, which was founded separately in 1889. Also state-supported is the Citadel, the Military College of South Carolina, which came under legal attack during the 1980s and 1990s for its refusal to admit women. In all, the state has 12 public four-year colleges and 21 two-year colleges. In addition, there are 20 private four-year colleges, including Furman University, an independent university founded in 1826, and Bob Jones University, a fundamentalist Christian school founded in 1927. There are also 11 private two-year colleges.

References: EB; CHE; *Two Hundred Years of the S.P.G.: An Historical Account of the Society for the Propagation of the Gospel in Foreign Parts, 1701–1900*, C. F. Pascoe (1901).

South Dakota The 40th state to join the Union, in 1889, South Dakota opened its first school in 1860. The strong Indian (largely Sioux) presence in the state—more than 50,000 in a population of almost 700,000—continues to influence public education, with four institutions of higher education, one of them a tribally controlled university. The tribal colleges are relatively small, rural institutions with no residence facilities. Oglala Lakota College, for example, has 1,100 full-time men and women commuter students, all of them Native Americans. Founded in 1971 by the Oglala Sioux Tribal Council, it offers programs in business, teaching and human services at 10 regional centers spread over 5,000 square miles of the Pine Ridge Indian Reservation in the southwest corner of the state, as well as at a central campus at Kyle. Sinte Gleska University was founded a year earlier in Rosebud, where it offers undergraduate programs in business, fine arts, professional training and technical studies. Like Oglala Lakota College, Sinte Gleska has no residence halls, but about 15% of its students are white, with the remainder either Native American or Eskimo. The average age of undergraduates is 31, and 90% graduate.

In the early 1990s, South Dakota had just under 800 public elementary and secondary schools, with a combined population of about 125,000. The public school system ranked above-average in the United States in educational quality, with a low student-teacher ratio of 15.4 (national average: 17.4), which elevated reading scores above the national average. The state had seven public and 10 private four-year institutions of higher learning and two two-year colleges, one public and one private. Each of the public, four-year colleges also operates two-year programs on their campuses.

References: CHE; EB; *Barron's Profiles of American Colleges* Long (updated annually).

Southeastern Community College v. Davis

A unanimous, 1979 U.S. Supreme Court decision that federally funded colleges were not required to admit all handicapped applicants or to make "extensive modifications" of their facilities to accommodate disabled students. The decision represented a narrow, albeit significant, modification of the Rehabilitation Act of 1973 (q.v.), which barred exclusion of an "otherwise qualified handicapped individual" from programs receiving federal aid. The Court interpreted the meaning of "an otherwise qualified person" as "one who is able to meet all of a program's requirements in spite of his handicap."

In the case in question, Frances B. Davis, a practical nurse with a severe hearing disability, had filed suit against Southeastern Community College, Whiteville, South Carolina, for rejecting her application to the school's registered nursing program. The Court backed the school's argument that her disability and her dependence on lip-reading would not allow her to function "sufficiently" as either a student or as a registered nurse. The college pointed out that lip-reading would be of no value in an operating room or other area, where personnel wore surgical masks, or with incoherent patients. The decision, however, only sought to modify and define more precisely the phrase "otherwise qualified person" and did nothing to undermine the vast reach of the Rehabilitation Act.

Reference: U.S. Supreme Court proceedings.

Southern Education Board A group of northern philanthropists and southern reformers who sought at the turn of the 20th century to restore the economy and social structure of the south by establishing universal public education. In addition to expanding public education, the board sought to make schools more useful socially and to the individual by introducing vocational education into the curriculum and improving teacher training.

The board was organized at the 1901 Conference for Education in the South, which brought together a group of Christian ministers and educators and a handful of northern progressive philanthropists such as Robert Curtis Ogden, George Foster Peabody and John D. Rockefeller Jr. (qq.v.) Financed by Rockefeller's General Education Board (q.v.), the Southern Education Board was designed to launch "a campaign of education for free schools for all the people" by flooding the press with news releases and feature articles, by attending meetings on education throughout the south and by pressuring legislators in every state. To keep conflict to a minimum, northern participants remained discreetly in the background, while southern board members led the struggle in the legislatures and communities of the south.

The board scored some notable successes. In Kentucky and Tennessee, it helped push through an assortment of laws in 1908 that established an enormously improved system of public schools and colleges. In Georgia it helped obtain passage of a constitutional amendment permitting local taxes to finance public schools. By 1912, the state had established a system of public elementary schools and was well on its way toward establishing a system of public high schools. North Carolina had on its own elected an "education" governor in 1898 and was establishing a public school system when the General Education Board began its campaign. The board did, however, serve a useful purpose in North Carolina by providing grants and loans to small communities to encourage the building of public schools. Similarly, public school proponents had already won control of a 1902 constitutional convention in Virginia, with the result that the state was already beginning to expand and modernize public schools. Nevertheless, the board was able to strengthen Virginia's new public school system with grants similar to those in North Carolina.

The board did not, however, meet with success on a universal basis, despite its political and financial power. In South Carolina, plantation and textile mill owners, who depended on child labor, controlled the legislature. Not surprisingly, it refused to vote funds to develop an adequate public school system that would have pulled children off the job and put them in classrooms. Moreover, even in states where the board did succeed in furthering the cause of public education, it did not succeed in getting education extended to blacks on an equal basis with whites. Indeed, a so-called "education" governor of North Carolina, who won election on a platform of universal education, explained quite clearly that he meant such education to be for white children only. Georgia's new public

school system was also reserved for whites only. And in Virginia, the constitutional convention that created an expanded, modernized system of public education specifically limited black public education to instruction in reading the Bible and little more. The convention noted, with some degree of anger, that 2,500 existing schoolhouses for blacks were producing tens of thousands of literate black voters who might one day take control of state government, and it rejected the notion of expanding black education.

Reference: *Origins of the New South, 1877–1913*, C. Vann Woodward (1971).

Spanish America   Those areas of the Americas controlled by Spain during the colonial era, prior to 1800. After establishing a foothold in South and Central America and the Caribbean during the first half of the 16th century, Spain founded what is now the oldest continuing settlement of European origin north of the Gulf of Mexico, at St. Augustine, Florida, in 1565. Seeking to protect their trade routes through the Caribbean, the Spanish captured what had been the embryonic French colony of Fort Caroline. Florida remained a Spanish possession until the Seven Years War in 1762. A British victory forced Spain to cede away Florida until 1783, when Spain repossessed it after siding with the American revolutionaries. By then, Spain had also acquired France's huge Louisiana territory, which, together, with its holdings in Mexico, California and the American West and Southwest, made New Spain the largest European-controlled area in the Americas. The mammoth size of these holdings did not translate into any immediate effect on American education, because of Spain's failure to establish large-scale civilian settlements.

Although the Spanish had explored California in the 1500s and 1600s, they did not establish their first permanent settlement there until 1769, in what is now San Diego. Interested primarily in exploiting mineral wealth, Spain limited education to Roman Catholic missionary efforts among the Indians. To that end, Spanish

Franciscans built a network of 21 missions in California, but even these lost their influence after newly independent Mexico assumed rule over the territory in 1822. After American settlers gained control of the area in the 1840s, the missions were forced to close. Elsewhere, the Spanish had ceded the Louisiana territory back to the French in 1800 and lost control of Florida to the United States in 1819—all without ever having established any permanent civilian colonies that would influence American culture east of the Mississippi. The most lasting and somewhat distorted Spanish influence on American education can still be seen in the Southwest and in large portions of California, where Mexican culture—a conglomeration of Spanish and Indian cultures—predominated until 1848, when Mexico ceded California to the United States following the Mexican War.
Reference: EB.

Sparks, Jared (1789–1866) American educator, author and historian, responsible for introducing history as a standard element of the American curriculum. Born in poverty and forced to educate himself, his success as an autodidact earned him a scholarship to Phillips Exeter Academy, in New Hampshire, at the age of 20. He earned his B.A. and M.A. at Harvard and became a Unitarian minister in Baltimore and then chaplain of the House of Representatives in 1821. He resigned in 1823 to move to Boston, where he bought the *North American Review,* which he transformed into the most influential literary magazine in North America. In 1825, he began collecting and studying historical materials, traveling across the United States and Europe to uncover, amass and publish an enormous body of research materials. The materials served as a foundation for one of the most remarkable bodies of historical studies ever produced and, in its time, certainly the most important.

Among the many historical works he wrote or edited were *The Life of John Ledyard* (1828), *The Diplomatic Correspondence of the American Revolution* (12 vols., 1829–30), *Life of Gouverneur*

Morris (3 vols., 1832), *Writings of George Washington* (12 vols., 1834–37), *Remarks on American History* (1837), *The Life of George Washington* (1839), *The Works of Benjamin Franklin* (1836–40) and *The Library of American Biography* (25 vols., 1834–47). In addition, he was editor of *Essays and Tracts on Theology.* His historical works ranked with the poetry of Longfellow, the essays of Emerson and the novels of Alcott as the most influential body of written work in early 19th-century American society.

A leader of the Unitarian-Transcendentalist intellectuals of his era, he was named professor of ancient and modern history at Harvard in 1839, the first professor of nonecclesiastical history at Harvard and, indeed, in the United States. He organized Harvard's history department and in 1849 was elected president of the institution. He served for four years in a somewhat less than successful term as a reactionary administrator for that era, advocating the lecture system of teaching and strongly opposing student electives. After his death, his histories gradually fell into disrepute as researchers learned that he had amended, omitted and rewritten whole passages attributed to historical figures. His aim, apparently, had been twofold: to avoid offending or sullying the reputation of historical figures he admired and to polish the writing of such figures.
References: BDAE; DAB; *The Life and Writings of Jared Sparks,* H. B. Adams (1893).

Spartan education A harsh, physically oriented form of education dispensed in an atmosphere of strict military or quasi-military discipline. Now usually limited to military school education in the United States, Spartan education of a sort pervaded American boarding school life throughout the 19th century and the half of the 20th.

It originated in the ancient Greek city-state of Sparta, a surprisingly small group of five simple villages at a pass leading to a rich, agricultural valley in the Greek Peloponnesus. Seeing themselves as defenders of the valley against other city states, the villages evolved into a military garrison by the 6th century B.C., and the villagers molded the upbringing of their children and their education into a system geared for war. Deformed children were abandoned and allowed to die. Girls remained at home to learn the domestic arts, while all boys began military training at seven. Assigned to barracks and trained by older men with military backgrounds, they spent the first two years as cadets, learning rudimentary military drill, the martial arts and politics. They spent the next 10 years in full-time military training, receiving full status as citizens of Sparta at 18 and then entering the military ranks at 20. Although permitted to marry, they lived in military barracks until the age of 30 and served in the military until the age of 60. Sparta defeated Athens in 404 B.C. and became the dominant Greek state until 371, when the Thebans defeated them, reducing Sparta to its original boundaries. Although Sparta seems to have prospered somewhat under Roman rule, it was destroyed by King Alaric and the Visigoths in 396 A.D.

References: EB; *The History of Western Education,* William Boyd and Edmund J. King (1975).

spatial imagery The reconstruction in the mind of the form, surrounding space and relationships of out-of-view objects that the eye has previously seen or the imagination has envisioned. Spatial images are seldom exact replicas of the actual objects. The variation between what the actual eye and the "mind's eye" see is usually an accurate reflection of the student's aptitude in architecture, art, design, drafting, engineering, geometry, shop, map making, mechanical drawing and other programs requiring well developed spatial imagery. A variety of nonverbal tests are available to measure aptitude for spatial imagery.

Reference: *The Mind's Eye,* Robert Sommer (1978).

Spearman rank difference correlation coefficient (Spearman's RHO) A mathematical method of relating two different sets of rankings—I.Q. rankings and rankings on a reading test, for example—for the same group of individuals. Using a complex formula, a teacher can determine whether student rankings on a particular test have a direct, inverse or no relationship with rankings on another test. Thus, a reading test whose student rankings are the reverse of their intelligence-test rankings may have little merit as a measure of reading skills. Rank correlations range from -1.00 to $+1.00$, with the former indicating an inverse correlation, 0.00 indicating no correlation and $+1.00$ a perfect correlation.

Reference: *Statistical Concepts for the Behavioral Sciences,* Harold O. Kiess (1989).

special education A broad range of instructional processes designed to help students with one or more mental, physical or emotional handicaps obtain the maximum amount of education compatible with their physical and intellectual potential. Special education can range from custodial institutional care, at one end of the spectrum, to simple oral or written exercises assigned to a student by a regular teacher in a conventional classroom to help the student overcome a specific deficiency. Between the two extremes are formal and informal programs designed to meet the specific needs of an infinite variety of handicapped, or, as they are euphemistically called, "exceptional" students. These programs include students with a range of deficiencies, including learning disabilities, mental retardation, hearing impairments, speech impairments, visual impairments, emotional disturbances, orthopedic or other disabling handicaps and multiple handicaps with combinations of any or all of the above (qq.v.).

Although special education dates from the 19th century, its expansion into a broad-based element of conventional education began in the 1970s, with the enactment of two federal laws that opened the doors of public schools to the handicapped and mandated their absorption to the greatest degree possible into normal life. In

1973, the Rehabilitation Act (q.v.) outlawed discrimination against handicapped persons in education and mandated the elimination of all architectural barriers that might prevent a handicapped youngster from attending school. Two years later, Congress revised the Rehabilitation Act with the Education for All Handicapped Children Act (q.v.), to improve public school education for the handicapped by underwriting a broad range of special education. Since then, teacher's colleges have staged a vast expansion of their training in special education, with regular classroom teachers, as well as those preparing to become specialists in the field, expected to learn aspects of special education.

The vast majority of special-ed students able to attend public schools are assigned to regular classrooms for all or part of the day to receive instruction from regular teachers. Depending on the particular student and the degree of disability, a special resource teacher may be assigned to the classroom to provide special help—especially with students who, for whatever reason, might disrupt the classroom routine and interfere with the learning process of other students. In many cases, too, resource teachers may work with special-ed students privately or in small groups for part of the day, in specially equipped resource rooms (q.v.) for the learning-disabled. Classrooms reserved for all other special-ed students are designated "special" classrooms.

Basically, there are eight placement options for special education students, and most schools constantly monitor the students' progress to move them into the least restrictive environment. In declining order of restriction and special education needs, these options are: the full-time residential school; full-time special day schools; full-time special classrooms devoted exclusively to special-ed students in a regular school; regular classroom attendance with part-time special education in a special classroom; regular classroom attendance with part-time help or tutoring in a resource room (usually for students with learning disabilities); full-time attendance in regular classrooms with occasional help from itinerant specialists; full-time attendance in regular classrooms with occasional help from the regular teacher.

Less than 12% of the 40 million American youngsters enrolled in public elementary and secondary schools received some form of special education in the 1990–1991 school year. About one-third received all special education in the regular classroom, another one-third received some of their special education in a resource room, and about 25% received all their education in special classrooms, apart from regular students, with whom they mingled only during free periods and some recreation periods. Of all disabled, school-aged youngsters, about 5% received their education in special day schools separate from regular schools, while just under 1% were in specialized residential facilities and an even smaller number were homebound or in hospitals. Of students receiving some form of federally funded special education, about 45% had specific learning disabilities such as dyslexia, and about 20% had speech or language impairments. About 11% had some degree of mental retardation and 8% had serious emotional disturbances. About 6% were physically disabled. The remaining 10% receiving federally funded special education were preschoolers, who received entirely different forms of special-ed because of their lack of literacy skills.

Special education services are available in conventional boarding schools as well as day schools, and all provide one or more of four basic services: specialized instruction by trained special-ed teachers; curricular flexibility and adaptation to the student's capabilities; special teaching methods by both regular and special-ed teachers, adapted to the special-ed student's limitations; and special instructional materials designed for the particular student's disability.

(See also DYSLEXIA.)

Reference: *The Special Education Handbook: A Comprehensive Guide for Parents and Educators,* Kenneth Shore (1986).

specialized institution of higher education

Any college or university that restricts its curricular or degree offerings to a limited number of fields or courses of study. The relatively few, specialized, four-year colleges and universities include the service academies, ahandful of engineering schools such as Massachusetts Institute of Technology, and several graduate schools of science such as Rockefeller University (qq.v.). In contrast, many two-year nonresidential community colleges tend to be specialized institutions that tailor their vocational offerings to meet the specific industrial and business requirements of the region they serve.

Academic specialization at the college and university level dates back to the middle ages, when institutions of higher education prepared students for but one profession: the Catholic clergy. The first college founded in the American colonies—Harvard (q.v.)—also began as a specialized institution, to prepare young men for the Protestant ministry. Yale, then and now its arch-rival, was also a specialized ministerial school. Diversity of academic offerings did not begin until the mid-18th century, with the opening of the College of Philadelphia (later, the University of Pennsylvania), which Benjamin Franklin founded as an academy to prepare young men for business, engineering and other professions needed to build a new society. Thomas Jefferson followed Franklin's example in founding the University of Virginia, with a broad-based curriculum of arts and sciences that conspicuously omitted theology.

Facing a declining interest in the ministry, Harvard, Yale and other colleges followed suit and began expanding their curricula at the end of the 18th century. By the middle of the 19th century, most offered a broad range of academic courses that included literature, the fine arts, mathematics, history, modern and classical languages, and a range of science courses that continued to expand with the development and growth of chemistry, physics, biology, zoology and other sciences. As the social sciences developed, they were added to the curriculum.

References: *American Education,* Lawrence Cremin (3 vols., 1970–87); *The Universities of Europe in the Middle Ages,* Hastings Rashdall (1936).

speech

The utterance of intelligible sounds and words in a sequence that effectively communicates thoughts to others. Once an integral part of elementary and secondary school curricula, speech instruction is now usually limited to special education by speech therapists or speech pathologists. Special education for speech disorders includes instructional programs for speech and hearing impaired students, speech therapy for children with cleft palates, and speech therapy for nonimpaired children with articulation problems such as stuttering, lisping, delayed speech, aphasia, voice problems and speech defects (see SPEECH PATHOLOGY). Until the last half of the 20th century, however, speech instruction had been a required element of education for all students since the Sophists began teaching oratorical skills in ancient Greece in the middle of the 5th century B.C. Under the rubric of rhetoric (q.v.), speech instruction included lessons in pronunciation, enunciation, public speaking and the careful fashioning of phrases.

Speech is a product of two elements: voice, or phonation, and articulation, with the former produced by expiring air through vibrating vocal cords in the larynx, and the latter produced by positioning of lips, tongue, teeth, jaw and palate. Voice produces variations in pitch, quality and intensity of speech, while articulation forms the unique sounds that differentiate letters, syllables and words from each other.

There are three types of sound produced in speech articulation: labials, labio-dentals and palatals. Pure labials, such as "p," "m," "b" and the "ooh" sound, are produced with the lips only; labio-dentals, such as "f," are produced by contact of lips and teeth; and palatals, such as "t" and "k," are created by contact of the tongue with the upper palate. Important in the teaching of foreign languages, palatals can be frontal or central, with the former involving exclusively the tip of the tongue in contact with the palate, as in the sound for "t." Central palatals are created by contact of the central part of the tongue only with the upper palate, as in the sound for "k."

Speech is a learned function, however, and physical or mental impairments that interfere with the learning process can produce speech impairments. Neuroses, psychoses and mental retardation often produce speech impairments, as do such physical impairments as brain damage, hearing loss, cerebral palsy and cleft palates.

Reference: *Speech Pathology,* William H. Perkins (1977); *Expression and Meaning,* J. R. Searle (1985); Patterns of English Pronunciation, Jean D. Bowen (1975).

speech pathology The study of communication disorders, including vocal, oral, auditory and comprehensive abnormalities. Among the many manifestations of such disorders are articulation problems such as stuttering, lisping, delayed speech, aphasia, voice problems and speaking defects, some of them congenitally generated, others born of trauma and still others the result of improper learning sequences. Neuroses, psychoses, mental retardation and brain damage are among the many causes of both congenital and acquired speech disorders. Physical disabilities such as cleft palates, cerebral palsy, hearing losses and paralyses also produce speech disorders. Speech impairment may, however, also result from unconscious imitation of poor speech by parents and other influences in early childhood.

Although speech pathology engages a wide range of researchers, clinicians, physicians and academicians, the speech therapist or speech pathologist associated with elementary and secondary school education is concerned solely with identification and remediation of student speech disorders. Speech therapists and pathologists in schools usually work with students on an indi-

vidual basis in resource rooms (q.v.) and with each student's teachers and parents to develop a broad remedial program. Because speech disorders can be the result of physical, neurological or psychological conditions, speech therapists and pathologists may also work with neurologists, otolaryngologists, psychiatrists or psychologists in treating speech disorders.

Reference: *Handbook of Speech Pathology and Audiology,* Lee Edward Travis (1971).

speed reading The perception, comprehension and intellectual integration of printed words and sentences at rates up to four times faster than the average individual's reading rate. The average reading rate of literate, English-speaking, American adults is 250 to 300 words a minute, while those who have acquired speed reading skills can absorb up to 1,000 to 1,200 words a minute. Speed reading is a learned skill limited only by the range and strength of individual peripheral vision. Instead of focusing on a single word, speed readers learn to use peripheral vision to incorporate words to the left and right of their central focus. Exceptionally gifted speed readers extend peripheral vision to both margins and even above and below their focal points to include blocks of print reaching from one page margin to the other. There are, however, physiological and psychological limits to the speed any individual can achieve, and for each individual there is a specific reading speed beyond which comprehension begins to decline.

There are a variety of speed reading methods, many of them self-taught, such as scanning and skimming. Scanning involves allowing the eye to travel rapidly across a page of print, without stopping to focus on individual words. Usually used when searching for a specific name, date or figure, scanning is used routinely to search through telephone books, dictionaries and other references and produces little or no comprehension or intellectual integration of materials. However, the techniques of scanning can, under professional tutelage, be used to develop speed reading skills. Indeed, skimming is nothing more than scanning at rates slow enough to achieve partial comprehension of the materials being scanned. Instead of searching for a single fact or figure, as in scanning, skimming involves allowing the eye to settle for a fraction of a second on key words and phrases significant enough to convey the general meaning of the entire sentence or paragraph. Considerable training is required in English composition and sentence and paragraph construction for students to obtain a significant degree of comprehension while skimming or speed reading. On average, skimming 800 to 1,000 words a minute has been found to reduce comprehension by 50% to 60%.

References: *Reading and Study Skills,* John Langan (1989); *The Psychology of Reading,* Keith Rayner and Alexander Pollatsek (1989).

speed test A standardized test designed to measure student ability to respond instantly in an anxiety-provoking situation—i.e., under pressure of examination. Speed tests consist of questions with low enough levels of difficulty to permit every student to respond correctly but not to complete the entire test—as in simple arithmetic computation tests in early elementary grades. Scores are based on the number of correct answers per minute, thus limiting the evaluation to speed rather than knowledge. Instant-response aptitude can affect performance on critical examinations of students of even the highest intelligence and degree of knowledge. An example is the battery of Scholastic Assessment Tests used by many colleges as admission tests. Remedial training can improve instant-response skills if started early enough in the elementary years.

(See also POWER TEST.)

Reference: *Psychological Testing,* Anne Anastasi (1988).

spelling The correct naming or writing of the letters of a word. Basic to reading and writing, the study of spelling, or orthography, has re-mained relatively unchanged since the Reformation, beginning with the learning of the alphabet, proceeding through the learning of syllabic sounds, and with the gradual learning of lists of words of increasing length, complexity and difficulty. In 1783, schoolmaster Noah Webster (q.v.) wrote and published the first spelling textbook in the United States, the first of three parts of his epic: *A Grammatical Institute, of the English Language, an Easy Concise, and Systematic Method of Education, Designed for the Use of English Schools in America.* In the tradition of English primers (q.v.), the Webster speller began with the alphabet, followed by a syllabarium and lists of words spelled in the English way. Webster was obsessed, however, with helping his new nation achieve cultural independence from England, as a companion to political independence. In 1806, he published *A Compendious Dictionary of the English Language,* containing 5,000 more words than the great dictionary of 1755 by Dr. Johnson. Of greater import, it contained the first Americanized spellings that eliminated the "k" in words like musick and the "u" in words like honour, and it phoneticized the spelling of words such as centre by reversing the "r" and the "e." Two decades later he published *An American Dictionary of the English Language* that completed the task of Americanizing the English language into the words students now learn to spell in the United States.

Spelling instruction has changed considerably since Webster's day. Most instruction now focuses more on words that students are likely to encounter than on esoterica aimed solely at open-ended vocabulary building. Depending on the instructional system, spelling instruction may or may not begin with mastery of the alphabet and the various sounds each letter can produce. When the alphabet is central to spelling instruction, students may then proceed either to mastery of the syllabarium (syllables) and then to whole words or go directly from alphabet mastery to study of whole words. In the first instance, teachers usually rely on phonics (q.v.), that is, the pronunciation or "sounding out" of the individual letter and syllable sounds of each word as they attempt to write it correctly. In the whole-word approach, teachers rely on the so-called "test-study-test" approach, in which students are asked to write words they have not studied before, then compare their personal, phonetic spellings to those on a master list and study any errors they may have made, before rewriting the words correctly.

(See also TOP-DOWN MODEL OF READING; WHOLE LANGUAGE.)

References: *Spelling Trends, Content, and Methods,* Ruel A. Albred (1984); *Teaching Reading in the Elementary School,* Eldon K. Ekwall and James L. Shanker (1989).

Spencer, Herbert (1820–1903)

English social philosopher, whose pronouncements on education had a broad impact on the course of American (and English) education during the last decades of the 19th century. They came at a time when Darwinism was racking the American educational establishment with fierce debates over what should be taught in schools and colleges and how to reconcile scientific knowledge with Christian beliefs in the creation of the world and man. Spencer's question, "What knowledge is of most worth?" lay at the center of the debate when he arrived for a lecture tour of the United States in 1882. His works had been published and widely circulated during the previous decades. His four essays published together under the title *Essays: Education, Moral and Physical,* described the most worthwhile knowledge in unequivocal terms: "To prepare us for complete living is the function which education has to discharge, and the only rational mode of judging of any educational course is, to judge in what degree it discharges such function." He divided "complete living" into five categories of activities designed to contribute to: self-preservation, the securing of the necessities of life, the rearing and disciplining of children, the maintenance of health, social and political relations, and the gratification of tastes and feelings. Complete preparation in each of these areas, he maintained, was possible only through the study of the sciences, both natural and social.

In effect, Spencer reignited the interest of leading American educators in the type of utilitarian education that Benjamin Franklin (q.v.) had espoused a century earlier in founding the academy that eventually evolved into the College of Philadelphia and the University of Pennsylvania. Most American educators of Spencer's era subscribed to the educational blueprint of Victorian England—namely, that the role of colleges was to provide the upper classes with a classical education based on languages, literature and theology, and that the primary role of elementary common schools was to teach children to read, study and believe in the Scriptures.

A student of evolution, Spencer reconciled the conflict between Darwinism and Christian beliefs by proclaiming the existence of two domains: the accessible domain of science and the domain of "the Unknowable," which was inaccessible except through worship. In establishing a credible duality between the knowable and unknowable, Spencer opened the door to the widespread study of the social sciences based on application of Darwinism to the psychological, social and political, as well as the physical, development of man.

Spencer's relatively simple philosophic separation of science from the world of the "Unknowable" provided a springboard for leading educators, led by Harvard President Charles W. Eliot (q.v.), to expand their practical and scientific academic offerings. Eliot would later write an introduction to the republication of Spencer's *Education.* Spencer himself contributed directly to that expansion by producing a body of knowledge that served as the basis for the new social science courses then developing. Among his many works were *Principles of Psychology* (1855), *A System of Synthetic Philosophy* (1860), *Principles of Biology* (2 vols., 1864–67), *Principles of Sociology* (3 vols., 1876–96), *Essays: Scientific, Political, and Speculative* (3 vols., 1891) and *Principles of Ethics* (2 vols., 1892–93).

References: *The Social and Political Thought of Herbert Spencer,* David Wiltshire (1987); *Herbert Spencer: The Evolution of a Sociologist,* J. D. Y. Peel (1971); *Herbert Spencer on Education,* F. A. Cavanagh, ed. (1932).

spiral curriculum A graphic term to describe a curricular design that constantly reviews previously mastered concepts while continually adding new ones. Unlike schedules of reinforcement (q.v.), which apply to lesson plans, spiral curriculum is a broader term referring to curriculum design, with each new course reviewing concepts of the course taken in the same subject a year (or semester) earlier.

Reference: *The Process of Education,* Jerome S. Bruner (1962).

Spock, Benjamin (1903–   ) American, psychiatrically trained pediatrician whose books on infant and child care transformed the upbringing of American children and indirectly affected the course of American education. A graduate of Yale College and Yale Medical School, Spock had acquired a national reputation as a New York pediatrician by the 1930s. Bemoaning the lack of any child-rearing manuals that combined ''sound pediatrics with sound psychology,'' he accepted an offer by Pocket Books, which had pioneered modern paperback publishing in 1939, to write such a book. The first printing of his *Baby and Child Care* appeared in 1946 and captured the minds and hearts of American parents, selling more than 500,000 copies in its first 10 months and about a million copies a year for decades thereafter.

Baby and Child Care revolutionized child care in the United States, warning parents not to take anyone's advice (including Spock's) too seriously, because books ''deal in generalities . . . [and] can't go into all the possible variations.'' His book challenged widely accepted child-rearing practices of not showing too much affection to children, feeding them according to a rigid schedule and using strict discipline to teach them proper behavior. Instead, he urged parents to ''trust yourself,'' show great affection and be ''natural'' with their infants and children. ''Trust yourself,'' he told parents, in making decisions about breast feeding. He urged parents to ignore thumb sucking and masturbation and to use pacifiers rather than restraints or punishment to discourage such behavior. Discipline, he said, should be administered as an expression of the family's love and concern, to foster the child's love, rather than as a form of punishment.

After 30 years and 30 million copies, Spock's guidance had changed the way Americans raised their children. Angry critics, however, insisted that he had spawned excessive permissiveness in American family life, which then spilled over into American elementary and secondary schools. His millions of followers retorted that he simply eliminated unnecessary cruelty and harshness from child-rearing. Despite his critics, Spock succeeded in reversing centuries of traditional, religiously based child-rearing methods based on ''beating the devil'' out of sinful children. Moreover, in training generations of parents to be more permissive at home, he taught them to demand that their surrogates in child-care institutions—namely teachers and school administrators—treat children in a similar fashion, with a maximum of warmth, patience and understanding.

Reference: *Doctor Spock: Biography of a Conservative Radical,* Lynn Z. Bloom (1972).

Sputnik The first artificial, Earth-orbiting satellite, launched into space on October 4, 1957, by the Union of Soviet Socialist Republics, then challenging the United States for global military, political and ideological supremacy. The Soviet success was particularly galling for American leaders who had publicly boasted for years about the technological supremacy of American capitalism over Soviet communism; officials had unhesitatingly predicted that the United States would be the first nation to send such a satellite into orbit. The no less boastful Soviet leadership had been conspicuously silent about any advances in space exploration until their sudden, dramatic announcement on October 5, 1957, that a 184-pound satellite was actually orbiting the Earth. The announcement stunned the American people, shaking their confidence in capitalist technological superiority and leaving them with a sense of imminent vulnerability to attack by the Soviets. After the initial shock abated, the presence of Sputnik in the skies above provoked a frenzy of congressional and public criticism of the American educational system's failure to train young Americans adequately in mathematics and the sciences. President Dwight D. Eisenhower called for a major federal investment to improve science and mathematics education, and the result was the National Defense Education Act of 1958 (q.v.), providing federal assistance to state and local school systems to strengthen instruction in science, mathematics, foreign languages and other subjects deemed critical to the ability to compete technologically with the Soviet Union and other potential enemies.

References: EB; DES.

SQ3R An acronym for the study technique consisting of survey, question, read, recite and review. SQ3R asks students to organize work assignments by following these steps: survey materials to be studied by scanning chapter headings and lead sentences; list important questions to be answered; read the material in depth, underlining key elements of each paragraph; recite answers to the questions raised in step 2; review all key, underlined materials read in step 3.

References: *Content Area Reading and Learning: Instructional Strategies,* Diane Lapp, James Flood and Nancy Farnan (1989); *Reading and Learning from Text,* Harry Singer and Dan Donlan (1989).

staff balance A euphemism for affirmative action (q.v.), and the attempt to build a school staff that reflects the racial, ethnic, age and gender makeup of the general population. Inspired by the Civil Rights Act of 1964 (q.v.), the staff balance concept has proved impossible to implement in most American public elementary and secondary schools, because the makeup of the teacher population in various communities does not necessarily reflect that of the general population. The concept has subsequently broadened to include establishing an equity of work load among staff members and attempting to balance curricular strengths and staff competency to avoid, for example, the teaching of five courses in biology and one in physics, or the staffing of one department with experienced teachers while another languishes with inexperienced newcomers.

References: *Personnel Administration in Education: Leadership for Instructional Improvement,* Ben M. Harris, et al. (1979).

staff development The fostering and furtherance of professional skills of teachers, school administrators and nonteaching personnel such as counselors, through a broad range of instruction. The latter is designed to improve the teacher's knowledge of subjects taught and to improve teaching, counseling or administrative skills and techniques. Among the activities available to achieve such goals are study leaves and sabbaticals, "development" conferences, peer teaching, work with outside consultants and pairing of less experienced teachers with more experienced mentor teachers.

References: American Association of School Administrators, Arlington, Virginia; *Staff Development: Problems and Solutions,* Stanley M. Elam, Jerome Cramer and Ben Brodinsky (1986); *Staff Development: Enhancing Human Potential,* Donald C. Orlich (1989).

Stafford Loans The largest and best known federal government program of educational loans to college students during the 1980s and 1990s. Officially renamed Federal Stafford Loans in 1993, the low-interest loans allowed any dependent student attending college at least half-time in the 1994–1995 school year to borrow up to about $23,000 over the four college years, regardless of family income. The total varied from year to year, with maximums set at $2,625 for dependent freshmen, $3,500 for sophomores and $5,500 a year for juniors and seniors. Emancipated students—that is, students not declared as dependents on their parents' income taxes—were eligible for additional annual loans of $4,000 for each of the first two undergraduate years and $5,000 for each of the last two years, up to the $23,000 maximum. Graduate and professional students were eligible for annual loans of $8,500 a year, up to a maximum of $46,000. Students actually borrowed the money from their local banks, but at interest rates well below that charged on ordinary bank loans, with the government making up the difference. By the mid-1990s, the government was paying more than $9 billion a year in such interest and was in the throes of eliminating banks as middlemen in the program and converting the program into direct loans, from the government to students.

Although students from any income level were eligible, students from families with annual incomes below $70,000 did not have to begin repaying the loans until six months after they completed their college or graduate school education. The government paid the interest due during those years. Students from families with income above $70,000 a year had to begin repaying their loans while still in college. Interest rates varied from year to year and were set each June, according to the rates for three-month Treasury Bills, with a ceiling of 8.25%. Rates were usually far lower, however —6.22%, for example, in the 1993–1994 school year.

Government-insured student loans were first authorized under the Guaranteed Student Loan Act of 1965 and expanded in 1973 and again in 1978, under the name Basic Educational Opportunity Grant (BEOG). "Stafford Loans" was one of the last in a series of names given to the program as it evolved over subsequent years from relatively small BEOG grants ($226 to $1,750 a year) into the Guaranteed Student Loan Program of 1980, with loans of up to $12,500, and, finally, the Federal Stafford Loan Program.

(See also STUDENT LOANS.)

References: *College Cost Book,* The College Board; *A Student's Guide to College Admissions,* Harlow G. Unger (1995).

standardized test Any examination for which a norm (q.v.) and associated scale have been calculated on the basis of the exam's results among a well-defined, statistically significant population sample. Once standardized, the test can be used to compare characteristics of individuals or groups of individuals with the original population sample. To qualify as a standardized test, however, conditions under which such tests are administered must be strictly controlled and virtually identical each time and in every way. Among the most commonly used standardized tests in education is the Scholastic Assessment Test I, which measures the verbal and mathematical skills of high school juniors and seniors.

Although designed to assure fairness to all test-takers, standardized tests seldom achieve that goal, because of a variety of uncontrollable factors. No group of test-takers can be identical in every way to the original group on which the test norms were based. Moreover, ethnic, racial and gender differences make it likely that otherwise identical test-takers will respond differently to the same questions. Administrators of the SATs have dealt with the first weakness by establishing a new norm—still scored as 500—for each year's SAT test-takers. The second weakness has proved more difficult to address: Women, who on average obtain higher high school and college grade-point averages than men, score lower than men as a group on the SATs, which are ostensibly designed to measure future academic performance at college.

References: *Using Standardized Tests in Education,* William A. Mehrens and Irvin J. Lehmann (1987); *Tests and Measurement,* W. Bruce Walsh and Nancy E. Betz (1985).

standard language The vocabulary, grammar and usage of a tongue, as set down in standard references and generally agreed upon by professional users of the language—i.e., orthographers, lexicographers, grammarians, editors and language teachers. Standard language may, depending on the language and the country in which it is used, differ substantially from nonstandard language, or the language commonly used in conversation by the average person in daily life. Indeed, many nonstandard languages, such as French argot, a slang with origins in the highwayman culture of the Middle Ages, differ so substantially from standard language as to be unintelligible to many speakers of the standard language. There are, however, a variety of nonstandard languages, including slang-based argots, or ''street languages'' (see BLACK ENGLISH VERNACULAR), and dialects, which can range from minor regional variations of the standard language (as in the American south) to well-developed, stand-alone mongrel languages such as Creole or Yiddish, which combine the words and grammar of several different languages.

(See also NONSTANDARD ENGLISH.)

References: *Learning to Read in a Multicultural Society,* Catherine Wallace (1988).

standard score A test score that has been converted to a common, specifically defined scale that permits comparison of a variety of scores from differently scored tests. There are a variety of standard scores, usually based on means or medians, such as 0.00, with a standard deviation of 1.00, or 50, with a standard deviation of 10. In either case, all raw scores from a variety of tests would be converted to standard scores for accurate comparisons. Scholastic Assessment Tests (SAT), for example, are scored quite differently from ordinary classroom tests, with SAT scores ranging from 200 to 800 based on a mean, or average, score of 500. Regardless of the correct number of answers on the tests — 60% correct, 68% correct or any other raw score) is always assigned 500 and the other SAT tests

are graded accordingly. Classroom tests, on the other hand, are often scored from 0% to 100%, based on the number of correct answers. Until both sets of scores are converted to a common scale, with standard scores, a valid comparison remains impossible. Once the SAT mean of 500 and, for example, a mean score of 75% on a standardized history test, are converted to a standard score of 50 on a common scale, scores from both tests can then be appropriately compared.

(See also SCALE.)

Reference: *Educational Measurement,* Robert L. Thorndike, ed. (1971).

Stanford Achievement Test One of the most commonly used standardized, norm-referenced and criterion-referenced tests for measuring such student skills as reading comprehension, vocabulary, spelling, language, math computation, math word problems, science and social studies. Designed for students in grades 1–9 and administered to groups rather than on an individual basis, the test evaluates actual student knowledge (criterion-based), while also comparing each child's scores with the norm for children in the same grade. Among other similar, widely used test batteries are the SRA (Science Research Associates) Achievements, the Iowa Test of Basic Skills, the California Achievement Tests and the Metropolitan Achievement Tests.

Reference: The Psychological Corporation, San Antonio, Texas.

Stanford-Binet Intelligence Test An individually administered test for measuring the intelligence quotient (q.v.) of children as young as two and adults. Of questionable value for adults of normal and superior intelligence, the Stanford-Binet Test was developed by Lewis M. Terman (q.v.), a psychologist and Stanford University professor of education who revised the Binet-Simon Intelligence Scale in 1916, by dividing the mental age, as determined by the

Binet-Simon Test, by the test-taker's chronological age. Terman called the result an Intelligence Quotient and developed a scale whereby the average I.Q. for a subject of any age was 100, with any I.Q. falling between 90 and 110 considered normal. Scores above 110 were superior and those below 90 inferior. Children whose I.Q.s ranged between 75 and 50, 50 and 25, and below 25, respectively, were categorized as educable, trainable and custodial. Administered under strictly controlled conditions, the test has been revised many times and remains heavily dependent on verbal and language skills.

Reference: Houghton Mifflin Company, Test Editorial Offices, Boston, Massachusetts.

Stanford University

A private, nonsectarian university generally considered the most academically demanding institution of its kind west of the Mississippi. Renowned the world over for its academic standards, Stanford was founded in 1885 by railroad magnate and former California governor and U.S. senator Leland Stanford, in memory of his only son, Leland Stanford Jr. The 15-year-old had died a year earlier from typhoid fever while the family was traveling in Europe. His father founded Leland Stanford Junior University with a gift of 9,000 acres, on which the family home was located, and an endowment of $21 million. Officially opened in 1891, the undergraduate school offers a broad-based curriculum in the arts, sciences and professions to more than 6,500 undergraduates. Among its seven graduate schools (with more than 7,000 students) is the famed Hoover Institution on War, Revolution and Peace, founded by president-to-be Herbert Hoover in 1919 as a center for advanced interdisciplinary study of 20th-century domestic and international affairs.

Reference: Stanford University Library Archivist, Stanford, California.

stanine

An interval on a scale of nine intervals. An acronym of the words standard nine, a stanine scale uses a mean of 5.00, with a standard deviation of plus or minus 1.96. A far broader, and therefore less precise, method of measuring a distribution of scores than percentiles (q.v.), the stanine distribution was developed during World War II by the Army Air Force Psychology Program as a broad method of grouping test scores into relatively comparable categories. Handy as a quick and easy way of evaluating test scores in the classroom situation, a bell-curve distribution of stanine-scale scores would see 20% of the population falling into the fifth or middle stanine, with 17% each in the fourth and sixth stanines, 12% each in the third and seventh, 7% each in the second and eighth stanines and 4% each in the first and ninth stanines.

References: Measuring and Evaluation School Learning, Lou M. Carey (1988); Principles of Educational and Psychological Measurement and Evaluation, Gilbert Sax (1989).

Starr, Ellen Gates (1859–1940)

American social reformer and co-founder, with Jane Addams, of Hull House (qq.v.), the flagship organization of the settlement house movement in the late 19th and early 20th centuries. Born in the Illinois wilderness and educated in a one-room schoolhouse, she and Addams met as students at Rockford Seminary, Rockford, Illinois, where they became close, lifelong friends. It was Addams who conceived the idea of Hull House and was its driving force, supplying most of the money and serving as chief administrator. Starr, however, provided Addams with the friendship and moral and emotional support needed to make the project succeed, and she made specific contributions that helped raise Hull House to national prominence as an educative institution.

For Starr, the liberal arts she had studied at Rockford held ennobling powers, and she was appalled at their absence in the common schools and daily life of the Chicago slums, where she and Addams founded Hull House. Astounded that immigrants had lost all their capacity to create folk art, she was determined to bring art, sculpture, literature and the other fine arts into the area. She organized reading clubs, decorated the walls of Hull House and nearby schools with murals and reproductions of great paintings, and she founded the Chicago Public School Art Society.

Life at Hull House amidst the poor, however, gradually changed her point of view. Abandoning the settlement house approach, she helped form an Illinois branch of the National Women's Trade Union League, determined to do battle against sweatshops, child labor and low wages. "The soul of man in the commercial and industrial struggle is in a state of siege," she wrote in 1895. "For the children of the 'degraded poor' . . . there is no artistic hope outside of a miracle." In 1896, 1910 and 1915, she walked the picket lines with striking textile and other workers. She organized mass rallies, collected money, delivered fiery speeches, protested to the press and public officials, and collected and carried food to the needy. Arrested for "interfering with a police officer in the discharge of his duty" in a 1914 restaurant workers' strike, she was acquitted by a jury that ruled the charges implausible, after seeing her fragile, bespectacled face and slight, 100-pound frame. Her activism caused considerable embarrassment for Addams, who tried to steer Hull House clear of politics and maintain an atmosphere of tolerance for all points of view. World War I brought an end to Starr's activism. She converted to Roman Catholicism and eventually joined a convent.

References: NAW; Ellen Gates Starr Papers, Sophia Smith Collection, Smith College, Northampton, Massachusetts; *Spearheads for Reform*, Allen F. Davis (1967).

state board of education A body responsible for supervising public education throughout a state. Often called a board of regents (q.v.), the state board of education's responsibilities and powers vary widely from state to state. In some states, boards have sweeping powers to direct virtually every detail of public education, including lesson plans and textbook selection. At the other extreme are states that leave all functional powers in the hands of local school boards and limit state board responsibilities to broad policy making. The majority of state boards, however, have certain common responsibilities. In addition to setting statewide educational policies and goals, they usually appoint the chief school officer in the state and determine the state department of education's budget. They also serve as a liaison with congressional committees and federal government agencies involved with education. Depending on the state, some boards have responsibility for supervising higher education as well as elementary and secondary education. Other states have separate boards for each, while some states have still another, separate board responsible for vocational education. Again depending on the state, board of education members may be appointed by the governor, publicly elected or serve ex officio, with length of service varying from two to 15 years, but usually running four to six years.

Reference: *State Departments of Education, State Boards of Education, and Chief State School Officers*, Sam Harris (1973).

state department of education A state agency charged with certification of schools, certification of teachers, distributing federal and state funds to school districts and educational institutions, recommending legislation affecting education to the governor and state legislature, and enforcing state education laws. Headed by the state's chief state school officer, who is variously known as the commissioner of education or state superintendent of education, the state department of education is responsible either to the state board of education or the governor, depending upon the state.

References: *State Departments of Education, State Boards of Education, and Chief State School Officers*, Sam Harris (1973).

state educational grants for students Any of a wide variety of direct awards totalling about $2.5 billion a year from state governments to all resident students who attend institutions of higher education in the state. Most states offer some form of aid to college students, some of it based on need, some on academic or other form of merit. Some carry provisos that the money be spent only at a college within that state or at a state-operated public college. Eight states offer "portable" scholarships for residents to use at out-of-state colleges. State grants range from as low as a token of several hundred dollars to as much as $5,000 a year, depending on need. In addition to universally available grants, special state grants are available to disabled and disadvantaged students.

References: *A Student's Guide to College Admissions,* Harlow G. Unger (1995)

state educational support The direct financial contributions of state government to public education in each state. In the early 1990s, the states provided more than 46% of all public and elementary school funding and more than 38% of all funding of public institutions of higher education.

State contributions to public elementary and secondary education varied between 45% and 50% during the last two decades of the 20th century. Only about 15% a century earlier, when public schools relied largely on local taxation for their revenues, the average state contribution climbed above 30% by 1940, reached 40% in 1970 and peaked at 49.7% in 1986. It dropped back to 46.4% in 1991, when 47% of school revenues were derived from local property taxes and 6.6% from the federal government. In 1993, however, the decline in the percentage of state contributions to public elementary and secondary schools halted and began reversing after a series of state-court decisions declared the traditional system of paying for schools with local property taxes unconstitutional. The courts held that the system automatically fed more funds into schools in wealthy areas, with higher property values, than in poor areas, with low property values, thus depriving poor children of equal educational rights guaranteed by most state constitutions. In response, Michigan in 1994 abandoned locally collected property taxes as a method of paying for schools. Instead, such taxes were paid directly to the state, which then redistributed them equally to each school district on a per student basis.

State contributions to public education, as a percentage of overall state spending, vary widely from year to year and from state to state, from a mere 8.5% in New Hampshire in the 1991–1992 school year, to 73.8% in New Mexico. From one year to the next, moreover, state contributions may rise or fall, depending on the commitment of the party in power to public education or the rise and fall of property values throughout the state or the change in personal income levels.

State governments provided about 38% of all funding of public institutions of higher education in the early 1990s and 2.5% of the funding of private colleges and universities. The latter represented an increase from 1.9% a decade earlier, while the former percentage represented a sharp decline from more than 45%, although state spending on higher education in actual dollars doubled to more than $39 billion during that period.

Reference: DES.

state education laws The state laws that, at a minimum, legislate the duration of compulsory education, attendance quotas, graduation requirements, teacher certification and funding procedures. Education laws, which dictate how education must be dispensed, are distinct from the basic principle guaranteeing all children the right to public schooling in each state, which is usually contained in the state constitution. A state education law, however, is usually what directly requires all children to obtain schooling and sets the minimum age at which they may legally withdraw.

The extent to which state laws determine local school operations varies widely from state to state, with some state laws giving state government control over the most minute elements of education, including even classroom lesson plans and textbook selection, and others leaving day-to-day operations to the discretion of local authorities. In general, the more elaborate and extensive the reach of state education laws, the more local authority, including that of school administrators and teachers in the classroom, is reduced. Educators agree that teachers with little authority to design individual lesson plans or select appropriate textbooks are seldom able to exert much authority over, or obtain the respect of, their students.

States with the most elaborate education laws that strip local schools of authority generally have the poorest student academic achievement. In 1973, the Education Commission of the States (q.v.) issued a *Model Legislation Report,* saying that state laws should be limited to broadly worded, policy-setting frameworks that define school functions, determine who can and must attend school and at what ages, set broad, statewide educational standards and requirements for entering and graduating, determine funding methods, and set requirements for becoming a teacher.

References: Education Commission of the States, Denver, Colorado.

states, educational comparisons Any of a variety of methods that rank the quality of each state's public elementary and secondary school instruction in relation to that of other states. There are two basic methods: a state-by-state comparison of student achievement in key subject areas and a comparison of a group of key characteristics of each state's public education system. The latter would compare such characteristics as spending per pupil, school spending as a percentage of all government spending, average teacher salaries, pupil-teacher ratios, graduation/dropout rates, teacher input and authority over educational policies, and the extent of student social problems such as substance abuse, teenage pregnancies and school violence. In 1991, only four states—Connecticut, Michigan, New York and Wisconsin—had school systems that ranked 10% or more above the average

for all school systems graded for those key characteristics. The school systems of Alabama, Arkansas, the District of Columbia, Hawaii, Idaho, Kentucky, Louisiana, Mississippi, Missouri, New Mexico, North Carolina, Oklahoma, South Carolina, Tennessee, Utah and West Virginia ranked more than 10% below the national average. The Louisiana, Mississippi, Hawaii, District of Columbia and Alabama school systems ranked as the five worst in the United States on the basis of key characteristics. School systems in 31 states ranked within 10% of the national average.

Comparison of scholastic achievement in the various states produced similar results at the low end of the scale, but substantially different results at the top. Average reading proficiency of fourth graders, for example, was substantially below the national average in five states, with the lowest scores registered in the District of Columbia, Mississippi, California, Hawaii and Louisiana, respectively. Average reading proficiency of fourth graders was substantially above the national average in only four states—New Hampshire, Maine, Iowa and Massachusetts. Fourth graders showed above-average proficiency in mathematics in four states—New Hampshire, Iowa, North Dakota and Wisconsin—and below-average proficiency in Mississippi, Louisiana and the District of Columbia, with D.C. children exhibiting the lowest level of proficiency. Mathematics proficiency of children in the District of Columbia, Louisiana and Mississippi showed no improvement by the time they reached eighth grade. Along with eighth graders in Alabama, they scored well below the national average, while eighth graders in Iowa, North Dakota and Minnesota scored above the national average.

References: DES; "What Did You Learn in School Today?" Harlow G. Unger (1991).

state superintendent of education The highest ranking educational officer in a state, with responsibilities as the chief executive officer of the state board of education and the chief administrative officer of the state department of education. Called the commissioner of education in some states, the state superintendent of education may be popularly elected, appointed by the board of education or appointed by the governor—for four years in most states.

Reference: *State Departments of Education, State Boards of Education, and Chief State School Officers,* Sam Harris (1973).

State University of New York (SUNY)

The world's largest university, spread over 64 campuses, with 30 two-year community colleges and 20 four-year institutions. State-supported, the university was established in 1948 by an act of the New York State legislature, which grouped a variety of existing, state-supported institutions (some dating back to the 1820s) under a single administrative umbrella and authorized funds for constructing new colleges to blanket the state with enough institutions to serve every area. SUNY's goals were and are "to educate the largest number of people possible at the highest level, including educationally and financially disadvantaged groups." Enrollment reached more than 400,000 in the early 1990s. With a faculty of more than 27,000, SUNY offers more than 1,500 programs leading to a bachelor's degree, more than 650 master's degree programs and more than 300 doctoral programs. Governed by a board of trustees and a chancellor who serves as chief administrator, SUNY delegates day-to-day administrative authority to the presidents of each college. SUNY is one of two major, public higher education systems in the state, the other being City University of New York (q.v.).

Reference: *Barron's Profiles of American Colleges* (updated annually).

Stead, William Thomas (1849–1912)

Crusading British journalist whose analysis of "the secret of American success" spurred the spread of universal public education in the United States and Britain. Publisher of the periodical *Review of Reviews,* Stead devoted the entire annual issue in 1902 to "The Americanization of the World." Predicting that the nation with the most efficient and effective education system would eventually dominate the world, Stead called American commitment to universal education one of America's three "secrets of success" (the others being production incentives and espousal of democracy). In defining universal education, Stead pointed out that the United States offered most communities not only elementary and secondary schooling, but also access to colleges, universities, libraries and technical institutes: "Until a change comes over the spirit of our country [Britain], and society . . . recognizes that unless our people are educated the game is up, we shall not see any material improvement."

Stead had overestimated the extent of universal education in America. At the time, only about 10% of American children ever completed high school. The vast majority were exploited in fields, mines and factories at abysmally low wages and under intolerably harsh working conditions. Stead's publication, however, had almost as wide a circulation in the United States as in Britain. Indeed, his jailing in England for exposing the outrages against women and children in the workplace made him somewhat of a hero among the growing number of social reformers crusading for women's suffrage and child labor laws in the United States. When *The Americanization of the World* reached social and education reformers, it served as an impetus for expansion of public education in both nations.

References: *The Americanization of the World; or, The Trend of the Twentieth Century,* W. T. Stead (1902); *The Life of W. T. Stead,* Frederick Whyte (2 vols., 1925).

Steiner, Rudolf (1861–1925)

Austrian social philosopher and scientist who developed a spiritual and mystical doctrine called anthroposophy, an outgrowth of which was the Waldorf school movement and the development of more than 400 Waldorf schools in more than 30 nations, including about 20 schools in the United States. Anthroposophy places man rather than God at the center of life, with knowledge a door and materialism a barrier to developing man's spiritual capacity, or "higher self."

Reference: Association of Waldorf Schools of North America, Fair Oaks, California.

Stevens Institute of Technology

The world's first college to offer a degree in mechanical engineering. The college was established in 1870, under the will of Edwin Augustus Stevens (1795–1868), a member of the most successful family of inventors in American history. Born in Hoboken, New Jersey, Stevens was a son of John Stevens (1749–1838), a pioneer in the development of steam engines who built a steamboat in 1803 (three years before Robert Fulton's *North River Steam Boat)* and launched the world's first oceangoing steamboat in 1808. In 1825, he built the first steam locomotive and in 1830 organized the first railway company in the United States, the Camden & Amboy Railroad and Transportation Company. To protect his inventions, he had convinced Congress to pass the first patent law, in April 1790. Both his sons worked with him during his lifetime and helped manage his vast business holdings, building the railway into one of the most successful enterprises in the United States. His older son Robert (1787–1856) invented the T-rail, the railroad track in use today throughout the world. Together, Robert and his younger brother Edwin designed and invented new types of ships, including some of the first ironclad ships for the United States Navy.

In willing money and his family's Hoboken land holdings to found Stevens Institute, Edwin was determined to raise the art of invention from a shop craft to a science. The founding trustees of the college coined the term "mechanical engineer" and designed the first curriculum leading to a bachelor's degree in that discipline. One member of the faculty founded the American Society of Mechanical Engineers in 1880. Now coeducational, Stevens Institute of Technology has more than 1,250 undergraduates enrolled in bachelor's degree programs in science, computer science, engineering and the humanities. There is one graduate school, with more than 1,500 students.

References: DAB; Stevens Institute of Technology, Hoboken, New Jersey.

Stiles, Ezra (1727–1795)

Connecticut-born scholar, educator, co-founder of the College of Rhode Island (later, Brown University) and president of Yale College during the turbulent Revolutionary War period. A Yale graduate and a tutor there, he was the son of a Congregationalist minister and was himself licensed to preach in 1749. In 1755, he became pastor of the Second Congregational Church of Newport, Rhode Island, where he quickly gained notoriety for his nontraditional views. Remaining an active scholar, he corresponded with such learned men as Benjamin Franklin. He became a leader of the American Philosophical Society, which Franklin had founded, and gained fame as a political and social radical.

An outspoken advocate of American independence from England, he also was an abolitionist (he freed his own slave) and ecumenist and associated freely with Jews and all denominations of Christians except Anglicans, whom he believed to be servants of the Crown. Forced by English authorities to flee Newport when the Revolutionary War broke out, he spent brief periods in Boston, Portsmouth, New Hampshire, and several other New England towns. In 1777, he accepted the presidency of Yale, which was in turmoil and, according to one Tory alumnus, a hotbed of "sedition, of faction and republicanism." Because of his own radicalism in favor of independence, Stiles was well received at Yale. At the time, many students had taken up arms to defend New Haven against British attacks.

The war and the removal of Yale to the countryside made it impossible for him to assume his duties fully until 1778, but he managed to calm student fervor and get them back to classes, most of which he taught himself. Although a prolific writer, he published little during his lifetime and earned a place in American education history largely because of his efforts to liberalize, secularize and Americanize college education and because of his influence on other college educators of the day. Many of his works were not published until 1901, in a three-volume work entitled *Literary Diary*, edited by F. B. Dexter.

References: Yale University Library Archives, New Haven, Connecticut.

stimulus-response theory A concept developed by Russian physiologist Ivan Pavlov that all behavior—both learned and unlearned—is the product of some stimulus. Central to the behaviorist school of psychology, the stimulus-response theory holds that each learned response is the result of adequate repetition of a specific stimulus, with physical stimuli usually producing automatic or unconditioned responses, and psychological stimuli usually producing unconditioned or learned responses. Pavlov repeatedly sprayed meat powder into a dog's mouth, producing the automatic, unconditioned, physical response of salivation. When a bell was sounded each time the meat powder was introduced, the dog gradually developed a conditioned or learned response of salivating at the sound of the bell alone. The stimulus-response theory conflicts with pleasure-pain theory whose proponents would argue that the dog's learning to salivate at the sound of the bell was the result of its association with the pleasure of the meat powder. Although each theory gave rise to its share of classroom teaching approaches, most modern teaching techniques attempt to take advantage of the best of all learning theories.

Reference: *Operant Conditioning Techniques for the Classroom*, T. Mark Ackerman (1972).

story telling In education, an age-old method of instructing children in language, communication and listening skills, as well as developing their appreciation of literature and imparting information about history, folklore, moral values and religion. An especially entertaining, and therefore effective, method of educating children and motivating them to read, story telling is considered an essential element of the daily curriculum in preschool, kindergarten and the early elementary grades in all effective schools and, indeed, is mandated in kindergarten education in a number of states. Led by a teacher or librarian, story telling may be accompanied by a variety of audiovisual materials, including recorded music, sound effects, film clips or live, dramatic acting out of various story elements. As they reach an appropriate age, students themselves often take turns reading stories to their classmates, to improve their reading and oratorical skills.

Reference: *Storytelling: Art and Technique*, Augusta Baker and Ellin Greene (1987).

Stowe, Calvin Ellis (1802–1886) Congregationalist minister, educator and pioneer in the public school movement. Born in Massachusetts, Stowe graduated from Bowdoin College, Maine, and Andover (Massachusetts) Theological Seminary, but entered teaching, first at Bowdoin, then at Dartmouth College, where he was professor of Greek. In 1832, he accepted the chair of biblical literature at Lane Theological Seminary in Cincinnati, Ohio, which was founded and directed by the famed American churchman Lyman Beecher, with whom he formed a deep and lasting friendship. He eventually became a member of the Beecher family, marrying Beecher's daughter Harriet and actively participating in the campaign by another daughter, Catherine, to Americanize immigrant children by establishing public schools throughout the west and training teachers to staff them. Stowe helped found the Western Literary Institute and College of Teachers to promote public education.

In 1836, the year he married Harriet Beecher, he was appointed by the Ohio state legislature to spend a year visiting and surveying schools in Europe and, most especially, Prussia, which was renowned for its effective system of universal public education. In 1837, his *Report on Elementary Instruction in Europe* became one of the most influential documents in the history of American public school education. The report detailed the advantages of the Prussian system, with state support of local schools, state-controlled teacher training and a state-determined curriculum. The Ohio legislature ordered 10,000 copies to distribute among all school districts in the state, and the legislatures of Massachusetts, Michigan, North Carolina, Pennsylvania and Virginia ordered enough reprints to do the same in their states. Carrying, as it did, the name of someone so closely tied to so prestigious a New England clergyman as Lyman Beecher, the report provided enormous impetus to the nascent public school movement in New England.

Stowe taught at Lane Seminary until 1850, then returned to Bowdoin to become a professor of religion for two years and, finally, returned to Andover Theological Seminary as professor of sacred literature. While at Bowdoin, his wife Harriet Beecher Stowe (q.v.), who had long supplemented her husband's meager income from teaching by writing stories and sketches for magazines, wrote *Uncle Tom's Cabin,* a work her abolitionist husband had strongly encouraged her to undertake. Ill-health forced his resignation and retirement from Andover in 1864, but income from Harriet's books afforded them a comfortable life of retirement, traveling twice to Europe and living in Hartford, Connecticut, and Mandarin, Florida, where they purchased a winter home.

References: DAB; BDAE; *Life of Harriet Beecher Stowe, Compiled from Her Letters and Journals,* Charles Edward Stowe (1891).

Stowe, Harriet Beecher (1811–1896)
American teacher, social reformer and author of what was perhaps the most politically explosive and influential novel in American history. Described during the Civil War (q.v.) by President Abraham Lincoln as "the little book that made this big war," *Uncle Tom's Cabin, or Life Among the Lowly* (1852) proved to be among the impor-

Harriet Beecher Stowe. (Library of Congress)

tant educative instruments of the mid-19th century. At a time when few Americans attended school, periodicals were the primary source of knowledge, and *Uncle Tom* first appeared in serialized form during 1851 and 1852 in the *National Era.* In it, Stowe described the trials, suffering and human dignity of Uncle Tom, an old black slave who dies after a beating by a transplanted Yankee plantation owner, Simon Legree. The story forced the world to examine the horrors of slavery—an institution that many of the most dedicated humanitarians had chosen to ignore until then.

In March 1852, the Boston publisher Jewett & Company published a two-volume edition. Within eight weeks, 50,000 copies were sold, an experience "without precedent in the history of this country," according to *Norton's Literary*

Gazette. Sales reached 120,000 in the Western Hemisphere by the end of the year and 180,000 (19 editions) in England. By the end of the year, it had been translated into 20 European languages; by the end of the following year, sales in the United States had reached 300,000—one copy for every 80 people in a nation with only 26 million. By the end of 1853, more copies of *Uncle Tom* had been sold than any other book in American history, save the Bible. No book other than the Bible had ever carried a message to as many people. Stage plays and children's books carried the story to every American of every age in every part of the country. In terms of its educative value, it explained slavery to all and solidified both North and South in their positions on slavery. Stowe said she believed her book converted many to abolitionism and inspired self-confidence, self-respect and hope among free blacks.

Born in Litchfield, Connecticut, Stowe was one of eight children of the firebrand Calvinist preacher Lyman Beecher (q.v.), who sired one of the most influential American families of the 19th century. Educated by her older sister, the great American educator Catherine Beecher (q.v.), Harriet taught at her sister's pioneering school for women in Hartford and remained an advocate of equal educational rights for women throughout her life. She joined her father and sister in moving to Cincinnati in 1832, where her father founded and headed the Lane Theological Seminary and her sister founded the Western Female Institute. Once again, Harriet served as a key instructor in her sister's school.

In 1836, she married Calvin E. Stowe, a minister/professor at Lane, and she began supplementing their meager income from teaching by writing stories and sketches for magazines. She published a collection of these in book form as *The Mayflower* in 1843. The Stowes moved to Maine in 1850, where her husband became a professor at Bowdoin, and she determined to join the cause of abolitionism and began work on *Uncle Tom*. It helped her launch a literary career that would take her to Europe several times and allow her and her husband to live the rest of their lives in comfort. They owned a summer home in Hartford, then a New England cultural and literary center, and a winter home in Mandarin, Florida. Throughout the 1850s and 1860s, she wrote dozens of stories for various periodicals and four more books and novels, including *A Key to Uncle Tom's Cabin*, a compilation of documentary evidence supporting disputed details in *Uncle Tom*, and *Dred: A Tale of the Great Dismal Swamp* (1856), another antislavery novel. In 1869, she and her sister Catherine tried, without success, to revive the Hartford Female Seminary, which Catherine had founded and where Harriet had been educated. With her sister, she coauthored *The American Woman's Home*, the most influential 19th-century book for mothers, detailing all aspects of housekeeping, family health and child care. A leading author and lecturer for the rest of her life, Stowe was elected to the Hall of Fame for Great Americans in 1910.

References: NAW; *Goodbye to Uncle Tom*, J. C. Furnas (1956); *Uncle Tom's Cabin*, Harriet Beecher Stowe (Kenneth Lyon, ed., 1962).

Strang, Ruth May (1895–1971) American educator and pioneer in the development of student counseling. A prolific author of texts for other educators, the New York–born Strang studied at Teachers College, Columbia University, where she earned her bachelor's degree in home economics and, later, her master's and Ph.D. degrees. She taught home economics in New York City schools until she joined the faculty at Teachers College in 1929, where she remained until her retirement in 1960. While there, she gained national renown for her research in the area of guidance and student counseling services. In addition to technical advances in the field, she was responsible for extending to teachers the counseling and guidance function that had hitherto been limited to specialists. Among her landmark books were *An Introduction to Child Study* (1930), *The Role of the Teacher in Personnel Work* (1932), *Personal Devel-*

opment and Guidance in College and Secondary Schools (1934), *Behavior and Background of Students in College and Secondary Schools* (1937), *Counseling Techniques in Colleges and Secondary Schools* (1937), *Educational Guidance: Its Principles and Practice* (1947); *An Introduction to Child Study* (1951), *The Role of Teachers in Personnel Work* (1953) and *The Adolescent Views Himself* (1957).
Reference: BDAE.

Strayer, George D. (1876–1962) Pennsylvania-born professor of education who developed the basic standards for educational administration in use today. A graduate of Columbia University, he taught at Teachers College-Columbia University from 1905 to 1943. Originally interested in mathematics teaching, he drifted into educational administration and eventually conducted more than 80 surveys to assess administrative efficiency of schools, concentrating especially on cost management. Author of more than 100 articles on school management, his books on education include *The Classroom Teacher* (1920) and *School Building Problems* (1927).
Reference: BDAE.

street academies Privately operated secondary schools for high school dropouts, established during the 1960s in disadvantaged areas of major cities such as New York, Chicago and Los Angeles. Forerunners of public, alternative schools, street academies were usually financed by philanthropic groups that set up classroom facilities in vacant stores or warehouses. Designed as college preparatory schools, many street academies operated on the theory that high, inner-city dropout rates at public high schools related to institutional rather than student failure and that most dropouts had quit school because of the lack of intellectual challenge. Street academies not only provided students with challenging academic activities and curricula, but also offered individual counseling and guidance that helped as many as 85% of their students graduate and enroll in college. College

completion rates, however, proved low, and many of the street academies began losing their private financial support by the mid-1970s. At that time, however, most public school systems were already establishing alternative schools with similar programs that gradually absorbed most of the street academy student population. Only a handful of such academies now remain.
Reference: *Alternative Learning Environments,* Gary Coats, ed. (1974).

strephosymbolia A perceptual disorder whereby the individual is unable to distinguish between various letters and symbols, seeing ''b,'' for example, as ''d,'' ''p'' or ''g.'' The term means twisted symbols and was coined in 1925 by psychiatrist Samuel Orton (q.v.), who was first to identify strephosymbolia, or dyslexia, as it was later called, as a learning disability possibly related to brain damage.
Reference: *Dyslexia,* Arthur L. Benton and David Pearl, eds. (1978).

Strong, Josiah (1847–1916) American religious leader who tried to unite American Protestant churches in a crusade to Christianize the United States, using education and the nation's schools as primary vehicles. Strong was born in Illinois, educated at Western Reserve College in Ohio, and ordained after studying at Lane Theological Seminary, in Cincinnati. Although Strong was a successful minister, he did not leap into the national spotlight until 1885, when he published his book *My Country,* which called for Christian action to solve the nation's burgeoning social problems. Warning that the immigrant tide from central and southern Europe—and the Mormon and Roman Catholic churches—were imperiling the nation's future, he called on Anglo-Saxon Christians to begin a massive conversion of America to create ''the largest liberty, the purest Christianity, the highest civilization.'' His goal was nothing less than the establishment of the Kingdom of God in the United States, and his instrument, he said, would be education.

In 1886, the Evangelical Alliance for the United States named him general secretary, a position that elevated him to international prominence. In 1893, he published a second book, *The New Era,* in which he expounded a new philosophy that he called Christian Socialism, a doctrine that called on Christians everywhere to engage in conversion-oriented social work among immigrants in city slums and among the unchurched. However, his program of collaboration between, and eventual unification of, Protestant churches began angering leaders of various conservative Christian sects, and he was forced to resign from the alliance in 1898. He formed a new organization, the League for Social Service, which in 1902 became the American Institute for Social Service and published his pamphlets and books and sponsored his lecture tours in the United States and abroad. His efforts to build the Sunday school movement and extend Christian teachings in public education peaked on the eve of American entry into World War I. His death in 1916, however, left Christian Socialism leaderless, and the mass disillusionment that followed the end of World War I essentially ended efforts to Christianize American schools—in all areas but the American South.

(See also SUNDAY SCHOOLS.)

References: "Josiah Strong and the Challenge of Social Christianity," Dorothea R. Muller (doct. th., New York University, 1955); *Our Country: Its Possible Future and Its Present Crisis,* Josiah Strong (1885).

Strong-Campbell Interest Inventory (formerly, Strong Vocational Interest Blank)

A paper-and-pencil test that attempts to measure occupational aptitudes by exploring the test-taker's general interests and comparing them with the interests of people in 124 various occupations. On the theory that people with common interests choose the same occupations, the test asks more than 300 questions relating to the test-taker's interests in seven broad areas: occupations, school subjects, activities, amusement, types of people, preferences on a list of paired items, and self-evaluative characteristics.

Reference: *The Mental Measurements Yearbook,* Buros Institute of Mental Measurements (published annually) .

structured overview A formal, graphically displayed outline of key words and concepts and their interrelationships in a course, textbook, classroom lesson or textbook chapter. A valuable form of advance organizer (q.v.), the structured overview not only gives the student a visible outline of the material to be covered and a guide for study and note taking, it also serves to hold the instructor accountable for covering specific materials. Usually represented graphically in pyramidal form, the structured overview has a single keyword for the major concept in the uppermost pyramid block. The top block, in turn, sits atop a tier of two or three blocks, each of which contains a keyword for a main idea supporting the main concept. Beneath each main idea are blocks containing keywords for supporting concepts, etc.

Reference: *Secondary School Reading Instruction: The Content Areas,* Betty D. Roe, Barbara D. Stoodt and Paul C. Burns (1983).

Structure of Intellect (SOI)

A complex of 90 different thinking skills that together make up a person's intellect and intelligence. Largely used to design an individualized curriculum for a gifted student, SOI attempts to measure the quality and degree of such intellectual skills as creativity, thinking and reasoning skills, higher-order thinking, and mathematical skills.

References: *Teaching the Gifted Child,* James J. Gallagher (1985); *Way Beyond the I.Q.,* Joy P. Guilford (1977); *The Basic SOI Manual,* Mary N. Meeker, Robert Meeker and Gayle Roid (1984).

student aid Funds from nonfamily sources to help students pay for their college and graduate school education. In the 1993–1994 school year, nearly half the more than 15 million college students in the United States availed themselves of student aid totaling $41.9 billion. Some 51% of such aid, or $21.2 billion, derived from subsidized Federal Family Education Loan programs, for which the federal government paid $9 billion a year in interest. These loans include Stafford Loans, Supplemental Loans for Students, and Parent Loans for Undergraduate Students.

Institutional grants, mostly from colleges and universities, but also from a few private foundations, accounted for 19% of student aid—a total of $82 billion. Pell grants (q.v.) represented 14% of all student aid, dispensing $5.7 billion a year to some 3.7 million college students. State grants to students accounted for $2.4 billion in student aid, or about 6%. Federal campus-based aid programs—usually work-study programs—accounted for 5% of student aid each year, totaling about $2.2 billion, while other, miscellaneous federal aid programs accounted for another 5% of student aid—about $2.3 billion in all.

Reference: U. S. Department of Education, Washington, D.C.

student behavior In education, the social and emotional response and interaction of students with other students and with teachers and administrators in the school situation. Student behavior may be guided and controlled indirectly and directly. Indirectly, schools and teachers attempt to affect behavior by distributing booklets to parents and students, outlining school rules and regulations. Direct controls come from both students and from teachers and administrators, through expressions of behavioral expectations and remonstrances or punishment in response to inappropriate or unacceptable behavior.

Almost all children misbehave periodically. Continuing, chronic misbehavior, however, may be a signal of socio-emotional disability—sometimes the result of undetected physical or learning disabilities that can be treated with special education or medications. School misbehavior may also result from the application of widely divergent standards at home and at school or from a wide difference between an individual's particular level of development and that of his or her classmates. Whatever the cause, socio-emotional disabilities usually evoke disruptive behavior in class and hostile relations with and alienation from both students and teachers.

Most school districts have a wide range of special programs for the socio-emotionally disabled, all of which begin with evaluation of the student and determination of the cause of the disability. Although above-normal and below-normal intelligence may be one cause of the student's behavior, most socio-emotionally disabled students are of normal intelligence. Often individual attention in small classes is enough to correct such behavior. Other students may require individual tutoring or remediation. A shift into vocational education often proves effective with some high school students unable to cope with traditional academic programs.

Depending on the size of the school district, a school may transfer socio-disabled students into alternative classes or schools, euphemistically called "opportunity classes." Although ostensibly temporary, such classes seldom see students return to regular school programs. Although such programs do help some students, they can exacerbate student behavioral disabilities because of the perception by both students and teachers that they represent a form of punishment. Dropout rates at alternative high schools are staggeringly high, reaching well above 75% in major cities such as New York.

Reference: *The Handbook of Special Education: Research and Practices,* Margaret C. Wang, M. C. Reynolds and Herbert J. Walberg, eds. (1988).

student council A group of students, usually in secondary schools, elected by the student body to serve as a form of representative self-government. Once ubiquitous at four-year colleges as well as high schools, student councils began disappearing after the age of majority was lowered from 21 to 18 in 1971, encouraging students to consider issues larger than those within the walls of a school. Student councils on most college campuses now restrict their activities to coordination of social and extracurricular activities.

At the high school level council activities are often far more encompassing. Depending on the school, the student council may fulfill any or all of the following functions: instruction of students in self-government; student discipline, through a student court that hears student violations of school rules and metes out appropriate punishment; dissemination of school news to students; coordination of student relations with the faculty and administration; participation in school administration; development of community service programs; and development and involvement in activities of benefit to the school, to the faculty and administration, to parents and to the students themselves (career-day and college-fair programs, homecoming programs, school clean-up and improvement programs, and so on).

The council's reach is determined solely by the school board and the chief school administrator, or principal, and its makeup varies from school to school. Some councils consist of an elected representative from each home room; others are made up of the chief officer or officers of each class; and still others may be elected by the entire student body from a list of individual candidates or candidate slates. The council president and other officers may be elected by council members, by the general student body or automatically named on the basis of membership in the senior class. Almost all councils have a permanent faculty advisor, either appointed by the school's chief administrator or elected by council members or the student body.

References: *The Student Council in the Secondary School,* National Association of Secondary School Principals; National Association of Student Councils, Washington, D.C.

Student Descriptive Form A standardized form published by the National Association of Secondary School Principals for teachers to use in evaluating each of their students on a variety of factors, including class participation, discussion skills, questioning skills, depth of understanding, independent study, responsibility and consideration of others.

Reference: National Association of Secondary School Principals, Reston, Virginia.

Student Descriptive Questionnaire An optional form for students taking the College Board Scholastic Assessment Tests. The questionnaire asks students for a variety of personal and demographic information to help colleges recruit applicants they consider good "fits" for their institutions. The questionnaires are never used for screening purposes and do not affect student applications. The questions asked concern ethnic identity, type of high school curriculum, size of high school, class rank, educational and career goals, housing preferences, financial or other aid that might be needed and academic and extracurricular interests. Students whose profiles match the typical student profile of any given college are automatically contacted by that college and invited to consider visiting and applying.

Reference: The College Board, Princeton, New Jersey.

student evaluation The determination of what a student has learned, is now learning and most likely will be able to learn in the future. There are three types of evaluation: criterion-referenced, norm-referenced and student-referenced. Criterion-referenced evaluations compare a student's knowledge to school expectations; norm-referenced evaluations compare individual student knowledge to that of other students; and student-referenced evaluations compare a student's knowledge after a period of instruction to his or her knowledge at the beginning of that period.

Determination of a student's accumulated knowledge is relatively simple, either with teacher-led evaluations or standardized tests. Teacher-led evaluations may be criterion-, norm- and child-referenced. These evaluations include a combination of homework assignments, oral recitations in class and a variety of written tests, some requiring thoughtful essays and others requiring short answers to objective questions. Standardized subject-based tests such as the College Board Scholastic Assessment Tests II and American College Testing Program examinations are both criterion- and norm-referenced, but seldom student-referenced.

Determinations of what a student is currently learning and his or her rate of progress are more complex. Tests that measure student rates of learning may be criterion- or norm-based. Thus, teacher-made tests reflecting the actual curriculum can provide a comparison of one student's progress with others in the same class. If, however, the curriculum is particularly undemanding, the results of such tests may be meaningless in terms of absolute rates of progress. Students might well be learning little and still obtain high test scores.

Standardized norm-referenced tests, on the other hand, offer a comparison of each student's progress with a national or statewide sampling of comparable students; but such comparisons may reflect teacher competence and the level of the school curriculum as well as the student's actual rate of progress. As a result, most American schools now rely on so-called basic skills tests (q.v.), which are standardized tests such as the California Achievement Test, the Iowa Test of Basic Skills, and the Comprehensive Test of Basic Skills (qq.v.). When compared with results from teacher-led evaluations, such skills tests quickly detect whether student performance at any given school or class is a reflection of teacher or school competence, as well as student progress. If, for example, teacher-led evaluations show students from a particular class performing at the upper end of the academic range, while standardized tests show them performing at the lower end, the results may well reflect teacher incompetence and render student academic progress suspect. Unfortunately, many students can be taught to achieve above-average results on standardized tests without acquiring the knowledge their scores would seem to reflect. Indeed, critics of basic skills testing maintain that many teachers spend an excessive amount of classroom time "teaching the test" (q.v.) while failing to teach students higher-order reasoning skills. Another criticism of standardized tests centers on the significantly lower scores obtained by poor and minority students—an indication to critics that test questions may be biased in some way or that schools in poor and minority areas are failing their students.

Determination of prospects for future student achievement, the third goal of student evaluation, is usually based on so-called readiness, proficiency or competency tests. Used to determine whether to promote a student to the next grade (or admit the student to college or graduate school), such tests are both criterion- and norm-referenced in that they demand that the student display a minimum body of knowledge considered essential for successful progress in the year ahead. At the same time, they measure student proficiency in certain areas, such as reading comprehension, writing and computation, and compare those skill levels with a national norm for students completing the same grade. Again, such tests are a constant target of criticism, especially because of the tendency of many schools to use them as a basis for rigid promotion policies that can see students promoted or held back, with only one point separating their scores. Because of different rates of development, many slower students who remain with their peers eventually catch up—often during the following year in the case of elementary school students. In contrast, studies show that students who are held back in the elementary years have above-average dropout rates in high school. As in the case of achievement tests, another criticism of competency tests is their disproportionately high tendency to retain poor and minority students—a factor that may contribute to the disproportionately high, school dropout rates for such students.

References: *Student Achievement Tests as Tools of Educational Policy,* Edward Haertel (1988); *The Effects of Standardized Testing,* Thomas Kellaghan, George F. Madaus and Peter W. Airasian (1985); *None of the Above: The Myth of Scholastic Aptitude,* David Owen (1986); *Flunking Grades,* Lorrie Sheppard and Mary Lee Smith (1988).

student government Any school-sanctioned program that extends to students the opportunity to control some aspect of their lives at school. An effective method of instruction in self-government, student government programs may range from a program of electing class officers to a school-wide system, with student-body officers or a student council (q.v.) elected by the entire student body. Student government not only teaches students the mechanics of democratic self-government, it also allows them to take responsibility for various aspects of their own learning. Student government may have partial or total control over student discipline, through a student court that hears student violations of school rules and metes out appropriate punishment. Student government can also serve as a liaison with the faculty and administration, disseminating school news to students and transmitting student views to the faculty and administration. Student government often serves as a faculty and administration advisory group on student relations. Student government may also be involved in developing a variety of activities that benefit students and the school, such as career-day and college-fair programs, homecoming programs, school clean-up and improvement programs, and community service. The extent of student government authority is determined solely by the school board and the chief school administrator, or principal, and varies from grade to grade and from school to school.

References: National Association of Elementary School Principals, Alexandria, Virginia; National Association of Secondary School Principals, Reston, Virginia; National Association of Student Councils, Washington, D.C.

Student Loan Marketing Association ("Sallie Mae") A federally chartered corporation, created in 1972 to provide liquidity to financial and educational institutions that originate federally guaranteed student loans (q.v.) for college and graduate school. Although the president of the United States appoints seven of its 21 directors, including its chairman, "Sallie Mae," as the company is called colloquially on Wall Street, operates as an investment bank. It buys student loans floated by commercial banks, colleges and the U.S. Government and, in turn, sells bond issues to the general public. Thus, Sallie Mae serves as a middleman, borrowing funds from the public to provide banks, colleges and the government with money to lend to students to pay for their college and graduate school education. In 1994, Sallie Mae's future grew uncertain when the government initiated a program of direct student loans that would bypass commercial banks, eliminating the cost of doing business with middlemen and obviating the need for Sallie Mae.

Reference: Student Loan Marketing Association, Washington, D.C.

student loans In education, a term usually referring to any of a variety of federal government loans or government-subsidized bank loans to help pay the costs of higher education for students enrolled on at least a half-time basis. A program costing more than $20 billion annually by the mid-1990s, the federal student loan program originated as a modest plan for needy students in 1963. An element of the Perkins Vocational Education Act of 1963 (q.v.), it provided about $16 million in loans to students from families below a certain income level, with two-thirds of the loans provided by the government and one-third by participating institutions of higher education. Students were forgiven all principal and interest payments until nine months after completion of their higher education, and interest rates were fixed at 5%. Repayment of Perkins loans was deferred for up to three years after graduation if students enrolled in graduate schools or were unable to find employment. Loans were entirely forgiven if, after graduation, students obtained full-time employment as teachers in public schools serving low-income students or if they became special education teachers, nurses, medical technicians, law-enforcement or corrections officers, staff members in Head Start programs, workers in public or nonprofit child-service or family service agencies, or became teachers of math, science, foreign languages or bilingual education.

In 1965, Congress passed and President Lyndon Johnson signed the Guaranteed Student Loan Act, in response to demands from middle-class families for relief from the rising costs of higher education. Never designed to be the massive program it eventually became, the original loans were limited to a range of about $250 to $1,500 a year. The program expanded in 1973, however, and loan limits were adjusted to account for inflation. In 1978 and 1980, it expanded once again, readjusting the maximum lending limits and finally evolving into Federal Stafford Loans (q.v.). By 1994, loan limits had climbed to $12,500.

The program allowed students to borrow from their banks at relatively low interest rates, without having to begin repayment of principle or interest until six months after they ended their higher education, either in college or graduate school. The federal government not only guaranteed to the banks the repayment of principal and interest, it also paid the interest due while the student remained at school and also paid banks the difference between the low student loan rates and the rates banks would normally have received from unsecured personal loans. At one point, eligibility was limited to students from families below a certain income level ($50,000, at one point; $75,000 at another). The program was then modified to force students from families with incomes above $75,000 to begin repaying the loans immediately, while they were still in college, and thus forgo government subsidies.

By 1993, a watershed year for the student loan program, Stafford Loans had grown to a total of about $17 billion, compared to $770 million in 1970, when, after several years in organizational delays, the program first got under way. Making 1993 so critical was the explosion of anger in Congress at the rate of student default. In the previous year, 22% of Stafford Loan recipients had defaulted on their loans, at a cost of more than $3.5 billion to taxpayers. A Department of Education study found that student default rates varied widely according to the type of institution. The rate was highest at proprietary trade and vocational schools where it reached 36%. Student default rates were 16% and 15%, respectively, at public and private two-year colleges and only 6% and 7%, respectively, at public and private four-year colleges.

The rate of default at proprietary trade and vocational schools had been a national scandal for many years. Usually appealing to the poorest, least educated high school students or to high school dropouts, trade schools advertised promises of quick-and-easy instruction leading to immediate job placement—at no cost to students. Students had only to sign government student loan forms, with which the schools obtained funds covering student fees. In fact, most trade school education was found to be substandard, with the vast majority of students dropping out before completing their studies and leaving loan monies in the pockets of school proprietors. Although students were legally responsible for repaying the loans, the cost of tracking down poor, mobile, semi-literate students of the type that enrolled in such programs proved prohibitive. As of the mid-1990s, the lobbying organization for trade schools was proving strong enough to thwart all congressional efforts to strip them of eligibility for student loans.

In an attempt to reorganize the program, Congress created a new, direct student loan program for the U.S. Department of Education to phase in over several years as a replacement for Stafford Loans. The idea behind the program was to give government—and its law enforcement agencies—direct control over student loans. In 1994, the first year of the program, banks loaned $18.25 billion in government-guaranteed Stafford Loans, while the government loaned $456 million to students directly. The Perkins Loan program (q.v.) for needy students remained unchanged. Under tight government controls, the Perkins Loan total had grown to only $158 million in 1994, compared to $16.1 million in 1965, while defaults remained relatively insignificant.

References: CHE; NYT; U.S. Department of Education, Washington, D.C.

Student Nonviolent Coordinating Committee (SNCC)

Originally, a group of African-American college students in the south, dedicated to ending racial segregation and obtaining constitutional rights for blacks. Formed in 1960, the first SNCC effort saw four college students enter and sit down at a whites-only lunch counter. Beaten and arrested, they nevertheless triggered a movement that swept the south and eventually led to thousands of black and white college students and adults boarding "freedom rides" on buses to the south. In addition to freedom rides, SNCC also sponsored massive voter-registration efforts and election campaigns for black candidates. In 1964, more than 1,000 SNCC members were arrested, eight were severely beaten and six were killed. Their well-publicized protests—and their sacrifices—provoked passage of the Voting Rights Act of 1965, which outlawed all devices such as literacy tests that white authorities had traditionally used to deprive blacks of the right to vote.

References: *Years of Discord: American Politics and Society, 1961–1974,* John Morton Blum (1991); *A Dictionary of Contemporary American History, 1945 to the Present,* by Stanley Hochman and Eleanor Hochman (1979).

student publications Any of a variety of periodicals, tracts and leaflets published for circulation to students, by students, either independently or under school or college auspices. Publications vary widely, depending on the student age group and level of school. The most common, however, are daily, weekly or periodical newspapers; monthly, quarterly, semiannual or annual literary magazines; and student annuals, or yearbooks. The latter are compilations of photographs, individual biographies and future plans of the graduating senior high school, college or graduate school classes, with summaries of the school's various activities. Similar in both high school and college, most tend to be owned by the institution, student staffed but with faculty advisors, and funded largely by advertisements and student subscriptions.

Among periodicals, daily newspapers are found only at large universities. They operate either as independent student enterprises, with total editorial freedom (within the framework of the laws of libel), or as college-owned organizations (often as adjuncts of the journalism department or school), staffed by students operating under faculty guidance. Most colleges also see the appearance each year of a host of "alternative" newspapers sponsored by a variety of student advocacy groups.

At the secondary school level, student publications are almost all school-owned, though student-operated under relatively strict faculty guidance. Students have no legal right to editorial freedom, although faculty advisors usually try to help develop such publications as an important conduit for the civil expression of faculty, administration and student views.

At the elementary school level, publications are usually limited to computer-produced compilations of student stories and poetry. Content of secondary school literary magazines is similar, although format and style are more sophisticated, often comparable to commercial magazines. Funded by a combination of school grants and paid advertisements, secondary school literary magazines usually fall under the purview of the English department. College literary magazines, like newspapers, may originate from a variety of sources, including advocacy groups. Most colleges have at least one, traditional literary magazine devoted to serious short stories, poetry and essays. Originally college-owned and under the direction of the English department, some are now independent student enterprises, although no less dedicated to the publishing of serious literature. Such ventures are usually funded by advertisements and student and faculty subscriptions. The advent of desk-top publishing, however, has permitted the appearance of a flock of "alternative" quasi-literary publications on virtually every college campus in the United States, with a range of quality stretching from childishly absurd and outrageous to highly professional.

Reference: Columbia University Graduate School of Journalism, New York, New York.

student record   All data relating to a student's academic, extracurricular and behavioral performance at school, along with significant information about the student's development and academic progress, physical and emotional condition, standardized test results, and attendance records. Elements of such data can be found, at various times, in the classroom teacher's records, but cumulative records are maintained in the school office, the district office or the college registrar's office.

A cumulative record, however, does not necessarily transfer into a permanent record. Under the Family Educational Rights and Privacy Act of 1974 (popularly known as the Buckley Amendment) parents have the right to examine all school records of their minor children, while students 18 and older have the right to examine their own records. The law gives parents and students of age the right to challenge and demand the removal of any data they can prove inaccurate and to write into the record any extenuating circumstances relating to what they consider an unfair or detrimental evaluation. As a student's record accumulates through elementary and secondary school and college, materials no longer considered relevant are, in the interests of space, discarded. By the time a student enters the world of work, little is retained other than a transcript of academic grades and, perhaps, a listing of extracurricular activities and honors.

References: *Introduction to Educational Administration,* Roald F. Campbell et al. (1977); *Handbook of College and University Administration,* Asa S. Knowles, ed. (1970).

student rights   A far-reaching, albeit vaguely defined term referring to the legal and constitutional freedoms of students. Students' rights differ sharply depending on their age and the schools they attend. At the college level, they have the same rights as any adults anywhere, to go and come at will, dress and groom themselves as they please, speak in any public place and conduct themselves in any way they please, so long as their conduct does not violate local or state laws or disrupt normal college operations.

Although protected by the Constitution, minors do not have adult rights in elementary and secondary schools, if those schools have clearly stated policies outlining acceptable and unacceptable student conduct. The key to student rights in an elementary or secondary school seems to lie in a broad area of school or classroom disruption, a phenomenon that cannot always be defined in legal terms. In *Tinker v. Des Moines Independent School District* (q.v.), the U.S. Supreme Court forced the school district to withdraw threats of suspension against students wearing black armbands to protest the Vietnam War. "Students in school as well as out of school," said the Court, "are 'persons' under our Constitution . . . The Constitution does not stop at the schoolhouse door like a puppy waiting for his master."

The ruling—that school authorities had overreacted to what was essentially a very personal, quiet protest, involving no speeches, proselytizing or any other disruption of school routine—was a limited victory for student-rights advocates. In general the courts have upheld the right of schools to dictate student dress and grooming codes, hair styles and the students with whom they may associate, denying students freedom of expression, freedom of association, freedom of expression, and a host of other rights constitutionally guaranteed to adults. Moreover, state courts have granted elementary and secondary schools increasing discretionary powers to impose and enforce regulations that school authorities deem necessary for maintaining a stable school atmosphere. The courts have insisted, however, that school authorities make rules and regulations clear to all students and parents, in the form of clearly written booklets whose contents are carefully explained to each student and parent to avoid future misunderstanding and possible litigation. Thus, any student violating the school's written dress or grooming code may, in most communities, be sent home and suspended until the student conforms to the school's written rules. Similarly, most school authorities have the right to suspend students guilty of behavior that disrupts normal classroom or school activities.

As for a student's constitutional guarantees, the courts have ruled that even these may be suspended in appropriate situations, where the welfare of other students is threatened. Indeed, some state courts have ruled that school authorities have the right to search student desks and lockers, which are legally the property of the school, when they suspect the presence of dangerous chemical substances or guns. Some states insist that such searches be conducted only with student permission and with the student and at least one adult witness present. Most states require that schools include in their published school rules their policy with regard to desk and locker searches.

The first, somewhat definitive U.S. Supreme Court decision in which the Court took up the question of searches of a student's person and property came in 1985, in *New Jersey v. T.L.O.* (q.v.). In that case, the Court ruled it legally permissible for public school officials and teachers to search a student's property as long as the scope of the search was proper and there were "reasonable grounds" to believe the search would yield evidence of a violation of the law or school rules. Although the Court said that students were covered by Fourth Amendment protection against "unreasonable searches and seizures," it also said that school officials could conduct certain types of searches without a warrant as long as they fulfilled two important prerequisites: (1) they based their searches on reasonable grounds of suspicion; and (2) the scope of the searches was appropriate to the circumstances.

In the case of "T.L.O" (the initials of a girl whose name was kept confidential), the student was caught smoking in the school bathroom. School officials searched her pocketbook and found drug paraphernalia and evidence of recent drug sales. They called the police, and she was arrested. She challenged her eventual conviction on the grounds that the evidence against her had been seized illegally, but the Court ruled against her. Noting that violent crime and drug use in schools had become "major social problems," the Court declared that "the school setting requires some easing of the restrictions to which searches by public authorities are ordinarily subject." The Court failed, however, to provide specific, in-school, search-and-seizure rules and left most educators unclear about the extent of their authority in this area. "The legality of a search of a student," said the Court, "should depend simply on the reasonableness, under all the circumstances of the search."

In general, after a decades-long experiment in liberalized student rights that led to near anarchy in many schools by the end of the 1970s, many public school authorities determined to restore order and discipline in the 1980s. With the "T.L.O." decision as a guideline and the support of lower courts, they systematically undertook to remove drugs, alcohol and guns from schools. Many schools also required adolescents to dress and groom themselves in conformity with generally accepted adult standards.

References: National Education Association, Washington, D.C.; *What Every Teacher Should Know About Student Rights,* Eve Cary (1975); *Student Discipline and the Law,* Eugene T. Connors (1979); *The Legal Rights of Students,* Thomas J. Flygare (1975); *Legal Handbook for Educators,* Patricia A. Hollander (1978); *The College Students and the Courts,* D. Parker Young and Donald Gehring (1977); U.S. Supreme Court proceedings.

Students' Army Training Corps

A short-lived program established on October 1, 1918, that drafted students who were potential officers but kept them in college until called for active duty. In addition to their regular college curriculum, however, they were expected to participate fully in standard military training for the Army. The program was designed to increase the pool of potential Army officers, while allowing men's colleges to preserve their enrollments and avoid total shutdowns. Launched amidst a flurry of publicity, the program was quickly dismantled after the Armistice a month later.

Reference: "Non-Military Education in the United States Army and Air Force, 1900–1960," Rudolph Schwarts (doct. th., New York University (1963).

Students for a Democratic Society (SDS)

A leading group in many student protests during the 1960s. An outgrowth of the Student League for Industrial Democracy of the mid-1930s, the organization had little impact on the workers' rights movements of that era and lay relatively dormant until 1962, when its members issued their radical platform at Port Huron, Michigan.

By 1966, its role in the student Free Speech Movement protests at the University of California, Berkeley, had won it more than 5,500 supporters on about 150 campuses. In April and May 1968, it led the so-called Siege of Morningside Heights, protesting Columbia University plans to build a gymnasium on adjacent city parkland used by nearby black residents. By then, its membership had expanded to more than 35,000 students on 250 college campuses, but its membership varied from marginally sympathetic liberal students to fanatic, dues-paying members. By the end of the decade, as the entire student protest movement began waning, SDS split into three organizations, one of which was the radical Revolutionary Youth Movement, which became better known as the Weathermen. Their name from a Bob Dylan lyric—"You don't need a weatherman to know which way the wind blows,"—the Weathermen, or Weather Underground, were eventually responsible for a series of arsons, robberies, murders and bombings, some at major universities, before their members were arrested and the organization dissolved.

References: *Years of Discord: American Politics and Society, 1961–1974,* John Morton Blum (1991); *A Dictionary of Contemporary American History, 1945 to the Present,* Stanley Hochman and Eleanor Hochman (1979).

student-teacher ratio

The relationship between the number of students and the number of teachers in an academic setting—that is, a class, school, district and so on. Often called the pupil-teacher ratio, the ratio was 17.2 elementary and secondary school students for every teacher in the United States in 1994, with the ratio for elementary schools 18.6:1 and the secondary school ratio 15.0:1. The overall public school student-teacher ratio was 17.6:1, with a ratio of 19.0:1 in elementary schools and 15.4:1 in high schools. The ratios for all private schools were 15.0:1, with elementary schools having a ratio of 16.5:1 and high schools 11.4:1. Often related to student achievement and educational quality, student-teacher ratios determine the individual attention a teacher can provide each student. Student-teacher ratios also reflect the amount of money a state or school district is willing to spend on teacher salaries and on education generally.

Reference: DES.

student teaching   A program akin to an apprenticeship in teaching, during the last year of college-level teacher training. The student teacher is assigned to work with a master teacher in a public or private school classroom, observing the master teacher, providing help and cooperation when required, and eventually designing lesson plans and conducting classes under the supervision of the master teacher. Unpaid and visited regularly by an advisor or supervisor from the college, the student receives full academic course credit for successful completion of student-teaching work, which usually lasts a semester and is required for teacher certification in most states.

References: *Successful Student Teaching: A Handbook for Elementary and Secondary Student Teachers*, Fillmer Hevener Jr. (1981); *Student Teaching and Field Experiences Handbook*, Betty D. Roe, Elinor P. Ross and Paul C. Burns (1984).

student-team learning   An approach to learning that groups four or five students, usually quite mixed in ability, gender and ethnicity, into teams to prepare each other academically for a particular learning unit; divided into five distinct phases: the class presentation by the teacher; team study of notes of the teacher's lecture and of appropriate required and recommended readings; cooperative preparation for quizzes, through group discussion of worksheet problems, comparison of solutions and correction of each other's work; calculation of individual improvement scores; and determination of the best performances among the various teams. The students take their quizzes individually, with scores compared to each individual's previous work to determine individual improvement. Individual scores within each team are then averaged to obtain a team score. In addition to enjoying the camaraderie of work, students learn a sense of responsibility to others. Academically, the more gifted students learn through teaching, while serving as role models for the slower students. Moreover, team competition lends excitement to student studies and academics. Careful selection of each team's participants is essential, however, to keep competition relatively even and prevent any single team from consistently dominating and, therefore, discouraging other participants.

Reference: *Using Student Team Teaching*, Robert E. Slavin (1986).

student unrest   The chronic disruption of regularly scheduled school or college activities by unruly students. Student unrest and activism date to the earliest, medieval universities in Europe, where students were often responsible for hiring and firing their teachers. In the American colonies, student unrest first appeared at Harvard College with bitter debates that began in 1725 over the question, "Is civil government originally founded on the consent of the people?" By 1760, the debate had escalated to "Is an absolute or arbitrary monarchy contrary to right reason?" and by 1769 it had evolved into the near-treasonous question: "Are the people the sole judges of their rights and liberties?" Students at the College of New Jersey (later, Princeton), the College of Philadelphia (later, University of Pennsylvania) and the College of Rhode Island (later, Brown) joined the spreading student unrest against the English Crown in the 1760s. By 1773, students at Harvard, Yale and the College of New Jersey regularly boycotted tea and burned it, along with British effigies. Students actually seized control of Harvard and Yale in 1776 and 1777 (and did battle with British troops), until those institutions named pro-independence presidents to restore calm.

Although the Civil War disrupted student life at both northern and southern colleges, the disruptions were not the result of student unrest per se. In the North, student abolitionists simply left school and marched to war, while students in southern schools joined regiments to protect their native soil. When the war ended, most southern schools and colleges had been destroyed.

The turn of the century saw some socialist activism at American universities, and World War I prompted minor student unrest at a handful of colleges. But student life remained relatively calm in the United States until 1960, when four black college students in Greensboro, North Carolina, sat down to be served at a variety store luncheon counter reserved for whites. After the four were beaten and arrested, other young blacks in the south began staging comparable sit-ins in restaurants and lunch counters. Within a year, they were joined by white and black college students from the north and west, who staged massive "freedom rides" to challenge racial segregation on interstate buses, trains and public facilities throughout the south.

The worldwide television publicity of the subsequent outrages suffered by student freedom riders at the hands of local police and white mobs succeeded in shaming federal government agencies into enforcing desegregation laws dealing with interstate transportation and federally regulated facilities. Amazed by their strength and effectiveness in provoking social change, myriad campus groups, formed originally as temporary ad hoc groups to fight racial segregation in the south, evolved into permanent student organizations determined to combat whatever they perceived as injustice. In so doing, they began a 30-year era of student unrest unparalleled in the history of American education. Student protests ran the gamut from reasoned discussion to class boycotts to campus shutdowns, sometimes lasting for weeks, and even to the bombing of university buildings. In the two years beginning in May 1967 alone, there were 25 bombings, 46 cases of arson, 207 buildings occupied and more than 6,000 arrests

on American college campuses. Few campuses were exempt, and none remained unchanged.

Some of the campus activist organizations merged to form national organizations such as the Student Nonviolent Coordinating Committee (SNCC) and the Students for a Democratic Society (SDS) (qq.v.), with SNCC a major force in recruiting college students for freedom rides in the south. Both SNCC and the Students for a Democratic Society also engineered demonstrations on many northern campuses, demanding that colleges end racially discriminatory admission policies. Of little import initially, the campus demonstrations gained worldwide attention after activists at the University of California at Berkeley demanded the right to use a public area of the campus to recruit students for freedom rides and off-campus demonstrations. University authorities had first refused, then relented, and then modified their stand, banning only recruitment for illegal causes. When student demonstrators were arrested for staging a civil rights demonstration at a local hotel, the demonstration spilled over onto the campus, where students melded the idea of civil rights for black people to civil rights for young people.

In effect, they demanded a greater share in university decisions and an end to the traditional university doctrine of in loco parentis, with university authorities acting in place of parents as legal guardians of students, with full authority to govern their lives. The age of majority at the time was 21, and most undergraduates were minors. In December 1964, thousands of students occupied Sproul Hall, the campus administration building. Eventually ejected by police, who arrested 800, the Berkeley students forced the university to accede to their demands, provoking similar demonstrations on other major college campuses across the United States.

In 1964, the passage of the Civil Rights Act (q.v.) outlawed all forms of racial segregation in public facilities, thus opening all college doors to blacks and eliminating one cause of the continuing student protests. But the war in Vietnam was escalating and provoking anger and distress among Americans of draft age. Because all students were eligible for a temporary injunction from compulsory military service to complete their higher education, college enrollments spiraled. Many blacks, however, were unable to afford college, and inordinately high numbers of them were drafted for service in Vietnam. The Rev. Martin Luther King Jr. began leading protests against the war and the inequities of military conscription. King's assassination on April 4, 1968, triggered a wave of riots that left whole areas of New York, Washington and other major cities aflame for days. The riots spilled over onto some campuses, where blacks demanded that white institutions do more for the black community.

In 1968, black students supported by members of the Students for a Democratic Society seized five Columbia University buildings to block construction of a new $10 million gymnasium on parkland leased from the city and normally used by children in the adjacent black slum. In California the same year, black college students at San Francisco State College rioted after their demands for admission of more blacks and the introduction of more courses on black history were rebuffed. Intermittent strikes and rioting led to 453 arrests in January 1969. In December 1968, armed black students seized an administration building at Cornell University. In all the demonstrations, blacks were initially supported only by radical white students and faculty members, but the eventual use of armed police to end the demonstrations ultimately radicalized large segments of moderate students.

When President Richard M. Nixon expanded the Vietnam fighting in 1969—after winning election on a campaign to end the war—radicalized American college students had a new cause around which to rally. Nixon incensed them even more by charging that ''anarchy'' was stalking American campuses. In the spring of 1969, Harvard student protesters shut down the undergraduate campus for the entire spring term. Like students at other campuses, they were protesting the questionable constitutional legitimacy of the Vietnam War and Harvard's sponsorship of the Reserve Officers Training Corps (q.v.) on campus to train future officers for the military.

The protests at Harvard and elsewhere resumed in even greater intensity in the fall of 1969. They reached a peak early the following May, after President Nixon revealed that he had ordered U.S. troops in Vietnam to invade Cambodia. On May 2, militants at Kent State University (q.v.) in Ohio burned down the ROTC building. At the request of Kent's mayor, Ohio Governor James Rhodes transferred exhausted National Guard troops from riot duty in the Cleveland-Akron area, with orders to break up all student demonstrations. On May 4, the troops ordered a group of student war protesters to disperse. The students began taunting the troops and hurling rocks at them, and the troops began firing, hitting 13 protesters, four of them fatally.

The killings set off a nationwide debate over the rights of the young. Some political leaders pointed out that American society had imposed the harshest obligations of citizenship on the young without giving them commensurate representation in the decision-making process. It was a plaint that had sparked the Revolutionary War, and by 1970 there were too many intelligent, young, college-educated Americans—both black and white—who were witnessing or suffering iniquities they had been taught by their elders did not exist. They had seen years of television news film documenting the brutal treatment of blacks in the south. Additional materials appeared about the deprivations of Mexicans, Puerto Ricans, American Indians, Asians and other minority groups. And by 1970, they had seen a decade of devastating coverage of cruelties in Vietnam: an hysterical little girl running naked, her body aflame in napalm; a police chief summarily shooting a suspected enemy soldier in the head; and the remnants of a massacre by U.S. soldiers of an estimated 109 to 567 unarmed men, women and children in My Lai. And in Kent, Ohio, 13 young Americans had been shot by American troops because they—along with the majority of Americans—wanted their government to abandon the war to which they, the young, would be sent to die.

Agreeing that Americans who are old enough to be drafted are also old enough to vote, Congress and the state legislatures overwhelmingly approved passage of the Twenty-sixth Amendment to the Constitution the following year. The amendment lowered the voting age (and age of majority) from 21 to 18, the age at which Americans reached draft status. Two years later, American military involvement in Vietnam came to an end, as did the draft. Although student unrest subsided, activist campus organizations remained in place on many campuses and continued to serve as vehicles for a wide variety of protests. Starting in the late 1970s, students at many private colleges protested against South African apartheid and demanded that their colleges cease investing funds in companies that profited from trade with or operations in South Africa. At a parochial level, demonstrators on some campuses demanded, variously, more black-studies courses, more women's-studies courses, fewer or no core curriculum requirements, the right of students to opt for pass-fail grading, lower tuition, gay and lesbian rights, and numerous other student rights.

The endless protests contributed to many permanent changes in higher education in the United States. The protests (along with the Twenty-sixth Amendment) ended the centuries-old doctrine of in loco parentis at college campuses. Students, not parents, became entirely responsible for their financial, academic, social and legal obligations on almost all college campuses. Colleges can no longer legally send grade reports or have any other direct formal relationship with parents without student consent. Campus rules governing personal conduct are generally limited to the usual community ordinances and laws governing vandalism, assault and underage consumption of alcoholic beverages. In the area of academics, few colleges require students to take any specific courses to qualify for graduation,

although all require a specific number of total courses, with the choice left to students. Most colleges permit enormous flexibility in the choice of majors, allowing students to combine two or more majors into inter-departmental programs if each department chair approves.

References: *Years of Discord: American Politics and Society, 1961–1974*, John Morton Blum (1991); *A Dictionary of Contemporary American History, 1945 to the Present*, Stanley Hochman and Eleanor Hochman (1979).

Student Volunteer Movement for Foreign Missions (SVM)

A massive evangelistic effort involving more than 8,000 American college students, who served as volunteer missionaries to Christianize and Americanize India, the Middle East, Southeast Asia, China, Japan, Africa and Latin America. Founded in 1888, SVM was an outgrowth of fundamentalist preacher Dwight L. Moody's (q.v.) conferences in Northfield, Vermont, where he called on young Americans to pledge themselves to the "evangelization of the world in this generation." With an executive committee drawn from the Moody-influenced YMCA and YWCA (qq.v.) organizations, SVM was placed under the leadership of John R. Mott (q.v.), the student head of the Cornell University YMCA. Mott became the founding chairman of SVM in 1888. In 1900, he wrote the widely circulated *The Evangelization of the World in This Generation*, and by 1910 he succeeded in organizing 2,000 SVM on-campus and off-campus study groups, with a total enrollment of 25,000 students.

Obsessed with Christianizing China, he wrote in 1911, "It is Western education that the Chinese are clamoring for, and will have. If the Church can give it to them, plus Christianity, they will take it; otherwise they will get it elsewhere, without Christianity—and that speedily." His appeal sent American student missionaries swarming across China, and by 1925 SVM had founded several hundred primary schools and about 90 secondary schools—boarding schools, high schools and seminaries—plus about

100 theological schools, medical schools and nursing schools. The colleges, which included Yale in China, had a total enrollment of 3,500 students, the secondary schools about 26,000 students and the primary schools about 250,000 students. All were American-style schools, teaching the English language, English literature, Western history, American science and mathematics and, of course, biblical and Christian theology.

Most SVM missionaries were from church-going Presbyterian, Methodist, Congregationalist and Baptist families and had attended denominational and theological colleges. A disproportionate number came from Denison and Yale colleges, among men's schools; Mount Holyoke and Rockford, among women's colleges; and Oberlin and Grinnell, among coeducational schools. Together, they surrendered their material ambitions and dedicated their lives to God's service. For whatever reasons, they believed that the spiritual needs of the non-Christian masses abroad—in China, India, Africa and elsewhere—presented a more urgent task in the eventual establishment of the Kingdom of God than the plight of millions of American poor.

Once abroad, they did more than attempt to Christianize the world through Bible instruction and preachments. Aside from ministers, there were physicians and nurses, who taught cleanliness and hygiene and established clinics and hospitals, albeit adorned throughout with Christian symbolism. Agronomists taught scientific farming methods and Western diets; and, in the most primitive areas, missionary wives taught what they believed was the sinfulness of nakedness and the virtue of wearing clothes. Central to these efforts, however, was the establishment of American-style schools that taught literacy and numeracy, as well as Christianity. Unfortunately, graduates of such schools emerged with skills that allowed them to live comfortably within the growing Christian compounds created by SVM, but they were seldom prepared to return to their own societies except as Christian missionaries who often found themselves scorned as traitors to their cultures.

In China and elsewhere, moreover, there were growing nationalistic demands for local control over educational institutions. Meanwhile, a post-World War I mood of disillusionment was sweeping across most U.S. college campuses, dissipating enthusiasm for SVM. Mott, who shared the Nobel Prize for peace in 1946, stepped down as SVM chairman in 1920, and the movement gradually declined in the face of the materialism of the 1920s, the economic depression of the 1930s and, finally, World War II. SVM nevertheless had an enormous impact on the non-Western world and on American education in the United States. Not only did SVM introduce Eastern, Mideastern and African cultures to American values, the American arts and sciences and American technology, it also created a sizable force of American intellectuals versed in Asian and African affairs. When they eventually returned to the United States, they became the leading scholars and interpreters—at American colleges and universities, in the diplomatic service, in journalism and in the world of letters—of the lands where they had lived.

References: *John R. Mott, 1865–1955: A Biography,* C. Howard Hopkins (1951); *The Evangelization of the World in This Generation,* John R. Mott (1900); *The Student Volunteer Movement for Foreign Missions: Some Personal Reminiscences of Its Origin and Early History,* Robert P. Wilder (1935).

study abroad programs Any of a variety of programs for American high school or college students, who take an approved leave to pursue studies in foreign schools or colleges and receive appropriate course credits in their home institutions. Some study abroad programs are arranged by American institutions, some by the student. Some study abroad programs arrange for students to live with host families; others simply arrange for living quarters at the foreign educational institution itself. A handful of study abroad programs involve study at a foreign branch of the American institution. Many American colleges have specific Junior Year

Abroad programs (q.v.) as acceptable elements of their four-year program, and a few colleges actually require students to spend one semester studying abroad at allied foreign universities.

(See also AMERICAN FIELD SERVICE.)

Reference: *Study Abroad*, UNESCO, Paris, France (published annually).

study hall A special classroom, usually in secondary schools, reserved for silent, independent pursuit of study or preparation of written assignments. Never held in libraries, study halls are usually supervised by one or more faculty members, whose primary responsibility is to ensure silence. Unlike resource classrooms, study halls are not designed to provide students with extra help. Study halls were originally designed to sequester and supervise students with no regularly scheduled class or activity. Many schools continue to require students whose grade-point averages fall below a certain level to attend study hall during their free periods. Once a standard part of student schedules at most secondary schools, study halls in many schools have recently given way to specific classroom or resource room assignments, where smaller groups of students can obtain individualized study help or practice computer skills.

Reference: *Instruction in Today's Middle and Secondary Schools*, Kenneth W. Hoover (1976).

study skills A variety of methods students can be taught to facilitate acquisition of knowledge in class and from textbooks. Among the variety of study skills that elementary and secondary school teachers try to teach their students are listening skills, speed reading (qq.v.), note-taking skills, test-taking skills, use of the library and research skills, and adapting the student's environment to facilitate learning (improved lighting, proper room temperature, proper seating and desk space, study regularity, elimination of distractions, etc.). Many elementary, middle, and high schools require entering students to take a specific minicourse in study skills at the beginning of each year.

Reference: *Reading and Study Skills*, John Langan (1989).

stuttering A speech disability that blocks the smooth transition from one syllable to another, manifesting itself in either abnormally long pauses or oral stoppages, prolongations of the previous sound or repetitions of the same sound. Some speech therapists differentiate among stuttering, stammering and cluttering, with the first referring to speech repetition, the second to speech blockage and the third to garbling of syllables. The causes of each remain undefined and varied, and few therapies have proved universally successful.

Stuttering occurs in about 1% to 3% of preadolescent children. Emotions such as fear, embarrassment, hostility and excitement can produce stuttering and stammering in even the most fluent individuals and have usually been cited as a cause of chronic stuttering. Although there is no evidence of any cerebral association, there is some evidence that stuttering may result from some form of neurological disorder "downstream" from the brain. For example, stutterers do not usually stutter when talking to themselves, their toys or their pets. Thus stuttering may relate to the timing of the muscular mechanisms involved in utterances. Therapies, such as psychotherapy, drugs, relaxation techniques and breath control, have scored uneven successes.

References: *Diagnosing Learning Disorders*, Bruce F. Pennington (1991); *Stuttering: Theory and Treatment*, Marcel E. Wingage (1976).

subject-centered curriculum A rigid curriculum, based on specific courses, with specific amounts of material to be covered over specific periods of time—regardless of student abilities or interests. Also known as a scholiocentric curriculum, subject-centered curricula assign greatest importance to the subject matter rather than students. Student failure to absorb the required material to an acceptable degree results in retention. The traditional approach to education for several centuries, subject-centered curricula were gradually modified and blended with a more child-centered approach to education, when progressive education was introduced in the late 1800s.

Few elementary schools remain subject-centered, with students forced to concentrate for an extended period on a single subject, before turning to the next subject. Younger children simply do not have the attention span to absorb any single body of material, say mathematics, beyond a specific amount of time. Indeed, the most academically successful elementary schools tend to present an amorphous, child-centered approach to learning during the elementary years, with all materials presented on the basis of student interest and then used as springboards to learning such traditional subjects as reading, writing, computation, history and science. A class might embark on a cooking project, but, in the course of their ostensible amusement, learn measuring, arithmetic, reading (from recipes), chemistry, and perhaps even some social studies, depending on the origin of the recipe.

Secondary school education continues to be relatively subject-centered, especially for college-bound students who must study a core curriculum of English, mathematics, a foreign language, social studies and the sciences to gain admission to college. The absolute coverage of each subject, however, is usually flexible enough to adapt to the abilities and interests of students, and it is rare to see graduates of different secondary schools who have studied identical materials in every subject.

(See also education, history of.)

Reference: *Curriculum Development,* Daniel Tanner and Laurel N. Tanner (1980).

subject correlation The teaching of two or more subjects in tandem, when materials of one relate to and help instruction of materials of the other. Thus, the study of *A Tale of Two Cities* by Charles Dickens or *The Scarlet Pimpernel* by Baroness Orczy, in English literature class, plunges younger students into personally felt adventures in what might otherwise be a rather dry approach to the study of the French Revolution in history class. Similarly, the study of the pyramids in history and the geometry of the cube and pyramid or the physics of their construction are eminently correlated topics. A standard pedagogical technique in the early elementary grades, the correlating of two or more subjects only gradually began working its way into the middle school and high school curricula in the 1960s, as academically progressive schools began discovering the benefits of team teaching (q.v.), with several or even all teachers in a specific grade attempting to coordinate and correlate the materials they taught and provide students with a unified picture of what they were learning.

Reference: *Curriculum Development,* Daniel Tanner and Laurel N. Tanner (1980).

subjective testing The nonempirical evaluation and grading of test results on the basis of the marker's judgment of what is acceptable or unacceptable work. Unlike most mathematics tests, where there is an absolute ''correct'' or ''incorrect'' answer to each question, essay-style questions in literature or social studies tests often offer opportunities for responses that are poor, good, better or best, with absolute grades assigned on the basis of teacher judgment.

Reference: *Improving Marking and Reporting in Classroom Instruction,* Norman E. Gronlund (1974).

substitute teacher A certified teacher who serves as a temporary replacement for a regular member of the faculty. Substitute teachers may replace a teacher for a day or more during a regular teacher's temporary absence or for an entire year, while a regular teacher is on leave. Regardless of the length of service, substitute teachers are required to fulfill all the administrative duties of regular teachers (recording attendance, grading papers, etc.) and to strictly follow the regular teacher's lesson plan. In addition, substitute teachers are expected to provide a written summary for regular teachers of the day's activities and to report to the principal at the beginning and end of the day. Substitute teachers may be on permanent assignment to a particular school or serve as "floaters," reporting to different schools throughout a district as needed.

Reference: *Getting Better Results from Substitute Teachers, Teacher Aides, and Volunteers,* Bryce Perkins and Harry A. Becker (1966).

subvocalization In reading, the movement of lips, the forming of words with the lips, or the whispering of word sounds while trying to read silently. Normal for young, beginning readers, subvocalization can become an impediment to silent reading at normal rates and even a learning disability if it persists beyond a reasonable age, into the upper elementary school years.

Reference: *Reading Difficulties: Their Diagnosis and Correction,* Guy Bond and Miles Tinker (1979).

suicide Intentional self-inflicted death. A major problem among school-aged children and adolescents in the 1980s and 1990s, suicide was the third leading cause of death for 15-to-24-year-olds, after motor vehicle accidents and death from firearms. In all, 4,650 Americans aged 15 to 24 died of suicide in 1992, along with 310 children aged 14 and under. Far more males committed suicide than females—3,970 males, as opposed to 690 females, among 15-to-24-year-olds, and 220 boys under 14, compared to 90 girls. Far more whites committed suicide than blacks—3,950 versus 500, in the older age group, and 290 white children 14 and under, as opposed to only 10 black children of that age. Of white suicides aged 15 to 24, 3,360 were male and 580 were female, while 460 of the 500 black suicides of that age group were male.

Of children 14 and under who committed suicide, 210 of the 290 white children and all 10 of the black children were male. Because so few young suicides undergo psychotherapy, little scientific or epidemiological evidence is available about them. Many psychologists, however, have been able to interview youngsters who have

attempted suicide. One such study found that, in contrast to the better than five-to-one ratio of male suicides to female, 90% of all adolescent suicide attempts are by females. The finding can be interpreted in many inconclusive ways. Psychologists list six broad bases for suicide attempts: grief following loss of a love object, whether real or fantasized (such as a famous star whom the near-suicide did not even know); self-punishment; an effort to obtain help from agencies outside the family; retribution against another person; psychotic instability; and suicide games, such as Russian roulette, excessive drinking or automobile racing, which are not atypical of high-risk adolescent behavior.

Reference: *Suicide: Theory and Clinical Aspects,* L. D. Hankoff and Bernice Einsidler (1979).

Summerhill A child-centered, private school established in England after World War I as an experimental, nontraditional approach to educating children with a variety of behavioral or learning disabilities. An outgrowth of the British infant school movement (q.v.), Summerhill School in Leiston, Suffolk, was founded by English educator A. S. Neill (1883–1977), who scorned the widely held religious notion of original sin. Believing that children were born innocent and inherently good, he established Summerhill as an environment where adults lavished students with tenderness and love and imposed a minimum of constraints. The goal was to allow children's innate interests to provide the motivation for learning in an environment designed to cultivate the affective domain (q.v.), where development of emotions, feelings, beliefs and attitudes had priority over intellectual and physical skills. Although his books *The Problem Child* (1926) and *The Problem Parent* (1931) gained his methods a considerable following in the 1930s, interest waned in the decades that followed. The 1960s, however, saw a revival of interest in progressive and open education, and Summerhill once again gained the attention of American educators, with the publication in 1962 of Neill's book *Summerhill.*

Extreme in its reliance on affective development, Neill's ideas and the Summerhill concept nevertheless served as a balance to traditional education based on strict discipline, religion, rote learning and adherence to a rigid curriculum and daily class schedule. Most academically successful schools have blended techniques from both extremes into modern pedagogy.

References: "Whatever Happened to Summerhill?" William Matthias, *Childhood Education* (April-May 1979); *Summerhill: For and Against,* Harold H. Hart, ed. (1970); *Summerhill: A Radical Approach to Child Rearing,* A. S. Neill (1977).

summer jobs For full-time students, paid employment during school or college summer vacation months. Relatively difficult to obtain, summer jobs for adolescents are generally not available in numbers sufficient to meet the demand, and an estimated 28% of teenaged students are each summer. The unemployment percentages often vary sharply according to gender (22% for males, 18% for females); race (19% for whites, 27% for blacks, 20% for Hispanics, 24% for Asians, 29% for American Indians); socioeconomic status (21% for low status, 18% for middle-low, 17% for middle-high, 24% for high); and school location (21.5% for urban, 19% for suburban and 20.6% for rural). Unemployment figures for adolescents, however, are notoriously unreliable because of untold thousands who perform odd jobs and even work full-time for cash that goes unreported. In an effort to ease high unemployment among economically disadvantaged youth, Congress enacted the Comprehensive Employment and Training Act in 1973, which eventually created more than 1 million summer jobs for young people 14 to 21. The program proved too cumbersome to maintain; indeed, the job application process proved so complex that many applicants were not notified of their acceptance for a job until the summer had ended and they had returned to school.

Of high school seniors whose income was reported in 1992, 9.9% earned less than the minimum wage at that time of $4.25 an hour; 77.5% earned between $4.25 and $6.00 an hour; 7.7% earned $6.01 to $8.00 an hour; and 5% earned $8.01 or more an hour. Only 1.7% worked more than 40 hours a week; 6.8% worked 31 to 40 hours; 18.1%, 21 to 30 hours; 18.9%, 16 to 20 hours; 14.9%, 11 to 15 hours; 11.5%, 6 to 10 hours; and 8%, 1 to 5 hours. Food service jobs offered the most opportunities for high school seniors in 1992, absorbing 24% of that work force, while 14.5% worked as grocery clerks or cashiers, 11.8% as sales personnel and 6.9% in office or clerical jobs. Other jobs open to high school seniors included lawn work (2.2%), delivery work (1.6%), babysitting and child care (4.3%), camp counselor and lifeguard (0.7%), farm work (2.2%), mechanic (1.4%), beautician (0.2%), house cleaning (0.9%), construction (2.0%), health service (1.6%) and warehouse work (2.1%). Some 23.5% of high school seniors were engaged in job categories lumped together as "other."

Summer jobs are of considerable importance in the college application process in the United States. To be eligible for scholarships and government grants, college and graduate students are expected to contribute at least 10% of the cost of their higher education from their own earnings, accumulated from summer work and work on campus during the school year—usually about half from each. Moreover, the most academically selective private colleges expect applicants from even the highest income families to have worked most summers during their high school years, at least in volunteer, if not paying, jobs. These colleges view the ability to obtain and keep a summer job as an indication of initiative and maturity, both of which are among the most desirable personality traits they seek among their applicants.

References: DES; *A Student's Guide to College Admissions,* Harlow G. Unger (1995); U.S. Department of Labor Bureau of Labor Statistics, Washington, D.C.

summer school A formal semester of school or college held during the traditional summer vacation months, between the end of the previous school year and the beginning of the next. Held at secondary schools and colleges, summer school allows students to repeat work they failed during the regular school year or take additional courses for extra credit, for remedial purposes or for their own edification. At the college level, summer school offers an opportunity to add one semester's credits to each calendar year, thus permitting candidates for a four-year bachelor's degree to graduate in three years.

Reference: *Summer School: A New Look,* John W. Dougherty (1981).

Sumner, William Graham (1840–1910)

American social scientist and educator, who "fathered" the introduction of the social sciences into the classic college curriculum in the United States. A convert to the philosophy of England's Herbert Spencer (q.v.), Sumner became the consummate social Darwinist, insisting that wealth, status and all other achievements of man were the result of evolution and natural selection that provide each individual with a specific set of abilities and capacities. Natural selection in the social sense, he insisted, improved society, much as natural selection in the physical sense produced stronger animals and plants and eliminated the weak. To allow sentimentality to interfere with social and economic evolution, he believed, would undermine progress.

A champion of social and economic laissez-faire, Sumner was born in Connecticut and educated at Yale College and at the universities of Geneva, Göttingen and Oxford in Europe before being ordained a minister in the Episcopal Church in 1869. Tired of clerical life, he joined the Yale College faculty as professor of political and social science in 1872, a post he held until his death. A charismatic teacher, he gained a national reputation as a social Darwinian and an authority on Spencer, whose works, by then, had become the intellectual rage in American education. In addition to fame as a scholar, Sumner gained considerable notoriety as one of the few outspoken opponents of the massive charitable movements sweeping the country in the last decades of the 19th century (to combat such social ills as poverty, unemployment, illiteracy and child labor).

Sumner believed that almost all social ills were the result of social evolution and natural selection, which would in time eliminate the weak and strengthen American society. His lecture "The Absurd Attempt to Make the World Over" won him a national audience, as did his written work, *What Social Classes Owe to Each Other* (1883). In that book he castigated welfare movements and government programs that drained the pockets of the hardworking, middle-class "forgotten man." An opponent of inflationary fiscal policies and protective tariffs, Sumner was a prolific author. Among his many influential books were *A History of American Currency* (1874), *American Finance* (1875), *Protectionism* (1885), *A History of Banking in the United States* (1896) and *Folkways* (1906), his magnum opus on customs and mores. *The Science of Society* (1927–28), a posthumously edited version of his notes and drafts on the entire range of sociology, became a classic text for many years.

Reference: *William Graham Sumner,* Harris E. Starr (1925).

Sunday schools

The school systems and local schools maintained and operated by churches, synagogues and a few other organizations to provide sectarian religious instruction to children on Sundays, independently of their regular, day-to-day education. A relatively recent educational institution, the first Sunday school opened in 1780, in Gloucester, England, where the British religious leader Robert Raikes (1735–1811) sought to provide both secular and religious education to lower-class children who worked in factories during the week and could not attend secular common schools. Under Raikes's leadership, the movement spread across England, enrolling an estimated 250,000 children within 10 years.

By 1799, the first Sunday schools were springing up in the United States; over the next 30 years, they became common, serving different purposes for children of different classes and in different communities. On the frontier, where churches were the first public buildings erected in new communities, Sunday schools were often the only schools, and therefore provided both secular and religious education to all children in the community, much as the church had been the only source of education for children in early colonial settlements. As communities grew large enough or rich enough to build common schools and libraries, the role of Sunday schools gradually receded into the religious sector. "Let Sabbath schools be established wherever it is practicable," suggested the Indiana Sabbath School Union in 1827. "They will answer the double purpose of paving the way for common schools, and of serving as a substitute till they [common schools] are generally formed."

In cities and most industrial towns, Sunday schools continued fulfilling their original purpose of providing secular and religious instruction to poor children forced to work in mines, factories and fields during the week. Sunday schools retained that role until states began enacting compulsory education laws, beginning in the 1850s. The influence of Sunday schools over American education, however, has waxed and waned since the formation of the American Sunday-School Union in 1824. Founded as a publisher of moral and religious texts for children, it soon became a major force in the founding of Sunday schools across the United States. Generally nondenominational, it was on the brink of bankruptcy and extinction during the 1850s, when a leading officer absconded with nearly $90,000 of organization funds, just as the Civil War was about to divide the nation and further disrupt the movement.

Rescued by the fundamentalist religious leaders Dwight L. Moody and John Heyl Vincent (qq.v.), the union soon created a uniform curriculum for all Christian Sunday schools, and by the end the 19th century was at the center of a vast, Christian revivalist movement that seemed so likely to engulf American public schools that the Roman Catholic Church decided to establish its own school system to prevent the Protestantization of Roman Catholic children. The movement's domestic efforts seemed to lose momentum, however, as growing numbers of missionaries turned their attention away from the education of American children and to the establishment of foreign missions to convert Asian, Middle Eastern and African children. In 1889, the first World's Sunday School Convention was held in London, and in 1907 the American Sunday-School Union, which had changed its name to the International Sunday School Union, helped form the World Sunday School Association. Inthe meantime, the growth of secular public school systems throughout the United States was gradually weakening the influence of Sunday schools in the area of secular education. By the end of World War I, their influence had receded to the confines of their churches.

Today's American Sunday schools vary according to religion, Although most of the Sunday schools of each Protestant denomination have uniform, system-wide curricula and are often run on a national or international basis, Roman Catholic and Jewish Sunday schools are generally organized on a local basis. Both Roman Catholic and Jewish Sunday schools are designed to provide religious education to students who would not obtain it elsewhere. Catholic students who attend parochial schools and Jewish students who attend Jewish schools during the week usually do not attend Sunday school. Only Reform and Conservative Jewish synagogues have Sunday schools, however. Orthodox Jewish synagogues, which require children to attend religious schools during the week, have no Sunday schools. Neither Catholic nor Jewish Sunday schools restrict instruction to Sundays; both hold classes at other times. By the mid-1980s, the vast majority of Sunday school enrollment was in the United States, with 29.7

million children. The Southern Baptist Convention had the largest group of students—7.9 million.

References: *The World Sunday School Movement: The Story of a Broadening Mission,* Gerald E. Knoff (1979); *The Big Little School: Sunday Child of American Protestantism,* Robert W. Lynn and Elliott Wright (1971); *The Encyclopedia of Sunday Schools and Religious Education,* John T. McFarland, Benjamin S. Winchester, R. Douglas Fraser and J. William Butcher, eds. (3 vols., 1915); *The Sunday-School Movement, 1780–1917, and the American Sunday-School Union, 1817–1917,* Edwin Wilbur Rice (1917).

superintendent of schools The chief administrative officer of a public school district. Usually hired by the district school board, the superintendent implements board policies in each district school and coordinates all school programs within the district. The first school superintendents were appointed in Louisville, Kentucky, and Buffalo, New York, in 1937, after the number of schools in each district grew too numerous for the board to supervise directly and assure that each principal adhered to board policies. School superintendents are appointed for their administrative skills rather than for any skills or background as educators. Turnover among superintendents in the United States is notoriously high, because most are hired on a contract basis that limits percentage raises for each contract renewal. By negotiating new contracts elsewhere, successful superintendents can assure themselves substantial pay increases with each move to a new district.

References: *The American School Superintendency,* American Association of School Administrators; *The Organization and Control of American Schools,* Roald F. Campbell et al. (1980).

supervising principal A virtually obsolete title for a school administrator with supervisory authority over a specific school within a larger district. In a district with, say, three elementary schools, each might be headed by a supervising principal, with a single principal for the entire elementary school sector based in the largest or most central of the schools. Often a part-time teacher, the supervising principal virtually disappeared by the end of the 1970s.

Reference: *Elementary School Organization and Administration,* Henry J. Otto and David C. Sanders (1964).

supervisor A term variously used in American public school systems to mean school superintendent or, more often, assistant superintendent for instruction and curriculum development. Usually an educator rather than an administrator, a supervisor may be hired by the school board as superintendent or simply as administrator in charge of developing curricula, coordinating academic programs and working with teachers to improve instruction.

Reference: *Supervision of Instruction: A Developmental Approach,* Carl D. Glickman (1985).

Supplemental Educational Opportunity Grants (SEOGs) A program of federal grants for exceptionally needy college students. Officially called Federal Supplemental Educational Opportunity Grants, a fixed number of SEOGs of up to $4,000 a year are distributed on a college-by-college basis for apportionment to eligible students on a first-come, first-served basis. Once each college's allocation has been distributed, latecomers are excluded from the program, regardless of need.

Reference: *A Student's Guide to College Admissions,* Harlow G. Unger (1995).

supplementary readers Books, periodicals and other printed reading materials used as adjuncts to enrich and augment the regular, required reading materials in a class or subject area. Usually optional and pursued by the more gifted students, supplementary reading materials may be suggested in every subject area.

Reference: *Curriculum Planning and Development,* James A. Beane, Conrad F. Toepfer Jr. and Samuel J. Alessi Jr. (1986).

supplementary school A 19th-century term referring to special, separate institutions that compensated for the "deficiencies" of youngsters then considered ineducable. These children included the orthopedically handicapped, blind, deaf, mentally retarded, incorrigible and delinquent youngsters, along with all black and Indian youngsters deemed unfit to attend regular classrooms. Somewhat akin to some of today's alternative schools (q.v.) for children with behavioral problems, supplementary schools were usually operated under private or quasi-public auspices, with a separate school usually established for each category of deficiency. In most instances, local or state laws gave children little choice but to attend such schools when so assigned. In 1838, the father of Mary Ann Crouse of Philadelphia charged the city with violating her Sixth Amendment rights (to a speedy trial and to confront her accusers) by committing her to the House of Refuge. He lost the case—*Ex Parte Crouse*—with the court holding that the city had the right to serve as "the parens patriae, or common guardian of the community." Similarly, in *Roberts v. City of Boston,* the father of a black child, Sarah Roberts, was unsuccessful in his effort to enroll his child in a primary school near his home rather than in a distant, black primary school to which the city had assigned her. The state court denied his claim that the assignment violated educational guarantees of the Massachusetts constitution, saying that the city of Boston had the right to maintain "separate but equal" facilities for blacks.

Supplementary schools all but disappeared following enactment of the Education for All Handicapped Children Act of 1975 (q.v.) and its amendments in 1983 and 1986, guaranteeing almost access to free public education for all the 1 million handicapped children who had hitherto been excluded from public schools.

References: *Children in Urban Society: Juvenile Delinquency in Nineteenth-Century America,* Joseph M. Hawes (1971); *A History of the Care and Study of the Mentally Retarded,* Leo Kanner (1964); "The Roberts Case: Source of the 'Separate but Equal' Doctrine," Leonard Levy and Harlan B. Philips, *American Historical Review* (LVI: 1950–51, pp. 510–18).

suspension   The temporary expulsion of a student from school for one or more days for violating school rules and regulations. Most frequently used at middle schools and high schools, suspensions may be short-term (10 days or less), long-term (10 days to a full school year), indefinite (without any fixed term, ranging from one day to a year) and extracurricular (required attendance in classes, but deprived of the right to participate in nonacademic activities). Unlike the disciplinary nature of most suspensions, indefinite suspensions are usually used to remove a student from a situation deemed dangerous to the student or to other students.

Used routinely as the most severe form of discipline short of expulsion, suspensions were the center of a legal struggle in 1975 that sharply modified and curtailed their use. In the case of *Goss v. Lopez* (q.v.), the U.S. Supreme Court reaffirmed a lower court's affirmation of a public school student's constitutional right, under the Fourteenth Amendment (q.v.), to due process in school disciplinary actions. "Young people do not shed their rights at the schoolhouse door," wrote Justice Byron R. White for the majority, in the 5–4 decision. The case involved nine Columbus, Ohio, students suspended in 1971 during demonstrations arising from racial disorders. State law then permitted the school to suspend students summarily for up to 10 days without granting those students any recourse or appeal.

The lower court had held that suspended public school pupils had the right to notice of charges against them and an opportunity to defend themselves against such charges. In its decision, the Court added that pupils had an "entitlement" to education in states that guaranteed its residents free, primary and secondary education and that states "may not withdraw that right on grounds of misconduct, absent fundamentally fair procedures to determine whether the misconduct has occurred." It held that students "must be given some kind of notice and afforded some kind of hearing," albeit an informal one, before being suspended.

Suspension without a hearing deprived the students of their property (the statutory right to an education) and liberty (slurring their school records without proof). As a result of the decisions, most states now require an informal hearing for short-term, indefinite suspensions and extracurricular suspensions, and a formal hearing for long-term suspensions.

References: *Student Discipline and the Law,* Eugene Connors (1979); U.S. Supreme Court proceedings.

Sustained Silent Reading (SSR)

A program that originated in the 1960s to encourage interest in reading by designating a regularly scheduled time for everyone in a school to halt all other activities and read, uninterruptedly, in total silence, for a designated period of time. Adopted by many schools across the country and designed to encourage an improved adult, as well as student, attitude about reading as a leisure activity, SSR required everyone in the school—students, teachers, staff, administrators and custodians—to relax and read whatever materials they selected. No materials were assigned, although students could use assigned readings if they chose. To eliminate clock watching, timers and bells were used to signal the beginning and end of each reading period, which were often of indefinite (albeit realistic) length. SSR permitted no interruptions.

Reference: *The Individualized Reading Program: A Guide for Classroom Teaching,* Lyman C. Hunt (1967).

Suzuki Method

An approach to formal instrumental education of preschool children as young as three. Largely limited to violin and piano instruction, the method begins in infancy, with constant exposure of the child to recorded music and integration of music as an element of the family environment. At three, or thereabouts, formal lessons begin, with the child first learning technique and memorizing musical pieces. The student listens, learns and memorizes a melody by ear, then imitates the teacher's motions and gradually learns to play the piece. Developed by Japanese music educator Dr. Shi-nachi Suzuki, the Suzuki Method was originally designed for private violin lessons requiring the presence and constant participation of at least one parent, who learned the violin along with the child. Only after rote learning of a sizable repertoire of melodies is the youngster exposed to reading music.

The method did not gain widespread acceptance in the United States until 1964, when Dr. Suzuki and 10 of his Japanese students—many of them beginners—amazed a Music Educators National Conference with their skills. Since then, American music educators have adapted the method to piano instruction and to group instruction for both violin and piano. Ironically, the heart of the Suzuki Method—rote learning—was (and is) nothing new to music education. Generations of musically illiterate boys throughout the mountain regions of the South and West have learned to play an instrument by ear, many of them acquiring remarkable artistic skills without being able to read a note of music.

References: *Talent Education and Suzuki,* John Kendall (1966); *Contemporary Music Education,* Michael L. Mark (1978); *The Suzuki Violinist,* William Starr (1976).

Swann v. Charlotte-Mecklenburg Board of Education

A landmark U.S. Supreme Court decision in 1971 that required a North Carolina school board to bus students across district lines to achieve racial integration in public schools. The decision was one of four key Supreme Court decisions that followed passage of the Civil Rights Acts of 1957, 1960 and 1964 (q.v.), outlawing racial segregation in public facilities and translating into law the momentous 1954 High Court decision in *Brown v. Board of Education of Topeka* (q.v.). Although that decision had outlawed racial segregation in public schools, hundreds of southern school districts resisted and, indeed, evaded the spirit and often the letter of the law. Federal government grants of about $15 billion to southern school districts had coaxed some into compliance with the Court's order that desegregation take place "with all deliberate speed." Two surveys of southern schools in 1967 and 1968 by the U.S. Commission on Civil Rights, however, found that some districts were continuing to resist desegregation, while others used de facto segregation of school districts to perpetuate racial segregation by virtue of the racial composition of various neighborhoods.

It was the first of these reports, *Racial Isolation in the Public Schools*, that exposed vast de facto segregation of public schools in both north and south. It took four major legal cases, however, to enforce the *Brown* decision and the various federal civil rights acts. *Swann v. Charlotte-Mecklenburg Board of Education* was the last and, in a sense, the most sweeping decision, crushing the last vestiges of resistance to racial integration by outlawing de facto segregation of schools and forcing school districts to bus their children to other districts to achieve racial balance in schools.

In the previous three decisions, the Court had defined desegregation in clear terms and imposed time limits for school districts to desegregate. In *Green v. County School Board of New Kent County* (q.v.), in 1968, the Court outlawed a free-choice plan in New Kent County, Virginia, that gave students of each race the choice of where to attend schools. The Court ordered the district "to take whatever steps might be necessary to convert to a unitary system in which racial discrimination would be eliminated root and branch."

In *Alexander v. Holmes County Board of Education* the following year, the Court angrily defined "with all deliberate speed" as meaning "at once," ordering school districts in Mississippi "to terminate dual school systems" and "to operate new and hereafter only unitary schools." And in *United States v. Montgomery County Board of Education* the same year, the Court established racial ratios for teacher assignments in Alabama and numerical goals for pupil assignments. Together with *Swann*, the four decisions ended official resistance to desegregation by local school boards and political leaders.

By 1972, a year after *Swann*, 91.3% of all southern black pupils attended biracial schools, compared with only 76.4% in border states and 89.1% in the north and west.

References: *Racial Isolation in the Public Schools: A Report of the U.S. Commission on Civil Rights,* U.S. Government Printing Office (1967); *Twenty Years After Brown: A Report of the United States Commission on Civil Rights,* U.S. Government Printing Office (1977); U.S. Supreme Court proceedings; *The Burden of "Brown": Thirty Years of School Desegregation,* Raymond Wolters (1984).

Sweatt v. Painter A 1950 U.S. Supreme Court decision that refused to review its previous decision ordering the all-white University of Texas Law School to admit Herman Marion Sweatt, a Negro. The order was based on the failure of the state of Texas to provide "separate but equal" law school facilities for blacks—a failure that "deprived him [Sweatt] of equal protection of the laws guaranteed by the Fourteenth Amendment." In response to the Court's previous order in 1946, the state had opened a law school for negroes, but, the Court found, "the law school for negroes . . . had no independent faculty or library. The teaching was to be carried on by four members of the University of Texas Law School faculty . . . [and] the school lacked accreditation."

In contrast, the University of Texas law school for whites was staffed by a faculty of 16 full-time and three part-time professors. The library contained over 65,000 volumes. Among the other facilities available to the students were a law review, moot court facilities and scholarship funds. "We cannot conclude," the decision went on, "that the education offered petitioner is substantially equal to that which he would receive if admitted to the University of Texas law school." The Court concluded that "the Equal Protection Clause of the Fourteenth Amendment requires that petitioner be admitted to the University of Texas Law School."

The decision was remarkable in that it ordered racial integration of a particular educational institution without overturning the half-century-old *Plessy v. Ferguson* (q.v.) decision that upheld the constitutionality of "separate but equal" facilities for blacks and whites. What Sweatt said was that the racially separate law school facilities of the state of Texas were not "equal" and, therefore, were unconstitutional. It went a step further by stating that "the law school to which Texas is willing to admit petitioner excludes from its student body eighty-five per cent of the population of the State . . . With such a substantial . . . segment of society excluded, we cannot conclude that the education offered petitioner is substantially equal to that which he would receive if admitted to the University of Texas Law School."

Thus, for the first time the Court concluded that separate educational facilities, simply by virtue of racial separation, were inherently unequal. The decision marked a major shift in the foundation of court decisions that had upheld the constitutionality of racial segregation for more than five decades. In fact, *Sweatt,* along with three other cases—*Missouri ex rel. Gaines v. Canada* (1938), *Alston v. School Board of the City of Norfolk* (1940) (qq.v.) and *McLaurin v. Oklahoma State Regents* (1950)—was one of a carefully planned series of lawsuits filed by the National Association for the Advancement of Colored People to build a foundation of precedents that would lead to the momentous 1954 Supreme Court decision in *Brown v. Board of Education of Topeka* (q.v.), declaring racial segregation of schools unconstitutional and thus overturning *Plessy v. Ferguson.*

References: *Simple Justice: A History of "Brown v. Board of Education" and Black America's Struggle for Equality,* Richard Kluger (1975); U.S. Supreme Court proceedings.

Swett, John (1830–1913) American educator and "father" of public school education in California. Born and educated in New Hampshire, he graduated from a normal school and taught in district schools from 1847 to 1851, when he joined the California Gold Rush, sailing around Cape Horn. A year later, however, he

returned to teaching, becoming a school principal in San Francisco, where he served for nine years before becoming California state superintendent of public instruction in 1862. In that capacity and until 1867, he not only coaxed the legislature into establishing a tax base for supporting public schools, but also wrote the state's first workable school law, established a teacher-certification system with statewide examinations, and provided for uniform textbooks for all state schools. He also established the state teachers' association, and in 1863 helped found the *California Teacher,* the first professional journal for educators in the west. After ending his work at the state level, Swett served variously as a San Francisco school principal, deputy superintendent of San Francisco public schools, principal of the state teachers' college and San Francisco superintendent of public schools. He collaborated in writing several language-arts and geography textbooks and was author of a number of important books, including *History of the Public School System of California* (1876), *Methods of Teaching* (1880), *American Public Schools: History and Pedagogics* (1900) and *Public Education in California* (1911). An innovative teacher, Swett changed California schooling from "keeping school" to "teaching school."

References: BDAE; DAB; *John Swett, the Biography of an Educational Pioneer,* W. G. Carr (1933).

syllabication (syllabification) A method of teaching enunciation, spelling, reading and vocabulary skills by dividing a word into its constituent syllables. Derived from the Greek *syllambanein,* to gather together, a syllable is the next larger speech unit after a phoneme (q.v.) and always contains the sound of at least one vowel. There are two broad types of syllabication: phonic and structural, with the former referring solely to word sounds and the latter referring to word structure and the division of words by prefixes, roots and suffixes.

Until the development of acoustical phonetics in the late 19th century and the subsequent development of phonics, children in the

Western world almost universally learned to read with the use of a syllabarium. An appendix to the first speller, with its printed alphabet, the syllabarium provided an almost endless list of frequently used syllables in alphabetical order—all of which had to be committed to memory. The introduction of phonics—the "sounding" out of individual letters, letter combinations and whole words—ended the necessity of learning syllables by rote.

Reference: *Language Skills in Elementary Education,* Paul S. Anderson and Diane Lapp (1979).

syllabus A detailed description of an academic course, including the main topics to be covered, a week-by-week or even day-by-day schedule of subtopics, the required textbooks and readings, recommended readings and homework requirements.

Reference: ERIC.

Syms School The first school founded in England's southern colonies, in what is now Virginia. The first free school in the Americas (albeit not "public" in the modern sense), the school was the result of a bequest in 1635 from Benjamin Syms, a planter who left 200 acres of land and eight cows to produce income for a free school "to educate and teach the children of the adjoining parishes of Elizabeth City and Poquoson" (just north of present-day Hampton, near Chesapeake Bay). The schoolhouse was built in 1643 with the proceeds from eight years' crops and calves. The Syms bequest called for proceeds in subsequent years to be used to pay for the education of poor students. Aside from its importance as the first school in the area, the Syms School stood as a symbol of settler determination to remain permanently in what had been, until then, a highly inhospitable land. An Indian massacre in 1622 ended previous initiatives by the Virginia Company and English investors to establish such permanent institutions as schools, and the Syms school was the first effort by the settlers themselves to build a permanent settlement.

Reference: "The Syms and Eaton Schools and Their Successor," Helen Jones Campbell, *William and Mary* Quarterly (2d ser., XX: 1940).

synagogue A house of worship and communal center for Jews. Derived from the Greek word *synagoge,* meaning assembly, the earliest synagogues were indeed meeting places in Greek-controlled Israel during the first century B.C. Imitating the Greek custom of the era, the Israelites established synagogues not as places of worship but as meeting places for study and "for the reading of the Law and the teaching of the commandments," according to a 1st-century B.C. Greek inscription. In contrast, the Jerusalem Temple was the center for prayer, and it was only after its destruction in 70 A.D. that local synagogues began to house religious services. Synagogues remain centers of learning as well as prayer, with adjacent community centers used as sites for regular Sunday school sessions throughout the traditional American school year and for mid-week instruction for youngsters preparing for the Bar and Bat Mitzvah and confirmation rites. Touro Synagogue is the oldest synagogue in the United States, built in Newport, Rhode Island, in 1763.

Reference: EB.

syntax The rules of grammar that determine sentence structure, including the structures of constituent phrases and clauses, word order, word relations and word forms.

Reference: *Reading Instruction,* Barbara B. Stoodt (1989).

T

tachistoscope A mechanical device to improve a learning-disabled student's perception and reading speed by exposing single letters, words or phrases for limited periods of time.
References: *Corrective Reading,* Miles V. Zintz (1977).

tactile learning Any form of knowledge acquisition acquired primarily through touch. Widely used in teaching the sight and hearing impaired, tactile learning is essential for all students, from infancy well into adulthood. In infancy, tactile learning is essential for teaching the difference between temperatures and textures. "Touching zoos" that encourage children to touch animals teach children differences between species. For the visually handicapped, tactile reading with the Braille system opens the world of books and periodicals. The visually impaired often depend entirely on tactile learning to establish the facial characteristics, or "look," of those with whom they associate. For the hearing impaired, tactile learning is essential for learning to read lips by feeling the lips of the speaker, the mouth, facial and neck positions. Many reading teachers include tactile learning as an essential element of the multisensory approach to reading instruction. In addition to seeing, saying and hearing a new letter, the student is asked to trace the letter's shape on the paper while reading it aloud.
Reference: *Handbook of Reception: Feeling and Hurting,* Edward C. Carterette and Morton P. Friedman (1978).

talking book Originally, a recording of a book for the blind to play at home on turntables. With the advent of audiocasettes, thousands of books are now available on tape for easy listening by the sighted as well as visually impaired.

Reference. The Lighthouse, New York, New York.

talking typewriter A curious, short-lived device that spelled out in sound as well as type the letters that children punched on a keyboard. Designed to help them learn to read and write faster, with a minimum of effort, the device was one of many new "teaching machines" that were tried in American classrooms following the Soviet Union's leap into space ahead of the United States in 1957. The Sputnik satellite so embarrassed the American government and American educational establishment that hundreds of millions of dollars flowed from the government and private foundations to develop technologically advanced teaching machines that would impart knowledge more quickly. The talking typewriter was no more successful than many other devices of the era, and it was soon abandoned.
Reference: *High School,* Ernest L. Boyer (1983).

Talmud Torah school A Jewish educational institution of the late 19th and early 20th century for poor boys to attend after school or work, on afternoons and Sundays, to prepare for their Bar Mitzvahs. Devoted to study of the Talmud (law and commentary) and Torah (the Pentateuch, or first five books of the Old Testament), the two most sacred works of the Jewish religion, Talmud Torah schools were supported by contributions and membership fees. Talmud Torah schools were but one of a variety of Jewish educative institutions in the United States at the turn of the century. Jewish congregational schools met three or four times a week for children of synagogue members. Jewish charitable organizations, settlement houses and orphanages also operated institutional schools for Jewish children, while independent, entrepreneurial teachers operated private day schools called heders (cheders), or Hebrew schools. Together, the schools might have formed the basis of an extraordinary, independent religious school system, akin to the one Roman Catholics were building. By 1920, however, a wave of prosperity swept across the United States, and Jews fanned out across the nation, enrolling in secular public or private schools and relegating religious education to the home or synagogue.

References: *Zion in America: The Jewish Experience from Colonial Times to the Present,* Henry L. Feingold (1974); *American Judaism,* Nathan Glazer (1972).

Tappan, Henry Philip (1805–1881) Pioneer American educator who, as president of the University of Michigan, helped transform university education in the United States from a fixed curriculum to one that permitted students a choice of electives. Born in upstate New York, Tappan taught for two years before entering Union College, where he studied under the college president, Eliphalet Nott (q.v), one of the most progressive innovators in early 19th-century higher education. Nott had introduced medical studies, along with courses in agriculture, foreign languages and engineering—all of them practical innovations later adopted by almost all but the most elitist, private American colleges such as Harvard and Yale.

After studying for the ministry and becoming pastor of a Pittsfield, Massachusetts, Congregational church, Tappan returned to teaching in 1832—at the University of the City of New York (later, New York University). He retired to full-time writing in 1838, but was named first president of the University of Michigan in 1852. He stunned the world of education by organizing the school along German lines, providing a wide range of elective courses that permitted students to follow their own interests instead of being tied to a single, impractical, fixed classical curriculum. Science was raised to equal status with classical courses, and the number of courses in other disciplines was increased to make the university a truly comprehensive educational institution. Students were treated as adults, with freedom to enter and leave the campus as they pleased. Tappan's work drew nationwide attention, and, within a decade, universities across the United States were adding some elements of the Michigan model to their institutions. In 1863, Tappan was forced to resign after a bitter dispute with the regents over what they considered his overly liberal policies. A prolific writer on religious and philosophical topics, his one notable secular work was *Elements of Logic* (1944).

References: BDAE; *A Memorial Discourse on the Life and Services of the Reverend Henry Philip Tappan,* Henry S. Frieze (1882).

taxonomy A system of orderly scientific classification, with items classified from the simplest to the most complex or from lower-order to higher-order species. In education, University of Chicago psychology professor and educator Benjamin S. Bloom and his colleagues developed the first taxonomy for learning, dividing learning into three domains: cognitive, affective and psychomotor. Each domain was then divided into numerically coded classifications. Thus, the cognitive domain was subclassified and coded as follows: knowledge (1.00); comprehension (2.00); application (3.00); analysis (4.00); synthesis (5.00); and evaluation (6.00). Each class, in turn, was divided into coded subclasses, such as 2.10 for translation (within the 2.00 comprehension classification), 2.20 for interpretation (again, within the 2.00 comprehension classification). The purpose of such a breakdown was to pinpoint the goals of a class or institution and to use it as a foundation for rebuilding the curriculum to meet those goals.

References: *Taxonomy of Educational Objectives,* Benjamin S. Bloom et al., eds.

Taylor, Harold A. (1914–) Canadian-born educator whose 1971 criticism of American education helped provoke a bitter, nonproductive debate over the condition of American higher education. After earning his B.A. and M.A. at the University of Toronto and his Ph.D. at the University of London, he taught philosophy at the University of Wisconsin in Madison from 1939 to 1945. He was president of Sarah Lawrence College from 1945 to 1959, also serving on the faculty of the New School for Social Research from 1947 to 1949. A prolific author of books and essays that examined and criticized higher education, Taylor gained considerable notoriety in 1971 with his work *How to Change Colleges*. In it he charged:

> . . . what is wrong with the [American] university as a teaching institution is precisely this: It has no philosophy of learning, no unifying principle around which reforms can be made, either to meet the problems of student unrest or to engage the students in their own learning.
>
> It has instead a system of administrative conveniences. The whole apparatus of departments, divisions, institutes, lectures, research, grades, examinations, academic credits, classes and faculty appointments is based on an administrative plan for dealing with students and academic subject matter, not a philosophy.

References: BDAE: *On Education and Freedom* (1954) and *A University for the World: The United Nations Plan* (1975), Harold A. Taylor.

teacher   In the broadest sense, anyone who imparts information or knowledge to another. Parents are usually their children's earliest teachers. At two or even earlier, the role is shared somewhat with one or more part-time or full-time child-care aides, including relatives, babysitters, nannies or governesses. At four, preschool workers and peers assume teaching roles, until at five, in the kindergarten, the child encounters his or her first professionally trained teacher. Thereafter, trained teachers will dominate the instructional process through elementary and secondary school, college and graduate school, providing an ever increasing proportion—at times a dominant proportion—of the data and knowledge presented to the individual. In contrast, the parent's role as teacher will gradually diminish, while peer teaching influences will fluctuate widely, according to the individual student's own knowledge, personality, age and environment.

Professional teacher training and certification has varied widely over the centuries, with the first teachers in the Western world having been clergymen—exclusively Catholic until the Protestant Reformation. Ordination as a priest or minister was tantamount to certification as a teacher. Similarly, among Jews, the rabbi was the teacher of all school-aged children in the congregation.

The first certification, or licensing, of teachers in the Western world came with two pieces of Elizabethan legislation, the Act of Supremacy and the Act of Uniformity. Both gave the English monarch authority to appoint all churchmen and forced those who would teach to take an oath declaring the supremacy of the queen in all matters secular and religious. The laws mandated the rites and ceremonies of the Book of Common Prayer as the official liturgy of the Church of England. They ordered that "every parson, vicar, and curate shall upon every holy day, and every second Sunday in the year, hear and instruct all the youth of the parish for half an hour at the least before evening prayer, in the Ten Commandments, the Articles of the Belief, and in the Lord's Prayer, and diligently examine them, and teach them the catechism set forth in the book of public prayer."

The same laws applied to teachers in the American colonies, but the spread of the population into the wilderness necessitated more and more secular teaching, with the task joined by parents, itinerant teachers and older literate students. Many mothers organized so-called "dame schools" in their kitchens, where, for a fee, they instructed their own as well as their neighbors' children in reading, writing, calculating and Scripture.

Ministers, however, remained the primary teachers in most communities, gathering children of all ages into the church on Sundays and on some evenings when children were not working. Licensing of such ministers remained the purview of the church. In New Netherland, schoolmasters were appointed by the classis of Amsterdam. In 1664, the licensing of teachers passed over to the British governor, who relied on the archbishop of Canterbury for approval of all teachers. In 1683, the Virginia governor, under instruction from Charles II, ordered every schoolmaster teaching in the colony to obtain a license to teach, either from the bishop of London or from the governor himself. Three years later, the governor ordered schoolmasters to appear before the general court at Jamestown to present evidence of their intellectual competence, uprightness and sobriety, and general conformity to the doctrines of the Church of England—or face removal.

In the century that followed, population expansion required more teachers than the churches could supply. The result was a vast growth in secular schools, usually taught by devout laymen who laced their instruction with Protestant liturgy and prayer. By the late 1600s, many renowned secular teachers had founded their own schools and were earning modest salaries by making teaching a full-time profession. As control of the church over education waned, so did control over teacher licensing. By the middle of the 18th century, teachers had become an amorphous group whose members ranged from semiliterate itinerants, in isolated, rural one-room schoolhouses, to highly educated churchmen in cities such as Boston and New York. Bnt only Harvard, William and Mary, Yale and Princeton could boast traditional faculties, licensed by appropriate clerical authorities.

Formal teacher training did not begin in the United States until 1805, when New York City's Mayor (later, governor) De Witt Clinton organized a course of six to eight weeks to train teachers to work in the city's charity schools. In the early 1820s, Catherine Beecher and Emma Willard opened female seminaries to train women to become teachers. The first state-operated "teacher's college" in the United States to train teachers for public school education opened in Lexington, Massachusetts, in 1839, founded by Horace Mann (q.v.), the founder of public school education in Massachusetts.

Following the Civil War, an acute shortage of teachers forced the emergence of teacher training schools, or normal schools, as they were called. The equivalent of vocational secondary schools, the normal schools were largely established for girls, who were being trained to replace men in classrooms. Men had made up 90% of all teachers in the United States before the Civil War, but thousands died in battle, and those that returned were lured into higher paying jobs in industry. By 1888, 63% of all teachers were women, compared to fewer than 10% 50 years earlier.

As the scope of the teaching curriculum expanded, so did the scope of teacher training, which grew from two-year normal schools into four-year teachers colleges, granting bachelor's degrees in the arts, sciences and education. Later, the curriculum expanded into graduate studies, with the granting of master's degrees and doctorates in education. By the mid-1990s, there were just under 4 million teachers in the United States, with about 78% in elementary and secondary education and the rest in higher education. Projections for the year 2000 call for a total of just over 4 million teachers, with 83% expected to be in the public sector and 27% in the private sector. About 79% of all teachers are expected to be in elementary and secondary school teaching, with 21% in higher education. Within the elementary and secondary school sector of 3,179,000 teachers, 60% are expected to teach in elementary schools in the year 2000— 85% in public schools and 15% in private schools. Of the 40% expected to teach in secondary schools, more than 90% will be in public schools and just over 9.5% in private schools. At the higher-education level, nearly 70% of the projected 892,000 college and university teachers are expected to teach in public schools, with just over 30% in private colleges and universities.

Qualifications for teaching vary widely, with many of the finest private elementary and secondary schools and colleges requiring no state certification or even teaching experience. The most academically selective private schools and colleges tend to rely wholly on the prospective teacher's knowledge of the subject to be taught and on academic credentials. Public elementary and secondary schools in every state, however, require strict, though often undemanding, licensing procedures, many of which focus on knowledge of educational psychology and pedagogy rather than knowledge of the material to be taught. Many states do not require a degree in the subject in which the teacher plans to instruct. A 1983 study by the U.S. Department of Education found that half of the math, science and English teachers hired at the time were unqualified to teach those subjects. The study found that fewer than one-third of public school physics courses were taught by qualified teachers, and that 20% of all American public school teachers admitted having been assigned to teach subjects they were not qualified to teach.

In an effort to raise teaching standards, many states have stiffened teacher certification tests. During the early 1980s, virtually all applicants for teaching positions in public schools had finished in the bottom half of their classes at college, and certification tests did not challenge them to perform better. In 1987, however, a group of leading educators established a National Board for Professional Teaching Standards. Comparable to national certification boards in the medical and legal professions, the board's functions were to set high national standards, to hold extensive examinations and teacher evaluations, and to test teacher knowledge beyond the minimum standards set by state certification boards. The first such national certification tests took place at the end of 1994. The program was expected to help revolutionize teaching and teacher certification across the United States.

North Carolina was first to respond to the new tests by promising an automatic 4% salary increase (and fee reimbursements) to all teachers who earned their national certificates. Iowa, North Carolina, New Mexico, Oklahoma, Massachusetts and Ohio waived state certification requirements for nationally certified teachers. Universal acceptance of the national certification program was expected to raise national standards of teaching and help establish national educational standards in public schools. National certification was also expected to cut the high cost of administering public education by eliminating state bureaucracies in charge of the cumbersome state licensing procedures.

References: National Board for Professional Teaching Standards, Washington, D.C.; National Education Association, Washington, D.C.; *The American Teacher: Evolution of a Profession in a Democracy,* Willard S. Ellsbree (1970); *The American Teacher: 1776–1976,* Merle B. Marks (1976).

teacher associate A special teaching position proposed in 1983 in a school-reform scheme of Ernest L. Boyer, educational reformer and president of the Carnegie Foundation for the Advancement of Teaching. Under the scheme, teachers would complete five years of teachers' college and then pass written examinations in English proficiency and subject matter competence before receiving teaching credentials. These credentials, however, would qualify them only for the title of associate teacher. Although associate teachers would carry a full, conventional teaching load, they would work under the constant tutelage and supervision of experienced, specially trained mentors. Associate teachers would earn the title teacher after serving two years and passing review procedures conducted by the mentor, other school personnel and students.

Reference: *High School,* Ernest L. Boyer (1983).

teacher burnout A stress/fatigue syndrome that often leads to sleeplessness, moodiness, jumpiness, irritability and unprovoked anger toward students, colleagues and family members. Causes have been variously related to conflicting, multidirectional pressures (from children, parents, peers and administrators), excessive noninstructional chores, diminishing satisfaction and sheer boredom from spending so many hours isolated from adults and with demanding, immature people. Most public schools have no faculty lounges for teachers to gather together in adult company and share problems. Few secondary school teachers have permanent classrooms or even a desk, let alone private offices. Shortages of teaching materials also contribute to teacher frustration. In the last decades of the 20th century, the threat of violence has emerged as yet another factor leading to teacher burnout. More than one-fourth of teachers polled by the *New York Times* in the early 1980s said that they had been assaulted in the halls, parking lots or classrooms of their schools. The figure was one-third in New York City.

Still another factor in teacher burnout is the repetition of the same materials, year after year, with none of the excitement of moving to another area of a teacher's expertise. Burnout, however, is not limited to the teaching profession: Its emergence in many occupational fields during the 1980s and 1990s has made it so fashionable a syndrome that some psychologists are beginning to question its validity as a verifiable illness.

References: NYT; *Burnout in the Public Schools,* Gary Dworkin (1987); *Overcoming Executive Midlife Crisis,* Home R. Figler (1978).

teacher centers   Independent, educative organizations that provide teachers with in-service programs, conferences and other professional development opportunities in a nonthreatening environment away from their schools or colleges. Originally established in England as autonomous teacher-run centers for other teachers to turn to for professional help, their equivalents in the United States are federally funded and can only be 51% operated by teachers. Unlike English centers, American centers are open to administrators, parents, university professors, teacher's aides and even students, as well as teachers, with the goals of each center varying according to local needs.

References: *Teacher Centers and Inservice Education,* Harry H. Bell and John W. Peightel (1976); *Teachers' Centers,* Robert Thornbury, ed. (1974); National Education Association, Washington, D.C.; National Foundation for the Improvement of Education, Teacher Center Project, Washington, D.C.

teacher competency tests   A variety of examinations aimed, on the one hand, to test teacher teaching skills and, on the other, to determine the depth of teacher knowledge of the course he or she will teach. The first type of test asks teachers to demonstrate specific, predetermined teaching behaviors and responses considered essential to good teaching. The second battery simply measures knowledge and ability to use materials from the courses the teacher will teach. Both are elements of national teacher certification tests developed in 1994 by the National Board for Professional Teaching Standards.

References: *Competency-Based Teacher Education: Progress, Problems, and Prospects,* W. Robert Houston and Robert B. Howsaw (1972); National Board for Professional Teaching Standards, Washington, D.C.

Teacher Corps   A program started under the Higher Education Act of 1965 (q.v.), when shortages of qualified teachers were threatening the quality of public education across the United States. The Teacher Corps was created to underwrite the expansion of teacher training programs, enlarge the teacher pool in disadvantaged areas and encourage minority group members to enter teaching. Initially, the Teacher Corps underwrote programs that produced junior-level teaching interns who received two years of combined classroom and field training under the supervision of participating teacher training institutions. In 1974, however, the teacher shortage all but disappeared, and the Teacher Corps was converted into a retraining program for teachers on the job. With little direction and no legal authority to affect standards of education, the Teacher Corps was gradually phased out of existence in the 1980s. During its existence, it trained 11,000 interns and retrained 8,000 teachers at an average annual cost of $26 million.

Reference: *Teacher Corps Evaluation,* James P. Steffensen et al. (1978).

teacher education   The formal and informal instruction and training required for entry into the teaching profession. In almost all American states, a bachelor's degree is a minimum requirement for teaching in elementary and secondary schools and in some colleges. Colleges, however, usually require teachers to have a master's degree and, in many cases, a doctorate.

Public elementary and secondary schools require teachers to complete a minimum number of courses in the field of education, in addition to completing their work for a bachelor's degree. More simply, teachers may obtain a bachelor's degree in education, completing a four-year program of general education study, which includes teaching methods courses, field experiences, student teaching and so-called content courses involving in-depth study of specific courses the future teacher intends to instruct. In addition to a degree, teachers must pass examinations in each state to obtain a state teaching certificate or license to teach in public schools. A few states also require teaching certificates for private school teachers. In the mid-1990s, a new movement got under way to establish a national teaching certificate. More than 1,500 four-year colleges offer undergraduate and graduate degrees in some form of teacher education. Teacher education does not stop with the acquisition of a teacher certificate, however. In-service education, or continuing training in workshops, seminars, field activities and advanced coursework and degree programs, is generally required throughout a teacher's career—to acquire the latest teaching skills and qualify for salary increases and promotions to master teacher status.

Despite the complex requirements to obtain the right to teach in American public schools, the quality of students entering teaching has been notoriously low for decades. Indeed, the Carnegie Foundation for the Advancement of Teaching found that, in 1983, most public school teachers had graduated "from the lower half of their college classes," which they had entered with the lowest average SAT scores. Nor did any state require any minimum college grades or standardized test scores to teach a particular subject or run a school. Even more disturbing was the lack of any requirement that teachers have degrees in the subjects they taught. A U.S. Government study in 1983 found that half the math, science and English teachers hired at that time were not qualified to teach those subjects. Fewer than one-third of U.S. public high school physics courses were taught by qualified teachers, and 20% of American teachers admitted that they had been assigned to teach subjects they were not qualified to teach. By 1991, more than one-fourth of all newly hired teachers were not fully qualified for their jobs, according to the National Commission on Teaching and America's Future. As late as 1991, 15% of all public schools in the United States and 23% of all inner-city schools had vacancies they could not fill with qualified teachers.

Particularly at higher levels of instruction, most teachers have traditionally taught subjects they knew and enjoyed. It was not until the 17th and 18th centuries, as mass education began spreading across Western Europe and the American colonies, that society began demanding specific skills in instruction that required some formal training. In 1685, the French priest Jean Batiste de la Salle (later canonized) established the first formal teacher training school in Reims. Called the Institute of the Brothers of the Christian Schools, it was followed by a host of other church-sponsored teacher training schools in France and Germany. In almost all cases, teachers were taught that ignorance was the result of the devil and that infliction of pain was the most effective means of "beating the devil" out of children and allowing knowledge to seep into their minds. The first radical change in teacher education came in 1794, again in France, where the world's first government-sponsored teacher training school was built. Using the principles of Jean-Jacques Rousseau (q.v.) as a basis for training teachers, the school taught future teachers to concern themselves primarily with the mental and physical development of students and only secondarily with subject matter. The principle remains the basis of teacher education to this day.

Although the German-born teacher Christopher Dock (q.v.) published a volume on teacher training in 1770, it was not until 1839 that Horace Mann (q.v.) established the first formal training school for public school teachers in the Americas, in Lexington, Massachusetts, to staff the public school system he had founded in the state. By 1875, however, most state legislatures had passed laws establishing similar public school systems and teacher training schools to furnish them with instructors. Called "normal" schools (derived from the Latin *norma*, or standard), most were two-year programs designed to follow secondary school. As educators developed various theories of pedagogy, and psychology expanded to include various theories of learning, normal schools gradually expanded into four-year teachers' colleges. The arrival of John Dewey and other theoreticians into the field of pedagogy so expanded the study of education that it evolved into a broad field of specialties, including preschool education, elementary education, early adolescent and late adolescent education, special education, education of the severely handicapped, etc., with a wide variety of undergraduate- and graduate-level courses and degrees available in each area.

Although graduate-level courses were established in many specialized areas, no standards were ever set for educating teachers to teach such conventional courses as elementary, middle and high school mathematics, English, history, modern languages and science. In 1986, the Carnegie Corporation of New York drew up a sweeping plan for reforming education, calling for the elimination of undergraduate teacher-education programs and the forcing of future teachers to study the liberal arts and sciences as undergraduates in college—and then major in a particular subject in which they would gain the specialized knowledge needed to teach it. The foundation recommended that teacher education itself become a master's program, followed by internships and residencies such as those required of doctors. In 1991, educator John Goodlad (q.v.) implemented the foundation's recommendations by establishing eight pilot programs at graduate schools of education across the United States to train future teachers already equipped with bachelor's degrees in the arts or sciences, but not in education.

References: Center for Educational Renewal, University of Washington, Seattle, Washington; *Colleges of Education: Perspectives on Their Future,* Charles W. Case and William A. Matthes, eds. (1985); *A Place Called School,* John I. Goodlad (1984); *Critical Studies in Teacher Education: Its Folklore, Theory and Practice,* Thomas S. Poppewitz, ed. (1987).

teacher evaluation Any of a variety of formal and informal programs for assessing the competence and effectiveness of an instructor. Designed to improve instruction as well as to rid schools of incompetent teachers, teacher evaluations usually depend on one or more of six approaches. Formal, written ratings by students are commonly used to evaluate teachers at many colleges. Though not ignored at the primary and secondary school level, student opinions about teachers are seldom solicited, although universal likes or dislikes eventually filter through any school system to the administration. A more common evaluation system in elementary and secondary schools is classroom observations by principals, teacher supervisors, outside teacher consultants or teaching peers. Another widely used form of teacher evaluation is so-called product evaluation, whereby year-to-year student-achievement test results and other measurements of student academic growth are compared to those of similar students under the guidance of other teachers. A fourth type of teacher evaluation is based on self-evaluative forms filled out by teachers themselves, while a fifth type of teacher evaluation relies almost entirely on objective observation instruments. The Flanders Interaction Analysis System (q.v.), for example, relies on recording selected classroom events such as teacher activities and pupil responses.

Although evaluation procedures vary widely from school to school, almost all attempt to objectify procedures by providing printed criteria listing desirable teacher competencies and student behavior and responses, along with printed forms for noting appropriate classroom observations. Teachers usually receive one written evaluation each year, and they are usually able to provide a written rebuttal or file grievances against what they consider to be inappropriate evaluations.

Reference: *The Teacher Evaluation Handbook,* Renfro C. Manning (1988).

teacher noninstructional chores A variety of paid and unpaid activities, unrelated to teaching, that are arbitrarily assigned to teachers. A source of bitterness between teachers and administrators, noninstructional chores vary from school to school, depending on school budgets. Among such chores are monitoring of halls and lunchrooms; chaperoning and supervising student extracurricular activities; coaching sports; driving buses and vans on various class and school trips; filing reports and other paperwork on absent and tardy students and on student academic progress; verifying student identification cards, checking passes and excuses; and counseling students. With the average student to guidance counselor ratio in American public high schools at more than 300:1, students invariably turn to their favorite teachers for counsel. Depending on the school, noninstructional activities can consume as much as 20% of the time teachers spend on campus.

Reference: *High School,* Ernest L. Boyer (1983).

teacher recognition and rewards Any of a variety of forms of recompense for instructional achievement. Most teacher recognition and rewards are either extrinsic, ancillary or psychological, with the first usually in the form of earnings, special awards, status and authority. Ancillary rewards usually include job security, spare time, convenient schedules, freedom from rivalries and pleasant working conditions. Psychic rewards come from job satisfaction and the pleasure of reaching students and success in helping them learn. Although more than 86% of American public school teachers responded to a 1982 survey by the Carnegie Foundation for the Advancement of Learning that psychic rewards were the most important of the three types, more than 73% reported that "student attitudes toward learning had a negative effect on their job satisfaction" and that many students "don't like to study anymore," "aren't interested in learning" and "don't seem to care about school." Others reported "subtle disrespect many adults have for teachers" as another source of dissatisfaction with their work.

References: *High School,* Ernest L. Boyer (1983); *Schoolteacher,* Dan Lortie (1975).

teacher's aide A paraprofessional school worker, usually assigned to one or more teachers to perform noninstructional duties such as clerical work or supervision of students who have been isolated in quiet areas to do their work. The first teacher's aide was introduced into Bay City, Michigan, schools in 1953, to ease the nonteaching burdens of teachers in overcrowded classrooms. The teacher's aide movement subsequently spread to schools with similar problems across the United States. As their numbers and responsibilities increased, community colleges began offering formal training and associate degrees in the new field. Today, responsibilities of teacher's aides in many schools have extended into tutoring, especially with bilingual children. **Reference:** *Paraprofessionals in Education Today,* Alan Gartner et al., eds. (1977).

teacher salaries The wages paid to instructors in elementary and secondary schools and institutions of higher education. Historically, a survey of actual dollar figures is relatively meaningless because of the constant inflation that has lowered the real purchasing power of the U.S. dollar. In current dollars, for example, the average annual salary of teachers in public elementary and secondary schools climbed more than 300% from about $8,600 in the 1969–1970 school year to about $36,000 in the 1993–1994 school year. In constant dollars based on purchasing power, however, the climb was only 7.7%, from the equivalent of $33,389 to $35,958. In other words, the $8,600 a teacher earned in 1969–1970 bought what $33,389 would have bought 25 years later. From another perspective, the $8,600 a teacher earned in 1969–1970 compared to an average annual wage of $6,100 for production workers, while the average annual teacher wage in 1993–1994 of $36,000 compared to an average annual wage of $19,300 for production workers that year.

Private school teachers earned 35% less than public school teachers, but they worked a shorter school year and faced less classroom stress because private school admissions selectivity minimizes the number of unstable students. Women teachers earned nearly 16% less than men in public schools and more than 26% less than men in private schools, but the differential was largely due to there being more women than men in lower-paying, elementary school jobs and more men than women in higher-paying, high school jobs. High school teaching jobs pay 11% more than elementary school jobs in public schools and 28% more in private schools. In general, teachers younger than 30 years old earn about 26% less than the average professianal wage for their age bracket. Teachers 30 to 40 years old earn about 10% less than the professional average, but see their wages reach 7.5% above the average when they reach the 40-to-49-year-old age range and 15% above the average when they reach 50.

Teacher salaries vary widely from state to state, with Connecticut public school teacher salaries 38% above and Mississippi teacher salaries 30.4% below the national average during the 1992–1993 school year. In the 1993–1994 school year, the 10 states that paid the highest teacher salaries were Connecticut ($50,389), Alaska ($47,902), New York ($45,772), New Jersey ($45,550), Michigan ($45,218), the District of Columbia ($43,014), Pennsylvania ($42,411), California ($40,636), Maryland ($39,475) and Illinois ($39,416).

Here, according to the National Education Association, are the percentage differences from the national average in each state in the 1992–1993 school year:

Alabama	−23.0%
Alaska	31.4
Arizona	10.5
Arkansas	−21.7
California	14.3
Colorado	4.2
Connecticut	38.0
Delaware	3.4
D.C.	10.5
Florida	−11.0
Georgia	−14.2
Hawaii	4.1
Idaho	−22.8
Illinois	10.3
Indiana	0.0
Iowa	−14.0
Kansas	−6.2
Kentucky	−11.1
Louisiana	−21.2
Maine	−13.6
Maryland	10.6
Massachusetts	9.1
Michigan	24.5

Minnesota	0.2%
Mississippi	− 30.4
Missouri	− 16.1
Montana	− 21.2
Nebraska	− 17.9
Nevada	− 2.6
New Hampshire	− 3.1
New Jersey	21.9
New Mexico	− 24.3
New York	28.5
North Carolina	− 16.3
North Dakota	− 28.0
Ohio	− 1.5
Oklahoma	− 26.0
Oregon	2.4
Pennsylvania	17.7
Rhode Island	8.3
South Carolina	− 16.6
South Dakota	− 30.7
Tennessee	− 17.3
Texas	− 14.5
Utah	− 22.2
Vermont	− 0.6
Virginia	− 7.8
Washington	2.1
Wisconsin	− 13.5
Wyoming	− 14.1

On a global scale, average salaries of American public school teachers ($36,000) ranked with British school teachers as sixth best in the world in the early 1990s, behind Switzerland ($80,000), Hong Kong ($58,000), Ottawa, Canada ($47,000), Japan and the Netherlands ($45,000 each) and Germany ($43,000). Compared to other professions in the United States, teacher salaries of $38,000 a year averaged more than those of armed services personnel ($24,000) and computer operators ($30,000), but behind accountants ($45,000), scientists, architects, surveyors and engineers (all $48,000), lawyers and judges ($82,000) and doctors and other health diagnosis professionals ($92,000).

In higher education, the average salary for all teachers was just under $44,000 in the early 1990s, or about 22% higher than the average salary for elementary and secondary school teachers. Within the college-university framework, average teacher salaries at all public institutions—both two-year and four-year—were about 0.5% below the national average for all college teachers, while average salaries at private institutions were about 1.2% above the national average. In general, salaries at all public colleges, both two-year and four-year, were higher than those at private colleges. Salaries at public four-year colleges were 4.1% above the national average for all colleges, while average teacher salaries at private four-year colleges were only 2.1% above the national average. Salaries at public two-year colleges were 11.2% below the national average for all college teachers, while salaries at private two-year colleges were 43.5% below the national average. Within the professorial ranks, professors at public four-year colleges earned 44.7% more than the national average for all college teachers, while professors at private colleges earned 72.3% more. Associate professors at public four-year colleges earned 0.2% less than the national average for all college teachers, and assistant professors earned 11.3% less. Associate professors at private colleges earned 17.8% above the national average for all college teachers, and assistant professors earned 0.4% less than the national average.
Reference: DES.

teachers' institutes Intensive, multi-day or week-long training programs for teachers. Usually limited to lectures or seminars on specific topics such as mathematics or reading instruction, teachers' institutes originated in the early 19th century as a form of teacher training prior to the establishment of teachers' colleges. Henry Barnard (q.v.) organized the first such institute in Hartford, Connecticut, in 1839, and their use as training vehicles spread across the United States. By the early 20th century, state and county school superintendents scheduled training institutes on a regular basis, requiring all public school teachers to attend training programs dealing with their specialties. Especially useful for teachers in rural schools, institutes provided an efficient, inexpensive substitute for in-service training and continuing education at distant teachers' colleges.

Reference: *Public Education in the United States: A Study and Interpretation of American Educational History,* Edward P. Cubberly (1962).

teacher strikes Short- or long-term work stoppages by the instructional staff at a school or college, often resulting in the closing of the institution and cessation of educational services. Elementary and secondary public schools whose teachers are unionized are the targets of almost all teacher strikes. Like strikes by other public employees, teacher strikes are illegal in almost all states, and school boards have a variety of remedies for forcing teachers back into their classrooms. These include court-imposed fines levied against a union and its leaders and the jailing of union leaders. The ill-will created by imprisonment of professionals has made most school boards reluctant to resort to such tactics, with the net result that the more militant union locals—usually in major cities such as New York or Chicago—often strike with impunity when their contracts expire.

Reference: *Understanding Collective Bargaining in Education: Negotiations, Contracts and Disputes Between Teachers and Boards,* Robert C. O'Reilly (1978).

teacher turnover The ratio of new teachers hired to those departing from a school or college staff. Teacher turnover rates usually reflect teacher satisfaction or dissatisfaction with their working conditions at a given institution and often hint at the quality of education at that institution. Although low teacher turnover can be an indication of relative stability in the life of an institution, it can also be an indication of curricular and pedagogic stagnation. On the other hand, high teacher turnover invariably produces institutional instability and a decline in educational quality. In addition to dissatisfaction

with working conditions, teacher turnover can result from the same factors—such as retirement, illness, death, better job offers and desire or need to obtain additional professional training or education—that produce turnover in any industry. In general, academically successful schools have faculties composed one-third of teachers with one to five years' service, one-third with five to 10 years' service and one-third 10 years' or more service, with turnover rates of 5% or less.

Reference: National Education Association, Washington, D.C.

teacher unions Labor organizations made up of teachers and other school staff members that engage in collective bargaining with school boards and boards of trustees. There are three major teacher unions, all of them national: the American Federation of Teachers, with about 850,000 members; the National Education Association, with about 2 million members; and the American Association of University Professors, with 43,000 members at 900 public and private two-year and four-year colleges. Neither NEA nor AAUP are labor unions in the strictest sense. While AFT began in 1971 as an entity within the huge American Federation of Labor, NEA and AAUP began as professional organizations and remain so to this day. Local chapters of each organization, however, began assuming collective bargaining responsibilities for their members in the 1950s. Their bargaining powers are somewhat limited because of laws in most states that ban strikes by public employees, including teachers at public schools and colleges. In general, all three organizations represent teachers in negotiating salaries, fringe benefits and working conditions. The bargaining goals of AAUP chapters, however, are more far-reaching in that they include many of the loftier aims of the national organization, namely, guarantees of academic freedom and shared governance with the administration and trustees over major college and university policies. About half the AAUP act as collective bargaining agents.

Because of costly competition for members and bargaining rights, and the recognition that they had many common goals, the AFT and NEA began merger talks in the mid-1970s and again in the mid-1990s, but merger at the national level seemed unlikely. On the other hand, there was evidence that local and state affiliates were drawing closer to each other and that they might form local working partnerships while maintaining their affiliation to their national organizations.

(See also AMERICAN ASSOCIATION OF UNIVERSITY PROFESSORS; AMERICAN FEDERATION OF TEACHERS; and NATIONAL EDUCATION ASSOCIATION.)

References: American Association of University Professors, Washington, D.C.; American Federation of Teachers, Washington, D.C.; National Education Association, Washington, D.C.

teacher warranty program A teacher-support system offered by various colleges of education to help ensure the success of their graduates during their first year as probationary teachers. In effect, warranty programs assure employer school districts that the new, inexperienced teachers they hire out of teachers' colleges will have such professional support services as telephone consultations, on-site evaluation and remediation and special workshops that many schools cannot afford to provide. Started in Nebraska in 1984, the teacher warranty program is especially effective in poorer, rural school districts that cannot afford master teachers to serve as mentors for inexperienced, first-year teachers.

Reference: ERIC.

teaching assistant (TA) In higher education, a graduate student hired as a part-time aide to a full-time professor and charged with a range of instructional duties that vary from course to course. These duties might include directing laboratory sections of science courses, leading small discussion groups following professorial addresses in lecture courses, grading student papers and, in recent years, teaching freshman- and sophomore-level courses. Paid a minimum stipend that seldom covers the cost of their own tuition, TAs have been at the center of controversy in the 1980s and 1990s at major, private eastern universities such as Yale and Harvard, which expanded the use of TAs to cut escalating salary costs in professorial ranks. In the meantime, students were charged between $25,000 and $30,000 a year for tuition, room and board, only to be taught by inexperienced TAs not much older than themselves.

Reference: *A Student's Guide to College Admissions,* Harlow G. Unger (1995).

teaching load A vague term, variously used to refer either to the total number of "contact hours" a teacher spends in the classroom or to the total amount of time a teacher spends in all school-related activities, including preparation, student counseling, grading papers and tests, and noninstructional chores such as lunchroom or bus duty and committee meetings. Regardless of which definition is used, the term remains somewhat meaningless because of the wide variations in teaching conditions, including the number of students in each class, the types of courses taught (for example, laboratory or non-laboratory) and the types of students enrolled in those courses.

Reference: *Introduction to Educational Administration,* Roald F. Campbell et al. (1977).

teaching machine Any of a wide variety of mechanical, electric and electronic equipment for displaying programmed instruction (q.v.) for self-teaching. Unlike audiovisual equipment, teaching machines are designed for (and operated by) the individual student rather than student groups. Moreover, they present data at a speed adjusted to the student's own pace of learning. They also require student responses and, in turn, provide the student with immediate feedback about the accuracy of the responses. Hand-operated mechanical devices when they first appeared in the 1920s, teaching machines are now standard computers designed to operate a variety of learning programs for the full range of academic courses.

(See also COMPUTER-ASSISTED INSTRUCTION.)

References: ERIC; *A Handbook of Computer-Based Training,* Christopher Dean and Quenton Whitlock (1988).

teaching method Any of a variety of systematic instructional techniques that can be applied to a broad range of academic subjects. The most common teaching methods are the lecture method, the Socratic or discussion method, the tutorial method and computer-assisted instruction (qq.v.). Although all have extensive application, there is no consensus on the advantages of one method over another. Effectiveness varies according to factors that include class size, student abilities and teacher skills.
Reference: ERIC.

teaching the test A colloquialism for a teacher's tendency to focus instruction on preparing students for standardized tests rather than on imparting a broad, in-depth understanding of the subject. Indeed, commercial test-preparation companies do nothing but "teach the test" in preparing students for such examinations as the College Board's Scholastic Assessment Tests and various graduate school entrance examinations. Teaching the test in conventional schools begins as early as first grade where annual student achievement tests are required, either by the school or by state law. Student performance on such tests is often used to evaluate individual teacher performance, thus contributing to the tendency of some teachers to teach the test rather than the subject. In addition to focusing instruction on specific topics most often covered by such tests, teaching the test also includes instruction in test-taking skills, such as whether and how to guess on multiple-choice questions, quick estimation techniques and question-hopping to score as heavily and as quickly as possible on those questions whose answers the student knows immediately.

Reference: *Making the Best of Schools,* Jeannie Oakes and Martin Lipton (1990).

team teaching Any of several forms of classroom instruction involving two or more teachers with complementary instructional responsibilities that depend on different sets of teacher skills. Team teaching at the middle school or high school level generally refers to faculty coordination of course curricula and lesson plans for a particular grade, to assure strong, interdisciplinary instruction with materials studied in each course related to materials in every other course. Eighth grade students might, for example, begin the academic year studying ancient Egypt in history class, the geometry of cubes and pyramids in mathematics, the problems of mass and leverage (using pyramid construction) in physics class, hieroglyphics and the history of art or languages in art class or language arts class.

In elementary school instruction, where a single generalist instructs a class in a variety of subjects throughout the day, team teaching generally refers to a form of dual instruction. The lead teacher in such programs generally handles conventional academics, while a specialist works with individual students or small groups on related special projects in a separate area of the classroom. Projects may range from specialized academic instruction to remedial instruction, depending on student needs.
Reference: *Team Teaching: Organization and Administration,* Leslie J. Chamberlain (1969).

technical college (technical institute) A post-secondary institution offering courses and training in a variety of non-academic, vocational skills. Often operated as entrepreneurial, profit-making schools, technical colleges usually offer no liberal arts or science courses and are colleges only in the sense that they serve a post-high school student population. Educational programs at technical colleges range from short-term instruction in clerical skills to complex, multi-year instruction in various crafts, production skills and semiprofessional technologies such as

computer programming, electronics and instrumentation.
Reference: ERIC.

tech-prep program An approach to vocational education that links the last two years of high school to continuing, post-secondary vocational instruction or training at a community college, technical institute or industrial or business facility. Usually a comprehensive four-year curriculum, tech-prep programs are most often organized by faculty or training aides at the post-secondary facility, with the cooperation and participation of a high school's own instructors. Because it is a comprehensive continuing program linked to post-secondary training or education, high school seniors must work seriously and assiduously throughout their senior year or risk failing the entire program. In addition to the link with post-secondary education, tech-prep programs differ from traditional vocational education in that they require students to focus entirely on nonvocational academics and acquire the same academic skills as college-bound students during their first two years of high school. Tech-prep students begin vocational training in their junior year with the same reading and comprehension skills, analytical skills, computer literacy, problem-solving and decision-making skills, and human relations and communications skills as students in the academic track.

(See also TWO-PLUS-TWO PROGRAM.)

References: *But What If I Don't Want to Go to College,* Harlow G. Unger (1992).

teenage pregnancy In education, a growing social problem that disrupts the educational routine of classmates as well as pregnant students. Although the vast majority of pregnant teenagers are forced to take voluntary leaves of absence or drop out of school, many schools automatically suspend or expel pregnant girls. Others segregate their pregnant girls into separate classrooms, while some school districts send pregnant teenagers to alternative schools to attend special classes for dysfunctional students. In 1991, the Centers for Disease Control reported 62.1 births for every 1,000 females aged 15 to 19. There were no national teenage pregnancy rates that include births and abortions, because of the refusal of 10 states to report abortions. Among the states that did release such figures, Georgia had the highest teenage pregnancy rate, with 110.6 pregnancies per 1,000 teenagers in 1990, followed by Nevada with 107.4 and North Carolina with 105.8. The lowest was North Dakota, with 56.4 pregnancies per 1,000.

Reference: Centers for Disease Control, Atlanta, Georgia.

telelecture Live instruction delivered to television monitors at remote locations via telephone or cable lines. Called teleconferencing in the business and financial world, telelectures permit two-way audiovisual communication between lecturer and students, with questioners seen and heard by all participants in the telelecture. Telelectures have proved particularly useful (and economical) for simultaneous, specialized instruction of small groups of students at remote, rural schools, which individually might not have enough students to warrant the cost of a teacher in a specific course—a foreign language, for example. At the university level, telelectures often result in significant savings by permitting guest lecturers from one university to address student audiences at other campuses without incurring any travel time, extra lecture time or other costs.

Reference: American Teleconferencing, New York, New York.

television The transmission over wires or through space of sound and images. Invented in the 1920s by scientists at General Electric Co., Westinghouse Electric Corp. and elsewhere, television technology was not converted into a commercial medium until April 10, 1939, when Radio Corporation of America broadcast a speech by President Franklin D. Roosevelt at the opening of the New York World's Fair. RCA's

National Broadcasting Co. subsidiary began broadcasting daily programs in New York, and Columbia Broadcasting Corp. and Dumont Corp. soon followed suit. World War II, however, postponed development of the medium until 1945. The number of stations grew dramatically—from 30 at the end of 1946 to 104 by 1950 and nearly 600 a decade later. The number of households with television sets mushroomed from 8,000 in 1946 to 5 million in 1950 and nearly 46 million, or 80% of American households, in 1960. By 1995, 98% of American households had at least one television set, and 64% had two or more sets.

From its beginnings, television programming combined many of the most effective techniques of radio, cinema, stage, circus, newspapers, magazines and aggressive salesmanship to produce the most influential medium and educative institution during the second half of the 20th century, surpassing even formal schools and colleges in its educative reach and influence. Offering the greatest variety of educative materials and entertainment of any medium in history, it carried both on-the-scene and after-the-fact news to audiences of unprecedented size, reaching an estimated 600 million for the live telecast of Neil A. Armstrong and Edwin Aldrin Jr. stepping from their space vehicle onto the surface of the moon in 1969.

Both commercial and educational television were often brilliant in fulfilling their obligation to serve the public interest. They educated and informed millions who had never had and would never have had access to documentaries, theater, concerts, opera, movies and dazzling variety shows. Television reached the illiterate, the homebound, the newly arrived immigrant and most especially the poor. Television taught disenfranchised Americans their constitutional rights and was in part responsible for the success of the civil rights movement that ended school segregation and assured millions of African Americans of the right to vote. Battlefield television news reports were a major factor in changing public perception about and attitude toward the war in Vietnam.

But television has also been responsible for much miseducation by filling home screens with a ceaseless barrage of commercials, violence and mindless entertainment. Targeting impressionable children as well as adults, commercials portray junk food as nutritious, junk toys as educational and garish vehicles as necessities. Television soap operas and prime-time dramas portray vulgar and violent behavior as justifiable, parents and the elderly as stupid, silly and helpless, uninhibited sexual activity as a healthy norm, semi-literate sports participants as "scholar-athletes," and criminal entertainers as beloved icons. Newton D. Minow called commercial television programming a "vast wasteland" in 1961, when he was chairman of the Federal Communications Commission, in charge of regulating licensing procedures but with no power to control programming. More than two decades later, Lawrence A. Cremin, president of Teachers College Columbia University, charged that television "was failing to inform, educate, and entertain the public at the highest levels of quality and . . . was proffering an indefensible potpourri of violence, escapism, and pap that moved the young to aggressive behavior and their parents to intellectual and moral somnolence."

Similar criticisms have been leveled, at one time or another, at virtually every other public medium, including magazines, newspapers and radio, and at producers of film, concert, stage and other productions. Unfortunately, the growth of the influence of television has been accompanied by a dramatic growth in juvenile crime and other dysfunctional student behavior in the United States, along with a perceived decline in the influence of schools on American children. As a vague, faceless institution, television has proved an easy scapegoat for parents, teachers and political and civic leaders to use to deny any responsibility for the problems of young Americans.

(See also CORPORATION FOR PUBLIC BROADCASTING; EDUCATIONAL TELEVISION.)

References: *Tube of Plenty: The Evolution of American Television,* Erik Barnouw (1975); *The Age of Television: A Study of Viewing Habits and the Impact of Television on American Life,* Leo Bogart (1972); *American Education: The Metropolitan Experience, 1876–1980,* Lawrence A. Cremin (1987); *Equal Time: The Private Broadcaster and the Public Interest,* Newton Minow (1964).

Tennessee The 16th state to join the Union, in 1796. A sparsely settled frontier state, Tennessee had an agricultural economy until the mid-20th century. Although the state's first colleges, the University of Tennessee at Knoxville and Tusculum College at Greeneville, were founded in 1794, the state did not establish a public school system until a century later, in 1873. It now has about 1,500 public elementary and secondary schools, with a total enrollment of more than 800,000, but a level of educational quality that ranks among the lowest in the United States. The state has 10 four-year and 14 two-year public institutions of higher education. It has 42 four-year and 21 two-year private colleges. The private colleges, including several historically black institutions, including Fisk University, graduate one-third of all college graduates in Tennessee. Among other notable private institutions are Vanderbilt University, in Nashville, and University of the South, in Sewanee.

References: CHE; DES.

Tenth Amendment That section of the Constitution that effectively vests control over education inter alia to the states. The amendment, the last of those grouped as "The Bill of Rights," is short and to the point: "The powers not delegated to the United States by the constitution, nor prohibited by it to the states, are reserved to the states respectively, or to the people." A handful of American leaders—notably John Adams, Thomas Jefferson, James Madison, Benjamin Franklin and Benjamin

Rush (qq.v.)—had urged the Constitutional Convention of 1787 to make universal public education a constitutional right of all Americans. Their appeal was rejected by representatives of the powerful textile lobby, whose cotton and cotton goods provided one of the economic mainstays of the new republic. The northern cotton mill owners depended on child labor to keep wages down, while southern plantation owners depended on slave labor, including children, to pick the cotton that fed northern mills. Both feared that universal public education would force children out of the mills and fields and into classrooms and create labor shortages that would drive wages up. In addition, southerners feared that universal public education would also mean educating black children and would lead to manumission.

References: *The Constitution of the United States,* Floyd G. Cullop (1984).

tenure A status granted to teachers protecting them from dismissal for other than contractually specified reasons. These are usually limited to "cause" (incompetency, immorality, criminal acts or inappropriate conduct) or unforeseen and unavoidable upheavals in the workplace (a lack of students for a particular subject or staffing reductions because of a consolidation of schools). Tenure (derived from the Latin verb *tenere,* to hold) was first granted to American public elementary and secondary school teachers in Massachusetts in 1886. It was designed to protect them against unjust dismissal and undue influence and control by political and religious groups and other noneducational interests. At the time, Massachusetts public schools had become a battleground between fundamentalist Christian groups that held Protestantization to be essential to the Americanization of the immigrant children then crowding American public schools. By granting tenure to public school teachers, the state legislature sought to ensure the secularization of public education. Most states subsequently granted their public school teachers tenure status, usually after a three-year probationary period, during which teacher contracts are renewed on a year-to-year basis, with no cause needed for nonrenewal. Tenure is often granted, as well, to nonteaching public school personnel, such as coaches, guidance counselors, assistant principals and principals.

Most public and private colleges and universities also grant tenure, usually after three to seven years. Tenure is seldom granted to nonteaching personnel, such as college presidents, who serve at the pleasure of the board of trustees, or to assistant presidents, deans of admission and coaches, who are hired by and serve at the pleasure of the college president. At the higher education level, tenure dates back to the Middle Ages, when European universities were run by consortia of scholars, comparable to the partnerships that run modern law firms. When admitted to such a group, a scholar was granted membership for life. United States higher education did not adopt tenure until the late 19th century, when Harvard sought to upgrade its instruction by replacing itinerant tutors with full-time professors. To lure two distinguished European professors to Harvard, the college offered them life positions rather than the three-year contracts that had hitherto been common.

Now a ubiquitous part of campus life, tenure at the higher education level has come under increasing attack in the closing decades of the 20th century, as the cost of undergraduate education has soared to $30,000 a year at the most prestigious private universities. In general, tenure is granted in two ways: as a reward to junior faculty who have successfully worked at a college for five to 10 years; and as a means of luring an outside faculty member whose fame and work will bring prestige to the university. Defenders of tenure claim that it gives professors ultimate academic freedom to express minority views and pursue independent research without fear of reprisal or dismissal and that it entices scholars to forgo higher monetary rewards in private industry in favor of a campus life. Opponents of tenure respond by pointing out that

academic freedom in the United States is protected by the constitutional right to free speech and also by the Fourteenth Amendment guarantee of due process, which protects professors against summary dismissal for expressing dissenting views.

Tenure proponents have become a diminishing minority since the passage of federal and state laws prohibiting mandatory retirement solely on the basis of age. Such laws all but guarantee that tenured professors may continue working long after they are no longer productive and when they may actually have begun to hurt academic quality by blocking the entry of younger replacements. The result "is the fossilization of any given department," according to Chester Finn, an assistant secretary of education in the Reagan administration and later a tenured professor of education at Vanderbilt University. "You end up with people who haven't had an idea in 15 years. There is no room for energetic, fresh thinkers." Moreover, the freedom that tenure grants on campus, say critics, allows tenured professors to ignore teaching responsibilities in favor of research that will produce fame and royalty-producing books. Students complain that they never have access to tenured "superstars," whose salaries are underwritten by the very students being ignored.

Several studies support such contentions. The Carnegie Foundation for the Advancement of Teaching found that the average college teacher spent only 9.8 to 10.5 hours in class with students in the early 1990s, and this figure was inflated by the schedules of community college teachers who spent 15 to 16 hours a week in classrooms. At four-year colleges and universities, many faculty members have two or three days when they never enter the classroom. Most faculty said they spend only an hour a week preparing for each hour of teaching. In all, they acknowledged spending a total of only 20 hours a week on instruction and preparation, often using the same notes for several years. About 90% of faculty said they gave no more than eight hours a week to counseling students or attending meetings, and more than half gave less than four hours a week to those tasks. Even more damning, almost half the full-time faculties admitted spending no more than four hours a week on research and scholarly writing, which is usually used as their excuse for not doing more teaching. Moreover, 45% of the entire professorial profession had not had any professional writing accepted or published during the previous two years.

A growing number of universities are responding to abuses of the tenure system by reducing the amount of tenure they grant and, instead, extending probationary periods for junior faculty and increasing the use of visiting lecturers, part-time or adjunct instructors and professors, and offering full-time professors limited-year, renewable contracts of five or 10 years. Some newer colleges have begun their existence by never offering tenure. About 64% of American university professors are tenured—a figure that has remained stable for the last decade and one that only attrition will gradually reduce. In the meantime, colleges have increased the number of part-time professors from 230,000 to 300,000.

References: American Association of University Professors, Washington, D.C.; American Federation of Teachers, Washington, D.C.; Carnegie Foundation for the Advancement of Teaching, New York, N.Y.

Terman, Lewis (1877–1956) American professor of education and psychology, whose seminal work, *The Measurement of Intelligence* (1916), introduced the Stanford-Binet Test (q.v.), the first widely used intelligence test, for which he developed the term "Intelligence Quotient," or "I.Q." Born and raised in Indiana, Terman earned his B.A. at Central Normal College, a teachers' college in Danville, Indiana, and at Indiana University. He taught in rural Indiana schools for two years, became a high school principal for three years and then enrolled at Clark University, in Worcester, Massachusetts, where he earned his Ph.D. in 1905. He became a professor of psychology and pedagogy

at the California State Normal School (later, University of California at Los Angeles) until 1910, when he joined the education faculty at Stanford University, where he also headed the psychology department until his retirement in 1942.

In addition to revising the Simon-Binet scale (q.v.) and developing the Stanford-Binet intelligence test, Terman designed and pursued one of the most remarkable longitudinal studies in the history of the social sciences: a 30-year study of gifted children with I.Q.s above 140. Initiated in 1921 with 1,528 subjects aged 3 to 18, the study carefully detailed almost all aspects of their lives through college, graduate school and into the workplace. Four definitive works emerged from the study: *Genetic Studies in Genius* (with others, vol. 1 [1925], vol. 2 [1926], vol. 3 [1930]); *Mental and Physical Traits of a Thousand Gifted Children* (1925); *Gifted Child Grows Up* (coauthored with Melita H. Oden, 1946); and *The Gifted Child at Mid-Life* (with Melita H. Oden, published posthumously, 1959).

Prior to beginning his study, Terman had served on the U.S. Army Committee on the Classification of Personnel during World War I. When Congress passed the Selective Service Act of 1917, the Army found a startlingly high number of illiterate, though often skilled and otherwise intelligent, registrants. It asked Terman to develop intelligence tests to help place recruits in jobs appropriate to their intelligence and skills. He developed the Army Alpha and Beta tests (q.v.)—one requiring literacy, the other, a nonverbal test for the roughly 25% of recruits who were illiterate.

A pioneer in the introduction of health and hygiene into elementary school administrative concerns, Terman wrote *The Teacher's Health* in 1914; *Health Work in the Schools* (with E. B. Hoag) in 1914; and *The Hygiene of the School Child*, also in 1914. His other important works included *Sex and Personality: Studies in Masculinity and Femininity* (with Catherine Cox Miles, 1936); *Measuring Intelligence* (with Maud Merrill, 1937); and *Marital Happiness* (1938).

References: BDAE; DAB; *A History of Psychology in Autobiography,* Carl A. Murchison, ed. (1930); *Terman and the Gifted,* May V. Seagoe (1975).

test battery   A type of examination made up of several sub-sections, each of which measures a different type of knowledge and skill, or aptitude. The Scholastic Assessment Test I, used by many colleges as an entrance examination, is a test battery consisting of a verbal sub-test, to measure reading and writing skills, and a mathematics sub-test, to measure computational skills. The score of a test battery may be reported as a composite score, as individual scores for each sub-test, or both.

Reference: *Educational Measurement,* Robert L. Thorndike (1971).

testing out   An evaluation process whereby students may omit a course or move from a lower-level course to a more advanced course and continue to advance at whatever pace their abilities permit. Many gifted students are often able to graduate from high school or college a year earlier than they ordinarily would by testing out of lower-level courses. Through a variety of school-college partnerships (q.v.), thousands of gifted high school students can take college-level courses at their own high schools or at nearby colleges, while remaining to graduate with their high school classmates. They nevertheless earn college credits that permit them to skip lower-level courses when they enroll at college. The College Board's Advanced Placement (q.v.) courses and examinations for high school students are a comparable program, often allowing students with high scores to bypass freshman-level college courses and enroll immediately into advanced college work.

Reference: *"What Did You Learn in School Today?"* Harlow G. Unger (1991).

testing preschoolers   A highly controversial practice that uses standardized, nonverbal examinations to determine the readiness of a preschooler to enter kindergarten. The widely used Gesell School Readiness Screening Test (q.v.) asks kindergarten applicants to copy a series of geometric shapes freehand. Although 97% of 4½-year-old girls and 92% of same-age boys can draw a figure that resembles a circle, only 35% of the girls and 25% of the boys can produce a well-proportioned circle. The square is more difficult, with only 65% of girls and 60% of boys able to draw a figure that appears to be a square, and only 15% of girls and 5% of boys able to draw a well-proportioned square. Vertical and horizontal diamonds are virtually impossible for 98% of pre-kindergarten children to copy in recognizable form.

A second element of the Gesell test is the Incomplete Man, a round-headed stick figure with missing body parts—both eyes, one ear, half his hair, one arm and one leg. The test measures how well a student completes the figure. A kindergarten-ready girl should add a few hairs by the time she is four years old; boys, when they are 4½. Most children add the missing ear by the time they are three, but placement is erratic until they are five. Some 70% of three-year-old girls and 55% of three-year-old boys add the missing arm, and 75% of three-year-old girls and 62% of the boys add the missing leg. Although placement and length of the added limbs are erratic at age three, they should meet the body line by the time the children are of kindergarten age.

Critics of the Gesell test and comparable examinations maintain that such evaluations are invalid. Usually administered by untrained kindergarten administrators, they can produce widely varying results for the same child on different days, depending on the child's mood. Moreover, rates of development of preschoolers are so rapid, in comparison, say, with high school seniors, that a test given several weeks before a child-applicant's prospective entry into kindergarten can show very different results when kindergarten opens. In the meantime, a poor score several weeks earlier may well have left the child rejected by the kindergarten and forced to wait another year before gaining admission. In contrast, a high school senior's college admission test scores seldom change more than one percentage point or two over a six-month period.

Thus, say critics, the use of kindergarten admission tests is not only invalid, but also grossly unfair. Moreover, the tests are certifiably biased against poor and minority children with less access to visual experiences and instructional playthings such as drawing boards and coloring books that help develop the very skills measured by the tests. As such, the tests are educationally destructive by denying kindergarten admission to many children who most need the skill-training that kindergarten provides. Still another criticism leveled at such testing concerns the deep anxieties and possible emotional trauma it can produce in impressionable youngsters, who readily feel and internalize the exaggerated parental hopes for their success.

References: *School Readiness—Behavior Tests Used at the Gesell Institute,* Francis L. Ilg (1978); *The School-Smart Parent,* Gene L. Maeroff (1989); "Uses and Abuses of Developmental Screening and School Readiness Testing," Samuel J. Meisels, *Young Children* (January 1987); *Making the Best of Schools,* Jeannie Oakes and Martin Lipton (1990).

Test of English as a Foreign Language (TOEFL) A standardized examination to evaluate English-language skills of students whose native tongue is other than English. Routinely used to evaluate foreign students applying for admission to colleges and universities in the United States, TOEFL is a test battery, with six sub-tests that measure listening skills, comprehension skills, knowledge of English language structure and syntax, reading comprehension and writing skills.

Reference: College Entrance Examination Board, Princeton, New Jersey.

tests In education, any of a wide variety of instruments designed to evaluate a student's aptitudes, skills, knowledge or intelligence. Tests may be oral or written, objective or subjective, and norm-referenced, criterion-referenced (qq.v.) or student-referenced. Norm-based tests

compare the student's scores to the average scores for other comparable students; criterion-based tests compare the student's score to the scores that the teacher or school had expected; and student-based tests compare the student's most recent score with his or her score at the beginning of the instructional unit.

The origin of tests in the schools of the Western world lies in the catechism, a manual of Roman Catholic doctrine, drawn up in question-and-answer form and used for religious instruction of the young since the first such manual was compiled by the English scholar Alcuin in the 8th century. Although many similar catechisms followed, they did not grow into universal importance in the Christian world until Martin Luther stressed the importance of instructing the young and published his own primer, *A Brief Explanation of the Ten Commandments, the Creed, and the Lord's Prayer,* in 1520. Although largely taught at home, the catechism entered the classroom in the early colonies, as churchmen were charged with secular, as well as religious, instruction of the young. Catechetical testing in secular subjects was a logical extension of the approach to religious training.

A routine element of school life ever since, tests have never been totally free of insoluble controversies. Can a single test truly determine a youngster's accumulated knowledge? Can a teacher grade a subjective test objectively? How does individual student anxiety affect test scores and how can scoring be adjusted to avoid any student-to-student scoring differences due solely to anxiety and not to lack of knowledge, skills or intelligence? A host of arguments—and attempts at solutions—have been developed for each of these and many other questions about testing. One of the most recent innovations is the development of student portfolios (q.v.) as a primary means of evaluating student achievement, thus relegating test scores to but one factor of many in an overall evaluation of a student's entire work for a specific period. To address the problem of student anxiety, many secondary schools require students to take minicourses in test-taking. Moreover, many objective tests penalize students for wrong answers to discourage random guessing by aggressive, "testwise" (see "TESTWISENESS") test-takers with inadequate knowledge of the subject on which they are being tested.

In addition to serving as an evaluative tool for teachers, traditional classroom testing serves as a classic application of learning theory (q.v.). The prospect of a test (or the fear of occasional unannounced surprise, or "pop," quizzes) is, in theory, a stimulus to study and the development of regular study habits, while the eventual test grades serve as either a reward or punishment for careful or careless preparation—and a valuable indication to the student of his or her strengths and inadequacies. Most schools begin some testing in the early elementary years. As students progress to the later elementary and middle school years, the frequency of testing increases, along with its weight as an evaluative instrument. Test routines vary widely, depending on the teacher's inclination and sense of the class. One classic routine, designed to encourage daily study, includes daily 10-minute quizzes on the previous day's class work and overnight homework, capped by a longer 30-minute or full-period test at the end of the learning unit and full-period final examination at the end of the quarter or semester. Other teachers prefer once-a-week testing, while still others rely on the surprise "pop" quiz, which encourages students to develop daily study habits because of the possibility of being tested at any time, without warning.

A multitude of test formats range from the objective test, with its multiple-choice and true-false questions, to the essay-style subjective test. The former yields only a single right or wrong answer for each question, while the latter requires substantial argumentation and logical discussion that is important less for its "rightness" or wrongness" than for its exposition of the degree of student familiarity with the subject matter and, therefore, the effort the student

invested in study and preparation for the examination.

Reference: *Evaluating Pupil Growth: Principles of Tests and Measurement,* Stanley J. Ahmann and Marvin D. Glock (1979); *The Development, Use and Abuse of Educational Tests,* Edward Burns (1979).

Tests in Print The definitive and most complete bibliography of commercially available tests, test reviews and data on specific tests, published annually by the Buros Institute of Mental Measurements, along with the equally definitive, biennial *Mental Measurements Yearbook.* Developed and for years edited by the late Oscar Krisen Buros, *Tests in Print* was first published in 1961 as a guide and index to the first five editions of *The Mental Measurements Yearbook.* Current editions include bibliographies of all known tests for English-speaking people; an index for *The Mental Measurements Yearbook,* which contains critical reviews of tests; descriptions of the construction, use and validity of each test; a list of tests that have gone out of print; and a directory of test publishers, with extensive cross-indexing to make the work an easy-to-use directory for teachers, administrators and other educators.

Reference: Buros Institute of Mental Measurements, University of Nebraska Press, Lincoln, Nebraska.

"testwiseness" A colloquialism referring to skills and instincts that can often give one student an advantage in a test over other students with identical intelligence and knowledge, but lacking test-taking skills. Many of these skills can be learned. At the simplest level, a cursory study of the meanings of basic prefixes and suffixes, for example, can provide a student with the ability to guess the meanings of many words in vocabulary tests. Training in mathematical estimation can also improve "testwiseness." Teachers can also help students develop testwiseness by teaching the test (q.v.)—focusing instruction on areas the teacher plans to test extensively or, in the case of commercially prepared standardized tests, focusing on topics and types of questions that such tests have usually stressed in the past.

Instinctual testwiseness is difficult to acquire. In general, educational psychologists have found two broad-based student responses to normal test anxieties: aggressive risk-taking and cautious, passive withdrawal from risks. The aggressive response is characterized by assertive guessing, even when the student has no idea of the answer; the cautious student responds to anxiety by refusing to risk a guess to questions whose answers he or she does not know. Given two equally knowledgeable and intelligent students, the risk-taker will normally produce higher test scores.

References: *Educational Psychology* (1977) and *Essentials of Psychological Testing* (1984), Lee J. Cronbach.

Texas The 28th state to join the Union, in 1845. The Spaniards explored Texas shortly after the Columbus voyages and more extensively in the late 1530s. A French explorer, however, claimed Texas for France in 1684; to counter the claim and to Christianize the native Indians, the Spanish founded missions in east Texas in 1690, establishing the first educative institutions of the region. Although officially a province of Spain, Texas remained sparsely settled borderland into the 19th century, with only one genuine school, founded in 1746 in the settlement of San Antonio. By 1820, on the eve of Mexican independence and almost 300 years after the first Spanish explorations, there were only about 2,000 settlers in Texas, but the area developed rapidly under Mexican rule, luring more than 24,000 Anglo-Americans, including 4,000 slaves. In 1839, three years after Texas became an independent nation, it organized a public school system, with each county receiving lands to be used for schools. It was not until after the Civil War that a new state constitution called for establishment of free public schools for all children. The state now has almost 6,000 public elementary and secondary schools, with a combined enrollment of well over 3 million students. One of four students is Hispanic or of Hispanic origin. Educational quality, as measured by most standard elements, is below average for the United States.

The state has 172 institutions of higher education—40 public four-year and 65 public two-year institutions, and 57 private four-year and 10 private two-year institutions. The state-controlled University of Texas and Texas A & M land-grant systems have the largest endowments of any public university systems in the world, largely because they have built huge private fund-raising arms to supplement revenues from state funds. The state's public colleges include two historically black institutions, Prairie View A & M and Texas Southern universities. In 1992, a state court found the public universities guilty of discrimination against Hispanic students from the southern parts of the state. Among the state's notable private institutions are Southern Methodist, Texas Christian, Baylor and Rice universities.

References: CHE; EB.

textbook Any bound volume of didactic literature that presents the principles of a subject and is deemed relevant to the study of that subject. Usually associated with books required in school, textbooks date from the organization of the earliest universities in Europe in the Middle Ages, where scriptural texts served as textbooks. As knowledge expanded and the works of ancient Greek scholars were rediscovered, the range of textbooks expanded to include manuals on medicine, law, politics, surveying, agriculture and conduct. To these were added works of poetry, drama, history and even fiction in the centuries that followed. At the primary and secondary school level, individual teachers and priests who served as teachers generally devised their own primers and early readers for children. As advances in printing permitted increased production of such books, standard versions of primers could be distributed to an ever increasing number of classrooms.

It was Isaiah Thomas (q.v.) who first recognized the potential of a captive "mass market" in education after the Revolution, and he became the first modern textbook publisher in the United States, producing textbooks for schools throughout New England. With an eye for high standards, Thomas recognized the superiority of Noah Webster's (q.v.) speller and grammar, Nicholas Pike's arithmetic, and works of literature appropriate for schoolchildren. Thomas launched what became a golden age of publishing, with education at its core. Of 2.5 million books printed in 1820, 750,000 were schoolbooks. The industry total climbed to 3.5 million in 1830, with schoolbooks accounting for 1.1 million; to 5.5 million in 1840, with schoolbooks accounting for 2.6 million; and to 12.5 million in 1850, with schoolbooks accounting for 5.5 million. Education had become the heart of publishing and publishing the heart of education.

Samuel Griswold Goodrich (q.v.) replaced Thomas as the leading American textbook publisher, dominating the field from 1816 until his death in 1860. Goodrich published myriad textbooks and children's works, including the Peter Parley books and a series of anthologies for children. Like the printers of earlier times, Goodrich authored many of the books he printed, commissioned others and reprinted popular British and European works.

Although they had started as conventional publishers of fictional and nonfictional works, the brothers James, John, Wesley and Fletcher Harper eventually borrowed a then-popular British publishing practice of producing series called "libraries." Recognizing that a lack of public schools and child labor practices had produced a generation of illiterate Americans, the Harper brothers fed an unquenchable, national thirst for education by producing the Family Library (187 titles), the Classical Library (37 titles), the Library of Select Novels (36 titles), the Boy's and Girl's Library (32 titles), the Theological Library (9 titles), the Dramatic Library (5 titles), and the School District Library, which fed schools with six different series with a total of 295 titles. In effect, they established educational curricula for homes, libraries, churches and schools, and they educated hundreds of thousands of Americans, bringing them the works of Bacon, Locke, Paine and other philosophers, along with works of history, biography, science and literature.

The value of textbooks varies widely according to the individual book, the author, the publisher, its use in the classroom, the instructor and those who select it. In many college courses, students are expected to study textbooks independently, as a complementary element of the professor's lecture. In other courses, the materials in the textbook are integrated with oral instruction. At the secondary school level, teacher classroom presentations are usually integrated with textbook materials. Some teachers, however, have a tendency to skip sections about which they have little knowledge. Indeed, the textbook is selected as often for the indoctrination of students as it is for their edification.

There are few textbooks that can be called unbiased, even in the empirical sciences and mathematics; authors invariably belong to one school of thought or another and seldom present all schools of thought in a balanced way. Most textbooks are designed to obtain maximum sales in as many school districts as possible across the United States. The result is often a product that skirts all controversies and is therefore a bland, uninteresting and, in effect, uninformative product. Many schools, school districts and states limit the use of textbooks to those that either omit or have been cleansed of political, sexual and religious references deemed by authorities to be unacceptable for young minds. Thus, new, rewritten versions of Shakespeare's plays, including *Romeo and Juliet,* are often published with no erotic references. Even more insidious has been the introduction in many school systems of pseudo-textbooks that purvey utter falsehoods in science, social studies, history and other courses. Some teach so-called "creation science," others invent civilizations that never existed in black Africa, still others present theories of racial superiority, and still more deny the existence of historical events such as the Holocaust.

(See also PUBLISHING.)

References: *The Brothers Harper: A Unique Publishing Partnership and Its Impact upon the Cultural Life of America from 1817 to 1853,* Eugene Exman (1965); *The Book in America: A History of the Making and Selling of Books in the United States,* Hellmut Lehmann-Haupt et al. (1951); *Samuel Griswold Goodrich, Creator of Peter Parley: A Study of His life and Work,* Daniel Roselle (1968); *Isaiah Thomas: Printer, Patriot and Philanthropist, 1749–1832,* Clifford K. Shipton (1948); *A History of Book Publishing in the United States,* John Tebbel (1972).

T-Group A small training group organized to explore interpersonal and intrapersonal relations by learning about group members, how they affect others and how they might interact more effectively with others. A form of group therapy, T-Groups are often called sensitivity training, which is used in schools to help students learn about and overcome racial, religious, gender and other forms of prejudice.

Reference: *T-Groups,* Cary L. Cooper and I. L. Mangham, eds. (1971).

Thayer, Sylvanus (1785–1872) Military leader, educator and "father" of West Point and modern military education. Born in Massachusetts, he graduated from Dartmouth College in 1807 and, after only a year, from West Point as well. After serving with the Corps of Engineers building fortifications along the New York and New England coasts for the War of 1812, he was assigned to tour Europe to study military education and compile a library of about 1,000 books and supplies for West Point. In 1817, he was appointed superintendent of West Point, with a mandate to change the institution from an ineffective, second-rate school into an effective, respected institution.

Borrowing much from the French model at the Ecole Polytechnique, he immediately raised academic standards and methods of assessing student achievement and broadened and strengthened the engineering and scientific curriculum. In addition, he broadened the general curriculum, adding chemistry, general history, moral philosophy, law, geography and ethics. He attracted the finest faculty available, both military and nonmilitary, and soon built the school into an outstanding academic, technical and scientific institution and the world's premier engineering school. In 1824, Rensselaer Polytechnic Institute (q.v.) used the West Point model to establish the first civilian engineering college; in the decades that followed other colleges such as Harvard and Yale established engineering departments along similar lines.

During his 16-year tenure, Thayer also introduced what remains today's strict academic and physical discipline at "the Point." Classes were small, averaging 10 to 14 students, with each student required to take each subject and to participate in each class. He instituted tough examinations, rigid military discipline and a code of honor. In 1818, students rebelled against his harsh ways. He court-martialed and dismissed five ringleaders. His unyielding discipline provoked another student revolt on Christmas Day, 1826, and rioting broke out on the campus. The bitterness between the cadets and Thayer intensified until 1833, when President Andrew Jackson reinstated several cadets that Thayer had ordered dismissed. Thayer resigned and spent the next 30 years as chief army engineer in charge of New England coastal fortifications and harbor improvements. He retired in 1863 and in 1867 endowed the Thayer School of Engineering at Dartmouth College.

Reference: *Duty, Honor, Country: A History of West Point,* Stephen E. Ambrose (1966).

thematic teaching An instructional approach that focuses on the study of a particular theme or topic, but indirectly forces students to study elements from a variety of traditional academic and scientific courses. Used at all levels of instruction, thematic teaching is akin to team teaching (q.v.), whereby instructors in different disciplines coordinate the materials they teach each week to promote interdisciplinary studies. Thematic teaching is based on the same principle, with an ostensibly non-academic rather than academic theme used as the centrality around-which students will amass applicable elements from as many academic and scientific courses as they can. Thus, thematic teaching might select "love" as a topic for study. Depending on the age group, the theme would provoke student forays into psychology, sociology, biology and zoology, physiology, literature, music and art—at the very least. Team teaching, on the other hand, selects a more finite academic or scientific topic—the study of the ancient Egyptian pyramids in history class, for example—and then obtains cooperation from all other teachers instructing the same grade to use the pyramids as a springboard for instruction in geometry, art history and language arts.

Reference: *Thematic Units in Teaching English and the Humanities,* Sylvia Spann and Mary Beth Culp (1977).

theology The study of God, his relationship to the world and to man, along with man's relationship to God and concomitant religious faiths, practices and experiences. Originally the core of higher education in the American colonies, today's theological education is unlike any other professional education in the United States, because the sheer number of different religions and religious sects mitigates against any set of universal standards of professionalism. Theology is a relatively minor course of study in today's overwhelmingly secular undergraduate four-year colleges. Even many Protestant-affiliated colleges, which dominated American higher education in the 18th and 19th century, often relegate theology to graduate school work, usually for students preparing for service in the ministry.

Roman Catholic educational institutions, on the other hand, usually integrate theology into the academic curriculum from kindergarten through secondary school and college. Students bound for the priesthood normally attend post-secondary or post-college seminaries. Theology studies for Orthodox Jews begin in the earliest elementary grades, with rabbinical studies beginning in secondary school and continuing through college. Jews bound for the Conservative and Reform rabbinate usually attend conventional, secular schools and colleges, before beginning their rabbinical studies at the graduate school level at either the Jewish Theological Seminary (Conservative) (see SOLOMON SCHECHTER) or Hebrew Union College/Jewish Institute of Religion (q.v.) (Reform).

Theology's roots reach back to ancient Greece and the Greek philosophers who invented the word theology, literally, the study of God. Greek pantheistic theology was a rational approach to God, based on the mythology of the Greek poets who told of continuing appearances of the gods on Earth, to interact with man. The Greek rational approach spawned the Christian theological approach of revelation as the source of theological truth. The role of Scripture, or sacred writings, appeared first with Judaism, then with Christianity. Usually accepted as revelatory works by the founders of the religion or as told by the founders to scribes or disciples, Scripture has emerged as a source of deep divisions in virtually every Western religious sect. In broadest terms, conservative Christian fundamentalists and Orthodox Jews view Scripture and sacred texts as the divinely inspired, infallible word of God, while liberals and reformers view religious texts as fallible, human assumptions and attestations of revelation, but not actual revelation. The split between the two camps grows even wider when scriptural passages are unclear and require human interpretation. The latter can vary so widely as to provoke endless divisions between members of virtually every sect, Christian and non-Christian alike.

Theology was the basis of all curricula when the first universities were founded in the Middle Ages. The thrust of theological thinking traveled from the concrete to the conceptual, accepting God as concrete and proceeding to define God in conceptual terms for the student to understand, using analogies, symbols and metaphors as vehicles for such understanding. The 13th-century Italian St. Thomas Aquinas and the 20th-century Swiss Karl Barth both insisted on the study of theology as a science that required the use of orderly, critically intellectual procedures to study God. Both agreed that, unlike objects of study in science, the object of their study—i.e., God—is not accessible to empirical study. They start from different points of view, however, with Aquinas asking whether God exists and setting out to prove it, while Barth begins with the assumption that revelation proves the existence of a self-communicating God. Barth's studies aim at determining the interrelationship between man and God.

There is, however, no single, universal methodology in theology, and the prevailing methodology changed dramatically throughout the Middle Ages, the Renaissance and, finally, the Reformation, when the study of theology was most extensive. Luther extended theological studies to the beginning reader, publishing specific texts and a primer for youngsters, *A Brief Explanation of the Ten Commandments, the Creed, and the Lord's Prayer,* in 1520. John Calvin published texts introduced an unquestioned sovereignty of God and the doctrine of predestination, whereby God had picked out each person's station in life.

Calvinism (q.v.) became the basis of the curriculum at Harvard College (q.v.), when it was founded in 1636 as a school to prepare ministers—the first college in the colonies. Although organized around the traditional trivium (grammar, rhetoric and logic) and quadrivium (arithmetic, music, geometry and astronomy), the entire thrust centered on theology, with several hours a week devoted to Greek, Latin and Hebrew studies of divinity. Theological studies began losing sway in the academic community from the beginning of the 18th century and with the growth of the empirical sciences and the beginning of the industrial revolution. By the middle of the 18th century, Benjamin Franklin had opened an academy in Philadelphia (later known as the College of Philadelphia (q.v.) and eventually as the University of Pennsylvania) that totally omitted theology as a course of study, replacing it with mechanics, arithmetics, agriculture, commerce and other practical courses that he believed were more needed than theology to build and expand a new nation. Thomas Jefferson followed Franklin's example in founding the University of Virginia early in the 19th century. Again, not a course in religion could be found in the curriculum. By the mid-20th century, theology had but disappeared from the undergraduate curricula of most liberal arts and science colleges. Colleges that continued to offer theology simply included it in their curricula as a subject with no greater status than any other liberal arts subject. In some areas of the country, Christian fundamentalists responded to the secularization of traditional colleges by opening bible colleges that taught nothing but theological and divinity courses.

In 1883, Harvard President Charles Eliot upgraded theological training for traditional Protestant Christian churches to the professional level by creating a three-year graduate school program, comparable to professional training for law and medicine. In so doing, he established as a prerequisite for admission the successful completion of a rigorous undergraduate pre-divinity program, comparable to undergraduate premedical studies required for admission to medical school. Predivinity studies included Greek, Latin and Hebrew, to permit study of Scripture in the languages in which it was originally written or translated. In addition, pre-divinity students were required to take courses in English literature, psychology, political science, history, German (to study Luther) and the natural sciences.

Once admitted to the Harvard Divinity School, future ministers were required to take courses in Semitic studies, New Testament criticism and exegesis, ecclesiastical history, comparative religion, psychology, ethics, philosophy of religion, systematic theology and homiletics, and engage in practical work in "charitable and reformatory methods, and the contest of Christian society with licentiousness, intemperance, pauperism, and crime.'' With some variations, this blend of scholarship and ministry remained the basic approach to theological studies at Harvard and other comparable institutions for the next century.

References: EB: Harvard University Library Archives; *A Handbook of Christian Theologians,* Martin Marty and Dean Peerman, eds. (1984).

Theory X and Theory Y and Theory Z

Three of many new approaches to education that have emerged from the observations of individual theoreticians. Often based on personal insights rather than costly, tightly controlled longitudinal studies, such theories frequently ring true enough in enough minds to become virtual education cults. Theory X and Theory Y can really be thought of as one theory that dichotomizes students (indeed, all humanity) into Theory X types, who dislike work, prefer direction and can perform only under tight control of superior authorities, and Theory Y types, who find physical and mental work as satisfying as play and willingly exercise self-direction once committed to a goal, if promised adequate ego-satisfaction/gratification and rewards. Theory Y types are the better able to learn and accept responsibility and display creativity and ingenuity.

Theory Z, which originated in Japan, ignores the personality characteristics of Theories X and Y and simply introduces effective technological equipment to transform every student, A through Z, into one capable of achieving his or her potential.

References: *The Z Theory School: Beyond Effectiveness,* Paul S. George (1983); *School Administration and Supervision: Important Issues, Concepts and Case Studies,* Richard A. Gorton (1980).

thinking A vague, all-encompassing term usually summed up colloquially as ''using one's brain.'' In education, the term generally refers to higher-level processes emanating from the brain and providing such phenomena as memory, imagination and ability to solve problems. Until the 1970s, few schools taught students how to think. What they concentrated on was teaching students to memorize facts, but not necessarily how to use the arsenal of facts thus accumulated to solve problems. Such higher-order thinking skills and how to teach them became the new goal for American education. They cannot be taught (although they may be implied) through haphazard, conventional, day-to-day teaching that simply plods through the curriculum. Educators agree that learning skills can and must be taught as part of an essential element of the curriculum of every class, from kindergarten through the college years.

Many children acquire higher-order thinking skills intuitively or by imitation. The systematic approach now used in elementary schools to assure maximum development of higher-order thinking skills is to help the child identify the problem clearly by discarding all extraneous materials presented as part of the problem but actually unrelated to its heart. The next step is a memory search for solutions used for comparable problems, the evaluation of each, and the implementation of the most likely. Even if the student does not arrive at the correct or best solution with the first effort, the key to teaching critical thinking is not a summary rejection of a wrong answer, as in ''That's wrong! Anyone else with an idea?'' To teach critical thinking, the child with a wrong answer must be helped to step backward, examine the reasons for choosing that solution and the reasons for not choosing alternatives and eventually, point by point, discover why one solution has more advantages than the alternatives. Then, having found the solution, the student must be taught immediately to generalize by exploring similar problems for which the same solution might be valid—and problems for which the incorrect solutions might have proved correct. Teaching thinking, in other words, requires a vast exploratory effort and enormous teacher patience.

There are many successful, systematic programs for teaching thinking skills, among them "Philosophy for Children" and "Instrumental Enrichment." The former was developed at Montclair (New Jersey) State College, using specially written short novels as a basis for extensive student discussion. Students learn to recognize irrelevant questions; to avoid jumping to conclusions; to employ analogy and syllogism in reasoning; to discover underlying assumptions; to detect ambiguities; to discover contradictory statements; and to discover causal relations.

Philosophy for Children tests thinking skills of elementary school students with questions such as the following:

1. If it's true that only animals are cats, then it's also true that:
   (a) all cats are animals
   (b) all animals are cats
   (c) neither of the above
   (The correct answer, "a," tests the ability to sort out statements of inclusion and exclusion.)
2. Glenn said, "Here comes a police car racing down the highway. There must be an accident." Glenn is assuming that:
   (a) when police cars speed along the highway, it's usually to chase criminals
   (b) when police cars speed along the highway, it's to get to an accident
   (c) when there's been an accident, police cars speed along the highway
   (The correct answer, "b," tests the ability to find underlying assumptions.)
3. All cats that cry are in pain. All cats are suffering creatures. Therefore:
   (a) all suffering creatures are cats that cry
   (b) all cats in pain are cats that cry
   (c) all cats that cry are suffering creatures
   (The correct answer, "c," tests syllogistic reasoning ability.)

The teaching of reasoning skills does not, however, require formal programs such as Phi-

losophy for Children. Many teachers are intuitively skilled in performing the job as they progress through the standard curriculum. There are six keys to teaching thinking skills: the use of questioning to provoke profound thinking rather than short answers; introduction of student-centered learning that encourages students to pursue knowledge on their own instead of relying on lectures and teacher answers; use of essay questions that require thoughtful answers rather than the memory responses of short-answer tests; extensive writing assignments, in and out of class, based on lessons, independent observations and thoughtful questions; discussions of strategies for problem solving; teacher display and instruction of how he or she goes about solving particular problems.

The College Board lists five reasoning skills it considers essential for higher education: the ability to identify and formulate problems and propose and evaluate solutions; the ability to recognize and use inductive and deductive reasoning and to recognize fallacies in other forms; the ability to reach and defend conclusions from written, oral, tabular or graphic data; the ability to comprehend, develop and use concepts and generalizations; and the ability to distinguish between fact and opinion. To achieve these skills requires enormous educational groundwork in elementary and secondary schools, usually laid down through carefully planned programs rather than by allowing these skills to develop on a catch-as-catch-can basis in traditional day-to-day teaching.

References: *Human Characteristics and School Learning,* Benjamin Bloom (1982); *Thinking Critically,* John Chaffee (1985); *Academic Preparation for College: What Students Need to Know and Be Able to Do,* The College Board (1983); *The School-Smart Parent,* Gene I. Maeroff (1989); "Teaching Thinking: Louis E. Raths Revisited," by Selma Wasserman, *Phi Delta Kappan* (February 1987).

Third Plenary Council of Baltimore An 1884 convention of Roman Catholic leaders in the United States to establish a unified system of education for Roman Catholic children. At the time, Catholic leaders were facing threats to the future of their church. On the one hand, divisions were arising among loyal congregants with different ethnic backgrounds who sought priests who spoke their own language. German Catholics wanted German priests; Irish Catholics, Irish priests; Polish Catholics, Polish priests. The higher Catholic leadership sought to build an American Catholic Church based on unity among all these groups and had purposely assigned priests to preach to congregations of ethnic backgrounds different from their own.

Meanwhile, another threat to church survival emerged from the public school systems, which absorbed Catholic children and promptly sought to Protestantize as well as Americanize them. The answer to both threats, the Catholic hierarchy concluded, was the creation of its own, independent school system, with a parochial elementary school at each parish, a high school in each diocese and, atop the entire structure, the Catholic University of America. All were to teach Americanism, using the English language to prepare subsequent generations of Roman Catholic Americans for places of leadership in the nation and in its communities.

References: *A History of the Councils of Baltimore: (1791–1884),* Peter Guilday, ed. (1932); *Catholic Education in America,* Neil G. McCluskey (1964); *A History of Catholic Higher Education in the United States,* Edward J. Power (1958).

Thomas, Isaiah (1749–1831) American patriot, printer and "father" of modern American publishing. Born in Boston to ne'er-do-wells, he was apprenticed to a Boston printer after only six weeks of formal schooling. Released from his indenture, he traveled abroad, but returned to Boston in 1770 to form a partnership with his former master. Together they published a Whig newspaper, the *Massachusetts Spy.* After becoming sole owner, Thomas took up the patriot cause, becoming a hero among the patriots but anathema to the British, who forced him to flee Boston in 1775. He set up shop in Worcester, became the official patriot

printer and resumed issuing the *Spy.* By then, the paper had gained a far-reaching reputation and produced enough income for Thomas to expand his publishing business to include magazines, almanacs and, eventually, books. By 1790, he had opened offices throughout Massachusetts and employed about 150 workers in his Worcester facility alone.

Recognizing the value of mass sales, Thomas was among the first to produce Bibles and take advantage of mass circulation through his chain of offices throughout the state. Thomas was also first to recognize the potential of a "mass market" in education after the Revolution, and he began producing textbooks for schools throughout New England. Rather than publishing any available primers or dictionaries, he sought out superior products and quickly obtained the rights to publish Noah Webster's (q.v.) speller and grammar, Nicholas Pike's arithmetic, and works of literature appropriate for schoolchildren, such as *Goody Two-Shoes, Mother Goose* and *Robinson Crusoe.* The consummate publisher, Thomas had a gift for selecting books of quality as well as salability. In 1789, he decided to publish *The Power of Sympathy,* by William H. Brown, the first novel by a Native American ever published in the United States. An author himself, he compiled the two-volume *Printing in America* in 1810, a work that remained the definitive shop manual to the trade for more than a century. In 1812, he founded and became first president of the American Antiquarian Society.

References: *The Book in America: A History of the Making and Selling of Books in the United States,* Hellmut Lehmann-Haupt et al. (1951); *Isaiah Thomas: Printer, Patriot and Philanthropist, 1749–1832,* Clifford K. Shipton (1948); *A History of Book Publishing in the United States,* John Tebbel (1972).

Thorndike, Edward Lee (1874–1900) American psychologist, educator and "the father of educational psychology." Born in Massachusetts and educated, successively, at Wesleyan, Harvard and Columbia universities,

Edward L. Thorndike. (Library of Congress)

Thorndike taught psychology at Teachers College, Columbia University from 1899 until 1940 and developed a host of refined intelligence tests to measure aptitudes in arithmetic, handwriting, spelling, drawing, reading and language skills.

A confirmed Darwinian, Thorndike sought to expand the use of the nascent Binet (q.v.) and Simon intelligence scales to convert education into a pure science. By measuring the intelligence, aptitude and achievement levels of each student, Thorndike developed tests as educational diagnostic tools with which to sort students into ability groups whose instruction could be tailored to their needs. Although considered progressive at the time, sorting, or tracking (q.v.), as it's now called, deteriorated

into one of the more regressive educational trends in modern education. What Thorndike failed to consider was the differences in rates of childhood development that might allow a slower five-year-old to leap ahead of his or her peers the following year. Instead of providing the less skilled with remediation that could raise their skill levels, sorting trapped them in their relatively low educational stations, often condemning them to lives of educational deprivation and consequent economic hardship.

Despite the failure of his sorting theories, Thorndike nevertheless made enormous contributions to education and educational psychology. His development of such standard testing devices as the maze, the puzzle box and various signal-and-choice mechanisms laid the groundwork for investigation of animal learning and, in turn, human learning. He conducted some of the earliest experiments on the influence of inheritance on intellectual functioning and character. He also used intelligence testing to study and develop practical teaching techniques for enhancing memory, rates of learning, adult learning and conditions of efficient learning. Many of these studies formed the basis of his seminal three-volume *Educational Psychology* (1913–14), the work that created the science of educational psychology. Author of more than 500 articles and books, he made several important contributions to elementary and secondary education by authoring *The Teachers Word Book of 30,000 Words* (1921), *The Thorndike Century Junior Dictionary* (1935) and *The Thorndike Century Senior Dictionary* (1941). The first two works were unique for their era in that they were designed from their inception for youngsters rather than representing a simplification of adult books.

References: *Psychology and the Science of Education: Selected Writings of Edward L. Thorndike* (1962) and *The Sane Positivist: A Biography of Edward L. Thorndike* (1968), Geraldine Joncich.

TIAA/CREF The Teachers Insurance and Annuity Association/College Retirement Equities Fund, which provide pensions and retirement benefits for employees of colleges, universities, independent private schools and a number of other educational institutions. Although now closely associated, TIAA (1918) and CREF (1952) began as (and, technically, remain) separate, nonprofit annuity companies. Founded by the Carnegie Foundation for the Advancement of Teaching, TIAA relies on a combination of employee and employer contributions to fund its investments, which are largely limited to mortgages, bonds and other fixed-income securities. Income from investments is paid out in fixed-dollar life pensions, based on a percentage of the retiree's former salary. In contrast, CREF is a mutual fund, with a broadly diversified portfolio of common stocks designed to protect TIAA fixed-income pensions from the effects of inflation. Like all mutual funds, CREF sells shares, or units, to investors, who are limited to TIAA members. Together, CIAA/CREF had assets totaling $135 billion at the beginning of 1995.

Reference: Teachers Insurance and Annuity Association/College Retirement Equities Fund, New York, New York.

Ticknor, George (1791–1871) American educator and originator of departmental curricular organization. Born in Boston, Ticknor was a child prodigy, passing the entrance examination at Dartmouth College at the age of nine, enrolling in the junior class at the age of 14 and graduating two years later. He went on to study Greek, Latin and the law, which he practiced briefly in 1813 and 1814. After extensive travels in Europe, he was appointed professor of French and Spanish at Harvard University in 1817; there, in the 1820s, he proposed broadening the curriculum, dividing the college into departments of related subjects and granting students the right to choose a number of elective subjects to complement the basic required curriculum. Considered radical for the day, his proposals were only partially adopted. After several years of campus infighting, he resigned, complaining, "I have been contending, against a constant oppo-

sition, to procure certain changes which should make the large means of the College more effectual for the education of the community. In my own department I have succeeded entirely, but I can get these changes carried no further . . .''

His proposals were eventually adopted, but not until after he left Harvard, in 1835. He spent the next three years in Europe, gathering materials for his *History of Spanish Literature* (1849), a three-volume work that took him 10 years to complete. A founder of the Boston Public Library, he spent 1856–57 touring Europe to acquire books for the library, to which he later donated his own extensive collection of Spanish literature.

References: *Remarks on Changes Lately Proposed or Adopted in Harvard University,* George Ticknor (1825); *Life, Letters and Journals of George Ticknor* (2 vols., 1876); *George Ticknor and the Boston Brahmins,* David B. Tyack (1967).

Tinker v. Des Moines Independent Community School District A 1969 U.S. Supreme Court ruling that public school officials cannot arbitrarily deprive students of their First Amendment rights to nondisruptive free speech. The case marked the first time the Court extended certain constitutional rights to minors.

Tinker involved the suspension in 1965 of three high school students, aged 13, 15 and 16, for wearing black armbands to protest the Vietnam War. Except for their armbands, they made no other attempt to protest the war on campus, and the Court ruled that "the Constitution does not stop at the public school doors like a puppy waiting for its master, but instead, it follows the student through the corridors into the classroom, and onto the athletic field." Pointing out that school officials routinely allowed students to wear political buttons, the Court said that the suspension of the students for wearing armbands was based solely on official disagreement with the political opinions of the students and not because the students had disrupted school routine in any way. The Court made it clear that its decision applied only to "symbolic speech" and not to demonstrative protests or conduct that might disrupt discipline or interfere with the rights of others. Nor did the decision in any way strip public schools of their inherent right to regulate student conduct. Further defining the extent of student freedom of speech in 1988, in *Hazelwood School District v. Kuhlmeier* (q.v.), the Court ruled that schools can maintain editorial control over student articles in school-owned publications and that, in effect, students do not have unlimited freedom of expression.

Reference: U.S. Supreme Court proceedings.

Title A heading of a particular section in a law. Often, a particular title in the law has such far-reaching effects that the title's number—usually a Roman numeral—is commonly used to refer to the particular section and its consequences. Although many laws have various titles, two titles in education are of particular importance:

- **Title I.** The best known of six titles in the Elementary and Secondary Education Act of 1965 (q.v.), a broad piece of legislation designed to improve the quality of American public school education. Title I provided for the special education needs of an estimated 5 million to 6 million educationally deprived, low-income students, furnishing funds to local educational agencies and schools for such services as remedial reading, remedial mathematics and special summer programs.
- **Title IX.** The commonly used, abbreviated name for the section of the Education Amendments of 1972 (q.v), prohibiting discrimination on the basis of gender. "No person in the United States," it reads, "shall, on the basis of sex, be excluded from participation in, be denied the benefits of, or be subjected to discrimination under any education program receiving federal financial assistance."

  Enactment of Title IX had shattering effects on educational traditions in the United States, forcing formerly all-male and all-female institutions to open their doors to students of the opposite gender and to provide equal facilities for each gender, including equal athletic facilities, equal numbers of teams and equal time and access to all practice facilities. A protection against discrimination for males as well as females, Title IX applied to all educational institutions from preschool through higher education and adult education, with the exception of certain types of religious schools, sororities and fraternities, and youth organizations such as the Boy Scouts and Girl Scouts. By the mid-1990s, almost all educational institutions had complied with Title IX provisions except a handful of all-male military schools and colleges in the south.

Reference: *Title IX: How It Affects Elementary and Secondary Education,* Norma Raffel (1976).

top-down model of reading A system of reading instruction in which children learn the meanings of entire words by sight—by recognizing the distinctive shape and context of each word in a sentence. Top-down reading instruction contrasts with the bottom-up model (q.v.), which depends on piecing together small parts, or phonic sounds, to form letter, syllabic and eventually word sounds. In the top-down model, children learn the whole word first, then take it apart to learn each letter and its individual sound. Most children instinctively use both methods in learning to read, and few teachers rely entirely on one approach in reading instruction. Most preschoolers, for example, have already used the top-down model in learning to read, but not spell, such words as "CORN FLAKES," which they have seen on signs and packages since infancy. Developmental, and perhaps hereditary, differences often see some children more adaptable to one model than the other. Many children are almost incapable of learning from the top down and are almost totally dependent on "sounding out" words, letter by letter, from the bottom up.

Reference: *Helping Children Learn to Read,* Patrick J. Finn (1985).

total communication An all-encompassing approach to teaching the hearing-impaired, by using a combination of oral speech, lip reading, signing and finger spelling. By using all available methods of teaching, the approach obviates the debate among some educators of the hearing-impaired on the advantages of manual over oral teaching methods and vice versa.

Reference: *Educating the Deaf: Psychology, Principles, and Practices,* Donald F. Moores (1978).

tracking A system of grouping students in classes according to ability and curriculum. Introduced in Britain in the 1920s as "streaming," tracking by ability became ubiquitous in U.S. public schools after World War II, when stricter enforcement of child labor laws and waves of immigration produced a vast expansion of the public high school student population. The elementary and middle school tracking system grouped children by ability, with faster or slower classes in each grade. At the high school level, tracking was organized on two levels: On one level, students were grouped according to curriculum (academic, general and vocational), and on the second, students on each track were grouped in classes according to ability.

The theory behind tracking maintains that children of nearly equal abilities should be grouped together for learning because they absorb knowledge at the same rate, making instruction more efficient. The theory fails to take into account different rates of development, however, and ample studies have proved tracking to be one of the most debilitating approaches to education ever devised. Studies by the Johns Hopkins Center for Social Organization of Schools show that mixed-ability groupings have no ill-effect on high achievers and actually improve the performance of low achievers. In contrast, when students are grouped by ability, low-ability groups get slower instruction, face lower teacher expectations, exhibit increased behavior problems and turn low achievement into a self-fulfilling prophecy.

With the exception of academic-vocational tracking, ability grouping has proved of benefit only to the most gifted students, while limiting and even impeding the educational progress of average and slower students and, most especially, of poor, minority students. Indeed, critics of tracking say it is nothing more than an insidious form of economic discrimination that is resegregating American students by race in the guise of improved education. According to a 1994 study by the Rand Corporation, advanced classes made up 34% of the math and science curriculum at heavily white schools, while making up only 12% of the curriculum at schools whose students are 90% or more black.

In 1988, the U.S. Department of Education's National Center for Educational Statistics conducted a National Longitudinal Study of 14,000 eighth grade students in public schools and obtained revealing data on ethnic and racial profiles grouping in English and math classes. About 40% of Asians, 32% of whites, 18% of Hispanics, 15% of blacks and 9% of American Indians were placed in high-ability English classes, and 47% of Asians, 35% of whites, 18% of Hispanics, 15% of blacks and 10% of American Indians were placed in high-ability math classes. In contrast, only 16% of Asians and 14% of whites, but 29% of Hispanics, 34% of blacks and 35% of American Indians were placed in low-ability English classes, while 17% of Asians, 15% of whites, 25% of Hispanics, 35% of blacks and 34% of American Indians were placed in low-ability math classes. On the socioeconomic scale, 39% of the top socioeconomic quarter of the students were placed in high-ability classes, while only 13% of the lowest socioeconomic quarter were placed in high-ability classes.

The department's findings have provoked a heated debate over whether placements reflect student abilities or whether student abilities reflect the effects of placement. The debate remains unresolved, but there is little doubt that, with ability grouping already in place at preschool levels, educators have little opportunity to prove that mixed-ability groupings might hold an answer to higher student achievement in later grades. Because gifted children from higher socioeconomic levels make up the majority of the student population in high-ability groupings, it is unlikely that affluent communities will willingly abandon a system that favors their children.

Ostensibly, each of the three broad curricular tracks at the high school level—academic, vocational and general—was designed to accommodate students according to their interests, but, in fact, placement on each track is usually determined by school authorities whose decisions are normally final and mandatory. Gifted students and academic achievers are usually assigned to the academic track; academically slower but manually skilled students are placed on the vocational track; and the slowest, most unskilled and, usually, most unmotivated students are consigned to the general track.

The academic track harbors a range of college-bound students, with ability groupings within the track absorbing students of differing intellectual abilities. The most gifted usually enroll in honors classes to prepare for academically selective four-year colleges. Most others on the academic track tend to enroll in less selective four- or two-year colleges, most with open-enrollment admission policies. The vocational track harbors a startlingly heterogeneous student population. Although consistently unmotivated academically, students on the vocational track are not necessarily slower than students on the academic track. They range from students with superior manual skills, who are extremely motivated to learn an industrial craft, to behaviorally dysfunctional students placed in vocational education by school psychologists hoping to use the track as a form of occupational therapy.

Between the extremes in vocational education is a broad range of students with widely varying degrees of motivation and intellectual ability. Like the academic track, the vocational track of many high schools is often divided into classes based on student abilities. Those at the upper end of the ability/motivational scale are usually clustered in so-called two-plus-two, tech-prep programs (qq.v.)—four-year courses of study beginning in junior year of high school and continuing through two years of an affiliated community college. Where no such programs are available, higher-level vocational track students usually enroll in cooperative programs (q.v.) with nearby industries, spending a half-day at school and a half-day at a cooperating firm that offers students on-the-job training as part of the total vocational-education package.

Of the three broad tracks, the general track has the least direction and has proven to be a national disaster in public education in the decades since World War II, producing two-thirds of all high school dropouts in the United States. More than one-third are unable to find work and join the chronically unemployed. A dumping ground for the unmotivated, the slow, the troubled, the behaviorally dysfunctional and too many of the learning disabled, the general track grants one-fourth of its credits for work outside school, personal improvement courses and physical and health education. The remainder of the program consists of childishly simplified versions of conventional academic courses—usually called general science, general social studies, general math and general English, with the last consisting of remedial work in reading and writing. Dale Parnell, the longtime president of the American Association of Community and Junior Colleges, described the high school general education program as "the academic and vocational desert of American education. [It] relates to nothing, leads to nothing and prepares for nothing." Indeed, it leaves the majority of its students semi-literate, without the intellectual and academic skills to obtain higher-level education in either the skilled or semi-skilled trades.

Some school systems began abandoning the academic track in the late 1970s in favor of separate, free-standing "alternative" schools (q.v.), where educational specialists could work with dysfunctional youngsters in small groups, while school psychologists worked with them on an individual basis. The development of alternative schools, however, progressed extremely slowly because of the high cost of such individualized education. By the mid-1980s, 80% of American secondary schools and 60% of elementary schools used some form of ability grouping; by 1994, studies by the Rand Corporation indicated that such tracking had actually increased, rather than decreased, as the socioeconomically powerful demanded special, advanced classes for their children.

Tracking is not, of course, limited to elementary and secondary education. Higher education has long had widely accepted forms of tracking, with slower and faster sections in many subjects, including the sciences and modern languages. Tracking at the college or university level for intellectually developed students, however, has far fewer social implications than it does at the elementary and secondary school levels.

Reference: *Making Inequality: The Hidden Curriculum in High School Tracking*, James E. Rosenbaum (1976).

transcendentalism In American education, an early 19th-century literary and philosophical movement in New England that rejected Puritan values and the doctrine of original sin and extolled the beauties of the individual as an element of the natural world. The movement not only produced a body of still-influential literature, it also was responsible for three utopian communities whose methods of instruction continue to influence American education.

Transcendentalism's roots go back to ancient Greece and the philosopher Plato's affirmation of the concept of absolute goodness, an indescribable quality known only intuitively, but evident when sensed. Religious philosophers extended the concept to God, in that God is indescribable and exists outside the realm of nature and human understanding. Later, the concept was extended to include the soul, truth and a number of other concepts that, once again, were beyond finite human experience.

The New England movement began in 1836 as an intellectual rebellion against Puritanism, Calvinism and all other dogmatic, ritualistic religious institutions, which, in effect, espoused the concept of man's worthlessness in the absence of church affiliation. Extolling the beauties of nature and humankind, the New England transcendentalists insisted that divinity permeated everything in the universe, both animate and inanimate, turning all into divine objects, filled with beauty, truth and goodness. Intuition was therefore superior to reason as a human faculty because, unlike self-inspired reason, intuition was divine in origin.

In 1836, a group of New England philosopher-educators, all of them dreamers, idealists and romantics, formed what became the Transcendental Club in Boston. There they spent long nights in discussion, produced *The Dial*, a periodical that recorded their thoughts, and planned the establishment of a variety of utopian communities. Their leaders included essayist Ralph Waldo Emerson, educator Bronson Alcott, philosopher William Ellery Channing (qq.v.), author Nathaniel Hawthorne (1804–64) and author-naturalist-philosopher Henry David Thoreau (1817–62). Transcendentalists founded two utopian communities. Neither outlasted their founders, but both had immediate, lasting influences on American education: Brook Farm and Fruitlands.

Brook Farm was a cooperative community established in West Roxbury, Massachusetts, in 1841 by Alcott, Channing, Emerson, Hawthorne and other transcendentalists. Officially known as the Brook Farm Institute of Agriculture and Education, the venture was a 200-acre farm, owned by a joint stock company, whose members were to contribute and share equally in all aspects of farm activities. The community's school offered free education to all who would enroll. Instruction was based on benevolence and affection and included nature study, dancing, music, vocational training and other nontraditional studies, in addition to basic academics. Abandoned in 1847, it was the setting of

Hawthorne's novel *The Blithedale Romance* (1852).

Fruitlands, described in Louisa May Alcott's *Little Women,* was founded by her father, the innovative, though undisciplined, teacher Bronson Alcott, who believed firmly in universal public education. Parents of students at his Boston school withdrew their children after he admitted a black child, and in 1842 he founded Fruitlands, a farm in Concord, Massachusetts, where he lazed through the summer days, philosophizing aimlessly with his friends Emerson, Hawthorne and Thoreau. Alcott's teaching methods, however, eventually helped revolutionize American pedagogy. Believing that each child's character was a gift of God, he did away with corporal punishment and introduced play, gymnastics and a school library that gave children freedom to choose their own books. In class, he dispensed with textbooks and, instead, introduced the Socratic method of teaching, used by Plato to teach students through gentle, persuasive conversations. His conversations produced scores of innovative and now-classic learning devices and teaching techniques. Alcott codified his teaching techniques in a manual of instruction, which, like a similar manual produced at Brook Farm, influenced educators for decades thereafter.

In contrast to the social utopias at Brook Farm and Fruitlands, Thoreau sought community with nature on the shores of Walden Pond, where he settled for two years, by himself, in a house he built in 1845. Although he never produced an instructional manual for teachers, his immortal journal, *Walden, or Life in the Woods,* served as a guide for discovering one's true self through solitude and communion with nature.

References: *The Flowering of New England, 1815–1861,* Van Wyck Brooks (1970); *Main Currents in American Thought: The Romantic Revolution, 1800–1860,* Vernon Louis Parrington (1927).

transcript An official, printed record of a student's academic grades and school or college performance, usually carrying an explanation of the school's grading system and a raised seal or other certification of authenticity. Although available to students, transcripts are usually not accepted as proof of previous academic performance unless posted directly from the certifying institution to the recipient institution.

Reference: ERIC.

transformational generative grammar In education, a term borrowed from linguistics and applied to a "bottom-up" approach to understanding and teaching grammar by using the deep structure of a sentence —a simple noun and simple verb—as a base, or foundation, on which a wide variety of surface structures may be constructed. The opposite of diagramming (q.v.), or parsing, sentences, transformational grammar uses an almost mathematical approach, based on strict, explicit rules, to generate sentences and transform their meaning. Thus, "cat plays" may constitute the deep structure of a sentence, whose superficial structure might consist of any of a wide variety of adjectives, adverbs and other words such as "the," "soft," "hungry" and "vicious," which can transform the meaning of the deep structure as they generate a complex sentence structure. "The cat plays with its food," for example, is a structure based on the same deep structure as "The cat plays with the mouse." A traditional form of teaching grammar, along with diagramming, transformational generative grammar has largely been replaced by the whole language (q.v.) approach to teaching grammar in most American schools.

References: *Syntactic Structure,* Noam Chomsky (1957); *Transformation-Generative Grammar,* Bert Jacobsen (1977); *Transformational Grammar and the Teacher of English,* Owen Thomas and Eugene R. Kantgen (1974).

transition school An organizational structure that links the curriculum of the last two years of high school with two or more years of study at an affiliated institution of higher education. A phrase coined in the 1980s by Ernest L.

Boyer, the president of the Carnegie Foundation for the Advancement of Teaching (qq.v.), transition schools ideally would provide programs in which only half of each student's time would be spent completing the traditional, academic core curriculum (English, science, mathematics and social studies). The other half of the time would be spent studying an "elective cluster" of courses, with each cluster carefully designed for each student's individual long-term needs. Thus, many vocational students now participate in so-called tech-prep or two-plus-two (qq.v.) programs, a course of study leading to certification in a specific craft or vocation after completion of four years of linked study that includes the last two years of high school and two years of study at an associated community college. Transition programs at some schools offer advanced, college-level courses during the last two years of high school that permit students to move directly into sophomore or even junior year of college.

Although used to refer to linked high school-college programs, the phrase transition school also refers to a handful of experimental schools that combine the last two years of high school with the first two years of college in a single, independent institution. Pasadena (California) City College was first among these in 1920, but Simon's Rock of Bard College, at Great Barrington, Massachusetts, admits students immediately after they have completed the 10th grade of high school and awards them associate degrees two years later and bachelor's degrees after they successfully complete four years of study.
Reference: *High School,* Ernest L. Boyer (1983).

trimester One-third of an academic year. Although traditionally organized into two parts, or semesters, the academic year is sometimes divided into three parts that condense materials in each course somewhat, but permit students to study a larger number and broader range of courses. Although used at a handful of private secondary schools, the trimester is more common at colleges.

Reference: *Handbook of College and University Education,* Asa S. Knowles, ed. (1970).

Triple-T Program A short-lived effort by the U.S. Office (now Department) of Education (q.v.) to reform teacher education. Funded under the National Defense Education Act (q.v.), the Training of Teacher Trainers program, as Triple-T was officially named, consisted of 58 university programs involving hundreds of schools and 42,000 students during its five-year existence, from 1968 to 1973. Although Triple-T did produce some minor improvements in teacher training by involving college liberal arts faculty in teacher education, the overall program lacked a unifying policy. The result was a disjointed program of independent projects that produced no overall changes in the national approach to teacher education.
Reference: *The Grand Experiment,* Malcolm M. Provus (1975).

trivium and quadrivium The two categories of the seven liberal arts, as taught in the first European universities during the Middle Ages. The trivium, a Latin word for the meeting of three roads, consisted of grammar, which included the study of literature; dialectic, or logic; and rhetoric, which included the study of law. Students received bachelor's degrees after successfully completing the trivium and then went on to earn their master's degrees by studying the quadrivium, meaning a crossroads, or meeting of four roads. The quadrivium was made up of arithmetic; geometry, which included geography and natural history; astronomy, which usually included astrology; and music, almost all of it church-related.

The term liberal arts dates from ancient Greece, where Plato and Aristotle (qq.v.) made a distinction between the liberal arts, for development of intellect and morality, and the practical arts. Although the Roman scholar Marcus Terentius Varro wrote of the liberal arts during the 1st century B.C. and of such utilitarian arts as medicine and architecture, the breakdown of the liberal arts into the seven specific subject areas of grammar, logic, rhetoric, geometry, arithmetic, astronomy and music seems to have awaited the writings of a group of 5th-, 6th- and 7th-century A.D. scholars that included the Carthaginian-born writer Martianus Capella, the Roman historian Flavius Magnus Cassiodorus and the Spanish scholar St. Isidore of Seville. The further breakdown into the elementary trivium and advanced quadrivium came with the founding of the first universities in the Middle Ages.

References: EB; *The Universities of Europe in the Middle Ages,* Hastings Rashdall (1936).

Troops to Teachers

A program sponsored by the Department of Defense to encourage qualified retiring members of the armed services to serve as teachers or aides in low-income school districts suffering shortages of qualified personnel. Started in 1994, the program provided such districts with more than 6,000 former members of the armed services, as qualified teachers, counselors and administrators to schools in 30 states. The program matches retiring service personnel, according to their background in specific subjects, organizational skills or counseling skills, with the needs of school districts facing staff or teacher shortages.

The Pentagon pays retiring service personnel up to $5,000 for the cost of obtaining teaching certificates. To make the program attractive for schools, it pays up to half the teacher's salary for five years, or a total of $50,000 per teacher. Troops-turned-teachers must agree to teach for five years. Because of the disproportionately high number of retiring military personnel who are black and Hispanic, the program has brought strong minority male and female role models into the inner-city neighborhoods most in need of the program. Of all inner-city schools, 23% had vacancies they could not fill with qualified teachers when the Troops-to-Teachers program was started. In high schools with large minority enrollments, only 50% of all students were taught by qualified mathematics or science teachers. In addition to former troops, the program is open to retiring civilian employees of the Defense and Energy departments, as well as civilians who worked for military contractors such as General Dynamics or McDonnell Douglas.

Reference: U. S. Department of Defense, Washington, D.C.

truancy Unexcused absence from elementary or secondary school, in violation of state education laws. Although local schools, school districts and state and federal education authorities compile careful statistics on student absentee rates, there are no specific statistics on truancy as an element of absenteeism (q.v.), largely because it is often difficult to prove unless a student or group of students is actually apprehended by police. Parents can easily convert truancy into a simple—and legal—absence from school by fabricating an excuse that the student was needed at home for personal family reasons. Moreover, many students apprehended by police as truants have legitimate reasons for not being in school. Some have been excused for medical or other reasons, and others simply attend private schools whose vacation periods and holidays often fail to coincide with those of public schools. Thus, random arrest of school-aged children on the street during school hours often produces serious civil rights complications.

Attempts to combat truancy have ranged from police sweeps to arrest all school-aged children on the street to the fining of parents for violation of compulsory education laws. The former has proved somewhat effective in low-income neighborhoods of major cities. Police sweeps in San Jose, California, in 1993 picked up 6,000 truants. The city reported a 35% decline in daytime burglaries and an increase in daily school attendance rates to 98.5%, compared to an average of 90% for the nation and 81% for California.

Prosecution of parents has proved less successful than truant arrests as a means of combating unlawful absenteeism. Authorities reason that parents of chronically truant children usually did little to supervise their children when they were young and responsive, and they are probably as ill-equipped as school authorities to control such behavior once the children reach adolescence. In smaller towns, fining parents has proved somewhat successful, especially where parents are forced to post hefty, refundable bonds until they bring their children under control and ensure their school attendance. Hamilton, Ohio, for example, lifted school attendance from 88% to 92% with this system in 1993.

Truancy, however, usually relates to serious mental, intellectual, academic, emotional, psychological or social problems and dysfunctions requiring therapy and counseling. Unfortunately, the vast majority of truancy occurs in the poorest areas of the United States, where schools lack the funds to provide the needed services to combat truancy. The result is an overreliance on law-enforcement authorities that produces little lasting effect on the problem. More often than not, truancy is simply ignored after it becomes chronic, and individual truants are simply allowed to drift away from school and integrate into society as best they can.

References: ERIC; NYT.

true-false test One of the most common forms of objective testing, with questions stated as declarative sentences that demand a simple student response of "correct" or "incorrect." Easy to construct and to score, true-false tests can give teachers quick indications of superficial student knowledge about a topic. On the other hand, the simplicity gives each child at least a 50% chance of guessing the correct answer for each question, thus skewing test results in favor of aggressive students who guess the answer to every question, while more anxious students leave blank answers to questions about which they may be unsure.

Reference: *Educational Testing and Measurement: Classroom Application and Practice,* Tom Kubiszyn and Gary Borich (1987).

Truman, Harry S (1884–1972) Thirty-third president of the United States, whose dedication to education helped convert American colleges and universities into instruments of universal education for the entire American people. A champion of civil rights, Truman was the first American president to demand an end to racial, religious and other forms of segregation in education and other areas of American life. Ignored by Congress, Truman nevertheless desegregated the American armed services by executive order in 1948.

A farmer's son from Missouri, he managed to finish high school but had no funds for college and went to work as a bank clerk and later as a farmer. After serving in World War I, he set up a clothing store in Kansas City, but he and his partner went bankrupt in 1921, and he drifted into local government jobs that served as a springboard to local political office and, eventually, the U.S. Senate. Named President Franklin D. Roosevelt's vice presidential running mate in 1944, he succeeded to the presidency after Roosevelt's death in April 1945, only three months after assuming the vice presidency.

Truman was an obsessive autodidact who made up for his lack of college education by studying history to a depth seldom reached by previous presidents or even by many scholars. In 1946, he established a Commission on Higher Education (q.v.) to study the possibility of universalizing higher education to give less affluent Americans the same educational opportunities and benefits as the affluent elite then attending college. The commission's report, *Higher Education for American Democracy* (1948), marked a turning point in American higher education and in civil rights. Five months after appointing his Commission on Higher Education, Truman appointed a Committee on Civil Rights (q.v.) "to safeguard the civil rights of the people." Both the commission and the committee declared "separate-but-equal education grossly unequal" and urged immediate enactment of "fair educational practices laws for public and private educational institutions, prohibiting discrimination in the admission and treatment of students based on race, color, creed, or national origin.'' In addition, the Commission on Higher Education urged an immediate doubling of higher education enrollments, an expansion of community colleges, and the establishment of federal scholarships for needy undergraduate and graduate students.

Congress ignored the two committee reports, refusing even to hold hearings on the proposals, but states—especially in the north—responded by expanding the number of community colleges and at least partially opening the doors of higher education to blacks. More important, however, the work of the two Truman groups provided the nation with a vision of the future and a program for the inevitable democratization of education that would follow in the ensuing two decades.

References: DAB; EB; *To Secure These Rights: The Report of the President's Committee on Civil Rights,* U.S. Government Printing Office (1947); *Higher Education for American Democracy: A Report of the President's Commission on Higher Education,* Harper Brothers (5 vols., 1948); *Public Papers of the Presidents of the United States: Harry S. Truman, 1948,* US. Government Printing Office.

truth-in-testing legislation A group of state laws that give students the right to see the actual results and scoring methods of standardized college and graduate school admission tests. First enacted in New York State in 1979, truth-in-testing legislation followed widespread complaints by students that they could not obtain the results on standardized admission tests in order verify the accuracy of scoring and of their eventual grades. As a result, New York enacted a law requiring administrators of such standardized examinations as the Scholastic Aptitude Tests (now, Scholastic Assessment Tests), the American College Testing Program, the Graduate Record Examination, the Medical College Admission Test and the Law School Admission Test to make public all statistical information on such tests. In addition, they must make available to each student his or her answer sheet and a

scoring key to allow students to verify their eventual grades. Until truth-in-testing legislation was passed, students would simply receive their grades on each test by mail and have no way of verifying their accuracy.

References: CHE; ERIC.

tuition The cost of formal instruction at an educational institution. Free at public elementary and secondary schools, some tuition is generally imposed on students at all colleges, public or private. Tuition does not cover any element of room costs, board or student extracurricular activities fees. Although levied at the beginning of each semester at most private elementary and secondary schools and colleges, tuition fees at public colleges and universities are often assessed on a course-credit basis, thus allowing students to pay only for the courses they actually take and extend the time they take to obtain their higher education.

In the 1993–1994 academic year, tuition at four-year private colleges averaged about $11,000—more than four times the tuition at public colleges, where such costs are subsidized by public monies. Tuition and fees account for only 17.1% of revenues at public colleges, with state government revenues providing 38.3% of total funding. Private colleges, which receive a mere 2.5% of their revenues from state governments, depend on tuition for more than 40% of their annual revenues. The sharp differences in tuition costs between private and public colleges forced a swelling in applications at public colleges and a decline in applications to many private colleges, as costs of private education, including tuition, room, board and other required student fees, climbed to between $20,000 and $30,000 a year in the early 1990s.

In an effort to reverse the trend, many universities began offering discounts to compete with public colleges. Tuition at four-year public colleges averaged about $3,000 a year in the mid-1990s, compared with average tuition of $12,000 at private colleges. Rochester University, a private institution, actually marked down its tuition $5,000 for New York State residents in 1995 to stem a decline in applications, and other private universities began following suit—though with somewhat less publicity. LehighUniversity, in Pennsylvania, Stevens Institute of Technology, in New Jersey, and Clark University, in Massachusetts, each began offering a fifth year of free study, while Oberlin College in Ohio offered a three-year program leading to a bachelor's degree at a saving of almost 25% of the cost of a four-year program. Susquehanna University in Pennsylvania and Clarkson University in New York started offering four years of courses for the price of three years' tuition, allowing students to cut tuition costs (though not the cost of room and board) by 25%.

Michigan's private Mercy College agreed to give out-of-state students outright grants that match what the state gives Michigan resident students. Lehigh and other comparable colleges also expanded the number of merit scholarships, offered on the basis of academic merit rather than need and designed to attract brighter students who might otherwise opt either for lower-cost public colleges or Ivy League schools, which, for a higher price, provide more prestigious names, albeit no better an education. More than 60% of students who had been accepted to Lehigh but chose to go elsewhere had indicated they would have selected Lehigh had they received merit scholarships.

References: DES; NYT.

tuition payment plan   A school, college or privately sponsored program whereby tuition costs for elementary, secondary or higher education may be paid in monthly, interest-free installments instead of a large lump sum at the beginning of the semester or academic year. Parents and students can thus pay tuition with income instead of capital. To cover lending costs and earn a profit, the payment plans usually charge a modest annual origination fee and begin collecting monthly installments for the following year's tuition four months in advance. By investing the advance payments, the plans can earn

interest on collected funds before having to pay the educational institutions. Tuition payment plans are usually membership plans involving only a specific group of participating schools or colleges.

Reference: *How to Pick a Perfect Private School,* Harlow G. Unger (1993).

Turner, Asa (1799–1885)   American clergyman, educator and co-founder of the famed "Yale Band" (q.v.), which was instrumental in bringing public education and colleges to the west. Born in Massachusetts, he attended and was ordained at Yale in 1830. While there, he joined an association of seven theology students who pledged to carry education westward by founding an institution in Illinois. There, they hoped to train preachers and teachers who would fan out across the rest of the west to establish more churches and schools. Playfully called the Yale Band (they played no instruments), the group sent Turner to establish a church in Quincy, Illinois, in 1830. He followed that triumph by helping to co-found Illinois College. He spent the next eight years tirelessly encouraging the growth of education in Illinois, establishing a public school in Quincy, soliciting funds for the college and assisting in the establishment of new congregations. In 1838, he moved to Denmark, Iowa, where he established another church and obtained a charter to found a new institution called Denmark Academy. He then joined members of an "Iowa Band" that had formed at the Andover Theological Seminary (q.v.) to campaign for the establishment of public schools and to found Iowa College, which later merged with Grinnell College.

Reference: *Asa Turner: A Home Missionary Patriarch and His Times,* George F. Magoun (1889).

Tuskegee Institute (now, Tuskegee University)   Historically, one of the most important institutions of African-American education in the United States. The first college operated entirely by African Americans, Tuskegee Institute stood as proof positive that blacks were the intellectual equals of whites in a state where it had been against the law even to teach blacks, who were regarded as subhuman.

Founded at Tuskegee, Alabama, in 1881, by an African-American educator and former slave, Booker T. Washington (q.v.), Tuskegee started out in an old shanty and a dilapidated church, whose roof leaked so badly that a student had to hold an umbrella over Washington's head as he attempted to teach. At the time, there were no schools in Alabama for blacks, and the level of poverty and illiteracy discovered in Alabama "left me [Washington] with a heavy heart. The work to be done in order to lift these people seemed beyond accomplishing."

He nevertheless opened the doors of his school to 30 students "about equally divided between the sexes," but limited enrollment to students older than 15 who could already read. From the beginning, Washington hoped to train his students to be teachers and leaders who would educate other African Americans. But his students were former slaves from plantations and were so poor that he had to do "something besides teach them mere books." He had to teach them basic hygiene. "We wanted to teach the students how to bathe; how to care for their

The first three buildings owned by Tuskegee. A cabin, henhouse and stable were all that remained on the plantation that Booker T. Washington purchased in Alabama in 1882 for $500 and eventually tansformed into Tuskegee Institute. (Library of Congress)

teeth and clothing. We wanted to teach them what to eat, and how to eat it properly, and how to care for their rooms."

In addition, Washington wanted to teach them as many trades as possible, so that they could teach others to become needed members of their communities. He believed that "the whole future of the Negro rested largely upon . . . whether or not he should make himself, through his skill, intelligence and character, of such undeniable value to the community in which he lived that the community could not dispense with his presence." Any individual, said Washington, "who learned to do something better than anyone else—learned to do a common thing in an uncommon manner—had solved his problem, regardless of the color of his skin."

Washington proceeded to make work an essential part of student and faculty life at Tuskegee. In addition to agricultural and domestic work, students learned all aspects of construction, including design, architecture, masonry, carpentry and roofing. They learned to harvest trees, mill their own lumber, manufacture their own bricks, make their own clothing, mattresses, bedding and upholstery, and build their own desks, chairs and furniture. They soon cleared the land and began growing food, some to eat themselves and some to sell, to repay the $500 Washington had borrowed to buy land for the college. Washington expanded the farm to include livestock, which soon produced enough to feed the faculty and students and even generated extra funds that permitted students to attend school full-time, without holding down jobs outside school.

At the beginning of the second year, Washington raised funds to build a large central building. Again, students dug out and laid the foundation and, with the faculty alongside, erected the superstructure. Washington marveled that "only sixteen years before . . . no Negro could be taught from books without the teacher receiving the condemnation of the law." Over the next 19 years, 40 buildings rose on the

Tuskegee campus, all but four of them products of student-faculty labor. "Hundreds of men are now scattered throughout the South," Washington later reminisced, "who received their knowledge of mechanics while being taught how to erect these buildings. Skill and knowledge are handed down from one set of students to another in this way, until at the present time a building of any description or size can be constructed wholly by our instructors and students, from the drawing of the plans to the putting in of electric fixtures, without going off grounds for a single workman."

Student skills soon earned money for the school. The kiln they built to make bricks became an important industry at the school. After 20 years, Washington could say that "our students manufacture twelve hundred thousand [1,200,000] bricks, of a quality suitable to be sold in any market. [White people] who had no contact with the school, and perhaps no sympathy with it, came to us to buy bricks, because they found out ours were good bricks. They discovered that we were supplying a real want in the community." The school had the same experience building wagons, carts and buggies. "The man who learns at Tuskegee to build and repair wagons and carts is regarded as a benefactor by both races in the community," said Washington. "The individual who can do something that the world wants done will, in the end make his way, regardless of race."

In 1896, Washington expanded the school by bringing in George Washington Carver to head the school's agriculture department, and Carver's work brought world renown to Tuskegee. When Washington died in 1915, he left behind him a monument of more than 100 buildings, spread over 25,000 acres, where more than 1,500 students trained each year in more than 300 trades and professions. At the time of Washington's death, the entire student body and faculty of 300 were African Americans and almost all were the descendants of former slaves. No longer a trade and agricultural institute,

Like almost all other buildings at Tuskegee Institute, the Old University Chapel was designed by faculty and built by students, in 1889, eight years after Booker T. Washington founded the school. It burned down in 1957. (Tuskegee University Archives, Hawkins Studio)

Tuskegee University is now a coeducational professional and technical institution offering undergraduate and graduate programs to more than 3,000 students, most of whom are African American, in liberal arts and sciences, agriculture, business, education, engineering, health professions and veterinary medicine.

References: Tuskegee University Archives, Tuskegee, Alabama; *Up From Slavery, An Autobiography,* Booker T. Washington (1901) .

tutor A teacher, usually private, who instructs students individually or in small groups. A traditional method of educating the children of the nobility in Britain, tutoring was common in America before the growth of public and private schools. Except at the university level (see TUTORIAL METHOD), a tutor is now often a special-education teacher who works with slower or learning-disabled students during free hours at school or after school hours and on weekends. Some families also use traditional tutors to help their children improve work at school with individualized compensatory instruction and critiques of written work.

Reference: *How to Tutor,* Samuel L. Blumenfeld (1973).

tutorial method A method of instruction commonly used in English universities, where teachers meet individually with students for intensive discussions about a topic based on materials the student has been assigned to study. Although some American universities and academically selective private schools use the tutorial method, most American colleges have refashioned the tutorial into seminars and so-called discussion groups, where a graduate student conducts in-depth conversations with students who have studied a particular topic and also absorbed the professor's lecture on the material.

Reference: *The Tutorial System and Its Future,* Will G. Moore (1968).

two-plus-two program A four-year, cooperative, vocational education program that begins in the junior year of high school and continues through senior year of high school and two years at an associated community college. Usually administered and taught by college teachers or specially trained high school teachers, the program is designed to professionalize vocational education by bringing college-level instruction into the high school. By creating a four-year continuum, the program does not permit students the luxury of the usual academic let-down during the spring of senior year as they prepare for high school graduation; graduation at high school does not guarantee promotion of two-plus-two students to the third year of the program at the community college. Also called tech-prep programs (q.v), two-plus-two programs create a separate, transition school that coincidentally uses the classrooms of two separate institutions but is, in effect, a four-year school, running from eleventh grade to fourteenth grade, with its own requirements for graduation and receipt of a professional certificate and an associate degree.

Reference: *But What If I Don't Want to Go to College?* Harlow G. Unger (1992).

U

underachievement In education, an often vague term referring to failure to perform academically at levels commensurate with a student's potential as measured by intelligence and other standardized tests. In general, educators consider high scores on standardized tests—e.g., I.Q. tests and Scholastic Assessment Tests—and low classroom grades an indicator of underachievement. Where such evidence is manifest in the elementary and early secondary school years, teachers, counselors and school administrators attempt to ferret out some of the most frequent causes, such as poor educational or socioeconomic background; psychological, emotional or medical problems, including learning disabilities; developmental differences; poor study habits; lack of parental support; lack of interest or motivation, generated by cultural background not conducive to academic pursuits; premature or inappropriate tracking of a student with high potential in low-ability classes, with low teacher expectations; unidimensional classrooms (q.v.), where teachers assume that a single classroom strategy is equally effective with all students; boredom resulting from above-average intelligence and teacher or school failure to provide adequately challenging materials.

The causes of underachievement, however, are often difficult to pinpoint. In many instances, a lack of aptitude in one subject area may produce discouragement that spills over into other areas. Low conceptual aptitudes in specific areas such as abstract thinking may also have a general effect on overall performance. In many instances, too, teachers may label a student an underachiever by misinterpreting a winning personality or social sophistication as an indicator of above-average intelligence and setting their expectations at levels far higher than the student's actual ability or potential. But the harshest criticism of the concept of underachievement is its philosophical foundation: that standardized tests do, indeed, measure each student's potential accurately and that every student can and therefore should be able to produce classroom grades commensurate with his or her scores on standardized tests. The universality of such an assertion has yet to be proved.

References: ERIC; *Giftedness, Conflict, and Underachievement,* Joanne R. Whitmore (1980).

unidimensional classroom A sociological term referring to the application of a single teaching strategy to all students in a given classroom. Although the introduction of computers has individualized teaching somewhat, most teachers in most public school classrooms continue—for practical reasons—to assign one task at a time to all students, on the assumption that all should be capable of completing it. Relative student performance in such classrooms generally remains constant, with the top students at the beginning of the year remaining at the top at the end of the year and the poorest students seldom raising their performance levels. Some teachers continue to conclude, as a result, that student failure is self-inflicted, the result either of an unwillingness to work hard enough or of congenital deficiencies. Despite ample evidence that instruction tailored to each student's developmental and aptitudinal needs can alter academic performance, the exigencies of large classrooms in many public schools make individualized instruction all but impossible and the unidimensional approach almost inevitable.

Reference: *Making the Best of Schools,* by Jeannie Oakes and Martin Lipton (1990).

unified phonics method A highly structured method of reading instruction based on the learning of 70 phonograms, or sounds, before actual reading begins. Developed in the late 1960s and often called the Spalding Method, the technique calls for oral recitation and memorization of the sounds in each phonogram (one or more letters that produce a unique sound that creates a word or word element). For example, although the phonogram ''at'' is itself a word, it is but one element in such words as ''cat attack.'' Students label, learn and write each phonogram by its complete sound, then learn basic spelling rules and eventually use phonograms to build words from a specific word list developed for the program. Only after students have learned an adequate number of words do they begin reading whole sentences.

(See also BOTTOM-UP MODEL OF READING; PHONICS; TOP-DOWN MODEL OF READING.)

Reference: The Writing Road to Reading, by Ronalda B. Spalding and Walter T. Spalding (1969).

Unitarianism A loosely knit, non-trinitarian Christian religion whose rejection of the Calvinist concept of predestination changed the course of American education in the early 19th century. Although anti-trinitarian movements, such as the Monarchian belief in the undivided unity of God, date from the early church of the 2nd century, the Unitarianism that so influenced American education was an outgrowth of 17th-century Arminianism. Named for the Dutch Calvinist and professor of theology Jacobus Arminius (1560–1609), Arminianism affirmed the existence of human free will. American Unitarianism of the early 19th century, as defined and articulated by Boston pastor William Ellery Channing (q.v.), conceived of a loving God who provided man with dignity and offered him the possibility of perfectibility.

The concept was nothing less than heresy to the Calvinist Puritans, whose Congregational churches had dominated New England politics, education and thought for nearly two centuries. As Unitarians took charge of Harvard College, then primarily a Congregational ministerial school, conservative Congregationalist leaders left for Andover, Massachusetts, in 1808 to found the rival Andover Theological Seminary. Their move not only split the ranks of Congregationalist leaders, it also shattered Congregationalism from its position as the official church

of several New England states (and therefore as the foundation of American education). Hardly mentioned in today's United States, Unitarianism was without question the most powerful religio-philosophical movement in the early 19th century. Indeed, many of its then-revolutionary concepts—especially that of human perfectibility through knowledge and education—were so totally absorbed into the national American psyche that they, and not Congregationalism, became the basis for building the American system of public education.

As pastor of the Federal Street Church of Boston, Channing became the most influential spokesman for Unitarianism, which he did not see as the new religion, but simply as a redefinition of traditional Congregationalism and a reinterpretation of Scripture. If man was indeed created in the image of God, then it followed that ''in ourselves are the elements of Divinity'' and, therefore, the distinct possibility of perfectibility and salvation. He envisioned formal education as a basis for achieving the Unitarian ideal of human perfectibility. Although recognizing the role of parents, ministers and institutions in education, Channing and his supporters saw schools, teachers and a public, common school system as essential to the ''flowering'' of the American child and American culture. ''The child,'' he said, ''is not put in the hands of parents alone. It is not born to hear but a few voices. It is brought at birth into a vast, may we say an infinite, school. The universe is charged with the office of its education.'' Teachers, he said, were primarily responsible for educating American children and, as such, their office was ''the noblest on earth.'' Channing and the Unitarians, along with the closely allied Transcendentalists (q.v.), became champions of universal public education and teacher training schools. In 1836, Horace Mann (q.v.), a Channing disciple, was instrumental in establishing the first state public school in the United States in Massachusetts.

Ironically, Unitarians were truer to the original Puritan-Congregationalist polity than the more orthodox Congregationalists in that they believed in complete congregational independence—the concept that caused the original split between the English Puritans and the Church of England. In 1961, the Unitarians (officially known as the American Unitarian Association) merged with the Universalist Church of America to form the Unitarian Universalist Association. Although it counts 172,000 members in more than 900 churches, the organization has no official statement of faith and does not require any specific religious belief or practice. Individual congregations remain completely independent, and the umbrella association simply serves as a coordinating body for women's federations, service committees and religious education.

References: American Unitarian Association, Boston, Massachusetts; *The Flowering of New England, 1815–1865,* Van Wyck Brooks (1936).

United Federation of Teachers

United Federation of Teachers The New York City local of the American Federation of Teachers (q.v.), a national labor union for teachers.

(See ALBERT SHANKER.)

Reference: United Federation of Teachers, New York, New York.

United Nations International School

United Nations International School A unique coeducational college-preparatory day school founded by parents working at the United Nations in New York, to give their children an international education while preserving their individual, cultural heritages. Accredited by the New York State Board of Regents and the Ministere de l'Education Nationale de France, it offers a curriculum of English, French, music, art, science, mathematics, social studies and physical education, along with preparation for the International Baccalaureate (q.v.), which is recognized by universities throughout the world. English is the medium of instruction, with French the second language. Teachers of English as a Second Language (q.v.) provide special instruction for students lacking English-

language skills. Classes in some mother tongues are held after school if there is enough demand and extra funds are provided.

The late United Nations Secretary General U Thant called the United Nations International School "an experiment in cultural understanding . . . [where] students who face each other across a laboratory bench today may, in a few years' time, face each other across an international conference table. The lessons they learn today are the foundations upon which a significant contribution to international cooperation may be made tomorrow."

Reference: United Nations International School, New York, New York.

United Negro College Fund

United Negro College Fund An organization founded in 1944 to raise funds for a group of more than three dozen, largely southern, independent four-year colleges for African Americans.

Reference: United Negro College Fund, New York, New York.

United States Air Force Academy

United States Air Force Academy A unit of the Department of the Air Force for educating and training officers for the United States Air Force. Located north of Colorado Springs, Colorado, the academy was established as an all-male institution by an act of Congress in 1954, with the first class graduating in 1954. The first women were admitted in 1976. Procedures for nomination to the applicant pool are identical to those of the United States Military Academy (q.v.). In addition to scholastic aptitude, as measured by the Scholastic Assessment Tests, applicants are judged on character, physical aptitude and condition, and prior academic record and extracurricular activities. About 1,500 cadets from an applicant pool of more than 9,000 are admitted each year. All educational and living expenses at the academy are paid by the U.S. Government. Cadets also receive annual salaries, commensurate with their rank in the U.S. Air Force. In addition to the arts and sciences, students obtain a general education in airmanship, including Air Force flying. Graduates receive a B.S. degree and are commissioned as second lieutenants in the regular Air Force. Physically qualified graduates receive pilot training after graduation. All graduates must serve at least six years in the armed forces.

Reference: Department of the Air Force, U.S. Department of Defense, Arlington, Virginia.

United States Armed Forces Institute A unique educative institution that provided correspondence courses to more than 600,000 American servicemen and women during World War II. The institute also provided classroom instruction on army posts and aboard ship and even in theaters of operation throughout the war and during the occupation of Germany and Japan. The institute's program supplemented a massive, service-wide educational program necessitated by the high illiteracy and low skill rates of draftees. By mid-1942, the Army was forced to provide specialized training to 63 of every 100 men; a year later, the figure rose to 90 of every 100. Limited to only a few weeks during each serviceman's basic training, the educational effort had to turn illiterates into literates and then train them to be auto, truck and aircraft mechanics, bookkeepers, carpenters, medics and pharmacists' mates, quartermasters, signalmen, torpedomen and a host of other specialists. Even the most literate and often well educated draftees still needed some form of specialized education in engineering, meteorology, navigation, language translation and trauma medicine.

The institute's work produced one of the most massive educational programs ever mounted by any nation in history. It included literacy courses at reception centers across the United States and technical schools operated by the military at every base. In addition, the armed services established contractual arrangements with vocational schools, colleges and universities to provide servicemen with specialized training in foreign languages, engineering, medicine, dentistry, military government and other professional skills. Once trained and assigned to per-

manent duty, servicemen could then turn to the Armed Forces Institute to supplement the education acquired in their earlier training.

Reference: *Classrooms in the Military: An Account of Education in the Armed Forces of the United States,* Harold F. Clark and Harold S. Sloan (1964).

United States Bureau of Education The first federal office created to give Washington a role in American education. Established in 1867 by an act of Congress, the bureau was to have served as a national center, to collect and disseminate information about education. Its first director, however, was Henry Barnard, a leader and outspoken advocate of the growing public school movement, which sought to establish universal public education and statewide public school systems in every state. After he turned the bureau into an advocacy organization for public schools, Congress abolished the bureau the following year, forcing Barnard to resign and transferring the bureau's data collection functions to a new Office of Education in the Department of Interior. In 1953, the office became part of the new Department of Health, Education and Welfare. In 1979, Congress created the U.S. Department of Education (q.v.), an executive department headed by a cabinet-level secretary.

Reference: EB.

United States Children's Bureau A federal office established by an act of Congress in 1912 to collect and disseminate information on "all matter pertaining to the welfare of children and child life" in the United States. Headed by Julia Lathrop (q.v.), the bureau aggressively gathered data on infant mortality, birth rates, orphanages, juvenile justice, desertion, accidents and diseases of children and child labor, in the belief that the collation and presentation of facts would force reform.

Establishment of the bureau was the result of 10 years of lobbying by the National Congress of Mothers and the Parent-Teacher Association (qq.v.), and a network of women from the social settlement movement (q.v.) who had helped

The United States Children's Bureau exposure of factory exploitation of young children led to passage of the first federal child labor law in 1916. (Library of Congress)

found the National Child Labor Committee to try to outlaw child labor (q.v.). Lathrop had been a resident of Hull House and was a close friend and associate of social activists Jane Addams, Florence Kelley and Lillian Wald (qq.v.). Once in office, Lathrop's investigation of infant mortality led to the establishment of uniform birth registration procedures. The bureau's subsequent studies of child labor led to enactment of the first federal child labor law in 1916. Lathrop formed the Child Labor Division within the bureau to enforce the new law and named a former Hull House resident, Grace Abbott (1878–1939), to head it. When Lathrop retired in 1921, Abbott took charge of the entire Children's Bureau and managed it for the next 13 years.

In 1918, the Supreme Court declared the child labor law an unconstitutional infringement on personal rights of children to work, but the bureau and its Child Labor Division continued to expose the outrages of child labor. A year before she left the bureau, Abbott succeeded in getting Congress to raise the minimum age for workers in most industries to 16 (to 18 in hazardous industries) as part of the National Industrial Recovery Act of 1933. Raising of the minimum working age had an immediate and widespread impact on education, forcing public schools across the United States to expand to accommodate a huge influx of new students who had formerly gone to work, sometimes as young as five. Southern industries, mines and farms had been especially dependent on child labor and had stalled formation of the Children's Bureau in the early 1900s and then successfully led the court battle that overturned the first federal child labor law in 1916. Their eventual agreement to a higher minimum working age came only after the mass unemployment of adult workers during the Great Depression of the 1930s began threatening the internal security of the republic. By eliminating children from the work force, Congress hoped to open up more jobs for adult workers.

In addition to its role in combating child labor, the Children's Bureau had a dramatic effect on child-rearing methods in the United States. This educative role was the result of three pamphlets it published, all written by Mary Mills West: *Prenatal Care* (1914), *Infant Care* (1915) and *Child Care: The Preschool Age* (1918). Together, the three pamphlets helped modernize child-rearing methods. The 41-page *Prenatal Care* taught mothers—especially immigrant mothers from relatively backward societies—the necessity of "perfect cleanliness" and the importance of putting oneself under the care of a doctor as early in pregnancy as possible. It also advised women to have their children delivered at hospitals, by doctors, instead of at home, by midwives, friends or relatives, as was common in that era. Covering all aspects of prenatal care, from the first signs of pregnancy to nursing the baby, the pamphlet asserted that "the first duty of every mother" was to nurse her baby, because "mother's milk was the perfect infant food."

Infant Care also stressed cleanliness and the duty of mothers to nurse their babies, and it offered 87 pages of instruction on food, clothing, training, discipline, health and hygiene. *Child Care: The Preschool Age* was 88 pages long and instructed parents on health, hygiene, food, clothing, exercise and play, discipline and education. It broke new ground by explaining that play was "a fundamental instinct" and "the foundation for a healthy adult life." The booklet urged parents to abstain from harsh punishment and suppression of children's basic instincts. It called the patient answering of children's constant questions "boundless opportunities [for parents] to lay the foundations of a broad and practical education." Although the first and last pamphlets had respectable circulation, *Infant Care* became one of the most influential publications in the history of American publishing. From the time of its issue, demand was unprecedented. By 1955, circulation had reached 35 million, making it the most widely circulated government publication in history, surpassing even the most widely circulated Department of Agriculture bulletins. By 1961, the total had reached 45 million, and by 1972, 59 million. Only the arrival of Dr. Benjamin Spock's (q.v.) *Baby and Child Care* in 1946 began to slow its distribution and gradually displace it as the most influential publication on child care.

One reason for the popularity of *Infant Care* was the constant updating by Children's Bureau researchers to keep the booklet abreast of the latest developments in child-care research. The original *Infant Care* urged teaching good habits through obsessive regularity, with the infant to be fed, bathed and put to sleep at the same time each day. Crying—especially after the infant was put to bed—was to be ignored. Parents were to begin toilet training infants in their third month, and they were not to tolerate thumb sucking, which the pamphlet called a source of disease. Pacifiers were forbidden, and thumb-sucking was to be eradicated by pinning or sewing the infant's sleeves to prevent its putting its thumb in its mouth. Even more dangerous than thumb-sucking, according to the pamphlet, was the "injurious practice" of masturbation. Moreover, the pamphlet warned that the child was "to know no other way than to do what he is told." Eventually, *Infant Care* relented on most of these proscriptions and subscribed to the child-rearing methods advocated by Dr. Spock.

Although West, the author, had no medical training, she was a widow with five children and had trained as a researcher at the University of Minnesota. In writing the pamphlets, she was careful to reflect the accepted medical advice of the era, and the pamphlet's succeeding editors continued to follow that practice.

References: *Children and Youth in America: A Documentary History,* Robert H. Brenner et al., eds. (3 vols., 1970–74); "Save the Children: A History of the Children's Bureau, 1903–1918," Nancy Pottishman Weiss (doct. th., University of California at Los Angeles, 1974).

United States Coast Guard Academy

An institution founded in 1876 to educate and train young men and, since 1975, women to be officers in the United States Coast Guard. Located in New London, Connecticut, since 1932, the academy is a four-year institution offering a full curriculum in the humanities, social sciences, physical sciences and engineering, along with required studies in seamanship and navigation. Professional training at sea is required in summer aboard the three-masted bark *Eagle* and on Coast Guard cutters. Except for a $1,500 entrance fee, the federal government pays all costs of attending by providing a monthly allowance of $525 plus a daily food allowance. Unlike the other service academies, the Coast Guard Academy selects cadets from a nationwide competition on the basis of standardized test scores, high school academic performance, participation in extracurricular and community activities, and desire to be a cadet. Any physically qualified, unmarried U.S. citizen may apply. All graduates are commissioned as ensigns in the Coast Guard.

Reference: United States Coast Guard Academy, New London, Connecticut.

United States Commissioner of Education

The chief executive officer of the United States Bureau of Education (later, Office of Education), established by an act of Congress in 1867. Rendered defunct in 1980 by the establishment of the Department of Education, with its secretary a member of the cabinet, the education commissioner was formerly appointed by the president with the approval of the Senate. The first such appointee was Connecticut's champion of public education, Henry Barnard, who immediately subverted the role of his office by making it an advocate of universal public education instead of an agency for collection and dissemination of information about American education. A year after his appointment, Barnard resigned the post, and the commissioner and bureau were transferred to the Department of Interior, where the bureau was renamed the Office of Education. In 1953, the office and its commissioner were transferred to the new Department of Health, Education and Welfare, where they remained until 1979.

References: EB; United States Department of Education, Washington, D.C.

United States Constitution

The document that outlines the principles, laws, powers and organization of the U.S. Government. Adopted in 1788, the Constitution leaves to the states all powers not specifically assigned to the central government in the document. The word education is not mentioned in the Constitution and, by design, was left entirely to the states to regulate. The decision to do so was not a casual one. Indeed, a large group of powerful and widely respected American leaders—among them Thomas Jefferson, James Madison, Benjamin Franklin and Benjamin Rush (qq.v.)—favored including universal public education as a fundamental constitutional right. Moreover, they envisioned establishing a national public educational system, directed by the central government, with a common school in each community, a secondary school in each county, a college in each state and a national university, from which graduation would be required for the right to hold public office. The scheme was defeated by a coalition of southern agricultural and northern industrial interests that depended on a combination of slave and child labor to produce cotton and textiles at prices low enough to compete on world markets.

References: EB; *American Education, The National Experience: 1783–1876,* Lawrence A. Cremin (1979); *The Constitution of the United States,* Floyd G. Cullop (1984).

United States Department of Agriculture

An executive department of the government that conducts research, maintains service activities and administers regulatory laws in the broad field of agriculture. Created as a small office in 1836 to distribute plants and seeds to farmers, it became a department in 1862 and was raised to cabinet status by Congress in 1889. Its myriad functions have expanded to include research, conservation, forestry, marketing, credit, food distribution, export expansion, production controls, grading and inspection, rural development, and a wide variety of education and education-related programs. Responsible since 1946 for administration of the National School Lunch Program (q.v.), the department has been a major provider of education to farmers and the men, women and children of farm communities since passage of the Smith-Lever Act (q.v.) in 1914. At the time, American agriculture was in the grip of a self-destructive process that had seen farmers deplete the soil of all its nutrients. Working in cooperation with land-grant colleges, the department established experiment stations and demonstration farms to teach farmers how to use fertilizers and pesticides and how to rotate crops.

The department's efforts to modernize American agriculture were so successful that farms were producing enormous food surpluses when the Great Depression of the 1930s sent prices tumbling and plunged hundreds of thousands of farmers into bankruptcy. The department's services were then reorganized to buy and store surplus foodstuffs and help maintain prices at levels high enough to make farming a viable industry. The department continues to regulate production and prices through a variety of market mechanisms.

The department's educational functions, however, reached well beyond the bounds of commercial agriculture. In the first half of the 20th century, its extension service helped teach several generations of farm women to run their households efficiently and feed their families at minimum cost by maintaining kitchen gardens and small livestock runs for chickens, pigs and the like. Its huge publications division taught rural adults how to build every type farm structure, how to raise every kind of domestic animal, how to make and repair clothes, cook, preserve foods, and conduct every conceivable activity designed to make a person self-sufficient in isolated rural areas. In addition to adults, the department's educational services reached millions of children through various programs such as the 4-H Clubs (q.v.). Ultimately, the department reached tens of millions of rural Americans and helped teach them how to modernize American agriculture and make it the largest revenue producing industry in the United States in the years following World War II—a position it maintained as late as 1960.

Because of the relative price stability maintained by the Department of Agriculture, other unregulated industries subsequently displaced it as leading revenue producer. In the last decades of the 20th century, the department's educative role declined somewhat as huge "agracorporations" took over the majority of American farmland from small farmers. In the 73 years from 1920 to 1993 the number of farms in the United States plunged from a high of about 6.8 million to about 2.1 million, while the average acreage of each farm soared from 155 acres in 1935 to 468 acres in 1992.

Reference: United States Department of Agriculture, Washington, D.C.

United States Department of Defense

An executive branch of the government charged with directing and controlling the American armed forces and assisting the president in safeguarding the nation's security. Created by the National Security Act of 1947, the department unified all branches of the armed services under a single, central command, with a civilian, cabinet-level secretary at its head. In the area of education, the department is responsible, through its various branches, for administering the various military service academies, the Army War College and the Command and General Staff School (qq.v.). Until 1981, it was also responsible for providing and administering elementary and secondary schools for children of military personnel and civilian workers on military bases in the United States and throughout the world. Authority over such dependents' schools (q.v.) was subsequently transferred to the Department of Education.

At the higher education level, the department underwrites the huge Army, Navy and Air Force reserve officers' training programs (qq.v.) that provide thousands of students with a free college education in return for their subsequent service as officers in the armed forces. It also provides grants to help underwrite the Servicemen's Opportunity Colleges Program (q.v.) that makes two-year and four-year college programs available to more than 250,000 servicemen.

Reference: United States Department of Defense, Arlington, Virginia.

United States Department of Education

The cabinet-level executive department charged with administering all federal programs relating to formal education in the United States. Created in 1979, the department is a successor to the Bureau of Education, which was founded in 1867 to gather and disseminate information on education. The Department of Education continues to perform that role through its Office of Educational Research and Improvement, which publishes the annual *Digest of Education Statistics,* the most complete publication of statistics on American education. The department has also assumed authority for a variety of educational programs that had been scattered in other executive departments, such as the departments of Defense, Agriculture, Labor and Justice.

The department dispenses nearly half the $70 billion spent by the United States government on education each year. Among its many responsibilities are enforcement of civil rights laws in the educational sector; oversight of vocational rehabilitation programs; administration of U.S.

Department of Defense dependents' schools (q.v.); administration of the National Institute for Education, the National Center for Education Statistics, the Fund for the Improvement of Secondary Education and the Institute for Museum Services; and indirect oversight of four special institutions: Howard and Gallaudet universities (qq.v.), the National Technical Institute for the Deaf and the American Printing House for the Blind. Most recently, the department assumed control of the huge guaranteed student loan program (see STUDENT LOANS), with students now able to borrow funds for their college education directly from the department instead of from commercial banks. Under the old program, students obtained low-interest loans from banks, with the government paying the banks the difference between the interest charged and the rates of conventional personal loans.

Almost since its creation, the department has been under attack. When Ronald Reagan assumed the presidency in 1981, he pledged to abolish the department and return its various functions to the agencies that had originally controlled them. He had support from a not inconsiderable number of conservative constitutionalists and educators who pointed out that the framers of the Constitution specifically left control of education to the states. By failing even to mention the word education, the Constitution delegated absolutely no authority over education to the federal government. The department had been a result of a campaign pledge by Jimmy Carter to the National Education Association (q.v.) in return for its support in the 1976 presidential election. It was Congress, however, that created the department and passed the various laws establishing the programs and institutions that it now controls. Interestingly, President Reagan wholeheartedly approved and signed into law the Education of the Handicapped Acts of 1983 and of 1986, which extended the Education for All Handicapped Children Act of 1975 (q.v.) and led to the federal government's deepest incursions into public school education. The two laws forced public schools across the United States to admit and provide appropriate education (and physical access to school facilities) for more than one million handicapped children who, until then, had been excluded.

Reference: United States Department of Education, Washington, D.C.

United States Department of Health, Education, and Welfare (HEW)

A now-defunct cabinet department that included the Office of Education. Created in 1953, HEW's constituent elements grew too large to administer efficiently in a single department. In 1979, Congress authorized a reorganization that converted the Office of Education into the autonomous Department of Education (q.v.) the following spring. HEW was renamed the Department of Health and Human Services.

Reference: United States Department of Education, Washington, D.C.

United States Department of Labor

An executive department of the federal government, headed by a cabinet secretary and created by Congress in 1913 "to foster, promote and develop the welfare of the wage earners of the United States, to improve their working conditions and to advance their opportunities for profitable employment." Among its myriad agencies are several directly related to education, including the Employment and Training Administration, which oversees job training and placement programs. Its Bureau of Apprenticeship and Training, created under the National Apprenticeship Act of 1937, establishes and promotes industry standards for on-the-job training and provides official accreditation of state standards that match its own. Most states have adopted the bureau's apprenticeship training standards.

In 1973, Congress assigned the department another educational function by creating the Comprehensive Employment and Training Act (CETA), which authorized the department to establish training and job opportunities for the unemployed, the disadvantaged and the under-employed whose skills or jobs had been rendered obsolete by automation and advanced technology. CETA also provided more than one million summer jobs for disadvantaged youths aged 14 to 21. Still another education function of the department is the certification of sheltered workshops for the handicapped.

Reference: United States Department of Labor, Washington, D.C.

United States Department of State

A cabinet-level executive department created in 1789 to implement the president's foreign policies. Its Office of Overseas Schools supports American international schools abroad both academically and administratively through a variety of services. These include sending consultants to visit such schools to ensure that they keep their curricula and student counseling and college advisory services attuned to those of comparable schools in the United States. American international schools are private institutions offering American-style education, from grades K through 12, to children of American civilians living overseas.

Reference: Office of Overseas Schools, United States Department of State, Washington, D.C.

United States Merchant Marine Academy

A publicly supported, four-year institution of higher education offering maritime, military and engineering programs to train officers for the United States merchant marine and the maritime industry in general. Administered by the United States Maritime Commission, the academy was founded at King's Point, New York, by President Franklin D. Roosevelt in 1943, after attacks by German and Japanese ships forced the United States to arm its merchant fleet for carrying troops and supplies overseas. Roosevelt's goal for the institution was to provide merchant ships and the transportation industry with a corps of well-trained professional officers, adept at commanding ships in peace as well as war.

Applicants to the academy must be nominated by a member of Congress. They must be U.S. citizens between the ages of 17 and 25 and in excellent physical condition. Once admitted, they must take a core curriculum of mathematics, science, English, humanities, history, naval science, physical education, ship's medicine and computer science. Students must also pass summertime sea-project courses while living aboard ship, and then must pass the U.S. Coast Guard licensing and certification examination. They must spend five months at sea on U.S. flagships during their junior and senior years and serve five years on a merchant vessel and eight years in the Naval Reserve after graduation. Upon graduation, students receive a bachelor of science degree and a license as a deck officer, an engineer or a dual officer.

With only about 1,000 students, the need for the academy came under question in the face of a massive downsizing of the U.S. merchant fleet, which had declined to fewer than 1,000 ships by the early 1990s, with only about 200 of them government-owned. Although the government held about 400 vessels in the so-called Ready Reserve Fleet and Sealift Command for emergency operations, many of the ships were obsolete and rapidly deteriorating from non-use. Moreover, five coastal states—California, Maine, Massachusetts, New York and Texas—had sea-grant colleges (q.v.) that duplicated the training of the academy, and many congressmen questioned whether the federal government should continue underwriting the cost of training officers for private industry.

Reference: United States Merchant Marine Academy, King's Point, Long Island, New York.

United States Military Academy

The national military college for soldiers at West Point, New York. Operated by the Department of the Army to educate and train young men and women to be officers in the United States Army,

Cadets on parade at the United States Military Academy, at West Point, New York. (Library of Congress)

West Point was founded by Congress in 1802 and became the first school of engineering in the United States. It admitted its first women cadets in 1976. All cadets must study a rigorous four-year curriculum in engineering, military science, the social and natural sciences and the humanities. Military training is conducted during summer sessions. Upon graduation, cadets receive the B.S. degree and commissions as second lieutenants in the regular army, where they must serve no less than six years.

The maximum strength of the cadet corps was authorized at just over 4,000 in the early-to-mid-1990s, with women making up about 105 of that number. Candidates for admission must be U.S. citizens and at least 17 but not yet 22 years old on the day of admission. (Qualified young men and women from allied nations are also admitted under special conditions.) They must be physically fit, of high moral character and have demonstrated superior academic skills in school and on standardized college entrance examinations. Qualified students with a deep desire to become a cadet must obtain a nomination by contacting their congressman. Five nominations each are allocated to the vice president, every senator, every representative and the congressional delegate from the District of Columbia. Territorial governors may each make one nomination, and the resident commissioner of Puerto Rico may make six. Military service nominations are distributed as follows: president, as commander in chief, 100; members of the regular army and members of the army reserves, 85 each; graduates of certain types of military and naval schools (called honor military schools) and Reserve Officers Training Corps, 20; children of deceased or severely disabled veterans, 10; children of Medal of Honor winners, unlimited (although there are few such candidates).

More than 10,000 students apply each year, and only about 1,200 are accepted. Tuition, room and board are paid by the federal government, which also provides students with a monthly stipend for books, uniforms and personal expenses. The unique curriculum and system of training at the academy was the work of Sylvanus Thayer (q.v.), who was appointed superintendent of the academy in 1817, after spending two years in Europe on behalf of the government to study military education and defense systems. Thayer's influence over the next 18 years converted the academy from a military drill school into a superior educational institution. Thayer expanded the science and arts curriculum and introduced engineering as a science, making that department the best in the world. He expanded the faculty, added courses, restructured students into a cadet corps and instituted the tough examinations and rigid student discipline that remain hallmarks of West Point's educational system.

Reference: United States Military Academy, West Point, New York.

United States Naval Academy A four-year college administered by the U.S. Navy to prepare young men and women to be officers in the U.S. Navy and U.S. Marine Corps. Founded by Secretary of the Navy George Bancroft (q.v.) in 1845 as the Naval School in Annapolis, it moved to Newport, Rhode Island, for the duration of the Civil War. Procedures for nomination to the applicant pool are identical to those of the United States Military Academy. Of the more than 4,000 students, about 500 are women. The Navy pays for tuition, room and board, and medical and dental care of students and provides midshipmen with a salary to cover the cost of uniforms and supplies and other expenses. In addition to wide-ranging studies in the liberal arts and sciences, students receive professional training in aviation, engineering and various military, maritime and technical fields. Candidates must be nominated under the same process as applicants to the United States Military Academy (q.v.). Unlike the other military academies, Annapolis has a graduate school for advanced studies in ordnance, mechanical engineering, radio, shop management, naval architecture and civil engineering."

Reference: United States Naval Academy, Annapolis, Maryland.

United States Office of Education A federal agency and forerunner of the Department of Education, originally founded as the Bureau of Education in 1867 to gather and disseminate statistics on education in the United States. The bureau's first commissioner, Henry Barnard, proved so strong an advocate of universal public education that he alienated southern cotton planters and northern textile mill owners, who depended on child labor. Within a year, their representatives in Congress emasculated the bureau, turning it into an agency of the Department of Interior, and forced Barnard to resign.

Relatively ineffectual for most of the next century, its importance grew as education reached more and more people. Eventually, the office was transferred to the Department of Health, Education and Welfare, and in 1979 it became an independent, executive department headed by a cabinet secretary and renamed the Department of Education.
Reference: Department of Education, Washington, D.C.

United States territories Partially self-governing geographic areas under the control of the United States government, but without the status or prerogatives of statehood. The most important territories of the United States are the Virgin Islands of the United States in the Caribbean and Guam and American Samoa in the Pacific Ocean. Puerto Rico was a territory from 1898 until 1952, when its population voted for commonwealth status and self-rule within a framework of U.S. federal laws. American Samoa has about 160 primary village schools, 30 public secondary schools, 6 private schools and one community college. Education is compulsory for children aged 6 to 18. The Virgin Islands have about 70 public elementary and secondary schools, with nearly 30,000 students. Education is compulsory for children 5½ to 16. The College of the Virgin Islands has an enrollment of 2,500.
Reference: EB.

United States v. Montgomery County Board of Education A U.S. Supreme Court decision in 1969 establishing racial ratios for teacher assignments in Montgomery, Alabama, public schools. The case was significant as the last of three Supreme Court decisions that effectively ended the massive resistance of states in the south to the Court's 1954 decision in *Brown v. Board of Education of Topeka* (q.v.), which declared racial segregation of public schools unconstitutional. In the two earlier decisions, *Green v. County School Board of New Kent County* (1968) and *Alexander v. Holmes County Board of Education*

(1969) (qq.v.), the Court had outlawed so-called free-choice plans that allowed students to select whatever schools they wanted to attend, and it ordered all public school districts everywhere to end all delays of racial integration and to desegregate schools by the beginning of the following school year.
Reference: U.S. Supreme Court proceedings.

unit of instruction The smallest subdivision of a subject or course, consisting of a specific problem or topic or group of closely interrelated problems and topics. In teacher lesson plans, each unit of instruction is normally accompanied by a carefully outlined instructional approach and associated student exercises. Thus, at the simplest level, a unit of instruction in beginning mathematics might consist of adding pairs of single-digit numbers in every possible combination. A breakdown of instruction into units is considered essential to the development of a logical sequence in the learning process, with each successive unit directly tied to knowledge accumulated in the previous unit.
Reference: *Teaching and Learning in the Elementary School,* John Haolimek and Clifford D. Foster (1985).

university An all-encompassing institution of post-secondary education and research, usually consisting of one or more four-year undergraduate schools, or colleges (q.v.), which confer bachelor's degrees, and one or more graduate and professional schools, which confer master's degrees and doctorates. The university can trace some of its roots to the academies of ancient Greece and similar institutions that emerged in Babylonia, Persia and Arabia, between the 6th century B.C. and the 9th century A.D. In 859, Al Qarawiwyn University was established at Fez, Morocco, and in 970, Al-Azhar University opened in Cairo. At the end of the 8th century, Charlemagne brought the cleric and educator Alcuin of York to Aix-la-Chapelle (Aachen) to establish a palace school. Alfred the Great, himself a scholar, turned his palace into a center of learning in Britain about a century later and ordered monks to expand the educational function of their monasteries. At the same time, the Moors swept into Spain and reopened what had been a Roman university at Cordoba, which became a center of philosophy and brought to Europe the long-lost works of Aristotle, Justinian, Galen, Hippocrates, Euclid and Ptolemy.

Beginning in the 12th century, the university movement spread northward into Europe proper. Northern universities in Paris, Oxford and Cambridge tended to be organized and administered by professors, while southern universities, such as the one in Bologna, Italy, were run by students. University students largely came from elite families who could afford to allow their children to spend their time learning—usually in preparation for the learned professions, that is, medicine, law and the church. The embryonic university was usually formed by theological scholars, philosophers, teachers of law and teachers of medicine, who formed groups analogous to medieval tradesmen to protect their interests and establish standards for their professions. When these standards obtained recognition either from a pope or king or by general consensus, they earned the title *studium generale,* or center of learning for all. Oxford emerged as a *studium generale* by the end of the 12th century, and Cambridge followed suit in 1209. As early university course offerings expanded to include grammar, arithmetic, music, geometry, astronomy, natural, moral and mental philosophy, medicine, theology and civil and canon law, the institution widened its scope to universal proportions and earned the name university, derived from the Latin *universitas,* meaning universe. In the Middle Ages, it came to mean society, guild or corporation and was applied to academic institutions, or *universitas magistrorum et scholarium.* Within each university, smaller colleges formed, often as common living quarters (the university offered no housing or maintenance), and individual colleges began to specialize in particular areas of study, attracting student masters with similar scholastic interests.

Like its English predecessors, the first college in America, Harvard, was founded in Massachusetts in 1636 for the specific purpose of training ministers of American Puritanism. Yale followed suit 65 years later. In founding Harvard and Yale, New Englanders were trying to strengthen their church and produce the spiritual and intellectual leadership needed to help them create a "promised land" amid inhospitable surroundings. The ministers who emerged from such colleges also served as local instructors of the young, teaching them to read, write and calculate, as well as learn the catechism.

In the mid-18th century, however, a new generation of practicalists emerged, insisting that universities leave lessons of the heavens to the church and concentrate on teaching young men the practical skills and crafts to survive on Earth and carve out a new nation from the American wilderness. To this end, Benjamin Franklin founded Franklin's Academy in Philadelphia (later, the College of Philadelphia, and now, the University of Pennsylvania). Not a word of theology was taught. A generation later, in 1819, Thomas Jefferson founded the University of Virginia. Like Franklin, he omitted theology and offered students the opportunity to choose from a broad curriculum in eight different "schools" that were comparable to modern "majors."

In New England, tiny Amherst College, in Massachusetts, pioneered the shift in college curricula from classical to practical education after Amherst science and mathematics professor Jacob Abbott (q.v.) prodded the faculty to add a new academic program with "a more modern and national aspect" than the traditional curriculum. Requirements for admission—competence in Greek and Latin—remained unchanged, and the four-year classical and scientific course leading to the bachelor's degree continued to be offered to those who sought such a curriculum. To satisfy "the taste and future pursuits of a large class of young men," however, Amherst added a new curriculum of liberal education, which unfortunately offered no degree as an incentive. It substituted French and German for Greek and Latin and added more courses in English literature, modern history, civil and political law and the natural sciences. In addition, Amherst added two new departments: one, for science and the art of teaching, was to train schoolmasters; the other offered theoretical and practical mechanics that would not only "afford exercise and amusement to many of the students," but also be profitable to the school by "keeping all the buildings and furniture in constant repair." Introduced in 1827, the radical new curriculum produced a rush of initial interest—until students learned that it did not lead to the degree that had become so essential to postcollegiate success. Although Amherst abandoned the program in 1829, it did not go unnoticed by other educators. Harvard and the University of Vermont reorganized their curricula into departments and permitted students a wider choice of subjects. Union College, in Schenectady, New York, did much the same, adding more courses in modern languages and the natural sciences.

All, however, represented modest reforms compared to those that were underway at Brown University, the University of Nashville and the University of Michigan. At Brown, Francis Wayland (q.v.) had taken over the presidency in 1827, following several years of riots by students demanding an expanded curriculum and more freedom to choose what they might study. Over the next two decades, he introduced "that kind of education which will be of the greatest use to . . . the prosecution of useful industry." A strong believer in the free-market economy, Wayland sought to adapt Brown's curriculum "to the wants of the whole community" by expanding the traditional curriculum to include chemistry, physics, geology, English language and rhetoric, political economy, history, law, the science of teaching, the principles of agriculture and a wide range of arts. In addition to expanding the curriculum to meet the needs of society, Wayland sought to

open Brown to all classes of society and offer students a choice of programs, courses and educational goals.

In Nashville, meanwhile, Philip Lindsley (1786–1855) was trying to reorganize Cumberland College into the University of Nashville, which he hoped to make into the keystone of a complete system of formal education in Tennessee, from infant schools through colleges, universities and professional schools of law, divinity, medicine, military and naval science, agriculture and architecture, with each branch of learning taught to an appropriate degree at each educational level. The university was to be "the means of teaching all the sciences, and everything, indeed, which it is desirable for any man to know." Its libraries would contain "one or more copies of every valuable book extant in any language, ancient or modern," and its laboratories would contain "specimens, living or preserved, of every vegetable and animal and mineral, peculiar to the earth, the air and the waters of our planet." He called for expansion of the university to include botanical gardens, astronomical observatories, models of machines and useful inventions and works of the noblest artists (or reproductions thereof). Lindsley's model of the university differed from Wayland's in that it offered the widest possible education regardless of market demand.

A third model for university reform came from the University of Michigan, whose president, Henry Philip Tappan (q.v.), proposed a comprehensive system of education for the entire state—not unlike the one proposed by Lindsley in Tennessee, but concerned as well with extending "the boundaries of human knowledge and understanding" through research. It was the element of research that made the Tappan model unique.

As it turned out, none of the three would-be reformers lived to see his vision incorporated into lasting, working institutions Although Brown adopted Wayland's reforms in 1851, his successor abandoned them as too impractical.

Lindsley, meanwhile, was unable to raise the funds needed to transform Nashville into a university, and in Michigan, the regents forced Tappan to resign in 1863. Nevertheless, the reforms envisioned by Wayland, Lindsley and Tappan would eventually be adopted by every major American university. The demand for practical skills gradually relegated theology to a minor role at most universities. Even the most traditional colleges, such as Yale, Harvard and Princeton, eagerly expanded into larger, more universal institutions. To that end, they began to found or combine with law schools and medical schools. They also expanded departments such as mechanics (engineering), which in turn became separate schools or colleges within the university.

The modern university is a conglomerate of disassociated schools, each often housed in its own building and teaching courses unrelated to those in other schools. Their affiliation to a central umbrella institution provides many advantages unavailable to any of the individual units acting singly. Chief among these is the reduction in administrative costs, with a single president, vice president, treasurer, secretary, bursar, registrar and staff to handle the bureaucratic functions of all divisions, leaving the dean of each school free to spend his entire time on curricular and academic affairs. A second source of enormous savings is derived from the sharing and multiple use of physical facilities, such as classrooms and laboratories that might otherwise remain underutilized.

The first practical model for the modern American university originated in October 1869, when the new, 35-year-old president of Harvard, Charles W. Eliot (q.v.), delivered his inaugural address. Considered a turning point in the history of American education, the address outlined a new scheme for a quintessentially American university. Within 20 years, he had accomplished his goals, separating and expanding the law department into a proper law school and the medical department into a medical school, each with its own faculty, granting professional, postgraduate degrees after completion of a much expanded and far more rigorous curriculum. Divinity studies moved into their own, separate graduate school. Undergraduate studies were also expanded, with the sciences incorporated into the core curriculum required for a bachelor's degree. In 1872, he established a graduate school of arts and sciences, offering master's and doctoral degrees; and in all these schools, a system of rigorous examinations was introduced as a requirement for graduation. By 1894, 25 years after taking office, Eliot had created the prototypical American university. Columbia, Princeton, Yale and, soon, most other independent universities followed the example of Harvard.

In the century that followed, universities evolved in ways that Eliot and his disciples at other universities could never have imagined. At the time Eliot took charge of Harvard, total enrollment of the university was 500, with a faculty of 23. When Nicholas Murray Butler joined the Columbia faculty in 1885, there were only 200 students; even after student ranks increased tenfold under his presidency in the early 1900s, he never faced the sort of explosive expansion that changed the complexion of universities following World War II.

From 1947 to 1992, total enrollment in institutions of higher learning climbed from 2.3 million to 14.5 million students. Their arrival overwhelmed most campuses, forcing huge physical expansions. Separate buildings were needed for a host of new graduate schools. Many undergraduate departments grew too large to share facilities with other departments. Some needed their own, new, separate buildings, with specialized facilities and equipment, such as laboratories and interactive computers. Moreover, the university curriculum had mushroomed unexpectedly, from fewer than 100 courses in the late 19th century, to well over 100 majors, with several thousand courses, a century later (see Appendix B).

No longer was a single central registrar, bursar or other administrator able to cope with the needs and demands of faculties and students from so many far-flung departments and graduate schools. At the typical large university, each graduate school gradually assumed responsibility for its own administration, establishing, in effect, a separate institution that shared only the streets, pathways, a few library services and a university president. The result was an organizational anarchy that saw each graduate school take charge of its own finances, tuition collection and fund-raising and share little with the central university or its undergraduate college. Operating like geographically connected but independent city states, graduate schools at some universities succeeded in building prosperous institutions, while core, undergraduate institutions faltered and accumulated substantial operating deficits. Indeed, most undergraduate colleges were forced to revert to 19th-century Lancasterian methods (q.v.) originally designed to educate poor children in orphanages by using unpaid older students to teach their younger inmates. The modern universities modified the system somewhat by hiring low-paid graduate students, with no teaching experience, to teach undergraduate students in lieu of high-salaried professors, whose time the graduate schools monopolized.

Many question whether the university, as conceived by Eliot, may now be so unmanageable as to warrant a Balkanization of its individual units, with a return to the 19th-century system of independent undergraduate and graduate colleges. That concern reached a peak in 1994—ironically at Harvard, where its president, the Renaissance literature scholar Neil L. Rudenstine, was forced to take a leave of absence because of "severe fatigue and exhaustion." Social scientists reacted quickly, calling any university presidency "a nearly impossible job," because of the conflicting constituencies. Famed social scientist David Riesman explained that faculties had become "unreasonable" and that

students had changed radically, from passive vessels to active consumers. In addition to the frustration of mediating conflicts between the university's various constituencies, university presidents like Rudenstine also faced the impossible task of traveling across the face of the nation raising billions of dollars in contributions to cover operating deficits and costs of maintenance and repair of huge, aging infrastructures. At least some of the deficits, however, can be traced to spiraling salaries, benefits and bonuses paid to university faculty and administrators. To compete with private industry, some universities had raised presidential salaries to nearly $500,000 a year and salaries of some graduate school professors (particularly at law and medical schools) to $600,000 or more.

References: NYT; *American Education,* Lawrence A. Cremin (3 vols., 1970–87).

university curriculum The curriculum, or courses, offered at a university. Once limited to theological studies and classical studies and numbering several dozen courses, university curricula have undergone an explosive expansion over the last two centuries. The practical and social needs of the latter half of the 20th century forced American colleges and universities to add thousands of courses leading to degrees in several hundred majors, ranging from accounting to zoology. They include virtually every imaginable vocational, preprofessional and professional area, as well as the liberal arts, the sciences and the social sciences. Depending on the college or university, the level of study in various courses may range from elementary, as in beginning foreign-language courses, to doctoral-level research and independent studies. (Appendix B lists the more than 100 undergraduate majors now available at accredited American colleges and universities.)

Reference: *Barron's Profiles of American Colleges* (updated annually).

university extension movement A 19th-century shift in the goals of major universities from educating the wealthy elite to servicing society at large by offering access to education to any and all who wished to avail themselves of it. The movement began at Oxford and Cambridge universities in England in the 1850s and 1860s, after critics attacked the publicly supported institutions for their self-imposed isolation from the rest of society. The institutional church and the social settlement (qq.v.) were two responses to such criticism, but a third response came in 1867, when scholars at Cambridge began offering courses to local groups of working men and women, including lawyers, ministers and teachers.

The informal offerings soon developed into a formal series of lectures, syllabi, homework assignments, discussions and examinations that university authorities eventually organized into an adult-education curriculum leading to university credits. By 1875, Cambridge was enrolling more than 7,000 students in extension courses. Oxford followed suit and by 1887 was enrolling about 13,000 students. The movement immediately spread to the United States, where the American Society for the Extension of University Teaching, in Philadelphia, organized similar programs at various local schools, colleges and universities. The University of the State of New York quickly emulated the Philadelphia example, and the Association of College Alumnae (later, the American Association of University Women) organized similar programs in Indiana.

University extension did not become a formal university program in the United States until William Rainey Harper and John D. Rockefeller drew up plans to open the University of Chicago in 1890. Believing that the university was the "keeper" of democracy and had a responsibility to disseminate knowledge to the widest possible audience, Harper included an aggressive, autonomous extension division, with its own faculty, into his initial plans for the new university. The division was to be organized into six departments offering, respectively, lecture study, classroom work, correspondence study, books and publications, examinations, and teacher training for the extension division. Although it never materialized as Harper had planned, it nevertheless served as the basis for a sizable number of correspondence courses and became a model for other universities, such as the University of Wisconsin (q.v.) and the University of Kansas, to use in establishing important extension programs in agriculture for local farmers. The University of Wisconsin so expanded the Harper model as to become the world's preeminent university in terms of outreach to the general public and service to the community.

By the beginning of World War I, the university extension program had become an integral part of American higher education, with scores of colleges and universities offering correspondence courses, lecture courses, short courses, club study, training institutes, community forums and library service programs. Columbia University had 2,000 adult students attending its extension courses for credit. Pennsylvania State University had 4,800 students enrolled in correspondence courses leading to B.A. degrees. The University of Michigan boasted an enrollment of 70,000 men and women at more than 300 lectures in its extension program.

References: *The University Extension Movement*, W. S. Bittner (1920); *University Extension in the United States*, Louis E. Reber (1914).

university finances The revenues and expenditures of institutions of higher learning. These differ somewhat between public and private institutions, with the former on average obtaining more revenue from government sources than from students and private sources. Here is a comparison of the percentage of revenues received from various sources by public and private institutions for the 1991–1992 academic year. The percentages have not changed substantially since then:

Revenue source	Public	Private
Tuition and fees	17.1%	40.7%
Federal government	10.6	15.3
Appropriations	1.6	0.4
Unrestricted grants/ contracts	1.4	2.1
Restricted grants/ contracts	7.3	7.0
Independent operations	0.2	5.8
State governments	38.3	2.5
Appropriations	35.8	0.5
Unrestricted grants/ contracts	0.2	0.2
Restricted grants/ contracts	2.2	1.8
Local governments	3.7	0.7
Appropriations	3.2	<0.05
Unrestricted grants/ contracts	0.1	0.1
Restricted grants/ contracts	0.4	0.5
Private gifts, grants and contracts	4.0	8.3
Unrestricted	0.6	3.8
Restricted	3.3	4.5
Endowment income	0.6	4.8
Unrestricted	0.2	2.2
Restricted	0.3	2.6
Sales and services	23.2	23.3
Educational activities	2.9	2.6
Auxiliary enterprises	9.5	10.3
Hospitals	10.9	10.3
Other sources	2.6	4.4

In the 1990s, university and college financing began to incur increasingly large deficits. On the one hand, returns on endowment investments began declining just as most institutions had to raise faculty and administration salaries to compete with private industry. Salaries of university presidents began approaching $500,000 a year, while some medical school professors were earning as much as $600,000. Most universities compensated for rising faculty salaries by hiring more teaching assistants—graduate students—to teach undergraduate courses for modest stipends, usually equivalent only to their own graduate school tuition costs. In addition, most schools instituted far-reaching, cost-cutting programs that included cuts in student aid, reductions in the number of courses offered (and, therefore, the number of faculty) and reductions in the number of sports and extracurricular activities.

References: DES; NYT.

university-in-the-school A school-college partnership (q.v.) which a college or university sends its own instructors, or trains high school instructors, to teach freshman-level college courses for college credits to advanced high school students in their own high school.

(See also PROJECT ADVANCE.)

References: American Association for Higher Education, Washington, D.C.; *"What Did You Learn in School Today?"* Harlow G. Unger (1991); *Linking America's Schools and Colleges,* Franklin Wilbur and Leo M. Lambert (1991).

University Microfilms A widely used commercial printer of doctoral dissertations and other scholarly works, in accordance with the standard presentations and formats for such documents as required by almost all American colleges and universities. Dissertations submitted to University Microfilms, which was acquired by Xerox Corporation in 1972, are microfilmed and available for purchase in both abstract and complete form. Most universities require that completed dissertations be submitted to and published by University Microfilms after presentation for inclusion in the student's university library. In 1973, Xerox University Microfilms published the *Comprehensive Dissertation Index, 1861–1972,* a 37-volume compilation of more than 400,000 abstracts of 400,000 available dissertations, and the company continues to update the index with annual supplements. Before the advent of computer technology, the company stored each dissertation on microfilm, which it distributed to libraries and which libraries could reproduce into full-sized manuscripts.

Reference: Xerox University Microfilms, Ann Arbor, Michigan.

University of the American Expeditionary Forces in France An institution of higher education established by General John J. Pershing in Beaune, France, in March 1919, for American servicemen. The commander-in-chief of American forces during World War I, Pershing found himself heading a large, idle army after the armistice and cessation of fighting on November 11, 1918. He quickly moved to set up schools on each post to provide elementary and secondary education for soldiers who lacked such schooling. He also set up educational centers at the corps and division level to provide more advanced education and technical education. The University of the AEF offered still more advanced training than these schools, offering about 200 courses taught by officers and enlisted men with appropriate training and experience. About 6,000 students enrolled in the college, which also offered teacher-training courses and the opportunity to serve as student teachers in post schools. The Pershing educational system was unique in that it was the first effort to make education and training an integral part of military life. In 1920 and 1921, however, Congress authorized sharp cutbacks in troop strength and military spending. The entire system, including the university, was abandoned, leaving the American armed forces totally unprepared for the educational effort they were forced to mount two decades later at the outbreak of World War II.

(See also UNITED STATES ARMED FORCES INSTITUTE.)

Reference: *Classrooms in the Military: An Account of Education in the Armed Forces of the United States,* Harold F. Clark and Harold S. Sloan (1964).

University of California One of the world's largest university complexes, with nine campuses and more than 7,000 faculty serving more than 150,000 students in 565 baccalaureate, 250 master's and 200 doctoral programs on campuses at Berkeley, Davis, Irvine, Los Angeles, Riverside, San Diego, Santa Barbara and Santa Cruz. State-run, it represents one of three levels of higher education in the state of California, which also operates 20 California State University campuses for students not academically qualified to enroll at the nine University campuses, and more than 100 two-year community colleges.

(See also CALIFORNIA.)

Reference: CHE.

University of California Regents v. Bakke One of the most complex U.S. Supreme Court cases in the history of American higher education. Handed down in 1978 by the narrowest possible, 5–4, majority, the case dealt with a charge by Allan P. Bakke, a 38-year-old white engineer, that the University of California Medical School had rejected him because of his race. In effect, Bakke charged he had been the victim of ''reverse'' racial discrimination. At the time, universities and other American organizations were desperately attempting to comply with affirmative action laws and executive orders passed in the 1960s and 1970s requiring them to broaden the racial and social composition of their organizations to compensate for historic discrimination. In accordance with its affirmative action plan, the University of California's medical school at Davis was then reserving 16 of 100 places in each year's freshman class for minority students. Bakke had twice been rejected when he charged the school with violating both his Fourteenth Amendment right to equal protection under the law and his rights under Title VI of the 1964 Civil Rights Act (qq.v.), outlawing all discrimination based on race, color, religion, sex or national origin.

The two-pronged approach was unique, and the U.S. Supreme Court decided to address the issue after California courts had handed down conflicting decisions. There was little question that the concept of affirmative action was in conflict with both the Fourteenth Amendment and Title VI of the Civil Rights Act, yet no one on the Court doubted the necessity and justice of affirmative action. The Court walked a legal tightrope in handing down what was, in effect, a two-part decision that attempted to redress Bakke's legitimate grievances, while leaving affirmative action and the Civil Rights Act in place. What the Court did, on the one hand, was to uphold the legality of affirmative action programs, because of the diversity they provided student bodies at schools such as the University of California. On the other hand, it struck down the use of fixed numerical quotas, and it ordered the medical school to admit Bakke, adding that he had been barred solely on the basis of race, in violation of Title VI. The justices ruled, however, that schools could take race or ethnicity into account in admitting students, so long as no predetermined, fixed quota was in place or used as the basis for admission. In effect, the Court left all the laws in place, while gaining Mr. Bakke admission to medical school and, eventually, helping him obtain his M.D.

References: *Bakke and the Politics of Equality: Friends and Foes in the Classroom of Litigation,* Timothy J. O'Neill (1984); U.S. Supreme Court proceedings.

University of Cambridge The second oldest university in England, six of whose 31 independent colleges emerged from monasteries and affiliated schools in the 13th and 14th centuries. Cambridge, like the University of Oxford, was instrumental in serving as a source of educators for the early American colonies: John Harvard, who helped found America's first college in 1636, was a Cambridge graduate, and the Massachusetts city where Harvard University stands today took its name from the seat of Cambridge University. Apart from Harvard, the University of Cambridge, like Oxford, had a direct and far-reaching effect on early American education in providing many ministers, teachers, doctors, lawyers and merchants who came to the colonies in the early 1600s with the training and education that assured the colonies of their ultimate success and stability.

Of the 130 university men who joined the Great Migration of Puritans to New England before 1646, 100 had attended Cambridge and 32 had attended Oxford, with some having attended both. Of the 130, 87 had B.A. degrees, 63 had M.A.s, 98 were ministers, 27 became public officials, 15 became teachers, five entered business, three practiced medicine and almost all were part-time farmers. Forty-three eventually returned to England permanently, but the rest remained and helped renew the strength of the colonies by sending their own sons back to Cambridge and Oxford to bring back still more skills and knowledge to assure the growth of the colonies. It was this second generation of Cantabrigians that was responsible for the building and growth of great institutions such as Harvard.

References: "Harvard Men in England, 1624–1714," William L. Sachse, *Publications of the Colonial Society of Massachusetts* (XXXV: 1951, 119–144).

University of Chicago One of the most unique institutions of higher education in the United States, founded in Chicago in 1890 with $35 million from John D. Rockefeller and the leadership and vision of educator William Rainey Harper (q.v.). Harper was already a renowned adult educator on the Sunday school and Chautauqua (qq.v.) circuits when he and Rockefeller developed their plan to build a "Harvard of the West." Unlike the original Harvard, the new university in Chicago was to be egalitarian and disseminate knowledge to as wide a constituency as possible. Harper envisioned adult education, or "extension," as the heart of the new university. His initial plan called for organizing the university into six departments, with regular degree credit available from each upon completion of an examination. Study could be on campus, in the classrooms of cooperating institutions nearby or at home through the first home-study correspondence course ever established by an accredited university. Harper established a new type of academic year for resident students, lasting a full calendar year and divided into four quarters, permitting those who needed to work to do so or, if they could afford it, to accelerate and finish their degree work in three years.

When Robert Maynard Hutchins became president in 1929, he reorganized the college, replacing the undergraduate college and the single graduate school with a college for general education and four graduate divisions, each devoted to research and advanced study in the social, physical and biological sciences and in the humanities. In addition, he established seven professional schools. Upon admission, undergraduates took placement tests that often reduced their degree requirements. To earn their bachelor's degrees, students had to pass 14 comprehensive examinations in the humanities, social sciences and physical and biological sciences. It made little difference when they passed such exams; if they had enough knowledge to pass them after two years, they did so, and qualified for their degrees. Hutchins banned campus sports at the university because he believed athletics would be a distraction.

Although students today may still earn advanced standing through placement tests, the college is more conventional, with most students completing four years of undergraduate study. To graduate, students must pass 42 quarter courses, including a core curriculum of year-long sequences in humanities, social sciences, biological and physical sciences, civilization and foreign languages. In addition, two quarters of mathematics, one of art, one of music and one of noncredit physical education are required for graduation. Organized sports are still absent from campus life. The college has about 1,900 men and 1,400 women, and the graduate schools more than 4,500 men and nearly 3,000 women. The university has graduate schools of business, divinity, law, medicine, public policy and social service administration, and it offers graduate degrees in each of these schools as well as in its divisions of the biological sciences, humanities, physical sciences and social sciences.

Reference: University of Chicago, Chicago, Illinois.

University of Chicago Laboratory Schools A unique educational institution, where children study subject matter that relates to and emerges from their needs and interests in the world around them. Founded as a single school in 1896 by American educator and philosopher John Dewey (q.v.), the school encouraged the intellectual, physical and social growth of children by challenging them to develop independence and investigate the world around them, on their own or in concert with others. Using children's instincts to play, build, cook and create, the school converted each child-instigated game or activity, from playing house to building furniture, into a learning experience that indirectly taught the child to read, write and calculate at remarkably rapid rates. Children emerged from the laboratory school at the sixth grade level nearly two years younger than their public school peers.

The school opened with just 12 pupils (all of them children of University of Chicago faculty or friends) and two teachers from the University of Chicago School of Education faculty. Their approach focused "on discovering how to learn, and on developing a love for learning," Dewey explained. "We believe that education at all levels, from nursery school on, is not simply preparation for life, but an integral part of living. Our students pursue a . . . curriculum in reading, writing, mathematics and science, and begin in early grades to study foreign languages, music and the arts. In the process of acquiring academic skills, our students learn to be responsible and independent in their studies, and to work and play both on their own and with others." Aside from developing a new approach to teaching and incorporating all the pedagogical advances developed in Europe by Johann Heinrich Pestalozzi (q.v.), the Laboratory School was a center of educational research, with its faculty continually developing new teaching techniques by studying the development and learning processes of their students.

Although Dewey and his wife, who was principal for a time, left the Laboratory School in 1904, they developed methods of instruction, collectively called progressive education, that sparked the opening of more than 200 other laboratory schools (q.v.) across the United States. By mid-century, many of the techniques developed at the Laboratory School had been incorporated into standard teaching methods throughout the United States and, indeed, much of the Western world. Dewey's original school eventually developed into three units, from preschool through high school. Still a remarkable school and made up of four units, the Laboratory School maintains a nursery school with about 120 three- and four-year-olds in five sections and a teacher-pupil ratio of 1:8. The lower, or elementary, school has about 500 pupils attending kindergarten through fifth grade. Grade levels are organized into home rooms of about 25 students each, with each room a self-contained classroom equipped with specialized learning areas for each subject. The middle school has about 350 sixth, seventh and eighth grade students, while the high school offers a strong college-preparatory program for more than 400 students. The schools have two types of after-school program: one is a child-care program for children of working parents; the other, a program of enrichment classes where students can develop particular interests and talents.

Reference: University of Chicago Laboratory Schools, Chicago, Illinois.

University of Chicago School Mathematics Project

A kindergarten to twelfth grade mathematics curriculum developed between 1980 and 1986 to give students of average mathematical ability a firm foundation in computational skills. An outgrowth of the educational reform movement of the early 1980s, the curriculum replaced the new math (q.v.) approach to teaching mathematics with a reality-based, problem-solving approach to mathematics. Designed to prepare students to function successfully in college, regardless of whether or not they were in a college-preparatory track in secondary school, the curriculum reverted to a traditional sequence of mathematics instruction: arithmetic, pre-algebra and pre-geometry through seventh grade; algebra and statistics in eighth grade; geometry in ninth grade; advanced algebra in tenth grade; functions, trigonometry, statistics and computer science in eleventh grade; and pre-calculus an option for twelfth grade. The use of calculators and computers was thoroughly integrated into the curriculum throughout the elementary and secondary school years.

Reference: The College Board, Princeton, New Jersey.

University of Edinburgh

A Scottish institution of higher learning founded in 1583 and the alma mater of many leading educators in the American colonies. Like Cambridge and Oxford in the previous century, Edinburgh and, to a lesser extent, its older counterpart in Glasgow, produced the leading Presbyterian ministers and thinkers of the 18th century, including philosopher Thomas Reid (1710–96), philosopher-historian David Hume (1711–76) and minister-teacher John Witherspoon (q.v.). Witherspoon moved to the colonies and reshaped the fledgling College of New Jersey into Princeton College. There, he taught and prepared for public office the principal shapers of the new American republic, including one president (James Madison), one vice president (Aaron Burr), 10 cabinet officers, 60 members of Congress and three justices of the U.S. Supreme Court.

In addition to Witherspoon, Edinburgh gave the colonies such teachers as William Tennent, who founded the Log College (q.v.), and Francis Alison, who reshaped Benjamin Franklin's Academy of Philadelphia into the College of Philadelphia (later, the University of Pennsylvania). What made Edinburgh and the training it gave its students important to American education is that Edinburgh, unlike English universities, did not cater to an elite class. Indeed,

Edinburgh and other Scottish institutions provided students with a practical as well as classical education, at affordable fees, regardless of economic class or social standing. Men like Witherspoon, Tennent and Alison had been educated in an atmosphere of social tolerance, and they brought that tolerance to the New World.

Like Cambridge and Oxford in the 17th century, the universities of Edinburgh and Glasgow also served as centers for advanced studies in the professions for Americans who had completed work for their baccalaureate at colonial colleges. Edinburgh's medical school was recognized as the world's finest in the mid-18th century, drawing students from all parts of the world. John Morgan (q.v.), who later founded the first American medical school, studied medicine at Edinburgh after earning his bachelor's degree at the College of Philadelphia.

References: EB; *Man and Society: The Scottish Inquiry of the Eighteenth Century,* Gladys Bryson (1945).

University of the Pacific

The first chartered institution of higher education in California. Founded in Santa Clara in 1851 by Methodist ministers, the College of the Pacific, as it was called until 1961, later moved to Santa Clara and in 1924 to its present location in Stockton. The college opened the first medical school in the west in 1858 (now a part of Stanford University) and was first in the west to elevate teacher training from a two-year, post-secondary "normal school" program to upper-division college and graduate school studies. Still affiliated with the Methodist faith, the university has more than 3,500 students enrolled in its eight undergraduate schools and more than 500 students in its graduate school.

Reference: University of the Pacific Library, Stockton, California.

University of the South

The first university founded in the south in response to the inclusion of abolitionism as a centrality in the teaching of religion, history and political science in northern universities. Founded in Sewanee, Tennessee, in 1857—and colloquially known as Sewanee rather than by its formal name—the University of the South was established by Episcopal Bishop Leonidas Polk, a Louisiana native and a graduate of the U.S. Military Academy at West Point. At the time, northern colleges and universities had become abolitionist in sentiment and active in hiding and transporting runaway slaves along the underground railway. The University of Michigan, Oberlin College, Franklin College, Illinois College and New York College had all gained reputations as "abolitionist seminaries."

Earlier in the century, many sons of southern plantation owners had traveled north for their formal education, simply because the few colleges in the south, such as the College of William and Mary and the University of Virginia, could not accommodate their numbers. As northern colleges turned abolitionist, the desire for more southern colleges with a proslavery philosophy increased, and Bishop Polk, who would later serve as a Confederate general, helped found the University of the South, where sons of southern planters could study a curriculum that accommodated the legitimacy of slavery in an academic climate friendly to southern values.

The university was destroyed during the Civil War, along with the fortunes of its benefactors, but gifts from southern sympathizers in England allowed it to reopen in 1868. Although it once included a medical school and law school, it now has but two divisions, an undergraduate college of arts and sciences and a graduate school of theology. Still affiliated with the Protestant Episcopal Church in the mid-1990s, its more than 1,000 students remain 96% white. Since 1892, the university has published the renowned literary quarterly, the *Sewanee Review,* containing short fiction, poetry, essays and reviews.

Reference: University of the South, Sewanee, Tennessee.

University of Virginia

The first American university to offer a comprehensive curriculum of the arts and sciences that would serve as an archetype for future American universities for much of the 19th century. Chartered in 1819 and opened in 1825, the University of Virginia was described by essayist Ralph Waldo Emerson as the "lengthened shadow of one man"—its founder Thomas Jefferson (q.v.). After leaving national office in 1809, Jefferson had returned to his home in Monticello, Virginia, where, as a behind-the-scenes power in Virginia politics, he continued pressing for a state system of free, universal public education. Indeed, he often remarked that if he had been forced to choose between establishing a statewide system of public primary schools or a great university, he would have chosen the former. Fearing that universal public education would mean an end to child labor and even manumission, the state legislature gave him the reverse, in January 1818. And so in August, a gubernatorial com-

mission chaired by Jefferson selected Central College in Charlottesville as the site for the new institution and adopted an organization and program that Jefferson had drawn up the previous year.

As stated in his report, Jefferson's goal for the new university whose buildings and lawns he designed was:

> To form the statesmen, legislators and judges, on whom public prosperity and individual happiness are so much to depend;
>
> To expound the principles and structure of government, the laws which regulate the intercourse of nations, those formed municipally for our own government, and a sound spirit of legislation, which, banishing all arbitrary and unnecessary restraint on individual action, shall leave us free to do whatever does not violate the equal rights of another;

Artist's rendering of the original buildings at the University of Virginia. Founder Thomas Jefferson designed the buildings and the school's original curriculum. (Library of Congress)

To harmonize and promote the interests of agriculture, manufactures and commerce, and by well-informed views of political economy to give a free scope to the public industry;

To develop the reasoning faculties of our youth, enlarge their minds, cultivate their morals, and instill into them the precepts of virtue and order;

To enlighten them with mathematical and physical sciences, which advance the arts, and administer to the health, the subsistence, and comforts of human life;

And, generally, to form them to habits of reflection, and correct action, rendering them examples of virtue to others, and of happiness within themselves.

Jefferson's curriculum—by far the broadest of any university in the United States (and in most of the world) at the time—did away with divinity studies and offered 10 broad areas of study: "ancient languages (Latin, Greek, Hebrew), modern languages (French, Spanish, Italian, German, Anglo-Saxon), pure mathematics (algebra, fluxions, geometry, architecture), physico-mathematics (mechanics, statics, dynamics, pneumatics, acoustics, optics, astronomy, geography), natural philosophy (chemistry and mineralogy), botany (including zoology), anatomy (including medicine), government political economy (the law of nature and nations, and history), municipal law, and ideology (grammar, ethics, rhetoric, belles lettres and the fine arts)."

Jefferson's curriculum reflected his general distaste for organized religion, his disdain for the English class system inherent in the Anglican Church, and his rejection of Puritan concepts of predestination. He believed that man could, through education, by his own free will, rise above his class. "Education," he said ". . . engrafts a new man on the native stock and improves what in his nature was vicious and perverse into qualities of virtue and social worth. And it cannot be but that each generation succeeding to the knowledge acquired by all those who preceded it, adding to it their own acquisitions and discoveries, and handing the mass down for successive and constant accumulation, must advance the knowledge and well-being of mankind, not infinitely, as some have said, but indefinitely, and to a term which no one can fix and foresee."

A skilled architect, Jefferson turned his dream for a great university into plans that were translated into an architectural reality over the next six years, and Jefferson was named rector, or chairman, of the board of visitors, or trustees. The 10 chairs he originally envisioned were reduced to eight, with law and government combined into one school and physico-mathematics abandoned. In addition, various Christian denominations were invited to establish theological seminaries outside the perimeter of the university; but the university itself, which he called an "academic village," remained a public, secular institution. It also offered students the widest measure of academic freedom then available in the world, with each student free to choose from the eight schools of the university. In a sense, each school was a precursor of the modern "major."

Jefferson died in 1826, just after completion of the last buildings of the original campus. He left behind a university that became the archetype of every major public university that would ever be built in the United States. The Land Grant College Act of 1862 would later create a new type of public college dedicated to practical skills needed in agriculture and industry, but as the great public universities emerged, they would be founded on the principles of "Mr. Jefferson's University." The University of Virginia today offers undergraduate programs in architecture, arts and sciences, commerce, education, engineering and applied science, and nursing. The six undergraduate schools enroll more than 11,000 students; the eight graduate schools, more than 6,000 graduate students.

Reference: University of Virginia Archives, Charlottesville, Virginia.

University of Wisconsin

University of Wisconsin A pioneer institution of higher education in the area of public service and adult education through its extension services. Now made up of 26 campuses, with a total enrollment of more than 150,000, the university's origins go back to 1849 and the founding of the tiny College of Wisconsin, in Madison. Later a land-grant institution, the university was swept up in the fervor of progressive political and economic reform that gripped the state in the 1890s. Several years of poor crops and dust storms had devastated American agriculture and helped plunge the nation into a financial panic. In Wisconsin, public discontent exploded with the discovery of rampant bribery and corruption among the Republican leadership that had controlled the state's politics since the end of the Civil War.

In 1900, Robert M. La Follette was elected governor on a platform of radically progressive reforms, including direct primaries for nominating candidates, establishment of a state civil service, and state regulation and equitable taxation of railroads and other corporate entities. Called the "Wisconsin Idea," it included government recruitment of expert advisors from the University of Wisconsin, whose equally progressive president, Charles Van Hise (q.v.), was quick to convert the university into a partner of state government in the rebuilding of the state economy and body politic.

A former professor of geology, Van Hise had conducted detailed studies of mineral-bearing areas of the Lake Superior region as a service to the state. As president of the university, he believed the obligation of a public institution of higher education was to use science to improve every aspect of the life of the state's citizens. He proposed to implement his goal in three ways: through faculty research to expand knowledge and develop as many practical uses as possible for such knowledge; by sending faculty experts to collaborate with government officials in improving agriculture, developing industry and solving social and economic problems; and by creating and expanding the university's extension program to bring knowledge to every citizen. "I shall never be content," said Van Hise, "until the beneficent influence of the University reaches every family in the state. This is my ideal of the state university."

Van Hise went on to strengthen the university's research programs and train experts in agriculture, engineering, medicine, law, politics, economics and history to advise state administrators. Dozens of professors served on state regulatory and investigating commissions and helped draft progressive legislation that shaped the "Wisconsin Idea." Van Hise also expanded the extension division into the most comprehensive, farthest reaching such unit of any university in the world. If, as educators contend, Charles W. Eliot had made Harvard the archetype of private universities, Van Hise, in his turn, built Wisconsin into the archetype of public universities. Word of his accomplishments spread through magazine articles and, eventually, through Charles McCarthy's widely circulated book, *The Wisconsin Idea* (1912). Delegations of educators from universities across the United States and from overseas flocked to Madison to study what Van Hise had accomplished and to take back with them what they could. The University of Wisconsin was hailed as the world's finest by English educators, and the author Lincoln Steffens declared Van Hise to be "in a class by himself among college presidents." As president from 1903 to 1918, Van Hise established a model for university-government cooperation that has become a uniquely American concept, with the university retaining academic freedom while working with government to provide the citizenry with the benefits of government-sponsored university research. In addition, he expanded the public service and educative functions of American universities by making university extension and other outreach services an integral part of every public university's basic functions.

The university today serves as the state's research center, and more than 120,000 people per year continue to avail themselves of the university's continuing education programs. Among the public service facilities on the Madison campus are the Space Science and Engineering Center, the Physical Science Laboratory, a museum of art, an arboretum, agricultural experiment stations and hospitals.

References: BDOE; EB; University of Wisconsin Library Archives, Madison, Wisconsin.

university press A publishing company owned by a university and devoted to the production of scholarly works, often, though not exclusively, by the university's own faculty. Usually nonprofit, university presses were first established in the 15th and 16th centuries at the Sorbonne, in Paris, and at Oxford and Cambridge universities, in England. Cornell University established the first university press in the United States in 1869, followed by Johns Hopkins University in 1878.

References: Book Publishing in America, Charles A. Madison (1966); A History of Book Publishing in the United States: The Expansion of an Industry, 1865–1919, John Tebbel (2 vols., 1975).

unobtrusive (nonreactive) measures Any examination of an individual or group of individuals that takes place without their knowledge and, therefore, permits them to perform free of the normal anxieties associated with test-taking. Thus, observation through one-way glass is one common method of studying behavior unobtrusively. The theory behind unobtrusive examinations and measures is that test-takers, regardless of age, invariably fail to perform to their potential because of anxieties associated with test-taking that necessarily invalidate their scores. On the other hand, the concept of unobtrusive testing violates every precept of privacy built into the concepts of American democracy.

Nevertheless, many psychological tests are fraught with unobtrusive measures, because it is believed that the necessity for valid diagnosis outweighs test-taker rights to privacy. Indeed,

the tendency of the emotionally disturbed not to reveal inner feelings represents one of the most self-destructive blockages to successful therapy. One standard method is to construct a test that appears to measure one characteristic while actually measuring another. A group of teenagers might, for example, be told that a test is measuring their preference in music, but the carefully constructed set of questions might actually be measuring their tolerance for violence. Still another element of the unobtrusive test is the promise of anonymity. While answer sheets of such tests require no names or other written identification, a variety of coding methods (such as a hidden numeral corresponding to each desk in a classroom) permit post-test identification of each test-taker. Because of a number of Supreme Court decisions in recent years guaranteeing the privacy rights of minors as well adults, test administrators have become reluctant to use unobtrusive measures without the permission of a parent or guardian (for minors) or a court order (in the case of adults).

Reference: Unobtrusive Measures: Nonreactive Research in the Social Sciences, Eugene J. Webb et al. (1966).

unskilled workers Members of the labor force with a level of intellectual, manual or physical training that is inadequate to meet the long-term needs or demands of potential employers and assure permanent employment. A disproportionate percentage of the unskilled are men and women who, for whatever reason, drop out of or fail to complete high school. About 25% of American students fell into that category in the 1980s and 1990s, and about 36% remained chronically unemployed, with unemployment rates twice the national average. Those who found employment earned median incomes about 50% below the median income for all American workers.

A high school diploma, however, constituted no guarantee of adequate skill levels for the marketplace as the United States approached the end of the 20th century. Unemployment rates among workers with a high school diploma, but no college, were consistently 11% to 12% higher than the national average. Workers with associate degrees from two-year institutions had unemployment rates about 23% below the national average, and workers with bachelor's degrees had unemployment rates nearly half the national average. However, studies by the Department of Labor indicate that the plight of the unskilled relates less to any decline in the quality of American secondary school education than to the disappearance of jobs for the unskilled and a sharp increase in skill requirements of existing and new jobs. At the simplest levels, a variety of earth-moving equipment has replaced the American day laborer who used to build American roads, automation has forced millions off factory production and assembly lines, and computers have left equally large numbers of clerical workers unemployed. Unlike skilled tradesmen, such as carpenters, plumbers and electricians, assembly-line workers and office clerks have few manual skills that they can carry to other jobs.

According to the Department of Labor, new opportunities for workers with no more than a high school degree have been falling sharply since the end of World War II. Machinery that semiliterate but mechanically adept workers could operate and even repair because of the visibility of all working parts, was replaced by equipment with microprocessors and other electronic components that require the ability to decode complex manuals and diagrams. By 1987, workers with no more than a high school diploma qualified for only 54.6% of new jobs, and projections indicated that the figure would drop to 46.5% by the year 2000. A 1989 U.S. Department of Labor study, *Workforce 2000*, found that average young adults 21 to 25 years old were reading at a level significantly below that demanded by the average job available five years earlier, in 1984. The study used a scale of 1 to 6 to rank required language skills, with a reading skill level of 6 required for scientists, lawyers and engineers, who need to read scientific and technical journals, and 1 the level required for manual labor. The study found that the 105 million nonmilitary jobs in 1984 required an average language proficiency of 3.0—equivalent to the language skills of retail salespeople and skilled construction workers. By the year 2000, however, the projected skill level of those same was seen as reaching 3.6; most new jobs were expected to be created in the hospitality industry, health-related occupations, construction, education, computer and data-processing services, government, legal services and finance. The average reading skill levels of a sample of 3,600 young adults in 1989 was only 2.6, the level required by farming and transportation work.

References: DES; *Occupational Outlook Handbook*, U.S. Department of Labor, Bureau of Labor Statistics; U.S. Department of Labor, Bureau of Labor Statistics, Washington, D.C.

upper division college A degree-granting institution of higher education limited to the last two years of the traditional four-year program. Unlike community and junior colleges, which limit their programs to freshman- and sophomore-level college work and confer associate degrees, upper division colleges offer junior- and senior-level studies and confer bachelor's degrees. College of the Pacific (now University of the Pacific) created one of the first upper division colleges in the United States in 1924, when it established its School of Education. The school was designed to elevate teacher training to a four-year, bachelor's degree program requiring study of college-level liberal arts and sciences before embarking on studies of pedagogy. At the time, most teacher training was limited to two-year, "normal" school programs that followed high school graduation.

Reference: *The Upper Division College*, Robert A. Altman (1970).

Upward Bound A federally supported program to supplement the secondary school education of the socioeconomically deprived and prepare them for college. Created under the Higher Education Act of 1965 (q.v.), Upward Bound provides grants to organizations and educational institutions that provide one-to-one tutoring, remedial instruction, cultural experiences, counseling and supplementary classes to participating students. Designed to instill motivation, as well as academic skills, Upward Bound offers two types of program: one, a six-to-eight-week summer session usually held on a college campus, and the other, an after-school and Saturday program during the school year. Most student participants attempt to combine the two. Although a federal study found that Upward Bound students have a significantly higher rate of enrollment in post-secondary education than nonparticipants, there are no satisfactory statistics of college-completion rates.

Reference: United States Department of Education, Washington, D.C.

usage The way in which language customarily communicates ideas. Most individuals learn and use several language varieties and are able to shift automatically—either consciously or unconsciously—from one consistent usage to another. Some grammarians cite seven overlapping categories of modern English usage: socioeconomic-educational, stylistic, gender-based, methodological, historical, occupational and geographic. Examples of socioeconomic-educational usage are standard English (that taught in schools) and nonstandard English (that used in specific communities, such as black English). Stylistic English ranges from casual (I'm, you're, etc.) to formal (I am, etc.), while gender-based English is evident in obscenity-laced, locker room chatter. Methodological usage depends on the method of communication (oral, written and so on). Historical usages are evident in the differences between Elizabethan, 19th-century and 20th-century English. Occupational usage is tied to the jargon of the individual's work, while geographic usages are evident in the varieties of English spoken in the American east, west, north and south.

Reference: *The Child and the English Language Arts,* Mildred R. Donoghue (1979).

Utah The 45th state to join the Union, in 1896. Utah was settled by Mormons in 1846, when the area was still controlled by Mexico. The Mormons established the first school there a year later, in the Salt Lake Valley. Education remained under the tight control of the Mormon Church (officially, The Church of Jesus Christ of the Latter-day Saints) even after the legislative assembly empowered city councils to establish secular common schools in 1895. A century later, the state had more than 700 public elementary and secondary schools, with a combined enrollment of more than 425,000 students. Although banned as unconstitutional by the Supreme Court, prayer in school remains the rule in many Utah public schools—especially in rural schools in virtually all-Mormon communities. Because of the deep involvement of the church with public school education and the tendency to lace scientific truths with biblical "truths," the quality level of Utah public schools ranks well below the national average, although the quality of public school mathematics education and college-level business education is above the national average.

The state has four public and two private four-year institutions of higher education and five public and four private two-year colleges. Its most notable private institution is Brigham Young University, founded by and still closely tied to the Mormon Church and the alma mater of many of the state's most prominent business and political leaders. BYU's mission statement describes as "inadequate" any education that does not emphasize Jesus Christ. In 1992, perhaps inevitably, Phi Beta Kappa, the national honor society, rejected Brigham Young's application for membership, saying that the university's religious philosophy was incompatible with academic freedom.

In the public sector, Utah State University has strong space and agricultural research departments, while the University of Utah has a renowned medical center and has been a leader in research on artificial organs and genetics. The University of Utah lost considerable standing in the scientific community, however, after a 1991 claim that its scientists had produced cold nuclear fusion in the laboratory could not be substantiated. The state was subsequently forced to shut its National Cold Fusion Institute.

References: CHE; EB.

V

vaccination programs In education, the immunization of school-aged children to prevent and control the spread of communicable childhood and other diseases, such as smallpox, diphtheria, measles, pertussis (whooping cough), poliomyelitis, rubella (German measles), scarlet fever and tetanus. Most states require children to receive appropriate vaccinations and to present evidence such as a doctor's or hospital certificate before enrolling in school each year. Despite such requirements, an estimated one-third of the children in the United States—most of them poor children of immigrant families—remain uninoculated. Although parents belonging to certain religious groups have attempted to bypass vaccination requirements on religious grounds, the U.S. Supreme Court has twice ruled (in 1920 and 1922) that state legislation requiring vaccination for admission to schools does not constitute an unconstitutional invasion of personal rights. The courts have also upheld the right of school boards and boards of health to require inoculations during epidemics.

Reference: *The Law and Public School Operation,* Leroy J. Peterson et al. (1978).

V-A-K-T method A multisensory approach to the teaching of reading that combines sight, speech, sound, movement and feel. The theory underlying this method is that the more senses that are involved, the greater the degree of learning. V-A-K-T—an acronym for visual, auditory, kinetic and tactile—was originally developed for the learning disabled, but is now commonly used in most elementary school classrooms. Developed at a University of California laboratory school in the 1920s by Grace Fernald and others (see FERNALD METHOD), the method calls for students to trace the letters of a word they have copied, while saying the word aloud, bringing into play visual, tactile, motile, oral and aural senses. After several repetitions, the student is then asked to write the word without using the copy. Eventually, the student learns to write the word without the tracing procedure and can begin recognizing parts of new words that contain elements of the first words learned.

References: *Remedial Techniques in Basic School Subjects,* Grace M. Fernald (1943); *Teaching Reading to Slow and Disabled Learners,* Samuel A. Kirk et al. (1978).

valedictorian The high school or college student who delivers the valedictory *(vale,* the Latin for farewell; *dictus,* from the Latin verb *dicere,* to say) address at graduation ceremonies. The speaker is usually chosen by virtue of having attained the highest academic rank in the graduating class. Valedictories first became a part of graduation ceremonies in England in the mid-17th century, as professors said farewell to their students. The leading student academic's reply began as a short expression of thanks to the faculty. The valedictory and the recognition bestowed on the valedictorian evolved into a prominent element of American (more than British) graduation ceremonies in the 19th and 20th centuries.

Reference: *Webster's Ninth New Collegiate Dictionary,* Merriam-Webster Inc. (1988).

values In education, the principles, morals and ethics learned in the home and at school. Values are bipolar—i.e., negative, as well as positive—and usually determine, consciously or unconsciously, student social behavior. Students enter preschool and the school system with a partially developed set of values, which will gradually be solidified or modified by teacher, peer and other influences. Values are usually somewhat amorphous and subject to change, often radical, throughout a student's development and throughout life. The teaching of values has brought elementary and secondary education into continual conflict with parents and religious groups that insist schools should limit teaching to academics—a difficult goal in the face of constant social interaction that often requires conflict resolution between students and teachers, school staff and other students.

Although some schools have responded by attempting to eliminate values from the curriculum, others have introduced programs of so-called value clarification, a teacher-neutral approach that tries to help students identify and define their own values. Value clarification, according to the program, is based on recognizing alternative values, choosing one's own values independently of external pressures, recognizing the consequences of behavior based on each value, and prizing one's choice and willingly affirming it publicly.

In one of the few studies relating adult values to level of education, a series of surveys of 77,000 individuals between 1949 and 1971 found a lasting correlation between level of schooling and the humaneness of a person's values, commitment to civil liberties and freedom of information, belief in due process of law, and readiness to grant equal opportunities to minority groups.

References: *Education's Lasting Influence on Values,* Herbert H. Hyman and Charles R. Wright (1979); *Elementary and Middle School Social Studies,* David T. Naylor and Richard E. Diem (1987); *Value Clarification: A Handbook of Practical Strategies for Teachers and Students,* Sidney Simon et al. (1972).

vandalism In education, any deliberate damage to school property, ranging from spraying graffiti to burning down buildings. Between 300,000 and 400,000 instances of school vandalism are reported in the United states each year. Police authorities claim most vandalism is committed by people under 18, with 12-to-15-year-olds the modal group. Schools represent particularly attractive targets for young vandals because they are unoccupied much of the time and are particularly resented by many youngsters as an enforcer of discipline and order. Alarm systems and uniformed patrols have done little to reduce school vandalism in recent years, and all prospects are for a rise in

vandalism as budget-conscious school boards cut back on security.

Reference: *School Vandalism: Strategies for Prevention,* Michael D. Casserly, Scott A. Bass and John R. Garrett (1980).

Van Hise, Charles R. (1857–1918) American geologist, educator and university president who expanded the role of the public university to include adult education and service to the state. Born and educated in Wisconsin, he spent his entire adult life at the University of Wisconsin—first as a student, then as professor of metallurgy and geology from 1879 to 1903, and then as president from 1903 until his death. Granted the university's first Ph.D., he was deeply devoted to the concept of public service and was responsible for surveys of the iron-bearing areas of Lake Superior to help the area's economic development. At the time, the state had suffered a decade of poor crops, and a financial panic in 1893 had left the entire United States in a deep depression.

In Wisconsin, public discontent exploded with the discovery of rampant bribery and corruption among the Republican leadership that had controlled the state's politics since the end of the Civil War. In 1900, Robert M. La Follette was elected governor on a platform of radically progressive reforms, including direct primaries for nominating candidates, establishment of a state civil service, state regulation and equitable taxation of railroads and other corporate entities. Called the "Wisconsin Idea," the program was not implemented until 1903, when La Follette finally obtained a majority in the statehouse.

The Wisconsin Idea was based in part on the government's use of academic experts in all fields relating to government. Van Hise, who had just become president of the University of Wisconsin, quickly redirected that institution's resources to help government rebuild the state's economy and body politic. He sent faculty experts to collaborate with government officials in improving agriculture, developing industry and solving social and economic problems.

Under his direction, dozens of University of Wisconsin professors were soon serving on state regulatory and investigating commissions and helped draft progressive legislation that eventually shaped the "Wisconsin Idea." Van Hise established a model for university-government cooperation that has become a uniquely American concept, with the university retaining academic freedom while working with government to provide the citizenry with the benefits of government-sponsored university research.

Van Hise believed the obligation of a public institution of higher education was to use science to improve every aspect of life for the state's citizens. He fulfilled that goal by encouraging faculty research to expand knowledge and develop as many practical uses as possible for such knowledge and by creating and expanding the university's extension program to bring knowledge to every citizen. During his administration, Van Hise increased the faculty fourfold, doubled student enrollment, increased state appropriations for the university almost fivefold and doubled the university's land holdings to permit construction of new buildings. In his most stunning accomplishment, he carried university education to the people of his state by expanding the extension program. He appointed a special assistant to redesign and popularize courses and convince farmers and other ordinary citizens to avail themselves of "their" university's educative services. Van Hise and his university set standards for extension education that drew educators from around the world to study and carry home elements of the process to their own universities. Educators who had hailed Charles W. Eliot for converting Harvard into the archetype of the private university, now hailed Van Hise for converting Wisconsin into the archetype of the public university. The University of Wisconsin was called the world's finest by English educators, and author Lincoln Steffens declared Van Hise to be "in a class by himself among college presidents."

While president of the university, Van Hise himself participated in public service as chairman of the Wisconsin State Conservation Commission and State Board of Forestry, and he served education as a trustee of the Carnegie Foundation for the Advancement of Teaching. He was author of a number of scientific books on geology and metallurgy and an important work on conservation, *The Conservation of Natural Resources in the United States* (1910). He also contributed scores of papers to scientific journals.

References BDOE; DAB; *The University of Wisconsin: A History, 1848–1925,* Merle Curti and Vernon Carstensen (1949); *University Extension in the United States,* Louis E. Reber (1914).

Van Rensselaer, Stephen (1764–1839)

American soldier, public official and founder of the first private technical school in the United States, the Rensselaer School, which was later renamed Rensselaer Polytechnic Institute. The aim of the school, said Van Rensselaer, was to apply science to "the common purposes of life." He opened the school as a specialized teacher training school that would sent its graduates to instruct the children of farmers and mechanics "on the application of experimental chemistry, philosophy, and natural history to agriculture, domestic economy, the arts, and manufactures." The school was the nation's first to train civilian engineers, although the United States Military Academy had already started training military engineers to build roads, bridges and other installations in wartime.

Except for underwriting his school, Van Rensselaer had no other connection with education. He had inherited his wealth and vast estates near Albany, New York, when he was five. A graduate of Harvard College, he was assigned the rank of major general largely because of his station in life. After an undistinguished command in the War of 1812, he entered politics, served in the state legislature for nine years, was lieutenant governor for one term and served a term in the United States House of Representatives. He was a major force behind the construction of the Erie Canal.

Reference: DAB.

varsity The principal team representing a college or school against other colleges and schools in a given sport or other competition. An English corruption of the last three syllables of the word university, the term dates from the 17th century and the beginning of competition among debating clubs from England's "versities."

Reference: *Webster's Ninth New Collegiate Dictionary,* Merriam-Webster Inc. (1988).

Vassar College A nonsectarian, coeducational institution founded as a woman's college in Poughkeepsie, New York, in 1861, during what had become a national frenzy to expand higher education and the number of Americans with superior training. From 13 colleges in 1783, the number of institutions of higher education had grown to 119 by 1850, not including 44 theological seminaries, 36 medical schools and 16 law schools. Colleges were opening for every conceivable special purpose: to train engineers, farmers, blacks and, of course women. Although several institutions—all of them called "seminaries" or "academies"—had opened earlier in the century offering college-level education for women, many had digressed into teacher training.

The English-born philanthropist Matthew Vassar (1792–1868), who had made a fortune in the United States from a brewery and a variety of other enterprises, was determined to build a true college for women, with a curriculum equal to that of any men's school. In 1861, he founded and endowed Vassar Female College. He advertised it across the United States, and, when it opened in 1865, it attracted a large student body. Vassar's high-quality education—for the first time at any women's institution, equal to that at Yale, Harvard and the nation's best men's colleges—proved instrumental in destroying the myth that women were not as academically capable as men. Indeed, Vassar's success led to a score of other women's colleges that eventually gained women educational equality with men at the undergraduate level.

Vassar dropped the "Female" from its name in 1867, and a century later, in 1969, it followed the example of many all-male colleges and became coeducational. It now has more than 2,000 students, about 40% of them male.

References: EB; DAB; Vassar College Library, Poughkeepsie, New York.

Vermont The 14th state to join the Union, in 1791, after 14 years as an independent republic. Its constitution as a republic called for establishment of primary schools in each town and a grammar school in each county. In 1823, the first formal teacher-training school in the United States was founded in Concord; it was, however, a private school. Unlike neighboring Massachusetts, where the first public teacher-training school was founded in 1839, Vermont would remain a bastion of private education until after World War II. Even the University of Vermont was a private institution until 1955, and to this day it is still tuition driven, receiving less than 15% of its budget from the state. The university is one of only four public four-year institutions of higher education. In contrast, the state has 13 private four-year colleges, including Bennington College; Norwich University, a private military college founded in 1819; and Middlebury College, a prestigious private institution founded in 1800 and the first American college to grant a degree to a black man, Alexander Lucius Twilight, in 1823. Vermont has five two-year colleges, two public and three private.

The state's more than 300 public elementary and secondary schools have about 85,000 students. Below-average quality of education spurred the state's schools to introduce radical reforms in 1991, when it became the first state to experiment with outcome-based education (q.v.). Outcome-based education uses the portfolio (q.v.) as a basic evaluative tool. The portfolio approach, in turn, requires more writing than conventional public schools in and out of class, more homework, and the production of a body of work indicative of a student's mastery of

a subject. Each piece of work becomes part of a record of development rather than an end in itself and can be compared to national norms that help students recognize the quality of their work in far broader terms. Portfolio assessment and comparison to national norms also help teachers to assess the quality of their own teaching. After five years, however, the reforms had produced few substantial improvements in student achievement in Vermont public schools.
References: EB; CHE; NYT.

vernacular learning In education, a highly controversial approach to inner-city classroom teaching, using the vernacular (from the Latin *verna,* meaning household-born slave) or language of the streets, with which most children are more familiar. Proponents of vernacular learning maintain that many inner-city children automatically translate standard English into their own vernacular, but that the necessity to translate slows the learning process and often blunts children's motivation to learn. Critics, on the other hand, maintain that classroom reinforcement of the vernacular automatically impedes children from assimilating into mainstream society by depriving them of standard English language skills. In spite of the controversy, inner-city schools have attracted so many teachers who are themselves products of the inner city that teaching and learning in the vernacular has gradually crept into the classroom of many such schools.

(See also BLACK ENGLISH; MULTICULTURAL EDUCATION.)
Reference: *Creative Communication,* Lillian M. Logan et al. (1972).

vesting A guarantee that an employee will receive all accumulated retirement benefits at the normal retirement age, even if the employee does not remain with the organization until then. The vast majority of school and college teachers contribute to vested pension plans. Under a vested plan, a teacher might, for example, leave the profession after 12 years, but

would still be entitled to 12 years' retirement benefits upon reaching the normal retirement age.

Beneficiaries may be partially or fully vested. They normally become vested after working in the organization for a prescribed number of years and if they do not withdraw any retirement contributions. More than 20 states require teachers to work for five years to be vested—the same number of years usually required for vesting in the private sector. Twenty states, including New York, New Jersey, Pennsylvania and Michigan, require teachers to work for 10 years to be vested. West Virginia requires teachers to work for 20 years, Alaska eight. Five states require less than five years of teaching for vesting. Although beneficiaries of vested pension funds cannot collect whatever is due them until they reach the normal retirement age, whatever benefits they have accrued while with the organization must be paid them upon retirement.
Reference: National Education Association, Washington, D.C.

vicarious learning A second- or third-hand learning process, whereby an individual learns from the experiences or purported knowledge of others. Elementary and secondary school children are especially subject to unquestioned, vicarious learning, from parents, peers, television programs, movies and other sources. Vicarious learning may or may not be based on accurate data. If unsubstantiated by subsequent firsthand research, vicarious learning can interfere with accurate assessment and acquisition of classroom knowledge. Racial and religious prejudice, for example, is typically the result of vicarious learning, and even the most skilled teachers are hard put at times to correct the ill effects of this type of vicarious learning.
Reference: *The Cognitive-Developmental Basis of Human Learning,* Barry Gholson (1980).

viewbooks Descriptive brochures issued by most private secondary schools and almost all colleges and graduate schools, with extensive photographs and information about their institutions. Many schools, colleges and graduate schools also provide videos with much the same data. Although they vary from institution to institution, viewbooks generally include information on life at each school, the range of courses and extracurricular activities, a profile of the most recent freshman class and of the most recent graduating class. Although extremely informative, viewbooks nevertheless portray each institution at its best—with photographs of the campus in full bloom and students universally enjoying themselves at work and play. Mention is seldom made of such matters as crime rates, drug and alcohol abuse, and the percentage of courses taught by untrained teaching assistants rather than professors. Negative data on any given school is usually attainable only through direct inquiry.

Reference: *A Student's Guide to College Admissions,* Harlow G. Unger (1995).

Vincent, John Heyl (1832–1920) American religious leader and educator who established a uniform Sunday-school curriculum for American Protestant churches. He was also responsible for expanding an annual meeting of Sunday-school teachers at Lake Chautauqua, New York, into one of the greatest national adult-education programs in history. Born in Alabama, he grew up in Pennsylvania and was ordained a Methodist minister in New Jersey in 1855. He moved to Illinois, serving as pastor for a number of churches, before moving to Chicago, where in 1872 he joined the evangelist Dwight L. Moody in taking control of and reorganizing the International Sunday School Union. At the time, almost every Protestant Sunday school had its own, individual approach to educating its children. After visiting the Holy Land and studying how Jewish schools taught religion, Vincent developed a rationally ordered curriculum, with the Bible as a textbook, and with a syllabus and a carefully worked out series of lessons for each Sunday in the school year, with home readings and questions of gradually

increasing complexity. The result was that the "Babel of courses" that Protestant churches had taught for 50 years was replaced with a single system. For the ensuing 50 years, each participating Protestant Sunday school in the United States taught the same passage from Scripture and the same classroom lesson every Sunday.

In addition to creating a universal curriculum, Vincent also introduced professional teacher training into the Protestant Sunday-school system. He published a monthly professional journal, *The Sunday School Teacher,* and organized an interdenominational convention, where Sunday-school teachers met for several days to hear lectures on the Bible, on pedagogy and on practical aspects of Sunday-school work, such as expanding their reach to adults. With the help of a wealthy inventor and lay Sunday-school teacher, Vincent also established the Chautauqua Assembly as a resident summer institute for Sunday-school teachers, but he soon expanded its educational reach into other areas, such as literature and science, and organized a book club and correspondence courses for teachers to study at home. Its success bordered on the phenomenal, attracting thousands when only a few hundred had been expected.

Sensing an insatiable thirst for knowledge among a people who had been denied a basic education by having been forced into child labor, Vincent expanded the program into a summer study and training institute with an educational scope that went well beyond teacher training for Sunday schools. By 1878, he expanded the program into the Chautauqua Literary and Scientific Circle (q.v.), a four-year program that combined correspondence courses and formal summer studies in the arts and sciences, followed by an examination and the granting of a college-type diploma.

Within a few years, the Chautauqua phenomenon spread across the northern part of the nation, with local study groups formed in thousands of communities and regional gatherings that lasted from a week to a month, offering lectures, concerts, courses and recreational activities. Vincent founded an appropriate publishing enterprise, the Chautauqua Press, to furnish Chautauqua participants with books, pamphlets, magazines and study guides. Vincent led both the Sunday School Union and the Chautauqua movement until 1888, when he was elected bishop of his church, the Methodist Episcopal, and served at a succession of posts in the United States and, from 1900 until his retirement in 1903, as bishop of all of Europe. Vincent was the author of a number of books, including *The Chautauqua Movement* (1886), *The Modern Sunday School* (1900) and *Family Worship for Every Day in the Year* (1905).

References: BDOE; DAB; *John Heyl Vincent: A Biographical Sketch*, Leon H. Vincent (1925).

violence In education, the use of force by a student, with or without a weapon, to cause injury to another student, teacher or member of the school staff. At the end of the 1980s, more than 40% of eighth graders and 34% of tenth graders in the United States had been involved in physical fights at school during the academic year. About 38% of eighth graders and 29% of tenth graders had been threatened by other students at school, while 16% of eighth graders and 8% of tenth graders had been attacked. Nearly 14% of eighth graders carried a knife to school and almost 2% carried a handgun, while 15% of tenth graders carried a knife and 1.6% carried a handgun. About 10% of both eighth graders and tenth graders had been robbed at school during the school year, half of them two or more times. About 8% of urban junior and senior high school students miss at least one day of school a month because they are afraid to go. Although only 4% of teachers say they have been physically abused or threatened by students, 24% of teachers report that violence against teachers is a problem in their schools and more than 35% say they feel unsafe at school. Some 44% of all teachers report that student-to-student violence is a problem in their school.

Educators and psychologists agree that the breakdown of traditional family structure is one cause of violence among children. In 1991, the Bureau of the Census reported that more than 60% of children under 18 and born in the United states had spent, were spending or would most likely spend some time in a single-parent household before they reached 18—a phenomenon that was unprecedented in American history and one that was having direct effects on American education. A study by the National Association of Elementary School Principals found that only 17% of children from single-parent households ranked as high academic achievers, compared to 30% of children from households where both parents were present. Only 23% of two-parent children ranked as low achievers, while 38% of one-parent children ranked as low achievers. One-parent students had higher rates of absenteeism and truancy than two-parent children and had twice the dropout rate. The Bureau of Justice Statistics found that 70% of the juveniles in state reform institutions, along with 75% of adolescent murderers, grew up in single-parent families or in institutions away from other parents.

To combat school violence, districts across the United States have adopted a host of programs, some of them preventive, others punishment-oriented and still others treatment-oriented. The first group of programs includes installation of metal detectors, through which all arriving students and staff must pass as the enter school. Other schools have hired uniformed security staff to patrol hallways. Among punishment-oriented responses to school violence has been the passage of a number of laws, including a federal ''schoolyard drug law'' (subsequently found to be unconstitutional by the courts) stipulating heavy penalties for drug trafficking within 1,000 feet of any campus. California passed an anti-youth gang law that calls for the arrest of parents who fail to ''exercise reasonable care, supervision, protection, and control over a minor child.'' Such parents may be subject to fines of up to $2,500 and imprisonment for up to one year. Among treatment-oriented programs are a variety of behavioral training schemes. Some schools provide one-to-one mentor programs, whereby trained volunteers serve as counselors, "friends," and academic tutors of elementary and secondary schoolchildren. Many elementary schools also have formal violence-prevention programs in each classroom, to train children how to deal with anger and other feelings and teach them nonviolent solutions to interpersonal problems and provocations. Hopeful of reducing the rising cost of violence in the United States, some insurance companies have developed "mediation kits" for distribution to classroom teachers.

References: DES; *The Condition of Teaching,* The Carnegie Foundation for the Advancement of Teaching.

Virginia (Commonwealth of) Tenth of the original 13 states to join the Union, in 1788. Site of the first permanent English community established in North America—Jamestown, in 1607—Virginia was also the site of the first free school in the Americas, the Syms School (q.v.), which was founded in 1635 and endowed with a bequest from planter Benjamin Syms. Efforts at establishing educational facilities had begun earlier, however—at least as early as 1619, when Sir George Yeardly, the newly appointed governor, set off from London with instructions from the Virginia Company of London to lay the foundation for "a flourishing state," which included reserving 10,000 acres at Henrico for the endowment of a college to train the children of the infidels (i.e., American Indians) "in true religion, moral virtue and civility and for other godly uses."

At the same time, the chaplain of the *Royal James I,* a ship in the East India Company fleet, was attempting to establish a school in Charles City for the children of settlers. The Virginia Company "conceived it most fit to resolve for the erecting of a public free school . . . for the education of children and grounding of them in principles of religion, civility of life and humane learning." It recommended that the school be called the East India School and "have dependence upon the college in Virginia which should be made capable to receive scholars from the school into such scholarships and fellowships as the said college shall be endowed withal for the advancement of scholars as they arise by degrees and deserts in learning." Thus started what almost became the first vertically integrated public school system in the United States—from primary school through college. An Indian massacre on March 22, 1622, ended the entire Henrico college project, and settlers abandoned formal education as a priority in favor of the problems of self-defense, agriculture and sheer survival.

Virginia nevertheless remained in the forefront of education during the colonial and early national era. In 1693, the College of William and Mary became the second college founded in the American colonies. Thereafter, the state produced many of the great minds of the colonial era, including George Washington, Thomas Jefferson, James Madison and James Monroe (qq.v.). In 1779, Thomas Jefferson, as governor, submitted to the state legislature a "Bill for the More General Diffusion of Knowledge," which called for universal public education in Virginia—the first such effort in the United States. Jefferson's bill was defeated by rich planters who rejected the idea of paying taxes to educate the poor. Virginia would wait until it drafted a new constitution in 1851 to open its first free, public primary schools. In 1819, however, Jefferson did succeed in convincing the legislature to establish the nation's first public university, at Charlottesville, "to form the statesmen, legislators and judges, on whom public prosperity and individual happiness are so much to depend." When it opened, the University of Virginia (q.v.) offered by far the broadest curriculum of any university in the United States.

Virginia now has a total of 15 public and 33 private four-year colleges, including the College of William and Mary, Hampden-Sydney College (1776), the University of Virginia, James Madison University (1908), Old Dominion University (1930), Randolph-Macon College (1830),

Sweet Briar College (1901) and Virginia Military Institute (1839). The state has 24 public and 11 private two-year colleges. As in the rest of the south, blacks and whites attended separate public schools in Virginia until the 1960s, when federal courts forced them to desegregate. By the early 1990s, the state had more than 1,750 public elementary and secondary schools, with a total enrollment of nearly one million. In addition, more than 70,000 students were attending private schools. Quality of education in the public schools was about average for the nation. **References:** CHE; EB.

Virgin Islands A self-governing territory of the United States, consisting of three islands and 50 largely uninhabited islets in the Lesser Antilles chain of the West Indies. Purchased from Denmark in 1917, the largely black population has about 70 elementary and secondary schools, with a total enrollment of fewer than 30,000 students. Education is compulsory for all children between the ages of 5½ and 16. The islands have one college, the College of the Virgin Islands, which opened in 1962 and has an annual enrollment of about 2,500 students. **Reference:** EB.

visiting teacher An archaic term for a school social worker—invented, apparently, to couch the social worker's role in neutral terms and spare students the stigma of requiring the social worker's services. **Reference:** *Schools and Social Work,* Margaret Robinson (1978).

VISTA An acronym for Volunteers in Service to America, a federal program established in 1964 as part of President Lyndon B. Johnson's War on Poverty. Often called "the domestic Peace Corps," VISTA volunteers provide a variety of educative services in seven broad fields: community service, economic development, knowledge skills (including the tutoring of out-of-school non-English-speaking immigrants), health and nutrition, legal rights, housing and energy conservation. As in the Peace Corps (q.v.), volunteers live in the communities they serve and receive a small stipend for their services. To qualify, they must be 18 and have complete command of a required skill. After a brief training period, volunteers must serve one year. **Reference:** Volunteers in Service to America, Washington, D.C.

visual discrimination The ability to recognize differences in form, between objects, letters, numbers and words. Visual discrimination is essential to successful mastery of reading and calculating skills. Lack of such discrimination may be a sign of either a learning disability or cultural deprivation. Preschool and early elementary school education includes a variety of exercises to enhance and reinforce visual discrimination. There are four basic approaches: distinguishing concrete objects, distinguishing similar-looking letters, distinguishing similar-looking words, and matching exercises. Exercises for preliterate children ask them to match round-, square- and other-shaped pegs with appropriate holes and to draw a circle around the one object pictured on a page that is different from all other objects.

Visual discrimination exercises among beginning readers might ask them to underline the letter that is different in the series "a,a,e,a," or "d,d,b,d." Slightly more advanced students might be asked to distinguish the word that is different in a short list such as "bat, bat, but, bat." Still more advanced drills add matching exercises that show students a column of pictures on one side of a paper and ask them to draw a line to the correct, written name in a list on the other side of the paper. **References:** *How to Increase Reading Ability,* Albert J. Harris and Edward R. Sipay (1985); *Principles and Practices of Teaching Reading,* Arthur W. Heilman, Timothy R. Blair and William H. Rupley (1986).

visual impairment In education, blindness or partial sightedness, with blindness defined as a condition requiring the use of Braille (q.v.) to read, while partial-sighted students can read large print.

Reference: *Exceptional Children: Introduction to Special Education,* Daniel P. Hallahan and James M. Kauffman (1988).

vocabulary development The growth, through a variety of exercises and activities, of the number of words an individual can spell, define and use routinely in conversation and writing. Word lists, made up of progressively complex words, whose spellings and meanings students must learn at home each week, are the most common, formal vocabulary-development exercise. In-class vocabulary-development exercises usually occur during oral reading, with the teacher stopping periodically to ask students to define each new word they encounter. Instruction and encouragement in the use of reference works, such as dictionaries, encyclopedias and thesauri, are another basic method of in-school vocabulary development.

Vocabulary development begins, however, long before a child enters school, or even pre-school. Parents' careful identification of objects by their proper names (as opposed to calling them "things," "bow-wow," "choo-choo" and so on) is a major thrust in early vocabulary development of preliterate youngsters. Indeed, many educators consider the role of the parent, even when talking to infants who are too young to respond, pivotal in the child's vocabulary development. Reading to preschoolers is still another impetus to vocabulary development.

Vocabulary development, continues through life, both in and out of home and school. Experiential learning, during field trips and other cultural experiences, including some films and plays, is an important spur to positive vocabulary development. In contrast, slang, obscenities, and other vernacular commonly heard in school-yards, during street play, on television and in many films may encourage negative vocabulary development, with single verb forms, such as

"ain't," replacing entire conjugations, and even meaningless words or phrases, such as "cool" or "ya know," substituting for precise locution.

References: *How to Increase Reading Ability,* Albert J. Harris and Edward R. Sipay (1985); *Principles and Practices of Teaching Reading,* by Arthur W. Heilman, Timothy R. Blair and William H. Rupley (1986).

vocational counseling The process of providing advice and guidance to help individuals make successful career choices. Although vocational counseling may be based solely on one-to-one interviews, it can be far more extensive and include lectures by representatives of a variety of professions and occupations or batteries of tests (psychological, personality, vocational interest, skill, intelligence and aptitude). In the end, vocational counseling aims at helping the individual make a realistic assessment of his or her goals, personal strengths and weaknesses, interests, skills and aptitudes, and to use that assessment in making appropriate career choices in the light of market needs.

The profession of vocational counseling requires formal training and education, sometimes at the graduate school level, and, in most states, certification. Most public secondary school guidance departments include at least one member trained in vocational counseling. At the high school level, vocational counseling also involves helping students select the right curriculum to prepare for the vocations they intend following. Vocational counselors also serve in independent and government agencies to advise adults already in the work force and help them obtain retraining, if necessary, or additional education to reinforce existing skills.

References: *History of Vocational Guidance: Origins and Early Development,* John M. Brewer et al. (1942); *Vocational Guidance and Career Development: Selected Readings,* Herman T. Peters and James C. Hansen (1977).

vocational education Instruction and training in preparation for entry into crafts and trades not requiring a college degree for entry-level positions and ultimate career advancement. Vocational education in U.S. public schools begins as early as the first year of high school and includes instruction and training in a wide variety of fields, including agriculture, business, office jobs, health-related occupations, home economics, trade and industrial education, technical education, and education in various skills and crafts related to construction and mechanics.

Until the mid-19th century, vocational education was conducted through the apprenticeship system (q.v.) under which children were indentured to master craftsmen. The master served as a surrogate parent for five or more years, teaching the apprentice to read, write and calculate, to know Scripture and to practice a craft with which to earn an independent living. In exchange, the apprentice served as the master's assistant.

Vocational education, as a mass instructional process away from the shop floor, became a necessity as the Industrial Revolution progressed during the 19th century. As mass production developed, the individual craftsman became obsolete. Production of goods shifted from the small shop to huge factories, where hundreds of workers shared the task of production, each performing only one small task and none

The first public vocational education schools offered manual training in skilled trades such as carpentry. (Library of Congress)

learning the entire spectrum of skills required to make a finished product. For a while, children learned from older workers, but as factories grew larger, production became too complex and dangerous to permit novice workers roaming around plant floors. Some companies established vocational schools—some of them astoundingly elaborate—in or near their own plants. Called "vestibule schools," the first such schools offered future workers formal classroom training before they actually assumed their duties. Although vestibule schools taught new workers basic skills, they did little to overcome high rates of worker illiteracy that resulted from the lack of compulsory education in the United States. At the time, worker errors stemming from illiteracy and innumeracy were deemed a major factor in the decline in quality and sales of American products on world markets.

In 1882, the Hoe Company, a pioneer manufacturer of printing machinery, became the first company to establish a formal school to train new employees in job-related skills. In 1892, department store magnate John Wanamaker went a step further by organizing the John Wanamaker Commercial Institute in Philadelphia, to give his workers "a working education in the arts and sciences of commerce and trade." The curriculum included reading, writing, arithmetic, English, spelling, stenography, commercial geography, commercial law, and business methods and administration." New employees attended two mornings a week, while advanced employees spent two evenings a week in school. Wanamaker's success encouraged other major companies to set up similar schools for workers at all levels. In 1900, General Electric Research Laboratory set up an educational program for its scientific and technical workers. Westinghouse Research Laboratory followed suit in 1903, as did American Telephone and Telegraph Co. in 1907. Bell Telephone Company, meanwhile, sponsored a host of vestibule schools to train telephone installers and operators in what was then the radically new telephone technology.

In 1908, International Harvester Company, the big farm equipment manufacturer (now Navistar) , started a school for apprentices that soon included courses ranging from mechanical drawing to shopwork. The school willingly taught any course for which five or more employees enrolled. By 1913, there were enough corporation-operated schools to form a National Association of Corporation Schools. Although their growth was halted by World War I, they proliferated in the 1920s. Bell Laboratories, the research arm of American Telephone & Telegraph, expanded its vestibule schools into a mammoth, company-wide human resources department, with an annual budget in the billions of dollars and facilities that ranged from individual classrooms in local telephone company offices to a university-style campus in Lisle, Illinois.

After World War II, General Motors Corporation carried the corporation school concept a step further by building the degree-granting General Motors Institute in Flint, Michigan. The institute (now, the independent GMI Engineering and Management Institute) enrolls more than 2,500 students in its five-year programs leading to bachelor of science degrees in engineering, with specialties in manufacturing, mechanical engineering, industrial engineering and electronic engineering. Students alternate 12 weeks on campus and 12 weeks on the job. About 25% of the students are women.

Although corporation schools provided exceptional vocational education to hundreds of thousands of workers, such education was limited to employees of the largest, most elite members of American industry. Smaller firms could hardly afford to establish similar educational facilities, and it became clear to academicians and industrialists alike that schools would be needed to educate workers in various trades and skills. The first such school was established in 1868—in Russia. Called the Moscow Imperial Technical School, it was headed by Victor Della Vos, who had developed an entirely new pedagogical approach to industrial education. He and his colleagues had analyzed the skills required for each basic craft and trade and organized them in order of ascending difficulty so that they could then be taught to students in that order. Using drawings, models and tools, teachers at the institute taught each trade, step by step, putting students through a series of graded exercises until they arrived at a basic skill level that would allow them to enter apprenticeships.

The Della Vos method of manual training, as vocational education was called, was first displayed abroad in the Russian exhibit at the Philadelphia Centennial Exposition in 1876. At the time, American educators had been searching for ways to introduce vocational education into the school curriculum to help prepare students for the industrial age. The two leaders of the vocational education movement were Massachusetts Institute of Technology President John D. Runkle and Washington University Professor Calvin M. Woodward. Both found in the Della Vos exhibit "the philosophical key to all industrial education," and they became the chief proponents of the new branch of education called "manual training." Urging its introduction into every high school curriculum, they envisioned the Della Vos system as a means of making schools meet the changing needs of an industrial society. They also saw it as a way of making schools more attractive to the huge number of children of immigrant laborers arriving in the United States, whose educational ambitions pointed them toward skilled trades and immediate, paying jobs rather than long, extended periods of study in academies and universities.

In 1880, St. Louis public high schools were first to respond, and the first schools devoted exclusively to manual training appeared four years later. The term manual training began to disappear in the 1930s, as vocational schools extended their curricula beyond individual crafts, such as woodwork and metalwork, to industrial instruction requiring multiple skills, as

in the aviation and automotive trades. Although enrollment in secondary school vocational education climbed during the economic depression of the 1930s, it began declining after World War II. In 1982, nearly 16,000 public high schools offered vocational education, but only 26.9% of high school students were enrolled in vocational education programs. And by 1992 the figure had plunged to less than 12%. Moreover, the outlook for the future of vocational education was even grimmer, as fewer than 8% of high school sophomores enrolled in such education.

There seemed to be two basic reasons for the decline. According to a 1984 report by the National Commission on Secondary Vocational Education, one was American society's obsession with higher education. Secondary schools, the report said, reflected that obsession by focusing educational efforts on the college-bound, while downgrading vocational education and often demeaning students who enroll in it—despite the fact that 80% of all jobs in the United States do not require college degrees. In neglecting vocational education, most comprehensive high schools permitted vocational equipment to become obsolete and of little value in training students for the existing marketplace. Knowing this, many vocational-education students either dropped out of school or enrolled in academic courses for the college-bound. The result, said the report, was an unacceptably high dropout rate of 28% at high school and an absurdly high dropout rate of more than 50% at four-year colleges.

Ironically, the market for skilled workers requiring vocational education was and is expanding. Indeed, the U.S. Labor Department forecasts creation of about five million new jobs for skilled workers by the year 2005, and in the mid-1990s major cities across the United States reported acute shortages of skilled workers. As a result, the Commission on Secondary Vocational Education recommended abandoning the traditional public school tracking system that mandates curricula and diplomas for vocational education that are different from those for college-bound students. It urged merging the two curricula and inviting industry to update school curricula and career education. The commission's recommendation did not fall on deaf ears, and a revolution in American vocational education has been taking place since then. Ironically, it is this very revolution that is the second reason for the decline in high school vocational education courses.

Almost all industrial trades and skilled crafts have become so complex that they now require the full complement of high school academic courses in the language arts, mathematics, computer science and the natural sciences required by the college bound. The net result is that an ever-increasing number of vocational education students are enrolling in the academic track at high school and postponing vocational training until after high school, when they can enroll in the more than 1,000 two-year community colleges (and several hundred four-year colleges) that have made advanced vocational education their specialties.

High schools are not abandoning vocational education, however. In the late 1980s and throughout the 1990s, many comprehensive high schools and specialized vocational schools upgraded their programs, requiring vocational education students to take a full academic course during the first two years of high school. Then, in their last two years, they may enroll in intensive vocational education curricula called two-plus-two or tech-prep (qq.v.) programs. Usually tied to a local community college, such programs are, in fact, four-year programs that lead to both a high school diploma and an associate degree or certificate in a particular field. In a variation on two-plus-two, many high schools have established cooperative vocational education programs (q.v.) that tie vocational education during the last two years of high school to training or apprenticeship programs at local industries, some of them federally financed.

In some cases, companies set up vocational training programs at nearby community colleges, thus making two-plus-two training a three-way partnership among vocational high schools, community colleges and industry.

In addition to school- and college-sponsored vocational education, more than 5,000 private, for-profit, proprietary or entrepreneurial schools (q.v.) offer vocational training—usually in a single field, for jobs such as barbering or bartending that require several weeks of intensive study to prepare for the workplace. And, despite the growth of formal instruction in schools, vocational education still goes on in thousands of in-plant, employer- and union-sponsored apprenticeship and industrial training programs. Most require about 2,000 hours of on-the-job training plus related study in classrooms, by correspondence or through self-instruction. More than 800 categories of apprenticeship programs are officially recognized and accredited by the Labor Department's Bureau of Apprenticeship and Training and by the 50 states.

References: *Corporate Classrooms: The Learning Business,* Nell P. Eurich (1985); *American Education and Vocationalism: A Documentary History,* Marvin Lazerson and W. Norton Grubb, eds. (1974); *The Neglected Majority,* Dale Parnell (1989); *Vocational and Practical Arts Education: History, Development and Principles,* Roy W. Roberts (1971).

Vocational Education Act of 1963 A federal law that called for expansion of existing high school vocational education programs, the creation of new ones and the creation of work-study programs available for full-time vocational education students. Unfortunately, the act remained underfunded for two decades and had little effect on vocational education in the United States until 1984, when Congress passed the Perkins Vocational Education Act, which provided more than $800 million in grants to the states for vocational education.

Reference: *Vocational and Practical Arts Education: History, Development and Principles,* Roy W. Roberts (1971).

vocational rehabilitation The training or retraining of the physically or mentally disabled to adapt their capabilities to appropriate jobs in the workplace. Vocational rehabilitation includes diagnosis, medical care, physical and psychological therapy, vocational counseling (q.v.), testing, training for a specific vocation, tuition for formal education and training, books and equipment, and, if needed, transportation, housing, supervision and special aides. A host of privately operated social service agencies and hospitals offer specialized vocational-rehabilitation services, as do governmental agencies in all 50 states and several U.S. government departments, including the Department of Defense.

Reference: *Readings in Career and Vocational Education for the Handicapped,* Stephen J. Feldman, ed., (1979).

vo-tech (vocational-technical) school A specialized, two-to-four-year high school where all students concentrate on some form of vocational education. Although all students receive the same, fundamental academic instruction of conventional high schools, vo-tech schools offer far more intensive, in-depth training by skilled craftspeople than conventional vocational education programs in comprehensive high schools. Vo-tech students emerge more skilled in academics as well, continually studying applied variations of English, mathematics, science and other academic subjects in conjunction with their vocational education (see applied studies). Employers, as a result, generally respect the credentials of vo-tech graduates more than they do those of students in conventional high school vocational-education programs.

Often called "technology academies," vo-tech schools usually maintain strong job-placement programs and close ties to local and regional employers. Student self-esteem in vo-tech schools is usually higher than that of students in vocational education in comprehensive schools, because the entire administration and faculty focuses entirely on technical studies. In comprehensive high schools, vocational educa-

tion is often held in low esteem by administrators, who tend to assign less able teachers to vocational education students than to students in the academic, college-preparatory track.

Still another advantage of vo-tech education over conventional vocational education is the time and opportunity to sample many trades and occupations before deciding on a specialty. Superior vo-tech schools offer a score of prevocational courses that offer students an in-depth look at "career clusters," such as agriculture, manufacturing, public service and other broad categories, and students then examine hundreds of specific jobs within each cluster. A result is that vo-tech graduates tend to be more committed to and skilled in the trades they select, and to undersand the nature of those trades in the larger environment. Unfortunately, there are, only about 500 vo-tech schools across the United States. Most communities have none and seem unwilling to commit as much funding to vocational education as they do to academic education.

Reference: *But What If I Don't Want to Go to College?–A Guide to Successful Careers through Alternative Education,* Harlow G. Unger (1992).

vouchers In education, a form of credit against school taxes, transferred from one school district to another or to private schools, permitting children to attend schools other than the those in the school district where they legally reside. Vouchers are a central element in the controversy over whether to give parents a choice of public schools for their children.

(See SCHOOL CHOICE; SCHOOL VOUCHER.)

V-12 A World War II, U.S. Navy program that permitted college students drafted into the military to finish their undergraduate and graduate education before entering military service. Designed to provide the Navy with a much needed corps of officers, doctors, engineers and other specialists, V-12 was an accelerated, year-round program that combined education with on-campus training, akin to that of the U.S. Naval Academy (q.v.), at Annapolis, Maryland. During World War II, American colleges and universities contracted to be associated either with the Navy V-12 or the Army Specialized Training Program (q.v.). The two programs were virtually identical, except for the military training and the ultimate service destination for trainees. Depending on whether they were training to be future soldiers or sailors, students transferred with their soldier/sailor classmates to colleges that had been taken over by one or the other service. Regardless of the college they eventually attended, they received degrees from the colleges where they had originally enrolled.

Like ASTP, V-12 offered 22 programs of study during its existence, including engineering, medicine, dentistry, personnel psychology and foreign languages. Those who completed bachelor's degree programs either entered the Navy as ensigns or continued their graduate studies to become doctors, lawyers or engineers before serving in the Navy in those capacities. Like ASTP, which was a progenitor of the post-World War II Army Reserve Officers Training Corps (q.v.), V-12 eventually became the Naval Reserve Officers Training Corps (q.v.).

Reference: U.S. Department of the Navy, Arlington, Virginia.

W

Wald, Lillian D. (1867–1940) American public-health nurse and social reformer. A pioneer in special education, Wald founded New York's first settlement house and was responsible for establishing the world's first public nursing program. Born in Cincinnati, Ohio, she applied for admission to Vassar at age 16, but was rejected as too young. Instead, she attended a course in nurses' training at New York Hospital and studied at Woman's Medical College, both in New York City. While there, she helped set up nurses' classes for immigrants on the Lower East Side, but was so appalled by the area's poverty, its lack of public-health care and its hordes of idle youngsters roaming the streets, that she and a companion obtained funds from philanthropist-banker Jacob H. Schiff to found the Nurses' Settlement in 1895.

At first, the role of the Nurses Settlement was limited to training immigrants in nursing and social work, but it soon expanded to meet the needs of area residents for public nursing services. The first settlement house in New York, it was renamed the Henry Street Settlement (q.v.) and once again responded to neighborhood needs by expanding services to include day care, recreation programs, clubs for children and educational programs in citizenship and English. At the time, there were an estimated 200,000 homeless children in New York, and Wald discovered untold thousands more uncared-for children locked in apartments by fearful immigrant parents who worked 12 or more hours a day, seven days a week and wanted to protect their children from the streets. Wald's project was an overwhelming success, with thousands of parents flocking to Henry Street for care. The Henry Street Settlement subsequently grew into one of the major, private social-service agencies in New York City, with far-reaching educational programs for children and adults of all ages, day-care programs, senior citizens' centers, home-care services, theater groups, arts programs and a host of other social services reaching beyond the immediate neighborhood into deprived areas throughout the city.

In 1902, Wald extended public nursing from the settlement house into a nearby public school. The project was so successful that Wald was able to influence the New York City Board of Health to establish a citywide public school nursing program—the world's first. A close friend of philosopher and educator John Dewey at Teachers College–Columbia University, she was influential in the establishment of a department of nursing and health at that institution. She also succeeded in convincing the New York Board of Education to establish special, un-

Lillian Wald. (Library of Congress)

graded classes—the forerunners of special education—in public schools, in which learning-disabled students might proceed at their own pace.

A pioneer in the movement to establish public playgrounds (q.v.), she was a vocal supporter of children's rights and woman suffrage, and, with Florence Kelley, originated the idea for the United States Children's Bureau (q.v.) to serve as a federal advocate for children. She was also active in the peace movement during World War I and a staunch supporter of women's labor unions. She wrote two books—*The House on Henry Street* (1915) and *Windows on Henry Street* (1934)—both of them autobiographical.

References: BDOE; DAB; NAW; Henry Street Settlement, New York, New York.

Waldorf schools A group of more than 500 independent schools in 32 countries, founded on the principals outlined by Austrian scientist and philosopher Rudolf Steiner (q.v.). Although unaffiliated, all have some common characteristics, and the more than 90 schools in North America are affiliated with an umbrella service organization, the Association of Waldorf Schools of North America. The Waldorf school "movement" originated in 1919, in Stuttgart, Germany, where the owner of the Waldorf Astoria cigarette factory asked Steiner to establish and operate a school for the children of company employees. Steiner agreed, but insisted on four conditions considered radical for that era, namely, that the school be coeducational; that it be open to all children, regardless of social class; that it be a unified 12-year school; and that it be controlled entirely by teachers, free of influence by the state or economic interests.

Steiner held to a rather vague, mystical philosophy in which learning is the product of a child's natural, human spirit and various degrees of learning take place to the extent that the child's spirit remains unfettered by externally imposed restrictions, including religion. Steiner's legacy for today's Waldorf schools is an educational approach that leaves preschoolers and kindergartners completely free to play and explore in surroundings that encourage "meaningful imitation" and "creative play." Rich with toys, games and equipment that feed their creative urges, Waldorf nursery-kindergartens essentially teach through indirection, allowing children to play at whatever they choose and learn from such activities as cooking, building houses, singing, painting, coloring and role playing. Waldorf elementary schools focus on the child's imagination as a primary vehicle for learning—even to the extent of using students in costume to represent numbers in skits about various arithmetic functions. "Whatever speaks to the imagination and is truly felt," says a Waldorf schools brochure, "stirs and activates the feelings and is remembered and learned. The elementary years are the time for educating the 'feeling intelligence.'"

One radical element in Waldorf elementary education is the continuing relationship between a class and its main teacher from year to year—whenever possible—and throughout the elementary school years. The lasting relationship between students and their teacher over six to eight years helps form a strong child-teacher-parent bond and a stable emotional and intellectual foundation during critical years of development. The long-lasting relationship is also beneficial to teachers, who can teach new materials and escape the tedium of repeating the same lessons year after year.

Still another unusual aspect of Waldorf elementary education is the presentation of the curriculum. Instead of giving each topic equal time each day throughout the school year, the day begins with a long, uninterrupted lesson focusing on one subject in depth. Running as long as two hours, the main lesson ties one topic to as many disciplines as possible. Only after the main lesson does the teacher conduct shorter lessons in other subjects. The main lesson may deal with the same subject for several days, before it turns to another subject and relegates the first topic to the shorter lessons of the day.

At the high school level, specialist teachers take over student education, but the curriculum continues to be built around a long lesson each day, focusing on a single subject for several weeks. Designed as a "spiral curriculum," the year progresses with in-depth study for several weeks of, say, mathematics, tying it peripherally each day to allied topics—physics, chemistry, home economics and consumerism—each of which is studied separately in shorter classes later in the day. After a few weeks, one of the peripheral topics becomes the main topic, with peripheral ties to all other subjects studied. The result is that all subjects are studied in relation to all other subjects. Students learn what historic events were occurring as Shakespeare wrote *Hamlet*, what music Newton might have listened to as he made his discoveries, and what scientific developments were occurring as Jefferson drew up plans for the University of Virginia. The curriculum is, in effect, integrated, with no subject taught in a vacuum.

References: American Waldorf Schools of North America, Fair Oaks, California; *The Education of the Child*, Rudolf Steiner (1965).

Wallace v. Jaffree A 1985 United States Supreme Court decision that declared unconstitutional an Alabama law authorizing a daily, one-minute period of silence in public schools "for meditation or voluntary prayer." The law was challenged by Ishmael Jaffree, of Mobile, an agnostic who objected to the exposure of his children to religious practices in public schools. The Court agreed that the Alabama law endorsed religion as a "favored practice" and declared that such an endorsement is not consistent with the established principle that the government "must pursue a course of complete neutrality toward religion."

Reference: U.S. Supreme Court proceedings.

Wanamaker, John (1838–1922) Businessman, merchant and pioneer in corporation-sponsored vocational education. Born in Philadelphia, he started working as a delivery boy at 14, entered retailing at 18 and, with his brother-in-law, founded a clothing store at 23. Within a

decade, John Wanamaker and Company of Philadelphia had become the leading men's clothier in the United States. In 1876, he expanded into an old freight depot and invited merchants in other, non-clothing lines to set up small specialty shops under the same roof and create "a new kind of store." They refused, and he established the shops himself a year later, introducing the world's first department store.

In 1896, he bought a store in New York, replicated the Philadelphia store and, after adding more branches, built one of the world's largest retail empires. By then he was hiring so many new employees that he decided it would be in his own and their interest to assure their knowledge of retail operations. What started as training classes for clerks at the Philadelphia store quickly evolved into the John Wanamaker Commercial Institute, a school of business methods "giving daily opportunities to obtain a working education in the arts and sciences of commerce and trade." The first school of its kind in the United States, it had a faculty of 24 teachers to teach a curriculum that included reading, writing, arithmetic, English, spelling, stenography, commercial geography, commercial law and business methods. New workers spent two mornings a week in school and more advanced employees two evenings a week, after eating a free supper in the employee cafeteria. Boys and girls were organized into drill teams to learn "discipline, organization, precision and obedience" while obtaining "health lessons of muscular training that give bodily strength without which successful mental work is impossible." Wanamaker boasted that the institute paid for itself. "Unintelligent and wasteful labor has lessened. The wisdom of cooperation and mutual helpfulness has been recognized. Knowledge of merchandise, its production, distribution and uses has been increased. Principles of control and government and organization have developed."

Wanamaker's paternalistic training program combined with relatively generous fringe benefits and security to build a level of employee efficiency, loyalty and longevity on the job that few companies could claim. His success inspired companies such as General Electric, Westinghouse, American Telephone & Telegraph, International Harvester and Bell Laboratories to set up similar worker schools. By 1913, there were enough corporation-operated schools to form a National Association of Corporation Schools; although their growth was halted by World War I, they proliferated in the 1920s. "Corporations are realizing more and more the importance of [worker] education in the efficient management of their business," said the National Association of Corporation Schools statement of objectives. "The Company school has been sufficiently tried out as a method of increasing efficiency to warrant its continuance as an industrial factor." Ironically, after American companies began abandoning the paternalistic Wanamaker formula during the depression of the 1930s, Japanese industry would later adopt it in the years following World War II and make it a cornerstone of superior performance.

References: DAB; *Corporate Classrooms: The Learning Business,* Nell P. Eurich (1985); "The John Wanamaker Commercial Institute—A Store School," John Wanamaker, *Annals of the American Academy of Political and Social Science* (XXXIII: 1909).

Ward, Lester Frank (1841–1913) American sociologist and educator, considered by many the "father" of modern sociology. Born in Illinois and raised in poverty on farms in Illinois and Iowa, he was self-taught until he reached college age, when he enrolled in a series of colleges, eventually earning a law degree at Columbia University in New York. Although working as a paleontologist and geologist, he published the seminal two-volume work *Dynamic Sociology* in 1883, in which he proposed education as the "great panacea" for the social ills of the day. He called on government to make education its highest priority and declared that the final stage in the evolution of a truly democratic state would depend on "a system for extending to all the members of society such of the extant knowledge of the world as may be deemed most important."

Ward's book drew little notice at first, with fewer than 500 copies of the first edition sold. But a decade later, in an era when the questions of educating women and the children of the poor were at the center of heated debates among educators and political leaders, *Dynamic Sociology* was rediscovered in 1896, and the second edition made Ward a standard-bearer for egalitarianism and elevated him to the status of prophet in the fields of sociology and education. The book was the first to offer a scientific basis for the burgeoning social reform movement under way in the United States and for the growing demands for an end to child labor, compulsory education through adolescence, educational rights for women and woman suffrage.

Ward's book stated unequivocally that there were no race, gender or social-class differences in intellect. Going a step further, he unveiled a theory that not only expounded the intellectual and social equality of women with men, but even suggested that women might well be superior to men. The book became a "bible" of sorts for progressivists. Hailed by sociologists for raising their subject to the scientific level, he was named president of the Institut International de Sociologie in 1903, and when the American Sociological Association was organized in 1905, Ward was elected its first president. Ward was named the first professor of sociology at Brown University the following year, and his work continued to influence social and educational thought throughout the early years of the 20th century.

References: DAB; BDOE; *Dynamic Sociology,* Lester Frank Ward (1883); *Young Ward's Diary,* Bernhard J. Stern, ed. (1935).

War on Poverty A far-reaching program of federal legislation developed in the mid-1960s by the Lyndon B. Johnson administration to reduce poverty. The program expanded educational opportunities to the poor on a scale never before seen in the United States, opening up preschool education to millions of economically and educationally deprived children and expanding opportunities for vocational education and higher education to millions of poor adolescents and adults.

Johnson declared an "unconditional war on poverty" in his State of the Union address to Congress on January 8, 1964, "not only to relieve the symptoms of poverty, but to cure it and, above all, to prevent it." Planning for the war had actually started two years earlier, when President John F. Kennedy had asked his Council of Economic Advisors to obtain data on the "poverty problem." At the time, *The Other America: Poverty in the United States,* a book by Michael Harrington, had shocked the nation by contradicting the popular notion of the United States as an "affluent society." It presented indisputable evidence that between 40 million and 50 million people—about 25% of American society—lived in poverty.

After Kennedy's assassination, Johnson picked up the banner of the antipoverty movement as his own and spurred the Council of Economic Advisors to accelerate its studies and recommend legislation. The first result was the Economic Opportunity Act of 1964, followed a year later by the Elementary and Secondary Education Act and the Higher Education Act (qq.v.). The Economic Opportunity Act created the Job Corps, Upward Bound, the National Youth Corps and VISTA (qq.v), the last a domestic equivalent to the Peace Corps and the other programs designed to provide job training and work for unemployed, socioeconomically deprived adolescents. The act created myriad education and job-training programs for adults and work-study (q.v.) programs that would allow college students from low-income families to earn money from on-campus jobs. Beyond these efforts, the Economic Opportunity Act also created community-action programs, the most far-reaching of which was Head Start (q.v.), which provided preschool education to millions of children in low-income areas across the United States.

The Elementary and Secondary Education Act, inter alia, provided remedial and other special education to socioeconomically deprived youngsters, while the Higher Education Act created the Teacher Corps (q.v.) to improve the quality of teaching in schools in economically deprived areas.

Although the War on Poverty produced many permanent, far-reaching changes in American education, it had virtually no success in reducing poverty. A decade later, the program's administrative bureaucracy, the Office of Economic Opportunity, was disbanded and many of its programs abandoned. Those that survived were placed under the jurisdiction of other departments.

Reference: *The Great Society's Poor Law: A New Approach to Poverty,* Sar A. Levitan (1969).

Washburne, Carleton Wolsey (1889–1968)

American educator who pioneered the development of preschool education, programmed instruction, ability-graded children's books and advanced teacher training. Born in Chicago, Washburne was educated in the University of Chicago and Hahnemann Medical School laboratory schools directed by famed educators John Dewey and Francis Parker. Both were also personal friends of Washburne's mother, a child-study lecturer with a deep interest in education, which she passed on to her son.

After earning his B.A. at Stanford University and Ed. D. at University of California, Washburne taught in a rural school in California before becoming the science department head at San Francisco State College for Teachers in 1914. In 1919, he assumed the superintendency of schools in Winnetka, Illinois. Over the next quarter-century, Washburne gained a national reputation as an educational innovator. Under his direction, Winnetka's school system became the first in the United States to make widespread use of programmed instruction (q.v.). With the help of his faculty, he introduced the nation's first public, prekindergarten, early-education programs for three- and four-year-olds and established the nation's first guidance programs, complete with school psychologists, psychiatrists and psychometrists, for elementary school children. He introduced individualized reading instruction, which helped slower and learning-disabled students keep up with their peers. He published the school's educational materials at the local Winnetka Education Press, which adopted his system of age-grading children's books according to ability levels. Other children's book publishers quickly adopted the system.

He also founded and obtained a charter for the Graduate Teachers College of Winnetka, where he trained graduates of liberal arts colleges for teaching. His program led to the establishment of similar master's degree programs in education at large universities across the United States. During World War II, he worked with the United States Army and the Department of State, then with the United Nations Educational, Scientific and Cultural Organization. He was director of the teacher education program at Brooklyn College from 1949 to 1960 and Distinguished Professor of Education at Michigan State University from 1961 to 1967. He was the author of *Adjusting the School to the Child* (1932).

References: BDOE; *Leaders in American Education,* Robert J. Havighurst (1971).

Washington The 42nd state to join the Union, in 1889. Although the first school was established in 1832 at Fort Vancouver, Washington was largely a hunting, trapping and fur-trading area until after the U.S. and British claims to it were settled in a treaty in 1846. Separated from Oregon in 1853, Washington had only about 4,000 white inhabitants. A public, territory-wide school system for white children was established in 1881, and the current state public school system was established in 1895.

The state now has more than 1,800 public elementary and secondary schools, with a total enrollment of nearly 600,000 students. Quality of education is about average for the nation. An additional 60,000 students attend private elementary and secondary schools. Washington has been a continual innovator in the area of higher education, having created five two-year, vocational-technical institutions of higher education to supplement the state's 22 public community colleges. There are also four private two-year colleges. The University of Washington and Washington State and Central Washington universities—three of the six public four-year colleges—opened five branch campuses in the heavily populated Vancouver, Spokane and Puget Sound regions in 1990 to deliver education more efficiently to the people of the state. The state has 20 private four-year institutions of higher education, including the University of Puget Sound and Gonzaga University.

References: EB; CHE.

Washington, Booker T. (1856?–1915)

Pioneer African-American educator, founder of Tuskegee University (q.v.) and tireless negotiator for peace between the races in the United States, for which he became known as the "Apostle of Accommodation." Washington wrote that he was "born a slave of a plantation in Franklin County Virginia. I am not sure of the exact place or exact date of my birth, but . . . I suspect I must have been born somewhere and at some time." After Union troops freed him and his mother in 1863, they moved to West Virginia, to a cluster of former slave quarter cabins surrounded by "intolerable . . . filth." Working in nearby salt mines from 4 A.M. to 9 A.M., he managed to attend school for a few hours each day before returning to the mines for a second two-hour shift in the afternoon. When he enrolled in school, he realized that, like many slaves, he did not know his last name. He simply chose the most impressive one he could think of—Washington. (He later learned from his mother that his family name was Taliaferro, which became his middle name.)

Booker T. Washington. (Library of Congress)

At 16, he overheard a group of miners "talking about a great school for colored people somewhere in Virginia" and decided to find it. After a trek of many weeks, he arrived, unbathed, in rags and penniless, at the Hampton Institute (q.v.), a vocational school founded by General Samuel Armstrong (q.v.) to give former slaves the necessary education and skills to earn a living. Handed a broom and asked to sweep a classroom as a measure of his willingness to work, Washington described the experience in his autobiography as "my college examination, and never did any youth pass an examination for entrance into Harvard or Yale that gave him more genuine satisfaction." In addition to learning basic academic skills at Hampton, he discovered what he called "a new world . . . The matter of having meals at regular hours, of eating on a tablecloth, using a napkin, the use of the bathtub and tooth brush, as well as sheets upon the bed, were all new to me."

Washington graduated from Hampton in June 1875, at the head of his class, and returned to West Virginia to open a "colored school." It remained open day and night, seven days a week, teaching blacks of all ages. After two years, he went to Washington, D.C., for a year of study of advanced academics before returning to Hampton to teach. In 1881, he was asked to start a normal school to train black teachers in Tuskegee, Alabama. Within a year, he raised $500 to buy an old plantation, with a kitchen, a stable and a hen house. Washington's classroom leaked so badly that a student held an umbrella above his head to permit him to teach when it rained. Planning to train his students to be teachers and leaders who would educate other African Americans, he found his students so poor and uneducated he had to teach "something . . . besides books. We wanted to teach [them] how to bathe; how to care for their teeth and clothing. We wanted to teach them what to eat, and how to eat it properly, and, how to care for their rooms."

In addition, Washington taught his students as many trades as possible, saying "the whole future of the Negro rested largely upon . . . whether or not he should make himself, through his skill, intelligence and character, of such undeniable value to the community in which he lived that the community could not dispense with his presence." Any individual, he wrote, "who learned to do something better than anyone else—learned to do a common thing in an uncommon manner—had solved his problem, regardless of the color of his skin." He told his students that they would find honor and respect to the extent that their knowledge and skills "added something to the wealth and comfort of the community."

Washington made work an essential part of student and faculty life at Tuskegee. In addition to agricultural and domestic work, students learned every aspect of construction, from design and architecture to masonry, carpentry and roofing. They learned to harvest trees, mill their own lumber, manufacture their own bricks, make their own clothing, mattresses, bedding and upholstery, build their own desks, chairs and furniture, grow their own food and raise and slaughter their own livestock.

Within months, Tuskegee Normal and Industrial Institute, as it was first called, was a self-sufficient community with enough profit from surplus production to allow students to attend school full-time, without working at off-campus jobs. Over the next 40 years, 40 buildings rose on the Tuskegee campus. All but four were "almost wholly the product of student labor." A brilliant public speaker, Washington traveled the nation raising millions of dollars to expand Tuskegee and provide scholarships for those who sought an education there. Thousands flocked to his and other, similar schools that were rising throughout the south. "It was a whole race trying to go to school. Few were too young, and none too old to make the attempt to learn. As fast as any kind of teachers could be secured, not only were day schools filled, but night schools as well."

Everywhere he traveled and to everyone who listened, Washington carried the same message: The path to political and social equality for African Americans lay in industrial education, development of skills, land ownership, hard work, and development of good habits such as thrift, cleanliness, ethical and moral behavior, patience and good manners. His inspiring speeches and the logic of his social and educational theories earned him national and, eventually, worldwide attention. Called the "Negro Moses" for leading his people toward a "promised land," he attracted huge sums for his institution—$20,000 from steel magnate Andrew Carnegie; $50,000 from a railroad tycoon.

In 1895, Washington's influence reached its peak, and he was invited to make one of the opening day speeches at the Cotton States International Exhibition, a commercially sponsored world's fair in Atlanta, Georgia, in a region that was desperately seeking to emerge from an eco-nomic depression by promoting international trade. It was the first time in American history that an African American sat, stood and spoke on the same platform with white southern men and women. Called the "Atlanta Compromise," his speech became the most momentous proclamation on race relations since the Emancipation Proclamation itself. Reminding his audience that African Americans made up one-third of the south's population, he warned that "nearly 16 millions of hands will aid you in pulling the load upward, or they will pull against you the load downward. We shall constitute one-third and more of the ignorance and crime of the South, or one-third of its intelligence and progress."

He pledged that if they received educational opportunities, African Americans would stand by their country "with a devotion that no foreigner can approach, ready to lay down our lives, if need be, in defense of yours, interlacing our industrial, commercial, civil, and religious life with yours in a way that shall make the interests of both races one. In all things purely social we can be as the fingers, yet one as the hand in all things essential to mutual progress. There is no defense or security for any of us except in the highest intelligence and development of all."

After his speech, crowds of white dignitaries rushed to shake his hand. Newspapers across the United States, Canada and western Europe published his speech in full. Counteracting the terrifying (to whites) calls from some black leaders for social revolution, Washington had called for economic and social evolution. While calming the fears of whites, he had offered a way for blacks to fulfill their hopes through education and job opportunities. "It is important and right," he said, "that all privileges of the law be ours, but it is vastly more important that we be prepared for the exercises of these privileges. The opportunity to earn a dollar in a factory just now is worth infinitely more than the opportunity to spend a dollar in an opera house."

Following the Atlanta speech, Harvard University awarded Washington an honorary master of arts degree, the first ever conferred on an African American. Washington called it "a recognition that had never entered into my mind, and it was hard for me to realize that I was to be honored by a degree from the oldest and most renowned university in America. As I sat . . . with this letter in my hand, tears came into my eyes. My whole former life—my life as a slave on the plantation, my work in the coal mine, the times when I was without food or clothing, when I made my bed under a sidewalk, my struggles for an education . . . the ostracism and sometimes oppression of my race—all this passed before me and nearly overcame me." Washington and his wife were subsequently invited to visit diplomats and royalty in Europe and Britain, where he attended Parliament and met Queen Victoria. In 1901, President Theodore Roosevelt invited him to be the first African American to dine at the White House.

Despite its impact on some Americans, Washington's "Atlanta Compromise" failed to halt the race riots and lynchings plaguing the south. In the face of government inaction, voices of other black leaders called for equal political and social rights. Rather than learning skilled trades that would leave them in the service of whites, blacks must obtain academic and professional education, said such activists as W. E. B. Du Bois (q.v.). The Du Bois-Washington debate grew into a bitter controversy. Washington railed against the political agitation that Du Bois was fomenting.

Northern sentiment continued to support Washington. By late 1915, he had built Tuskegee's endowment to about $2 million and its physical plant to more than 100 buildings, spread over 25,000 acres, with a faculty of nearly 300 and a student body of more than 1,500, learning more than three dozen trades. Tuskegee served as a model for 40 other such colleges and universities that continue to educate African Americans. Washington also founded the National Negro Business League to give African Americans the training to set up their own businesses. The south, however, refused to accept the Atlanta Compromise. Where employers offered work to blacks, they paid sub-par wages that put whites out of work, inflamed racism and led to riots and uninhibited assaults and persecution of blacks, whom white law enforcement authorities refused to protect. After Washington's death, most blacks also began abandoning the principles of the Atlanta Compromise. Discouraged by oppression, they turned instead to the activism that, at the time, was personified by W. E. B. Du Bois.

References: BDOE; DAB; *Booker T. Washington,* Louis R. Harlan (1972); *Up From Slavery, An Autobiography* (1901) and *My Larger Education* (1911), Booker T. Washington.

Washington, George (1732–1799)

First president of the United States and an advocate of the much-debated principal of the need for universal education in a society of self-governing people. Though hardly outspoken in support of pro-education at the time of the Constitutional Convention, Washington did, in 1796, advocate establishing a national university in the capital city to train those bound for public office. The concept of a national university had been proposed earlier by Thomas Jefferson, James Madison and others who had unsuccessfully battled for constitutional guarantees of universal public education. Although Washington had little influence over education during his two terms in office, from 1789 to 1797, he did undertake "rational experiments" for imparting the "blessings of civilization" to Indians. Backed by congressional passage of several "trade and intercourse acts," he appointed agents to live among Indians to teach them agricultural and domestic skills and help them establish and maintain factories and trading houses. Aimed also at protecting them from exploitation by illegal traders, Washington's program sought to teach Indians the "discipline" of private ownership and agriculture in order "to promote civilization among the friendly Indian tribes and to secure the continuance of their friendship."

References: DAB; *The Writings of George Washington from the Original Manuscript Sources, 1745–1799,* John C. Fitzpatrick, ed. (39 vols., 1931–44).

Watson, Elkanah (1758–1842)

Businessman, banker, agriculturalist and founder of the Berkshire Agricultural Society, a vital educative institution at a time when there were no agricultural colleges. Born in Massachusetts, Watson had made and lost several fortunes as a merchant, a developer of canal transportation and as a banker. It was in this last calling that he finally found success in the early 19th century as founder of the Bank of Albany and the New York State Bank. His earnings allowed him to retire and "seek the satisfactions of rural felicity" in Pittsfield, Massachusetts, where he purchased a large farm at the age of 50.

Deciding on experimenting with the latest principles of English scientific agriculture, he purchased a pair of prized Merino sheep, whose wool was of such exceptionally high quality that he decided to display them in the public square in Pittsfield. "Many farmers, and even women," he wrote, "were excited by curiosity to attend this first novel, and humble exhibition. It was by this lucky accident, I reasoned thus: If two animals are capable of exiting so much attention, what would be the effect on a larger scale, with larger animals? The farmers present responded to my remarks with approbation." The result was the idea of the modern agricultural fair, according to Watson. After three years of cooperative, scientific breeding, Watson and 26 of his neighbors sponsored the Berkshire Cattle Show, which became a heavily attended annual event. A year later, in 1811, they formed the Berkshire Agricultural Society, which expanded the annual show into an agricultural fair, with a wide variety of displays of livestock and agricultural products. Patriotic and religious oratory, marches, processions and dances were added to make it more festive, but Watson's original purpose of educating farmers by teaching them to use scientific principles remained the fair's central purpose. Entertainment encouraged farmers to come to the fair with their families, but the exhibits taught them how to improve their farms. Watson began writing letters and pamphlets and traveling the country to promote the "Berkshire plan" and encourage the establishment of similar agricultural societies across the United States. His efforts eventually made the agricultural fair a perennial fixture in American life and an important element in the continuing education of the American farmer.

References: *The Agricultural Fair,* Wayne C. Neeley (1935); *History of the Rise, Progress, and Existing Conditions of Canals in the State of New-York . . . , Together with the Rise, Progress, and Existing State of Modern Agricultural Societies on the Berkshire System, from 1807, to . . . 1820,* Elkanah Watson (1820).

Watson, John Broadus (1878–1958)

American psychologist and founder of the behaviorist school of psychology that held personality, behavior and learning to be the result of training and conditioning rather than heredity. A major influence on education, Watson's theories implied that any child who is not born brain-damaged could be trained and taught to do and be anything.

Born and raised in South Carolina, he graduated from Furman University in Greenville, went to the University of Chicago to earn his doctorate in 1903 and remained there as an instructor in experimental psychology for five years. He then became a professor of experimental and comparative psychology at Johns Hopkins, where in 1913 he published the paper that created the behaviorist school: "Psychology as the Behaviorist Views It." Until then he had studied conditioned learning, with rats in mazes, and learning by imitation among monkeys. In 1917, however, he began studying infants to prove his theories of learning, but the experiments were cut short when the publicity of a bitter divorce suit forced him to resign. He went into advertising. Applying his theories of learning, he scored so many successes that, by 1924, he was named a vice president of the J. Walter Thompson Company, one of the world's leading advertising agencies. Although he continued writing on behaviorism and lecturing at the New School for Social Research, his efforts to return to university life were continually blocked. In spite of this rebuff, behaviorism remained a major force in experimental psychology and in education during the remainder of his life.

References: BDOE ; DAB; *The Great Psychologists*, Editors of Lippincott (1971); "John Broadus Watson, Behaviorist," B. F. Skinner, *Science* (January 29, 1959).

Watts, Isaac (1674–1748)

Watts, Isaac (1674–1748) English theologian, educator, hymn writer and author, whose works were highly influential in shaping American education during the early 18th century. Born to a nonconformist family, which, like other Puritans, suffered persecution, he was an assiduous student of the works of John Locke. He served as a tutor to the children of well-to-do dissenters and as pastor of one of London's most exclusive independent congregations. A victim of chronic illness, he spent the last 40 years of life in productive semi-retirement, writing a host of hymns, essays on educational policy, devotional works for children and textbooks on logic and pedagogy that became standard in the colonies as well as in many English academies. Often asked to screen teaching candidates for academies in England and the colonies and to design courses and write textbooks, he engaged in continual and active friendships and correspondence with colonial educators, including Cotton Mather (q.v.). He contributed to the libraries of Harvard and Yale (qq.v.) and helped found and fill the Hollis professorship of mathematics at Harvard. He was active in raising funds for educational and missionary programs among the Indians.

All of his writings—even his hymns—were innovative for the times and had particular appeal to colonial parents and educators bent on educating children to build a new society in a new world. His hymns and works for children presented a benevolent Deity, and his texts emphasized a gentle approach to pedagogy. His *Logick* (1725) and *The Improvement of the Mind* (1741, 1751) were standard texts, with the former explaining the meaning of reason and its use in acquiring knowledge. The latter, which was first published as part of *Logick* and later published posthumously as a separate work, gives the principles of communicating knowledge to others, explaining the differences between teaching and preaching, along with various styles of instruction and principles for writing books. It was the most popular tract on the subject in 18th-century America.

A third work, *A Discourse upon the Education of Children and Youth* (also published posthumously, in 1753), became the standard guide to pedagogy for parents and educators in 18th- and early 19th-century America. Espousing a universal approach to education, he suggested a curriculum for all children that would include training in six broad areas: religion; understanding, memory, judgment, reasoning and conscience; reading, spelling, and writing; conduct of human life and the art of self-government; appropriate trades, businesses or professions; the ornamental arts, including history, poetry, painting and similar subjects, to add pleasure to their lives.

Reference: *Isaac Watts: His Life and Works*, Arthur Paul Davis (1943).

Wayland, Francis (1796-1865)

Wayland, Francis (1796-1865) American educator and theologian who was one of the leaders in the reform of higher education during the first half of the 19th century. Born in New York City, he graduated from Union College, Schenectedy, New York, and went on to earn his medical degree, but never practiced. Having experienced a religious conversion, he went instead to Andover (Massachusetts) Theological Seminary and became pastor of the First Baptist Church of Boston. In 1826, he returned to Union College as a professor of mathematics and natural philosophy, and, a year later, became president of Brown University, a post he held for the next 25 years.

Wayland took over Brown at a time when student rioting had forced his predecessor to resign, and his first presidential moves hardly reflected the liberating philosophy he would later espouse for higher education. Indeed, he immediately obtained power to dismiss any students who violated school rules and ordered all members of the faculty to live on campus to oversee student living quarters. The residence requirement led to the closing of the medical school, whose faculty refused to relinquish their lucrative off-campus practices.

Although he did expand the curriculum somewhat, Wayland instituted a set of conservative academic reforms at Brown that related primarily to increased academic and behavioral discipline. He increased the number of required daily student recitations and banned textbooks, to force faculty to teach and make students learn and display their knowledge in discussions. "It is the action of mind upon mind, exciting, awakening, showing by example the power of reasoning and the scope of generalization, and rendering it impossible that the pupil should not think; this is the noble and the ennobling duty of the instructor." Wayland also expanded the library and developed a system of cumulative grades to inform parents of their sons' educational achievement. He personally taught moral philosophy to seniors, visited students and established a ubiquitous presence on campus.

With order restored, he gradually developed a new theory of the role of learning in an American university, dictated by the needs of an emerging industrial society rather than by classical tradition tied to theology. He gradually converted the science curriculum from one based on theory to one of "adopting the course of instruction . . . to the wants of the whole

community. The abstract principles of a science, if learned merely as disconnected truths, are soon forgotten," he said. "If combined with application to matters of actual existence, they will be remembered." In addition, he recognized the need for broadening the reach of education. If education, he wrote, "is good for one class of the community, it is good for all classes. Not that the same studies are to be pursued by all, but that each one should have the opportunity of pursuing such studies as will be of the greatest advantage to him in the course of life which he has chosen."

Combining his ideas on the connections between theory and practice and the universal need for education, he developed a program for higher education in his highly influential tract, *Thoughts on the Present Collegiate System of the United States,* which was published in 1842. Wayland expanded that document in an 1850 report on "proposed alterations in the course of study" to the Brown trustees and in a subsequent address at Union College in 1854 called "The Education Demanded by the People of the United States." Together, the three essays helped convert American higher education into a unique curriculum that differed substantially from the traditional English system in that it catered to a new class of individuals with special educational needs. "It is manifest to the most casual observer," he wrote in his report to the Brown trustees, "that the movement of civilization is precisely in the line of the useful arts. Steam, machines and commerce, have built up a class of society which formerly was only of secondary importance. The inducements to enter the learned professions have become far less, and those to enter upon the active professions, vastly greater."

Wayland called on institutions of higher education to broaden their curricula to meet the needs of all classes of society, to open their doors to all classes of society and to give students free choice among the programs, courses and educational offerings at those colleges. Moreover, he urged colleges to reach out to the community at large, opening their doors to adults as well as students of traditional college age. Each college, he said in his oration at Union College, should become "the grand center of intelligence to all classes and conditions of men, diffusing among all the light of every kind of knowledge and approving itself to the best feelings of every class of the community." During the quarter-century before the Civil War, in an era in which demands for reform of education were triggering campus riots, Wayland's program became the best known and most influential program of reforms. It eventually formed the basis for creating the public land-grant colleges in the last half of the century.

References: BDAE; DAB; *Francis Wayland: Political Economist as Educator,* Theodore Rawson Crane (1962); *Francis Wayland: A Neglected Pioneer of Higher Education,* William G. Roelker (1944).

Webster, Noah (1758–1843) American patriot, educator, author, lexicographer, lawyer and journalist who, more than any other single American, forever shaped the course of American education after the founding of the Republic. Often referred to as "Schoolmaster to America" and "our greatest schoolmaster," he not only produced his famous dictionary, which Americanized the spellings of the English language, he also fathered an American philosophy of education that was as different from the traditional English approach as the new language would be. Where the monarchy had used education to implant in the minds of students an acceptance of one's class, American republican education would teach men independence and motivate them to choose to act, of their own free will, in the public rather than the private

Noah Webster and the books he wrote that created the "American" language. (Library of Congress)

interest. "Unshackle your minds and act like independent beings," Webster called out to his countrymen. "You have been children long enough, subject to the control and subservient interest of a haughty parent. You have now an interest of your own to augment and defend: you have an empire to raise and support by your exertions and a national character to establish and extend by your wisdom and virtues. To effect these great objects, it is necessary to frame a plan of policy and build it on a broad system of education."

Unlike English education that served an elite, Webster's vision of American education was one of universality and utility. He believed that the new natural sciences of botany, chemistry and geology would enhance the development of agriculture, trade and industry, and that the social sciences of history, economics and political science would ensure the beneficial conduct of domestic and foreign affairs.

Born in comfort in West Hartford, Connecticut, he attended Yale University, left to serve in the Connecticut militia in the Revolutionary War and returned to graduate in 1778. He taught school part-time while obtaining a law degree; although admitted to the bar in 1781, he decided to teach full-time. His dissatisfaction with the curriculum and the texts used to teach it, provoked his plan to develop a radically new American "system of instruction," complete with new texts that would meet the needs of the new nation and educate "all ranks of society." The result was a three-part work, published between 1783 and 1785: *A Grammatical Institute, of the English Language, Comprising, an Easy, Concise, and Systematic Method of Education, Designed for the Use of English Schools in America.*

Fortunately, the three texts were far easier and more concise than their title. The first part was a speller, which in the classical tradition consisted of the alphabet, followed, respectively, by a syllabarium, lists of words of increasing syllabic length, and readings made up of definitions, maxims, geographical information and a brief chronology of "remarkable events in Amer-

ica" from 1492 to 1783. What made the speller unique was its emphasis on a single—New England—pronunciation "to destroy . . . differences of dialect . . ." Its openly stated goal was to promote cultural independence for the new nation. "It is the business of Americans to . . . diffuse a uniformity and purity of language—to add superior dignity to this infant Empire and to human nature." The second part of the *Grammatical Institute* was a traditional grammar, but the third part—a reader—was made up entirely of writings by Americans such as Thomas Paine, Timothy Dwight (qq.v.) others. "In the choice of pieces," Webster wrote, "I have not been inattentive to the political interests of America. Several of those masterly addresses of Congress, written at the commencement of the late revolution, contain such noble, just and independent sentiments of liberty and patriotism, that I cannot help wishing to transfuse them into the breasts of the rising generation." Thus began the first system of truly American education, linking political independence with cultural independence. Webster's system touched virtually every child in every school in the United States. His "American" speller became standard, as did its American spellings. By 1850, annual sales of his spellers reached one million, and by 1890 more than 60 million had been sold.

It was soon after the initial publication of his speller that Webster thought of "compiling a dictionary, which should complete a system for the instruction of the citizens of this country in the language." However, not until 1806 did he publish *A Compendious Dictionary of the English Language,* in which he Americanized English spellings and replaced nonphonetic English spellings with phonetic American spellings, dropping the "k" in words like "musick" and the "u" in words like "honour" and reversing the "re" in words like "centre." The *Dictionary* attempted to impose a uniformity of pronunciation, and its spellings were quickly incorporated into the speller he had written earlier.

Fired by the success of his earlier *Grammatical Institute,* Webster became a fierce advocate of universal public education and the need to make that education uniquely American. In 1785, Webster published a 48-page pamphlet called *Sketches of American Policy,* which called for "education or a general diffusion of knowledge among all classes of men" to develop a uniquely American character befitting an independent nation. "An American ought not to ask what is the custom of London and Paris; but what is proper for us in our circumstances and what is becoming our dignity." Two years later, as the states were debating the U.S. Constitution (q.v.), he published a series of articles declaring that "it is an object of vast magnitude that systems of education should be adopted and pursued which may not only diffuse a knowledge of the sciences but may implant in the minds of the American youth the principles of virtue and liberty and inspire them with just and liberal ideas of government and with an inviolable attachment to their own country."

A believer in utilitarian education, Webster designed a multi-part curriculum to teach children to speak, read and write American English correctly and uniformly. The basic universal curriculum included arithmetic, American history, American geography and American political science. Following completion of this core curriculum, students were to study what they needed to prepare them for their ultimate work: agriculture for future farmers; modern languages, mathematics, and the principles of trade and commerce for those destined for the business world; the classics for those bound for the learned professions. Women, he suggested, should learn poetry and literature. Webster attacked the study in elementary schools of Latin and Greek and the use of the Bible as a school textbook as impractical for a people building a new nation. He called for establishment of statewide public school systems where each community's best educated men would instruct "young gentlemen" at least four months a year. "Here children should be taught the usual branches of learning, submission to superiors and to laws, the moral or social duties, the

history and transactions of their own country, the principles of liberty and government. Here the rough manners of the wilderness should be softened and the principles of virtue and good behavior inculcated."

Beyond formal schooling, he called on parents and periodicals to complete their sons' education. "To educate a child well is one of the most important duties of parents and guardians," he declared. Webster flooded the American press with essays and articles and traveled widely, lecturing Americans on the need for a distinctly American education and culture. To enhance that outcome, he wrote an enormous number of textbooks, which, like his *Grammatical Institute,* became standard in most American schools throughout most of the 19th century. These texts included *Elements of Useful Knowledge* (1801–12), with volumes on history, geography and zoology; *Biography for the Use of Schools* (1830); *A History of the United States* (1832); *The Teacher* (a manual for using the spelling book, 1839); and *A Manual of Useful Studies* (a one-volume home encyclopedia, 1839). To disseminate his views on education, he founded the *American Magazine* in New York City in 1787, but its failure forced him to return to Hartford to practice law. He returned to New York in 1793 to found and edit two strongly Federalist newspapers, selling them 10 years later, after the success of his speller allowed him to retire.

He moved to New Haven, Connecticut, where he completed work on his *Dictionary,* which contained 5,000 more words than Dr. Johnson's and other dictionaries of the day, and included nonliterary words as well as Americanisms. He wrote in his preface that the work was preparatory to an even greater dictionary that would be forthcoming; and after more than 20 years of continued labor, he issued the *American Dictionary of the English Language.* Published in 1828, it contained 70,000 excellent definitions in two volumes, and once again called for uniformity of language as a cement of national unity. Its spellings and definitions became the foundation of American English, while many of its spellings displaced English spellings even in England.

Ironically, although Webster successfully coaxed state legislatures into passing copyright laws to protect the revenues from his *Grammatical Institute* and other textbooks, after his death, his name passed into the public domain. Although his estate sold the rights to his dictionary to Charles and George Merriam—and their Merriam-Webster publishing company continues to produce *Webster's Dictionary*—his name appears on many other dictionaries and reference works that have no lineal connection to Webster or his books. Equally ironic has been introduction of multilingual education into American public schools, two centuries after Webster first enunciated his concept of uniformity of language as the cement of national unity and the basis of public education.

Unlike Benjamin Franklin, Thomas Jefferson (qq.v.) and other proponents of universal public education of his era, Webster had little association with higher education until he experienced a religious conversion and in 1820 was instrumental in the founding of Amherst College (q.v.), as a theological school to train ministers in orthodox Congregationalism.

References: BDAE; DAB; *The American Language: An Inquiry into the Development of English in the United States, Together with Supplements I and II,* H. L. Mencken (3 vols., 1936–1948); *Noah Webster,* John S. Morgan (1975); *Noah Webster: Pioneer of Learning,* Ervin C. Shoemaker (1936); *A Bibliography of the Writings of Noah Webster,* Emily Ellsworth Ford Skeel and Edwin H. Carpenter Jr. (1958); *Noah Webster: Schoolmaster to America,* Harry R. Warfel (1936); *On Being American: Selected Writings, 1783–1828,* Noah Webster (Homer D. Babbage Jr., ed., 1967).

Wechsler-Bellevue Intelligence Scale An individually administered intelligence test developed by Dr. David Wechsler for his adult patients at Bellevue Hospital in New York City in 1939. The first such test developed specifically for adults, it was a forerunner of a battery of individual intelligence tests developed for both adults and children. Among them are the following:

- Wechsler Adult Intelligence Scale, for people older than 16. The test yields three scores, a verbal I.Q., a performance I.Q. and a full-scale I.Q. The verbal section of the test measures nonabstract thinking skills—breadth of knowledge, comprehension, arithmetic skills and vocabulary. The performance scale measures abstract and spatial skills with digit-symbol questions, picture completion, block design, picture arrangement and block assembly.

- Wechsler Intelligence Scale for Children, for children six to 16. Revised in 1974, the test is the most commonly used I.Q. test for this age group. It has 12 sub-tests grouped into verbal and performance sections that produce verbal, performance and full-scale I.Q. measurements. The verbal section consists of general information, general comprehension, arithmetic, similarities and vocabulary. The performance section consists of picture completion, picture arrangement, block design, object assembly and coding or maze exercises.

- Wechsler Preschool and Primary Scale of Intelligence, for children four to 6½. The test is derived from the Wechsler Intelligence Scale for Children, with 10 sub-tests and one optional sub-test grouped in verbal and performance sections, with categories of questions virtually identical to those of other Wechsler scales. The level of complexity, however, is lower, and it can be administered in two sessions to accommodate the shorter attention spans of younger children.

References: The Psychological Corporation, San Antonio, Texas; *The Measurement of Adult Intelligence* (1944), *Wechsler Adult Intelligence Scale Manual* (1955), *Wechsler Intelligence Scale for Children* (Revised, 1974) and *Manual for the Wechsler Preschool and Primary Scale of Intelligence* (1967), David Wechsler.

weighted classroom unit An archaic method of measuring per pupil costs and financial needs in elementary schools. Also known as a weighted elementary pupil unit, the weighted classroom unit was calculated on a base of 1.0, with adjustments made according to transportation costs, students per classroom, and differences in living costs in each district. The method has been replaced by the full-time equivalent (q.v.) method of calculating costs.

Reference: *The Measurement of Educational Need,* by Paul R. Mort (1924).

Welch, William Henry (1850–1934)

American physician and educator who devised the model for modern medical school education. One of the most important and influential figures in American medicine, Welch was born in Connecticut, the son and grandson of doctors. He did his undergraduate work at Yale University and earned his M.D. at the College of Physicians and Surgeons (now part of Columbia University), in New York. After studying in Germany under several leading scientists, he returned to New York in 1879 to become professor of pathology and anatomy at Bellevue Hospital Medical College, where he founded the first pathology laboratory in the United States.

In 1884, he was appointed professor of pathology at Johns Hopkins University, a relatively new institution that was pioneering new approaches to higher education. At the time, medical education consisted of a combination of apprenticeships, textbook study and one to three years of formal lectures at one of the myriad proprietary medical schools organized by local practitioners. Welch developed a new, formal, four-year medical-school curriculum—the first in the United States. It consisted of two years of laboratory study of preclinical subjects, such as anatomy, physiology, pharmacology and pathology, followed by two years of in-hospital study of the clinical subjects of medicine, surgery and obstetrics.

Welch helped found both the Johns Hopkins Hospital in 1889 and its medical school in 1893, of which he was the first dean. He linked the school inextricably to the hospital by recruiting such distinguished physician-researchers as Sir William Osler (1849–1919) and the renowned surgeon William S. Halsted (1852–1922) to staff both institutions—as professors in the medical school and as heads of their departments in the hospital. The appointments made them responsible for delivery of medical services as well as medical instruction, and the arrangement created the first so-called teaching hospital in the United States.

While making the hospital's physician-teachers central to the life of the medical school, Welch also made the medical school's laboratory and library facilities equally central to the research needs of the hospital and its physicians. Their combined duties forced physician-professors to integrate advanced medical education with practical hospital routine, as they led their students on daily rounds of hospital wards, applying textbook and laboratory knowledge. The teaching standards and methods—and the four-year medical degree—made Johns Hopkins a model for teaching hospitals that sprang up in cities across the United States.

In 1896, Welch founded the *Journal of Experimental Medicine,* the first journal to publish the results of major medical experiments. Still at Johns Hopkins in 1901, he helped found the Rockefeller Institute for Medical Research (now, Rockefeller University), in New York, and served as chairman of its board of scientific directors. In 1926, he became the director of the Johns Hopkins School of Hygiene and Public Health, the first school of its kind in the world. He also became the university's first professor of the history of medicine in that year. The author of many medical papers on pathology and bacterial infections, he served at one time or another as president of almost all the leading medical and scientific organizations in the United States, including the Association of American Physicians (1901), the American Medical Association (1910) and the National Academy of Sciences

(1913–16). During World War I, he served with the surgeon general of the United States, earning the rank of brigadier general.

References: BDAE; DAB; *William H. Welch and the Rise of Modern Medicine,* Donald Fleming (1954).

Westinghouse Science Talent Search A nationwide program to encourage the study of science in the United States by identifying the most scientifically talented high school students in the country each year and rewarding them with college scholarships totaling more than $200,000. The program traces its its roots to a discussion at the 1939 New York World's Fair between a representative of Westinghouse Corporation and the director of Science Service, a nonprofit organization in Washington. Both men lamented the lack of science education in the United States and the fact that fewer than 1,000 of the 25,000 American high schools at that time had trained science teachers or even rudimentary science courses. Three years later, Westinghouse agreed to grant $25,000 to cover scholarships and costs for the first "search," in 1942. Since then, the company has provided more than $3 million in scholarships and cash awards to more than 15,000 semi-finalists and 2,000 finalists, in what have become the nation's most prestigious science awards for secondary school students. Science Service continues to administer the program, with all funding flowing from Westinghouse Electric Corporation.

The search brings together the brightest, most creative science students in the United States. STS finalists have gone on to win more than 100 of the world's most coveted science and mathematics awards and honors, including five Nobel Prizes and nine MacArthur Foundation Fellowships. Fifty-six have been named Sloan Research Fellows and 30 have been elected to the National Academy of Sciences. More than half the former search winners are in either teaching or research positions at colleges and universities.

More than 100,000 students have competed in the awards since their inception. Each student must submit a written report on an independent research project in the physical sciences, behavioral and social sciences, engineering, mathematics, or biological sciences (excluding live vertebrate experimentation). An entry must include verification from school officials and a teacher or mentor, along with official high school transcripts and any available standardized test scores such as SATs or ACTs. The competition is open only to students who will be seniors during the academic year in which that year's competition falls. Awards consist of one $40,000 college scholarship ($10,000 a year for four years); one $30,000 scholarship ($7,500 a year for four years); one $20,000 scholarship ($5,000 a year for four years); three $15,000 scholarships ($3,750 per year for four years); four $10,000 scholarships ($2,500 per year for four years); and 30 $1,000 scholarships, payable upon matriculation.

Deadlines for entries are early December of each year, with the names of 300 semifinalists announced in mid-January and those of the 40 finalists announced in late January. The 300 semifinalists receive certificates of commendation, along with recommendations from Westinghouse to colleges and universities, urging each student's admission, with appropriate financial assistance if necessary. In early March, the 40 finalists are awarded a five-day, all-expenses-paid trip to the Science Talent Institute in Washington, D.C., for the final judging. Their research exhibits are displayed and viewed by thousands of visitors, including members of the government and scientific community. Winners, whose names are announced at a culminating awards ceremony, meet the president, the vice president and distinguished science advisers.

References: Science Talent Search, Washington, D.C. 20036; Westinghouse Electric Corporation, Corporate Public Relations Department, Pittsburgh, Pennsylvania.

West Point The popular name for the United States Military Academy (q.v.), which is located on a rocky outcropping known as West Point, on the west bank of the Hudson River, approximately 60 miles north of New York City.

West Virginia The 35th state to enter the Union, in 1863, after its secession from Virginia, which had joined the confederacy at the beginning of the Civil War. Although peopled by a large Confederate minority, West Virginia was so overwhelmed by Union military victories in the summer of 1861 that separatist leaders organized what they called a restored Virginia government in Wheeling to make peace with the North. Two years later, they petitioned for statehood.

From the time its first white settlers arrived in the mountainous wilderness in the 1750s, western Virginia remained physically, culturally and economically apart from the genteel plantations of eastern Virginia. What education existed prior to statehood was largely provided by churchmen. With statehood came the establishment of public schools; but the isolation of so many mountain families left most children unaffected by formal education until well into the 20th century.

By the early 1990s, the state had about 1,000 public elementary and secondary public schools, with a total enrollment of more than 300,000. Quality of education ranks among the poorest in the United States—largely because of the deep belief of many West Virginians that formal education serves little purpose in a mountainous terrain where most adults either become self-sufficient or work in coal mines. One-third of the state's population has not completed high school. The lack of interest in formal education has affected the state's higher education, which is perennially short of funds. Chronically depressed economically, West Virginia has long been forced by its impenetrable geography to duplicate academic and technical programs in colleges throughout the state. There are a total of 28 colleges and universities—12 public and nine private four-year institutions and four public and three private two-year colleges. In an effort to avoid duplication and to systematize higher education, the state divided its colleges into two systems in 1989: the University of West Virginia System for research universities, and the State College System for the other institutions. The reorganization has improved teacher education and cooperative-education links between colleges and high schools, and helped introduce and expand Advanced Placement (q.v.) course offerings at many high schools.
References: CHE; EB.

Wheelock, Eleazar (1711–1779) American religious leader and educator, who founded the town of Hanover, New Hampshire, and Dartmouth College. Born in Connecticut, Wheelock graduated from Yale College and became the Congregationalist pastor in Lebanon, Connecticut, where he augmented his income by taking in boarders to tutor in preparation for college. One was Samson Occom, a Mohegan Indian who was later ordained and inspired Wheelock to educate and convert other Indians and thus promote peace between the two races.

Determined to found a free school to educate whites and Indians together, he obtained the use of Colonel Joshua Moor's house in Mansfield, Connecticut, in 1754 and founded Moor's Charity School with funds raised by Occom during a trip to England. Although it had a large attendance, the school failed four years later, and Wheelock accepted an offer of a township of land from the governor of New Hampshire. In 1770 he moved northward with 30 students and other settlers to found the town of Hanover and Dartmouth College, for which he had obtained a charter from King George III the previous year. He spent the remainder of his life teaching, supervising construction of new buildings and raising funds. His son, John Wheelock (q.v.), graduated from Dartmouth's first class, in 1771, and after his father's death in 1779 became Dartmouth's second president.

References: *Eleazar Wheelock*, J. D. McCallum (1939); *History of Dartmouth College*, Leon Burr Richardson (1932).

Wheelock, John (1754–1817)

American educator who succeeded his father, the founder and first president of Dartmouth College, to the presidency of that institution in 1779. Born in Lebanon, Connecticut, where his father had opened his first school and had taught and converted Indians to Christianity, the young Wheelock was educated by his father and, after attending Yale, transferred to Hanover to become a member of the first graduating class at Dartmouth, in 1771. He became a tutor at Dartmouth, then served in the New Hampshire Assembly and joined the Continental Army in 1777, rising to the rank of lieutenant colonel.

During the first 25 years of his presidency, he achieved noteworthy success by expanding the institution's physical plant and curriculum, by raising considerable funds, by reviving his father's program of educating Indians and by lecturing and conducting prayer services. In 1798, he founded the medical school. Unfortunately, his virtually lifelong relationship with Dartmouth began to unravel bitterly in 1815, when his largely Federalist board of trustees dismissed him in a power struggle over pedagogical and administrative policies.

He appealed to the Democratic state legislature, and in 1816 a Democratic legislature declared the charter issued by George III invalid and replaced it with a new one, naming a new board and reinstating Wheelock. The old board sued and, after it lost its case in a state court, obtained the services of Daniel Webster and appealed to the U.S. Supreme Court. In 1819, the Court ruled that Dartmouth was a "private eleemosynary corporation" and that its charter issued by the English Crown was a valid contract. It ruled the New Hampshire law reinstating Wheelock a violation of Article 1, Section 10 of the Constitution, forbidding any state legislation that impairs a contractual obligation. The decision restored the original board to power, but by then Wheelock had died.

References: BDOE; DAB; *History of Dartmouth College*, Leon Burr Richardson (1932).

white citizens' councils

Ad hoc groups of townspeople formed throughout the South in the 1950s to resist racial desegregation of schools and what they called the "mongrelization" of the Caucasian race. The first white citizens' council was formed in Indianola, Mississippi, in the summer of 1954, less than two months after the United States Supreme Court had declared racial segregation of public schools unconstitutional, in its landmark decision, *Brown v. Board of Education of Topeka* (q.v.).

The formation of the Indianola council set off a white citizens' council movement throughout the south to fight desegregation by whatever means possible and to purge schools of "liberal" teachers and "liberal" books. The councils also sought to purge the south of the National Association for the Advancement of Colored People, which had led the legal battle that produced the *Brown* decision. Southern governors, senators and representatives flocked to support the citizens' councils, which they called a democratic "grass roots" movement, despite the secrecy that cloaked the identities of many council members. Senators Harry Byrd of Virginia and James Eastland of Mississippi resurrected the doctrine of interposition, first enunciated by John C. Calhoun before the Civil War as a fundamental right and obligation of the states to interpose themselves between the federal government and the people.

In addition to outright defiance of the 1954 Supreme Court decision, southern states passed laws to ensure perpetuation of segregation. They repealed compulsory education laws and passed laws denying funds to biracial schools and providing tuition grants to white students to attend segregated private schools. Other laws gave individual school districts authority to transfer and assign students to various schools arbitrarily and to support "white academies." In 1955, the white citizens' councils united to form a Federation for Constitutional Government to coordinate the battle against desegregation and the Supreme Court. They established allegedly private, white academies throughout the south, and in March 1956 organized a group of 101 southern congressmen and senators to issue a "Declaration of Constitutional Principles" that declared *Brown* invalid and inaugurated a program of "massive resistance."

The citizens' councils' resistance to desegregation, however, involved not only white parents' refusal to send their children to school with black children, but also violence against, and intimidation of, tens of thousands of black men, women and children throughout the south. The council-movement program of massive resistance reached a climax in Little Rock, Arkansas, in 1957, when Governor Orval Faubus prevented entry of black students to Central High School, claiming he was acting to maintain public order. As mobs of white supremacists milled about the school, President Dwight D. Eisenhower federalized the Arkansas National Guard and sent units of the 101st Airborne Division to Little Rock to enforce the Supreme Court's orders.

There were several subsequent gubernatorial attempts in Mississippi and Alabama in the early 1960s to "interpose" between the federal government and the people of the two states. Swift action by Washington, along with a spate of decisions by the Supreme Court, finally ended such official, state-government efforts. The white citizens' councils continued their campaigns of violence and intimidation until 1964, when passage of the Civil Rights Act gave the Federal Bureau of Investigation the power to investigate and arrest "citizens" for violating the civil rights of African Americans.

Reference: *The Deep South Says "Never,"* John Barlow Martin (1957).

whole language A pedagogical approach to the teaching of reading and writing by extensive use of themes from children's literature and children's own experiences and stories. A thematic program based on authentic children's literature, whole language extracts themes from across the curriculum and asks students to explore and articulate them through a variety of media, including acting out, discussion, recitation and other forms of direct participation. Integrated into the maelstrom of activity are a form of reading and writing instruction, with students asked to recite and/or write a similar story (or a personal reaction) to the one they've just heard.

The theory behind whole language is that learning is facilitated by the interactive use of all language cueing systems in unison—namely phonology, orthography, morphology, syntax, semantics and pragmatics. The basis of actual learning is the immediate and fulfilling use of meaningful language rather than the series of meaningless, guttural sounds used in phonics instruction. The learner leaves the whole language class able to articulate whole, useful words and sentences that can be put to immediate use in life outside the classroom.

In kindergarten, children's writing is largely personal and phonetic, but students nevertheless experience the excitement of translating words into writing and vice versa. Training in penmanship, spelling and the rules of grammar is postponed in favor of reinforcing the pleasure of listening to and telling stories. Students do, nevertheless, gradually learn to read and write correctly through an evolutionary process based on imitation, as the teacher writes words from the story material just narrated in large, bold, carefully shaped letters on the chalkboard, repeating each word aloud and asking students to join in by repeating the words and sentences in unison and then trying to write what they see and have just said.

Although somewhat complex to organize, the whole language approach to learning makes the story central to skill learning rather than the reverse. Instead of endless, repetitive writing exercises, whole language capitalizes on children's instinctive fascination with and ability to invent stories long before they can read or write. It thus uses a pleasurable activity on which to build skills. By watching the teacher write the story and eventually reading and writing it themselves, students learn the "whole language"— the stories and related communication skills — while engaging in an activity they enjoy.

Essentially an ultimate form of top-down reading (q.v.) instruction, the whole language approach has many obvious advantages and an army of proponents among educators. Like most approaches to reading instruction, it also has its critics, who point out that it often fails to compensate for individual developmental differences of children four, five, six and seven years old. Not only do children learn at different rates, they also learn in different ways. Each has different interests, a different background and a different style of learning, and any classroom with only one kind of reading program can fail some of its students. Despite exaggerated claims for virtually every type of reading program— phonics, whole word, whole language, etc.—no reading program has yet proved perfect for all.

References: *The Elementary School Handbook,* Joanne Oppenheim (1989); *What's Whole in Whole Language?* Kenneth Goodman (1986); *Whole Language: Theory in Use,* Judith Newman (1985).

Widmar v. Vincent A U.S. Supreme Court ruling in 1981 affirming the constitutional right of student organizations at public colleges and universities to hold religious services on campus property. The University of Missouri's Kansas City campus had barred such student groups from university buildings, saying such activity violated the constitutional doctrine of separation of church and state. The university, meanwhile, permitted indiscriminate use of its buildings by nonreligious student groups. The Court held that in barring religious groups, the university had violated the First Amendment rights of students by depriving them of their right to free association and by excluding religious speech from the otherwise free speech permitted in its buildings. The Court held that the doctrine of

separation of church and state would have had application only if the university itself had been responsible for the religious speech addressed to the students.

Reference: U.S. Supreme Court proceedings.

Wieman v. Updegraff A 1952 U.S. Supreme Court decision that declared unconstitutional an Oklahoma law requiring state employees to take a loyalty oath as a condition of employment. The case involved the dismissal in 1951 by Oklahoma Agricultural and Mechanical College of seven teachers who had refused to swear that they had not been members of the Communist Party within the previous five years or members of any group deemed by the U.S. Government to be a "Red Front" or subversive organization. Calling test oaths "notorious tools of tyranny," the Court ruled that the Oklahoma law violated the individual's constitutional right of free association and denied jobs to people "solely on the basis of organizational membership . . . regardless of their knowledge of the organizations to which they had belonged. But membership may be innocent," said the Court. "Indiscriminate classification of innocent with knowing activity must fall as an assertion of arbitrary power. The oath offends due process . . ."

Reference: United States Supreme Court proceedings.

Wiley, Calvin H. (1819–1887) American educator who defied violent anti-education sentiment in his native North Carolina to establish universal public education in the state and to keep most schools running during the Civil War. A graduate of the University of North Carolina in 1840, he was admitted to the bar the following year and, after eight years of practicing law, was elected to the state legislature. When the law establishing the office of state superintendent of common schools was passed, Wiley was elected to that post in 1853. He held the office until April 26, 1865, when, after the surrender of the Confederacy, a Union Army directive declared all state offices vacant. But during his 12 years in office, he had laid the foundation for the future of public education in the state. He had organized the state education association, had helped establish teacher training schools, had established standards and examining boards for teachers, had instituted required annual certification of teachers, had organized county school units, with school superintendents and school boards, and had promoted universal education as a means for assuring the state's economic recovery.

References: BDAE; *The Problems, Policies and Achievement of Calvin H. Wiley,* H. C. Renegar (1925).

Willard, Emma Hart (1787–1870)

America's first woman educator and founder of the first school for women that offered a curriculum equivalent to that of men's academies and colleges. Born Emma Hart, she was one of 17 children of the wealthy landed family for whom Connecticut's capital city of Hartford had been

Emma Willard. (Emma Willard School)

named. Her father and mother were among the most cultured and influential people in Hartford; unlike most parents of that era, they routinely spent evenings in deep, animated philosophical discussions with their children. As a youngster, Emma attended common schools, but at 13 learned philosophy, literature, geometry and arithmetic on her own. At 15 she enrolled in the then-famed Berlin (Connecticut) Academy for girls and did so well that the town appointed her to head the district public school.

Throwing away whips and rulers, she maintained order and stimulated learning by developing imaginative new teaching methods that are now part of the foundation of modern teaching. Hart abandoned rote learning in favor of Socratic questions and answers that taught her students to reason logically. The results astounded parents and students alike, and word of her methods traveled across New England. She was named to teach at the Berlin Academy in 1806, where she had been a student two years earlier—all the while continuing her own studies and adding to her vast knowledge. Prestigious girls' academies in New York, Massachusetts and Vermont invited her to teach. Not yet 21, she moved to Middlebury, Vermont, to teach at the girls' academy there.

In 1809, she met and married her husband, the prominent, wealthy physician John Willard, who helped his wife study all his scientific and medical books, along with philosophical works on individual liberty and equal rights. In 1814, she decided to enroll in nearby Middlebury College, which, like all the world's colleges then, was open only to men. She met with a swift, immediate and humiliating rejection. She converted her anger and bitterness, however, into a design for a woman's boarding school that would make "an important change in education by the introduction of a grade of schools for women higher than any heretofore known." She had already taught herself most college courses, and disguising her school with the title Middlebury Female Seminary, she proceeded to introduce a curriculum that was virtually identical to that of Middlebury's, with a full range of classical and scientific studies. Prior to this, female seminaries had taught only "domestic and ornamental arts" to train women as housekeepers, wives and mothers.

The school's fame spread quickly and, within two years and with her husband's help, drew 70 students and required expansion. Knowing the Vermont legislature would reject any request for state support, she wrote instead to New York State's Governor De Witt Clinton, a strong advocate of universal public education and the education of women. Although a supporter of the then-growing women's rights movement, Willard decided on diplomacy in her appeal to the all-male New York State legislature, saying that it was in their best interests and that of all men to see that their sons were not taught by ignorant, uneducated women. "Our sex need but be considered in the single relation of mothers," she said. "In this character, we have the charge of the whole mass of individuals who are to compose the succeeding generation . . . How important a power is given by this charge."

Although backed by Governor Clinton and a vast following of parents, Willard was unable to obtain official funding from the state legislature. At her own expense, she published a pamphlet called *An Address to the Public: Particularly to the Members of the Legislature of New York Proposing a Plan for the Improvement of Female Education.* Educators across the United States and Europe hailed the proposal as one of the most important documents on education of its time. It won praise from President James Monroe and former presidents Thomas Jefferson and John Adams, as it did from Governor Clinton. But hordes of conservatives charged that Willard was a radical who would upset the social order and destroy the American family by making women so ambitious that they would leave their families.

Furious "almost to frenzy," she continued touring the United States, speaking to groups of parents. The people of Troy appropriated money to buy a three-story building to found a new school, and they agreed to raise enough

money to renovate it and endow it. Convinced the area would become an important commercial and cultural center after the opening of the Erie Canal, Willard founded her Troy Female Seminary in 1821, four years before the opening of the canal and five years before the opening of the first public high schools for girls in the United States. It was the first school in the world to teach women science, philosophy, history and other subjects hitherto reserved for men. Only 34 years old on opening day, the regally dressed Willard watched 90 women from seven states march through the doors of her new school. Willard's husband abandoned his medical practice to help his wife, and together they broke new ground in academics and pioneered changes in school administration that would eventually sweep the nation. She introduced student government, appointing student monitors to inspect rooms and report violations. Students shared double rooms, with each taking turns cleaning every other week.

Instead of a whip to "beat the devil" out of miscreants as at most schools, Willard spent hours talking with each child, probing to find the emotional roots of any youngster's misconduct—35 years before the birth of Freud. By 1831, 10 years after its opening, Troy Female Seminary had become world-renowned, enrolling more than 100 boarding students and 200 day students each year. Many were from some of the most prominent families in the United States and Europe. Willard educated the daughters of several governors, the nieces of the American author Washington Irving and, in what was a triumph for so gallant an advocate of women's rights, the niece of England's Mary Wollstonecraft, who in 1792 had written the world's first major work on women's rights, *A Vindication of the Rights of Women.* Published in Philadelphia in 1794, it is generally credited with having planted the seeds for the woman suffrage movement and the demand for equal educational rights for women. The book deeply influenced Willard, who believed wholeheartedly in Wollstonecraft's proclamation that only a good education stood in the way of women becoming the equals of men. Women, Willard said, were the natural equals of men, and "the subjugation of women was not the law of nature but simply an injustice inflicted by men."

Willard's curriculum astonished administrators at men's colleges. As one student described her course of study to an astonished family friend, "We had reading, writing, spelling, arithmetic, grammar, geography. history, maps, the globe, algebra, geometry, trigonometry, astronomy, natural philosophy, chemistry, botany, physiology, mineralogy, geology, and zoology in the mornings; and dancing, drawing, painting, French, Italian, Spanish and German in the afternoon. Greek and the higher branches of mathematics were only studied by the tall [older] girls." The school's worldwide reputation earned it a visit from France's General Lafayette in 1824, during his triumphal return to the country he had helped free during the American Revolution. A few years later, when Willard visited France as a representative of the American government to an educational conference, Lafayette escorted her to court balls, to the French parliament and to the most famous French schools for girls. Willard became as well known in Europe as in the United States and helped pioneer women's education there as well, by raising thousands of dollars to found a teachers' training school in Athens, Greece.

Willard also pioneered new teaching methods that made it easier for young minds to understand complex facts. To that end, she wrote a number of widely used textbooks, including a groundbreaking geography textbook that included maps, which, for the first time, tied geography to history and showed how nations had changed shape in each era. Among her other classic texts were *History of the United States* (1828) and *Astronomy* (1853). She also wrote a book of poems, the best known of which was "Rocked in the Cradle of the Deep." Admired by her students, she inspired more than 200 to become teachers themselves. As her school grew, she made it the first to offer scholarships for

intellectually gifted women who could not otherwise have afforded to attend.

In 1824, Willard's beloved husband and helpmate died, and she was forced to run the school by herself. Gradually, her son and daughter-in-law assumed responsibilities for running the school. In 1838, alone at 51, she shocked admirers and detractors alike by turning the school over to her son and marrying Christopher Yates, an Albany ne'er-do-well who soon left her penniless. Willard returned to her childhood home near Hartford and threw herself into Henry Barnard's (q.v.) campaign to establish universal public education in Connecticut. Fortunately, she had trained her son and daughter-in-law as skilled administrators and teachers. By 1850, they had not only maintained the school's reputation as the finest women's school in the world, they had also it the academic equal of the finest men's academies.

In the meantime, Willard wrote articles, toured Connecticut, trained teachers and became superintendent of four district schools in Hartford—the first woman superintendent of schools in the United States. In 1844, Willard returned to Troy to lead the campaign for improvement of public schools in New York State. Traveling 700 miles across the state by stagecoach and barge, she managed to train more than 500 teachers as she went and helped hundreds of towns establish public schools. In 1846, she set out on a two-year, 8,000-mile trek across the west and south to carry her message of universal public education and gender equality across America.

In 1854, Willard and Barnard went to England for a world educational conference and were both honored by the British House of Lords. When she returned to the United States, she settled in a small house near her son and daughter-in-law on the campus in Troy. She spent the rest of her life there, editing and updating her books, writing new ones, and sharing her wisdom with educators and students. In 1870, after decades of continual, rude rejections of her pleas for educational funds for women's education, the all-male New York State Legislature finally expressed appreciation for what she had done for her country by passing a solemn resolution of praise for her work in education. Unfortunately, she was dead; but the school's name was changed to the Emma Willard School. Still a school for girls, it prepares students from ninth through twelfth grades for the most prestigious colleges and universities in the United States.

References: *Great Women Teachers,* Alice Fleming (1965); *Pioneers of Women's Education in the United States,* Willystine Goodsell; *Emma Willard, Daughter of Democracy,* Alma Lutz (1964); *Founders: Innovators in Education, 1830–1980,* Ernest Stabler (1980).

William Penn Charter School The first school founded by the Society of Friends, or Quakers, in the United States. Established in Philadelphia in 1689, the school was a response to the call of William Penn to his fellow Quakers to found schools wherever they settled. "There is scarcely any one thing," Penn wrote in 1679, "that so much needs the wisdom of the nation in the contrivance of a new law as the education of our youth . . ." Because they refused to pay tithes and to recognize the priesthood and sacraments of the Church of England, Quakers had been perceived as unpatriotic and atheistic. The result was a wave of persecution that sent them fleeing to the American colonies in the 1660s, settling first in New Jersey. After William Penn was granted the Pennsylvania colony, some 7,000 Friends migrated into the Philadelphia area to escape persecution in other states.

Starting with the Friends' Public School in 1689 (now the William Penn Charter School), the society established more than 40 schools in the next 70 years, giving Pennsylvania the largest school system of any American colony. Penn Charter remains one of the nation's most prestigious primary-secondary schools, with a total enrollment of more than 800 students attending kindergarten through high school. Although still affiliated with the Society of Friends, it offers a completely secular curriculum of arts and sciences and a college preparatory program that feeds its graduates into the nation's finest colleges and universities.

References: *Early Quaker Education in Pennsylvania,* Thomas Woody (1920); *Literature and Education in Early Quakerism,* Luella M. Wright (1933).

Wing Standardized Test of Musical Intelligence A battery of tests to measure acuity of musical hearing and sensitivity to musical performance. Designed in 1939 as a test for children eight years old and older, it is seldom administered to less than gifted children and is intended largely to help determine whether they should embark on a specialized musical education. It measures the ear's ability to discriminate rather than any factual knowledge about music. The seven sub-tests measure acuity with questions on chord analysis, pitch change, memory, rhythmic sensitivity, harmony, intensity and phrasing. The test is one of several measurements of musical aptitude, the very first of which was developed by Carl E. Seashore, who pioneered musical aptitude testing in 1919. The Seashore Measures of Musical Talents tests student discrimination of pitch, rhythm, time, timbre, loudness and tonal memory. Other musical aptitude tests include the Gaston Test of Musicality and the Gordon Musical Profile.

Reference: Tests in Print, Buros Institute of Mental Measurements, University of Nebraska Press, Lincoln, Nebraska.

Winnetka Plan One of the many innovative educational experiments that American teachers and school administrators were attempting in the wake of John Dewey's seminal work in the University of Chicago Laboratory School (q.v.). Dewey's work inspired a whole generation of imaginative teachers to break the mold of traditional pedagogy and attempt other, newer methods of teaching children. Introduced in 1919 in the Chicago suburb of that name, the Winnetka Plan was the creation of superintendent Carleton Washburne (q.v.), who sought to individualize elementary school instruction by dividing the curriculum into two parts. One part concentrated on instruction in basic skills that all students would have to master, i.e., reading, writing, language usage and spelling. Such subjects would be taught on a largely individualized basis that would permit each student to progress at his own developmental rate and finish the program whenever he could. Each student had to record his rate of progress on worksheets that would permit classwide comparisons.

The second part of the curriculum was made up of cultural and creative experiences taught in group settings, where no grading took place but each child was expected to absorb as much as he or she enjoyed, and then participate in group discussions from which children were to learn from one another.

Reference: *Winnetka: The History and Significance of An Educational Experiment,* Carleton W. Washburne and Sydney P. Marland Jr.

Winthrop, John (1714–1779)

American-born heir to one of the most preeminent colonial families, and the most distinguished teacher, scholar and scientist of the colonial or provincial era. Born in Boston, he was a descendant of John Winthrop (1588–1649), the first governor of the Massachusetts Bay Colony. He graduated from Harvard in 1732, but devoted the next six years to private study in his father's house, emerging in 1738 prepared to accept the distinguished Hollis Professorship of Mathematics and Natural Philosophy at Harvard, a chair founded by Isaac Watts (q.v.) and filled earlier by Winthrop's own teacher, Isaac Greenwood. Winthrop remained at Harvard until his death, amassing the most distinguished academic career in the colonies and a reputation and body of scientific discovery that earned him world renown. His initial work was in the field of astronomy, where he was among the first scientists to study sun spots and to track the transits

of Mercury and Venus. And his inquiries into the natural history of earthquakes and his mathematical calculations on the reach of a New England earthquake in 1775 are credited with having created the science of seismology.

At Harvard, Winthrop was responsible for a vast expansion in the breadth and quality of the science and mathematics curriculum, introducing calculus and developing a series of lectures on the laws of mechanics, heat, light and electricity. His work was instrumental in transforming Harvard from a theological institution to one that focused increasingly on secular academics and sciences. In addition to expanding the curriculum, in 1751 he established the first American laboratory of experimental physics at Harvard, to house a vast array of equipment for demonstrations during instructional lectures. A deep believer in Sir Isaac Newton's principles and doctrines, he taught four decades of Harvard graduates and, through a lengthy correspondence, had considerable influence on the work and thinking of Washington, Franklin and John Adams. He was a fellow of the Royal Society and the American Philosophical Society and was awarded honorary degrees by the University of Edinburgh, Scotland, and by Harvard.

References: BDAE; DAB; Harvard College Archives, Cambridge, Massachusetts; Massachusetts Historical Society, Boston, Massachusetts.

Wisconsin

The 30th state to join the Union, in 1848. Always a leader in American education, with education a top priority for the majority of its citizens, Wisconsin established its first public elementary school in 1845, its first public high school in 1849, and in 1856 the first kindergarten in the United States. By the end of the 19th century, the state had one of the best-developed public education systems in the United States. In 1911, Wisconsin established the nation's first statewide vocational education system, while the University of Wisconsin (q.v.) established the first statewide adult educational network. As the end of the 20th century approached, the state had more than 2,000 public elementary and secondary schools, with more than 350,000 students and a quality of education that ranked among the top 10% of American state school systems.

Reflecting the state's populist traditions, Wisconsin's university system serves more than 132,000 students on 26 two-year and four-year campuses and nearly a million other Wisconsinians through extension programs. A pioneer of adult education and still a national leader, the state has purposely built its higher-education system with a geographic breadth that allows it to reach almost every citizen in the state. The state has 28 private four-year colleges and universities, including Marquette and Lawrence universities and Beloit and Ripon colleges. There are three private two-year colleges in the state.

(See also CHARLES VAN HISE.)

References: CHE; EB; University of Wisconsin Archives, Madison, Wisconsin.

Wisconsin v. Yoder A 1972 ruling by the U.S. Supreme Court that gave the Amish religious sect a rare exemption from state compulsory education laws. The Court held that 300 years of unswerving dedication to their simple way of life entitled the Amish to be exempt from Wisconsin's (and, by extension, from every other state's) law requiring children to attend school until they were 16. The Amish traditionally withdraw their children from school after the eighth grade. The Court said that compulsory education laws violated their constitutional rights to free exercise of religion. The Amish believe that secondary schools teach children worldly values that are in conflict with their way of life.

The decision represented the first exemption of a religious group from compulsory education, and the Court warned that the ruling did not and would not apply to any other group that opposed formal education for whatever reason. "It cannot be overemphasized that we are not dealing with a way of life and mode of education by a group claiming to have recently discovered some 'progressive' or more enlightened process for rearing children in modern life."

Reference: U.S. Supreme Court proceedings.

withdrawal A vague term, which, in education, can mean everything from a student's transfer to another school, to a leave due to illness, forced expulsion or dropping out. Withdrawal can also refer to a personality characteristic that sees a student fail to participate in classroom discussions and activities; the student may then require referral to the school health office.

Reference: *Introduction to Psychology,* James O. Whittaker (1970).

Witherspoon, John (1723–1794) Scottish-born Presbyterian minister, educator, president of the College of New Jersey (now, Princeton) for 25 years and the only clergyman to sign the U.S. Declaration of Independence. Perhaps the most influential educator of his era, Witherspoon was educated at the University of Edinburgh and ordained and served in the Presbyterian ministry until 1768, when he was offered—and at first declined to accept—the presidency of the College of New Jersey. Established in 1746, the college was founded after a split in the New York Presbyterian Church between orthodox "Old Light" and more liberal, evangelical "New Light" factions. The New Light academy was moved to the home of Jonathan Dickinson, in Elizabethtown, New Jersey, then to the parsonage of Aaron Burr Sr. in Newark, and finally to Nassau Hall in Princeton, where Burr and three other evangelists turned it into a center for controversy with Old Lights in New York. A conservative, Witherspoon had little inclination to lead a New Light school that reportedly was losing enrollment and was in deep financial difficulty. After considerable coaxing from his friend Benjamin Rush (q.v.), he packed up 300 books to stock the college library, and he and his five children embarked for Princeton and Nassau

Hall, where students celebrated his arrival by illuminating Nassau Hall with candles in each window.

Touched by the warmth of his reception, he set to work rebuilding the school. He found students inadequately prepared, enrollment from the south in steep decline and a near-empty exchequer. He set off on trips through the colonies, preaching, recruiting students and gathering funds. An extremely erudite man, he combined strongly orthodox views with a deep belief in the "common sense" school of Scottish philosophy, holding many well-read persons to be "greatly inferior to more ignorant persons in clear, sound common sense." He promoted the college as a center of learning, and recruited students from some of the finest and wealthiest families. He encouraged the Madisons of Virginia to send him their son James, and he coaxed a gift of 50 gold guineas from his friend George Washington.

Committed to essential Calvinism, yet equally committed to the right of a congregation to appoint its own pastor independently of the mother church, Witherspoon combined the best of the old thinking from Scotland with the new thinking of a new nation. Building on his great popularity, he reshaped the college and, with it, many other leading American colleges. He added American education to the traditional classical education, broadening traditional classical and philosophical studies to include English- and French-language studies, history, oratory and eloquence. He opened a grammar school in the basement of Nassau Hall to provide young students with a better preparation for college. He even educated children not destined for college and, while at the college, coined the Latin word *campus* (Latin for field) to describe the bucolic setting. The word would become synonymous with the grounds of colleges and universities throughout the United States.

Externally, he redirected the effort of the college to community service; internally, he made clear to students that their work at college was to give them the education necessary to fulfill their ultimate obligation to serve the commonwealth and the church. Throughout his years at Princeton, Witherspoon played an active role in reorganizing the Presbyterian Church, emphasizing the need for an educated clergy. In his classes, he taught both politics and religion, constantly emphasizing the relationship and essential unity of piety and public service. An inspiration to his students, he wholeheartedly supported the national cause and became a leading member of the Continental Congress. His graduates included one president of the new nation, James Madison; a vice president, Aaron Burr; 10 cabinet officers; 60 members of Congress; and three Supreme Court justices. In effect, Witherspoon helped to shape the thinking of the leadership of a new nation and the type of education it would offer its children.

References: *John Witherspoon Comes to America,* L. H. Butterfield (1953); *History of the College of New Jersey, from Its Origin in 1746 to the Commencement of 1854,* John Maclean (1877); *The Works of the Rev. John Witherspoon* (4 vols., 1802).

Wolman v. Walter A complex 1977 U.S. Supreme Court decision that upheld the constitutionality of an Ohio law authorizing various forms of state aid to private schools. In rejecting such aid in previous decisions, the Court had held it unconstitutional for public schools to use taxpayer money to provide religious schools with materials or personal services that would, in effect, publicly support and further a religion. The Ohio law allowed specific forms of aid that could in no way be construed as furthering a religion. Loans of secular textbooks, for example, were included, along with such services as standardized testing and scoring, speech and hearing diagnostic services, and remedial and guidance services. The Court voted against the lending of classroom instructional equipment other than textbooks, and rejected a provision that would have allowed state financing of parochial school field trips. The key element in deciding which form of state aid was considered constitutional was whether the aid could be construed as "advancing religion." Far from a landmark case, the indecisive nature of the decision left school district officials in complete confusion over what equipment and services they could or could not share with or lend to parochial schools.

Reference: U.S. Supreme Court Proceedings.

Women's Armed Services Act of 1948 A federal law that made women permanent participants in all branches of the U.S. Armed Services. The act opened important avenues of technical and professional education and job opportunities that had hitherto been closed to women. Although admitted to the Armed Services during World War II, women had been confined to all-female units and assigned jobs traditionally associated with women's work—nursing, clerical duties, light transportation and low-level quartermaster functions. Moreover, servicewomen were often set apart in special, often physically isolated service organizations such as the WACs, WAVEs and WAFs. The act of 1948 represented a recognition of the essentiality of the work women had contributed during the war, and it sought to integrate women into the services to a degree that would make the military more attractive as a career.

Opposition to the integration of women into the Armed Services was more long-lasting than opposition to the integration of blacks, and it was not until the 1970s that barriers began disappearing and the number of women in the military began to increase substantially. Although still barred from combat roles, they gained access to almost the full range of even the most sensitive military operations as well as to the military academies and most postgraduate military colleges.

Reference: United States Department of Defense, Arlington, Virginia.

women's education The formal instruction of women—until relatively recently, limited to the "domestic arts" and centering around skills needed for nurturing infants and maintaining the household. In early civilizations, children were educated informally, within the family unit, in preparation for the roles they would play in later life—namely, man as hunter and fighter and woman as caretaker of infants and the home. God-centered religions indoctrinated their followers in the belief that women were naturally weaker and inferior to men. In the Christian Bible, St. Paul urged Christian wives to be obedient to their husbands. Hinduism promised virtuous women the reward of rebirth as men. Ancient Greece and Rome reserved education for men, although the Greek philosopher and teacher Plato advocated equal educational rights for women in *The Republic,* his concept of the ideal state.

The post-Babylonian Captivity Jews may have been the first to offer women equal opportunity for formal instruction, which was largely related to study of sacred texts. Some educational opportunities were extended to women of noble birth during the early Christian era and throughout the Reformation, although they tended to be limited to the domestic and ornamental arts. Martin Luther called for equal education for women, albeit in separate schools from men, and even appealed for civil support of such schools. The Roman Catholic Church echoed that appeal at the Council of Trent, from 1545 to 1563. The appeal had little practical effect, however, and education of women in the Western world changed little until the end of the 18th century and the beginning of the women's rights movement.

Even the expanded role of women necessitated by life in the American colonial wilderness did little to expand women's access to formal education. English common law was clear: "husband and wife are one, and man is the one." Girls, like boys, were the property of their fathers, and women became the property of their husbands, with no control of their persons or their children, no right to own land or money, and no access to an academic education. The domestic arts in which they received training were those required for raising children and running the household; the ornamental arts included singing, dancing and other skills needed to amuse husbands and "ornament" their households.

The accumulation of wealth in the colonies sowed the seeds of change, as families of means began sending their daughters to private academies, where they learned to read literature other than Scripture, as well as to write and to calculate. Among the books young women read in the wake of the American Revolution was Mary Wollstonecraft's *Vindication of the Rights of Woman*. Written in England in 1792, when popular demands for greater individual liberties were provoking uprisings throughout the Western world, it inspired such academy graduates as Catherine Beecher, Emma Willard and Mary Lyon (qq.v.) to launch the women's educational rights movement in the United States.

Beecher and Willard opened academies that offered women college-level education, and in 1837 Lyon founded the world's first college for women in Mount Holyoke, Massachusetts. By the end of the 19th century, women had taken control of the teaching profession in elementary schools, and outstanding women's colleges had been founded throughout the United States. Even all-male colleges, such as Harvard and Columbia, had established affiliated colleges for women. The state-by-state passage of compulsory education laws and the granting of woman suffrage after World War I provoked a vast expansion in women's education, but it remained different and inherently unequal to that afforded men. Few women's colleges offered courses in engineering, the advanced sciences, advanced economics and other studies that prepared men for careers at the highest levels of the professions, industry and government.

When Congress passed the Educational Amendments of 1972 (q.v.), prohibiting discrimination on the basis of sex in educational institutions receiving federal aid, universities

Troy Female Academy, founded in 1821, was the first school in the United States to offer women the same academic education as men in the arts and sciences. (Emma Willard School)

were forced to give women access to the same courses of study as men. By 1994, more than half of all college students were women, and their numbers had grown dramatically in medical, law, business and other traditionally male graduate schools (qq.v.). Despite equal access in higher education, many women still perceived that they were often not obtaining equal educational benefits at mixed-gender institutions—from kindergarten on. A number of studies tended to support that perception. One study found that teachers in elementary and secondary schools—even female teachers—tended to call on boys more often than girls. Other studies found that women at coeducational institutions felt pressured to study traditionally female subjects and eschew studies in mathematics, the sciences and engineering. In addition, many women reported concern over persistent sexual harassment at coeducational institutions.

For these and other perceived inequalities, a decline in enrollment at all-female schools and colleges that began in the 1970s with expanded coeducation had sharply reversed itself by the mid-1990s. By 1995, applications to the 84 women's colleges still functioning as single-sex institutions in the United States had climbed 14% to a 14-year high of 98,000 students, compared to 82,500 students in 1981. Although the number of students attending such colleges was a mere 2.5% of the 7.6 million women attending all two- and four-year institutions of higher education in the United States, women's colleges were graduating a disproportionately high share of scholars, professionals and business and government leaders. Graduates of women's colleges were more than twice as likely as graduates of coeducational institutions to receive doctoral degrees. Graduates of five all-women's colleges—Barnard, Bryn Mawr, Mount Holyoke, Smith and Wellesley—accounted for 43% of the math doctorates and 50% of the engineering doctorates earned by American women. One-third of the female board members of Fortune 500 companies were graduates of women's colleges, and 24% of the women in Congress in the early 1990s were graduates of women's colleges. The achievements of graduates of all-female colleges spurred a 6% growth in enrollments at all-girl primary and secondary schools from 1990 to 1995.

(See also GENDER DISCRIMINATION.)

References: EB; DES; NYT; *A History of Western Education,* James A. Bowen (3 vols., 1972–83); *A Century of Higher Education for American Women,* Mabel Newcomer (1959); *In the Company of Educated Women: A History of Women and Higher Education in America,* Barbara Miller Solomon (1985); Women's College Coalition, Washington, D.C.

women's studies Any of a variety of liberal arts courses that focus on the roles, history, productive and creative output, and contributions of women. Thus a literature course in a women's studies program would concentrate solely on the prose and poetry of women. Usually limited in high schools to individual courses in the senior year, women's studies may be grouped in a separate department at some colleges and universities and offered as a major.

Reference: ERIC.

Woodson, Carter G. (1875–1950) American historian and educator; cited in most reference works as the "father of Negro history in the United States." Born of former slaves in Virginia, he grew up in such dire poverty that his formal schooling was postponed until he was almost 20. He graduated from high school in 1896 and from Berea College in 1903. He earned his M.A. in history at the University of Chicago and went to Massachusetts to earn his doctorate at Harvard University in 1912, all the while teaching and writing to support his studies. In 1915, he founded the Association for the Study of Negro Life and History, to collect accurate data and publish information to educate black—and white—Americans about African-American culture and history.

Woodson founded the association to promote an alternative to the types of African-American education then being espoused by

Booker T. Washington and W. E. B. Du Bois. Washington and Du Bois had spent a decade in bitter debate over the advantages and disadvantages of industrial education and classical university education as a means for lifting African Americans out of poverty and illiteracy. Washington and his disciples called for massive programs of industrial education to give African Americans the skills to earn a living in white society. Du Bois, on the other hand, called for an equally massive program of classical education to give blacks the same civil and political rights as whites.

Woodson harshly criticized both positions, saying that industrial education tended to lag behind industrial progress and too often prepared blacks for jobs that were made obsolete by new industrial equipment before the blacks even graduated from school. He was equally harsh in attacking classical education, which he said taught the "educated Negro . . . to admire the Hebrew, the Greek, and the Latin and the Teuton and to despise the African." Woodson maintained that blacks would be unable to participate in American life on an equal basis with whites until they gained a complete knowledge and understanding of their own African-American heritage through black studies programs. Education as it existed in the United States, he said, had robbed blacks of their heritage and alienated them from their traditional values.

While still teaching at a Washington, D.C., high school, Woodson began publishing the *Journal of Negro History* to help teach blacks about their own history. In 1919, he became dean of the liberal arts college at Howard University, and a year later became dean at West Virginia State College for two years. In 1921, he organized Associated Publishers, Inc., which published works by black authors on black culture at a time when white publishers refused to publish such material. He himself concentrated on writing books on black history, of which the most notable were the widely used textbook *The Negro in Our History* (1922); *African Myths* (1928); *The*

Rural Negro (1930); *The African Background Outlined* (1936); and *African Heroes and Heroines* (1939). In 1926, he created the idea of Negro History Week, which has been observed annually ever since. In 1937, he began publishing the *Negro History Bulletin* for use in schools. It eventually formed the basis for the black studies curriculum that has been widely adopted in schools and colleges across the United States.
References: DAB; "Carter G. Woodson, The Negro History Movement, and Africa," Otey M. Scruggs, *Pan African Journal* (Spring 1974).

Wood v. Strickland A 1975 U.S. Supreme Court ruling that held a school board member liable for damages for violating the constitutional rights of students. By implication, the ruling applied to school administrators, teachers, counselors and, indeed, all public employees. In effect, it stripped teachers and school administrators of the traditional, arbitrary powers they had held over schoolchildren for centuries under the doctrine of in loco parentis (q.v.), whereby they acted on behalf of parents and were generally immune from retaliation for violating a child's constitutional rights. *Wood* stripped school representatives of that immunity and held them open to civil suits for damages. In *Wood,* the Court held a school board member liable for damages "if he knew or reasonably should have known that the action he took within his sphere of official responsibility would violate the constitutional rights of the students affected, or if he took the action with the malicious intention to cause a deprivation of constitutional rights or other injury to the student."
Reference: United States Supreme Court proceedings.

word-attack skills An essential methodology for deciphering the meaning of new and unfamiliar words. There are three sets of basic word-attack skills: structural analysis, phonic analysis and contextual analysis. Structural analysis breaks down words into their meaningful parts—roots, prefixes and suffixes—and presumes a basic knowledge of those word elements. Phonic analysis ties various sound elements of the unfamiliar word with the same sounds of a word whose meaning is known. Contextual analysis attempts to derive a meaning for an unknown word from the meanings of the surrounding words and phrases.

Reference: *Developmental Reading, K-8,* Daniel R. Hittleman (1988).

word book   A pedagogical tool for teaching and improving spelling and writing of first, second and third graders. Usually nothing more than an old-fashioned spiral stenographer's book with alphabetic tabs, a word book is a child's own, personal spelling book, or dictionary, to which he or she may refer. When a student needs a word to be spelled in class, he or she asks the teacher, then writes the word down in the spelling book on the page with appropriate tab, for future reference. The act of discussing the spelling of a word and recording it in one's personal word book tends to produce a memory construct that indelibly affixes the word and its spelling in the student's mind.

Reference: *The Elementary School Handbook,* Joanne Oppenheim (1989).

word family   A pedagogical method for helping children to remember spellings of large groups of words by linking them into artificial "families," each based on a rhyming sound, as in "bit, fit, hit, kit, lit, pit, sit, wit," all of which belong in the "it" family, or "bat, cat, fat," in the "at" family.

Reference: *Developmental Reading, K-8,* Daniel R. Hittleman (1988).

word lists   Any of a variety of compilations of words, arranged on the basis of increasing difficulty and used as an element of spelling instruction. Designed for students in elementary school, the first of the modern, comprehensive words lists was developed by American educator Edward Thorndike (q.v.) in *A Teacher's Word-book of 20,000 Words,* published in 1926 and later expanded to 30,000 words.

Reference: *Developmental Reading, K-8,* Daniel R. Hittleman (1988).

word processing   The production and editing of printed documents on a computerized system that includes a keyboard, video display, magnetic storage device, and software or operating system. Although many children are capable of learning word processing in preschool, formal instruction in schools is generally postponed until students are 10 or 11, because premature exposure to, and dependence on, word-processing equipment can interfere with the development of good penmanship and spelling skills. Once learned, word processing allows students to produce typewritten documents, complete with illustrations and complex layouts. The word processor speeds the entire process of writing, editing and completing school papers, allowing almost instant corrections, replacement, deletion, transfer and insertion of text.

References: *The Elementary School Handbook,* Joanne Oppenheim (1989); *The School-Smart Parent,* Gene I. Maeroff (1989).

words-in-color   An extension of the multisensory approach to the teaching of reading by adding the medium of color to the sounds of the English language. Developed in 1957 for teaching English as a second language (q.v.), the system uses 39 color shades to promote recognition of the 47 sounds in English. The process is somewhat akin to coloring each of the states or countries on a map a different color.

Reference: *Teaching Reading to Every Child,* Diane Lapp and James Flood (1978).

word wheel   An entertaining aid for teaching children to read. Word wheels are made up of two concentric, rotating cardboard wheels, with selected consonants printed near the rim of theouter wheel, much like the numbers on a clock. A smaller wheel, superimposed on the larger, is segmented like a pie, with each segment containing one of a related group of phonograms such as "at, ap, am" or "it, im, ip." By rotating the inner wheel the student can continually juxtapose the phonogram with a consonant that combines with it to make a word.

Reference: *Reading: Foundations and Instructional Strategies,* Pose Lamb and Richard Arnolds., eds. (1976).

work, transition to The link between formal education and specific job opportunities. One of the most highly criticized elements of American secondary school education is the poor preparation students in high school receive for the world of work, regardless of whether they are in the vocational, general education or academic track (see tracking). Moreover, the vocational track, despite its name, has a history of ineffective preparation of students for the job market. In 1992, for example, unemployment among high school graduates with no college education was about 25%, compared with an unemployment rate of just under 14% for graduates with associate degrees from two-year colleges and 6.5% for graduates of four-year colleges with bachelor's degrees. In an effort to strengthen the links between high school education and the world of work, many vocational education programs are now tying into so-called tech-prep or two-plus-two programs (qq.v.)—four-year vocational programs that combine the last two years of high school vocational education with two years of vocational education at associated community colleges.

Reference: *High School,* Ernest L. Boyer (1983).

workbook A textbook supplement containing exercises tied directly to materials discussed in the related text. Effective in early elementary education, workbooks force students to review all textbook materials and demonstrate an understanding thereof in a limited space that imposes language discipline by requiring terse answers that are to the point. In addition, the workbook serves as a portfolio of a student's work over an extended period, providing a visible measure of academic progress.

Reference: ERIC.

worker education Any formal or informal instructional program to improve employee vocational or academic skills. Worker education is as old as the skilled crafts themselves and first took the form of apprenticeships (q.v.), with master craftsmen teaching novice workers a manual craft and, in many cases, enough reading, writing and calculating skills to pursue a trade. In the American colonies and early years of the republic, apprenticeship training often included religious instruction. Formal worker education in the United States began after the passage of compulsory education (q.v.) laws in the mid-19th century. Factories dependent on child labor established in-plant classrooms, where child workers attended school for several hours a day, either in the morning or afternoon, before or after working a morning or afternoon shift in the factory. Toward the end of the 19th century, intensified competition and the threat of unionization in American industry forced companies to search for ways to improve worker efficiency and loyalty. Some companies found an answer in the establishment of company schools that not only improved worker skills but also taught workers an array of academic subjects. In the case of General Motors, the corporation school even provided a college education leading to bachelor's degrees.

With the emergence of labor unions at the end of the 19th and beginning of the 20th century, workers and their organizations also began organizing educational programs and institutions. At the time, fewer than 10% of American children were afforded a secondary education, and many children who had gone to work at the age of five or six lacked even a primary education. Many of the educative programs that emerged were tied to efforts by the Socialist Party and other reform movements to end child labor, improve working conditions and win more rights for workers. In major cities, such as New York and Chicago, the Socialist Party published books and pamphlets and sponsored lectures, study circles, discussion groups and formal classes for workers. Designed primarily to denounce the evils of capitalism and promote socialism, many of the classes evolved into instruction in reading and writing because few workers were literate enough to read and understand socialist propaganda. As early as 1906, the Rand School of Social Science in New York City was teaching courses in union organizing techniques and collective bargaining. In 1910, the International Ladies Garment Workers Union established its own educational department, while some colleges organized special programs for workers. In 1921, the Socialist Party organized a formal institution known as the Brookwood Labor College, in Katonah, New York, north of New York City. Based on the English Workingman's College in London, Brookwood remained open until 1937, offering courses in social history and philosophy, and practical instruction in the organizing of unions and strikes. It also offered courses in writing.

At a different level, Bryn Mawr College, the prestigious and private women's institution near Philadelphia, organized the Bryn Mawr Workers' Summer School in 1921 to offer working women a broader, non-labor-oriented education in literature, history, science and hygiene—an "education for life," as it was called. With the spread of the worker education movement came the need to coordinate programs and avoid costly duplication. In 1921, the Workers' Education Bureau of America was founded to act as a clearinghouse for labor education across the United States; after America's two largest unions merged into the giant AFL-CIO in 1955, it worked to centralize such education. In 1970, it opened the George Meany Center for Labor Studies in Silver Spring, Maryland, as a training institute for potential labor leaders.

Meanwhile, the other, older forms of worker education, such as labor colleges, began disappearing, as compulsory education and child labor laws forced every child under 16 into school and obviated the need for compensatory education later on. After World War II, tradi-

tional colleges and universities increasingly opened their doors to the general population, and also expanded their adult education programs, making separate worker education for older workers unnecessary.

References: AFL-CIO, Washington, D.C.; *Educational Experiments in Industry,* Nathaniel Peffer (1932); *The Apprenticeship System in Its Relation to Industrial Education,* Carroll D. Wright (1908).

Works Progress Administration (WPA)

A federal agency created in 1935, during the depths of the Great Depression, to provide the unemployed with the kind of work they were best fitted to do. During its eight years in existence, the WPA not only helped millions of Americans fend off starvation, it also proved to be one of the most remarkable educative institutions ever created by any American governmental entity.

For the unskilled, the WPA created jobs building and repairing country roads and city streets, improving parks and playgrounds and building flood-control and irrigation projects. The WPA hired skilled laborers such as carpenters, masons, plumbers, electricians and other construction workers to build or repair schoolhouses, libraries, city halls, courthouses and other public buildings. For out-of-work creative artists and scholars, the WPA created the Federal Art Project (q.v.), which served as an umbrella organization for four divisions that engaged the talents of artists, writers, actors, musicians and architects for the enrichment of the lives of millions of Americans who had never before been exposed to the arts. Out-of-work artists painted murals in public buildings across the nation; musicians and actors played concerts and gave theatrical presentations in schools, libraries, hospitals and community centers. Scholars organized and surveyed national, state and local archives and historical records and compiled oral and written histories.

When the work that the WPA offered to parents threatened to leave millions of preschool children unattended at home, WPA responded by creating a division of education that established nursery schools and parent education programs across the nation. By 1937, it was operating nearly 1,500 nursery schools (q.v.) for almost 40,000 children and conducting 3,270 parent-education classes with an enrollment of more than 50,000. The WPA came to an end in 1943, after World War II had created labor shortages that absorbed the unemployed and made the WPA's work unnecessary.

References: *Workers on Relief,* Grace Anderson (1939); *The Right to Work,* Nels Anderson (1938); *Educational Activities of the Works Progress Administration,* Doak S. Campbell, Frederick H. Bair and Oswald L. Harvey (1939); *Spending to Save: The Complete Story of Relief,* Harry L. Hopkins (1936).

work study A somewhat confusing term referring to on-campus job programs for needy students to earn part of the costs of tuition and room and board at college or university. Although there are many informal programs whereby a college or university offers students on-campus job opportunities, work study is also the diminutive name of a federal government program initiated as part of the Economic Opportunity Act of 1964 (q.v.). Officially called the College Work-Study Program, it provides some 700,000 needy college students with on-campus and off-campus jobs during each academic year. The jobs pay slightly more than $1,000 a year and range from clerical work to tutoring. Jobs are provided either by the college, in the case of on-campus jobs, or by approved, participating, nonprofit organizations off-campus. The U.S. Government pays 80% of the wages, with the college or off-campus employer paying the remainder.

Reference: United States Department of Education, Washington, D.C.

World of Work A secondary school course or series of courses designed to give students a broad understanding and overview of the adult workplace. Usually made up of two one-semester courses, the World of Work curriculum is designed for both preacademic and prevocational students. The first course explores so-called "job clusters," such as agriculture, manufacturing and health care, and explains the function of individual jobs within each cluster. A second course teaches students the basic elements of the job search: where and how to look for jobs, writing resumes, filling out job applications, how to conduct oneself in interviews, and handling all other aspects of looking for, finding and keeping a job. The course also teaches basic job skills such as promptness, proper behavior and the proper conduct of on-the-job relationships with coworkers, employers and clients.

Reference: *But What If I Don't Want to Go to College?* Harlow G. Unger (1992).

World's Christian Fundamentals Association (WCFA) An organization formed in 1919 by a group of leaders of various fundamentalist Protestant Christian sects to mount a massive, formal education effort to combat secular education in the United States. WCFA was organized at a time when disillusionment over the useless carnage of World War I had captured the national psyche. In addition, 3,600 strikes involving four million workers had brought the economy to a virtual halt. WCFA addressed the national fears by accusing "thousands of false teachers" of spreading "damnable heresies" and threatening the nation with "swift destruction."

Some 6,000 turned up for the first WCFA conference to "combat the heresy sweeping the nation" and to organize a "widespread revival in . . . the Word of God." To that end, it formed an education committee to encourage the founding of Bible institutes comparable to the famed Moody Bible Institute in Chicago (see MOODY, DWIGHT L.) to serve as alternative educational institutions to secular colleges and universities. By 1919, there were about two dozen such institutes, and with WCFA encouragement their number reached about 100 over the next several decades.

The WCFA education committee developed a common creed and broad curriculum to which Bible schools and institutes would have to subscribe to obtain WCFA endorsement. Endorsements were granted to virtually all applicants, however. Low in cost, the new Bible schools had few formal credit requirements for the degrees they offered, and many deteriorated into so-called degree (diploma) mills (q.v.). Precollegiate in terms of their formal curricula, they offered a variety of practical courses in Sunday school teaching, missionary work, evangelism, street preaching, fund-raising and a host of other subjects of interest to would-be fundamentalist preachers. In addition to formal education, the institutes were centers of informal activities, including prayer meetings, Bible conferences, shared spiritual pilgrimages and collective religious experiences. Bible institutes also sponsored scores of correspondence courses, radio (and eventually television) broadcasts and publishing enterprises.

In 1920, WCFA expanded its original mission by mounting a national campaign against secular education generally and the teaching of Darwinism in particular. It lobbied intensely for passage of state laws to bar the teaching of evolution; its efforts failed in Kentucky, North Carolina and Texas, but it succeeded in Oklahoma, Florida and Tennessee. To obtain broader popular support, WCFA enlisted the aid of William Jennings Bryan (q.v.), a thrice-defeated candidate for the presidency but nonetheless a popular national figure, who agreed to head WCFA's "Laymen's Movement" against modernism and evolution. In 1925, WCFA asked Bryan to represent it as cocounsel in the prosecution of John Thomas Scopes, a high school science teacher who had violated the new law against teaching evolution in Tennessee. Although Scopes was found guilty, Bryan and WCFA became the targets of worldwide mockery during and after the "Scopes Monkey Trial" (q.v.). Humiliated, Bryan died less than a week later, leaving the fundamentalist move-

ment splintered. Within a few years, WCFA had all but disappeared.

Reference: *Fundamentalism and American Culture: The Shaping of Twentieth-Century Evangelism, 1870–1925,* George M. Marsden (1980).

Wright, Carroll D. (1840–1909)

American educator and author of the first definitive government study of American vocational education. Born in New Hampshire, he became a schoolteacher to pay for his training in law. After enlisting as a private in the Civil War in 1862, he rose through the ranks and became a colonel in charge of his own regiment by 1864. After the war he practiced law in New Hampshire and Massachusetts, where he entered state politics and was named chief of the Massachusetts Bureau of Statistics for Labor in 1873. In 1885, President Chester A. Arthur appointed him the first commissioner of the Bureau of Labor (later, the Department of Labor), a post he held until 1905. While in that post, he resumed his teaching career, even becoming president of Clark College (now, Clark University), in Worcester, Massachusetts, in 1902.

In 1908, Wright produced a survey of the apprenticeship system in American industry for the United States Bureau of Education. Entitled *The Apprenticeship System in Its Relationship to Industrial Education,* the report criticized "the old apprenticeship system" for exploiting young people by paying substandard wages while locking them into apprenticeship status long after they had learned the skills to progress to higher-paid, journeyman status. Wright was equally critical of manual-training schools for inadequate and impractical instruction that taught young men few of the skills needed on actual production lines. Wright recommended establishment of a new "enlightened, coordinated system that shall secure all that can be gained from the apprenticeship system and all that can be gained from modern schools for trades and industrial education generally."

Wright cited as an example of ideal vocational

education the system then in place at the General Electric Company's Lynn, Massachusetts, plant, where a company-operated, four-year school combined academic instruction with shopwork. During the first two years, students concentrated on academics, learning arithmetic, elementary algebra and trigonometry, mensuration, elements of machines, power transmission, strength of materials, mechanics, elementary electricity, mechanical drawing, machine design, and jig and fixture design. Part of the day was spent on the shop floor, running errands and doing unskilled labor designed solely to give students a familiarity with shop-floor routine. In the last two years, students moved out of the classroom to the shop floor for advanced training, learning simple bench work and stock-keeping at first and progressing to toolmaking, diemaking and machine work.

Wright called the program "the most advanced of apprentice systems" and urged its adoption by American industry. Ironically, Wright's report had little impact, but the concepts he outlined would eventually become the heart of the cooperative vocational education (q.v.) movement that evolved in the 1970s, when American industry began establishing affiliations with vocational schools and colleges and integrating classroom vocational education with practical in-plant instruction. In addition to his seminal work on apprenticeship, Wright also wrote *The Industrial History of the United States* (1895).

References: DAB; Clark University Archives, Worcester, Massachusetts.

Wright v. Regan   A landmark, 1982 decision by the Circuit Court of Appeals for Washington, D.C., prohibiting the federal government from granting tax-exempt status to any private school that practices racial discrimination. Although racial discrimination had been banned at any school receiving any form of public funds, the decision extended that ban to schools receiving indirect government benefits in the form of tax exemptions that derived from their status as nonprofit organizations. The decision was appealed to and upheld by the U.S. Supreme Court.

Reference: U.S. Supreme Court proceedings.

writing   A method of human intercommunication by inscribing visible symbols on any of a wide variety of surfaces. Unlike copying, the skill of writing is inextricably tied to the ability to think and read. The mere copying of letters and words that are unintelligible to the copier does not constitute writing.

The earliest forms of writing were limited systems of pictography. From the earliest pictographic systems that represented only concrete objects, two modern, full systems of writing evolved that communicated abstract concepts through symbols: ideographic systems, in which each symbol represents a word, as in Chinese; and alphabetic systems, with each symbol representing a phoneme, or unit of speech, as in English.

The first full systems known appear to have developed among the Sumerians of Mesopotamia sometime before 3000 B.C. Full alphabetic writing that distinguishes between vowels and consonants was developed about 800 B.C. by the ancient Greeks. Like reading, however, writing as a means of mass communication had the potential for promoting popular disaffection; thus writing, like reading, remained a skill taught only to the ruling classes throughout the Greek and Roman eras and, during the early Christian era, only to aspiring members of the church hierarchy. Writing lagged behind reading in its development as a popular skill. In the English-speaking world, reading, as a popular skill, can be traced to John Wycliffe's translation of the Bible into English at the end of the 14th century. Writing, however, dates only to the expansion of schooling under the Tudors in 16th-century England. By the time settlers opened their first schools in the American colonies, writing and ciphering, along with reading, had become the foundation of all instruction.

In modern American education, writing instruction generally begins in kindergarten, with the teacher translating spoken words into print. Individual children orally describe an experience or relate an imaginary story, and the teacher carefully writes each word on the chalkboard in large letters. As the letters appear, the children gradually learn how letters and words are formed and, inevitably, begin imitating the process, both with the urging of the teacher and on their own. Individual progress is tied to the rate of development of each child's intellectual and motor skills.

Unlike earlier, traditional writing instruction, many schools now de-emphasize spelling and penmanship in early writing instruction. The theory is that children instinctively enjoy communicating, but their limited attention spans tend to make endless writing, rewriting and shaping of individual letters and words discouraging to the writing process. Instead of focusing on penmanship and motor skills, therefore, many reading programs emphasize storytelling as a basic form of communication to enhance children's thinking skills while postponing the development of mechanical writing skills.

Too narrow a focus on mechanics, say proponents of such programs, fails to teach children the primary reasons for writing—to express and understand ideas and to communicate to others. They support their criticisms of traditional writing instruction with results of the National Assessment of Educational Progress, which found American fourth graders scoring only about 200 on writing achievement tests (scored on a scale from 0 to 500, with 300 considered a minimum level of "adequate" proficiency). The average scores remained relatively unchanged in tests of 11 writing skills administered in 1984, 1988, 1990 and 1992. Scores of eighth graders ranged between 257 and 274 during those years, while scores of eleventh graders remained stable at about 287 out of a possible 500. Although there were significant differences in average scores in each grade on the basis of race, ethnicity, economic status, parental education, region and type of school, not a single group scored an average of 300 or better.

The poor performance provoked radical changes in the teaching of writing at some schools, to the so-called whole language (q.v.) method of instruction, with kindergarten children encouraged to write by using their own personal, phonetic spellings (and to read aloud what they write) rather than to copy letter after letter and word after word to improve their penmanship and spelling. Children write and read phonetically with amazing ease and not inconsiderable joy and a sense of accomplishment. Instead of rote learning, a type of evolutionary learning takes place, as students watch (and later imitate) the teacher slowly spell each word correctly on the chalkboard, with bold, carefully formed letters.

Unlike kindergarten, where children decide what they write, most first grade programs see teachers begin to assign specific writing tasks—usually related to social studies, science or class trips. Children are encouraged to illustrate their stories, making the important connection between the visual and the abstract letter symbols that describe the visual. Through the first grade, extended periods of time are set aside for students to express themselves on paper. Depending on content, stories are shared either privately with the teacher or publicly with the entire class. In almost all cases, the stories are edited and rewritten to improve spelling, content and organization. The emphasis, however, is always on content, until motor skills permit a shift toward legibility and spelling and students are mature enough to recognize the importance of standards in effective communication.

Many teachers in the early elementary grades now use so-called "process writing" as a basic pedagogical technique. Under the process-writing approach, students engage in "brainstorming" sessions, listing rough ideas or thoughts, with no concern for spelling or punctuation. Then they write rough drafts, edit them with their teachers and produce a "publishable" paper. Teachers say recording thoughts and wild stories without fear of being "wrong" liberates young minds and engenders a deep appreciation of writing and communication. Although the process-writing technique is effective throughout the elementary school years, most teachers gradually attempt to introduce discipline into the program by the third grade, when most students have developed motor skills sufficiently advanced to learn cursive writing, and the intellectual maturity and discipline to learn proper spelling, punctuation and rules of grammar.

(See also READING.)

References: *The School-Smart Parent,* Gene I. Maeroff (1989); *Making the Best of Schools,* Jeannie Oakes and Martin Lipton (1990); *The Elementary School Handbook,* Joanne Oppenheim (1989).

writing center A section of the elementary school classroom where students can engage quietly in original writing, apart from the rest of the class. In addition to writing and resource materials such as word processors, software, dictionaries and encyclopedias, the writing center features displays of student work, including poems, stories and other written materials.

Reference: *Writing Centers in the Elementary Schools,* Duane R. Tovey (1979).

Wygant v. Jackson Board of Education A 1986 United States Supreme Court ruling that a school board, in an effort to cut costs, could not preserve the jobs of black teachers by laying off white teachers. Although it ordered the school board to equalize its layoff procedures, the Court made it clear that the ruling applied only to racially based layoffs. It specifically reaffirmed the constitutionality of affirmative action programs to integrate teaching staffs.

Reference: U.S. Supreme Court proceedings.

Wyoming The 44th state to join the Union, in 1890. The first school was built at Fort Laramie in 1852, and in 1869, a year after Wyoming became a territory, the territorial legislature enacted a then-radical school law, providing for establishment and maintenance of schools through a system of general taxation. The legislature's forward-looking stance on education came at the same time that it made the state the Western world's first governmental entity to grant women the right to vote. Four years later, the legislature established a uniform curriculum for all elementary and secondary schools.

The least populated state in the United States, Wyoming now has about 400 public elementary and secondary schools, with a total student population of less than 100,000. Its relatively small classes give the system a level of educational quality that ranks above-average for the nation. The state has only one four-year institution of higher education, the University of Wyoming, a public institution in Laramie. There are seven public community colleges and one private two-year college. Wyoming is the only state with no private, nonprofit four-year colleges.

References: CHE; EB.

Wythe, George (1726–1806) American patriot, lawyer and educator and the first professor of law in any American college. Born in Virginia, he had little formal education but was tutored by his mother and studied law under the then-common clerk system, which was a form of non-indentured apprenticeship that preceded the establishment of law schools. Admitted to the bar in 1746, he practiced law for nearly a decade before involving himself in Virginia politics. A member of the House of Burgesses in 1754–1755 and from 1758 to 1768, he gained a reputation as one of the colony's leading legal scholars. Among the clerks he trained as lawyers were Thomas Jefferson (q.v.), who studied with him from 1762 to 1767, and James Monroe (q.v.).

A strong advocate of American independence, he drafted the initial Virginia protest of the Stamp Act and was elected to the Continental Congress in 1775. A year later, he signed the Declaration of Independence. After independence, he returned to Virginia to serve in the House of Delegates, then on Virginia's Court of Chancery and finally as chancellor, or chief judge, of the state. In 1779, he was appointed to the newly created chair for professor of law at William and Mary College (q.v.)—the first such professorship in the United States and the first sign of an approaching end to the traditional apprenticeship system of training for the bar.

In his 10 years at William and Mary he helped shape the course of formal legal education in the United States, supplementing his lectures with student-conducted moot courts and moot legislatures. Among his students was John Marshall, the future chief justice of the United States Supreme Court. In 1787, Wythe served in the federal Constitutional Convention and, the following year, led Virginia's ratifying convention. By 1790, age and the hardships of travel forced him to choose between his judicial post in Richmond and his teaching position at William and Mary. He chose Richmond, where he continued his work on the bench, and opened a private law school, where he trained, among others, Henry Clay (1777–1852), the future speaker of the House of Representatives. One of the earliest American abolitionists, he freed his own slaves after independence and provided for them in his will.

References: BDOE; DAB.

Y

Yale, Elihu (1649–1721) English colonial administrator who, between 1714 and 1721, bestowed so extensive a library of books and other gifts to the Collegiate School of Saybrook, Connecticut, that it changed its name to Yale College in 1718, two years after it moved to New Haven.

Born in Boston, he was the son of an American colonist who returned to England in 1651. He received his education in London and went to work for the English East India Company, which assigned him to a post in Madras, India, in 1670. Rising rapidly through the ranks, he amassed a personal fortune in private trade along the way. In 1687, he was named governor of Fort Saint George, but a scandal involving his administration led to his removal five years later. He continued in private trade in India until 1699, when he returned to England and became a governor of the East India Company. During those years, he had maintained a correspondence with his nephew in the colonies, a minister who had joined in founding the Collegiate School. The nephew prevailed on his uncle for a donation that eventually turned into the largest private gift ever made to a college at that time.

References: EB; Yale University Library Archives, New Haven, Connecticut.

"Yale Band" An informal association of seven theology students at Yale College who, before their ordination in 1830, pledged to devote their lives to "beating the drums for" and establishing formal education in the west. Asa Turner (q.v.), the Massachusetts-born leader of the "band," established a church in Quincy, Illinois, the same year and, with fellow band member Julian Monson Sturtevant (1805–86), became a founding trustee of Illinois College. He devoted the next eight years to educational causes in Illinois before moving to Iowa where he assisted an "Iowa Band" that had formed at Andover (Massachusetts) Theo-

logical Seminary to help bring public education to Iowa. The Iowa Band led the campaign to establish public schools in Iowa and founded Iowa College, which later merged with Grinnell College.

Reference: *The Founding of American Colleges and Universities Before the Civil War,* Donald G. Tewksbury (1932).

Yale College (and University) The third oldest institution of higher education in the United States, after Harvard and the College of William and Mary (qq.v.). Founded in 1701 as the Collegiate School, in Branford, Connecticut, it granted its first bachelor of arts degree in 1703 and moved to Saybrook (now, Old Saybrook), Connecticut, four years later. Like Harvard, Yale was a divinity school dedicated to the training of Congregationalist ministers who would perpetuate the Puritanism of their forebears. At the time, the colonies were suffering an acute shortage of ministers to serve their burgeoning populations, and the Connecticut population was growing especially quickly. The Puritans were a minority in England and could ill afford to send their pastors to the colonies, and Harvard was no longer able to supply the growing demand. Moreover, Harvard had become somewhat suspect for its religious liberalism. Clearly, Connecticut needed its own divinity school, and Yale was founded expressly for the "upholding and propagating of the Christian Protestant religion by a succession of learned and orthodox men."

In 1716, the college moved to New Haven, and two years later changed its name to Yale in honor of the Boston-born merchant Elihu Yale, who gave the college the largest gift it would receive until 1837, in the form of a sizable library and other goods. Together, Harvard and Yale supplied the colonies with 850 ministers between 1701 and 1740. By mid-century, however, a growing number of Yale students were

1093

The Harkness Tower at Yale University, New Haven, Connecticut. (Yale University Office of Public Affairs)

enrolling simply to take advantage of the education there: During the 1760s, only one-third of Yale's graduates entered the ministry, compared to well over half during the early part of the century. Class size seldom exceeded 30 students, but the proportion of ministers emerging was nevertheless declining, while the number of future physicians and lawyers was increasing—as it was at Harvard and other colleges that had started as divinity schools.

In the 1760s, Yale students were swept up in the fervor for national independence. After weeks of rioting, they forced the president of Yale to resign and the trustees to replace him with a professor more devoted to national inde-

pendence than to the church. By 1773, formal education all but ended at Yale (as well as at Harvard and Princeton), as students regularly boycotted, condemned and burned British effigies and crates of tea. By 1776, patriotic students, with the encouragement of acting president Naphthali Daggett, a popular divinity professor, controlled the institution, and a year later, the Rev. Ezra Stiles (q.v.), an ardent advocate of independence, was named president. By 1779, the faculty and students were engaged in the defense of New Haven against a British invasion, with Professor Daggett, armed with only a "fowling piece," emerging a hero by singlehandedly fending off an attack by a detachment of British regulars.

Yale reemerged as a leader in higher education in the years from 1795 to 1817, when its president, Timothy Dwight (q.v.), established Yale's first professional schools (including the medical school, in 1813) and converted the college into a university. By 1820, Yale was the country's largest and most influential college, with the most geographically diverse student body. Its graduates were founding new colleges and extending Yale's influence over higher education across the nation. In the forefront of the trend toward departmentalization, Yale officials grew somewhat alarmed by the increased introduction of nonacademic subjects such as mechanics and agriculture into higher education. With the famous Yale Report of 1828, they helped helped shape the curricula of American colleges and universities for the next 30 years, until the establishment of the first public land-grant colleges and state universities after the Civil War. The report urged traditional colleges and universities to limit their curricula to liberal arts programs and allow scientific and technical institutes and professional schools to teach engineering and other specialized subjects. It said the object of a college was "to lay the foundation of a superior education." It called the "study of the classics . . . the most effectual discipline of the mental faculties."

The emergence of land-grant institutions of higher education and the spread of public education undermined Yale's status as a pioneer educational institution during the latter half of the 19th century, although its graduates continued to exert influence in education, as well as in the arts, industry and government. In its first two centuries of existence, its graduates included Nathan Hale, Jonathan Edwards, Noah Webster, James Fenimore Cooper, Eli Whitney, Samuel F. B. Morse and William Howard Taft, along with a legion of men who headed schools and colleges that would grow into some of the nation's leading educational institutions.

During the second half of the 19th century, however, it was Yale's arch-rival Harvard that pioneered the major advances in private higher education. After Charles Eliot (q.v.) had made Harvard the model of the modern university at the turn of the century, Yale followed suit, and, along with Harvard, it remains one of the world's foremost universities. In addition to its undergraduate college of more than 5,000 students, Yale boasts some of the nation's foremost graduate schools of medicine, law, architecture, art, drama, music, forestry, business and divinity. Its library contains more than 7.5 million volumes, and the Yale University Art Gallery is the nation's oldest college-affiliated art museum. The Yale Center for British Art houses the largest collection of British art in the world outside of England, and the extraordinary Museum of Musical Instruments contains more than 800 rare instruments.

Reference: Yale University Library Archives, New Haven, Connecticut.

Yale-New Haven Teachers Institute A pioneer collaborative venture between Yale University and the public school system of the city of New Haven. Founded in 1978 and funded by the Carnegie Corporation, the College Board, the Ford Foundation, the National Endowment for the Humanities, a bank and a private foundation, the institute brought together public school representatives, a university advisory council, a national advisory committee and individual fellows in English, history, languages, art, science and mathematics in an effort to strengthen teaching and learning in the city's public middle schools and high schools. Largely populated by students from low socioeconomic backgrounds, the failing New Haven public school system was seen as a perfect laboratory in which to study new approaches to educating and motivating the growing inner-city student populations of the nation's cities.

Reference: Yale-New Haven Teachers Institute, New Haven, Connecticut.

yearbook (student) An annual high school, college or graduate school student publication, usually published in hardcover, to commemorate the events of the previous academic year. Produced by seniors, often in collaboration with a faculty adviser, the book is usually divided into several sections, the largest and most important of which contains individual photographic portraits of each graduating senior along with a biography detailing his or her school career and future plans. Other sections are devoted to athletic teams, extracurricular activities, the year's events and the faculty. Sold to students, parents, friends and faculty, yearbooks, or annuals, as they are often called, usually contain paid advertisements to defray publication costs.

References: *Managing the Student Yearbook*, Jim Nelson Black (1983); *Yearbook Planning, Editing, and Production*, N. S. Paterson (1976).

year-round school A school that operates a 12-month-a-year academic program to ensure maximum utilization of school facilities and accommodate a larger number of students without investing in plant expansion.

(See also SCHOOL CALENDAR.)

yeshiva (or, yeshivah) In American education, a generic term referring to any of a variety of Jewish day schools, depending on their sectarian sponsorship. Most day schools that bear the capitalized name Yeshiva are normally religiously-based Orthodox elementary schools. Conservative Jewish schools, while called yeshivas in the generic sense, seldom include the word yeshiva in their title. Conservative yeshivas are usually K-12 day schools that provide a combination of conventional secular American education and Jewish religious instruction comparable to the kind of religio-secular education given in Catholic parochial and diocesan schools. Although some Reform Jews send their children to religio-secular schools, the majority rely on nonsectarian schools and reserve Jewish education to synagogue-sponsored Sunday schools.

Originally, yeshivas (or, *yeshivot* in Hebrew) were European secondary schools, or academies, devoted exclusively to study of the Talmud, the huge and complex compilation of Jewish traditions and behavioral rules and regulations. Such talmudic study was in preparation for later study for the rabbinate. Although it now connotes a school, the word yeshiva does not actually mean school. Yeshiva is derived from the Hebrew root "to sit." A modern yeshiva in the literal sense, therefore, is simply a place to sit—and, presumably, to study.

Reference: Jewish Historical Society of New York, New York, New York.

Young Men's Christian Association (YMCA)

An international organization with 26 million members in 92 countries, sponsoring social, physical and educational activities for youths and adults of both genders as well as all religions, races and ethnic backgrounds. The YMCA was founded in London in 1844 by the British humanitarian Sir George Williams (1821–1905) to provide prayer meetings and Bible study for destitute young men on the streets of London. By 1851, the concept had spread to Europe and the United States, with the first unit in the United States founded in Boston in 1851. Similar groups formed in New York, Philadelphia and other cities, and by 1854 there were 26 associations in North America.

The American Civil War all but ended the movement, but a number of evangelists, including Dwight L. Moody (q.v.), managed to revive it in the late 1860s and 1870s, and a series of well publicized conventions spurred the formation and growth of a national movement. Inspired members fanned out into cities across the United States to preach on street corners in slums, distribute tracts in boarding houses, hospitals and jails, and conduct Bible classes and prayer meetings. The YMCA began putting up buildings with libraries, auditoria for lectures, and Spartan, albeit adequate hotel rooms to provide temporary housing for destitute young men. In the 1890s, it expanded its program to include regular evening classes, which soon became known as "a college of the people" and included courses in elementary school subjects for boys who had gone to work before they could obtain a basic education. Other courses in English and American citizenship were added in some cities to accommodate young immigrants; by the end of the century, the "Y" was even offering vocational education for boys who wanted to improve their lot by learning skilled trades.

By 1913, the association was enrolling nearly 75,000 students a year in courses ranging from accounting to public speaking to wireless telegraphy. In every major city, buildings rose to accommodate the Y's ever-expanding activities. By 1916, the Y had a membership of 600,000, and its buildings were complete with libraries, gymnasia, swimming pools and other facilities. It opened summer camps and pioneered physical education at a special school of physical education it established in Springfield, Massachusetts, to train teachers to promote physical fitness among the young. It was at this YMCA Training School that basketball and volleyball were invented. Now known as Springfield University, the YMCA Training School eventually made physical education the heart of YMCA activities.

The YMCA also trained thousands of students on college campuses to serve as missionaries overseas. In addition to missionary work, many established new YMCAs that were eventually turned over to local control. During World War I, it sponsored war relief activities, and in World War II it joined with six other organizations to form the United Service Organizations (USO) to provide entertainment and social services to millions of American servicemen around the world. As it reached out to more and more Americans, the YMCA evolved into an ecumenical, quasi-public organization, serving Catholics and Jews as well as Protestants and, by the 1950s, women as well as men. Its success as a universal service organization all but ended its original religious role. Among the main programs of today's YMCAs are swimming, aquatic exercise, aerobics, fitness classes, child care, day camps and youth sports. Many also provide emergency shelter, day care for the elderly, job training, rehabilitation classes for the disabled and youth counseling. Each of the more than 2,000 branches functions independently and is governed by volunteer board members who determine policy according to the needs of their community. Serving a total of 14 million people a year, the organization maintains a national council at its headquarters in Chicago.

Reference: National Board of YMCA, Chicago, Illinois.

Young Men's/Young Women's Hebrew Association (YM-YWHA)

Any of more than 500 local organizations that provide educational cultural, recreational, health, social and other services to Jewish people of all ages. With few exceptions, now called Jewish Community Centers, the YMHA was an outgrowth of informal Jewish literary associations that flourished in the United States during the mid-19th century. They grew into the more formal Young Men's Hebrew Literary Associations, about 70 of which were formed before the end of the 19th century.

The first formal YMHA was founded in Baltimore in 1854, and in 1888 the world-famous New York YMHA ("the 92nd Street Y") and auxiliary for women was founded. All these organizations merged to form the National Council of Young Men's Hebrew and Kindred Associations in 1913, and that organization merged with the National Jewish Welfare Board in 1921, which served as the umbrella association for the hundreds of Jewish Community Centers across the nation. It subsequently changed its name to the more appropriate Jewish Community Centers Association of North America.

Although open to non-Jews, YM/YWHAs and Jewish Community Centers normally serve Jewish residents of their local communities. Although some community centers are affiliated with adjacent or nearby synagogues, the term is a generic one, and the true Jewish Community Center of YM/YWHA is a lay organization devoted to the enhancement of Jewish family life, welcoming temple-goers and non-temple-goers alike. Jewish Community Centers offer a wide range of activities, including arts and crafts, dramatics, physical education, lectures and forums. Some sponsor day camps and summer camps and international exchanges with similar organizations in Israel. New York's 92nd Street Y has a world-class auditorium, where it sponsors the New York Chamber Music Orchestra and concerts by celebrated performers, along with dramatic readings by renowned authors. It also has a full program of educational activities for youths and adults.

References: Jewish Community Centers of North America, New York, New York; Young Men's/Young Women's Hebrew Association, New York, New York.

Young Women's Christian Association (YWCA)

An international organization dedicated to the personal, social and physical development of girls and women aged 12 and older. The oldest volunteer women's membership movement in the United States, the YWCA was inspired by the 1855 merger of two British women's organizations—the Prayer Union, which sponsored church-like activities, and the General Female Training Institute, founded as a home for nurses returning from the Crimean War. The new Women's Christian Association began serving the thousands of women who had flocked to cities during the industrial expansion of the late 1800s to find jobs—only to find poverty-level wages and unemployment. A similar phenomenon in the United States spurred the founding of the Ladies' Christian Association in New York City, to work for the "temporal, moral, and spiritual welfare of the self-supporting young woman." Later that year, a similar group calling itself the Young Women's Christian Association formed in Boston.

As YWCAs formed in other cities, they provided many of the services that YMCAs provided for young men: Christian spiritual guidance, housing facilities, recreation and physical training, and formal education, including classes in such academic subjects as reading and writing, penmanship, arithmetic, science and music, and such vocational subjects as sewing, needlework, dressmaking, typing, bookkeeping, clerical and secretarial work, telegraphy, interior decorating and commercial art. Like YMCAs, YWCAs recruited missionaries on college and university campuses, and established camping programs that provided inexpensive summer vacations for working girls.

Unlike YMCAs, however, YWCAs have always remained far more decentralized, with only loose ties to a National Board in New York City that was not even founded until the first decade of the 20th century. Moreover, YWCAs traditionally remained more committed for a longer

period of time to their evangelical mission than did YMCAs, whose early attraction to sports and physical fitness diluted their original mission. During the 1920s and 1930s, YWCAs concerned themselves with social service and with the training of women for jobs that had been inaccessible to them prior to woman suffrage and the development of the women's rights movement.

After World War II, as formerly all-male colleges and universities opened their doors to women and as the job market expanded and provided women with more opportunities, YWCA membership plunged by nearly 25%, and those branches that survived reached out to wider audiences, including many non-Protestants. Men and boys may now join as associate members. Like YMCAs, many YWCA branches have evolved into nonsectarian, quasi-public organizations. Branches remain totally independent, however, and are operated and funded by volunteers and are dedicated to a variety of widely varying activities designed to meet the needs of each particular community. Not all YWCAs are housed in formal structures. Many are simply member organizations that gather in private homes, churches, libraries, schools and colleges. Toward the end of the 1980s, there were about 400 community and student associations and some 4,000 actual Ys across the United States, with a total membership of about 2 million.

Reference: National Board YWCA of USA, New York, New York.

Z

zero-based budgeting A system of planning annual spending that disregards previous spending levels and creates each year's new budget from a base of zero. Developed at Texas Instruments Inc. in the 1960s and adopted by many corporations and government agencies as a cost-cutting measure, the process has found widespread use in many school districts. As in business, zero-based budgeting forces administrators to justify and rejustify each item of spending every year, thus eliminating the inertia that allows automatic reapproval of budget items that might well be eliminated or reduced. Zero-based budgeting has proved especially effective in cutting the cost of noninstructional services, where careful annual reconsideration often results in subcontracting of such services to private firms at reduced cost. Zero-based budgeting can, to some extent, reduce instructional costs by forcing annual reevaluation of the cost per student of each course and staff member.

Reference: *Financing Education in a Climate of Change,* Percy E. Burrup, Vern Brimsley Jr. and Rulon R. Garfield (1988).

zero reject A concept derived from the federal Education for All Handicapped Children Act of 1975 (q.v.) and subsequent court decisions requiring public school districts to provide all handicapped children with free, appropriate education. The act, in effect, reduced handicap-based student rejection rates to zero.

Reference: United States Department of Education, Washington, D.C.

zoological garden A nonacademic educative institution that displays live animals for public enjoyment, education, conservation, research and, often, for profit, depending on the financial status of the institution. Popularly known as zoos and a valuable adjunct to classroom studies of zoology, modern zoological gardens attempt to simulate the native habitat of each species, and often offer opportunities for threatened species to breed. Zoological gardens date from the earliest civilizations, and rulers in Egypt, China and elsewhere kept collections of animals for their personal enjoyment. In Europe, the first modern zoo—a collection of caged animals—was the Imperial Menagerie established in Vienna in 1752 and opened to the public in 1828. The Jardin des Plantes (Botanical Garden) was the first zoo to surround its cages with gardens. The oldest zoo in the United States is New York's Central Park Zoo, which opened in 1864. Until the 1970s, it followed the traditional practice of most zoos of housing their wide variety of beasts in bare steel cages that allowed animals only to pace endlessly in circles during their waking hours. In the final decades of the 20th century, the zoological organizations that operate zoos in New York and other major cities began doing away with cages in order to let animals roam free in large fields and forests surrounded by fences or moats too high or too deep for them to escape. For viewing purposes, many zoological gardens installed monorails or other forms of protected transportation that allowed visitors to safely watch the animals in their natural habitats.

Reference: EB

Zorach v. Clauson A 1952 United States Supreme Court decision that upheld a New York law permitting public schools to release students to attend religious instruction that took place outside public school grounds and did not require public financial support. The case represented a partial reversal of a 1948 ruling in *People of the State of Illinois ex. rel. McCollum v. Board of Education,* which is better known as the *McCollum* case (see MCCOLLUM V. BOARD OF EDUCATION). In that case, the Supreme Court had ordered the public schools of

Champaign, Illinois, to cease the practice of releasing students for religious instruction with clerics on public school grounds. A then-common practice in schools across the United States, the excusing of students from classes to attend religious instruction in public school facilities was deemed a violation of the establishment clause of the First Amendment of the Constitution, because it involved "too great" a cooperation between church and state. But the *McCollum* decision also interfered with First Amendment rights of students to free exercise of religion. *Zorach* resolved the conflict created by *McCollum* by letting students exercise their religious rights—but off publicly supported school property and without any public financial support, such as school transportation or extra tutoring for students to make up classroom work missed because of religious instruction.

Reference: U.S. Supreme Court proceedings.

BIBLIOGRAPHY AND REFERENCES

The bibliography is divided into 41 sections, each of which has been organized on the basis of the most likely needs of the student of education or professional educator. Thus, the bibliography for administration is divided according to administrative function and subfunction—elementary school administration, secondary school administration, student affairs, and so on, with works listed alphabetically by title. Biographies, on the other hand, are organized alphabetically according to the subject of each biography. The bibliography includes works of the broadest possible scope and does not replicate all the reference works cited in the body of the encyclopedia. Additional references may be found at the end of the articles on specific subjects. Because of their reach, certain works appear in more than one category. The addresses of professional associations and organizations have purposely been omitted because of the frequency with which they relocate. Their current locations can easily be obtained from the current edition of *The Encyclopedia of Associations*, available in most libraries.

Subject Guide to the Bibliography

1. ADMINISTRATION

College and University Administration

Colleges in Consort: Institutional Cooperation Through Consortia, by Franklin Patterson (1974).

Handbook of College and University Administration, Asa S. Knowles, ed. (1970).

Leadership, Goals, and Power in Higher Education, by Barry M. Richman and Richard N. Farmer (1974).

Managing the Academic Enterprise, by Elwood B. Ehrle and John B. Bennett (1988).

Managing Today's University, by Frederick E. Baldeston (1974).

Presidents, Professors, and Trustees, by W. H. Cowley (1980).

Elementary School Administration

Educational Administration: An Introduction, by Ralph B. Kimbrough and Michael Y. Nunnery (1976).

The Effective Principal: Perspective on School Leadership, by Arthur Blumberg and William Greenfield (1986).

The Elementary Principal's Handbook: A Guide to Effective Action, by Larry W. Hughes and Gerald C. Ubben (1989).

Elementary School Organization and Administration, by Henry J. Otto and David C. Sanders (1964).

Government Administration of Education

The American School Superintendency, American Association of School Administrators, Arlington, Virginia.

Educational Evaluation, by W. James Popham (1988).

Educational Legislation and Administration of the Colonial Governments, by Elsie W. Clews (1899).

Evaluations of Year-Round School Programs, by Debra D. Nygaard (1974).

Financing Education in a Climate of Change, by Percy E. Burrup, Vern Brimsley, Jr., and Rulon R. Garfield (1988).

Introduction to PERT, by Harry F. Evarts (1964).

The Organization and Control of American Schools, by Roald F. Campbell et al. (1980).

Organizing Schools for Effective Education, by Daniel E. Griffiths.

The Paradox of Progressive Education: The Gary Plan and Urban Schooling, by Ronald D. Cohen and Raymond A. Mohl (1979).

Performance Contracting in School Systems, by Roald F. Campbell and James E. Lorion (1972).

Politics, Markets and America's Schools, by John E. Chubb and Terry M. Moe (1989).

Profiles of Significant Schools: Schools Without Walls, Educational Facilities Laboratories, New York (1971).

Program Evaluation: Methods and Case Studies, by Emil J. Posavac and Raymond J. Carey (1989).

Pros and Cons of Merit Pay, by Susan M. Johnson (1984).

School Boards: Their Status, Functions and Activities, by Charles L. Reeves (1969).

School Finance: The Economics and Politics of Public Education, by Walter I. Garms et al. (1978).

The Schools-Within-A-School Program: A Modern Approach to Secondary Instruction and Guidance, by Robert D. Ramsey et al. (1965).

State Departments of Education, State Boards of Education, and Chief State School Officers, by Sam Harris (1973).

Student Achievement Tests as Tools of Educational Policy: Practices and Consequences, by Edward Haertel (1988).

Understanding Collective Bargaining in Education: Negotiations, Contracts and Disputes Between Teachers and Boards, by Robert C. O'Reilly (1978).

Professional Organizations for Administrators (See current edition of *The Encyclopedia of Associations* for current addresses)

National Association of Elementary School Principals.

National Association of Independent Colleges and Universities.

National Association of Independent Schools.

National Association of Secondary School Principals.

American Association of School Administrators.

American Association of School Superintendents.

National Association of State Boards of Education.

National Middle School Association.

National School Boards Association.

School Administration (General)

Analyzing Teacher Behavior, by Ned A. Flanders (1970).

The Delivery of Psychological Services in Schools, by Stephen N. Elliott and Joseph C. Witt (1986).

Educational Administration: A Management Approach, by Ronald W. Rebore (1985).

Educational Administration: An Introduction, by Ralph B. Kimbrough and Michael Y. Nunnery (1976).

The Effective Principal: Perspective on School Leadership, by Arthur Blumberg and William Greenfield (1986).

Handbook of Educational Administration: A Guide for the Practitioner, by Emery Stoops et al. (1975).

Intramural Administration: Theory and Practice, James A. Peterson, ed. (1976).

Introduction to Educational Administration, by Roald F. Campbell et al. (1977).

Legal Handbook for Educators, Patricia A. Hollander (1978).

Linking America's Schools and Colleges, by Franklin Wilbur, and Leo M. Lambert (1991).

Minimum Competency Testing, by Rodney P. Riegel and Irvin J. Lehman (1980).

The New School Executive: A Theory of Administration, by Thomas J. Sergiovanni and Fred D. Carver (1980).

Predicting School Enrollments, by Roscoe C. Brown, Jr. (1961).

The Principal: Creative Leadership for Effective Schools, by Gerald C. Ubben and Larry W. Hughes (1987).

Program Evaluation: Methods and Case Studies, by Emil J. Posavak (1989).

Redesigning School Health Services, by Annette Lynch (1983).

School Administration: Challenge and Opportunity for Leadership, by Richard A. Gorton (1976).

School Administration and Supervision: Important Issues, Concepts and Case Studies, by Richard A. Gorton (1980).

The Underachieving Curriculum: Assessing U.S. School Mathematics from the International Perspective, by Curtis C. McKnight *et al.* (1987).

School Business Administration

Practitioner's Guide to School Business Management, by John Greenhalgh (1978).

School Business Administration, by K. Forbis Jordan et al. (1985).

School Site Management, by Lawrence C. Pierce (1977).

School Planning and Construction

Educational Facilities: Planning, Remodeling, and Management, by Basil Castoldi (1977).

Educational System Planning, by Roger A. Kaufman (1972).

Guide for Planning Educational Facilities, Council of Educational Facility Planners, Columbus, Ohio.

Planning Physical Education and Athletic Facilities in Schools, by Kenneth A. Penman (1977).

Secondary School Administration

Innovations in Secondary Education, by Glenys G. Unruh and William M. Alexander (1974).

Secondary School Administration, by Lester W. Anderson and Lauren A. Van Dyke (1972).

Strategies for Instruction and Organization, by Carl Braun and Ted Giles (1976).

Staff Administration

Differentiated Staffing, by Richard A. Dempsey and Rodney P. Smith, Jr. (1972).

Educational Administration and Organizational Behavior, by E. Mark Hanson (1979).

Examining Departmental Management, John C. Smart and James R. Montgomery, eds. (1976).

Getting Better Results from Substitute Teachers, Teacher Aides, and Volunteers, by Bryce Perkins and Harry A. Becker (1966).

Organizational Behavior in Schools, by Robert G. Owens (1970).

The Organizational Climate of Schools, by Andrew W. Halpin and Don B. Croft (1963).

Personnel Administration in Education: Leadership for Instructional Improvement, by Ben M. Harris, et al. (1979).

The Personnel Function in Educational Administration, by William Castetter (1981).

The Role of the Special Education Paraprofessional, by Greg H. Firth (1982).

School Administrator's Guide to Flexible Master Scheduling, by Alexander M. Swaab (1974).

School Organization: Theory and Practice, by Marian P. Franklin et al. (1967).

Staff Development: Enhancing Human Potential, by Donald C. Orlich (1989).

Staff Development: Problems and Solutions, by Stanley M. Elam, Jerome Cramer, and Ben Brodinsky (1986).

Strategies for Instruction and Organization, by Carl Braun and Ted Giles (1976).

Supervision of Instruction: A Developmental Approach, by Carl D. Glickman (1985).

Student Affairs Administration

Flunking Grades, by Lorrie Shephard and Mary Lee Smith (1988).

Organization and Administration of Pupil Personnel Services, by Howard Lawrence Blanchard (1974).

School Discipline, by William C. Bagley (1976).

School Vandalism: Strategies for Prevention, by Michael D. Casserly, Scott A. Bass, and John R. Garrett (1980).

Truancy and School Phobias, by A. H. Denney (1974).

2. ADOLESCENCE

The Adolescent Society: The Social Life of the Teenager and Its Impact on Education, by James S. Coleman (1961).

Alternative Learning Environments, Gary Coats, ed. (1974).

Dropouts in America, by Andrew Hahn and Jacqueline Danzberger (1987).

Explaining Delinquency and Drug Abuse, by Delbert S. Elliott (1984).

Home, School, and Community in Adolescent Education, by Francis A. J. Ianni (1983).

Law Enforcement and the Youthful Offender, by Edward Eldefonso (1983).

Patterns of Juvenile Delinquency, by Howard B. Kaplan (1984).

The Practice of Social Work in Schools, by Wendy G. Winters and Freda Easton (1983).

School Vandalism: Strategies for Prevention, by Michael D. Casserly, Scott A. Bass, and John R. Garrett (1980).

Sexism: New Issue in American Education, by Pauline Gough (1976).

3. ADULT EDUCATION

Administration

Adult and Continuing Education: Theory and Practice, by Peter Jarvis (1983).

Adult Elementary Education (1956), by Angelica Cass and Arthur P. Crabtree.

Androgogy in Action: Applying Modern Principles of Adult Learning, by Malcolm S. Knowles and Associates (1984).

Building Bridges to the Public: New Directions for Higher Education, by Louis T. Benezet and Frances W. Magnuson (1979).

Helping Adults Learn, by Alan Boyd Knox (1986).

Agricultural Extension Programs

Extension Education and Rural Development, by Bruce Crouch and Shankarish Chamala (1980).

Federal Cooperation in Agricultural Extension Work, Vocational Education, and Vocational Rehabilitation, by Lloyd E. Blauch (1969).

The Reluctant Farmer: The Rise of Agricultural Extension to 1914, by Roy V. Scott (1970).

Corporation Sponsorship

Corporate Classrooms: The Learning Business, by Neil P. Eurich (1985).

Educational Experiments in Industry, by Nathaniel Peffer (1932).

History

The Adult Education Movement in the United States, by Malcolm S. Knowles (1962).

The American Lyceum: Its History and Contribution to Education, by Cecil B. Hayes (1932).

The American Lyceum: Town Meeting of the Mind, by Carl Bode (1956).

Chautauqua: An American Place, by Rebecca Richmond (1934).

The Chautauqua Movement, by John H. Vincent (1886).

Classrooms in the Military: An Account of Education in the Armed Forces of the United States, by Harold F. Clark and Harold S. Sloan (1964).

The State University, Its Work and Problems: A Selection from Addresses Delivered between 1921 and 1923, by Lotus Delta Coffman (1934).

Twenty Years at Hull House (1910) and *The Second Twenty Years at Hull House* (1930) by Jane Addams.

University Extension in the United States, by Louis E. Reber (1914).

The University Extension Movement, by W. S. Bittner (1920).

Workers' Education in the United States, Theodore Brameld, ed. (1941).

Reference Guides to Adult Education

But What If I Don't Want To Go to College?: A Guide to Successful Careers through Alternative Education (1992), by Harlow G. Unger.

Peterson's Guide to Two-Year Colleges (current edition).

Profiles of American Colleges, Barron's Educational Series, Inc.

The Educational Alliance, New York, New York.

Self-Directed

The Autobiography of Benjamin Franklin, Leonard W. Labaree, Ralph L. Ketcham, Helen C. Boatfield, and Helen H. Fineman, eds. (1964).

Bear's Guide to Earning Non-Traditional College Degrees, by John Bear (1982).

Campus-Free College Degrees, by Marcie Kisner Thorson (1989).

Defense Activity for Non-Traditional Education Support.

A Degree of Difference: The Open University of the United Kingdom, by Naomi E. McIntosh et al. (1977).

How to Read a Book: The Art of Getting a Liberal Education, by Mortimer J. Adler (1940).

Lifelong Learning: Formal, Nonformal, Informal, and Self-Directed (1982), by Donald W. Mocker and George E. Spear.

The Open University, by Walter Perry (1977).

4. AFRICAN-AMERICAN EDUCATION

Black Studies

Black Studies: Threat or Challenge, by Nick Aaron Ford (1973).

Black Studies Programs in Public Schools, by Raymond H. Giles, Jr. (1974).

Pride: A Handbook of Black Studies Techniques for the Classroom Teacher, by Clifford D. Watson (1971).

Desegregation/Integration

The Burden of "Brown": Thirty Years of School Desegregation, by Raymond Wolters (1984).

The Deep South Says "Never", by John Barlow Martin (1957).

Desegregation: How Schools Are Meeting Historic Challenge, National School Public Relations Association, Arlington, Virginia (1973).

From Brown to Bradley: School Desegregation 1954–1974, R. Stephen Browning, ed. (1975).

The Integration of American Schools, by Norene Harris et al. (1975).

Making of Massive Resistance: Virginia's Politics of Public School Desegregation, 1954–1956, by Robbins L. Gates (1964).

The NAACP's Legal Strategy Against Segregated Education, 1925–1950, by Mark V. Tushnet (1987).

The School Busing Controversy: 1970–1975, by Judith F. Buncher (1975).

School Desegregation, by Harold B. Gerard and Normal Miller (1975).

School Desegregation: Past, Present and Future, Walter G. Stephen and Joe R. Feagin, eds. (1980).

School Desegregation in the North, by Bentley Edwards and Frederick M. Wirt (1967).

Simple Justice: A History of "Brown v. Board of Education and Black America's Struggle for Equality, by Richard Kluger (1975).

Twenty Years After Brown: A Report of the United States Commission on Civil Rights (1977).

Higher Education

Black Colleges in America, by Charles V. Willie and Ronald R. Edmonds, eds. (1978).

The College-Bred Negro, W. E. Burghardt Du Bois, ed. (1900).

The Evolution of the Negro College, by Dwight Oliver Wendell Holmes (1934).

The Founding of Howard University, by Walter Dyson (1921).

Howard University: The First Hundred Years, 1876–1967, by Rayford W. Logan (1969).

United Negro College Fund, New York, New York.

History

An Appraisal of the Negro in Colonial South Carolina: A Study in Americanization, by Frank J. Klingberg (1941).

Black American Scholars: A Study of Their Beginnings, by Horace Mann Bond (1972).

The Education of the Negro in the American Social Order, by Horace Mann Bond (1966).

The Education of the Negro Prior to 1861, by Carter G. Woodson (1919).

The History of Black Americans, by Philip S. Foner (3 vols., 1975–83).

NAACP: A History of the National Association for the Advancement of Colored People, by Charles Flint Kellogg (1976).

Negro Education: A Study of the Private and Higher Schools for Colored People in the United States, by Thomas Jesse Jones (1916).

Northern Schools, Southern Blacks, and Reconstruction: Freedmen's Education, 1862–75, by Ronald E. Butchart (1980).

Reading, 'Riting, and Reconstruction: The Education of Freedmen in the South, 1861–1870, by Robert C. Morris (1981).

Reconstruction After the Civil War, by John Hope Franklin (1961).

Schools for All: The Blacks & Public Education in the South, 1865–1877, by William Preston Vaughn (1974).

Up From Slavery, by Booker T. Washington (1901).

W. E. B. Du Bois, by Patricia & Frederick McKissack (1990).

W. E. B. Du Bois: Negro Leader in a Time of Crisis, by Francis L. Broderick (1959).

Racism

Human Variation: Races, Types and Ethnic Groups, by Stephen Molnar (1991).

Race and Races, by Richard A. Goldsby (1977).

Racism in the United States: An American Dilemma, David M. Reimers, ed. (1972).

The Retreat of Scientific Racism, by Elazar Barkan (1992).

Social Problems

An American Dilemma: The Negro Problem and Modern Democracy, by Gunnar Myrdal (1944).

Dark Ghetto: Dilemmas of Social Power, by Kenneth B. Clark (1965).

Equal Educational Opportunity: More Promise Than Progress, Institute for the Study of Educational Policy, Washington, D.C.

Language in the Inner City: Studies in the Black Vernacular, by William Labov (1972).

Racial Isolation in the Public Schools: A Report of the U.S. Commission on Civil Rights, U.S. Government Printing Office, Washington D.C. (1967).

5. AMERICAN-INDIAN EDUCATION

American Indian Education, R. Merwin Deever et al., eds. (1974).

American Indian Education: Government Schools and Economic Progress, by Evelyn C. Adams (1946).

Church, State, and the American Indians: Two and a Half Centuries of Partnership in Missions Between Protestant Churches and Government, by R. Pierce Beaver (1966).

Education and the American Indian: The Road to Self-Determination Since 1928, by Margaret C. Stasz (1977).

John Eliot: "Apostle to the Indians," by Ola Elizabeth Winslow (1968).

The Indian in America, by Wilcomb E. Washburn (1975).

New England Frontier: Puritans and Indians, 1620–1675, by Alden T. Vaughan (1965).

The New England Company, 1649–1776: Missionary Society to the American Indians, by William Kellaway (1961).

Reference Encyclopedia of the American Indian, Barry Klein, Ed. (1978).

The Savages of America: A Study of the Indian and the Idea of Civilization, by Roy Harvey Pearce (1953).

6. COUNSELING

Career Counseling

A Model Career Counseling and Placement Program, by Andre G. Beaumont et al. (1978).

Vocational Guidance and Career Development: Selected Readings, by Herman T. Peters and James C. Hansen (1977).

Guidance Counseling

Counseling Students, by Preston L. Munter et al. (1988).

Fundamentals of Individual Appraisal: Assessment Techniques for Counselors, by Bruce Shertzer and James D. Linden (1979).

Group Counseling, by Merle M. Ohlsen (1977).

An Introduction to Guidance: The Professional Counselor, by E. L. Tolbert (1982).

The Schools-Within-A-School Program: A Modern Approach to Secondary Instruction and Guidance, by Robert D. Ramsey et al. (1965).

Using Role Playing in the Classroom, by John Thompson (1978).

Psychological Counseling

The Delivery of Psychological Services in Schools, by Stephen N. Elliott and Joseph C. Witt (1986).

The Practice of Social Work in Schools, by Wendy G. Winters and Freda Easton (1983).

School Psychologists Handbook, by Arthur A. Atwell (1976).

Schools and Social Work, by Margaret Robinson (1978).

Sensitivity Training: The Scientific Understanding of Individuals, by Henry C. Smith (1973).

T-Groups, Cary L. Cooper and I. L. Mangham, eds. (1971).

Truancy and School Phobias, by A. H. Denney (1974).

7. CURRICULUM

General

Academic Preparation for College: What Students Need to Know and Be Able to Do, The College Board, Princeton, New Jersey (1983).

Basic Principles of Curriculum and Instruction, by Ralph Tyler (1949).

Bilingualism in Education, by Jim Cummins and Merrill Swain (1986).

Contemporary Approaches to Moral Education: Analyzing Alternative Theories, by Barry Chazan (1985).

Curriculum Change Toward the 21st Century, Harold G. Shane, ed. (1977).

Curriculum Development: Theory into Practice, by Daniel Tanner and Laurel N. Tanner (1980).

Curriculum: A History of the Undergraduate Course of Study Since 1636, by Frederick Rudolph (1977).

Curriculum: Principles and Foundations, by Robert S. Zais. (1976).

Curriculum Planning and Development, by James A. Beane, Conrad F. Toepfer, Jr., and Samuel J. Alessi, Jr. (1986).

Curriculum Theory, Alex Molnar and John A. Zahorik, editors (1977).

From School to College: Articulation and Transfer, by Julius Menacker (1975).

Great Books, The Foundation of a Liberal Education, by Robert M. Hutchins (1954).

High School, A Report on Secondary Education in America, by Ernest L. Boyer (1983).

How to Measure Readability, by W. B. Gray, Jr. (1975).

Humanities and the Study of Civilization, by John Ferguson and Arthur Marwick (1970).

Ideology and Curriculum, by Michael W. Apple (1979).

James Madison Elementary School, A Curriculum for American Students, by William J. Bennett (1988).

James Madison High School, A Curriculum for American Students, by William J. Bennett (1987).

The Learning Center: Heart of the School, by Lowell Horton and Phyllis Horton (1973).

Making the Best of Schools, by Jeannie Oakes & Martin Lipton (1990).

Minimum Competency Testing, by Rodney P. Riegel and Irvin J. Lehman (1980).

Models of Moral Education: An Appraisal, by Richard H. Hersh et al. (1980).

Moral Education: Character, Community, and Ideals, by Betty A. Sichel (1988).

Multicultural Education: A Handbook of Activities, Information and Resources, by Pamela L. Tiedt and Iris M. Tiedt (1986).

Multicultural Education: A Teacher's Guide to Content and Process, by Hilda Hernandez (1989).

Multicultural Education in Western Societies, James A. Banks and James Lynch, eds. (1986).

A New System of Education, by B. Everard Blanchard (1975).

The Paideia Proposal (1982), *Paideia Problems and Possibilities* (1983) and *The Paideia Program* (1984), by Mortimer J. Adler.

The Process of Education, by Jerome S. Bruner (1962).

Self-Concept, Self-Esteem and the Curriculum, by James A. Beane and Richard P. Lipka (1984).

A Teacher's Handbook for Study Outside the Classroom, by Shirley A. Brehm (1969).

The Underachieving Curriculum: Assessing U.S. School Mathematics from the International Perspective, by Curtis C. McKnight *et al.* (1987).

"What Did You Learn in School Today?": A Parent's Guide for Evaluating Your Child's School, by Harlow G. Unger (1991).

Winnetka: The History and Significance of An Educational Experiment, by Carleton W. Washburne and Sydney P. Marland, Jr.

Council on International Educational Exchange.

Institute of International Education.

International Baccalaureate North America.

Note: Specific recommended or mandated curricula are available from the Boards of Education of the individual states.

Subjects

The Arts:

The Art Teacher's Resource Book, by Leslie A. Baker (1979).

Contemporary Music Education, by Michael L. Mark (1978).

The Eclectic Curriculum in American Music Education: Contributions of Dalcroze, Kodaly, and Orff, by Beth Landis and Polly Carder (1972).

Economics:

Joint Council on Economic Education, New York, New York.

Environmental Studies:

The Administration of Outdoor Education Programs, by Charles A. Lewis, Jr. (1975).

Outdoor Education, by Julian Smith et al. (1972).

Principles and Practices of Outdoor/Environmental Education, by Phyllis M. Ford (1981).

English:

Syntactic Structure, by Noam Chomsky (1957).

Transformation-Generative Grammar, by Bert Jacobsen (1977).

Transformational Grammar and the Teacher of English, by Owen Thomas and Eugene R. Kantgen (1974).

Thematic Units in Teaching English and the Humanities, by Sylvia Spann and Mary Beth Culp (1977).

Field Experience:

Implementing Field Experience Education, John Duley, ed. (1974).

Geography:

The Geography Learning of High School Seniors, Educational Testing Service.

Home Economics:

Home Economics: Past, Present, and Future, by Marjorie East (1980).

Foreign Languages:

Foreign Language in the Elementary School, by Theodore Andersson (1969).

Foreign Languages in Elementary School, by Marguerite Erikson, et al. (1964).

Speaking in Many Tongues, by Wilga M. Rivers (1976).

Teaching Modern Language, by David Webb (1974).

The World's Major Languages, Bernard Comrie (1990).

Language Arts:

An Experience-Based Approach to Language and Reading, Carl Braun and Victor Froese, eds. (1977).

The Language Arts: Teaching and Learning in the Elementary School, by Kean and Carl Personke (1976).

Teaching Language Arts, by Carole Cox (1988).

Teaching the Language Arts in the Elementary School, by Martha Dallman (1976).

Mathematics:

An Introduction to Modern Mathematics, by Nathan J. Fine (1965).

Science and Mathematics Curricular Developments Internationally, 1956–1974, J. David Lockhart, ed. (1974).

The Underachieving Curriculum: Assessing U.S. Mathematics from the International Perspective, by Curtis C. McKnight et al. (1987).

Morality:

Morals and Ethics, by Carl Wellman (1975).

Physical Education:

Planning Physical Education and Athletic Facilities in Schools, by Kenneth A. Penman (1977).

Problem Solving:

Thinking Critically, by John Chaffee (1985).

Safety Education:

Safety: Concepts and Instruction, by Alton L. Thygerson (1976).

Safety Education, by A. E. Floria, et al. (1979).

Science:

Science and Mathematics Curricular Developments Internationally, 1956–1974, J. David Lockhart, ed. (1974).

Teaching Elementary Science, by William K. Esler (1977).

Teaching Science through Discovery, by Arthur A. Carin and Robert B. Sund (1975).

Science Research Associates.

Sex Education:

Discussing Sex in the Classroom: Readings for Teachers, David R. Stronck, ed. (1982).

SIECUS.

Social Studies:

Elementary and Middle School Social Studies, by David T. Naylor and Richard A. Diem (1987).

Social Studies for Children in a Democracy: Recent Trends and Developments, by John U. Michaelis (1976).

The Social Studies, Howard D. Mehlinger and O. L. Davis, eds. (1981).

8. EARLY CHILDHOOD EDUCATION

Effects

As the Twig Is Bent: Lasting Effects of Preschool Programs, Lawrence Erlbaum Associates (1983).

Changed Lives, by John R. Berrueta-Clement et al. (1984, High/Scope Press).

Effectiveness of Early Education, by David Smith and Elizabeth Soper (1983).

Project Head Start: A Legacy of the War on Poverty, Edward Zigler and Jeannette Valentine, eds. (1979).

High Scope Educational Research Foundation, Ypsilanti, Michigan.

U.S. Department of Health and Human Services.

History

The Children's Cause, by Gilbert Y. Steiner (1976).

Contemporary Influence in Early Childhood Education, by Ellis D. Evans (1975).

Educational Activities of the Works Progress Administration, by Doak S. Campbell, Frederick H. Bair and Oswald L. Harvey (1939).

Finger Painting: An Outline of Its Origins and History, by Francis R. Fast (1945).

Preschool Education: A Historical and Critical Study, by Ilse Forest (1927).

Who's Minding the Children? The History of Politics of Day Care in America, by Margaret O'Brien Steinfels (1973).

Working Mothers and the Day Nursery, by Ethel Beer (1957).

Pedagogy

The Development of Language, Jean Berko Gleason, ed. (1985).

Early Childhood Education, by Marjorie L. Hipple (1975).

Early Childhood Education: An Introduction, by Carol Seefeldt and Nita Barbour (1986).

Education and Learning to Think, by Lauren B. Resnick (1987).

Getting Ready for School, World Book (1987).

Nursery Education: Theory and Practice, by William Blatz et al. (1935).

Play as Exploratory Learning, Mary Reilly, ed. (1974).

Play and Education, by Otto Weininger (1979).

ReQuest in Prereading Activities for Content Area Reading and Learning, by David W. Moor, John E. Readance, and Robert J. Rickelman (1982).

The Self-Contained Classroom, Edith R. Snyder, ed. (1960).

9. ECONOMICS OF EDUCATION

Barron's Handbook of American College Financial Aid (updated periodically).

The College Blue Book: Scholarships, Fellowships, Grants and Loans, by Lorraine Mathies and Elizabeth I. Dixon (updated periodically).

The Economics of Education, by Elchanan Cohn (1979).

The Economic Value of Education, by Theodore W. Schultz (1963).

Education and Economic Development, by W. Arthur Lewis (1964).

Financing Education in a Climate of Change, by Percy E. Burrup, Vern Brimsley, Jr., and Rulon R. Garfield (1988).

Knowledge and Knowledge Production, by Fritz Machlup (1980).

The Knowledge Industry in the United States, 1960–1980, started by Fritz Machlup and completed posthumously by Machlup's associates, Michael Rogers Rubin and Mary Taylor Huber (1986).

The Production and Distribution of Knowledge in the United States (1962).

Scholars, Dollars, and Bureaucrats, by Charles E. Finn, Jr. (1978).

School Finance in Transition: The Courts and Educational Reform, John Pincus, ed. (1974).

School Finance: The Economics and Politics of Public Education, by Walter I. Garms et al. (1978).

10. EDUCATION EQUIPMENT AND TECHNOLOGY

Audio-Visual Fundamentals: Basic Equipment Operation and Sample Materials Production, by John R. Bullard and Calvin E. Mather (1974).

The Children's Machine, Rethinking School in the Age of the Computer, by Seymour Papert (1993).

Computers in Education, by Bobbie K. Hentel and Linda Harper (1985).

Computers in Education, by Paul F. Merrill et al. (1986).

Fundamentals of Teaching with Audiovisual Technology, by Carlton W. H. Erickson and David H. Curl (1972).

A Guide to Programmed Instruction, by Jerome P. Lysaught and Clarence M. Williams (1963).

A Handbook of Computer-Based Training, by Christopher Dean and Quentin Whitlock (1988).

The Information Revolution: Education and Learning, by Walter Oleksy (1995).

Instructional Media and the New Technologies of Instruction, by Robert Heinich, Michael Molenda, and James D. Russell (1985).

Instructional Technology: Its Nature and Use, by Walter A. Wittich and Charles F. Schuler (1979).

The Language Laboratory and Language Learning, by Julian Dakin (1972).

Mediaware: Selection, Operation, and Maintenance, by Raymond Wyman (1976).

Planning, Producing and Using Instructional Media, by Jerrold E. Kemp and Don C. Smellie (1989).

Systems of Individualized Education, by Harriet Talmadge (1975).

The Teacher and Overhead Projection: A Treasury of Ideas, Uses and Techniques, by Morton J. Schultz (1965).

American Teleconferencing, New York, New York.

11. EDUCATION LAW

Court Decisions

The College Students and the Courts, D. Parker Young and Donald Gehring (1977).

The Courts and Education, Annual Yearbook, University of Chicago Press.

Landmark Supreme Court Decisions on Public School Issues, by Edward C. Bolmeier (1973).

Parochiad and the Courts, by Dale E. Twomley (1979).

School Finance in Transition: The Courts and Educational Reform, John Pincus, ed. (1974).

The Supreme Court and Education, by David Fellman (1976).

Legislation

Bakke and the Politics of Equality: Friends and Foes in the Classroom of Litigation, by Timothy J. O'Neill.

Educational Legislation and Administration of the Colonial Governments, by Elsie W. Clews (1899).

Education and the Law: Cases and Materials on Public Schools by William R. Hazard.

Employment Discrimination Law, by Barbara Lindemann Schlei and Paul Frossman (1983).

Free Appropriate Education, The Law and Children with Disabilities, by H. Rutherford Turnbull III (1986).

From Brown to Bradley: School Desegregation 1954–1974, R. Stephen Browning, ed. (1975).

The Law and Public School Operation, by Leroy J. Peterson et al. (1978).

The Law of Public Education, by Robert R. Hamilton (1976).

Legal Handbook for Educators, Patricia A. Hollander (1978).

The School Busing Controversy: 1970–1975, by Judith F. Buncher (1975).

Title IX: How It Affects Elementary and Secondary Education, by Norma Raffel (1976).

Equal Employment Opportunity Commission.

Student Rights

Constitutional Rights and Student Life: Value Conflict in Law and Education, by Frank R. Kemerer and Kenneth L. Deutsch.

Legality of Student Disciplinary Practices, by Edward C. Bolmeier (1976).

The Legal Rights of Students, by Thomas J. Flygare (1975).

Student Discipline and the Law, by Eugene T. Connors (1979).

What Every Teacher Should Know About Student Rights, by Eve Cary (1975).

12. EDUCATION QUALITY

Burnout in the Public Schools, by Gary Dworkin (1987).

The Condition of Teaching: A State-by-State Analysis, 1988, The Carnegie Foundation for the Advancement of Teaching.

Educational Evaluation, by W. James Popham (1988).

Guidelines for Using the National Teacher Examinations, National Teacher Examinations Policy Council, Princeton, New Jersey.

International Studies in Evaluation, International Association for the Evaluation of Educational Achievement, Ghent, Belgium (1976; available in U.S. educational reference libraries).

Measuring Educational Progress, by William Greenbaum (1977).

Metropolitanism: Its Challenge to Education, Robert J. Havighurst, ed. (1968).

Metropolitanism and Education: Teachers in Amsterdam, London, Paris and New York, by Max A. Eckstein and Harold J. Noah (1973).

The Miseducation of American Teachers, by James Koerner (1963).

A Nation at Risk: The Imperative for Educational Reform, U.S. Government Printing Office, Washington, D.C. (1983).

The Nation's Report Card, by Lamar Alexander and H. Thomas James (1987).

President's Commission on Foreign Language and International Studies: Background Papers and Studies, U.S. Department of Health, Education and Welfare/ Office of Education, Washington, D.C. (1979, U.S. Government Printing Office).

Program Evaluation: Methods and Case Studies, by Emil J. Posavac and Raymond J. Carey (1989).

The Underachieving Curriculum: Assessing U.S. Mathematics from the International Perspective, by Curtis C. McKnight et al. (1987).

National Assessment Governing Board.

National Congress of Parents and Teachers.

National Education Commission.

National Study of School Evaluation, Falls Church, Virginia.

U.S. Department of Education, National Center for Education Statistics.

13. EDUCATION REFORM

American Education: A National Failure, by Hyman Rickover (1963).

"The Carnegie Report—A Call for Redesigning the Schools," by Marc Ticker and David Madel, *Phi Delta Kappa*, Vol. 62, No. 1, 1986.

The Closing of the American Mind: How Higher Education Has Failed Democracy and Impoverished the Souls of Today's Students, by Allan Bloom (1987).

Defining the Basics of American Education, by Ben Brodinsky (1977).

Educational Vouchers: Concepts and Controversies, George R. La Noue, ed. (1970).

Educational Wastelands: The Retreat from Learning in Our Public Schools, by Arthur E. Bestor, Jr. (1953).

Education Vouchers: A Report on Financing Education by Payments to Parents, Center for the Study of Public Policy, Cambridge, Massachusetts (1970).

Evaluations of Year-Round School Programs, by Debra D. Nygaard (1974).

The Grand Experiment, by Malcolm M. Provus (1975).

Guidelines for Using the National Teacher Examinations, National Teacher Examinations Policy Council, Princeton, New Jersey.

High School, A Report on Secondary Education in America, by Ernest Boyer (1983).

Horace's Compromise: The Dilemma of the American High School, by Theodore S. Sizer (1984).

How to Start a School/Business Partnership, by Carol O'Connell.

Innovations in Secondary Education, by Glenys G. Unruh and William M. Alexander (1974).

In the Cause of True Education: Henry Barnard & Nineteenth Century School Reform, by Edith N. MacMullen (1991).

Linking America's Schools and Colleges, by Franklin Wilbur, and Leo M. Lambert (1991).

James Madison Elementary School, A Curriculum for American Students, by William J. Bennett (1988).

James Madison High School, A Curriculum for American Students, by William J. Bennett (1987).

Making Inequality: The Hidden Curriculum in High School Tracking, by James E. Rosenbaum (1976).

The Miseducation of American Teachers, by James Koerner (1963).

National Society for the Study of Education, Chicago, Illinois.

A Nation at Risk: The Imperative for Educational Reform, U.S. Government Printing Office, Washington, D.C. (1983).

The Nation's Report Card, by Lamar Alexander and H. Thomas James (1987).

Parenting Our Schools, A Hands-On Guide to Education Reform, by Jill Bloom (1992).

A Place Called School: Prospects for the Future, by John Goodlad (1984).

Places Where Teachers Are Taught, John I. Goodlad, Roger Soder, and Kenneth A. Sirotnik, eds. (1990).

Politics, Markets and America's Schools, by John E. Chubb and Terry M. Moe (1989).

The Purposes of Education in American Democracy, by the Educational Policies Commission, Washington, D.C. (1938).

School Finance in Transition: The Courts and Educational Reform, John Pincus, ed. (1974).

The School Fix, NYC, by Miriam Wasserman (1970).

The Reform of Secondary Education: A Report to the Public and the Profession, National Commission on the Reform of Secondary Education (1973).

The Schools-Within-A-School Program: A Modern Approach to Secondary Instruction and Guidance, by Robert D. Ramsey et al. (1965).

Spearheads for Reform, by Allen F. Davis (1967).

The Story of the Eight-Year Study, by Wilford M. Aikin (1942).

Swiss Schools and Ours: Why Theirs Are Better, by Hyman Rickover (1962).

Teachers for Our Nation's Schools (1990), by John I. Goodlad.

Winnetka: The History and Significance of An Educational Experiment, by Carleton W. Washburne and Sydney P. Marland, Jr.

Center for Educational Renewal, College of Education, University of Washington, Seattle, Washington.

Charles F. Kettering Foundation, Washington, D.C.

Holmes Group, East Lansing, Michigan.

14. EDUCATION RESEARCH

Education Index.

Educational Research: An Introduction, by Walter B. Borg and

Meredith D. Gall (1989).

The Encyclopedia of Associations.

A Guide to Sources of Educational Information.

Guide to Reference Books.

Phi Delta Kappan.

Statistical Abstract of the United States.

American Assembly of Collegiate Schools of Business.

American Association of School Administrators.

The American Association of University Professors.

American Association of University Women.

American Federation of Teachers.

American Library Association.

Bureau of Indian Affairs.

Carnegie Foundation for the Advancement of Teaching.

Charles F. Kettering Foundation.

The College Board.

Education Commission of the States.

Educational Research Information Center (ERIC).

Educational Research Service.

Ford Foundation, New York, New York.

Gesell Institute of Child Development.

Intergovernmental Advisory Council on Education.

W. K. Kellogg Foundation.

Library of Congress.

National Association of Elementary School Principals.

National Association of Independent Schools.

National Association of Secondary School Principles.

National Center for Research in Vocational Education.

National Collegiate Association.

National Commission for Cooperative Education.

National Council of Teachers of Mathematics.

National Education Association.

National Organization on Legal Problems of Education.

National Science Foundation.

National Society for the Study of Education.

National Study of School Evaluation.

Phi Delta Kappa Educational Foundation.

Research for Better Schools.

Rockefeller Foundation.

U.S. Department of Commerce Bureau of the Census.

U.S. Department of Defense.

U.S. Department of Education National Center for Education.

Statistics.

U.S. Department of Health, U.S. Department of Health and Human Services.

U.S. Department of Labor Bureau of Labor Statistics.

U.S. Department of Labor Employment and Training Administration Bureau of Apprenticeship and Training.

U.S. Department of State.

University archives.

15. EDUCATIONAL PHILOSOPHY

Education Movements

Back-to-Basics:

High School, by Ernest L. Boyer (1983).

James Madison Elementary School, A Curriculum for American Students, by William J. Bennett (1988).

James Madison High School, A Curriculum for American Students, by William J. Bennett (1987).

The Paideia Proposal (1982), *Paideia Problems and Possibilities* (1983) and *The Paideia Program* (1984), by Mortimer J. Adler.

Humanistic Education:
The Humanistic Education Sourcebook, Donald C. Read and Sidney B. Simon, eds. (1975).

Liberal Education:
Cultural Literacy and the Idea of General Education, Ian Westbury and Alan C. Purves (1988).
Orators and Philosophers: A History of the Idea of Liberal Education, by Bruce A. Kimball (1986).

Marxist Education:
Dare the School Build a New Social Order?, by George S. Counts (1932).
Education and the Class Struggle: A Critical Examination of the Liberal Educator's Program for Social Reconstruction, by Zalmen Slesinger (1937).
Toward A Reconstructed Education, by Theodore Brameld (1956).

Open Education:
Summary of Research on Open Education, by Heather S. Doob (1974).
The Teacher's Guide to Open Education, by Lilian S. Stephens (1974).

Perennialism:
Great Books, The Foundation of a Liberal Education, by Robert M. Hutchins (1954).

Progressive Education:
The Paradox of Progressive Education: The Gary Plan and Urban Schooling, by Ronald D. Cohen and Raymond A. Mohl (1979).
Progressive Education at the Crossroads, by Henry Boyd Bode (1938).
Progressive Education, From Arcady to Academe: A History of the Progressive Education Association, 1919–1955, by Patricia A. Graham (1967).
The Transformation of the School: Progressivism in American Education, 1876–1957, by Lawrence A. Cremin (1961).

Education Theorists

Felix Adler:
An Ethical Philosophy of Life, by Felix Adler (1921).
The Moral Instruction of Children, By Felix Adler (1892).

Mortimer J. Adler:
Paideia Problems and Possibilities, by Mortimer J. Adler (1983)
The Paideia Program, by Mortimer J. Adler et al. (1984).
The Paideia Proposal, by Mortimer J. Adler (1982).

John Dewey:
John Dewey, by Richard J. Bernstein (1981).
John Dewey: His Thought & Influence, John Blewett, ed. (1973).
John Dewey and American Democracy, by Robert B. Westbrook (1991).
John Dewey in Perspective, by George R. Geiger (1974).

Erasmus:
Erasmus of Christendom, by Roland H. Bainton (1969).
Erasmus: A Study of His Life, Ideals and Place, by Preserved Smith (1923).

William T. Harris:
The Theory of Education, by William T. Harris (1898).

Johann Friedrich Herbart:
General Principles of Pedagogy Deduced from the Aim of Education, by Johann Friedrich Herbart (1806).
The Outlines of Educational Doctrine, Johann Friedrich Herbart (1835).
The Science of Education, by Johann Friedrich Herbart (1892).

Robert M. Hutchins:
Great Books, The Foundation of a Liberal Education, by Robert M. Hutchins (1954).

William James:
The Philosophy of William James, by T. Flournoy (1917).

Alexander Meiklejohn:
Education Between Two Worlds, by Alexander Meiklejohn (1942).
The Experimental College, by Alexander Meiklejohn (1932).
Free Speech and Its Relationship to Government, by Alexander Meiklejohn (1948).
The Liberal College, by Alexander Meiklejohn (1920).
What Does American Mean?, by Alexander Meiklejohn (1935).

Maria Montessori:
American Montessori Society, New York, New York.

The Essential Montessori, by Elizabeth Hainstock (1986).

Maria Montessori: A Biography, by Rita Kramer (1976).

Montessori: A Modern Approach, by Paula P. Lillard (1972).

The Montessori Controversy, by John Chattin McNichols (1992).

The Montessori Method, by Maria Montessori (1st Eng. ed. 1912; reprinted, 1964).

A. S. Neill:

Summerhill: A Radical Approach to Child Rearing, by A. S. Neill (1977).

Summerhill: For and Against, Harold H. Hart, ed. (1970).

Johann Heinrich Pestalozzi:

Pestalozzi and American Education, by Thomas A. Barlow (1977).

Thomas Reid:

Essays on the Active Powers of Man, by Thomas Reid (1788).

Essays on the Intellectual Powers of Man, by Thomas Reid (1785).

Inquiry into the Human Mind on the Principles of Common Sense, by Thomas Reid (1764).

Jean-Jacques Rousseau:

Confessions, by Jean-Jacques Rousseau (posthumously, 1788).

Emile, ou l'Education, by Jean-Jacques Rousseau (1762).

B. F. Skinner:

The Analysis of Behavior, by B. F. Skinner (with James G. Holland, 1961).

Science and Human Behavior, by B. F. Skinner (1953).

The Technology of Teaching, by B. F. Skinner (1968).

Adam Smith:

The Theory of Education in the Political Philosophy of Adam Smith, by Charles Flinn Arrowood (1945).

Rudolf Steiner:

The Education of the Child, by Rudolf Steiner (1965).

Noah Webster:

A Bibliography of the Writings of Noah Webster, by Emily Ellsworth Ford Skeel and Edwin H. Carpenter, Jr. (1958).

On Being American: Selected Writings, 1783–1828, by Noah Webster (Homer D. Babbage, Jr., ed., 1967).

General

Conflicting Theories of Education, by Isaac L. Kandel (1938).

Education's Lasting Influence on Values, by Herbert H. Hyman and Charles R. Wright (1979).

Essays on Education in the Early Republic, Frederick Rudolph, ed. (1965).

Foundations of Vocational Education: Social and Philosophical Concepts, by John F. Thompson (1973).

Grandmasters of Educational Thought, by Adolphe E. Meyer (1975).

An Introduction to the Philosophy of Education, by Michael J. Demiashkevich (1935).

Introduction to the Philosophy of Education, by George Kneller (1971).

Main Currents in American Thought: The Romantic Revolution, 1800–1860, by Vernon Louis Parrington (1927).

Pioneers of Popular Education, 1760–1850, by Hugh M. Pollard (1957).

Profiles of Significant Schools: Schools Without Walls, Educational Facilities Laboratories, New York (1971).

The Purposes of Education in American Democracy, by the Educational Policies Commission, Washington, D.C. (1938).

Seeds of Liberty: The Genesis of the American Mind, by Max Savelle and Clinton Rossiter (1948).

The Social Ideas of American Educators, by Merle Curti (1935).

Turning Points in American Educational History, by David Tyack (1967).

16. EDUCATIONAL PSYCHOLOGY

Behavior and Evaluation, by Jean Piaget (1978).

Bias in Mental Testing, by Arthur R. Jensen (1979).

The Conditions of Learning, by Robert M. Gagne (1985).

Conflicting Psychologies of Learning, by Henry Boyd Bode (1929).

The Development of Thought: Equilibrium of Cognitive Structures, by Jean Piaget (1977).

Educational and Psychological Measurement, by George K. Cunningham (1986).

Educational Psychology, by Lee Cronbach (1977).

Educational Psychology, by Richard E. Mayer (1982).

Educational Psychology: An Introduction, by Gary S. Belkin and Jerry L. Gray (1977).

Educational Psychology: Mastering Principles and Applications, by Janice T. Gibson and Louis A. Chandler (1988).

Essentials of Psychological Testing, by Lee J. Cronbach (1984).

The Great Psychologists (J. B. Lippincott, 1971).

Group Dynamics: The Psychology of Small Group Behavior, by Marvin E. Shaw (1971).

The Growth of Logical Thinking from Childhood to Adolescence, by Jean Piaget (1958).

Guidelines for Test Use: A Commentary on the Standards for Educational and Psychological Tests, by Frederick G. Brown (1980).

Handbook of Psychology: Senses and Intellect, by James M. Baldwin (1989).

Hemisphere Function in the Human Brain, Stuart T. Dimond, ed. (1974).

A History of Psychology in Autobiography, Carl A. Murchison, ed. (1930).

How We Learn, by Henry Boyd Bode (1940).

Intelligence: Heredity and Environment, by Philip E. Vernon (1979).

The Intelligence Men: Makers of the IQ Controversy, by Raymond E. Fancher (1985).

Introduction to Psychology, by Clifford T. Morgan and Richard King (1975).

Introduction to Psychology, by James O. Whittaker (1970).

The Language and Thought of the Child, by Jean Piaget (1925).

Measurement and Evaluation in Psychology and Education, by Robert L. Thorndike and Elizabeth P. Hagen (1977).

Modern Educational Theories, by Henry Boyd Bode (1927).

Motivation and Personality, by Abraham H. Maslow (1954, 1970).

Motivation in Education, Samuel Bell, ed. (1977).

Nature of Human Intelligence, by Joy P. Guilford (1968).

Principles of Educational and Psychological Measurement and Evaluation, by Gilbert Sax (1989).

Psychologic Foundations of Education: An Attempt to Show the Genesis of the Higher Faculties of the Mind (1898), by William T. Harris.

Psychological Testing, by Anne Anastasi (1988).

Psychology and the Science of Education: Selected Writings of Edward L. Thorndike, by Geraldine Joncich (1962).

The Psychology of Intelligence, by Jean Piaget (1947).

The Third Force: The Psychology of Abraham Maslow, by Frank G. Goble (1970).

17. EDUCATIVE INSTITUTIONS (NON-ACADEMIC)

Adult Education

The American Lyceum: Its History and Contribution to Education, by Cecil B. Hayes (1932).

The American Lyceum: Town Meeting of the Mind, by Carl Bode (1956).

Chautauqua: An American Place, by Rebecca Richmond (1934).

The Chautauqua Movement, by John H. Vincent (1886, 1971).

Fairs

The Agricultural Fair, by Wayne C. Neely (1935).

The Great American Fair: The World's Columbian Exposition and American Culture, by Reid Badger (1979).

The Illustrated History of the Centennial Exhibition, by John D. McCabe (1876).

Government

Art for the Millions: Essays from the 1930's by the Artists and Administrators of the WPA Federal Art Project, Francis V. O'Connor, ed. (1973).

Culture & the City Cultural Philosophy in Chicago from the 1880s to 1917, by Helen Lefkowitz Horowitz (1976).

Federal Relief Administration and the Arts, by William F. McDonald (1973).

Muscles and Morals: Organized Playgrounds and Urban Reform, 1880–1920, by Dominick Cavallo (1981).

The Peace Corps, by Robert G. Carey (1970).

[Smithsonian Institution] *America's Castle*, by Kenneth Haffertepe (1984).

The Smithsonian Institution, 1846–1896: The History of Its First Half-Century, George Brown Goode, ed. (1897).

The Smithsonian Institution: Documents Relating to Its Origins and History, William J. Rhees, ed. (1979).

National Endowment for the Arts *and* National Endowment for the Humanities.

Smithsonian Institution.

Libraries

Encyclopedia of Library and Information Science, Allen Kent and Harold Lancour, eds. (1972).

Foundations of the Public Library, by Jesse H. Shera (1949).

The Library in America, by Paul Dickson (1986).

American Library Association.

The New York Public Library.

Museums

The Educational Philosophy and Practice of Art Museums in the United States, by Theodore Lewis Low (1948).

Merchants and Masterpieces: The Story of the Metropolitan Museum of Art, by Calvin Tomkins.

Museum Masters and Their Influence, by Edward P. Alexander (1983).

Palaces for the People: A Social History of the American Art Museum, by Nathaniel Burt (1977).

A Plan for a New Museum: The Kind It Will Profit a City to Maintain, by John Cotton Dana (1920).

Publishing

American Journalism: A History, 1690–1960, by Frank Luther Mott (1962).

The Book in America: A History of the Making and Selling of Books in the United States, by Hellmut Lehmann-Haupt et al. (1951).

The Brothers Harper: A Unique Publishing Partnership and Its Impact upon the Cultural Life of America from 1817 to 1853, by Eugene Exman (1965).

The Colonial Printer, by Lawrence C. Wroth (1938).

A History of Book Publishing in the United States, by John Tebbel (1972).

The History of Printing in America, With a Bibliography of Printers, by Isaiah Thomas (2 vols., 1874).

Joseph Pulitzer and the New York World, by George Juergens (1966).

Radio and Television

A History of Broadcasting in the United States, by Erik Barnouw (3 vols., 1966–1970).

To Serve the Public Interest: Educational Broadcasting in the United States, by Robert J. Blakely (1979).

Religious Organizations

The Administration of an Institutional Church: A Detailed Account of the Operation of St. George's Parish in the City of New York, by George Hodges and John Reichert (1906).

Soldiers Without Swords: The History of the Salvation Army in the United States, by Herbert A. Wisbeym, Jr. (1955).

Social Settlements

Spearheads for Reform: The Social Settlements and the Progressive Movement, 1890–1914, by Allen F. Davis (1967).

Twenty Years at Hull House (1910) and *The Second Twenty Years at Hull House* (1930) by Jane Addams.

Youth Organizations

Muscles and Morals: Organized Playgrounds and Urban Reform, 1880–1920, by Dominick Cavallo (1981).

Future Farmers of America.

Future Homemakers of America.

Girl Scouts of the U.S.A.

Jewish Community Centers of North America.

National Board of YMCA.

National Board YWCA of USA.

National 4-H Council.

Young Men's/Young Women's Hebrew Association.

18. EDUCATORS

Biographies (by subject)

Bronson Alcott, Teacher, by Dorothy McCuskey (1940); *A Critical Estimate of the Educational Theories and Practices of A. Bronson Alcott,* by George E. Haefner (1937).

Samuel C. Armstrong, by Edith A. Talbot (1904, reprinted 1969).

Henry Barnard, by Robert B. Downs (1977).

Catherine Beecher: A Study in Domesticity, by Kathryn Kish Sklar (1976).

Alfred A. Binet, by Theta H. Wolf (1973).

John Dewey, by Richard J. Bernstein (1981); *John Dewey and American Democracy*, by Robert B. Westbrook (1991); *John Dewey: His Thought & Influence*, John Blewett, ed. (1973); *John Dewey in Perspective*, by George R. Geiger (1974).

Life and Works of Christopher Dock, by Martin G. Brumbaugh (1908).

W. E. B. Du Bois, by Patricia & Frederick McKissack (1990); *W. E. B. Du Bois: Negro Leader in a Time of Crisis*, by Francis L. Broderick (1959).

Timothy Dwight, by Kenneth Silverman (1969); *Tim-*

othy Dwight, 1752–1817: A Biography, by Charles E. Cunningham (1942).

Jonathan Edwards: The Narrative of a Puritan Mind, by Edward H. Davidson (1968).

Charles W. Eliot: Founder of Harvard University, 1869–1909, by Henry James (2 vols., 1930).

John Eliot: "Apostle to the Indians," by Ola Elizabeth Winslow (1968).

Life of the Rev. Jos. Emerson, by Ralph Emerson [a second cousin; q.v.] (1834); *The Story of Byfield: A New England Parish*, by J. L. Ewell (1904).

[Ralph Waldo] *Emerson on Education*, by Howard Mumford Jones (1966).

Memoirs of Rev. Charles G. Finney, Written by Himself (1876), by Charles Grandison Finney; "The Life of Charles Grandison Finney," by James E. Johnson (doct. th., 1959).

Father Flanagan of Boys Town, by Fulton Oursler and Will Oursler (1949).

The Autobiography of Benjamin Franklin, Leonard W. Labaree, Ralph L. Ketcham, Helen C. Boatfield, and Helen H. Fineman, eds. (1964);

Benjamin Franklin, by Carl Van Doren (1938).

Friedrich Froebel, by Robert B. Downs (1978).

Charlotte Perkins Gilman: The Making of a Radical Feminist, 1860–1896, by Mary A. Hill (1980).

Samuel Griswold Goodrich, Creator of Peter Parley: A Study of His Life and Work, by Daniel Roselle (1968).

Luther Halsey Gulick, 1865–1918, by Ethel Josephine Dorgan (1934).

G. Stanley Hall: A Biography of a Mind, by Lorine Pruette (1926); *G. Stanley Hall: The Psychologist as Prophet*, by Dorothy Ross (1972).

[William Rainey] *Harper's University: The Beginnings; A History of the University of Chicago*, by Richard J. Storr (1966).

Yankee Teacher: The Life of William Torrey Harris, by Kurt F. Leidecker (1946).

Joseph Henry: His Life and Work, by Thomas Coulson (1950).

Autobiography of Thomas Jefferson, with an introduction by Dumas Malone (1959); *Jefferson and His Time*, by Dumas Malone (6 vols., 1948–81); *Thomas Jefferson & the New Nation: A Biography*, by Miller D. Peterson (1970).

William Heard Kilpatrick, by Samuel Tanenbaum (1951).

Seaman A. Knapp: Schoolmaster of American Agriculture, by Joseph Cannon Bailey (1945).

Mary Lyon, by Evelyn Banning (1965); *The Power of Christian Benevolence, Illustrated in the Life and Labors of Mary Lyon*, by Edward Hitchcock (1852).

Breadth and Depth in Economics: Fritz Machlup — The Man and His Ideas, Jacob S. Dreyer, ed. (1978).

Anne Sullivan Macy, by Nella Braddy (1933); *Teacher: Anne Sullivan*, by Helen Keller (1955, revised ed. 1966).

Horace Mann: A Biography, by Jonathan Messerli (1972).

Cotton Mather: The Puritan Priest, by Barrett Wendell (1891, 1963).

Increase Mather: The Foremost American, by Kenneth B. Murdock (1925).

McGuffey and His Readers: Piety, Morality, and Education in Nineteenth Century America, by John H. Westerhoff III (1978); *William Holmes McGuffey: The Schoolmaster to Our Nation*, by Benjamin F. Crawford (1963).

Margaret Mead: A Life, by Jane Howard (1984).

Dwight L. Moody: American Evangelist, 1837–1899, by James F. Findlay, Jr. (1969).

John Morgan: Continental Doctor, by William J. Bell, Jr. (1965).

John R. Mott, 1865–1955: A Biography, by C. Howard Hopkins (1951).

Eliphalet Nott, by Codman Hislop (1971); *The Old Time College President*, by G. P. Schmidt (1930).

The Life of Robert Owen Written by Himself (1857–1858), by Robert Owen; *Robert Owen's American Legacy*, Donald E. Pitzer, ed. (1972).

Robert Dale Owen, by Richard William Leopold (1940); *Threading My Way: Twenty-Seven Years of Autobiography*, by Robert Dale Owen (1874).

Walter Hines Page: The Southerner as American, 1855–1918, by John Milton Cooper, Jr. (1977).

Paine, by David Freeman Hawke (1974); *Tom Paine and Revolutionary America*, by Eric Foner (1976).

Colonel Francis W. Parker: The Children's Crusader, by Jack K. Campbell (1967).

The Life of Francis Daniel Pastorius, by Marion Dexter Learned (1908).

A Brief Sketch of George Peabody, and a History of the Peabody Education Fund Through Thirty Years, by J. L. M. Curry (1898).

The Peabody [Elizabeth and Mary] *Sisters of Salem*, by Louise Tharp (1950).

Charles Willson Peale, by Charles Colman Sellers (2 vols., 1947).

William Penn As Social Philosopher, by Edward C. O.

Beatty (1939); *William Penn's "Holy Experiment": The Founding of Pennsylvania, 1681–1701*, by Edwin B. Bronner (1962).

[Johann Heinrich] *Pestalozzi and American Education*, by Thomas A. Barlow (1977).

John D. Pierce: Founder of the Michigan School System, A Study of Education in the Northwest, by Charles O. Hoyt and R. Clyde Forst (1905).

[Richard Henry Pratt] *The Red Man's Moses*, by E. G. Eastman (1935).

[Franklin D.] *Roosevelt: The Lion and the Fox*, by James MacGregor Burns (1956); *FDR*, by Kenneth S. Davis (3 vols. 1985–86).

The Autobiography of Benjamin Rush, George W. Corner, ed. (1948); *Benjamin Rush: Philosopher of the American Revolution*, by Donald J. D'Elia (19740; *Benjamin Rush and His Services to American Education*, by Harry G. Good (1918); *Benjamin Rush: Physician and Citizen, 1746–1813*, by Nathan G. Goodman (1934).

[Edward A. Sheldon] *Oswego: Fountainhead of Teacher Education*, by Dorothy Rogers (1961).

William Smith: Educator and Churchman, by Albert Frank Gegenheimer (1943).

The Life and Writings of Jared Sparks, by H. B. Adams (1893).

Herbert Spencer on Education, F. A. Cavanagh, ed. (1932); *Herbert Spencer: The Evolution of a Sociologist*, by J. D. Y. Peel (1971); *The Social and Political Thought of Herbert Spencer*, by David Wiltshire (1987).

Doctor [Benjamin] Spock: Biography of a Conservative Radical, by Lynn Z. Bloom (1972).

Life of Harriet Beecher Stowe, Compiled from Her Letters and Journals, by Charles Edward Stowe (1891).

William Graham Sumner, by Harris E. Starr (1925).

John Swett, the Biography of an Educational Pioneer, by W. G. Carr (1933).

A Memorial Discourse on the Life and Services of the Reverend Henry Philip Tappan, by Henry S. Frieze (1882).

[Lewis] *Terman and the Gifted*, by May V. Seagoe (1975).

[Sylvanus Thayer] *Duty, Honor, Country: A History of West Point*, by Stephen E. Ambrose (1966).

Isaiah Thomas: Printer, Patriot and Philanthropist, 1749–1832, by Clifford K. Shipton (1948).

George Ticknor and the Boston Brahmins, by David B. Tyack (1967).

Asa Turner: A Home Missionary Patriarch and His Times, by George F. Magoun (1889).

John Heyl Vincent: A Biographical Sketch, by Leon H. Vincent (1925).

Booker T. Washington, by Louis R. Harlan (1972); *Booker T. Washington*, by Basil J. Mathews (1948); *Booker T. Washington*, by Emmett J. Scott and Lyman B. Stowe (1916); *Up From Slavery, An Autobiography*, by Booker T. Washington (1989; first published 1901).

Isaac Watts: His Life and Works, by Arthur Paul Davis (1943).

Francis Wayland: A Neglected Pioneer of Higher Education, by William G. Roelker (1944); *Francis Wayland: Political Economist as Educator*, by Theodore Rawson Crane (1962).

Noah Webster, by John S. Morgan (1975); *Noah Webster: Pioneer of Learning*, by Ervin C. Shoemaker (1936); *Noah Webster: Schoolmaster to America*, by Harry R. Warfel (1936).

Eleazar Wheelock, by J. D. McCallum (1939, reprinted 1969).

William H. Welch and the Rise of Modern Medicine, by Donald Fleming (1954).

The Problems, Policies and Achievement of Calvin H. Wiley, by H. C. Renegar (1925).

Emma Willard, Daughter of Democracy, by Alma Lutz (1964).

John Witherspoon Comes to America, by L.H. Butterfield (1953); *The Works of the Rev. John Witherspoon* (4 vols., 1802).

General Reference Works

Biographical Dictionary of American Educators.

The Classless Profession: American Schoolmen in the Nineteenth Century, by Paul H. Mattingly (1975).

Dictionary of American Biographies.

Founders: Innovators in Education, 1830–1980, by Ernest Stabler (1980).

Great Educators of Three Centuries: Their Work and Its Influence on Modern Education, by Frank P. Graves (1971).

Great Women Teachers, by Alice Fleming (1965).

Leaders in American Education, Robert J. Havighurst (1971).

Notable American Women.

Pioneers of Women's Education in the United States, by Willystine Goodsell (1970).

The Social Ideas of American Educators, by Merle Curti (1935).

19. ELEMENTARY EDUCATION

Administration

Educational Administration: An Introduction, by Ralph B. Kimbrough and Michael Y. Nunnery (1976).

The Effective Principal: Perspective on School Leadership, by Arthur Blumberg and William Greenfield (1986).

The Elementary Principal's Handbook: A Guide to Effective Action, by Larry W. Hughes and Gerald C. Ubben (1989).

Elementary School Organization and Administration, by Henry J. Otto and David C. Sanders (1964).

Handbook of Educational Administration: A Guide for the Practitioner, by Emery Stoops et al. (1975).

Introduction to Educational Administration, by Roald F. Campbell et al. (1977).

Legal Handbook for Educators, Patricia A. Hollander (1978).

Minimum Competency Testing, by Rodney P. Riegel and Irvin J. Lehman (1980).

Predicting School Enrollments, by Roscoe C. Brown, Jr. (1961).*The Laboratory School: Its Rise and Fall*, by William Van Til (1969).

Multicultural Education in Western Societies, James A. Banks and James Lynch, eds. (1986).

Promotion or Failure for the Elementary School Pupil? by Carleton M. Saunders (1941).

National Association of Elementary School Principals.

Curriculum Planning and Evaluation

The Elementary School Handbook: Making the Most of Your Child's Education, by Joanne Oppenheim (1989).

How to Pick a Perfect Private School, by Harlow G. Unger (1993).

James Madison Elementary School, A Curriculum for American Students, by William J. Bennett (1988).

"What Did You Learn in School Today?": A Parent's Guide for Evaluating Your Child's School, by Harlow G. Unger (1991).

Instruction

The Child from Five to Ten, by Arnold L. Gesell et al. (1977).

Classroom Behavior, by Don Bushnell, Jr. (1973).

A Handbook for Elementary School Teachers, by Kenneth H. Hoover and Paul M. Hollingsworth (1978).

How to Measure Readability, by W. B. Gray, Jr. (1975).

Multicultural Education: A Handbook of Activities, Information and Resources, by Pamela L. Tiedt and Iris M. Tiedt (1986).

Multicultural Education: A Teacher's Guide to Content and Process, by Hilda Hernandez (1989).

School Readiness, by Francis L. Ilg, Louise B. Ames et al. (1972).

The Self-Contained Classroom, Edith R. Snyder, ed. (1960).

Storytelling: Art and Technique, by Augusta Baker and Ellin Greene (1987).

Teaching and Learning in the Elementary School, by John Jarolimek and Clifford D. Foster (1985).

Kindergarten

Play and Education, by Otto Weininger (1979).

Play as Exploratory Learning, Mary Reilly, ed. (1974).

ReQuest in Prereading Activities for Content Area Reading and Learning, by David W. Moor, John E. Readance, and Robert J. Rickelman (1982).

Multicultural Education

Multicultural Education: A Handbook of Activities, Information and Resources, by Pamela L. Tiedt and Iris M. Tiedt (1986).

Multicultural Education: A Teacher's Guide to Content and Process, by Hilda Hernandez (1989).

School Subjects

The Arts:

The Art Teacher's Resource Book, by Leslie A. Baker (1979).

Creative Dance in the Primary School (1975), by Joan Russel.

Finger Painting: An Outline of Its Origins and History, by Francis R. Fast (1945).

Music in the Elementary School, by Robert E. Nye and Vernice T. Nye (1977).

Foreign Languages:

Foreign Language in the Elementary School, by Theodore Andersson (1969).

Foreign Languages in Elementary School, by Marguerite Erikson, et al. (1964).

The Language Laboratory and Language Learning, by Julian Dakin (1972).

Teaching Modern Languages, by David Webb (1974).

Language Arts:

Effective Communication: Language Arts Instruction in the Elementary School, by John F. Savage (1977).

An Experience-Based Approach to Language and Reading, Carl Braun and Victor Froese, eds. (1977).

The Language Arts: Teaching and Learning in the Elementary School, by Kean and Carl Personke (1976).

Language Skills in Elementary Education, by Paul S. Anderson and Diane Lapp (1979).

Teaching Language Arts, by Carole Cox (1988).

Teaching the Language Arts in the Elementary School, by Martha Dallman (1976).

Mathematics:

Cognitive Science and Mathematics Education, Alan Schoenfeld, ed. (1987).

Creative Teaching of Mathematics in the Elementary School, by Alvin M. Westcott (1978).

Elementary School Mathematics: Teaching the Basic Skills, by William Zlot (1976).

Mathematical Problem Solving, by Alan Schoenfeld (1985).

A Metric Handbook for Teachers, Jon L. Higgins, ed. (1974).

Successful Problem Solving Technique, by Carole E. Greenes et al. (1977).

Teaching Children Mathematics by Hunter Ballew (1973).

Teaching Modern Mathematics in the Elementary School, by Howard Fehr and Jo McKeeby Phillips (1967).

Media Center Skills:

The School Media Center: A Book of Readings, Pearl L. Ward and Robert Beacon, eds. (1973).

The Teaching Role of the School Media Specialist, by Kay E. Vandergroft (1979).

Reading:

Correction Reading Techniques for the Classroom Teacher, by Joan P. Gipe (1987).

Developmental Reading, K-8, by Daniel R. Hittleman (1988).

Directing Reading Maturity as a Cognitive Process, by Russell G. Stauffer (1969).

Direct Instruction Reading, by D. Carnine and J. Silbert (1979).

Distar Reading, by Siegfried Engelmann and Elaine C. Bruner (1977).

Helping Children Learn to Read, by Patrick J. Finn (1985)

How to Increase Reading Ability, by Albert J. Harris and Edward R. Sipay (1985).

Literacy: Reading the Word and the World, by Paolo Freire and Donaldo Macedo (1987).

The Management of Meaning, by Charles E. Osgood et al. (1957).

Principles and Practices of Teaching Reading, by Arthur W. Heilman, Timothy R. Blair, and William H. Rupley (1986).

Reading Comprehension: New Directions for Classroom Practice, by John D. McNeil (1987).

Reading: Foundations and Instructional Strategies, Pose Lamb and Richard Arnolds., eds. (1976).

Reading Improvement in the Elementary School, by Donald C. Cushenbery (1969).

Reading Instruction, by Barbara D. Stoodt (1989).

Semantic Mapping: Classroom Application, by Joan E. Heimlich and Susan D. Pittelman (1986).

Stages of Reading Development, by Jeanne Chall (1983).

The Story of the Initial Teaching Alphabet, by Maurice Harrison (1964).

Strategies of Reading in the Elementary School, by Clifford L. Bush and Mildred H. Huebner (1979).

Teaching Them to Read, by Dolores Durkin (1989).

Teaching Reading, by Estill Alexander, Jr., et al. (1979).

Teaching Reading in the Elementary School, by Eldon K. Ekwall and James L. Shanker (1989).

Teaching Reading in Today's Elementary Schools, by Paul C. Burns, Betty D. Roe, and Elinor P. Ross (1984).

Teaching Reading to Every Child, by Diane Lapp and James Flood (1978).

Teaching Reading Vocabulary, by D. D. Johnson and P. D. Pearson (1984).

The Writing Road to Reading, by Ronalda B. Spalding and Walter T. Spalding (1969).

Science:

Building Bridges, The American Chemical Society.

Teaching Children Science, by Joseph Abruscato (1988).

Teaching Elementary Science, by William K. Esler (1977).

Teaching Science through Discovery, by Arthur A. Carin and Robert B. Sund (1975).

Science Research Associates, Chicago, Illinois.

Social Studies:

Elementary and Middle School Social Studies, by David T. Naylor and Richard A. Diem (1987).

The Social Studies, Howard D. Mehlinger and O. L. Davis, eds. (1981).

Social Studies for Children in a Democracy: Recent Trends and Developments, by John U. Michaelis (1976).

Special Education:

Exceptional Children: Introduction to Special Education, by Daniel P. Hallahan and James M. Kauffman (1988).

An Introduction to Special Education, William H. Berdine and A. Edward Blackhurst, eds. (1985).

The Learning Disabled Child, by Sylvia Farnham-Diggory (1992).

Making the Best of Schools, by Jeannie Oakes & Martin Lipton (1990).

The Misunderstood Child: A Guide for Parents of Learning Disabled Children, by L. B. Silver (1988).

No Easy Answers: The Learning Disabled Child, by S. L. Smith (1987).

The Role of the Special Education Paraprofessional, by Greg H. Firth (1982).

The School-Smart Parent, by Gene L. Maeroff (1989).

The Special Education Handbook: A Comprehensive Guide for Parents and Educators, by Kenneth Shore (1986).

Writing:

Spelling Trends, Content, and Methods, by Ruel A. Albred (1984).

What's Whole in Whole Language? by Kenneth Goodman (1986).

Whole Language: Theory in Use, by Judith Newman (1985).

Writing Centers in the Elementary Schools, by Duane R. Tovey (1979).

20. EQUAL RIGHTS IN EDUCATION

Affirmative Discrimination: Ethnic Inequality and Public Policy, by Nathan Glaser (1975).

Bakke and the Politics of Equality: Friends and Foes in the Classroom of Litigation, by Timothy J. O'Neill.

Education and the American Indian: The Road to Self-Determination Since 1928, by Margaret C. Stasz (1977).

An Even Chance, N.A.A.C.P. Legal Defense and Educational Fund, Inc. (1971).

Federal Equal Employment Opportunity, by David H. Rosenbloom (1977).

Higher Education for American Democracy: A Report of the President's Commission on Higher Education (5 vols., 1948), Harper Brothers, New York.

The Integration of American Schools, by Norene Harris et al. (1975).

The Making of Massive Resistance: Virginia's Politics of Public School Desegregation, 1954–1956, by Robbins L. Gates (1964).

Simple Justice: A History of "Brown v. Board of Education" and Black America's Struggle for Equality, by Richard Kluger (1975).

To Secure These Rights: The Report of the President's Committee on Civil Rights (1947), U.S. Government Printing Office.

Twenty Years After Brown: A Report of the United States Commission on Civil Rights (1977).

National Association for Equal Opportunity in Higher Education.

21. EXTRACURRICULAR ACTIVITIES (NONATHLETIC)

Baird's Manual of American College Fraternities, National Interfraternity Council, Indianapolis, Indiana (published periodically)

The College Fraternity and Its Modern Role, by J. Robson (1966).

Fundamentals of Recreation, by Thomas S. Yukic (1970).

Implementing Field Experience Education, John Duley, ed. (1974).

Intramural Administration: Theory and Practice, James A. Peterson, ed. (1976).

Managing the Student Yearbook, by Jim Nelson black (1983).

A Teacher's Handbook for Study Outside the Classroom, by Shirley A. Brehm (1969).

Yearbook Planning, Editing, and Production, by N. S. Paterson (1976).

22. FEDERAL AID TO EDUCATION

Administering the National Defense Education Act, by Sidney C. Sufrin (1963).

A Decade of Federal Antipoverty Programs, by Robert H. Haveman (1977)

Practitioner's Guide to School Business Management, by John Greenhalgh (1978).

Scholars, Dollars, and Bureaucrats, by Charles E. Finn, Jr. (1978).

National Science Foundation.

Student Loan Marketing Association.

U.S. Department of Agriculture.

U.S. Department of Defense.

U.S. Department of Education.

U.S. Department of Health and Human Services.

U.S. Department of Labor.

23. GIFTED EDUCATION

Academic Acceleration of Gifted Children, by Eric D. Jones (1991.

The Basic SOI Manual, by Mary N. Meeker, Robert Meeker, and Gayle Roid (1984).

"Curriculum-Based Programs for the Gifted," by Byron L. Barrington, *Education* (Spring, 1986).

Different by Design: The Context and Character of Three Magnet Schools, by May Haywood Metz (1986).

Educating the Gifted: Acceleration and Enrichment, by William C. George et al. (1979).

Education of the Gifted and Talented, by Gary A. Davis and Sylvia B. Rimm (1989).

Genetic Studies of Genius: Mental and Physical Traits of a Thousand Gifted Children, by Lewis Terman et al. (1925), *Gifted Child Grows Up* (1947) and *The Gifted Group at Midlife* (1959), by John C. Flanagan et al. [a three-part longitudinal study].

The Gifted and the Talented: Their Education and Development, A. Harry Passow, ed. (1979).

Giftedness, Conflict, and Underachievement, by Joanne R. Whitmore (1980).

High School, by Ernest L. Boyer (1983).

The Hurried Child, by David Elkind (1988).

Linking America's Schools and Colleges, by Franklin Wilbur, and Leo M. Lambert (1991).

National Excellence: A Case for Developing America's Talent, U.S. Department of Education report (1993).

"*Odyssey of the Mind*" *Program Handbook: Instructional Manual for Teams and Coaches*, by C. Samuel Micklus and Carole Micklus (1989).

Studies in Giftedness, R. Sternbery and J. Davidson, eds. (1984).

Teaching the Gifted Child, by James J. Gallagher (1985).

Way Beyond the I.Q., by Joy P. Guilford (1977).

National Association for Gifted Children, Washington, D.C.

Project Advance, Center for Instructional Development, Syracuse University.

24. HANDICAPPED

General

Adapted Physical Education, by Arthur S. Daniels and Evelyn A. Davies (1975).

Free Appropriate Education, The Law and Children with Disabilities, by H. Rutherford Turnbull III (1986).

Learning and Behavior Characteristics of Exceptional Children and Youth, by William I. Gardner (1977).

The Least Restrictive Alternative: Principles and Practices, H. Rutherford Turbull, III, ed. (1981).

Minimal Brain Dysfunction in Children, by P.H. Wender (1971).

P.L. 94–142: Impact on Schools, by Roberta Weiner (1985).

Psychopathology of Childhood, by Steven Schwartz and James H. Johnson (1985).

Readings in Career and Vocational Education for the Handicapped, Stephen J. Feldman, ed. (1979).

Special Physical Education: Adapted, Corrective, Developmental, by Hollis F. Fait (1978).

Workshops for the Handicapped in the United States: An Historical and Developmental Perspective, by Nathan Nelson (1971).

Council for Exceptional Children.

U.S. Department of Education, Bureau of Education for the Handicapped.

Hearing Disabilities

Educating the Deaf: Psychology, Principles, and Practices, by Donald F. Moores (1978).

A Handbook of Readings in Education of the Deaf and Postschool Implications, Irving S, Fusfeld, ed. (1967).

Sign Language of the Deaf: Psychological, Linguistic, and Sociological Perspectives, I. M. Schlesinger and Lila Namir, eds. (1978).

Mentally Retarded

Residential Facilities for the Mentally Retarded, Alfred A. Baumeister and Earl Butterfield, eds. (1970).

A History of the Care and Study of the Mentally Retarded, by Leo Kanner (1964).

Labeling the Mentally Retarded, by Jane Mercer (1973).

Visual Disabilities

Exceptional Children: Introduction to Special Education, by Daniel P. Hallahan and James M. Kauffman (1988).

The Handbook of Special Education: Research and Practices, Margaret C. Wang, M. C. Reynolds, and Herbert J. Walberg, eds. (1988).

The Teaching of Braille Reading, by Randall K. Harley et al. (1979).

The Lighthouse.

25. HIGHER EDUCATION

Administration

Handbook of College and University Administration, Asa S. Knowles, ed. (1970)

Leadership, Goals, and Power in Higher Education, by Barry M. Richman and Richard N. Farmer (1974).

Managing Today's University, by Frederick E. Baldeston (1874)

Presidents, Professors, and Trustees, by W. H. Cowley (1980).

Admissions and Financial Aid

Barron's Handbook of American College Financial Aid

Barron's Profiles of American Colleges

Bear's Guide to Earning Non-Traditional College Degrees, by John Bear (1988).

The College Blue Book: Scholarships, Fellowships, Grants and Loans, by Lorraine Mathies and Elizabeth I. Dixon (updated periodically).

College Cost Book, The College Board, Princeton, New Jersey (updated annually).

A Student's Guide to College Admissions, by Harlow G. Unger (1995).

Federal Student Aid Information Center, Washington, D.C.

Adult Education

The University Extension Movement, by W. S. Bittner (1920).

University Extension in the United States, by Louis E. Reber (1914).

Colleges of Education

Colleges of Education: Perspectives on Their Future, Charles W. Case and William A. Matthes, eds. (1985).

The Upper Division College, by Robert A. Altman (1970).

Directories

Barron's Profiles of American Colleges.

Cass and Birnbaum's *Comparative Guide to American Colleges*.

College Admissions Data Handbook, Wintergreen Orchard House.

The College Board's *College Handbook*.

Peterson's Guide to Undergraduate Study.

General

Academic Degree Structures: Innovative Approaches, by Stephen H. Spurr (1970).

Academic Turmoil: The Reality and Promise of Open Education, by Theodore L. Gross (1980).

American Degree Mills: A Study of their Operations and of Existing and Potential Ways to Control Them, by Robert H. Reid, American Council of Education (1959).

American Higher Education: A Documentary History, Richard Hofstadter and Wilson Smith, eds. (1961).

The American University: How It Runs, Where It Is Going, by Jacques Barzun (1969).

College Sports Inc., by Murray Sperber (1990).

Harper's University: The Beginnings; A History of the University of Chicago, by Richard J. Storr (1966).

Instructional Techniques in Higher Education, by Robert B. Kozma et al. (1978).

Joseph Lancaster and the Monitorial School Movement: A Documentary History, by Carl E. Kaestle (1973).

The Laboratory School: Its Rise and Fall, by William Van Til (1969).

A Metropolitan University, by Henry Mitchell MacCracken (1892).

The Multiversity: A Personal Report on What Happens to Today's Students at American Universities, by Nicholas von Hoffman (1966).

The Open University, by Walter Perry (1977).

The Qualified Student: A History of Selective College Admission in America, by Harold S. Wechsler (1977).

The Student in Graduate School, by James Harvey (1972).

The Tutorial System and Its Future, by Will G. Moore (1968).

The Uses of the University, by Clark Kerr (1963).

National Collegiate Athletic Association.

Public Education

The End of Education: The Experience of the City of New York with Open Enrollment and the Threat to Higher Education in America, by Geoffrey Wagner (1976).

The Evolution of the Community College, by Robert Palinchak (1973).

A General Pattern for American Public Higher Education, by T. R. McConnell (1962).

Right versus Privilege: The Open Admissions Experiment at the City University of New York, by David E. Lavin,

Richard D. Alba, and Richard A. Silberstein (1983).

The State University, Its Work and Problems: A Selection from Addresses Delivered between 1921 and 1923, by Lotus Delta Coffman (1934).

Women's Education

A Century of Higher Education for American Women, by Mabel Newcomer (1959).

In the Company of Educated Women: A History of Women and Higher Education in America, by Barbara Miller Solomon (1985).

26. HISPANICS

Chicanos in a Changing Society: From Mexican Pueblos to American Barrios in Santa Barbara and Southern California, 1848-1930, by Albert Camarillo (1979).

East Los Angeles: History of a Barrio, by Ricard Romo (1983).

La Familia: Chicano Families in the Urban Southwest, 1848 to the Present, by Richard Griswold del Castillo (1984).

The Great School Wars, New York City, 1805-1973: A History of the Public Schools as Battlefield of Social Change, by Diane Ravitch (1974).

Language in the Inner City: Studies in the Black Vernacular, by William Labov (1972).

Learning to Read in a Multicultural Society, by Catherine Wallace (1988).

Puerto Rican Americans: The Meaning of Migration to the Mainland, by Joseph P. Fitzgerald (1971).

Puerto Rico: A Political and Cultural History, by Raymond Carr (1983).

27. HISTORY OF EDUCATION

American Education [3 vols.]: *The Colonial Experience, 1607-1783* (1970); *The National Experience, 1783-1876* (1979); *The Metropolitan Experience, 1876-1980*, by Lawrence A. Cremin (1987).

The American Language: An Inquiry into the Development of English in the United States, Together with Supplements I and II, by H. L. Mencken (3 vols., 1936-1948).

Children in Urban Society: Juvenile Delinquency in Nineteenth-Century America, by Joseph M. Hawes (1971).

Children and Youth in America: A Documentary History, Robert H. Bremner, ed. (3 vols., 1970-1974).

The Development of Academic Freedom in the United States, by Richard Hofstadter and Walter P. Metzger (1955).

Historical Statistics of the United States: Colonial Times to 1970, U.S. Bureau of the Census, Government Printing Office, Washington, D.C. (1975).

A History of American Education, by H. G. Good (1968).

A History of American Education, by Harry G. Good and James D. Teller (1973).

History of American Education, by B. Edward McClellan and William J. Reese (1988).

A History of the Care and Study of the Mentally Retarded, by Leo Kanner (1964).

A History of Western Education, by James A. Bowen (3 vol., 1972-1983).

The History of Western Education, by William Boyd and Edmund J. King (1975).

The Little Red School House, by Agnes deLima (1942).

A Nation of Learners, by Walter Wood (1976).

Private Schools: From the Puritans to the Present, by Otto F. Kraushaar (1976).

Turning Points in American Educational History, by David Tyack (1967).

Adult Education

The Adult Education Movement in the United States, by Malcolm S. Knowles (1962).

The University Extension Movement, by W. S. Bittner (1920).

Colonial Education

American Education: The Colonial Experience, 1607-1783, by Lawrence A. Cremin (1970).

The Charity School Movement in Colonial Pennsylvania, by Samuel Edwin Weber (1905).

Child Life in Colonial Days, by Alice Morse Earle (1899).

The Cultural Life of the American Colonies, by Louis B. Wright (1957).

The Dutch Schools of New Netherland and Colonial New York, by William H. Kilpatrick (1912).

Early New England Schools, by Walter Herbert Small (1914).

Early Quaker Education in Pennsylvania, by Thomas Woody (1920).

Educational Legislation and Administration of the Colonial Governments, by Elsie W. Clews (1899).

The Evening School in Colonial America, by Robert Francis Seybolt (1925).

The Glorious Revolution in America, Michael G. Hall, Lawrence H. Leder, and Michael G. Kammen, eds. (1964).

Home Life in Colonial Days (1898) by Alice Morse Earle.

Intercolonial Aspects of American Culture on the Eve of the Revolution, by Michael Kraus (1957).

Literature and Education in Early Quakerism, by Luella M. Wright (1933).

Our Colonial Curriculum, 1607–1776, by Colyer Meriwether (1907).

The Puritan Pronaos: Studies in the Intellectual Life of New England (1936), by Samuel Eliot Morrison.

The Pursuit of Science in Revolutionary America, 1735–1789, by Brooke Hindle (1956).

Two Hundred Years of the S.P.G.: An Historical Account of the Society for the Propagation of the Gospel in Foreign Parts, 1701–1900, by C. F. Pascoe (1901).

Source Studies in American Colonial Education (1925), by Robert Francis Seybolt.

Curriculum

Curriculum: A History of the Undergraduate Course of Study Since 1636, by Frederick Rudolph (1977).

Historical Foundations of Music Education in the United States, by Lloyd F. Sunderman (1971).

Political Science in American Colleges and Universities, 1636–1900, by Anna Haddow (1939).

The Early Republic

American Education: The National Experience, 1783–1876, by Lawrence A. Cremin (1979).

The Educational Significance of the Early Federal Land Ordinances, by Howard Cromwell Taylor (1922).

The Educational Work of Thomas Jefferson, by Roy J. Honeywell (1931).

Essays on Education in the Early Republic, Frederick Rudolph, ed. (1965).

Federalists in Dissent: Imagery and Ideology in Jeffersonian America, by Linda K. Ferber (1970).

Journal & Letters of Philip Vickers Fithian, 1773–1774: A Plantation Tutor in the Old Dominion, Hunter Dickinson Farish, ed. (1943).

Liberalism and American Education in the Eighteenth Century, by Allen Oscar Hansen (1926).

Noah Webster: Schoolmaster to America, by Harry R. Warfel (1936).

On the Education of Youth in America, by Noah Webster (1790).

Educative Institutions (Nonacademic)

Foundations of the Public Library, by Jesse H. Shera (1949).

Palaces for the People: A Social History of the American Art Museum, by Nathaniel Burt (1977).

Twenty Years at Hull House (1910) and *The Second Twenty Years at Hull House* (1930) by Jane Addams.

Higher Education

American Higher Education: A Documentary History, Richard Hofstadter and Wilson Smith, eds. (1961).

Curriculum: A History of the American Undergraduate Curriculum Since 1636, by Frederick Rudolph (1978).

The Evolution of the Community College, by Robert Palinchak (1973).

The Founding of American Colleges and Universities Before the Civil War, by Donald G. Tewksbury (1932).

The Founding of Harvard College and *Harvard College in the Seventeenth Century*, by Samuel Eliot Morison (2 vols., 1936).

The G. I. Bill, the Veterans, and the Colleges, by Keith W. Olson (1974).

Government Policy and Higher Education: A Study of the University of the State of New York, 1784–1948, by Frank C. Abbott (1968).

Harper's University: The Beginnings; A History of the University of Chicago, by Richard J. Storr (1966).

Harvard College in the Seventeenth Century, by Samuel Eliot Morison (2 vols., 1936).

History of the College of New Jersey, from Its Origin in 1746 to the Commencement of 1854, by John Maclean (1877).

A History of Oberlin College from its Foundation Through the Civil War, by Robert Samuel Fletcher (1943).

Land-Grant Universities and Their Continuing Challenge, G. Lester Anderson, ed. (1976).

The National University: Enduring Dream of the USA, by David Madsen (1966).

The Old Time College President, by G. P. Schmidt (1930).

Princeton College During the Eighteenth Century, by Samuel Davies Alexander (1872).

Science and the Ante-Bellum American College, by Stanley M. Guralnick (1975).

The State Universities and Democracy, by Allan Nevins (1962).

The University of the State of New York: History of Higher Education in the State of New York, by Sidney Sherwood (1900).

History of the University of Pennsylvania, by Edward P. Cheyney (1940).

Princeton, 1746–1896, by Thomas Jefferson Wertenbaker (1946).

Problems in the Transition from Elite to Mass Higher Education, by Martin Trow (1972).

Progressive Education, From Arcady to Academe: A History of the Progressive Education Association, 1919–1955, by Patricia A. Graham (1967).

Scientific Thought in the American Colleges, 1638–1800, by Theodore Hornberger (1945).

The Scottish Universities and the Colleges of Colonial America, by George S. Pryde (1957).

The Separation of College and State: Columbia, Dartmouth, Harvard, and Yale, 1776–1876, by John S. Whitehead (1973).

Three Centuries of Harvard, by Samuel Eliot Morison (1936).

The Universities of Europe in the Middle Ages, by Hastings Rashdall (1936).

University Extension in the United States, by Louis E. Reber (1914).

Minority Education

Adventure in Giving: The Story of the General Education Board, by Raymond B. Fosdick (1962).

The American People, by Bernard A. Weisberger (1971)

John Eliot: "Apostle to the Indians," by Ola Elizabeth Winslow (1968).

The Evolution of the Negro College, by Dwight Oliver Wendell Holmes (1934).

The Founding of Howard University, by Walter Dyson (1921).

A History of Catholic Higher Education in the United States, by Edward J. Power (1958).

A History of the Councils of Baltimore: (1791–1884), Peter Guilday, ed. (1932).

Howard University: The First Hundred Years, 1876–1967, by Rayford W. Logan (1969).

Northern Schools, Southern Blacks, and Reconstruction: Freedmen's Education, 1862–75, by Ronald E. Butchart (1980).

Reading, 'Riting, and Reconstruction: The Education of Freedmen in the South, 1861–1870, by Robert C. Morris (1981).

Schools for All: The Blacks & Public Education in the South, 1865–1877, by William Preston Vaughn (1974).

Simple Justice: A History of "Brown v. Board of Education and Black America's Struggle for Equality, by Richard Kluger (1975).

Zion in America: The Jewish Experience from Colonial Times to the Present, by Henry L. Feingold (1974).

Professional Education

American Medical Education: The Formative Years, 1765–1910, by Martin Kaufman (1976).

The American Teacher: Evolution of a Profession in a Democracy, by Willard Elsbree (1939).

Engineering in American Society, 1850–1875, by Raymond H. Merritt (1969).

Historical Foundations of Music Education in the United States, by Lloyd F. Sunderman (1971).

History of Medicine in the United States, by Francis R. Packard (2 vols., 1931).

Learning to Heal: The Development of American Medical Education, by Kenneth M. Ludmerer (1985).

The Litchfield Law School, 1775–1833, by Samuel H. Fisher (1933).

Medical Education in the United States and Canada: A Report to the Carnegie Foundation for the Advancement of Teaching, by Abraham Flexner (1910).

Professional Lives in America: Structure and Aspiration, 1750–1850, by Daniel H. Calhoun (1965).

Training for the Public Profession of the Law, by Alfred Zantzinger Reed (1921).

William H. Welch and the Rise of Modern Medicine, by Donald Fleming (1954).

Public Education

The Evolution of an Urban School System: New York City, 1750–1850, by Carl F. Kaestle (1973).

Free Schools: A Documentary History of the Free School Movement in New York State, Thomas E. Finegan, ed. (1921).

The Great School Wars, New York City, 1805–1973: A History of the Public Schools as Battlefield of Social Change, by Diane Ravitch (1974).

Henry Barnard's American Journal of Education, AMS Press, New York, n.d..

History of the Public School Society of the City of New York, by William Oland Bourne (1870).

History of the State Education Department, by F. P. Graves (Vol. IX, of *History of the State of New York*, 10 vols., 1937).

In the Cause of True Education: Henry Barnard & Nineteenth Century School Reform, by Edith N. MacMullen (1991).

Practical Observations Upon the Education of the People, Addressed to the Working Classes and their Employers, by H. Brougham (1825).

Preschool Education: A Historical and Critical Study, by Ilse Forest (1927).

Public Education in the United States: A Study and Interpretation of American Educational History, by Edward P. Cubberly (1962).

The Republic and the School: Horace Mann on the Education of Free Men, Lawrence A. Cremin, ed. (1957).

Schooled to Order: A Social History of Public Schooling in the United States, by David Nasaw (1979).

Secondary Schools at the Turn of Century, by Theodore S. Sizer (1964).

The Shaping of the American High School, by Edward A. Krug (1964).

The Shaping of the American High School, 1920–1941 (1972), by Edward A. Krug.

The Transformation of the School: Progressivism in American Education, 1876–1957, by Lawrence A. Cremin (1961).

Religion and Education

Church Cooperation and Unity in America: A Historical Review, 1905–1930, by Samuel McCrea Cavert (1970).

Early Quaker Education in Pennsylvania, by Thomas Woody (1920).

Evolution and Religion in Education: Polemics of the Fundamentalist Controversy of 1922–1925, by Henry Fairfield Osborne (1826).

The Great Awakening: A History of the Revival of Religion in the Time of Edwards and Whitefield, by Joseph Tracy (1942).

The Ministry in Historical Perspectives, by H. Richard Niebuhr and Daniel D. Williams, et al. (1956).

Protestantism and the Pagan World: The First Half-Century of the American Board of Commissioners for Foreign Missions, 1810–1860, by Clifton Jackson Phillips (1969).

Religion and the American Mind from the Great Awakening to the Revolution, by Alan Heimert (1966).

Religion in the Development of American Culture, 1765–1840, by William Warren Sweet (1952).

A Religious History of the American People, by Sydney E. Ahlstrom (1972).

The Teaching Office in the Reformed Tradition: A History of the Doctoral Ministry, by Robert W. Henderson (1962).

The War on Modern Science: A Short History of the Fundamentalist Attacks on Evolution and Modernism, by Maynard Shipley (1927).

Teaching

The American Teacher: Evolution of a Profession in a Democracy, by Willard S. Ellsbree (1970).

The American Teacher: 1776–1976, by Merle B. Marks (1976).

The Classless Profession: American Schoolmen in the Nineteenth Century, by Paul H. Mattingly (1975).

Textbooks

American Primers, Indian Primers, Royal Primers, and Thirty-Seven Other Types of Non-New England Primers Issued Prior to 1830, by Charles F. Heartman (1935).

The Evolution of American Secondary School Textbooks, by John Nietz (1966).

Guardians of Tradition: American Schoolbooks of the Nineteenth Century, by Ruth Miller Elson (1964).

History of American Schoolbooks, by Charles Carpenter (1962).

History of the Horn-Book, by Andrew W. Tuer (1897).

The New England Primer: A History of Its Origin and Development with a Reprint of the Unique Copy of the Earliest Known Edition and Many Fac-Simile Illustrations and Reproductions, by Paul Leicester Ford (1897).

The New England Primer Issued Prior to 1830, by Charles F. Heartman (1934).

Old Textbooks, by John Nietz (1966).

Vocational Education

American Apprenticeship and Industrial Education, by Paul H. Douglas (1921).

American Education and Vocationalism: A Documentary History, Marvin Lazerson and W. Norton Grubb, eds. (1974).

The Enforcement of English Apprenticeship: A Study in Applied Mercantilism, 1563–1640, by Margaret Gay Davies (1940).

English Apprenticeship & Child Labor, by O. Jocelyn Dunlop (1912).

A History of Agricultural Education in the United States, 1785–1925, by Alfred Charles True (1929).

History of Vocational Guidance: Origins and Early Development, by John M. Brewer et al. (1942).

Household Manufactures in the United States, 1640–1860: A Study in Industrial History, by Rolla Milton Tryon (1917).

Vocational and Practical Arts Education: History, Development, and Principles, by Roy W. Roberts (1965).

Women's Education

A Century of Higher Education for American Women, by Mabel Newcomer (1959).

In the Company of Educated Women: A History of Women and Higher Education in America, by Barbara Miller Solomon (1985).

28. LEARNING THEORY AND INTELLIGENCE

Intelligence

Intelligence: Heredity and Environment, by Philip E. Vernon (1979).

Nature of Human Intelligence, by Joy P. Guilford (1968).

The Psychology of Intelligence, by Jean Piaget (1947).

Learning

The Affective Domain in Education, by Thomas A. Ringness (1975).

Associative Learning: A Cognitive Analysis, James G. Greeno et al. (1978).

Behavior and Evaluation (1978), by Jean Piaget.

The Cognitive-Developmental Basis of Human Learning, by Barry Gholson (1980).

Concepts in Learning, by William L. Mikulas (1974).

The Conditions of Learning, by Robert M. Gagne (1985).

The Development of Thought: Equilibrium of Cognitive Structures, by Jean Piaget (1977).

Essentials of Learning for Instruction, by R. M. Gagne (1974).

The Growth of Logical Thinking from Childhood to Adolescence, by Jean Piaget (1958).

An Introduction to Theories of Learning, by B. R. Herganhahn (1988).

Itard, Seguin, and Kephart: Sensory Education — A Learning Interpretation, by Thomas S. Ball (1971).

The Language and Thought of the Child, by Jean Piaget (1925).

Taxonomy of Educational Objectives: Handbook I, Benjamin S. Bloom et al. (1956).

Taxonomy of Educational Objectives: The Classification of Educational Objectives, Handbook II, by David R. Krathwohl et al. (1964).

29. MINORITY EDUCATION

American Judaism, by Nathan Glazer (1972).

The American People, by Bernard A. Weisberger (1971) (history of minorities).

Bilingual and ESL Classrooms, by Carlos J. Ovando and Virginia P. Collier (1985).

Bilingualism in Education, by Jim Cummins and Merrill Swain (1986).

A History of Catholic Higher Education in the United States, by Edward J. Power (1958).

A History of the Councils of Baltimore: (1791–1884), Peter Guilday, ed. (1932).

Human Variation: Races, Types and Ethnic Groups, by Stephen Molnar (1991).

The Indian in America, by Wilcomb E. Washburn (1975).

Jewish Education in the United States, Lloyd P. Gartner, ed. (1969).

Language in the Inner City: Studies in the Black Vernacular, by William Labov (1972).

Learning to Read in a Multicultural Society, by Catherine Wallace (1988).

The Melting Pot, by Israel Zangwill (1909).

Mirror of Language: The Debate on Bilingualism, by Kenji Hakuta (1986).

New England Frontier: Puritans and Indians, 1620–1675, by Alden T. Vaughan (1965).

Race and Races, by Richard A. Goldsby (1977).

The Reform Movement in Judaism, by David Philipson (1931).

The Savages of America: A Study of the Indian and the Idea of Civilization, by Roy Harvey Pearce (1953).

Zion in America: The Jewish Experience from Colonial Times to the Present, by Henry L. Feingold (1974).

The Educational Alliance, New York, New York.

30. PARENTS AND EDUCATION

Baby and Child Care, by Dr. Benjamin Spock (1946).

The Child from Five to Ten, by Arnold L. Gesell et al. (1977).

The Elementary School Handbook: Making the Most of Your Child's Education, by Joanne Oppenheim (1989).

How Does Your Child Grow and Learn? A Guide for Parents of Young Children, Missouri Department of Elementary and Secondary Education, Jefferson City, Missouri (1982).

How Parent-Teacher Conferences Build Partnerships, by Robert L. Canady and John T. Seyfarth (1979).

Parent Conferences in the Schools: Procedures for Developing Effective Partnership, by Stuart M. Losen and Bert Diament (1978).

Parent Education: Toward Parental Competence, by Evelyn Pickarts and Jean Fargo (1971).

Parent Effectiveness Training, by Peter H. Wyden (1970).

Parents and Teachers: A Resource Book for Home, School and Community Relations, by Doreen Croft (1979).

"What Did You Learn in School Today?"—A Parent's Guide for Evaluating Your Child's School, by Harlow G. Unger (1991).

National Congress of Parents and Teachers.

31. PEDAGOGY (TEACHING METHODS)

Classroom Skills

Ah Hah! The Inquiry Process of Generating and Testing Knowledge, by John A. McCollum (1978).

Classroom Teaching Skills, by James M. Cooper (1982).

Discussing Sex in the Classroom: Readings for Teachers, David R. Stronck, ed. (1982).

Imagery and Related Mnemonics Processes: Theories, Individual Differences, and Applications, by Mark A. McDaniel and Michael Pressley (1987).

Improving Marking and Reporting in Classroom Instruction, by Norman Edward Gronlund (1974).

Involving Students in Questioning (1976), by Francis P. Hunkins.

Cooperative Learning

An Experiment in Cross-Age Peer Instruction, by Barry Nelson (1979).

Learning Together and Alone, by David W. Johnson and Roger T. Johnson (1975).

Learning Together and Alone: Cooperative, Competitive, and Individualistic Learning, by D. W. Johnson and R. T. Johnson (1987).

Peer Teaching, by Lilya Wagner (1982).

The Peer Tutoring Handbook: Promoting Cooperative Learning, by Keith J. Topping (1988).

The Pros and Cons of Ability Grouping; Learning Together and Alone: Cooperative, Competitive and Individual-istic Learning, by D. W. Johnson and R. T. Johnson (1987).

Using Student Team Teaching, by Robert E. Slavin (1986).

Discipline

Classroom Behavior, by Don Bushnell, Jr. (1973).

Positive Classroom Discipline, by Frederic H. Jones (1987).

Preventing Classroom Discipline Problems, by Howard Seeman (1988).

Elementary School

The Child and the English Language Arts, by Mildred R. Donoghue (1979).

Developmental Reading, K-8, by Daniel R. Hittleman (1988).

A Handbook for Elementary School Teachers, by Kenneth H. Hoover and Paul M. Hollingsworth (1978).

Play and Education, by Otto Weininger (1979).

Play as Exploratory Learning, Mary Reilly, ed. (1974).

Principles and Practices of Teaching Reading, by Arthur W. Heilman, Timothy R. Blair, and William H. Rupley (1986).

Spelling Trends, Content, and Methods, by Ruel A. Albred (1984).

Storytelling: Art and Technique, by Augusta Baker and Ellin Greene (1987).

Teaching and Learning in the Elementary School, by John Jarolimek and Clifford D. Foster (1985).

Teaching Them to Read, by Dolores Durkin (1989).

Teaching Reading in Today's Elementary Schools, by Paul C. Burns, Betty D. Roe, and Elinor P. Ross (1984).

General

Aptitudes and Instructional Methods, by Lee J. Cronbach and Richard E. Snow (1977).

The Art of Teaching, by Gilbert Highet (1989).

The Audio-Tutorial Approach to Learning: Through Independent Study and Integrated Experiences, by S. N. Postlethwait (1969).

Characteristics and School Learning, by Benjamin Bloom (1982).

Creative Communication, by Lillian M. Logan et al. (1972).

The Development of Language, Jean Berko Gleason, ed. (1985).

Dialectics: A Controversy-Oriented Approach to the Theory of Knowledge, by Nicholas Rescher (1977).

Education and Learning to Think, by Lauren B. Resnick (1987).

Essentials of Learning for Instruction, by R. M. Gagne (1974).

Flunking Grades, by Lorrie Shephard and Mary Lee Smith (1988).

Fundamentals of Teaching with Audiovisual Technology, by Carlton W. H. Erickson and David H. Curl (1972).

A Guide to Programmed Instruction, by Jerome P. Lysaught and Clarence M. Williams (1963).

The Guide to Simulations/Games for Education and Training, Robert E. Horn and Ann Cleaves, eds. (1980).

A Guide to Teaching Practice, by Louis Cohen and Lawrence Manion (1991).

A Handbook of Computer-Based Training, by Christopher Dean and Quentin Whitlock (1988).

Handbook of Reception: Feeling and Hurting, Edward C. Carterette and Morton P. Friedman (1978).

Imagery and Related Mnemonics Processes: Theories, Individual Differences, and Applications, by Mark A. McDaniel and Michael Pressley (1987).

An Introduction to Teaching: A Question of Commitment, by Ralph E. Martin, Jr., George H. Wood, and Edward W. Stevens, Jr. (1988).

An Introduction to Theories of Learning, by B. R. Herganhahn (1988).

Learning How to Learn, by Bob Gowan and Joseph Novak (1984).

The Management of Meaning, by Charles E. Osgood et al. (1957).

The Mind's Eye, by Robert Sommer (1978).

Reading-Language Instruction: Innovative Practices, by Robert B. Ruddell (1974).

Sensitivity Training: The Scientific Understanding of Individuals, by Henry C. Smith (1973).

Successful Problem Solving Technique, by Carole E. Greenes et al. (1977).

Teacher in America, by Jacques Barzun (1945).

The Theory of Reinforcement Schedules, William N. Schoefeld, ed. (1970).

Team Teaching: Organization and Administration, by Leslie J. Chamberlain (1969).

The Timeless Way of Building, by Christopher Alexander (1979).

Higher Education

Instructional Techniques in Higher Education, by Robert B. Kozma et al. (1978).

Individualized Instruction

A Guide to Programming Instruction, by Jerome P. Lysaught and Clarence M. Williams; (1963).

How To Tutor, by Samuel L. Blumenfeld (1973).

Individualizing Education by Learning Contracts, Neal R. Berte, ed. (1975).

Individualizing Instruction, by Carol M. Charles (1980).

Learning Packets: New Approach to Individualizing Instruction, by Patricia S. Ward and E. Craig Williams (1979).

Programmed Instruction, by the National Society for the Study of Education.

Systems of Individualized Education, by Harriet Talmage (1975).

The Teacher and Individually Guided Instruction, by Edward J. Nussel et al. (1976).

Lesson Planning

Operant Conditioning Techniques for the Classroom, by T. Mark Ackerman (1972).

Planning for Effective Instruction, by Madeline Hunter and D. Russell (1980).

Questioning Strategies and Techniques, by Francis P. Hunkins (1972).

Semantic Mapping: Classroom Application, by Joan E. Heimlich and Susan D. Pittelman (1986).

The Skills of Teaching: Lesson Planning Skills, by Robert R. Carkhuff et al. (1978).

Strategic Questioning, by Ronald T. Hyman (1979).

Mastery Learning

Implementing Mastery Learning, by Thomas R. Guskey (1986).

Mastery Learning in Classroom Instruction, by James H. Block and Lorin W. Anderson (1975).

Schools, Society and Mastery Learning, James H. Block, ed. (1974).

Multicultural Education

Multicultural Education: A Handbook of Activities, Information and Resources, by Pamela L. Tiedt and Iris M. Tiedt (1986).

Multicultural Education: A Teacher's Guide to Content and Process, by Hilda Hernandez (1989).

Preschool

Play and Education, by Otto Weininger (1979).

Play as Exploratory Learning, Mary Reilly, ed. (1974).

ReQuest in Prereading Activities for Content Area Reading and Learning, by David W. Moor, John E. Readance, and Robert J. Rickelman (1982).

Secondary School

Fundamentals of Secondary Classroom Instruction, by Earl J. Montague (1987).

The Industrial Arts Teacher's Handbook: Techniques, Principles, and Methods, by Donald A. Maley (1978).

Secondary and Middle School Teaching Methods, by Leonard H. Clark and Irving S. Starr (1976).

The Schools-Within-A-School Program: A Modern Approach to Secondary Instruction and Guidance, by Robert D. Ramsey et al. (1965).

Value Clarification: A Handbook of Practical Strategies for Teachers and Students, by Sidney Simon et al. (1972).

Special Education

Mainstreaming: A Practical Approach for Teachers, by Judy W. Wood (1989).

Reading Instruction: Diagnostic Teaching in the Classroom, by Larry A. Harris and Carl B. Smith (1976).

The Role of the Special Education Paraprofessional, by Greg H. Firth (1982).

The Resource Teacher: A Guide to Effective Practice, by J. Lee Wiederholt (1978).

Subject Areas

Art:

The Art Teacher's Resource Book, by Leslie A. Baker (1979).

Language Arts:

Effective Communication: Language Arts Instruction in the Elementary School, by John F. Savage (1977).

Language Skills in Elementary Education, by Paul S. Anderson and Diane Lapp (1979).

Teaching Language Arts, by Carole Cox (1988).

Teaching the Language Arts in the Elementary School, by Martha Dallman (1976).

Mathematics and Arithmetic:

Arithmetic Teacher; Cognitive Science and Mathematics Education, Alan Schoenfeld, ed. (1987).

Creative Teaching of Mathematics in the Elementary School, by Alvin M. Westcott (1978).

Elementary School Mathematics: Teaching the Basic Skills, by William Zlot (1976).

Mathematical Problem Solving, by Alan Schoenfeld (1985).

A Metric Handbook for Teachers, Jon L. Higgins, ed. (1974).

Successful Problem Solving Technique, by Carole E. Greenes et al. (1977).

Teaching Children Mathematics by Hunter Ballew (1973).

Teaching Modern Mathematics in the Elementary School, by Howard Fehr and Jo McKeeby Phillips (1967).

Media Center Skills:

The Teaching Role of the School Media Specialist, by Kay E. Vandergroft (1979).

Modern Languages:

The Language Laboratory and Language Learning, by Julian Dakin (1972).

Teaching Modern Languages, by David Webb (1974).

Reading, Writing and Vocabulary:

Content Area Reading and Learning: Instructional Strategies, by Diane Lapp, James Flood, and Nancy Farnan (1989).

Correction Reading Techniques for the Classroom Teacher, by Joan P. Gipe (1987).

Direct Instruction Reading, by D. Carnine and J. Silbert (1979).

Distar Reading, by Siegfried Engelmann and Elaine C. Bruner (1977).

Helping Children Learn to Read, by Patrick J. Finn (1985).

How to Increase Reading Ability, by Albert J. Harris and Edward R. Sipay (1985).

Principles and Practices of Teaching Reading, by Arthur W. Heilman, Timothy R. Blair, and William H. Rupley (1986).

The Psychology of Reading, by Keith Rayner and Alexander Pollatsek (1989).

Reading: Foundations and Instructional Strategies, Pose Lamb and Richard Arnolds., eds. (1976).

Reading and Learning from Text, by Harry Singer and Dan Donlan (1989).

Reading and Study Skills, by John Langan (1989).

Reading Comprehension: New Directions for Classroom Practice, by John D. McNeil (1987).

Reading Instruction, by Barbara D. Stoodt (1989).

Strategies of Reading in the Elementary School, by Clifford L. Bush and Mildred H. Huebner (1979).

Teaching Reading, by Estill Alexander, Jr., et al. (1979).

Teaching Reading in the Elementary School, by Eldon K. Ekwall and James L. Shanker (1989).

Teaching Reading in Today's Elementary Schools, by Paul C. Burns, Betty D. Roe, and Elinor P. Ross (1984).

Teaching Reading to Every Child, by Diane Lapp and James Flood (1978).

Teaching Reading Vocabulary, by D. D. Johnson and P. D. Pearson (1984).

Teaching Them to Read, by Dolores Durkin (1989).

Theoretical Models and Processes of Reading, Harry Singer and Robert B. Ruddell, eds. (1985).

The Writing Road to Reading, by Ronalda B. Spalding and Walter T. Spalding (1969).

Science:

Teaching Children Science, by Joseph Abruscato (1988).

Teaching Elementary Science, by William K. Esler (1977).

Teaching Science through Discovery, by Arthur A. Carin and Robert B. Sund (1975).

Social Studies:

Teaching Strategies for the Social Studies: Inquiry, Valuing, and Decision Making, by James A. Banks and Ambrose A. Clegg (1985).

Writing:

Spelling Trends, Content, and Methods, by Ruel A. Albred (1984).

What's Whole in Whole Language? by Kenneth Goodman (1986).

Whole Language: Theory in Use, by Judith Newman (1985).

The Writing Road to Reading, by Ronalda B. Spalding and Walter T. Spalding (1969).

32. PHYSICAL EDUCATION AND ATHLETICS

Adapted Physical Education, by Arthur S. Daniels and Evelyn A. Davies (1975).

College Sports Inc., by Murray Sperber (1990).

Foundations of Physical Education, by Charles A. Bucher (multiple editions).

A History of Sport and Physical Education to 1900, Earle F. Ziegler, ed. (1973).

Movement Education, by Robert E. Gensemer (1979).

Planning Physical Education and Athletic Facilities in Schools, by Kenneth A. Penman (1977).

Special Physical Education: Adapted, Corrective, Developmental, by Hollis F. Fait (1978).

National Association of Intercollegiate Athletics, Kansas City, Missouri.

National Collegiate Athletic Association.

33. RELIGION AND EDUCATION

General

American Education, by Lawrence A Cremin (3 vols., 1970, 1979, 1987).

The Centennial History of the American Bible Society, by Henry Otis Dwight (1916).

Church Cooperation and Unity in America: A Historical Review, 1905–1930, by Samuel McCrea Cavert (1970).

Education in Religion and Morals, by George A. Coe (1904).

The Encyclopedia of Sunday Schools and Religious Education, John T. McFarland, Benjamin S. Winchester, R. Douglas Fraser, and J. William Butcher, eds. (3 vols., 1915).

Home Mission on the American Frontier with Particular Reference to the American Home Missionary Society, by Colin Brummitt Goodykoontz (1939).

The Melting Pot, by Israel Zangwill (1909).

The Ministry in Historical Perspectives, by H. Richard Niebuhr and Daniel D. Williams, et al. (1956).

Protestantism and the Pagan World: The First Half-Century of the American Board of Commissioners for Foreign Missions, 1810–1816, by Clifton Jackson Phillips (1969).

A Religious History of America, by Edwin Scott Gaustad (1966).

A Religious History of the American People, by Sydney E. Ahlstrom (1972).

Religion in the Development of American Culture, 1765–1840, by William Warren Sweet (1952).

Religion and the American Mind from the Great Awakening to the Revolution, by Alan Heimert (1966).

The Sunday School Movement, 1780–1917 and the American Sunday School Union, 1817–1917, by Edwin Wilbur Rice (1917).

The Uneasy Boundary: Church and State, by Dean M. Kelly and Richard D. Lambert (1979).

The World Sunday School Movement: The Story of a Broadening Mission, by Gerald E. Knoff (1979).

Religious Groups

Anglican:

Two Hundred Years of the S.P.G.: An Historical Account of the Society for the Propagation of the Gospel in Foreign Parts, 1701–1900, by C. F. Pascoe (1901).

Dutch Reformed:

The Dutch Schools of New Netherlands and Colonial New York, by William H. Kilpatrick (1912).

Evangelist:

The Administration of an Institutional Church: A Detailed Account of the Operation of St. George's Parish in the City of New York, by George Hodges and John Reichert (1906).

Church, State, and the American Indians: Two and a Half Centuries of Partnership in Missions Between Protestant Churches and Government, by R. Pierce Beaver (1966).

Evangelical Religion and Popular Education: A Modern Interpretation, by John McLeisch (1969).

The Great Awakening: A History of the Revival of Religion in the Time of Edwards and Whitefield, by Joseph Tracy (1842).

Modern Revivalism: Charles Grandison Finney to Billy Graham, by William G. McLoughlin, Jr. (1959).

Revivalism in America: Its Origin, Growth and Decline, by William Waren Sweet (1944).

Trumpets of Jubilee, by Constance Rourke (1927).

Fundamentalist Christian:

Bryan and Darrow at Dayton: The Record and Documents of the "Bible-Evolution Trial", Leslie H. Allen, Ed. (1925).

Evolution and Religion in Education: Polemics of the Fundamentalist Controversy of 1922–1925, by Henry Fairfield Osborne (1826).

Fundamentalism and American Culture: The Shaping of Twentieth-Century Evangelism, 1870–1925, by George M. Marsden (1980).

God's Choice: The Total World of a Fundamentalist Christian School, by Alan Peshkin (1986).

Living in the Shadow of the Second Coming, by Timothy P. Weber (1983).

The Roots of Fundamentalism: British and American Millenarianism, 1800–1930, by Ernest R. Sandeed (1970).

The War on Modern Science: A Short History of the Fundamentalist Attacks on Evolution and Modernism, by Maynard Shipley (1927).

Jewish:

Jewish Education in the United States, Lloyd P. Gartner, ed. (1978).

The Reform Movement in Judaism, by David Philipson (1931).

Methodist:

The History of American Methodism, Emory Stevens Buckle, ed. (3 vols., 1964).

Presbyterian:

The Scottish Universities and the Colleges of Colonial America, by George S. Pryde (1957).

Protestant (general):

The Big Little School: Sunday Child of American Protestantism, by Robert W. Lynn and Elliott Wright (1971).

The Protestant Church as a Social Institution, by H. Paul Douglass and Edmund deS. Brunner (1935).

The Shaping of Protestant Education: An Interpretation of the Sunday School and the Development of Protestant Educational Strategy in the United States, 1789–1860, by William Bean Kennedy (1966).

Puritan:

Children & Puritanism: The Place of Children in the Life and Thought of the New England Churches, by Sandford Fleming (1933).

Puritanism in America: New Culture in a New World, by Larzer Ziff (1973).

The Puritan Pronaos: Studies in the Intellectual Life of New England in the Seventeenth Century, by Samuel Eliot Morison (1936).

Quaker:

Early Quaker Education in Pennsylvania, by Thomas Woody (1920).

Literature and Education in Early Quakerism, by Luella M. Wright (1933).

Reformed (Calvinist):

The Teaching Office in the Reformed Tradition: A History of the Doctoral Ministry, by Robert W. Henderson (1962).

Roman Catholic:

Catholic Education in America, Neil G. McCluskey (1964).

A History of Catholic Higher Education in the United States, by Edward J. Power (1958).

A History of the Councils of Baltimore: (1791–1884), Peter Guilday, ed. (1932).

34. SECONDARY EDUCATION

Counseling

Counseling Students, by Preston L. Munter et al. (1988).

Fundamentals of Individual Appraisal: Assessment Techniques for Counselors, by Bruce Shertzer and James D. Linden (1979).

Group Counseling, by Merle M. Ohlsen (1977).

An Introduction to Guidance: The Professional Counselor, by E. L. Tolbert (1982).

Curriculum

Advanced Placement Course Description, by the College Entrance Examination Board.

Creative Dance in the Secondary School (1969), by Joan Russell.

James Madison High School, A Curriculum for American Students, by William J. Bennett (1987)

The Language Laboratory and Language Learning, by Julian Dakin (1972).

"What Did You Learn in School Today?": A Parent's Guide for Evaluating Your Child's School, by Harlow G. Unger (1991).

Middle School

Elementary and Middle School Social Studies, by David T. Naylor and Richard A. Diem (1987).

The Exemplary Middle School, by William M. Alexander and Paul S. George (1981)

The Middle School: A Bridge between Elementary and High Schools, by Sylvester Kohut, Jr. (1988).

Toward Adolescence: The Middle School Years, Mauritz Johnson, ed. (1980).

Multicultural Education

Multicultural Education: A Teacher's Guide to Content and Process, by Hilda Hernandez (1989).

Multicultural Education: A Handbook of Activities, Information and Resources, by Pamela L. Tiedt and Iris M. Tiedt (1986).

Public High Schools

Different by Design: The Context and Character of Three Magnet Schools, by May Haywood Metz (1986).

The High School, by William N. Alexander et al. (1971).

High School, A Report on Secondary Education in America, by Ernest Boyer (1983).

Mainstreaming: A Practical Approach for Teachers, by Judy W. Wood (1989).

Making Inequality: The Hidden Curriculum in High School Tracking, by James E. Rosenbaum (1976).

A Place Called School, by John I. Goodlad (1984)

Secondary Education: An Introduction, by David G. Armstrong and Thomas V. Savage (1983).

The School Media Center: A Book of Readings, Pearl L. Ward and Robert Beacon, eds. (1973).

The Schools-Within-A-School Program: A Modern Approach to Secondary Instruction and Guidance, by Robert D. Ramsey et al. (1965).

The Shaping of the American High School, by Edward A. Krug (1964).

The Shaping of the American High School, 1920–1941, by Edward A. Krug (1972).

Summer School: A New Look, by John W. Dougherty (1981).

National Association of Secondary School Principals.

Private High Schools

How to Pick a Perfect Private School, by Harlow G. Unger (1993).

Preparing for Power: America's Elite Boarding Schools, by Peter W. Cookson, Jr., and Caroline H. Persell (1985).

National Association of Independent Schools.

Student Affairs

The Student Council in the Secondary School, National Association of Secondary School Principals

National Association of Student Councils, Washington, D.C.

National Merit Scholarship Corporation, Evanston, Illinois.

The White House Commission on Presidential Scholars, Washington, D.C.

Teaching

Arithmetic Teacher; Cognitive Science and Mathematics Education, Alan Schoenfeld, ed. (1987).

The Art Teacher's Resource Book, by Leslie A. Baker (1979).

Instruction in Today's Middle and Secondary Schools, by Kenneth H. Hoover (1976).

Mathematical Problem Solving, by Alan Schoenfeld (1985).

A Metric Handbook for Teachers, Jon L. Higgins, ed. (1974).

The Professional Teacher's Handbook: A Guide for Improving Instruction in Today's Middle and Secondary Schools, by Kenneth H. Hoover (1976).

Science Teaching in the Secondary School: A Guide for Modernizing Instruction, by Alfred T. Colletee (1973).

Secondary School Reading Instruction: The Content Areas, by Betty D. Roe, Barbara D. Stoodt, and Paul C. Burns (1983).

Secondary and Middle School Teaching Methods, by Leonard H. Clark and Irving S. Starr (1976).

Successful Problem Solving Technique, by Carole E. Greenes et al. (1977)

Teaching Modern Languages, by David Webb (1974).

The Teaching Role of the School Media Specialist, by Kay E. Vandergroft (1979).

Vocational Education

The Neglected Majority, by Dale Parnell (1989).

35. SOCIAL PROBLEMS AND EDUCATION

AIDS

Alternative Learning Environments, Gary Coats, ed. (1974).

Centers for Disease Control.

Dropouts

The Dropout Prevention Handbook: A Guide for Administrators, Counselors, and Teachers, by Nancy C. Myll (1988).

Dropouts in America, by Andrew Hahn and Jacqueline Danzberger (1987).

Illiteracy

Adult Illiteracy in the United States: A Report to the Ford Foundation, by Carman St. John Hunter and David Harmon (1979).

Language in the Inner City: Studies in the Black Vernacular, by William Labov (1972).

Learning to Read in a Multicultural Society, by Catherine Wallace (1988).

Literacy: Reading the Word and the World, by Paolo Freire and Donaldo Macedo (1987).

Innumeracy

Innumeracy: Mathematical Illiteracy and Its Consequences, by John Allen Paulos (1989).

Juvenile Delinquency

Children in Urban Society: Juvenile Delinquency in Nineteenth-Century America, by Joseph M. Hawes (1971).

The Child Savers: Juvenile Justice Observed, by Peter S. Prescott (1981).

Explaining Delinquency and Drug Abuse, by Delbert S. Elliott (1984).

House of Refuge: Origins of Juvenile Reform in New York State, by Robert S. Pickett (1969).

Law Enforcement and the Youthful Offender, by Edward Eldefonso (1983).

Patterns of Juvenile Delinquency, by Howard B. Kaplan (1984).

Prisoner Education, by Marjorie Seashore (1976).

Parental Abuse

Alternative Learning Environments, Gary Coats, ed. (1974).

The Practice of Social Work in Schools, by Wendy G. Winters and Freda Easton (1983).

Henry Street Settlement, New York, New York.

Hull House Association, Chicago, Illinois.

Poverty

A Decade of Federal Antipoverty Programs, by Robert H. Haveman (1977).

Equal Educational Opportunity: More Promise That Progress, Institute for the Study of Educational Policy.

The Great Society's Poor Law: A New Approach to Poverty, by Sar A. Levitan (1969).

The Homeless, by Christopher Jencks (1994).

Project Head Start: A Legacy of the War on Poverty, Edward Zigler and Jeannette Valentine, eds. (1979).

The Right to Work, by Nels Anderson (1938).

Spending to Save: The Complete Story of Relief, by Harry L. Hopkins (1936).

Workers on Relief, by Grace Anderson (1939).

Racism and Bigotry

An American Dilemma: The Negro Problem and Modern Democracy, by Gunnar Myrdal (1944).

Human Variation: Races, Types and Ethnic Groups, by Stephen Molnar (1991).

The Nature of Prejudice, by Gordon W. Allport (1954).

The Retreat of Scientific Racism, by Elazar Barkan (1992).

Race and Races, by Richard A. Goldsby (1977).

Racism in the United States: An American Dilemma, David M. Reimers, ed. (1972).

Sexism

Sexism: New Issue in American Education, by Pauline Gough (1976).

School Vandalism

School Vandalism: Strategies for Prevention, by Michael D. Casserly, Scott A. Bass, and John R. Garrett (1980).

Substance Abuse

Alternative Learning Environments, Gary Coats, ed. (1974).
The Practice of Social Work in Schools, by Wendy G. Winters and Freda Easton (1983).
Centers for Disease Control.

Teenage Pregnancy

Alternative Learning Environments, Gary Coats, ed. (1974).
The Practice of Social Work in Schools, by Wendy G. Winters and Freda Easton (1983).
Henry Street Settlement, New York, New York.
Hull House Association, Chicago, Illinois.

Teenage Suicide

Suicide: Theory and Clinical Aspects, by L. D. Hankoff and Bernice Einsidler (1979).

Truancy

Truancy and School Phobias, by A. H. Denney (1974).
The Practice of Social Work in Schools, by Wendy G. Winters and Freda Easton (1983).

36. SPECIAL EDUCATION
Diagnosis of Learning Disabilities

Characteristics of Children's Behavior Disorders, by James M. Kaufman (1977).
Diagnosing Learning Disorders: A Neuropsychological Framework, by Bruce Pennington (1991).
Diagnosis and Remediation: Classroom and Clinic, by William H. Rupley and Timothy R. Blair (1983).
Diagnostic and Remedial Reading for Classroom and Clinic, by Robert M. Wilson and Craig J. Cleland (1989).
Reading Difficulties: Their Diagnosis and Correction, by Guy Bond and Miles Tinker (1979).
Orton Dyslexia Society.

Learning Disabilities (General)

Exceptional Children: Introduction to Special Education, by Daniel P. Hallahan and James M. Kauffman (1988).
The Handbook of Special Education: Research and Practices, Margaret C. Wang, M. C. Reynolds, and Herbert J. Walberg, eds. (1988).

Human Exceptionality, Society, School, and Family, by Michael L. Hardman, et al. (1987).
An Introduction to Special Education, William H. Berdine and A. Edward Blackhurst, eds. (1985).
The Learning Disabled Child, by Sylvia Farnham-Diggory (1992).
Making the Best of Schools, by Jeannie Oakes & Martin Lipton (1990).
Minimal Brain Dysfunction in Children, by P. H. Wender (1971).
The Misunderstood Child: A Guide for Parents of Learning Disabled Children, by L. B. Silver (1988).
No Easy Answers: The Learning Disabled Child, by S. L. Smith (1987).
The School-Smart Parent, by Gene L. Maeroff (1989).
The Special Education Handbook: A Comprehensive Guide for Parents and Educators, by Kenneth Shore (1986).

Learning Disabilities (Specific)

Aphasia, by Frederic L. Darley (1982).
Aphasia and Brain Organization, by Ivar Rewvang (1985).
Attention-Deficit Hyperactivity Disorder, by Russell Barkley (1990).
Dyslexia, Arthur L. Benton and David Pearl, eds. (1978).
Dyslexia: An Annotated Bibliography, by Martha M. Evans (1982).
The Epilepsy Fact Book, by Harry Sands and Frances C. Minters (1977).
Handbook of Speech Pathology and Audiology, by Lee Edward Travis (1971).
Hyperactivity: Current Issues, Research and Theory, by Dorothea Ross and Sheila Ross (1982).
Children: Learning and Attention Problems, by Paula J. Caplan (1979).
Reading, Writing, and Speech Problems in Children, by Samuel T. Orton (1937).
Speech, Language, and Hearing: Normal Processes, by Paul H. Skinner and Ralph L. Shelton (1978).
Speech Pathology, by William H. Perkins (1977).

Teaching and Remediation

Activities for Developing Auditory Perception, by Polly Behrmann (1975).
Classroom Behavior, by Don Bushnell, Jr. (1973).
Collaboration in Special Education: Children, Parents Teachers and the IEP [Individualized Education Program], by Carol Downs-Taylor and Eleanor M. Landon (1990).

Corrective Reading, by Miles V. Zintz (1977).

Developing Individualized Education Programs, by Edward D. Fiscus and Colleen J. Mandell (1983).

Exceptional Children: Introduction to Special Education, by Daniel P. Hallahan and James M. Kauffman (1988).

Exceptional Children: An Introductory Survey of Special Education, by William L. Heward and Michael D. Orlansky (1988).

Free Appropriate Public Education: The Law and Children with Disabilities, by H. Rutherford Turnbull III (1986).

Improving Student Learning Skills, by Martha Maxwell (1979).

Introduction to Diagnostic-Prescriptive Teaching and Programming, by John Stellern et al. (1976).

Learning Disabilities: Educational Strategies, by B. R. Gearhart (1988).

Mainstreaming: A Practical Approach for Teachers, by Judy W. Wood (1989).

The Organization and Management of the Resource Room: A Cookbook Approach, by Howard Drucker (1976).

Placing Children in Special Education: A Strategy for Equity, K. A. Heller, W. H. Holtzman, and S. Messick, eds. (1982).

Reading Problems: Assessment and Teaching Strategies, by Margaret A. Richek, Lynn K. List, and Janet W. Lerner (1989).

Remedial Teaching for Children with Specific Disability in Reading, Spelling, and Penmanship, by Anna Gillingham and Bessie Stillman (1968).

Remedial Techniques in Basic School Subjects, by Grace M. Fernald (1943).

The Remediation of Learning Disabilities, by Robert E. Valett (1990).

The Resource Teacher: A Guide to Effective Practice, by J. Lee Wiederholt (1978).

Special Children: An Integrative Approach, by Bernard G. Suran and Joseph V. Rizzo (1979).

Speech Correction, by Charles V. Riper (1963).

Stuttering: Theory and Treatment, by Marcel E. Wingage (1976).

Teaching Reading to Slow and Disabled Learners, by Samuel A. Kirk et al. (1978).

37. SPECIALIZED EDUCATION

General

The Culture of Professionalism: The Middle Class and the Development of Higher Education in America, by Burton J. Bledstein (1976).

But What If I Don't Want to Go to College: A Guide to Successful Careers through Alternative Education, by Harlow G. Unger (1992).

The Semi-Professions and Their Organization: Teachers, Nurses, Social Workers, Amitai Etzioni ed. (1969)

Professional Education in the United States (3 vols., a survey of American professional education in 1899–1900, prepared by the College Department, University of the State of New York, Albany)

Professional Lives in America: Structure and Aspiration, 1750–1850, by Daniel H. Calhoun (1965).

Specializations

Agriculture:

Agricultural Science and the Quest for Legitimacy: Farmers, Agricultural Colleges, and Experiment Stations, 1870–1890, by Alan I. Marcus (1985)

Colleges for Our Land and Times: The Land-Grant Idea in American Education, by Edward Danforth Eddy (1957).

A History of Agricultural Education in the United States, 1785–1925, by Alfred Charles True (1929)

The Reluctant Farmer: The Rise of Agricultural Extension to 1914, by Roy V. Scott (1970).

Art:

Contemporary Music Education, by Michael L. Mark (1978).

The Eclectic Curriculum in American Music Education: Contributions of Dalcroze, Kodaly, and Orff, by Beth Landis and Polly Carder (1972).

Fine Arts in America, by Joshua C. Taylor (1979).

Historical Foundations of Music Education in the United States, by Lloyd F. Sunderman (1971).

The Kodaly Method: Comprehensive Music Education from Infant to Adult, by Lois Choksy (1974).

Music Talks: Conversations with Musicians, by Helen Epstein (1987).

Business:

Business Education Yesterday, Today, and Tomorrow, Ruth B. Woolschlager and E. Edward Harris (1976).

Engineering:

Engineering in American Society, 1850–1875, by Raymond H. Merritt (1969).

Health Care:

Handbook of Health Professions Education, Christine H. McGuire, et al. (1983).

A History of Health Education in the United States, by R. Means (1962).
American Medical Association.

International:
The Fulbright Program: A History, by Francis J. Colligan (1970).
The Fulbright Program: A History, by Walter Johnson and Francis J. Colligan (1969)
International Education and Exchange, by Steven E. Deutsch (1970).
Experiment in International Living, Brattleboro, Vermont.

Law:
Great American Lawyers, William Draper Lewis, ed. (1909).
The Law at Harvard, by Arthur Sullivan (1967).
The Litchfield Law School, 1775–1833, by Samuel H. Fisher (1933).
Training for the Public Profession of the Law, by Alfred Zantzinger Reed (1921).
American Bar Association, Chicago, Illinois.

Medical:
American Medical Education: The Formative Years, 1765–1910, by Martin Kaufman (1976).
Learning to Heal: The Development of American Medical Education, by Kenneth M. Ludmerer (1985).
Medical Education in the United States and Canada: A Report to the Carnegie Foundation for the Advancement of Teaching, by Abraham Flexner (1910).
William H. Welch and the Rise of Modern Medicine, by Donald Fleming (1954).
American Medical Association.

Military:
Classrooms in the Military: An Account of Education in the Armed Forces of the United States, by Harold F. Clark and Harold S. Sloan (1964).
Duty, Honor, Country: A History of West Point, by Stephen E. Ambrose (1966).
Education and Military Leadership: A Study of the ROTC, by Gene M. Lyons and John W. Masland (1959).
Handbook of Military Institutions, Roger W. Little, ed. (updated periodically).
Neither Athens Nor Sparta: The American Service Academies in Transition, by John P. Lovell (1979).
U.S. Department of Defense.

Teaching:
The American Teacher: Evolution of a Profession in a Democracy, by Willard Elsbree (1939).

The American Teacher: 1776–1976, by Merle B. Marks (1976).
Colleges of Education: Perspectives on Their Future, Charles W. Case and William A. Matthes, eds. (1985)
The Upper Division College, by Robert A. Altman (1970).

38. TEACHER TRAINING

The American Teacher: Evolution of a Profession in a Democracy, by Willard Ellsbree (1970).
The American Teacher: 1776–1976, by Merle B. Marks (1976).
Analyzing Teacher Behavior, by Ned A. Flanders (1974).
Colleges of Education: Perspectives on Their Future, Charles W. Case and William A. Matthes, eds. (1985).
Competency-Based Teacher Education: Progress, Problems, and Prospects, by W. Robert Houston and Robert B. Howsaw (1972). National Board for Professional Teaching Standards.
The Condition of Teaching, The Carnegie Foundation for the Advancement of Teaching.
Critical Studies in Teacher Education: Its Folklore, Theory and Practice, Thomas S. Poppewitz, ed. (1987).
The Evaluation of In-Service Teacher Training, by Euan S. Henderson (1978).
The Grand Experiment, by Malcolm M. Provus (1975).
Guidelines for Using the National Teacher Examinations, National Teacher Examinations Policy Council.
A Guide to Practice Teaching, by Louis Cohen and Lawrence Manion (1989).
Interaction Analysis: Theory, Research and Application, Edmond J. Amidon and John B. Hough, eds. (1979).
Master Teachers, by Richard W. Moore (1984).
Mentoring at Work: Developmental Relationships in Organizational Life, by Kathy E. Kram (1985).
Mentor Teachers: The California Model, by Roger G. Lowne (1986).
The Miseducation of American Teachers, by James Koerner (1963).
The National Education Association: The Power Base for Education, by Allan M. West (1980).
The National Education Association: A Special Mission, by Susan Lowell Butler (1987).
Paraprofessionals in Education Today, Alan Gartner, et al, eds. (1977).
A Place Called School, by John I. Goodlad (1984).
Portal Schools, Linda Lutonsky (1973).

Power to the Teacher, by Marshall Donley (1975).

The Reflective Practitioner: How Professionals Think in Practice, by Donald A. Schon (1983).

Schoolteacher, by Dan Lortie (1975).

Sensitivity Training: The Scientific Understanding of Individuals, by Henry C. Smith (1973).

Student Teaching and Field Experiences Handbook, by Betty D. Roe, Elinor P. Ross, and Paul C. Burns (1984).

Successful Student Teaching: A Handbook for Elementary and Secondary Student Teachers, by Fillmer Hevener, Jr. (1981).

Teacher Centers and Inservice Education, by Harry H. Bell and John W. Peightel (1976).

Teacher Corps Evaluation, by James P. Steffensen et al. (1978).

The Teacher Evaluation Handbook, by Renfro C. Manning (1988).

Teachers' Centers, Robert Thornbury, ed. (1974).

Understanding Collective Bargaining in Education: Negotiations, Contracts and Disputes Between Teachers and Boards, by Robert C. O'Reilly (1978).

The Upper Division College, by Robert A. Altman (1970).

American Association of University Professors.

American Federation of Teachers.

National Council for the Accreditation of Teacher Education.

National Education Association.

National Foundation for the Improvement of Education, Teacher Center Project.

National Writing Project, School of Education, University of California.

39. TESTING

Aptitudes

The Abuses of Standardized Testing, by Vito Perrone (1977).

The Effects of Standardized Testing, by Thomas Kellaghan, George F. Madaus, and Peter W. Airasian (1985).

None of the Above: The Myth of Scholastic Aptitude, by David Owen (1986).

The Psychological Corporation, San Antonio, Texas.

Educational

Applying Norm-Referenced and Criterion-Referenced Measurement in Education, by Victor R. Martuza (1977).

The Development, Use and Abuse of Educational Tests, by Edward Burns 1979).

Domain Referenced Testing, Wells Hively, ed. (1974).

Educational and Psychological Measurement, by George K. Cunningham (1986).

Educational Measurement, by Robert L. Thorndike (1971).

Evaluating Pupil Growth: Principles of Tests and Measurement, by Stanley J. Ahmann and Marvin D. Glock (1979).

Educational Testing and Measurement: Classroom Application and Practice, by Tom Kubiszyn and Gary Borich (1987).

Guidelines for Test Use: A Commentary on the Standards for Educational and Psychological Tests, by Frederick G. Brown (1980).

Measurement and Evaluation in Psychology and Education, by Robert L. Thorndike and Elizabeth P. Hagen (1977).

Measurement and Evaluation in Teaching, by Norman E. Gronlund.

Measuring and Evaluating School Learning, by Lou M. Carey (1988).

Modern Language Testing: A Handbook, by Rebecca M. Valette (1967).

Principles of Educational and Psychological Measurement and Evaluation, by Gilbert Sax (1989).

Student Achievement Tests as Tools of Educational Policy: Practices and Consequences, by Edward Haertel (1988).

Testing for Learning, by Ruth Mitchell (1992).

Tests and Measurement, by W. Bruce Walsh and Nancy E. Betz (1985).

Using Standardized Tests in Education, by William A. Mehrens and Irvin J. Lehmann (1987).

Intelligence

Assessment of Children's Intelligence, by Jerome M. Sattler (1974).

Manual for the Wechsler Preschool and Primary Scale of Intelligence (1967), by David Wechsler.

The Measurement of Adult Intelligence, By David Wechsler (1944).

The Measurement of Intelligence, by Lewis M. Terman (1916).

Wechsler Adult Intelligence Scale Manual, by David Wechsler (1955).

Wechsler Intelligence Scale for Children, by David Wechsler (Revised, 1974).

Psychological

Bias in Mental Testing, by Arthur R. Jensen (1979).

Educational and Psychological Measurement, by George K. Cunningham (1986).

Essentials of Psychological Testing, by Lee J. Cronbach (1984).

Measurement and Evaluation in Psychology and Education, by Robert L. Thorndike and Elizabeth P. Hagen (1977).

Perspective on Bias in Mental Testing, Cecil Reynolds and Robert T. Brown, eds. (1984).

Principles of Educational and Psychological Measurement and Evaluation, by Gilbert Sax (1989).

Psychological Testing, by Anne Anastasi (1988).

Unobtrusive Measures: Nonreactive Research in the Social Sciences, by Eugene J. Webb et al. (1966).

School and Program Evaluation

Minimum Competency Testing, by Rodney P. Riegel and Irvin J. Lehman (1980).

The Underachieving Curriculum: Assessing U.S. School Mathematics

From the International Perspective, by Curtis C. McKnight *et al.* (1987).

Specialized

Barron's How to Prepare for the High School Equivalency Examination, Barron's Educational Series, Inc., New York (updated annually).

Graduate Management Admission Test, Gino Crocette et al. (1987).

Guide to the Use of the Graduate Record Examinations, Educational Testing Service.

School Readiness — Behavior Tests Used at the Gesell Institute, by Francis L. Ilg (1978).

Test Directories and Organizations

A Guide to 85 Tests for Special Education, by Carolyn Compton (1990).

Mental Measurement Yearbook and *Tests in Print*, Buros Institute of Mental Measurements, The University of Nebraska Press, Lincoln, Nebraska.

The College Board, Princeton, New Jersey.

Educational Testing Service, Princeton, New Jersey.

40. VOCATIONAL EDUCATION

General

American Apprenticeship and Industrial Education, by Paul H. Douglas (1921).

American Education and Vocationalism: A Documentary History, Marvin Lazerson and W. Norton Grubb, eds. (1974).

The Apprenticeship System in Its Relation to Industrial Education, by Carroll D. Wright (1908).

But What If I Don't Want To Go to College?: A Guide to Successful Careers through Alternative Education (1992), by Harlow G. Unger.

Foundations of Vocational Education, by Rupert N. Evans and Edwin L. Herr (1978).

Foundations of Vocational Education: Social and Philosophical Concepts, by John F. Thompson (1973).

Handbook of Trade and Technical Careers and Training (Occupational Outlook Handbook), U.S. Labor Department Bureau of Labor Statistics.

The Industrial Arts Teacher's Handbook: Techniques, Principles, and Methods, by Donald A. Maley (1978).

The Neglected Majority, by Dale Parnell (1989).

Peterson's Guide to Two-Year Colleges (current edition).

Proprietary Vocational Education, by Stephen M. Jung (1980).

Readings in Career and Vocational Education for the Handicapped, Stephen J. Feldman, ed., (1979).

Vocational and Career Education: Concepts and Operations, by Calfrey C. Calhoun and Alton V. Finch (1976).

Vocational Guidance and Career Development: Selected Readings, by Herman T. Peters and James C. Hansen (1977).

The World of Construction and *The World of Manufacturing*, by Donald G. Lux and Willis E. Ray (1971).

Career College Association.

National Commission for Cooperative Education.

United States Chamber of Commerce Center for Workforce Preparation and Quality Education.

U.S. Department of Education.

U.S. Department of Labor.

Specialized

Agriculture:

Agricultural Science and the Quest for Legitimacy: Farmers, Agricultural Colleges, and Experiment Stations, 1870–1890, by Alan I. Marcus (1985).

Colleges for Our Land and Times: The Land-Grant Idea in American Education, by Edward Danforth Eddy (1957).

Federal Cooperation in Agricultural Extension Work, Vocational Education, and Vocational Rehabilitation, by Lloyd E. Blauch (1969).

A History of Agricultural Education in the United States, 1785–1925, by Alfred Charles True (1929).

History of Agriculture in the Northern United States, 1620–1860, by Percy Wells Bidwell and John I. Falconer (1978).

Business:

Business Education Yesterday, Today, and Tomorrow, Ruth B. Woolschlager and E. Edward Harris (1976).

Corporate:

Corporate Classrooms: The Learning Business, by Neil P. Eurich (1985).

Educational Experiments in Industry, by Nathaniel Peffer (1932).

Employee Training: A Study of Education and Training Departments in Various Corporations, by John Van Liew Morris (1932).

Mission Communications: The Story of Bell Laboratories, by Prescott C. Mabon (n.d.).

41. WOMEN'S EDUCATION

Catherine Beecher: A Study in Domesticity, by Kathryn Kish Sklar (1976).

A Century of Higher Education for American Women, by Mabel Newcomer (1959).

The Clubwoman as Feminist: True Womanhood Redefined, 1868–1914, by Karen J. Blair (1980).

Failing at Fairness: How America's Schools Cheat Girls, by Myra and David Sadker (1994).

Charlotte Perkins Gilman: The Making of a Radical Feminist, 1860–1896, by Mary A. Hill (1980).

Great Women Teachers, by Alice Fleming (1965).

"How Schools Shortchange Women: The A.A.U.W. Report," American Association of University Women.

A Hundred Years of Mount Holyoke College, by Arthur C. Coe (1940).

In the Company of Educated Women: A History of Women and Higher Education in America, by Barbara Miller Solomon (1985).

Mary Lyon, by Evelyn Banning (1965).

Anne Sullivan Macy, by Nella Braddy (1933).

Teacher: Anne Sullivan, by Helen Keller (1955, revised ed. 1966).

Title IX: How It Affects Elementary and Secondary Education, by Norma Raffel (1976).

Emma Willard, Daughter of Democracy, by Alma Lutz (1964).

American Association of University Women, Washington, D.C.

APPENDIX A: CHRONOLOGY

1607 First permanent English settlement established in the American colonies, in Jamestown, Virginia.

1621 Pilgrims establish first permanent settlement in the northern colonies, at Plymouth, Massachusetts.

1635 Boston Latin School is first school established in the Americas.

1636 First college opens in Cambridge, Massachusetts, as a Congregationalist divinity school, named after benefactor the Rev. John Harvard.

1643 First school in southern colonies, the Syms School, established in Virginia.

1647 Massachusetts passes "the Old Deluder Satan" law. A precedent for future American education, the law is first to make education compulsory and an obligation of government rather than the church.

1679 William Penn enunciates Quaker policy of universal public education in Pennsylvania.

1693 Anglicans found College of William and Mary, in Williamsburg, Virginia, to support Church of England and loyalty to Crown against Harvard's Congregationalist preachers from the North.

1701 Society for the Propagation of the Gospel in Foreign Parts founded in London to spread Christianity, build churches and spread education throughout the American colonies.

Yale University founded as the Collegiate School in Connecticut to meet New England's growing need for Congregationalist ministers.

1720 The Great Awakening begins as a religious movement, but inflames fervor for independence and universal education in the colonies.

1727 Benjamin Franklin founds first "public" library at the American Philosophical Society, Philadelphia.

1732 Benjamin Franklin begins publishing *Poor Richard's Almanack*, the first educative journal for "conveying instruction among the common people. . . ."

1746 College of New Jersey (later, Princeton) founded at Princeton, New Jersey, by Scottish Presbyterian "school of common sense." Early graduates form a core of founding fathers of the United States.

1751 Benjamin Franklin founds Franklin's Academy, the first secular educational institution in the American colonies tied to practical rather than theological learning.

1754 King's College (later, Columbia) founded in New York City to preserve Anglicanism and loyalty to the Crown in the northern English colonies.

1765 John Morgan establishes first formal program of medical education in the colonies, at College of Philadelphia (later, the University of Pennsylvania).

1774 Tapping Reeve opens first "law school" in American colonies, in Litchfield, Connecticut.

1776 American colonies declare independence from England.

1779 Virginia rejects Thomas Jefferson proposal to establish the first free, universal public education school system in the United States.

1783 Noah Webster begins publishing first "American system of instruction," to meet needs of new nation and educate "all ranks of society."

1789 The United States Constitution adopted as supreme law of the land. Universal public education voted down by southern proponents of slavery and northern advocates of child labor. Education omitted from final document and left to state controls.

1786 Artist Charles Willson Peale founds first public museum, in Philadelphia.

1795 North Carolina opens first state university.

1796 Thomas Paine's *The Age of Reason* calls for stripping the church of control over education and establishing universal public education.

1802 United States Military Academy founded at West Point, to train officers in military science and for the new profession of civil engineering.

1806 Noah Webster celebrates the American language with publication of *A Compendious Dictionary of the English Language*.

1811 Elkanah Watson founds Berkshire Agricultural Society, the precursor to the agricultural fair and adult education.

1821 Emma Willard founds Troy Female Seminary, the world's first academy offering a liberal arts and science education for women.

First publicly supported high school, the English Classical School (later, English High School), established in Boston.

1826 Josiah Holbrook founds American Lyceum, the first organized program of adult education and secular, public vocational education.

1830 Catherine Beecher urges American women to make the teaching profession their own. Due in large part to her efforts, over the next 50 years the teaching profession goes from being more than 90% men to more than 60% women.

1836 Horace Mann establishes first secular, state public school system in the United States in Massachusetts.

Mary Lyon founds world's first college for women, Mount Holyoke, in Massachusetts.

1838 Henry Barnard begins the American "public school movement," borrowing from Mann's work in Massachusetts to establish state public school systems, successively, in Connecticut, Rhode Island and Wisconsin.

1839 Horace Mann establishes first state-operated teacher-training school to meet needs of the Massachusetts public school system.

1841 Phineas T. Barnum opens the New American Museum, which begins the museum movement and transforms museums from private, scholarly preserves into public, educative institutions.

1851 Young Men's Christian Association begins campaign to Christianize the people of the United States; widespread poverty and unemployment eventually convert organizational goals to social welfare and vocational education.

1852 Massachusetts passes first compulsory education law in the United States.

1853 Horace Mann opens Antioch College, in Antioch, Ohio, as the first coeducational college in the United States, with both men and women attending the same classes and women on the faculty.

1861 Civil War begins.

1862 Congress enacts first Morrill Act, establishing land-grant colleges and first state university systems.

1863 President Abraham Lincoln signs the Emancipation Proclamation freeing all slaves held in states in rebellion against the federal government.

1868 Hampton Institute opens in Hampton, Virginia, as first educational institution for former slaves.

1869 Charles W. Eliot inaugurated as president of Harvard College; begins transformation of the American college into modern, secular, American university, with an undergraduate college and a variety of graduate professional schools.

1871 Johns Hopkins University opens as first institution of higher education devoted exclusively to graduate study and research, bringing research into the purview of American university functions for the first time.

1873 First public-school kindergarten established in St. Louis.

1874 John Heyl Vincent founds the Chautauqua adult education movement at Lake Chautauqua, New York.

1881 Booker T. Washington founds first black-operated educational institution at Tuskegee, Alabama.

1886 Social-settlements movement begins in the United States, to provide privately funded social welfare, health care, and basic secular education to unemployed immigrants and their children in American cities.

1887 Dwight L. Moody founds Moody Bible Institute in Chicago, to challenge secular education and lead national effort to Christianize American public education.

1896 United States Supreme Court deems separate-but-equal public facilities for the races constitutional in *Plessy* v. *Ferguson*.

1896 John Dewey opens University of Chicago Laboratory School, inaugurating age of progressive education.

1903 Charles R. Van Hise transforms University of Wisconsin into model of modern public, state university, serving the entire population of the state, with continuing education to serve adult population.

1912 United States opens U.S. Children's Bureau, the first federal agency devoted to advocacy of children's rights.

1914 United States Department of Agriculture establishes Extension Service to provide millions of rural Americans agricultural education.

1917 United States enters World War I. Armistice in 1918 spurs Gen. John J. Pershing to establish the University of the American Expeditionary Forces in France, the largest educative effort in military history.

1919 Nineteenth Amendment to the Constitution enacted, providing for women's suffrage.

1925 Five-year effort by Christian fundamentalists to ban teaching of evolution culminates in Scopes "Monkey Trial." Tennessee high-school teacher convicted for teaching Darwinism but trial makes fundamentalism a target of worldwide mockery that temporarily ends its influence over public education.

1929 Stock market crash marks beginning of worst economic depression in American history, with consequent expansion of education to improve worker skills and remove children from job market and expand opportunities for adults.

1933 United States passes child labor law making it a federal crime to employ workers younger than 16 in most nonfarming occupations and younger than 18 in hazardous industries.

1941 United States enters World War II and creates the most far-reaching military program in history of primary, secondary, college and professional education for millions of American servicemen.

1944 U.S. Government enacts "G.I. Bill of Rights," providing World War II veterans with free, higher education and opening higher education to all Americans, regardless of economic class.

1954 United States Supreme Court reverses *Plessy* v. *Ferguson* decision of 1896; rules racial segregation of public schools unconstitutional in landmark case of *Brown* v. *Board of Education of Topeka*.

1964 Congress enacts Economic Opportunity Act, declaring "war on poverty" and providing federally funded preschool education to millions of economically deprived children through "Operation Head Start."

1965 Congress enacts Guaranteed Student Loan Act, qualifying every American citizen, regardless of economic class, for loans to pay for higher education.

1972 Congress enacts Educational Amendments of 1972, prohibiting discrimination on the basis of sex in educational institutions receiving federal aid.

1975 Congress enacts Education for All Handicapped Act, requiring all public schools to provide free and appropriate education to all handicapped children.

1979 Congress establishes the Department of Education as a cabinet-level unit in the executive, to assume control over all federal programs related to American education.

1993 Congress establishes nationwide educational goals for the year 2000 and provides federal grants to states and local communities to reform the nation's educational system in an effort to achieve those goals. The "Goals 2000" program provides for the first national certification, albeit voluntary, of state and local education standards and assessments.

1994 Federal spending on education reaches nearly $70 billion, compared to less than $5.4 billion 30 years earlier. About half is spent on support of elementary and secondary education and 21% on support of postsecondary education, with 22% spent on research at educational institutions and the remainder spent on support of other forms of education.

Sources of Federal Government Funds for Education, by Agency, Fiscal Year 1994: Total Funds = $68.4 billion
Department of Education, 42.2%
Department of Health and Human Services, 17.1%
Department of Agriculture, 12.8%
Department of Labor, 6.6%
Department of Defense, 5.5%
Department of Energy, 3.9%
National Science Foundation, 3.3%
National Aeronautics and Space Administration, 2.1%
Department of Veterans Affairs, 2.0%
All other government agencies combined, 4.5%

APPENDIX B: SIGNIFICANT FEDERAL EDUCATION LEGISLATION, 1787–1993

1787 *Northwest Ordinance* authorizes land grants for the establishment of educational institutions.

1802 *An Act Fixing the Military Peace Establishment of the United States* establishes the U.S. Military Academy. (The U.S. Naval Academy is established in 1845 by the Secretary of the Navy.)

1862 First *Morrill Act* authorizes public land grants to the states for the establishment and maintenance of agricultural and mechanical colleges.

1867 *Department of Education Act* authorizes the establishment of the U.S. Department of Education. (Later known as the Office of Education, it becomes a cabinet-level department in 1980.)

1876 *Appropriation Act*, U.S. Department of the Treasury, establishes the U.S. Coast Guard Academy.

1890 Second *Morrill Act* provides for money grants for support of instruction in the agricultural and mechanical colleges.

1917 *Smith-Hughes Act* provides for grants to states for support of vocational education.

1918 *Vocational Rehabilitation Act* provides for rehabilitation through training of World War I veterans.

1919 *An Act to Provide Further Educational Facilities* authorizes the sale by the federal government of surplus machine tools to educational institutions at 15% of acquisition cost.

1920 *Smith-Bankhead Act* authorizes grants to states for vocational rehabilitation programs.

1935 *Smith-Bankhead Act* authorizes grants to states for agricultural experiment stations. *Agricultural Adjustment Act* authorizes 30% of the annual customs receipts to be used to encourage the exportation and domestic consumption of agricultural commodities. Commodities purchased under this authorization began to be used in school lunch programs in 1936. The National School Lunch Act of 1946 continued and expanded this assistance.

1936 *An Act to Further the Development and Maintenance of an Adequate and Well-Balanced American Merchant Marine* establishes the U.S. Merchant Marine Academy.

1937 *National Cancer Institute Act* establishes the Public Health Service fellowship program.

1941 Amendment to *Lanham Act of 1940* authorizes federal aid for construction, maintenance, and operation of schools in federally impacted areas.

1944 *Servicemen's Readjustment Act*, known as the GI Bill, provides funds for the education of veterans. *Surplus Property Act* authorizes transfer of surplus federal government property to educational institutions.

1946 *National School Lunch Act* authorizes grants-in-aid and other assistance to help states provide adequate foods and facilities for the establishment, maintenance, operation and expansion of nonprofit school-lunch programs.
Fulbright Act provided funds for international exchange of professors and students to promote international understanding. Scope expanded in 1961 under Fulbright-Hays Act, which provides funds for improved foreign language training and overseas study of foreign cultures.

1948 *United States Information and Educational Exchange Act* provides for the interchange of persons, knowledge, and skills between the United States and other countries.

1950 *Financial Assistance for Local Educational Agencies Affected by Federal Activities* provides funds for construction and operation of schools in federally affected areas.

1954 *An Act for the Establishment of the United States Air Force Academy and Other Purposes* establishes the U.S. Air Force Academy.

Cooperative Research Act authorizes cooperative arrangements with universities, colleges, and state educational agencies for educational research.

School Milk Program Act provides funds for purchase of milk for school-lunch programs.

1956 *Library Services Act* provides for extension and improvement of rural public library services.

1958 *National Defense Education Act* provides funds to state and local school systems for strengthening instruction in science, mathematics, modern foreign languages and other critical subjects.

Education of Mentally Retarded Children Act authorizes federal funds for training teachers of the handicapped.

1962 *Manpower Development and Training Act* provides training in new and improved skills for the unemployed and underemployed. Amendment to the *Communications Act of 1934* provides grants for the construction of educational television broadcasting facilities.

Migration and Refugee Assistance Act of 1962 authorizes loans, advances, and grants for education and training of refugees.

1963 *Health Professions Educational Assistance Act* provides funds to expand teaching facilities and for loans to students in the health professions.

Vocational Education Act of 1963 increases federal support of vocational education schools; vocational work-study programs; and research, training and demonstrations in vocational education.

Higher Education Facilities Act of 1963 authorizes grants and loans for classrooms, libraries, and laboratories in public community colleges, colleges and technical institutes, as well as undergraduate and graduate facilities in other institutions.

1964 *Civil Rights Act of 1964* authorizes the Commissioner of Education to arrange for support for institutions of higher education and school districts to provide in-service programs for assisting instructional staff dealing with problems caused by desegregation.

Economic Opportunity Act of 1964 authorizes grants for college work-study programs for students from low-income families; establishes a Job Corps and authorizes support for work-training programs to provide education and vocational training and work experience in welfare programs; authorizes support of education and training activities and of community action programs, including Head Start, Follow Through, and Upward Bound; and authorizes the establishment of Volunteers in Service to America (VISTA).

1965 *Elementary and Secondary Education Act* authorizes grants for elementary and secondary school programs for children of low-income families; school library resources, textbooks, and other instructional materials for children; supplementary educational centers and services; strengthens state education agencies; and provides educational research and training.

Health Professions Educational Assistance Amendments authorizes scholarships to aid needy students in the health professions.

Higher Education Act of 1965 provides grants for university community service programs, college libraries, library training and research, strengthening developing institutions, teacher training programs, and undergraduate instructional equipment. Authorizes insured student loans, establishes a National Teacher Corps, and provides for graduate teacher training fellowships.

National Foundation on the Arts and Humanities Act authorizes grants and loans for projects in the creative and performing arts and for research, training and scholarly publications in the humanities.

National Technical Institute for the Deaf Act provides for the establishment, construction, equipping, and operation of a residential school for postsecondary education and training of the deaf.

National Vocational Student Loan Insurance Act encourages state and nonprofit private institutions and organizations to establish adequate loan insurance programs to assist students to attend postsecondary business, trade, technical and other vocational schools.

Disaster Relief Act provides funds to local education agencies to help meet exceptional costs resulting from a major disaster.

1966 *International Education Act* provides grants to institutions of higher education for centers of research and training in international studies and the international aspects of other fields of study.

National Sea Grant College and Program Act authorizes establishment and operation of Sea Grant Colleges and programs initiating and supporting programs of education and research in various fields relating to development of marine resources.

Adult Education Act authorizes grants to states for adult education programs, including training of teachers of adults and demonstrations in adult education, (previously part of Economic Opportunity Act of 1964).

Model Secondary School for the Deaf Act authorizes establishment and operation, by Gallaudet College, of a model secondary school for the deaf.

1967 *Education Professions Development Act* amended the *Higher Education Act of 1965* to improve the quality of teaching and to help meet critical shortages of adequately trained educational personnel.

Public Broadcasting Act of 1967 establishes Corporation for Public Broadcasting to assume a major responsibility in channeling federal funds to noncommercial radio and television stations, program production groups and Educational Television networks; to conduct research, demonstration, or training in matters related to

noncommercial broadcasting; and to award grants for construction of educational radio and television facilities.

1968 *Elementary and Secondary Education Amendments of 1967* modifies existing programs, authorizes support of regional centers for education of handicapped children, model centers and services for deaf-blind children, recruitment of personnel and dissemination of information on education of the handicapped; technical assistance in education to rural areas; support of dropout prevention projects; and support of bilingual education programs.

Handicapped Children's Early Education Assistance Act authorizes preschool and early education programs for handicapped children.

Higher Education Amendments of 1968 authorizes new programs to assist disadvantaged college students through special counseling and summer tutorial programs and programs to assist colleges to combine resources of cooperative programs and to expand programs which provide clinical experiences for law students.

1970 *National Commission on Libraries and Information Services Act* establishes a National Commission on Libraries and Information Science to promote inter-library services.

Office of Education Appropriation Act provides emergency funding to help schools desegregate.

Environmental Education Act establishes an Office of Environmental Education to develop curriculum and initiate and maintain environment and ecology education programs at the elementary-secondary levels and provide training programs for teachers.

Drug Abuse Education Act of 1970 provides for development, demonstration, and evaluation of curricula on the problems of drug abuse.

1972 *Education Amendments of 1972* establishes the Education Division in the U.S. Department of Health, Education, and Welfare and the National Institute of Education; general aid for institutions of higher education; federal matching grants for state Student Incentive

Grants; Pell Grants; a National Commission on Financing Postsecondary Education; State Advisory Councils on Community Colleges; a Bureau of Occupational and Adult Education, and state grants for postsecondary occupational education; and a bureau-level Office of Indian Education. Title IX prohibits sex bias in admission to vocational, professional and graduate schools and public institutions of undergraduate higher education.

1973 *Older Americans Comprehensive Services Amendment of 1973* makes available to older citizens comprehensive programs of health, education and social services.

Comprehensive Employment and Training Act of 1973 provides for opportunities for employment and training to unemployed and underemployed persons.

1974 *Educational Amendments of 1974* establishes a National Center for Education Statistics.

Juvenile Justice and Delinquency Prevention Act of 1974 provides for technical assistance, staff training, centralized research, and resources to develop and implement programs to prevent dropouts in elementary and secondary schools; and establishes in the U.S. Department of Justice, a National Institute for Juvenile Justice and Delinquency Prevention.

1975 *Indian Self-Determination and Education Assistance Act* provides for increased participation of Indians in the establishment and conduct of their education programs and services.

Indochina Migration and Refugee Assistance Act of 1975 authorizes funds to be use for education and training of aliens who have fled from Cambodia or Vietnam. *Education for All Handicapped Act* provides that all handicapped have available to them a free appropriate education designed to meet their unique needs.

1977 *Youth Employment and Demonstration Projects Act of 1977* establishes a youth employment training program that includes, among other activities, promoting education-to-work

transition, literacy training and bilingual training, and attainment of certificates of high school equivalency.

1978 *Tribally Controlled Community College Assistance Act* provides federal funds for the operation and improvement of tribally controlled community colleges for Indian students.

Education Amendments of 1978 establishes a comprehensive basic skills program to improve pupil achievement (Replaced National Reading improvement Program); establishes a community schools program to expand use of public buildings.

Middle Income Student Assistance Act modified provisions for student financial assistance programs to allow middle-income as well as low-income students attending college or other post-secondary institutions to qualify for federal education assistance.

1979 *Department of Education Organization Act* establishes a U.S. Department of Education containing functions from the Education Division of the Department of Health, Education and Welfare, and other selected programs from HEW, the departments of Justice and Labor and the National Science Foundation.

1980 *Asbestos School Hazard Protection and Control Act of 1980* establishes a program for inspection of schools to detect hazardous asbestos materials and provide loans to assist educational agencies the containment or removal and replacement such materials.

1983 *Student Loan Consolidation and Technical Amendments Act of 1983* establishes an 8% interest rate for Guaranteeed Student Loans and extended Family Contribution Schedule.

Education for All Handicapped Act Amendments adds Architectural Barrier amendment and clarified participation of handicapped children in private schools.

1984 *Education for Economic Security Act* adds new science and mathematics programs for elementary, secondary and postsecondary education. The new programs include magnet schools, excellence in education and equal access.

Carl D. Perkins Vocational Education Act replaces the Vocational Education Act of 1963 and provides aid to states to make vocational education programs accessible to all persons, including the handicapped and disadvantaged, single parents and homemakers, and the incarcerated.

1985 *Montgomery GI Bill—Active Duty* creates a new GI Bill for individuals who initially entered active military duty on or after July 1, 1985.

Montgomery GI Bill—Selected Reserve created a GI Bill for members of the Selected Reserve (which includes the National Guard) who enlist, re-enlist or extend an enlistment after June 30, 1985, for a six-year period.

1988 *The Omnibus Trade and Competitiveness Act of 1988* authorizes new and expanded education programs in literacy, math-science, foreign language, vocational training, international education and technology training.

The Omnibus Drug Abuse Prevention Act of 1988 authorizes a new teacher-training program under the Drug-Free Schools and Communities Act, an early childhood education program and a pilot program for the children of alcoholics.

Tax Reform Technical Amendments authorizes an issuance of tax-exempt Series EE U.S. Government Education Savings Bond for the post-secondary educational expenses.

1990 *The Excellence in Mathematics, Science and Engineering Education Act of 1990* promotes excellence in American mathematics, science, and engineering education by creating a national mathematics and science clearing house and establishing regional mathematics and science education consortia and scholarship programs.

The Student Right-to-Know and Campus Security Act requires institutions of higher education receiving federal assistance to provide information on graduation rates, including those of student-athletes. The act requires institutions to certify the existence of a security policy and to submit a uniform, annual report of crime on campus to the Federal Bureau of Information for public dissemination.

The Children's Television Act of 1990 requires the Federal Communications Commission to reinstate restrictions on advertising during children's television and enforces the obligation of broadcasters to meet the educational and informational needs of the child audience.

The Americans with Disabilities Act of 1990 prohibits discrimination against persons with disabilities.

1991 *National Literacy Act* establishes the National Institute for Literacy, the National Institute Board and the Interagency Task Force on Literacy.

National Commission on a Longer School Year Act establishes the National Education Commission on Time and Learning and the National Council on Education Standards and Testing.

High-Performance Computing Act of 1991 directed the President to implement a National High-Performance Computing Program. The act provides for the establishment of a National Research and Education Network and the development of standards and guidelines for high-performance networks.

1992 *Ready-To-Learn Act* authorizes support for Ready-To-Learn television programming and support materials for preschool and elementary school children and their parents, child-care providers and educators.

1993 *Student Loan Reform Act* reformed default-ridden federal student loan programs by phasing in a system of direct government lending to students and a wider variety of repayment options.

National Service Trust Act establishes a Corporation for National Service that offered education grants of up to $4,725 a year for two years to people 17 years or older who perform community service before, during or after postsecondary education.

Goals 2000: Educate America Act establishes nationwide educational goals for the year 2000 and provides federal grants to states and local communities to reform the nation's educational system in an effort to achieve those goals. The act establishes a National Education Standards and Improvement Council to provide voluntary national certification of state and local education standards and assessments, and it establishes the National Skill Standards Board to develop voluntary national skill standards.

School-To-Work Opportunities Act provides funds to states and communities to develop programs that combine work-based and school-based learning, leading to a high school diploma (or its equivalent), a nationally recognized skill certificate, an associate degree (if appropriate) and appropriate career guidance.

Safe Schools Act authorizes award of competitive grants to local educational agencies with serious crime problems to implement violence prevention activities such as conflict resolution and peer mediation.

OERI Reauthorization authorizes the educational research and dissemination activities of the Office of Educational Research and Improvement (OERI), along with its regional educational laboratories and university-based research and development centers.

APPENDIX C: SIGNIFICANT U.S. SUPREME COURT DECISIONS IN EDUCATION

Abington School District v. *Schempp.* A 1963 decision that declares prayers and Bible readings in public schools unconstitutional — even when unwilling students were excused from such activities. The decision is a reaffirmation of *Engel* v. *Vitale*, handed down the previous year.

Aguilar v. *Felton.* A 1985 decision that declares it unconstitutional to use public employees to provide instruction and services to students in private religious schools.

Aguillard v. *Edwards* A 1987 decision that declares unconstitutional a Louisiana law which prohibited the teaching of the theory of evolution in public schools unless "creation science" (q.v.) is taught with it at the same time.

Alexander v. *Holmes County Board of Education (1969).* One of three of U.S. Supreme Court decisions to speed the pace of desegregation and outlaw all efforts to evade it. (*See also Green* v. *New Kent County, Virginia* (1968) and *United States* v. *Montgomery County Board of Education* (1969).

Alston v. *School Board of the City of Norfolk.* A 1940 ruling that upholds a lower court decision that a different salary schedule for equally qualified and similarly assigned black and white teachers in Norfolk, Virginia, schools violates the due process and equal protection classes of the Fourteenth Amendment to the Constitution. The case is the second in a 14-year series of five law suits sponsored by the National Association for the Advancement of Colored People (NAACP), the climax of which comes with the 1954 U.S. Supreme Court decision in *Brown* v. *Board of Education of Topeka* (q.v.) declaring racial segregation in schools unconstitutional. (*See also McLaurin* v. *Oklahoma State Regents, Missouri ex. rel. Gaines* v. *Canada, Sipuel* v. *Board of Regents of the University of Oklahoma* and *Sweatt* v. *Painter*.)

Barenblatt v. *United States.* A 1959 decision that upholds the constitutional right of congressional committees to conduct investigations in the field of education.

Board of Education of Central School District v. *Allen.* A 1968 decision upholding a New York State law requiring local school boards to purchase textbooks and lend them free of charge to students in private and parochial schools.

Board of Education v. *Rowley.* A 1982 ruling that reverses a lower court order forcing a public school to provide a free, sign-language interpreter for an 11-year-old deaf girl.

Board of Regents of State Colleges v. *Roth.* A 1972 ruling that a publicly employed teacher has the right to a hearing when discharged only if formal or *de facto* tenure has been conferred.

Bob Jones University v. *United States* and *Goldsboro Christian Schools Inc.* v. *United States.* A landmark 1983 decision that extends the principle of racial integration to private schools by ruling that the Internal Revenue Service has the power to deny tax exemptions to private schools that practices racial discrimination.

Bradley v. *Richmond School Board* (1965). The last of three U.S. High Court decisions between 1963 and 1965 that effectively end resistance to school desegregation in the South. The *Bradley* decision applies all previous desegregation rulings to public school teachers as well as students. (*See also Goss* v. *Board of Education* (1963) and *Griffin* v. *County School Board* of Prince Edward County(1964).

Briggs v. *Elliot.* One of four separate cases consolidated by the U.S. Supreme Court into the single landmark case known as *Brown* v. Board of Education of Topeka (q.v.) in 1954.

Brown v. *Board of Education of Topeka.* The landmark 1954 U.S. Supreme Court decision that outlaws racial segregation in American public schools and signals the end to racial segregation in all public facilities in the United States. The decision was a consolidation of four separate cases including *Briggs* v. *Elliot, Gebbart* v. *Belton* and *Davis* v. *County School Board.*

Camer v. *Eikenberry.* A 1983 ruling in which the High Court refuses to review a lower court decision that a public school has the legal right to establish minimum academic standards for entry into special programs such as honors programs and bar unqualified students.

Charles E. Stuart and Others v. *School District No. 1 of the Village of Kalamazoo and Others.* A precedent-setting case in 1874 that not only establish the right of town officials to raise taxes to pay for a public high school.

Cleveland Board of Education v. *LaFleur.* A 1974 decision that the Cleveland Board of Education violated the Constitutional rights of women by requiring pregnant teachers to take unpaid maternity leaves several months before and after childbirth.

Committee for Public Education and Religious Freedom v. *Regan.* A 1980 decision that New York State can reimburse private and parochial schools for the costs of state-mandated testing and other activities.

Cooper v. *Aaron.* A 1958 decision that denies a school board the right to delay racial integration of public schools.

Cramp v. *Board of Public Instruction of Orange County, Florida.* A 1961 decision that declares a Florida loyalty oath unconstitutional.

Davis v. *County School Board.* One of four cases in Kansas, South Carolina, Virginia and Delaware that the High Court consolidated into the landmark school desegregation decision *Brown* v. *Board of Education of Topeka* (q.v.).

Engel v. *Vitale.* A 1962 decision declaring as unconstitutional a New York State law giving public school officials the option to mandate a daily nondenominational prayer in school.

Epperson v. *Arkansas.* A unanimous 1968 decision declaring a 1928 Arkansas law unconstitutional for permitting the teaching of the Biblical story of man's creation while banning the teaching of any theory that "mankind ascended or descended from a lower order of animals."

Everson v. *Board of Education.* A landmark 1946 ruling that it is not a violation of the Establishment Clause of the First Amendment to reimburse parents of parochial, as well as private, school children for school bus costs.

Goss v. *Board of Education* (1963). The first of three Supreme Court decisions between 1963 and 1965 that effectively ends resistance to school desegregation in the South. *Goss* strikes down a Tennessee law intended to obstruct the progress of desegregation by allowing students to transfer from schools where their race is a minority into schools where their race is a majority. (*See also Bradley* v. *Richmond School Board* (1965)) and *Griffin* v. *County School Board of Prince Edward County* (1964) and

Goss v. *Lopez.* A 1975 decision reaffirming a lower court affirmation of a public school student's constitutional right, under the Fourteenth Amendment (q.v.), to due process in school disciplinary actions.

Green v. *County School Board of New Kent County.* A 1968 decision that strikes down a desegregation plan allowing black and white students in New Kent County to choose whether or not they wanted to attend formerly all-black or all-white schools.

Griffin v. *County School Board of Prince Edward County.* A landmark decision affirming the right of federal courts to levy taxes and raise funds to reopen public schools when local school boards fail to do so.

Healy v. *James.* A unanimous 1972 ruling that a college could not prevent students from forming a chapter of the Students for a Democratic Society or deny students the use of campus facilities without evidence that they intended to disrupt the local campus.

Hazelwood School District v. *Kuhlmeier.* A 1988 decision that gave a high school principal the right to delete from the student newspaper student articles he deems inappropriate.

Ingraham v. *Wright.* A 1977 ruling that spanking by school authorities does not violate the constitutional rights of students.

Irving School District v. *Tatro.* A 1984 decision that public school districts are obligated by the Education for All Handicapped Children Act of 1975 to render quasi-medical services to handicapped students.

Keyes v. *School District No. 1.* A landmark 1973 decision that orders the Denver, Colorado, school board to desegregate its entire school system "root and branch," using every possible device, including system-wide busing to redistribute Mexican, black and white pupils and affect "the greatest possible degree of actual desegregation." The decision is the first ever to deal with segregation in a "northern" city and the first involving an ethnic group. The decision extends the desegregation doctrine beyond race to every class of Americans.

Lau v. *Nichols.* A far-reaching 1974 decision that extends the obligations of American public schools to educate *all* children residing in the United States, including non-English-speaking, foreign-born children. The court holds that public schools must, if necessary, teach such children in their native languages.

Lee v. *Weisman.* A 1992 ruling that prayer at a school graduation is unconstitutional, calling it "pervasive" government involvement in religious activity that left students little choice but to participate.

Lemon v. *Kurtzman.* A 1971 U.S. Supreme Court decision that declares direct state support of parochial schools an unconstitutional violation of the Establishment Clause of the First Amendment (q.v.) which bans state support of any religion.

McCarthy v. *Philadelphia Civil Service Commission.* A 1976 ruling that upholds as constitutional Philadelphia's ordinance requiring city employees, such as teachers, to live within the city limits.

McCollum v. *Board of Education.* A 1948 ruling that orders the public schools of Champaign, Illinois, to cease the practice of releasing students for religious instruction by visiting clerics on school grounds.

Meek v. *Pittinger.* A 1975 decision that strikes down as unconstitutional a Pennsylvania law under which parochial and private schools were provided with loans of state-owned maps, projectors, films and other public school equipment, as well as with public school teachers for remedial and special learning courses.

Milliken v. *Bradley.* A controversial 1974 decision that effectively ends busing (q.v.) between independent school districts to achieve racial segregation.

Mills v. *District of Columbia Board of Education.* A landmark 1972 class-action suit that establishes the constitutional right of handicapped children to free, public school education. *Mills* opens the way towards the establishment of zero-rejection policies of American public schools.

Minnesota Board for Community Colleges v. *Knight.* A 1984 ruling giving the state the right to certify a single organization as the representative of college faculties in state schools and bar nonmembers of such organizations from policy discussions.

Missouri ex rel. Gaines v. *Canada.* A 1938 decision that holds the state in violation of the

Constitution by depriving its black citizens of the right to legal education and, therefore, the constitutional right to charge others and defend themselves in court. The case is the first in a series of six decisions over 16 years that culminated in 1954 with *Brown* v. *Board of Education of Topeka*, which ended racial segregation of public schools in the United States. (*See also Alston* v. *School Board of the City of Norfolk, McLaurin* v. *Oklahoma State Regents, Sipuel* v. *Board of Regents of the University of Oklahoma* and *Sweatt* v. *Painter.*)

Mueller v. *Allen.* A 1983 decision upholding the constitutionality of a Minnesota law that granted parents limited tax deductions for certain costs of secular education and educational services provided by private and parochial schools.

National Collegiate Athletic Association v. *University of Oklahoma.* A 1984 ruling that the National Collegiate Athletic Association (NCAA) violated federal antitrust law by preventing individual colleges and universities from negotiating the rights to football telecasts.

National Labor Relations Board v. *Catholic Bishop of Chicago.* A 1974 ruling that the National Labor Relations Board lacks the power to intervene in disputes between parochial schools that had refused to bargain with lay faculty unions.

National Labor Relations Board v. *Yeshiva University* and *Yeshiva University Faculty Association* v. *Yeshiva University.* A 1980 ruling that most faculty unions at private colleges and universities are not protected by federal labor law.

New Jersey v. *T.L.O.* A 1985 decision ruling it legally permissible for public school officials and teachers to search a student's property as long as the scope of the search is proper and there are "reasonable grounds" to believe the search will yield evidence of a violation of the law or school rules.

North Haven Board of Education v. *Bell.* A 1982 decision that extends the reach of a law prohibiting gender discrimination in federally funded education programs to school and college employees, as well as students.

Pennsylvania Association for Retarded Children v. *Commonwealth of Pennsylvania* (**PARC decision**). A landmark 1971 case that extends universal public education laws to retarded children as a Constitutional right.

Pickering v. *Board of Education of Township High School.* A 1968 decision that public school teachers cannot be dismissed for publicly criticizing school systems, even if some of the charges were wrong.

Pierce v. *Society of Sisters.* A unanimous 1925 decision that a 1922 Oregon law requiring children to attend public rather than private schools is unconstitutional.

Plessy v. *Ferguson.* An 1896 decision that holds separate-but-equal public facilities for different racial groups constitutional.

Plyler v. *Doe.* An historic 1982 ruling that public schools are constitutionally obliged to admit children of illegal aliens and provide them with tuition-free public education. It is the first time the court extends Constitutional protection to persons who were not U.S. citizens.

Rodriguez v. *San Antonio School District.* A 1974 decision upholding the right of states to finance public school systems with local property taxes. The decision is a setback for representatives of minority groups and the poor who contend that tax-based public-school funding leads to inequitable spending on education.

Schall v. *Martin.* A significant but little known 1984 decision in which the court holds it constitutional for states to hold juvenile criminal suspects in preventive detention before bringing them to trial.

School District of the City of Grand Rapids v. *Ball.* A 1985 decision that declares it unconstitutional to pay public school teachers from public funds to teach special programs in religious schools — even when the programs, such as remedial reading, are nonreligious.

Shelton v. *Tucker*. A 1960 decision declaring unconstitutional a 1958 Arkansas law requiring teachers to list all organizations to which they belonged in the previous five years.

Sipuel v. *Board of Regents of the University of Oklahoma*. A 1948 ruling that the state must provide opportunities for legal education for blacks and must do so for one race as soon as for the other. *Sipuel* is one of a series of five cases, from 1938 to 1954, that culminates in 1954 with *Brown* v. *Board of Education of Topeka*, which ends racial segregation of public schools in the United States. (*See also Alston* v. *School Board of the City of Norfolk, McLaurin* v. *Oklahoma State Regents, Missouri ex rel. Gaines* v. *Canada* and *Sweatt* v. *Painter*.)

Southeastern Community College v. *Davis*. A unanimous 1979 decision that federally funded colleges are not required to admit all handicapped applicants or to make "extensive modifications" of their facilities to accommodate disabled students.

Swann v. *Charlotte-Mecklenburg Board of Education*. A landmark decision in 1971 that requires a North Carolina school board to bus students across district lines to achieve racial integration in public schools.

Sweatt v. *Painter*. A 1950 ruling that leaves standing a previous High Court decision ordering all-white University of Texas Law School to admit Herman Marion Sweatt, a Negro. Together with *Alston* v. *School Board of the City of Norfolk* (1940) and *McLaurin* v. *Oklahoma State Regents, Missouri ex rel. Gaines* v. *Canada* and *Sipuel* v. *Board of Regents of the University of Oklahoma* (q.q.v.), *Sweatt* is one of a carefully planned series of law suits that reach a climax in 1954 in *Brown* v. *Board of Education of Topeka* (q.v.), in which the Supreme Court declares racial segregation of public schools unconstitutional.

Tinker v. *Des Moines Independent Community School District*. A 1969 ruling that public school officials cannot arbitrarily deprive students of their First Amendment rights to nondisruptive free speech.

Trustees of Dartmouth College v. *Woodward*. A still-controversial 1819 decision that holds charters—even those granted by the British king before U.S. independence—to be binding contracts protected by the Constitution.

United States v. *Montgomery County Board of Education*. A decision in 1969 establishing racial ratios for teacher assignments in Montgomery, Alabama, public schools. The case is significant in that it effectively ends the massive resistance of states in the South to the 1954 decision in *Brown v. Board of Education of Topeka* declaring racial segregation of public schools unconstitutional.

University of California Regents v. *Bakke*. A 1978 decision that upholds the claim of "reverse discrimination" by a white student who charged the University of California Medical School rejected him because of his race.

Wallace v. *Jaffree*. A 1985 decision that declares unconstitutional an Alabama law authorizing a daily, one-minute period of silence in public schools "for meditation or voluntary prayer."

Waters v. *Churchill*. A 1994 ruling that public employers have the right to dismiss employees whose speech, while constitutionally guaranteed, might disrupt normal operations in the workplace.

Widmar v. *Vincent*. A ruling in 1981 affirming the constitutional right of student organizations at public colleges and universities to hold religious services on campus property.

Wisconsin v. *Yoder*. A 1972 ruling that gives the Amish religious sect a rare exemption from state compulsory educational laws. The High Court holds that 300 years of unswerving dedication to their way of life entitled the Amish to be exempt from Wisconsin's (and, by extension, to every other state's) law requiring children to attend school until age 16.

***Wolman* v. *Walter*.** A 1977 decision that upholds the constitutionality of an Ohio law authorizing various forms of state aid to private schools.

***Wood* v. *Strickland*.** A 1975 ruling that holds a school board member liable for damages for violating the constitutional rights of students.

***Wygant* v. *Jackson Board of Education*.** A 1986 ruling that, in an effort to cut costs, a school board cannot preserve the jobs of black teachers by laying off white teachers.

***Zorach* v. *Clauson*.** A 1952 decision that upholds a New York law permitting public schools to release students to attend religious instruction that takes place outside public school and does not require public financial support.

APPENDIX D: GRADUATE SCHOOL OFFERINGS IN EDUCATION, UNDERGRADUATE EDUCATION MAJORS AND UNDERGRADUATE MAJORS AT AMERICAN COLLEGES

GRADUATE SCHOOL OFFERINGS IN EDUCATION

At the graduate school level, more than 500 universities offer master's and doctoral programs in administration and supervision, curriculum and instruction, elementary and secondary teaching, evaluation and research, foundations of education, guidance and counseling, health/physical education, history and philosophy of education, reading specialist, recreation, school psychology, special education, speech pathology and audiology, vocational/distributive/occupational education, early childhood education, extension education, and student personnel services.

Somewhat fewer graduate schools offer specialized post-college training and degrees in adult and community education, audio-visual education, community college teaching, computers in education, education of the gifted, English as a Second Language, learning disabilities, marriage and family counseling, recreation administration, safety education, school librarianship, sex education, teaching the culturally disadvantaged, teaching the emotionally disturbed, teaching the mentally retarded, teaching the physically handicapped and urban education.

UNDERGRADUATE MAJORS AND COURSES OF STUDY IN EDUCATION

agricultural education, art education, bilingual/bicultural education, business education, Christian education, computer education, curriculum and instruction, drama education, safety education, early childhood education, education, education of the deaf and hearing impaired, education of the emotionally handicapped, education of the exceptional child, education of the mentally handicapped, education of the multiple-handicapped, education of the physically handicapped, education of the visually handicapped, educational media, educational statistics and research, elementary education, English education, environmental education, foreign languages education, guidance education, health education, home economics education, industrial arts education, journalism education, marketing and distribution education, mathematics education, middle school education, music education, nursing education, nutrition education, physical education, psychology education, reading education, recreation education, religious education, science education, secondary education, social science education, social studies education, special education, teaching English as a second language or as a foreign language, technical education, trade and industrial education, and vocational education.

UNDERGRADUATE MAJORS OFFERED AT AMERICAN COLLEGES

In the last century, American colleges and universities have constantly expanded their curricula to meet the changing practical and social needs of their student constituencies. Those changes have seen curricula explode from a small selection of several dozen classical arts and science courses into a cafeteria of several thousand courses grouped in more than 100 majors, ranging from accounting to zoology. Here are the majors listed at more than 1,500 accredited four-year colleges and universities as the 20th century neared its end. Several annual college directories available at libraries and bookstores cross-reference each of the majors with the multitude of colleges that offer them. Listed among the following majors are educational majors, which have also been listed earlier, with a list of graduate-school offerings in education.

Accounting, actuarial science, addition studies, advertising, aeronautical engineering, aeronautical science, aeronautical technology, aerospace studies, African languages, African studies, African-American studies, agricultural business management, agricultural economics, agricultural education, agricultural engineering, agricultural engineering technology, agricultural mechanics, agriculture, agronomy, air traffic control, aircraft mechanics, airline piloting and navigation, allied health, American Indian studies, American literature, American studies, anatomy, anesthesiology, animal science. anthropology, apparel and accessories, apparel design, applied art, applied mathematics, applied music, applied physics, Arabic, archeology, architectural engineering, architectural technology, architecture, area studies, art, art education, art history and appreciation, art therapy, arts administration and management, Asian-American studies, Asian-Orien-tal studies, astronomy, astrophysics, athletic training, atmospheric sciences and meteorology, audio technology, automotive technology, avian sciences, aviation administration and management, aviation computer technology.

Bacteriology, banking and finance, behavioral science, biblical languages, biblical studies, bilingual/bicultural education, biochemistry, bioengineering, biology and biological science, biomedical engineering, biomedical science, biometrics and biostatics, biotechnology, botany, broadcasting, business administration and management, business data processing, business economics, business education, business law, business statistics, business systems analysis.

Canadian studies, Caribbean studies, cartography, cell biology, Celtic studies, ceramic art and design, ceramic engineering, ceramic science, chemical engineering, chemical technology, chemistry, child care and child-family studies, child psychology and development, Chinese, chiropractic, Christian education, Christian studies, city/community/regional planning, civil engineering, civil engineering technology, classical and ancient civilizations, classical languages, classics, clinical psychology, clinical science, clothing and textiles management/production/ services, cognitive science, commercial art, communications, communications technology, community health work, community psychology, community services, comparative literature, computer education, computer engineering, computer graphics, computer management, computer mathematics, computer programming, computer science, computer technology, conservation and regulation, consumer services, construction engineering, construction management, construction technology, corrections, counseling psychology, court reporting, crafts, creative writing, criminal justice, criminology, cross-cultural studies, curriculum and instruction, cybernetics, cytotechnology.

Dairy science, dance, dance education, dance therapy, data processing, dental hygiene, dental laboratories technology, design, developmental psychology, dietetics, drafting and design, drafting and design technology, drama education, dramatic arts, drawing, driver and safety education, Dutch.

Early childhood education, early childhood studies, earth science, East Asian languages and literature, East Asian studies, Eastern European studies, economics, education, education of the deaf and hearing impaired, education of the emotionally handicapped, education of the exceptional child, education of the mentally handicapped, education of the multiple-handicapped, education of the physically handicapped, education of the visually handicapped, educational media, educational statistics and research, electrical and electronics engineering, electrical and electronics engineering technology, electromechanical technology, electron physics, elementary education, elementary particles physics, emergency-disaster science, emergency medical technologies, energy management technology, engineering, engineering and applied science, engineering management, engineering mechanics, engineering physics, engineering technology, (teaching) English as a second or foreign language, English education, English literature, entomology, entrepreneurial studies, environmental biology, environmental design, environmental education, environmental engineering, environmental engineering technology, environmental health science, environmental science, equestrian science, Eskimo, ethics of politics and social policy, ethnic studies, European studies, evolutionary biology, experimental psychology.

Family and community services, family and consumer resource management, family and consumer studies. fashion design and technology, fashion merchandising, fiber and textiles weaving, film arts, fine arts, fire control and safety technology, fire protection, fire protection engineering, fire science, fish and game management, fishing and fisheries, fluid and thermal science, folklore and mythology, food production and management services, food science, food services technology, foreign languages education, forensic studies, forest engineering, forestry production and processing, forestry and related services, French, French language and literature, French studies, furniture design.

Genetics, geochemistry, geodetic science, geography, geological engineering, geology, geophysical engineering, geophysics and seismology, geoscience, German, German area studies, German languages and literature, gerontology, glass, graphic arts technology, graphic design, graphic and printing production, Greek (classical), Greek (modern), Greek studies, guidance education, guitar.

Hawaiian, Hawaiian studies, health, health care administration, health education, health science, Hebrew, Hispanic American studies, historic preservation, history, history of philosophy, history of science, home economics, home economics education, home furnishings and equipment management and production services, horticulture, hospice care, hospital administration, hospitality management service, hotel/motel and restaurant management, human development, human ecology, human resources, human services, humanities, humanities and social science, hydrology.

Illustration, Indic languages, industrial administration and management, industrial arts education, industrial design, industrial and organizational psychology, industrial engineering technology, industrial hygiene, information sciences and systems, institutional management, insurance, insurance and risk management, interdisciplinary studies, interior design, international agriculture, international business management, international economics, international public service, international relations, international studies, interpreter for the deaf, investments and securities, Islamic studies, Italian, Italian studies.

Japanese, jazz, journalism, journalism education, Judaic studies.

Korean.

labor studies, landscape architecture and design, land use management and reclamation, languages, laser electro-optics technology, Latin, Latin American studies, law, law enforcement and corrections, liberal arts/general studies, library science, life science, limnology, linguistics, literature, Luso-Brazilian studies.

management engineering, management information systems, management science, manufacturing engineering, manufacturing technology, marine biology, marine engineering, marine science, maritime science, marketing and distribution, marketing and distribution education, marketing management, marketing/retailing/merchandising, materials engineering, materials science, mathematics, mathematics education, mechanical design technology, mechanical engineering, mechanical engineering technology, media arts, medical laboratory science, medical laboratory technology, medical records administration and services, medical technology, medical science, medieval studies, mental health and human services, metal/jewelry, metallurgical engineering, metallurgy, Mexican American/Chicano studies, microbiology, Middle Eastern studies, middle school education, military science, mining and mineral engineering, mining and petroleum technology, ministries, missions, modern languages, molecular biology, museum studies, music, music business management, music education, music history and appreciation, music performance, music theory and composition, music therapy, musical theater.

Native American studies, natural resource management, natural sciences, naval architecture and marine engineering, naval science, Near Eastern studies, neuroscience, nuclear engineering, nuclear engineering technology, nuclear medical technology, nuclear technology, nursing, nursing education, nutrition, nutrition education.

occupational safety and health, occupational therapy, ocean engineering, oceanography, office supervision and management, opera, operations research, optical engineering, optics, optometry, organizational behavior.

Pacific area studies, painting, paleontology, paper and pulp science, paper engineering, paralegal studies, parks and recreation management, pastoral studies, peace studies, percussion, performing arts, personnel management, petroleum and natural gas engineering, pharmacy, philosophy, photography, physical chemistry, physical education, physical fitness and movement, physical sciences, physical therapy, physician's assistant, physics, physiology, piano and organ, planetary

and space science, plant genetics, plant pathology, plant physiology, plant protection and pest management, plant science, plastics engineering, plastics technology, Polish, political science and government, polymer science, Portuguese, poultry science, predentistry, preengineering, prelaw, premedicine, preosteopathy, prepharmacy, prepodiatry, preveterinary science, printmaking, printing technology, psychobiology, psychology, psychology education, public administration, public affairs, public health, public relations, publishing, purchasing and inventory management.

quantitative methods.

radiation therapy, radio and television technology, radiographic medical technology, radiological science, radiological technology, range and farm management, reading education, real estate, recreation and leisure services, recreational facilities management, recreation education, recreation therapy, rehabilitation therapy, religion, religious education, religious music, respiratory therapy, retailing, Romance languages, rural sociology, Russian, Russian and Slavic studies.

safety and security technology, safety management, Sanskrit and Indian studies, Scandinavian languages, Scandinavian studies, school psychology, science, science and management, science education, science technology, sculpture, secondary education, secretarial studies and office management, Slavic languages, small business management, social foundations, social psychology, social science, social science education, social studies, social studies education, social work, sociology, soil science, South Asian studies, Southwest American studies, Spanish, Spanish studies, special education, specific learning disabilities, speech correction, speech pathology and audiology, speech therapy, sports management, sports medicine, statistics, strings, studio art, survey and mapping technology, surveying engineering, systems analysis, systems engineering, systems science.

teaching English as a second language or as a foreign language, technical and business writing, technical education, technological management, technology and public affairs, telecommunication, textile engineering, textile technology, textiles and clothing, theater design, theater management, theological studies, third work studies, tourism, toxicology, toy design, trade and industrial education, transportation and travel marketing, transportation engineering, transportation management, transportation technology.

ultrasound technology, urban design, urban planning technology, urban studies.

veterinary science, video, visual and performing arts, vocational education, voice.

water resources, water and wastewater technology, welding engineering, western European studies, western civilization and culture, wildlife biology, wildlife management, winds, women's studies, wood science, woodworking.

Yiddish, youth ministry.

zoology.

INDEX

This index is designed to be used in conjunction with the extensive A-to-Z encyclopedia entries. Page references to titles, names and terms that have their own encyclopedia entry are **boldfaced** below; for additional references, see their text entries. Other titles, names and terms that are not the subjects of the A-to-Z entries are generally given fuller citations here. *Italicized* page references indicate illustrations.

A

Aaron v. McKinley, **1**
AASA. *See American Association of School Administrators*
AAUP. *See American Association of University Professors*
AAUW. *See American Association of University Women*
A.B. *See Bachelor of Arts*
abacus, **1**
Abbot, Edith, 708
Abbott, Grace, 1008
Abbott, Jacob, **1–2**, 66, 69, 1017
ABC. *See American Broadcasting Company*
ABE. *See Adult Basic Education*
ability grouping, **2**, 898
    age-equivalent scales, 36
    Detroit X-Y-Z Plan, **288**
    Goodlad's criticism of, 418
    homogeneous versus heterogeneous, **480**
    Thorndike's sorting theories, 989
    tracking and, 992–93
Abington School District v. Schempp, **2–3**, 196, 197, 747, **851–52**
abolitionist movement, 531, 687, 775, 930, 1027
absenteeism, **3**, 301
    class cutting, 3, 301
    and fear of violence, 1041
    single-parent home impact, 1041

truancy, 90, **997–98**, 1041
abstracts, **3**, 303, 325, 328
Academia di Disegno, 9
academic dress (academicals), **3–4**, 627
academic freedom, **4–6**, 9, 99, 349, 388, 976
academic officers, **21–22** *See also specific administrative positions*
academic quality, **6–8**, 429
academic rank, **8–9**, 19, 215
academy, **9–10**, 353, 468, 542, 868
Academy and Charitable School in the City of Philadelphia. *See Franklin's Academy*
Academy of Fine Arts, 674
Academy of Music, 729
Academy of Natural Sciences, 634, 635, 729
Academy of Plato, 9, 76, 210, 438, 733, 738
Academy of St. Luke, 9
Accelerated Schools Project, **10–12**, 334
acceleration, **12–13**, 775, 849
accommodation. *See assimilation and accommodation*
accountability, **13–14**
    school audits, **843**
accreditation, **14–15**, 327, 492, 843
accreditation associations, 14, **15**, 653, 777 *See also specific associations*

Accrediting Bureau of Health Education Schools, 462
achievement tests, **15–16**, 75, 972 *See also specific tests and testing programs*
Achievement Tests (SAT IIs), 841, 935
ACLU. *See American Civil Liberties Union*
acoustic phonetics, 732
acquisition learning phase, 545
ACT Assessment Program, **16**, 22–23, 736
acting out, **16**
Action (periodical), 53
active learning, **17**, 24, 447, 450, 892
Act of Supremacy (England), 961
Act of Uniformity (England), 961
ADA. *See average daily attendance*
ADAMHA. *See Alcohol, Drug Abuse, and Mental Health Administration*
Adams, John
    as Academy of Arts and Sciences founder, 50, 64, 902
    American Indian initiatives, 55
    Americanization and, 57–58
    as educational rights supporter, 281, 513, 895, 975
    Library of Congress appropriation, 554

as national education system advocate, 322, 531, 565, 654, 814, 832
    on Thomas Paine's impact, 706
    as women's education supporter, 1074
    mentioned, 198, 832, 1077
Adams, John Quincy, 50, 58, 64, 481, 571, 655
adapted (adaptive) physical education, **17**
adaptive programming, **17–18**
ADD. *See attention deficit disorder*
Addams, Jane, **18–19**, 1008
    as Chautauqua speaker, 180
    as Hull House founder, 449, 484, 900, 922, 923
    as NAACP supporter, 640
    as Nobel Prize winner, 18, 150
Address to the Public, An: Particularly to the Members of the Legislature of New York Proposing a Plan for the Improvement of Female Education (E. Willard), 1074
Adelphi University, 754
adjunct, **19**
Adler, Felix, **19–20**
Adler, Mortimer J., **20**, **127, 417**
    Great Books Program, 20, 433, 486–87, 520, 724
    Paideia Proposal, 20, 705, 893

O